Qlik

according to

HIC

by

Henric I. Cronström

ISBN 978-91-527-9926-0
First edition 2024
Published 2024 by mm förlag (www.mmforlag.se)
Layout by Dustobit Media (www.dustobit.se)
Script examples on www.qhic.se

Contents

Contents

Contents

Contents

Contents

Contents

Contents

Contents

Foreword

This book is aimed to help people better understand how to build apps using Qlik Sense or QlikView, and to better understand how the Qlik Associative Engine works. Much of the content is based on material I developed during my many years at Qlik but has been adapted for the new situation where Qlik Sense is the main analysis tool instead of QlikView. Most of the material has been published as blog posts on web sites, or as white papers, but by gathering it in one book the reader will get a better overview and a context.

The illustrations are sometimes from Qlik Sense, sometimes from QlikView. For you as a user, it should in most cases make no difference – the logic is the same in both products.

A blog post needs to be a small, digestible text. It should be possible to read it in a fairly short time, meaning that it is rarely longer than two pages or 500 words. I believe that this concept has great value when it comes to conveying information in an understandable way. *Less is more.*

Consequently, I have chosen to continue to use this format also in the book. Hence, the book contains a number of articles that have been or could have been blog posts. These articles are grouped into chapters based on the content of the article. Some sections are however longer since they are based on whitepapers.

I want to thank Qlik for letting me re-use the material. I also want to thank colleagues at Qlik and all Qlik developers I have met over the years for the discussions and sharing of knowledge. A special thanks to Håkan W. for making everything possible. Finally, I want to thank my wife for support and publishing.

HIC

Henric Cronström, Lund and Brussels, 2024

Foreword

In ignorance lost
the winding path of learning
knowledge dawns ahead

1

Business Intelligence

What is Business Intelligence?

Over the years, there have been many names of what today is called Business Intelligence, such as:

- Analytics
- Executive Information Systems (EIS)
- Management Information Systems (MIS)
- Online Analytical Processing (OLAP)
- Decision Support Systems (DSS)
- Ad hoc query and reporting
- Data discovery
- Data visualization

In this book, I choose to call it "Business intelligence", but I have no good argument why this is a better label than the other ones. It is just the most commonly used term today. But in fact, the word "business" is misleading. Analysis and visualization are just as useful in non-business situations.

There are slight differences in what the above terms mean, but they are small. So, I don't care to elaborate on what might set them apart. It is more interesting to see what they have in common: *They allow a user to dynamically look at data.* As opposed to "reporting" which is static, i.e. a report is a bunch of papers or a pdf document.

Most of the time, the methods and tools have been aimed at a small, select number of decision-makers, but I think that this has been a mistake: Decisions are made at all levels in a company.

Obviously, managers are decision-makers, but we sometimes forget that machine operators and receptionists also are decision-makers, albeit at a more local level. And they also need information to make good decisions.

I believe that information can change the world and that everyone should be able to easily view data, navigate data, and analyze data. Everyone should be able to experience that "a-ha" moment of finding knowledge in data.

Business intelligence is dynamic and empowering. And it is fun!

Welcome to the Qlik Design Blog

Originally posted in the Qlik Design Blog May 14, 2012

Eighteen years ago, I had just started a new job at QuikTech (no that's not a typo) and my boss – one of the two founders – dropped a shrink-wrapped FoxPro in my lap while saying: "You see, I have this idea about color coding information – green, white and grey. Can you see if you can achieve that with this database?"

At the same time, two other people in the company were given the same task but with other tools – *Excel* and a multimedia tool called *Authorware*. Neither of us succeeded very well, so we decided to call a really good developer that two of us knew from university and ask him if he could do something in C++.

A couple of months later we had the first version of QuikView, later renamed QlikView. It had list boxes and nothing else. No tables, no graphs, no aggregations, no numerical calculations. We sold these early versions to companies that needed logical visualization of data.

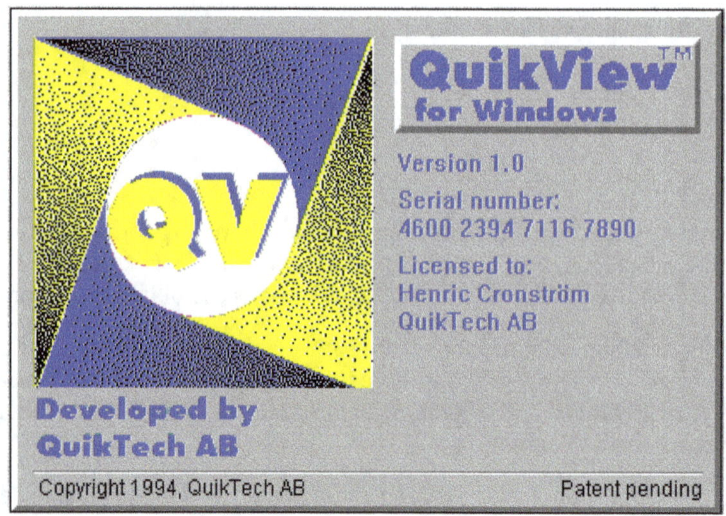

Many things have changed since, but the core in QlikView is still the same: ***The logical inference engine***; the user selects a field value and QlikView and Qlik Sense answer by indicating which other values are implied by the selection and which are excluded. QlikView was different from all other tools on the market in that it was not a number-crunching tool – it was a tool for visualizing logical relationships.

QlikView and Qlik Sense are still today different from all other tools in this regard. In fact, the logical inference engine is what enables the user to explore data freely without predefined search paths, which is the core of Qlik's Business Intelligence.

The first two years with QlikTech I had many hats. At one and the same time, I was the project manager, the product manager, the R&D manager, the technical writer and the pre-sales consultant. But we did not use these labels then. We did not have clear roles and flexibility was important.

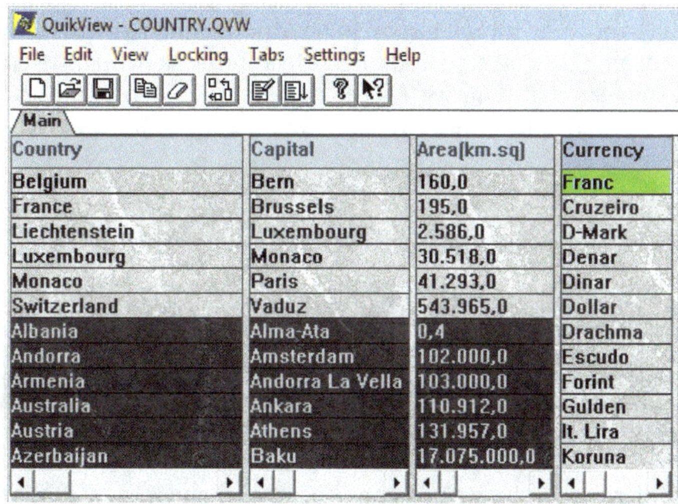

Since then, I have implemented numerous QlikView solutions and been heavily involved in defining new QlikView and Qlik Sense versions. Today, my responsibilities have moved toward communication about the product.

Hence, the Qlik Design Blog. Here, I and other "QlikTechies" will write about how to build Qlik solutions. We will write about scripting, visual design, extensions, server configuration, do's and don'ts, etc. It will sometimes be very technical and sometimes not.

Please give us feedback on the content. Send us questions and suggestions. We are here for you. Welcome to the Qlik Design Blog!

HIC

Interacting with Data

The classic picture of business intelligence is that the user has one or several questions, and that the data holds the answers. So, the problem boils down to creating a tool where the user can enter their questions, and the tool can return the answers.

However, this picture is incorrect. The truth is that the user initially rarely knows the question. Or rather, if the user knows the question, they often already know the answer. So, the first thing the tool should do is to help the user find the questions.

Finding the questions is a process that involves exploring the data. It involves testing what you suspect but don't know for sure. It also involves discovering new facts. Further, it involves playing with data, turning data around, looking at relationships from different angles: If A means B, does it also mean that B means A? You need to be able to play with the data before you can say that you understand it, and you need to understand the data before you can talk smartly about it.

You use your gut feeling as a source of ideas, and you use the data to refine the ideas into knowledge; or to discard the ideas if facts show that the ideas are wrong.

When you have formulated a relevant question, you also need to be able to conduct an analysis to get a well-founded answer to the question.

Finally, the process involves presenting the answer to the question to other people as a basis for a decision or an action. The tool must support the entire process of going from ignorance to insight.

Hence, the major differentiator between a good tool and the more old-fashioned tools is that the good tool supports the entire process—the process of coming from a blank mind, not knowing what you are looking for, all the way to attaining knowledge and taking action.

Qlik Sense and QlikView do exactly this.

The Unclearly Said

Posted on the Business Discovery Blog on Nov 27, 2012

> "What you cannot clearly say, you know not.
> With the thought, the word is born on a man's lips:
> the obscurely uttered is the obscurely thought."

These lines were part of an epilogue read by Esaias Tegnér at the Lund University graduation in 1820. The last line is famous in Sweden and has become a proverb in its own right:

> "Det dunkelt sagda är det dunkelt tänkta."

Picture *1*: *Esaias Tegnér.*

Tegnér was professor of Greek in Lund and one of greatest writers in Swedish history. The statue on the picture is found in central Lund, not far from the statue of Nothingness. (See "The Importance of Nothing").

He was at the time known not only in Sweden but also abroad. The American poet Henry Wadsworth Longfellow translated some of Tegnér's works to English and at Tegnér's death Longfellow wrote Tegnér's drapa, a poem that praised the man and his works.

Tegnér's words at the graduation were an attack on the Phosphorists, a neo-romantic group with metaphysical ideals. Tegnér himself was more down to earth and believed in observations of nature and a scientific approach.

So basically, Tegnér was telling the students not to trust unclear speech because it is a sign of dim thoughts or lack of facts. This message is simple enough and very relevant still today.

What has all this got to do with QlikView? At first glance, nothing. But in fact, quite a lot.

People all over the world tend to rightfully distrust obscure speech, irrespective of whether they have heard of Tegnér or not. Further, an implication of Tegnér's message is that you shouldn't speak or act until you get your thoughts and facts straightened out. And when putting it this way, the analogy becomes obvious: get your facts right, get your thoughts straightened out – only then are you ready to communicate what you're thinking. Only then can you act wisely.

In a professional situation where a database is a major source of information, you need to use the data not only to find facts and answers, but also to find the questions. You use your gut feeling to create ideas and you use the data to refine the ideas into knowledge. Or, to discard the ideas, if facts show that the ideas are wrong. You need to be able to play with the data, to turn facts around and look at them from different angles before you can say that you understand the data. And you need to understand the data before you can talk smartly about it.

This is what Business intelligence is all about: helping you to prepare before you speak, act, or make a decision. It is the process of going from the dark to the light, from the unknown to the known, from ignorance to insight. It is the process of going all the way from a blank mind to a substantiated allegation.

Because – what is unclearly said is unclearly thought.

The failure of traditional Business Intelligence

Users want the ability to explore data and ask questions on their own, but traditional business intelligence solutions are usually not well-suited for user demands. Instead, it is common that the BI solutions are created in an IT-centric manner, where system demands set the goals, rather than user demands. The solutions often have pre-configured dashboards, fixed drill-down paths, predefined queries, predefined views, and very little flexibility.

When analyzing data, the user wants to set filters – make selections – but with traditional tools, you often need to start at the top of a predefined hierarchy. So instead of selecting a customer directly, you may need to first enter the market to which the customer belongs, then the country, and only then can you specify the customer. This means that the users cannot follow their own train of thought.

Further, in a drill-down hierarchy, you are often limited to the choice of one or all. The possibility of choosing two or three specific customers doesn't exist unless this has been specifically predefined by the data model developer.

Numbers are often precalculated to ensure short response times, but this has a drawback that if the developer hasn't anticipated a specific calculation, the tool will not be able to make the calculation.

Further, the architecture of the tool is often made in three layers. The first layer is the ETL (Extract, Transform, Load) layer, the second is the database layer, and the third is the UI (User Interface). The three layers are often different pieces of software, sometimes delivered by different software vendors.

These three layers also demand different skillsets. Often the ETL expert knows little or nothing about the UI software, and the UI expert knows little or nothing about the ETL.

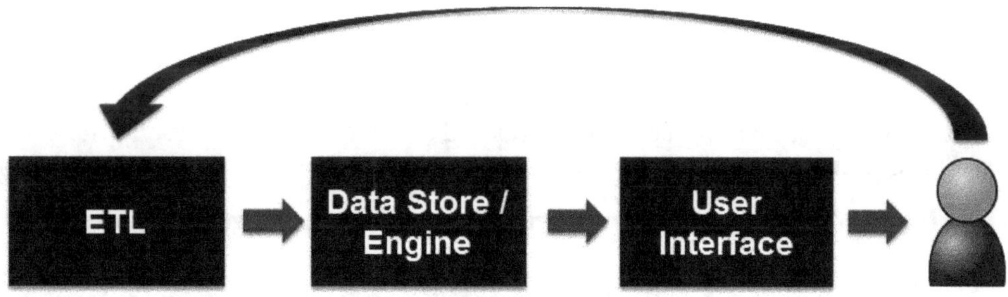

This architecture leads to problems. When an application is built, the feedback comes from users trying to use the application. It could be that metrics are incorrectly calculated or that dimensions or measures are missing. It could also mean that the user realizes that the initial requirements were incorrect or insufficient. The feedback could imply changes in the UI, or in the data model, or even in the ETL component.

This type of feedback is normal — it happens in all business intelligence projects. It only means that the development of applications is a process where you need to work iteratively. The expectation that you would be able to define an application completely and correctly prior to a prototype or an intermediate version is just unrealistic.

This is where the architecture leads to problems. For a project to be successful, change requests and new user demands need to be handled with short notice, and this can be difficult since there are three different pieces of software and three different groups of people involved. The distance between the user and the ETL component is just too great for efficient communication. Hence, traditional architecture often leads to a broken process.

The Qlik way

Qlik has tried to solve all the drawbacks discussed in the preceding section by doing things differently.

First of all, you click and view. You don't need to formulate your question or tell the system more specifically *what* you want to look at. You just click, and by that, you say "Tell me more about that…". Then you look at the metrics or fields that might be interesting.

The color coding defines the answer. Some things are associated with what you clicked on, and they remain white. Others that are not associated become gray. The color coding is for simplicity. The user quickly gets an overview and understands how things work.

Showing the excluded reveals the unexpected, creates insight, and creates new questions. Hence, the gray color is an important part of making the Qlik experience an associative one—a data dialog and an information interaction — rather than just a database query. Showing you that something is excluded when you didn't expect it means answering questions you didn't ask. This surprise creates new knowledge in a way that only a true data discovery platform can.

A user has total freedom to navigate through data and make any combination of selections. Any number of values can be selected. No drill-down paths need to be predefined. This allows the user to follow their own train of thought instead of someone else's. Start anywhere and just follow your intuition.

This total freedom when exploring data is really the core attribute of good business intelligence.

Further, no numbers need to be precalculated. QlikView and Qlik Sense calculate everything on demand, usually in a fraction of a second. The short response time allows the user to "have a conversation" with the data, where one answer leads to the next question, which in turn leads to next, and so on. Only this way can you interact with data so that you learn from it.

The developer does not need to anticipate all questions that the user will pose. All they need to do is to create a logical, coherent data model, and the Qlik engine will be able to answer the question correctly:

The stack (ETL-Data Store / Engine-UI) is replaced by a single integrated environment. This makes it possible to develop applications in close cooperation with the users, and it can often be done by the users themselves. Change requests are implemented instantaneously, and the changes can often be evaluated just seconds later. This shortens the development cycle and ensures that the application meets the user demands much sooner than it would otherwise.

This stepwise implementation is crucial for the success of a business intelligence project. It is also the core of modern agile methodologies that are used in all types of software development.

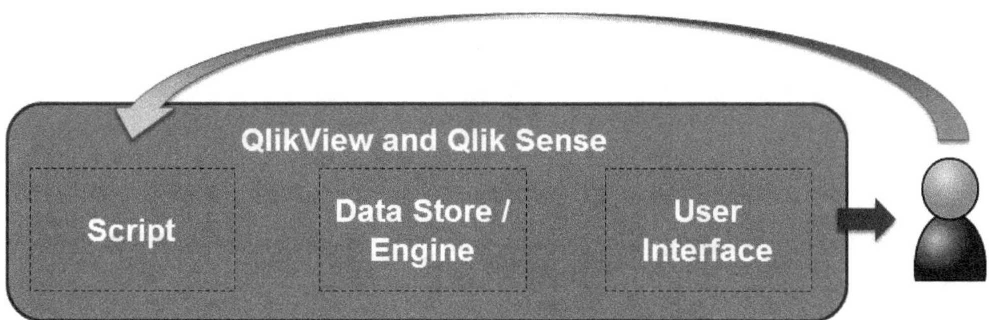

With Qlik Sense and QlikView, all BI stack functions are integrated into one tool.

Development of business intelligence applications must be done as close to the user as possible to enable user feedback and short development cycles. It does not necessarily imply self-service capability, although it is good if this capability exists.

Green is the Colour

Posted on the Business Discovery Blog on May 18, 2012

On the Pink Floyd album "Music from the Film More" (1969) there is a song "Green Is the Colour". It is a ballad typical of the early Pink Floyd. And it is still good. Listen to it, when you can.

Given the title, it could have been QlikView's song. There is no color so associated with QlikView as green. Green is the QlikView brand. Green is how you interact with QlikView, how you focus on a piece of information, how you ask questions. You click, and it turns green. And the answer to your question turns up in white. It is so easy.

Green and White. Everything is ordered, simple and beautiful.

Then – enter the black swan: Grey, the color that adds spice to QlikView. After all, green is just a query filter and white is just a query result. Anyone can do that! But *Grey* ...

Grey is the color that reveals the unexpected. Grey is the color that creates insight. Grey is the color that creates new questions. Grey is an important part of making the Qlik experience an associative one — a data dialogue and an information interaction, rather than just a database query. Showing you that something is excluded when you didn't expect it is answering questions you didn't ask. This surprise creates new knowledge in a way that only a true Business Discovery platform can.

One of the first prospects of QlikView was a pharmaceutical company where physicians wanted to analyze their clinical trials database. We connected QlikView to their database and were up and running in just a few minutes. I clicked on one of their coming products and we could see the countries where studies of this product were in progress. But one major European country was greyed out when I clicked ...

The audience was silent. This information obviously came as a surprise.

"Oh, it does not matter," someone said. "We can get the product approved there using the studies from other countries."

"No!" someone else said. "It is a large market. We need a study there for marketing purposes!"

Needless to say, they initiated a study also in that country.

Things have not changed. Qlik still helps people discover their data and their business. And grey is a crucial part of the discovery process. Therefore, I feel uneasy when I get questions like "How do I hide the grey values?" I always try to persuade the developer to leave the grey values visible, because my view on this is firm: Showing excluded values is an important part of the QlikView experience. Don't hide them!

Green may be the Colour, but *Grey makes the Difference*.

Which trends affect Business Intelligence?

Originally posted in the Business Discovery Blog on May 28, 2012

I've been thinking lately about IT trends that will have a major impact on how business intelligence is used in organizations. A few of my thoughts:

- **Mobile technology**
  Mobile is a buzz word that is sometimes misunderstood. "I am already mobile – I have a laptop and can connect wherever I am." Although it's true that the laptop is mobile, that's not really the thing. Mobile is rather about availability — that you bring your device wherever you are, that you can turn it on in a second, and that it is equipped with a touch screen. It's about connecting instantly to Internet-based apps and resources. Today, mobility is more about smartphones and tablets than it is about laptops. Everyone will soon have one. This will change the IT landscape completely and with this change comes the possibility of having your business analysis at your fingertips wherever you are.

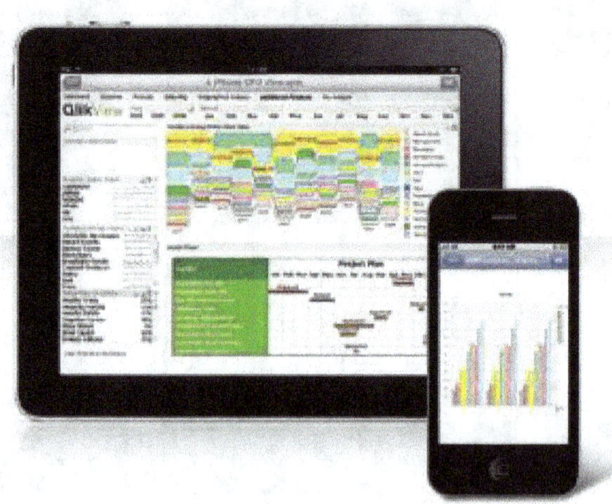

- **Big Data**
  We will continue to see more cases where we are talking about billions of records instead of just millions. We will also see more cases of analysis where data has been collected from the web, e.g., from social media or customer loyalty programs, or from machines. However, I am convinced that Big Data will not change the lion's share of BI apps for the foreseeable future. Most BI apps will still be analysis of sales, costs, purchases, suppliers, log files, finance data etc. Most apps will continue to utilize a more moderate amount of data: millions of records rather than billions — even when they include data from "Big Data" sources. The German magazine *Computerwoche* rightfully asked, "The question should not be, 'How much data can I analyze?' but rather, 'How can I use the data, so that I can make better decisions'"? Big Data becomes useful only when it is relevant for the business and in context with other data (e.g., enterprise data, cloud data).

- **Cloud and SaaS computing**
  Cloud computing, sometimes combined with software as a service (SaaS) licensing models, is another trend that we will see more of. Slowly but surely, more and more data is moving into the cloud. As a consequence, more analysis will be done over the Internet. But this change takes time, and most enterprise BI installations will for many years to come remain within the corporate network. Is your company using cloud computing for data that should be analyzed? If so, you should perhaps consider putting your BI platform there too.

- **Consumerization of IT**
  With this we usually mean how computers, mobile devices, and apps more and more are used in people's personal lives. But the same trend also exists within people's professional lives and here it is probably more correct to call it user empowerment. We are talking about a democratization of technology resulting in more and more people using data and needing tools to analyze and make sense of the data. This trend is in my mind the most important one and it is certainly also a driver for some of the above trends. Young people are today accustomed both to using electronic devices for almost anything and to solving problems themselves. They will expect that at work also.

I think the key to staying on top of the trends is user empowerment. If users are empowered to make decisions, they will also take an active part in assessing information, both internal and external. They will drive the need for analysis, and they will see which trends affect your business. Empower your staff, give them a good Business Discovery solution, and many needed business changes will come automatically.

QlikView and Qlik Sense

Originally posted in the Qlik Design Blog July 29, 2014

As most of you have noticed – I hope – we have now released a new product. *Qlik Sense.*

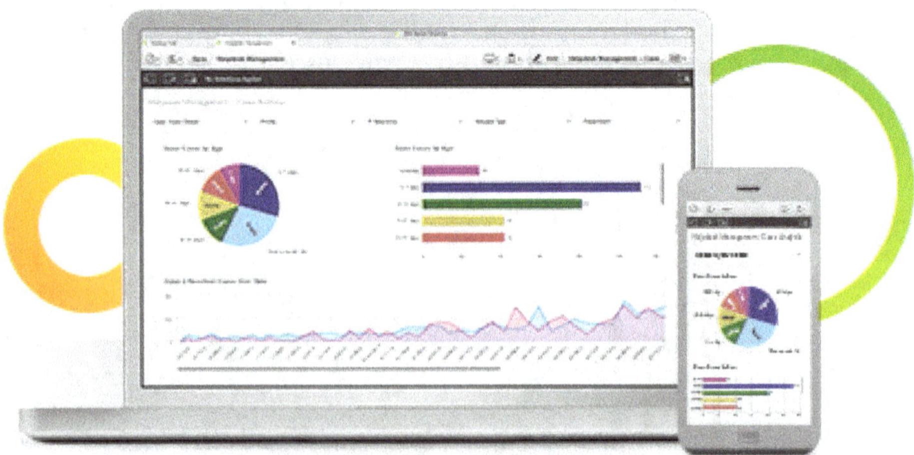

Qlik Sense is not just a new release of QlikView. Instead, it is something different. But there are still so many similarities between the two products, so I thought it would be appropriate to dedicate a blog post to differences and similarities between the two.

Basically, the two products are two different user interfaces to *the same analysis engine*. This means that old scripts and old formulae will (almost) always work exactly the same way as before. (There are some smaller differences in that Qlik Sense uses libraries and cannot always use relative paths for files.)

Hence, the two products both have the same Green-White-Gray logic; both use the same calculation engine; both have roughly the same response times; and you should use the same considerations for both when it comes to data modelling. This also means that many of the previous posts here on the Design Blog are just as relevant for Qlik Sense as for QlikView.

But the two products are still very different. And just as a parent cannot say that one child is better than the other, I cannot say that one product is better than the other. They are good at different things:

- *QlikView* is a tool for situations where you want prepared business applications, i.e. applications created by developers who put a lot of thought into the data model, the layout, the charts and the formulae; and deliver the applications to end-users who consume the applications. We call this *Guided Analytics*. The end-user has total freedom to explore data, select, drill down and navigate in the information, and can this way discover both questions and answers in the data. The end-user is, however, limited when it comes to creating new visualizations. This type of situation will without doubt be common for many, many years to come.

- **Qlik Sense** is a tool for situations where you don't want to pre-can so much. Instead, you want the user to have the freedom to create a layout of his own and in it, new visualizations; charts that the developer couldn't imagine that the user wants to see. You want *Self-service data discovery*, which means a much more active, modern, engaged user. In addition, Qlik Sense is much easier to use when you have a touch screen and is adaptive to different screen sizes and form factors. On the whole, Qlik Sense is a much more modern tool.

Qlik Sense today is only the first version of something that will evolve further and get more features and functions as time goes on. Some of the features and functions of QlikView have not yet been implemented in Qlik Sense – there just hasn't been time enough – but many of them will be implemented in coming versions.

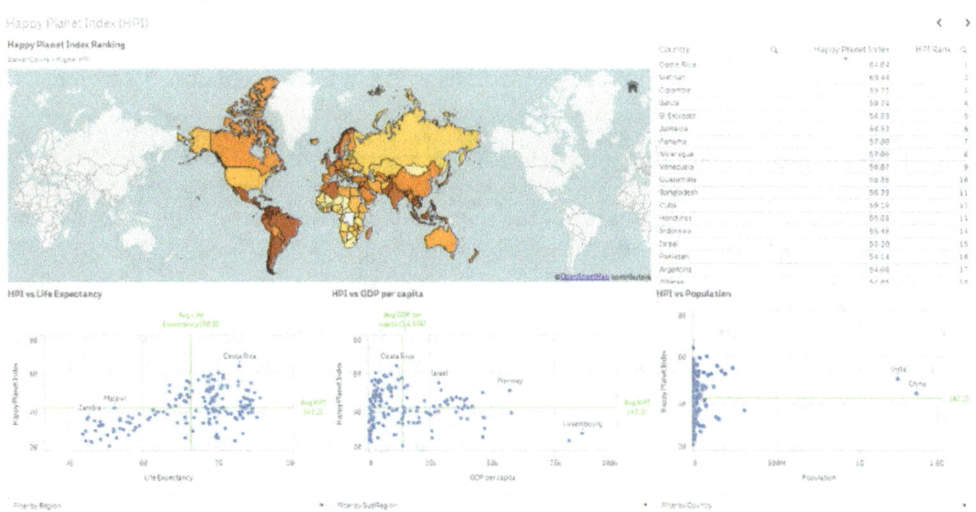

Also, QlikView is not yet a "final product". The product will be developed further, and most likely we will see some of the new functionality from Qlik Sense also in coming versions of QlikView. The goal is to use the same platform for both user interfaces.

With these two tools, we believe that we are well prepared for the future.

Self-service and the BI avantgarde

Self-service business intelligence is an approach that enables business users to access and explore data sets even if they don't have a background in BI or data mining and statistical analysis. Self-service BI tools allow users to load, transform, filter, sort, analyze and visualize data without involving an expert.

Organizations implemented self-service BI to make it easier for employees to get useful business insights from existing data. The primary goal was to drive more informed decision-making resulting in increased efficiency, better customer satisfaction and higher revenue and profits.

A self-service BI environment would enable executives, business analysts and other users to run queries themselves and create their own data visualizations, dashboards, and reports. Because some of those users may not be tech-savvy, it's imperative that the user interface is intuitive and easy to use.

Ten years ago, self-service business intelligence was on everybody's lips. The expectations were high. It was thought to liberate users from the shackles of slow and inefficient IT departments. "Guided analytics" – as the prepared apps were called – was on the way out.

The previous article describes well how the world as well as Qlik looked at self-service at the time.

But times have changed slightly since.

Self-service BI has since shown that it is *not* the magic bullet of business intelligence. A number of things prevents it from being the universal BI solution:

- **Many users don't have time**
  Many users, e.g. managers, have more important things to do than to build visualizations on their own. These users expect other people – experts – to prepare apps for them.

- **Supportability**
  In an environment where users create their own apps, it is very difficult to help the users when they run into problems. The Helpdesk can hardly answer any questions from the users.

- **Experts are needed for advanced analysis**
  Self-service can solve the problem of simple calculations, but to create advanced analysis, complex data models and complex calculations are needed. An average business user cannot create this.

- **One version of the truth**
  It can be difficult to enforce a single way of calculating a metric. Different users and different apps will calculate the same metric in slightly different ways.

However, I still claim that the need for self-service BI will grow. It will be increasing important to the sub-set of users that develop new apps, new concepts, and new metrics. This **BI avantgarde** will be the ones driving the development, and they need to be able to do all the above themselves.

The lion part of users will however continue to use prepared apps or reports. Which is good, since it solves their analysis need. Because the prepared apps are really not "guided" at all. The users still have complete freedom in navigating, exploring, and filtering data. As they should have.

This new landscape of a mixture between prepared apps and self-service is well reflected in Qlik's development. Qlik Sense is today much more capable of creating prepared apps than it was a few years ago. So, the goal of "only self-service" has been dropped. Also, Qlik's work on spaces, on a catalog service, and on governance and lineage supports a mixed environment where self-service and prepared apps will exist side-by-side.

2
Data

Some analysis challenges are general and independent of which tool you use. They pertain to *Data* as such, or to limitations in our computers.

- What classes of data are there?
- Which classes fit with which visualizations?
- How is data stored internally in a computer? And what limitations are there with this?

This chapter tries to describe some of these topics and will give you a high-level overview.

Scales of Measurement

Posted in the Qlik Design Blog on Sep 2, 2014

As you load data into a Qlik app, it is useful to ask the question: *What type of field is this? Which properties does it have?* Different categories of data have different properties:

The first category is **Nominals**. These are fields with discrete, qualitative values. There is no inherent quantitative difference between different values of a field. Examples: Product, Customer, Color, Gender, etc.

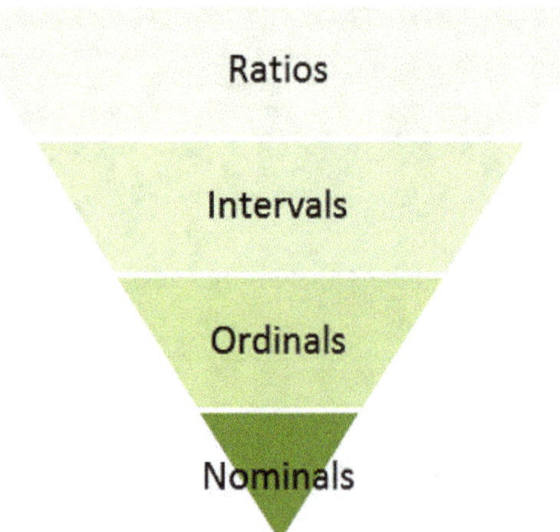

The second category is ***Ordinals***. These fields also have discrete values, but the fields differ from the Nominals in that they have an intrinsic order. Examples of ordinals:

- low, medium, high
- tiny, small, medium, large, huge
- XS, S, M, L, XL
- unsatisfied, neutral, satisfied

The ordinals can sometimes be numeric but should still not be thought of as numeric since the distance between one value and the next may differ from case to case. This means that you cannot calculate an average – but you can calculate a median.

The next category is numeric: ***Intervals***. These can be discrete or continuous. Examples: Date, Time, Longitude, Latitude, Temperature (°C or °F). What makes them different from Ordinals is that the difference between two values is well-defined: The difference between a temperature of 0 degrees and 10 degrees is the same as between 70 degrees and 80 degrees. Such fields always describe a position in time, in space or in some other dimension. I find the term "Interval" to be confusing, so I think of them as ***Coordinates*** instead.

Intervals are not additive, so you cannot sum them up. However, you can calculate a difference between two values and use this value for further calculations.

The last category is ***Ratios***. The Ratio category is the most informative one. It has all properties of the Interval category, with the additional property that zero is special: it indicates the absence of the quantity. Examples: Sales amount, Weight, Length, Order quantity, etc. Further, they are almost always additive. Since I think the term "Ratio" is misleading, I think of them as ***Amounts*** instead.

The above taxonomy was created by the psychologist S. S. Stevens in the early 1940s and is normally referred to as *Scales of Measurement*. Although it has been criticized from a scientific perspective, I find the classification useful, since a number of rules of thumb for visualizations can be tied to this model. For instance:

- *Nominals* should be sorted by a measure or alphabetically. Other categories should be sorted according to the intrinsic sort order.
- *Nominals* should never be used as first dimension in a Line chart, since this chart type implies an intrinsic sort order.
- Pie charts should not be used unless the dimension is a *Nominal*.
- Scatter charts are best if they have a *Nominal* or *Ordinal* as dimension.
- Continuous *Intervals* and *Ratios* should normally not be used as dimensions. Use Round() or Class() to make them discrete.
- *Ordinals* should not be used to calculate an average.
- *Intervals* should not be used to calculate a sum.
- The axis of a *Ratio* should start at zero and not be broken.

I am sure that some of you can find exceptions to the above "rules", but as I said – they are only rules of thumb.

The bottom line is that you should think about the field categorization before you create your visualizations.

Thank you, Michael Bienstein – R.I.P. – for the inspiration and discussions.

		as Dimension			as Measure	
		Sort order	Use e.g.	Do not use	Use e.g.	Do not use
Nominal		Alphabetical or by Measure	Bar chart, Pie chart, Scatter chart	Line chart	Count()	Average(), Median(), Sum()
Ordinal		by Intrinsic order	Bar chart, Line chart, Scatter chart	Pie chart	Count(), Median()	Average(), Sum()
Quantitative	Interval/ Coordinate	by Number	Bar chart, Line chart	Pie chart	Count(), Average(), Median()	Sum()
	Ratio/ Amount	by Number	Bar chart, Line chart, Histogram	Pie chart	Count(), Average(), Median(), Sum()	

Additive and non-additive measures

Posted in the Qlik Design Blog Feb 09, 2016

Measures in BI solutions are usually additive – but not always. To avoid mistakes, it is important to understand when you can sum the number, and when you cannot. This post will not only help you understand the problem, but also point out some possible ways to handle non-additive numbers.

Numbers fall into one of three categories:

- Fully additive numbers, which can be summed across any of the dimensions. Most transactional amounts are additive.

- Semi-additive numbers, which can be summed across some dimensions, but not all. An example is warehouse balances: these are amounts that are additive across all dimensions except time.

- Non-additive numbers, which cannot be summed over any dimension. An example is the gross margin for a product.

Additive numbers are straightforward to sum: Just use the Sum() function in your measure, and everything will work.

Semi-additive and non-additive numbers are however not as straightforward. These will be shown correctly *only* in a chart with exactly the same grain as the source data, i.e. if the chart dimension(s) is the primary key in the source table. In all other cases the sum function will potentially return incorrect results. In other words – these numbers are often unusable in a dynamic analysis app.

But there are ways to get around the problem:

Balances

Balances and other numbers describing a situation in time are usually semi-additive. They can be summed over all dimensions, except time. Adding the balance for one month with that of the next month would not make sense. But it *does* make sense to sum balances from different warehouses. So, for balances you need to adapt the expression to reflect this. If your data contains one balance number per month, you can often use an expression similar to one of the following:

```
Sum(Balance) / Count(distinct Month)                    // Average
FirstSortedValue(Aggr(Sum(Balance), Month), -Month) // Last value
```

The first expression will calculate an average over relevant numbers. The second will sort them and pick the last possible value.

In the table below, you can see the population for some countries during four years. By dividing the sum by the number of years, the semi-additive population can be used also in the total column.

Sum(Population) / Count(distinct Year)					
Country	Year	2011	2012	2013	2014	Total
Denmark		5 570 572	5 591 572	5 614 932	5 639 565	5 604 160
France		65 342 776	65 639 975	65 925 498	66 206 930	65 778 795
Germany		81 797 673	80 425 823	80 645 605	80 889 505	80 939 652
Italy		59 379 449	59 539 717	60 233 948	61 336 387	60 122 375
Netherlands		16 693 074	16 754 962	16 804 432	16 854 183	16 776 663
Spain		46 742 697	46 773 055	46 620 045	46 404 602	46 635 100
Sweden		9 449 213	9 519 374	9 600 379	9 689 555	9 564 630
United Kingdom		63 258 918	63 700 300	64 106 779	64 510 376	63 894 093
United States		311 721 632	314 112 078	316 497 531	318 857 056	315 297 074
Total		**659 956 004**	**662 056 856**	**666 049 149**	**670 388 159**	**664 612 542**

Ratios

Ratios, percentages and averages are usually non-additive numbers. Examples are the gross margin and the average order value. If you have such fields in your source data, it is likely that your data already has been aggregated once. Such fields are often calculated by dividing one number with another, e.g. by expressions similar to the following:

```
(Sum (Revenue) - Sum(CostOfGoods)) / Sum(Revenue) // Gross margin
Sum (OrderValue)  / Count (distinct OrderID)   // Avg order value
```

Note that the numerators and the denominators all are additive numbers!

Hence, if you have the original numerator and the denominator in your source data, you should use these to calculate your measures, instead of the pre-calculated ratios. In other words: Use the above expressions as measures in charts or gauges to define your gross margin and average order value. Do not use the pre-calculated ratios.

Mixed Units

In some cases, you have mixed units in a field, which makes the numbers non-additive. The most common case is that you have mixed currencies. This is a problem that is easily solved: Just convert the numbers to a common currency or common unit already in the script, by multiplying with the appropriate currency rate, e.g.

```
LocalCurrency * CurrencyRate as CommonCurrency,
```

Then you can use the common currency as an additive field. You may need a join or an Applymap() to get the correct currency rate into the fact table.

Incomplete Data

There is also the case of incomplete data, i.e. where you have the total number and the numbers for some parts, but data is missing for some other parts. For example, you may have the populations for Europe's ten largest countries along with a total for Europe. In such a case, you need to convert this source table to a complete set of data, e.g. by removing the "Total" record and introducing an "Others" record that is calculated from the total minus the sum of all known parts.

Bottom line: If you have semi-additive or non-additive numbers, you need to convert these to something usable using one of the methods described here. If you can't, the numbers are almost useless and you should use the Only() function when you display them, thereby preventing a summation.

AND and OR

Posted in the Qlik Design Blog Mar 18, 2014

In the Qlik engine, the logic of the selections is always an OR (a union) between values in the same field, and an AND (an intersection) between selections in different fields. Selecting e.g. two products and one customer is very much like the WHERE clause in the following SELECT statement:

```
SELECT ...
   WHERE (Product='Cap' OR Product='Tracksuit')
   AND    Customer='ACME'
```

Note the "OR" and the "AND".

Under some special circumstances, you can however in QlikView use something called AND-mode. With AND-mode you can select two different products and find the customers that bought both.

However, the AND-mode logic is quite different from a standard AND operator in a WHERE clause: And it does not work at all the same way as OR-logic. There are theoretical implications that do not exist for OR logic.

For example: If you select two products and demand an OR between them, the possible values of all other fields are immediately determined: Any field value implied by either of the products is marked as "possible".

But if you instead demand an AND between them, it is not clear what you mean: Do you mean "**Customers**" that have bought both products, or do you mean "**Months**" when both products have been sold? Or do you mean "**Countries**" where both products have been sold? Just specifying the two products is *not* enough to determine a result. You also need to specify the field that the AND-mode refers to.

The example shows that the AND-mode demands *an intermediate iterator*: The AND-mode always infers a second field for which the AND-logic is relevant. This is a theoretical problem that has nothing to do with how the logic is implemented in the software.

Let's look at SQL: In a standard SELECT statement, the conditions on either side of the AND operator almost always concern two different fields. It would not make sense to demand the following:

```
SELECT ...
    WHERE Product='Cap' AND Product='Tracksuit'
```

In a normalized database there are <u>no individual records</u> that fulfill that requirement: "**Product**" can only have one value at a time. But this is exactly the type of requirement that you have in AND-mode – however operating on a group of records instead of on a single record.

If you implement something similar to AND-mode in SQL, you will need to join a table with a copy of itself. The following will pick out customers that have bought both a Cap and a Tracksuit:

```
SELECT DISTINCT  Customer
    FROM         Orders      AS Orders1
    INNER JOIN   Orders      AS Orders2
    ON           Orders1.Customer=Orders2.Customer
    WHERE        Orders1.Product ='Cap'
        AND      Orders2.Product ='Tracksuit'
```

Again, an intermediate iterator is needed: Here it is "Customer" – the field used to join the two tables.

In the Qlik engine we have chosen to solve this problem by demanding a two-column table for AND-mode, where the first column defines the iterator (e.g. Customer), and the second is the field where the user makes the AND selection (e.g. Product).

So, the two-column table is not just an arbitrary limitation; it is instead a framework implied by the theoretical problem.

IEEE double binary

Internally in the Qlik engine most numbers are stored as double precision binary64, or more specifically, as IEEE 754 double-precision binary floating-point. This format is very common and has the advantage that there are many software libraries available for development. One example is the Cephes Mathematical Functions Library that the engine uses for many statistical functions.

The format uses 64 bits to represent a number. One bit for the sign, 11 bits for the exponent, and 52 bits for the mantissa (the significand).

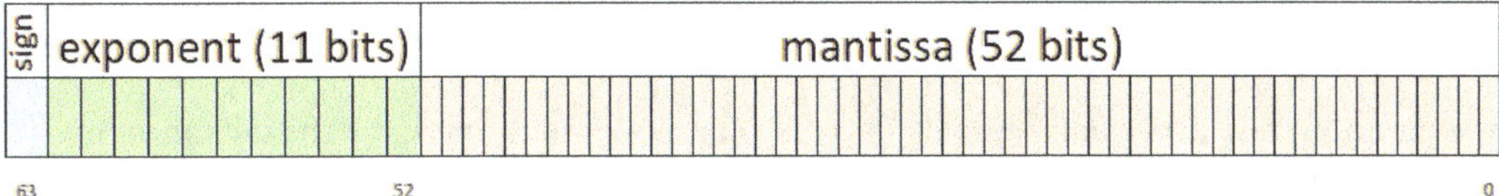

The mantissa is really 53 bits, since the first digit always is assumed to be 1 and isn't stored anywhere. It is just assumed.

This, however, means a limitation: The precision is limited to 14-16 decimal digits. This is usually not a problem though, since it is very rare that higher precision is needed.

An example: With 14 digits, all points in time between year 1547 and 2252 can be represented down to milliseconds.

A second example: The US gross domestic product is 23 trillion dollars (2021). This amount is not a problem for the Qlik engine. It fits within the 14 digits. Every dollar will be counted.

It should be noted that the range is not affected – just the precision. So, you can use timestamps long after year 2252, but you will then lose the millisecond precision. And you can use amounts that far exceed the US GDP, but you will then have to accept that small rounding effects will occur.

A consequence is that a Qlik script will not be able to correctly interpret numbers with more than 14 digits. You can however work around this problem by using the Evaluate function. The following will work fine, and a rounded number will be loaded:

```
Evaluate('123456789012345678890') as LargeNumber
```

But if you load the same string without the Evaluate function, the number interpretation will fail.

Internally, the Qlik engine will in most cases use 16 digits for the calculations.

A second consequence of the double binary format is that many decimal numbers cannot be represented exactly. But more about that in the next article.

Rounding Errors

Posted in the Qlik Design Blog Dec 17, 2013

> "If you use equality as a condition when comparing floats, I will flunk you!"

I can still hear the words of the Professor in my first programming class when studying for my engineering degree. The threat was very real – *he meant it* – and the reason was of course the fact that you cannot always represent decimal numbers in an exact binary form.

For example, we would never dream of writing a condition like

    If(x = 0.3333333 , ...)

when we want to test if x equals a third. *Never*. Because we all know that a third cannot be represented exactly as a decimal number. No matter how many digits we add to the number, it will still not be exact.

But it is not uncommon that people make comparisons with an exact decimal number, similar to

    If(x = 0.01 , ...)

thinking that it is a valid comparison, although it internally leads to *exactly* the same problem as the previous comparison! This becomes obvious if you look at the hexadecimal representation of 0.01:

    0.01 (decimal) = 0.028F5C28F5C28F.... (hex)

The sequence …28F5C… is repeated an infinite number of times, but since the Qlik engine uses a finite number of binary digits (all according to the IEEE standard), it will internally use a "rounded" number.

So, what are the consequences? Well, the Qlik engine will sometimes deliver the "wrong" number as result. Examples:

- Ceil(0.15, 0.01)   will return 0.16
- Floor(0.34, 0.01)   will return 0.33
- 0.175 * 1000 = 175   will return FALSE
- Time(Floor(Time#('04:00:00'),1/24/60/60))   will return 03:59:59

What you see are not errors in Qlik. And they are not errors in IEEE 754. Rather, they represent errors in the expectation and usage of binary floating-point numbers. Once you understand what binary floating-point numbers really are, it makes perfect sense. It's simply that some values cannot be exactly represented as binary numbers, so you get rounding errors. There's no way around it.

Should you want to investigate this yourself, I suggest you start with the following script that generates 100 numbers and their rounded counterparts. In five cases the Ceil() function rounds "incorrectly" and generates a "Diff" different from zero:

```
Load
   Num(Rounded,'(HEX) 0.000000000000000','.',' ') as RoundedHEX,
   (Round(100*Rounded) - PartsPer100)/100        as Diff,
   *;
Load
   Ceil(PartsPer100/100, 0.01)                    as Rounded,
   PartsPer100/100                                as OriginalNumber,
   *;
Load
   RecNo()                                        as PartsPer100
   Autogenerate 100 ;
```

So, what should you do?

First, you should realize that the rounding errors are small and usually insignificant. In most cases they will not affect the result of the analysis.

Further, you could avoid rounding with Floor() and Ceil() to sub-integer fractions.

Also, you could convert the numbers to integers, because the errors will only appear if the numbers can have sub-integer components. For instance, if you know that you always deal with dollars and cents, you could convert the numbers to (integer) cents:

```
Round( 100*Amount )      as Cents,
```

Or if you know that you never deal with time units smaller than seconds:

```
Round( 24*60*60*Time )   as Seconds,
```

And finally, you should _never_ use equality as a condition when comparing floats. Use greater than or less than. My professor isn't here to flunk you, but rest assured: *In his absence, the Qlik engine will do it for him.*

PS

Some of the above has been improved since this article was written. The Qlik engine today contains logic that removes some – but not all – of these effects.

Simpson's paradox

Data is multidimensional – meaning that it is possible to break it down in many ways. For example, sales numbers can be broken down by **Customer**, **Product**, **Sales campaign**, **Time**, etc. Often, you do not understand the data until you have seen it broken down by the relevant dimensions.

These dimensions are usually uncorrelated, and as long as they are, data is usually easy to understand.

But beware – if you have correlations between the different dimensions, the result can be counterintuitive, and you will be tempted to draw conclusions that aren't necessary true. One such example is *Simpson's paradox*.

Let's look at an example:

In the fall of 1973, a study was made at the University of California in Berkeley on gender bias among graduate school admissions. It found a statistically significant difference in admittance numbers between men and women: Men applying were more likely than women to be admitted.

Gender 🔍	Values	
	Applicants	Admitted
Totals	4526	39%
Men	2691	45%
Women	1835	30%

As you can see, there was a clear difference in admittance rate between men (45%) and women (30%). And the statistical sample is large – the statistical uncertainty for the percentages is only around ±1.3%, so the difference between 45% and 30% is certainly statistically significant.

*But the bias is still **<u>not</u>** there…*

The reason is that we haven't yet looked at other factors: There were different departments, and there was a correlation between the departments and the sexes: Men and women had different preference for what department to apply to.

If you use the same data, but break it down by department, you get a different picture:

Department 🔍	Gender 🔍	Values		
	Men		Women	
	Applicants	Admitted	Applicants	Admitted
Totals	2691	45%	1835	30%
A	825	62%	108	82%
B	560	63%	25	68%
C	325	37%	593	34%
D	417	33%	375	35%
E	191	28%	393	24%
F	373	6%	341	7%

Here you can see that some departments had low admittance rates – for *both* men and women – and these were departments preferred by women. See department C, D, E, and F. Whereas department A and B had high admittance rates and were preferred by men.

Women chose departments with low admittance rates.

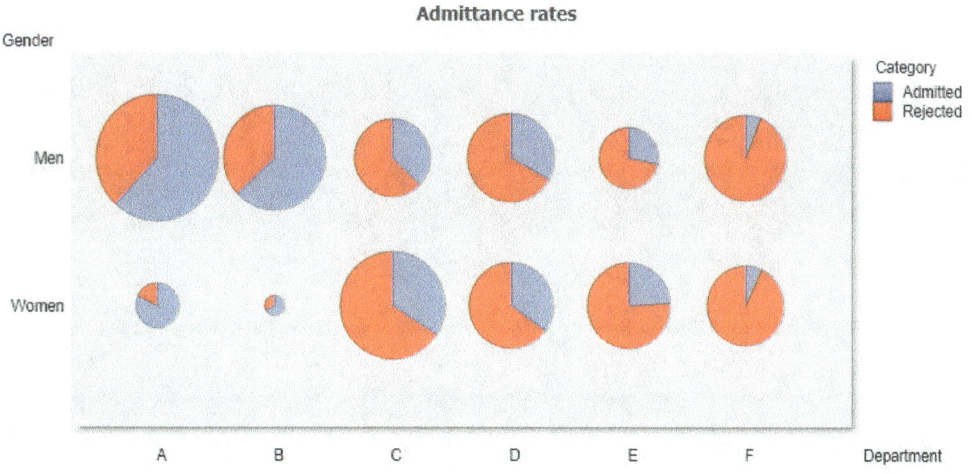

In other words: The bias that we see in the totals is caused by an innate correlation between **Gender** and **Department**; something we would never have discovered unless we make a chart with these two dimensions together.

What do we learn from this?

Well, correlations can deceive. We always try to look for reasons for correlations, and in this case, you may initially draw the conclusion that the correlation is caused by a bias in the admittance process. But it turns out that the bias has another reason.

So, the conclusion must be that you need to look at data from different angles, using different dimensions, before you can say that you understand it.

3

The Load Script

The first thing you need to do when you build an app is to load data into it. This is done by creating a load script that defines the tables and fields that should be loaded.

This chapter is about writing such scripts and how to solve many data challenges when doing so.

Graphical Script Generation

In Qlik Sense there is a graphical way of generating the script – the user can in a graphical UI define what to load and how to link tables. This has the important advantage that it helps the novices to get going and allows a broad group of normal users to create their own apps.

It can also help skilled users by speeding up the process of generating an initial script – a script that later can be manually modified, if necessary.

But the graphical script generation also has disadvantages: The graphical UI obscures what really happens behind the curtains and prevents the user from doing advanced things. Advanced transformations are either impossible or difficult to define. Most solutions described in this, and next chapter are not possible to achieve with graphical script generation.

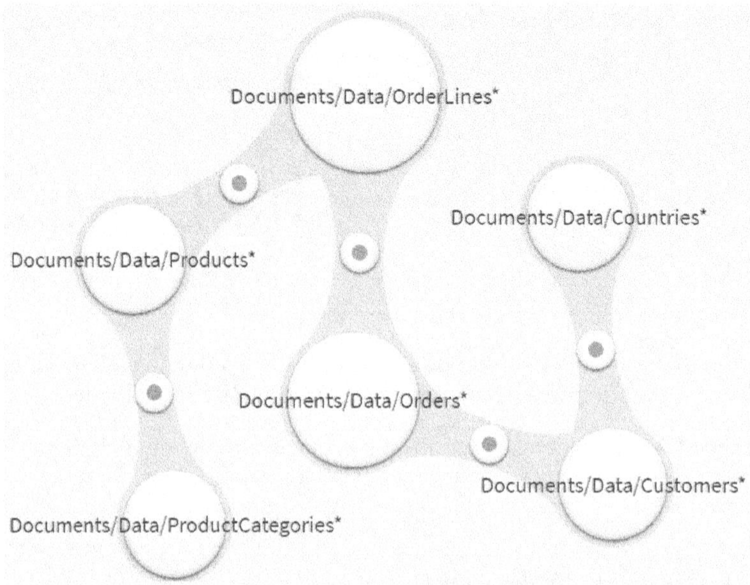

The first group of operations that is difficult to achieve, is transformations that need multiple steps:

- Loops
- Bespoke mapping tables
  If you need a mapping table used for data cleansing or to rename fields.
- As-of tables
  To handle accumulations, "As-of"-tables are sometimes needed.
- Temporary tables
  Transformations that need a second pass through a table often need the first table to be a temporary one – a table that must be dropped later in the script.

The second group of operations is advanced transformations that need prefixes:

- Crosstables
- Generic databases
- Hierarchies
- Slowly changing dimensions and IntervalMatch

Some of the above operations *are* in fact possible to achieve in a graphical UI, but I argue that the graphical UI does not make it easier: Rather, the UI obfuscates the needed transformations and makes the development process more difficult.

Further, the data load process must be manageable: It has to be possible to take an already defined load sequence and tweak it according to a given change request. And that is almost impossible with a graphical UI. So, in a governed, controlled environment, I cannot see how a graphical data load definition can be used in the long run.

Hence: If you want to do anything more that loading already well-structured, prepared tables, then you need to enter the script editor and start writing scripts.

So, I strongly recommend that you start using the Data Load Editor. Only then can you use temporary tables, load hierarchies, create "As-of"-tables, create canonical dates, and use dollar expansions.

Only then can you learn and use the full power of the Qlik load script.

Script basics

The first thing you need to do is to create a new app. In Qlik Sense, this is done by choosing "New analytics app" under the plus sign in the top bar. In QlikView, you choose "New" in the file menu.

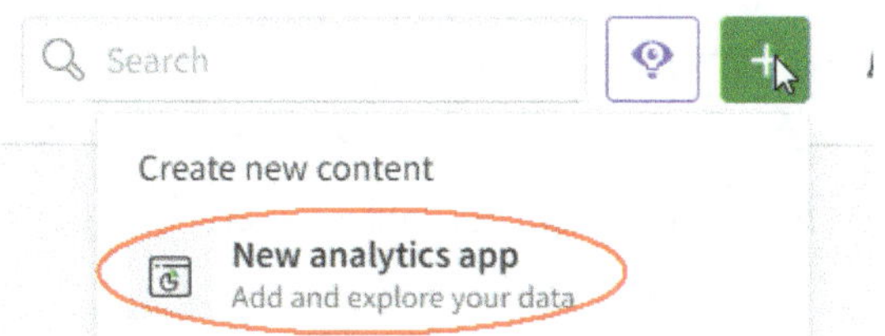

Once created, you need to open the Data Load Editor. This is done by choosing "Data load editor" under "Prepare" in the top bar. In QlikView, you choose "Edit Script" in the file menu.

Once in the script editor, you need to create a connection to a data source. This could be a database or a folder with files. Try the "Create new connection button" to find your data. I use a OneDrive connection, so I can use files stored in the cloud.

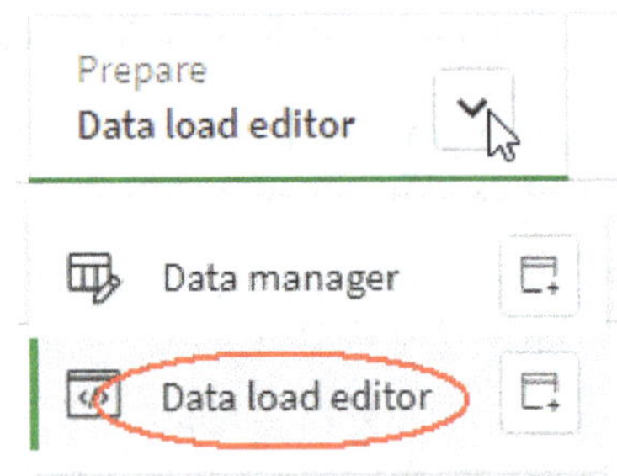

Once that is done, you can start loading your files. You can select a file by using the lower left button in your connection. The corresponding button in QlikView is called "Table Files…".

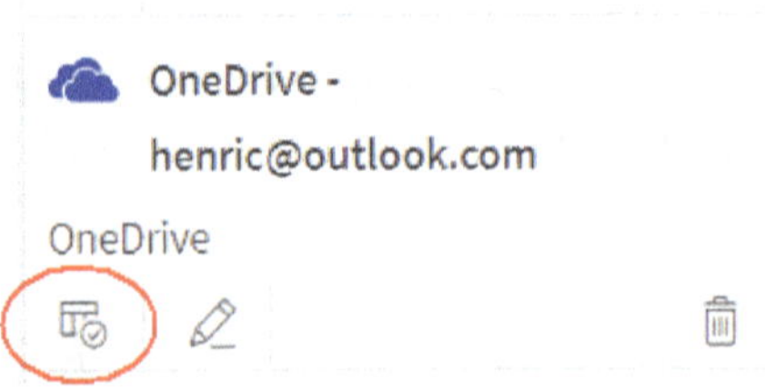

At this stage, it is up to you to start loading your tables, by creating Load or SELECT statements.

Some rules:

- **One Load statement – One table**
  Each Load or SELECT statement will normally create exactly one output table. Hence, if you want three tables in your data model, you need three load statements. However, there are some exceptions
  - **Auto-concatenation**
    If two Load statements result in identical sets of fields, the result of the second Load will be appended to the result of the first Load.
  - **Prefix**
    Some prefixes will invalidate the above rule, e.g. Join, Concatenate, and Generic.
- **Associations – not joins**
  A Qlik app can have a multi-table data model, where associations (links) are made between tables. So, usually, there is no need to make explicit joins in the script.

- **Automatic associations on field names**
  Tables are linked through field names, so if a field name exists in two or more tables, this field is considered a key. The association is always a natural join, i.e. the same value in both tables will link the records.

- **Connect statement**
  A Connect statement defines the default database and will affect all subsequent SELECT statements. A new Connect statement will cancel the previous one.

- **Directory statement**
  A Directory statement defines the default folder and will affect all subsequent Load statements. A new Directory statement will cancel the previous one.
  Example: (Note that the Lib-path is in the Directory statement, and not in the Load statement.)

```
Directory lib://OneDrive - henric@outlook.com/Data/ ;
Load * From [Orders.txt] (txt, utf8, delimiter is '\t') ;
Load * From [OrderLines.txt] (txt, utf8, delimiter is '\t');
```

- **Lib-paths vs File system paths**
  Qlik Sense must have Lib-paths. It cannot use file system paths, e.g. 'C:\Folder'. QlikView must have file system paths. It can currently not use Lib-paths.

With this, you have enough knowledge to start testing your own scripts.

Preceding Load

Originally posted in the Qlik Design Blog on Mar 4, 2013

A Qlik script feature that is poorly known and brilliant in its simplicity is the *Preceding Load*. If you don't know what it is, then I strongly suggest that you read this article and find out. Because it will help you in your Qlik scripting.

So, what is it?

It is a way for you to define successive transformations and filters so that you can load a table *in one pass* but still have several transformation steps. Basically, it is a Load statement that loads from the next Load/SELECT statement in the script.

Example: You have a database where your dates are stored as strings, and you want to use the Qlik date functions to interpret these. But the Qlik date functions are not available in the SELECT statement. The solution is to put a Load statement in front of the SELECT statement:

```
Load Date#(OrderDate,'YYYYMMDD') as OrderDate ;
SQL SELECT OrderDate FROM … ;
```

Note the absence of the keyword "From" or "Resident" in the Load statement.

What happens then is that the SELECT statement is evaluated first, and the result is piped into the Load statement that does the date interpretation. The fact that the SELECT statement is evaluated *before* the Load, is at first glance confusing, but it is not so strange. If you read a Preceding Load as

$$Load\ From\ (\ Select\ From\ (\ DB\_TABLE\ )\ )$$

and regard each pair of brackets as a table, then it becomes clearer.

Compare it with nested functions: How would you evaluate "Round(Exp(x))". You would of course evaluate the Exp() function first and then the Round() function. That is, you evaluate it from right to left.

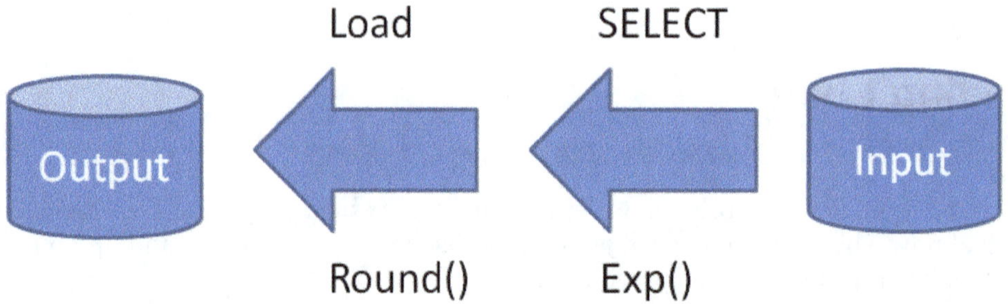

The reason is that the Exp() function is closest to the source data, and therefore should be evaluated first. It's the same with the Preceding Load: The SELECT is closest to the source data and should therefore be evaluated first. In both cases, you can look at it as a transformation that has an input and an output and to do it correctly, you need to start with the part of the transformation closest to the input.

Any number of Loads can be "nested" this way. The Qlik engine will start from the bottom and pipe record by record to the closest preceding Load, then to the next, etc. And it is *almost always* faster than running a second pass through the same table.

With preceding Load, you don't need to have the same calculation in several places. For instance, instead of writing

```
Load
    Age ( FromDate + IterNo() - 1, BirthDate )   as Age,
    Date( FromDate + IterNo() - 1 )              as ReferenceDate,
    *

    Resident Policies
    While IterNo() <= ToDate - FromDate + 1 ;
```

where the same calculation is made for both **Age** and **ReferenceDate**, I would in real life define my **ReferenceDate** only once and then use it in the **Age** function in a Preceding Load:

```
Load
    Age ( ReferenceDate, BirthDate )             as Age,
    *;
Load
    Date( FromDate + IterNo() - 1 )              as ReferenceDate,
    *

    Resident Policies
    While IterNo() <= ToDate - FromDate + 1 ;
```

This way I have only one place where I define my calculation.

The Preceding Load has no disadvantages. Use it. You'll love it.

Resident Load and Temporary Tables

In some situations, you need to use already loaded tables as a source. The Load statement has a syntax for this, called Resident Load. *This article is about how this is done.*

There are several cases when you want to use an already loaded table as a source for a second table. Then you should use a Resident Load. One common and simple case is the Master Calendar, where you want to create a separate table from the dates found in a larger transaction table:

```
Orders:
Load OrderID, Date, Amount                       From <SourceTable>;

MasterCalendar:
Load distinct Date, Year(Date), Month(Date), … Resident Orders ;
```

Note that the second Load statement uses the keyword "Resident" and not "From". The Load statement will then use the **Orders** table as input.

Another common case is when you want to calculate something that isn't possible to calculate directly when the source data is loaded. Then you may need to load the initial data into a temporary table, transform this, and subsequently load the relevant data from the temporary table. See e.g. *"How to populate a sparsely populated field"*.

Finally, the temporary table needs to be discarded. This is done through

```
Drop Table TempTable ;
```

Temporary tables can also be used to transform slightly unstructured data into something usable. For example, Excel files often have rows with section labels inserted between the data records, and these cannot be loaded directly.

For example, in the table to the right, you have a list of countries and the respective population. But you also have the continents inserted like section headers. How would you load this?

First, you would need to find a condition that defines the "Continent" rows. Here, we can see that only the "Country" records have a number in the "Population" column. The other rows are "Continent" rows.

You can use this information to separate the continent information from the country information when loading the data. First, you mark the record as either a "Country" record or a "Continent" record – the "IsCountry" field. Then you use this flag to conditionally define a new field "**Continent**":

	A	B
1	**Country**	**Population**
2	**Africa**	
3	Nigeria	206139589
4	South Africa	59308690
5	**Asia**	
6	China	1439323776
7	India	1380004385
8	Japan	126476461
9	**Australia and Oceania**	
10	Australia	25499884
11	New Zealand	4822233
12	**Europe**	
13	France	65273511
14	Germany	83783942
15	Sweden	10099265
16	United Kingdom	67886011
17	**North America**	
18	Canada	37742154
19	United States of America	331002651
20	**South America**	
21	Argentina	45195774
22	Brazil	212559417

```
tmpCountries:
 Load
   If( IsCountry, Peek(Continent), Country)      as Continent,
   * ;
Load
   If(Len(Population)>0, 1, 0 )                   as IsCountry,
   Country,
   Population
   From Populations.xlsx ;

Countries:
NoConcatenate Load
   Continent,
   Country,
   Population
   Resident tmpCountries
   Where IsCountry;

Drop Table tmpCountries;
```

This way you have created a new field "**Continent**" and you have removed the unnecessary records.

Note the prefix "**NoConcatenate**". It prevents the automatic concatenation of two tables. In this case, it is not necessary since the two tables have different sets of fields, but it is good practice to do so anyway. I cannot count the times that the auto-concatenation has kicked in without me realizing it, and the Drop statement has removed the table I wanted to keep…

Window functions

In SQL and many business intelligence tools, there are functions referred to as "window functions". These perform calculations using values from multiple rows to produce a value for each row separately. They can only be calculated once the entire table is read. Examples:

- Comparing an individual number with the average, max or min within the group

- Calculating the rank of an individual value, either within the group or within the entire table

The window functions do not change the number of records of the table but can still perform similar tasks as aggregation functions, or Qlik Relational functions and Range functions. One example is to calculate an aggregate, and assign this to each relevant row:

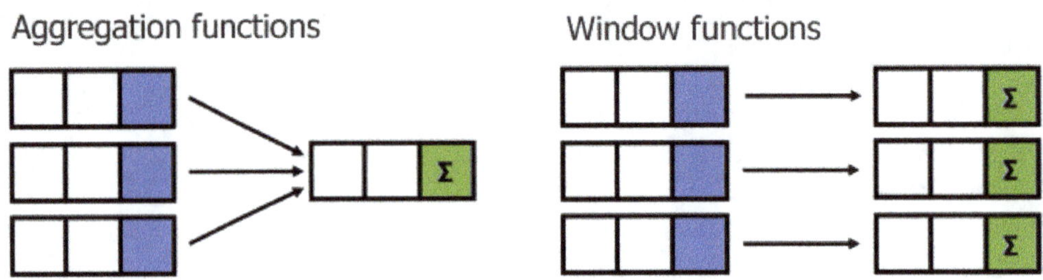

The left picture corresponds to a normal aggregation. In SQL this could be written e.g.

```
SELECT
    Department,
    AVG( Salary )                    AS AvgSalary
FROM Employees
GROUP BY Department ;
```

The right picture would correspond to a window function that assigns the same aggregate value to each row in the table, e.g.

```
SELECT
    Name,
    Department,
    Salary,
    AVG( Salary ) OVER
        ( PARTITION BY Department )    AS AvgSalary
FROM Employees ;
```

Both these statements calculate the average salary within a department, but the result is used in different ways. Note that

- The aggregation functions collapse many records into one, whereas the window functions do not.

- In the normal aggregation, the grouping is performed for the entire table (the "GROUP BY"), whereas it is performed on the field level for the windows functions (the "PARTITION BY").

Not all window functions perform aggregations. Some perform ranking and numbering. For example, the following will calculate the seniority among all the employees. It reorders the records by age, and assigns a row number so that the oldest employee gets seniority 1:

```
SELECT
    Name,
    ROW_NUMBER() OVER
        ( ORDER BY Age DESC )              AS Seniority
FROM Employees ;
```

The following will do the same, but now within each department:

```
SELECT
    Name,
    ROW_NUMBER() OVER
        ( PARTITION BY Department ORDER BY Age DESC )
                                    AS Seniority
FROM Employees ;
```

A SQL window function can hence contain either a partitioning or an ordering, or both.

Window functions have recently been added to the capabilities of the Qlik engine. See more in the Qlik help.

However, all of the above can be achieved in the Qlik script using a combination of temporary tables, resident loads, and joins. So, workarounds creating the relevant functionality can be achieved also in earlier versions of the Qlik engine. For example, the above example with average salary can be created by using a resident load and a join.

```
Employees:
Load Name, Department, Salary From Employees;
Join (Employees)
Load
    Avg(Salary) as AvgSalary,
    Department
    Resident Employees
    Group By Department;
```

And if you want to calculate the rank of something, like the seniority above, this can be achieved in a similar way:

```
Employees:
Load Name, Age From Employees ;
Join (Employees)
Load
    Name,
    RecNo() as Seniority
    Resident Employees
    Order By Age Desc;
```

And with this, I leave you to test window functions on your own.

Merging Data from Multiple Sources

Posted in the Qlik Design Blog Jan 14, 2014

A common situation in Business Intelligence is that you have data in different data sources. It could e.g. be that you have several data systems within your company or that you have some data in an Excel spreadsheet in addition to the data in your database.

In any case, you want to load data from several sources and view them in a coherent way. This is sometimes referred to as *merging data* or *blending data*.

Not all BI tools can do this – you sometimes have to rely on external tools or SQL to do this prior to loading the data into your BI tool. The Qlik engine, however, can do this easily.

If you have two different database systems, you need two different connect strings in the script:

```
ODBC CONNECT TO        Database_1  ;
SQL SELECT * FROM      TableA      ;
ODBC CONNECT TO        Database_2  ;
SQL SELECT * FROM      TableB      ;
```

At any place in the script, a SELECT statement will use the latest CONNECT string. In addition, LOAD statements will load data from files, disregarding the CONNECT statement. This way you can merge data from any number of databases and any number of files. Simple!

The next question is *how* to merge the two tables. In principle there are two ways to do this: Concatenating them (a union) or linking them (joining). Which one to use depends on the situation.

Customer	Country	CustomerID
Alfreds Futterkiste	Germany	ALFKI
Around the Horn	UK	AROUT
Berglunds snabbköp	Sweden	BERGS
Blondel père et fils	France	BLONP

Customer	Country	CustomerID
Bottom-Dollar Markets	Canada	BOTTM
Great Lakes Food Market	USA	GREAL
Hungry Coyote Import Store	USA	HUNGC
Laughing Bacchus Wine Cellars	Canada	LAUGB

Concatenation should be used, if you have two tables with basically the same type of entity, but different data sets: for example, "Customers in Europe" and "Customers in North America". In this case, you want both tables to be merged into one. See picture above.

The script then becomes:

```
ODBC CONNECT TO        Database_1  ;
SQL SELECT * FROM      Customers   ;
ODBC CONNECT TO        Database_2  ;
Concatenate
SQL SELECT * FROM      Customers   ;
```

But if you instead have a situation where the tables contain *different* entities, and a selection of an entity in one of the tables should imply one or several entities in the other table, then you should usually link the tables.

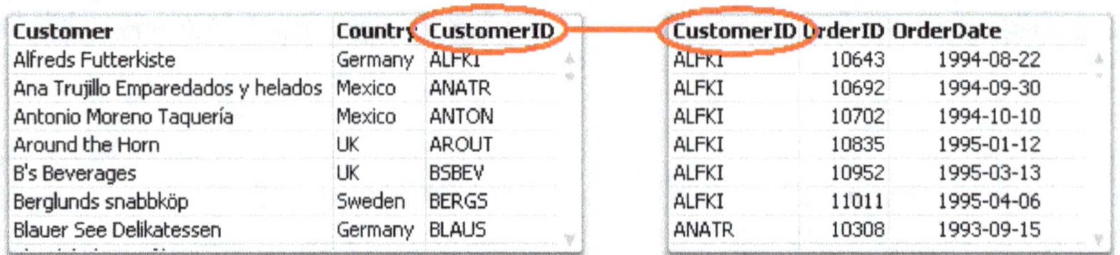

Customer	Country	CustomerID		CustomerID	OrderID	OrderDate
Alfreds Futterkiste	Germany	ALFKI		ALFKI	10643	1994-08-22
Ana Trujillo Emparedados y helados	Mexico	ANATR		ALFKI	10692	1994-09-30
Antonio Moreno Taquería	Mexico	ANTON		ALFKI	10702	1994-10-10
Around the Horn	UK	AROUT		ALFKI	10835	1995-01-12
B's Beverages	UK	BSBEV		ALFKI	10952	1995-03-13
Berglunds snabbköp	Sweden	BERGS		ALFKI	11011	1995-04-06
Blauer See Delikatessen	Germany	BLAUS		ANATR	10308	1993-09-15

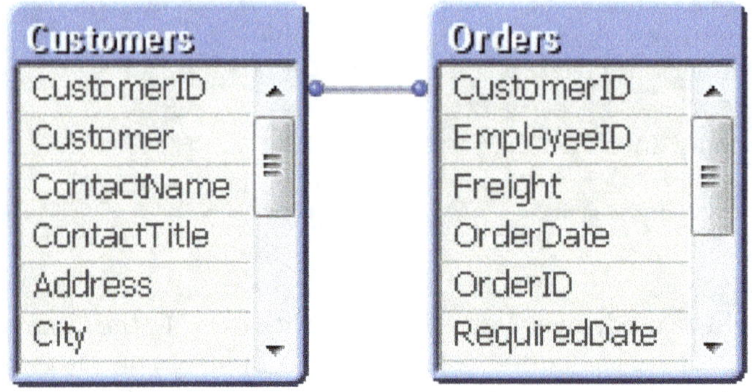

The script then instead becomes:

```
ODBC CONNECT TO      Database_1  ;
SQL SELECT * FROM    Customers   ;
ODBC CONNECT TO      Database_2  ;
SQL SELECT * FROM    Orders      ;
```

Linking tables is from a logical-mathematical perspective identical to an outer join, but the Qlik engine keeps the two tables separate. Keeping them separate has the advantage that calculations are made in the "right table".

Not all BI tools can perform an outer join as easily as this. I recently read an article about how to join an "**Opportunities**" table with a "**Leads**" table using a competing tool, and it was all but simple. But with the Qlik engine, it is straightforward: Just make sure that the linking key field is named the same in both tables (and that no other fields are) and it will work right away.

The ability of the Qlik engine to load data from any number of sources and merge it any way you want is one of the major strengths of Qlik and its script. Use it.

The Crosstable Load

Originally posted in the Qlik Design Blog on Mar 25, 2014

There are a number of prefixes in the Qlik script, that help you load and transform data. One of them is the **Crosstable** transformation.

Whenever you have a cross table of data, the **Crosstable** prefix can be used to transform the data and create the desired fields. A cross table is basically a matrix where one of the fields is displayed vertically and another is displayed horizontally. In the input table below, you have a cross table with one column per month and one row per product.

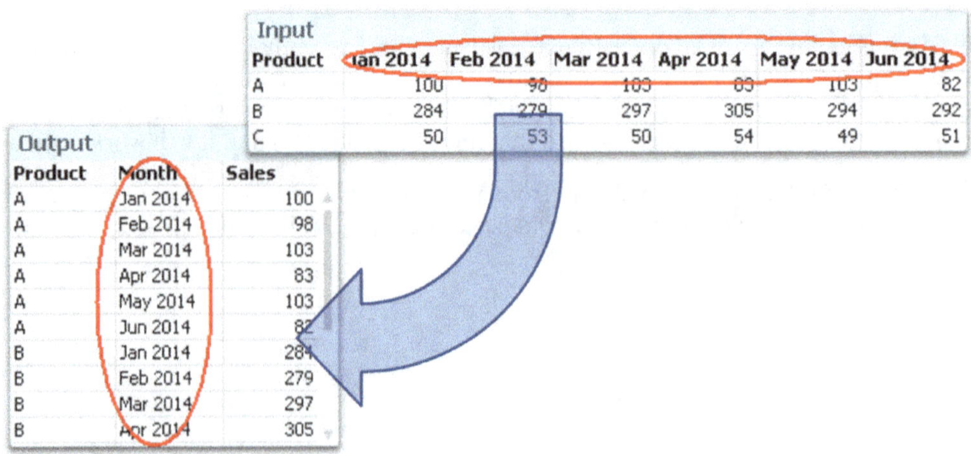

But if you want to analyze this data, it is much easier to have all sales numbers in one field and all months in another, i.e. in a three-column table. It is not very practical to have one column per month, since you want to use Month as dimension and Sum(**Sales**) as measure.

Enter the *Crosstable* prefix.

It converts the data to a table with one column for **Month** and another for **Sales**. Another way to express it is to say that it takes field names and converts these to field values. If you compare it to the **Generic** prefix, you will find that they in principle are each other's inverses.

The structure is

```
Crosstable (Month, Sales)
Load Product, [Jan 2014], [Feb 2014], [Mar 2014], … From … ;
```

There are however a couple of things worth noting:

- Usually, the input data has only one column as qualifier field; as internal key (**Product** in the above example). But you can have several. If so, all qualifying fields must be listed *before* the attribute fields, and the third parameter to the **Crosstable** prefix must be used to define the number of qualifying fields.

- It is not possible to have a preceding Load or a prefix in front of the **Crosstable** keyword. Auto-concatenate will however work.

- The numeric interpretation will not work for the attribute fields. This means that if you have months as column headers, these will not be automatically interpreted as dates. The work-around is to use the **Crosstable** prefix to create a temporary table, and to run a second pass through it to make the proper interpretations:

```
tmpData:
Crosstable (MonthText, Sales)
Load Product, [Jan 2014], [Feb 2014], [Mar 2014], … From Data;

Final:
Load Product,
    Date(Date#(MonthText,'MMM YYYY'),'MMM YYYY') as Month,
    Sales
    Resident tmpData;

Drop Table tmpData;
```

Finally, if your source is a cross table and you also want to display the data as a cross table, it might be tempting to load the data as it is, without any transformation.

But I strongly recommend that you don't. A **Crosstable** transformation simplifies everything, and you can still display your data as a cross table using a standard pivot table.

The Generic Load

Originally posted in the Qlik Design Blog on Apr 1, 2014

There are a number of prefixes in the Qlik script, that help you load and transform data. One of them is the **Generic** prefix.

Whenever you have a generic database, the **Generic** prefix can be used to transform the data and create the desired fields. A generic database is basically a table where the second last column is an arbitrary attribute and the very last is the value of the attribute. In the input table below, you have a three-column generic database.

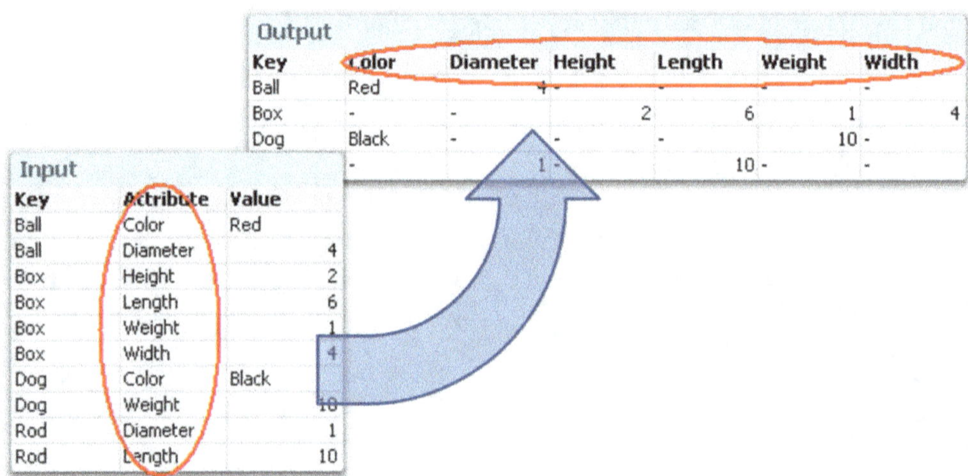

But if you want to analyze this data, it is much easier to have all attributes in separate fields so that you can make the appropriate selections. It is not very practical to have one single field for all attribute values, since you may want to make selections using different attributes at the same time.

Enter the *Generic* prefix.

It converts the data to a structure where each attribute is placed in a field of its own. Another way to express it is to say that it takes field values and converts these to field names. If you compare it to the **Crosstable** prefix, you will find that they in principle are each other's inverses.

The structure is

```
Generic
Load Key, Attribute, Value From … ;
```

There are however a couple of things worth noting:

- Usually, the input data has three columns: one qualifier field (**Key** in the above example), an **Attribute** and a **Value**. But you may also have several qualifying fields. If you have four or more columns, all columns except the two last will be treated as qualifying fields.

- The **Generic** prefix will create several tables: one table per attribute. This is normally not a problem. Rather, it is an advantage: It is the least memory-consuming way to store data if you have many attributes.

- If you have more than one key, this means that you will get a composite key – a synthetic key – in the data model:

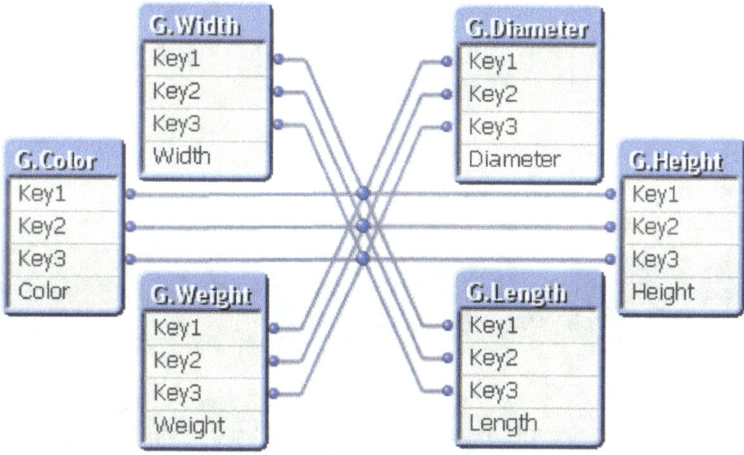

Although it looks ugly, this synthetic key is completely harmless. However, it may still be a good idea to replace it with a manually created concatenated key:

```
Autonumber( Key1 & '|' & Key2 & '|' & Key3 ) as Key,
```

Finally, I have seen many examples on QlikCommunity where a For-Next loop is used to join together all tables created by the Generic prefix, for example:

```
Set vListOfTables = ;
For vTableNo = 0 to NoOfTables()
    Let vTableName = TableName($(vTableNo)) ;
    If Subfield(vTableName,'.',1) = 'GenericLabel' Then
        Let vListOfTables = vListOfTables &
            If(Len(vListOfTables)>0,',')  &
            Chr(39) & vTableName & Chr(39) ;
    End If
Next vTableNo

CombinedGenericTable:
Load distinct Key
    From GenericDB ;

For each vTableName in $(vListOfTables)
    Left Join (CombinedGenericTable)
    Load *
        Resident [$(vTableName)];
    Drop Table [$(vTableName)] ;
Next vTableName
```

The result is one big table that contains all attributes; a table that often is sparse (containing many NULL values) and much larger than the initial tables. And very little performance has been gained… So, I can only say:

You should normally not do this – unless you have a specific reason to. There are, however, cases where you want to transform the data further and need the data in one, unified table. Then the above script can be used. Just change the names of the tables 'GenericLabel' and 'GenericDB'.

The **Generic** prefix creates a set of tables that store the data in an optimal way. In most cases you should not change this.

Loops in the Script

Originally posted in the Qlik Design Blog on Sep 3, 2013

Iterations – or loops – are constructions where a set of statements are executed zero or more times, until some condition is met. They are very common in all programming languages, and Qlik scripting is no exception.

First, the Load statement is in itself a loop: For each record in the input table, the field values are read and appended to the output table. The record number is the loop counter, and once the record is read, the loop counter is increased by one and the next record is read. *Hence – a loop.*

But there are cases where you want to create other types of iterations – in addition to the Load statement.

For - Next Loops

Often you want a loop *outside* the Load statement. In other words, you enclose normal script statements with a control statement e.g. a "For…Next" to create a loop. An enclosed Load will then be executed several times, once for each value of the loop counter or until the exit condition is met.

The most common case is that you have several files with the same structure, e.g. log files, and you want to load all of them:

```
Set Path = C:\Path\      ;   // QlikView
Set Path = lib://Path/   ;   // Qlik Sense

For each vFile in Filelist('$(Path)*.txt')
   Load *,
       '$(vFile)' as FileName
       From "$(vFile)";
Next vFile
```

Documents library
Logs

Name	Date modified	Size
Log_File_2012_09_18.txt	2013-08-22 22:20	42 KB
Log_File_2012_09_25.txt	2013-08-22 22:20	42 KB
Log_File_2012_10_02.txt	2013-08-22 22:20	51 KB
Log_File_2012_10_09.txt	2013-08-22 22:20	26 KB
Log_File_2012_10_16.txt	2013-08-22 22:20	9 KB
Log_File_2012_10_23.txt	2013-08-22 22:20	28 KB
Log_File_2012_10_30.txt	2013-08-22 22:20	46 KB

Another common case is that you already have loaded a separate table listing the files you want to load. Then you need to loop over the rows in this table, fetch the file name using the Peek() function, and load the listed file:

```
For No = 1 to NoOfRows('FileList')
    Let vFile =
        Peek('File',No-1,'FileList');
    Load *,
        '$(vFile)' as FileName
        From "$(vFile)";
Next No
```

FileList

Date	File
2012-09-18	Log_File_2012_09_18.txt
2012-09-25	Log_File_2012_09_25.txt
2012-10-02	Log_File_2012_10_02.txt
2012-10-09	Log_File_2012_10_09.txt
2012-10-16	Log_File_2012_10_16.txt
2012-10-23	Log_File_2012_10_23.txt

Looping over the same record – using While

You can also have iterations *inside* the Load statement. I.e., during the execution of a Load statement the same input record is read several times. This will normally result in an output table that has more records than the input table. There are two ways to do this: Either by using a **While** clause or by calling the Subfield() function.

One common situation is that you have a table with intervals, and you want to generate all values between the beginning and the end of the interval. Then you would use a **While** clause where you can set a condition using the loop counter IterNo() to define the number of values to generate, i.e. how many times this record should be loaded:

```
Dates:
Load
    IntervalID,
    Date( FromDate + IterNo() - 1 ) as Date
    Resident Intervals
    While IterNo() <= ToDate - FromDate + 1 ;
```

Intervals

IntervalID	Product	FromDate	ToDate	Price
1	A	2010-01-01	2011-01-31	20
2	A	2011-02-01	2011-10-31	22
3	A	2011-11-01	2013-12-31	30
4	B	2010-01-01	2011-12-31	50
5	B	2012-01-01	2012-09-30	45
6	B	2012-10-01	2013-12-31	60

Dates

IntervalID	Date
1	2011-01-29
1	2011-01-30
1	2011-01-31
2	2011-02-01
2	2011-02-02
2	2011-02-03
2	2011-02-04
2	2011-02-05
2	2011-02-06

Looping over the same record – using SubField

Another common situation is that you have a list of values within one single field. This is a fairly common case when e.g. tags or skills are stored, since it then isn't clear how many tags or skills one object can have. In such a situation you would want to break up the skill list into separate records using the Subfield() function. This function is, when its third parameter is omitted, an implicit loop: The Load will read the entire record once per value in the list.

```
[Individual Skills]:
Load
    [Employee No],
    SubField(Skills, ',') as Skill
    Resident Employees;
```

Employees

Employee No	Skills
159	Economics,Pharmacology
163	Marketing,Sociology,Spanish
174	Bookkeeping,Particle physics
210	Economics,Marketing
215	Economics,Law,Marketing
279	Law,Marketing,German
286	Finance,Marketing,French,German
300	Bookkeeping,Finance

Individual skills

Employee No	Skill
159	Economics
159	Pharmacology
163	Marketing
163	Sociology
163	Spanish
174	Bookkeeping
174	Particle physics
210	Economics
210	Marketing

Bottom line: Iterations are powerful tools that can help you create a good data model. Use them.

Counters in the Load

Originally posted in the Qlik Design Blog on Sep 17, 2013

Often when you create scripts, you need to create new fields, based on counters. There are several ways to do this. Some are simple, others are more complicated.

RecNo()

The RecNo() function simply counts the *input* records and returns the number of the current record. Simple, and very useful if you want to create a record ID. However, if you concatenate several input files, or use a **While** clause, the numbers will not be unique.

```
RecNo() as ID,
```

RowNo()

The RowNo() function is very similar to the RecNo(), but this instead counts the *output* records and returns the number of the current record. Also this counter is simple and useful, especially if you concatenate several input tables. In such a case, the function will return consecutive numbers for the output table.

```
RowNo() as ID,
```

AutoNumber()

The AutoNumber() function is useful if you want to put a number on a specific field value, or on an attribute that is a combination of field values. The attributes will be numbered, and their numbers re-used appropriately.

```
AutoNumber( Product & '|' & Date ) as ID,
```

Inline Peek() together with RangeSum()

This is the mother of all record counters. Anything can be numbered; it can be done conditionally, and anything can be used as condition. The idea is to fetch the counter value from the previous record and increase it only if some condition is fulfilled. Or reset it.

An example: For production quality control, some process indicator is measured, and the Quality Manager wants to track trends and trend shifts. Then it is important to see the number of consecutive days that this indicator has increased or decreased. It is also good if the series of consecutive days has a unique ID that can be used for selections and charts.

The following script creates these two fields: **TrendID** and **DaysWithTrend**.

```
Load
    If( SameTrendAsPrevious,
        Peek( TrendID ),            //  No trend shift: Same TrendID
        RangeSum(1,Peek(TrendID)) //  Trend shift: New TrendID
        )
                                        as TrendID,
    If( SameTrendAsPrevious,
        RangeSum(1,Peek(DaysWithTrend)),
        0
        )
                                        as DaysWithTrend,
    * ;
Load
    If(Change*Peek(Change)>0, 1, 0)     as SameTrendAsPrevious,
    * ;
Load
    Indicator,
    Indicator - Peek( Indicator )     as Change
    Resident Daily_TQM_Measurement
    Order By Date;
```

Bottom Load statement: This Load is the first to be executed, and here the change of the indicator value is calculated using the Peek() function.

First preceding Load: Here, the Boolean field **SameTrendAsPrevious** is calculated: The change of the current record is multiplied with that of the previous one. If the product of the two is greater than zero, the trend has been the same two days in a row.

Second preceding Load: Here, the **SameTrendAsPrevious** is used as condition in the If() functions. If true, the **TrendID** of the previous record is used (the Peek() function) and **DaysWithTrend** is increased by one.

But if **SameTrendAsPrevious** is false, the **TrendID** is increased by one and the **DaysWithTrend** is reset to zero.

When a counter is increased, normal addition cannot be used since the Peek() will return NULL for the very first record. Instead the addition is made using the RangeSum() function.

Summary: You can create any auto-incrementing counter in a QlikView script. Just choose your counter function …

The Great ODBC Confusion

Originally posted in the Qlik Design Blog on Feb 11, 2014

Before the ODBC interface to databases was developed in the late '80s and early '90s, it was difficult to connect to an arbitrary database and import data. But thanks to Microsoft and some other DB vendors, we got an open interface with which we still today can load data from almost any database.

But some aspects of the Windows ODBC implementation are confusing…

When ODBC was developed, computers were running DOS or Windows 3.1, i.e. 16-bit programs, and as a consequence, ODBC was also 16-bit. Then came 32-bit programs and it got messy: *You could not use the 16-bit ODBC with your 32-bit programs* – you had to use the 32-bit ODBC. But at least there were two icons for the two different ODBCs in the control panel, so it was clear what you needed to do to configure the right driver.

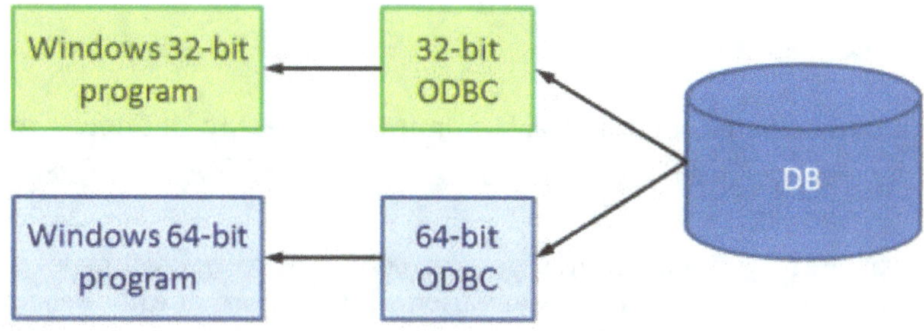

Today, with 64-bit operating systems, we have a similar situation: There are both 32-bit and 64-bit programs. But it has become even more confusing, because there is only one ODBC icon in the control panel. And many users do not know that this is just for the 64-bit ODBC.

Facts:

- A program needs the correct ODBC driver: A 64-bit driver for 64-bit programs, and a 32-bit driver for 32-bit programs.

- The 64-bit drivers are configured using *C:\Windows\System32\odbcad32.exe*
  (Can be started from the Windows control panel: Administrative Tools > Data Sources (ODBC))

- The 32-bit drivers are configured using *C:\Windows\SysWoW64\odbcad32.exe*
  (Cannot be started from the control panel)

And, no, there are no typos in the paths and the file names. They are really named like that. Trust me. The 32-bit administrator really is found in SysWoW64, and the 64-bit is found in System32. Microsoft cannot have had any usability tests here

To simplify things, QlikView has menu items for both ODBC administrators in the script editor:

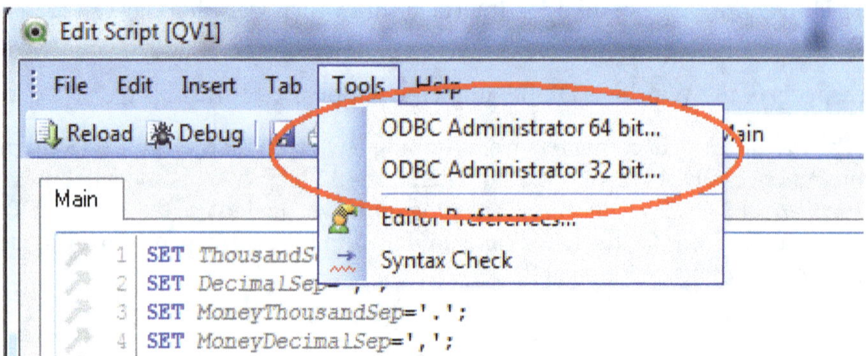

With these, you can open the correct ODBC Administrator easily. But note – the two administrators cannot run at the same time. *You need to close the open one* before you can open the other.

Further, when you create your data source, you can choose between creating a User DSN or a System DSN. The latter can be accessed by any user, while the former can be accessed only by you.

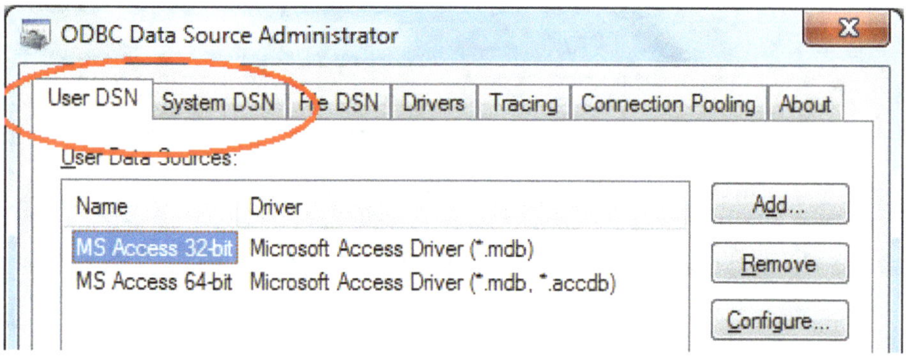

But unfortunately, that is not the only difference between the two. There is a second, confusing difference: The list of User Data Sources is a mixture between 32-bit and 64-bit User DSNs, so when you create the connect string, you will also see unusable data sources (see below). If you choose an unusable data source, you will get an error message that talks about an "architecture mismatch". To avoid mixed lists, you should *never create any User DSNs*. Always create System DSNs.

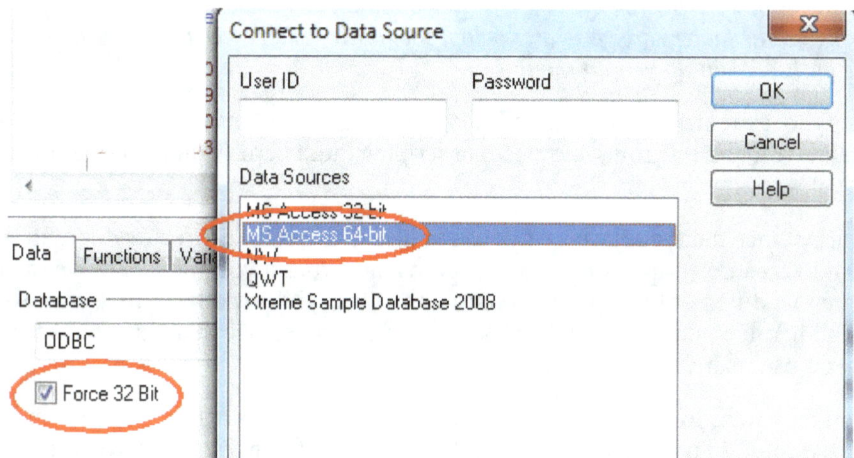

Finally, a couple of words on how it is that QlikView can use both 32- and 64-bit ODBC drivers: The QV.exe itself never connects to ODBC. Instead, it launches a separate process. Depending on whether CONNECT32 or CONNECT64 is used, QVConnect32.exe or QVConnect64.exe is launched, which connects to ODBC and streams the data in QVX format to the QV.exe.

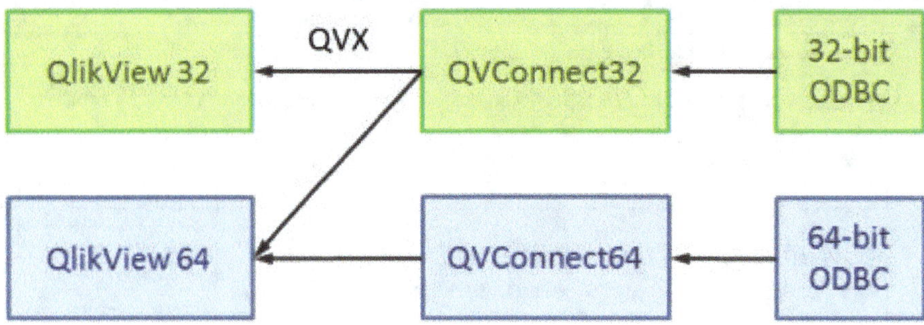

With this solution it is possible to use 32-bit ODBC drivers together with your 64-bit QlikView.

Relative Paths

Originally posted in the Qlik Design Blog on May 05, 2020

When creating a load script, you often use data from files, e.g. xls, csv, txt, or qvd. By default, absolute paths to the folders are generated when the library is created. But what if you want to use relative paths? What do you do then?

Relative paths are extremely useful. They allow you to create solutions that are robust, yet portable. They also allow you to create re-usable pieces of script without hard-coding physical file locations or library names too much.

Imagine for instance that you have many source files in a tree-like directory structure. It is easy enough to create a script using absolute paths, but what if you want to move the entire file structure to a different location? Or rename the library? The paths in the script would no longer be valid. You could in principle make a search-and-replace in all affected scripts, but it is easier if you use relative paths in the first place.

Further, you may want to use "Include" directives to refer to files containing pre-defined script entities. These could in principle contain explicit library references, but it would soon get very convoluted: First you need the library name in your Include directive – to refer to the script file itself – and then you would also need to use the library names inside the script file. No, better then to use relative paths and make the script files portable.

So, how do you use relative paths?

Directory statement

One solution is to use a "**Directory**" statement. It specifies a root folder that is used for all subsequent file references. This means that it is possible to use relative paths if files are stored in the root folder or in one of its sub-folders.

```
Directory C:\Path ;              // === QlikView
Directory lib://Scripts ;    // === Qlik Sense
```

In the following script, both the Include directives and the Load statements use relative paths: The Include macros load the scripts for some standardized components like environment variables and calendar.

```
Directory lib://Scripts ;
$(must_include=Environment en-EU.qvs) ;
$(must_include=Subroutine Standard Calendar.qvs) ;

Directory lib://Sales Data;
Customers:            Load * From [Customers.qvd]      (qvd);
Orders:               Load * From [Orders.qvd]         (qvd);
OrderDetails:         Load * From [Order Details.qvd] (qvd);
Products:             Load * From [Products.qvd]        (qvd);
ProductCategories:  Load * From [Categories.qvd]      (qvd);

Call Calendar( 'OrderDate' );
```

This method works both in QlikView and in Qlik Sense.

Path relative the qvw file

In QlikView there is a second way to use relative paths: If no Directory statement is used, the location of the qvw file is used as root folder. This means that relative paths work directly if files are stored in the same folder as the qvw or in a sub-folder.

Name	Date	Type
Data	2020-04-30 15:32	File folder
Scripts	2020-04-30 15:31	File folder
Sales Data.qvw	2020-04-30 15:31	QlikView Document

In the following script, both the Include directives and the Load statements use relative paths.

```
$(include=Scripts/Environment en-EU.qvs) ;
$(include=Scripts/Subroutine Standard Calendar.qvs) ;

Customers:          Load * From [Data/Customers.qvd]    (qvd);
Orders:             Load * From [Data/Orders.qvd]       (qvd);
OrderDetails:       Load * From [Data/Order Details.qvd] (qvd);
Products:           Load * From [Data/Products.qvd]     (qvd);
ProductCategories:  Load * From [Data/Categories.qvd]   (qvd);


Call Calendar( 'OrderDate' );
```

Note that the file paths contain the names of the sub-folders, without being absolute paths. Note also that you don't need to use backward slashes – you can always use forward slashes, although the file references refer to file system on a Windows drive.

This method, however, does not work in Qlik Sense.

sing variables

third way is to use a variable containing the path to the root folder:

```
Set RootFolder = Lib://Scripts ;
$(must_include=$(RootFolder)/Environment en-EU.qvs) ;
$(must_include=$(RootFolder)/Subroutine Standard Calendar.qvs) ;

Set RootFolder = Lib://Sales Data;
Customers:    Load * From [$(RootFolder)/Customers.qvd]    (qvd);
Orders:       Load * From [$(RootFolder)/Orders.qvd]       (qvd);
OrderDetails:Load * From [$(RootFolder)/Order Details.qvd] (qvd);
Products:     Load * From [$(RootFolder)/Products.qvd]     (qvd);
Categories:   Load * From [$(RootFolder)/Categories.qvd]   (qvd);

Call Calendar( 'OrderDate' );
```

e structure is similar to when you use a directory statement. The difference is that here you
ed to dollar-expand the variable in all paths. Strictly speaking, relative paths are not used
re – the dollar expansion creates an absolute path. But the solution allows you to create
ipts that are flexible and portable, since only the relative path is hard coded in the Load
tements.

is method works both in QlikView and in Qlik Sense.

summarize: Use relative paths to make your scripts more manageable.

lik Quoteology

iginally posted in the Qlik Design Blog on Apr 9, 2013

*all programming environments there is a need for quotation marks, and the Qlik script is no
eption. But which symbol should you use? " ", [ ], ` ` or ' '? This post will try to explain the
ferences between the different quotation marks.*

hen creating the script or an expression in QlikView or Qlik Sense, you need to reference
ds, explicit values and variables. To do this correctly, you sometimes need to write the
ing inside a pair of quotation marks. One common case is when a field name contains a
nbol that prevents QlikView from parsing it correctly, like a space or a minus sign.

For example, if you have a field called "Unit Cost", then

```
Load Unit Cost,
```

will cause a syntax error since the Qlik parser expects an "as" or a comma after the word "Unit". If you instead write

```
Load [Unit Cost],
```

the script will load the field "Unit Cost", which probably is what you want. Finally, if you write

```
Load 'Unit Cost' as ... ,
```

the script will load the text string 'Unit Cost' as a field value. Hence, it is important that you choose the correct quotation mark.

So, what are the rules? Which quote should I use? Single? Double? Square brackets?

There are three basic rules:

1. Single quotes are used to quote literals, e.g. strings that should be used as field values.

2. Double quotes are used to quote field references, i.e. names of fields. (In formulae, or to the left of the "as" inside a Load statement.)

3. Double quotes can always be substituted by square brackets or by grave accents.

	ASCII	Appearance
Single quotes	39	'string'
Double quotes	34	"string"
Square brackets	91,93	[string]
Grave accents	96	`string`

With these three rules, most cases are covered. However, they don't cover everything, so I'll continue:

4. In the script, but *outside* a Load statement, double quotes denote a variable reference and not a field reference. If double quotes are used, the enclosed string will be interpreted as a variable name and the value of the variable will be used.

A general rule in the Qlik engine is that field references inside a Load must refer to the fields in the input table – the *source* of the Load statement. They are *source field references* or *in-context field references*. Aliases and fields that are created in the Load cannot be referred since they do not exist in the source.

There are however a couple of exceptions: the functions Peek() and Exists(). The first parameters of these functions refer to fields that either have already been created or are in the output of the Load. These are *out-of-context field references*.

5. Out-of-context field references and table references, e.g. the parameters in NoOfRows() and Peek(), should be regarded as literals and therefore need single quotes.

6. Finally, in many places you are free to use any of the four quotation methods, e.g.

    a. Inside a Load statement, to the right of the "as"
    b. In places where the Qlik parser expects a file name, a URL or a table name
    c. Defining the beginning and end of an inline table
    d. For the first parameter of Peek() or Exists() when used inside a Load

I have deliberately chosen not to say anything about SELECT statements. The reason is that the rules depend on which database and which ODBC/OLEDB you have: The syntax is defined by the ODBC/OLEDB driver, and not by the Qlik engine. But usually, rules 1-3 apply there also.

With this, I hope that the Qlik quoteology is a little clearer.

Escape sequences

Originally posted in the Qlik Design Blog on Jun 9, 2015

Escape sequences are a general technique to represent characters that are not possible to represent directly. In the Qlik script the need is mainly for quotation marks, but in the general case it could also be strange characters, tabs, and newlines. How this is handled in the Qlik engine is explained in this post.

When writing a string in the Qlik script, it must usually be enclosed in single quotes. But what if you want to use a single quote inside the string? The following will <u>not</u> work:

```
Set Variable = 'This year's number';
```

The reason is that the apostrophe in the word '*year's*' will be interpreted as the single quote that ends the string. So, what should you do instead?

One solution that I have seen often in the community is to hard-code the apostrophe using the Chr() function:

```
Let Variable = 'This year' & Chr(39) & 's number' ;
Let Variable = Replace('This year#s number','#',Chr(39)) ;
```

Both these methods work fine, but they are maybe not very elegant. Instead, I would suggest one of the following methods. First, you can often use a different quoting symbol:

```
Set Variable = [This year's number] ;
```

As you can see, the **Set** statement can also use square brackets (or double quotes) as quotes. Hence, if you just use a quoting symbol that is different from what you have in the string, it will work. The same is true if you need to load from a file with a name that contains single quotes or square brackets. Just make sure you quote it using double quotes (which is a character that shouldn't exist in file names):

```
Load … From "This year's numbers [3].xlsx" ;
```

But there is a second way this problem can be solved. *An escape sequence:*

```
Let Variable = 'This year''s number' ;
```

Write the single quote twice, and the two characters will no longer be interpreted as a string delimiter, but instead as a single instance of the character itself.

The **Let** statement is different from the **Set** statement in that you *must* use single quotes as delimiter for literals. So, here you need to use an escape sequence instead. The same method can be used in other places also, e.g. in Set Analysis. The following expression is a correct one picking out the records from Robert's unit:

```
Sum( {1<Unit={'Robert''s unit'}>} Amount )
```

An escape sequence can be used for double quotes and square brackets, too. So, if you have a field name that contains double quotes, for instance **Name"5**, you can load it either by using square brackets or by escaping the double quote:

```
[Name"5]    as Field1,
"Name""5"   as Field2,
```

If the field name contains square brackets, e.g. a field called **Name[5]**, only the right bracket needs to be escaped. Such a field can be loaded in either of the two following ways:

```
"Name[5]"    as Field1,
[Name[5]]]   as Field2,
```

With this, I hope you got some ideas about how to deal with odd characters and strangely named fields.

Data Cleansing

Originally posted in the Qlik Design Blog on Jun 30, 2015

When building business intelligence solutions, one problem is that data usually contains errors, e.g. attributes are written in different ways so that data cannot be grouped correctly. The attribute could be written in upper case or not; it could be abbreviated or not; and sometimes several synonyms exist for the same thing.

For instance, 'United Kingdom' could be referred to as 'UNITED KINGDOM', 'United Kingdom', 'Great Britain', or just 'UK'.

Country	Person	Department
United Kingdom	Jose Perreira	Mechanical
UK	J.Perreira	MECHANICAL
Great Britain	J. Perreira	Mech. Dept.
…	…	…

As a consequence, what the users really think of as the same instance will appear on several rows in a list box or be displayed in several bars in a bar chart. This will cause problems in the data analysis, since selections and numbers displaying totals often will be incomplete.

But there are ways to solve this. The best way is of course to correct it in the source data. But this is not always possible, so it may be that the correction must be made elsewhere.

In QlikView and Qlik Sense there are several ways to do this. The most obvious – but not the best – is to use a hard-coded, conditional expression in the script:

```
If(Match(Country,'Great Britain','GB','UNITED KINGDOM','UK'),
    'United Kingdom',
    Country                                     ) as Country,
```

Similar constructions can be made using Replace() or Pick(). These all work and will do the job.

But they are not manageable.

Should you want to add more cases or change some previous ones, you will soon realize that this isn't a good method. The expressions will become too long, and they will be error prone. So, I strongly recommend _not_ doing this.

There is however a solution which is both manageable and simple: **Mapping Load**. The first step is to create a mapping table with all changes you want to make:

The Load Script

ChangeFrom	ChangeTo
US	United States
U.S.A.	United States
UK	United Kingdom
Great Britain	United Kingdom
MECHANICAL	Mechanical
Mech. Dept.	Mechanical
J.Perreira	J. Perreira
Jose Perreira	J. Perreira

The easiest approach is to do this in Excel, but you can also have it in a database. Then you load this table using the Mapping prefix:

```
MapTable:
Mapping Load ChangeFrom, ChangeTo From MapTable.xlsx ;
```

Now you can use this table in the script to correct all field values. The simplest way is to use the "Map" statement: Declare the mapping early in the script before any of the relevant fields are loaded, and the corrections will be made automatically:

```
Map Country, Department, Person Using MapTable ;
```

Alternatively, you can use either ApplyMap() or MapSubstring() when you load the field, which both will make a lookup in the mapping table and if necessary make the appropriate replacement, for example:

```
ApplyMap( 'MapTable', Country ) as Country ,
```

The mapping table will be discarded at the end of the script run and not use any memory in the final application.

Using a mapping table is by far the best way to manage this type of data cleansing in QlikView and Qlik Sense:

- It is easy to add new corrections and to change the old ones.

- The mapping table can be stored separately from the script, e.g. in an Excel sheet or in a database.

Good Luck!

How to Rename Fields

Originally posted in the Qlik Design Blog on Sep 25, 2012

Renaming fields in the script is something that all Qlik developers do, not only for creating links between tables, but also for making the often cryptic database field names understandable for the users. So how do you best do that? The question seems trivial, but there are in fact a number of things to say about renaming fields.

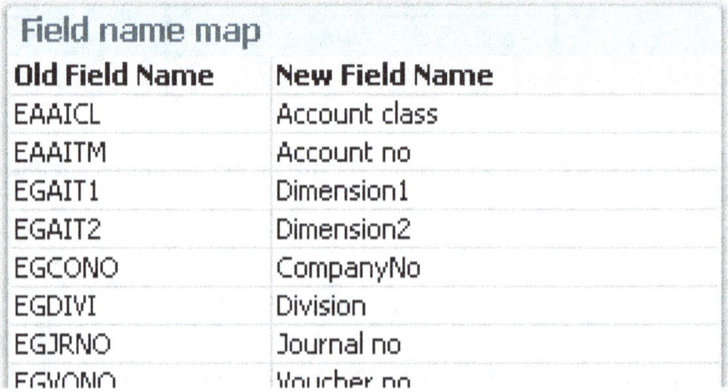

Field name map	
Old Field Name	**New Field Name**
EAAICL	Account class
EAAITM	Account no
EGAIT1	Dimension1
EGAIT2	Dimension2
EGCONO	CompanyNo
EGDIVI	Division
EGJRNO	Journal no
EGVONO	Voucher no

First, the most common way is to use aliases inside the Load or SELECT statements. If there are many fields to rename you may not want to do this, since it seems like tedious work having to enter all new field names manually in the script. But doing it has the advantage that it makes the script easy to understand for other developers.

```
CompanyName as CustomerName,
```

A second way is to use an **Alias** statement or a **Qualify** statement before the Load. These two statements are similar, in that they "silently" rename the fields in the output of the Load statement.

```
Alias CompanyName as CustomerName;
Load * From Customers;
```

However, a consequence of using the **Alias** or **Qualify** statement is that you cannot use a resident load that refers to an original field name – instead it must refer to the field name as defined in the **Alias** or **Qualify** statement. This is sometimes confusing – especially if the **Alias** statement is written earlier in the script, far from the Load statement. The **Alias** and **Qualify** statements will certainly make your script harder to understand for other developers.

A third way to rename fields is to use the **Rename** statement. This is a very good method if you want to rename all or some fields at the end of the script run. You can, however, not change the data model: You cannot merge two fields under one name.

The best way is to have a mapping table with the old and new field names and use this as follows:

```
FieldNameMap:
Mapping Load OldFieldName, NewFieldName From FieldNames ;
Rename Fields using FieldNameMap;
```

You can store the mapping table in your database or in an excel sheet so that it is easier to maintain.

Which methods do I use? I usually use aliases within the Load statements to define the data model. I never or rarely use the **Alias** or the **Qualify** statements.

In addition, I often end the script with a "Rename fields" statement to make the field names user-friendly. This way the script itself uses the database field names that are understandable for developers – who often are well familiar with the source database – while the app interface (list boxes, current selections, etc.) uses more user-friendly field names that are understandable for the users.

The result: I get the advantages of both naming schemes.

Semantic Load

Originally posted in HIC's blog on Wordpress on Apr 12, 2023

There is a rarely used feature in Qlik Sense called "Semantic Links". Here's how they work.

Normally, selections are made explicitly by clicking on the field values that are interesting. There is, however, also a way to make selections indirectly through *semantic links*. These are similar to field values, but with the difference that they describe the relations between the field values rather than the field values themselves.

A click in a normal field represents a selection in this field, whereas a click in a semantic field is a *selection in another field*. Say, for example, that you have a table listing the US presidents as your data source:

No	Name	Born	Deceased	TermFrom	TermTo	Party
1	George Washington	1732	1799	April 30, 1789	March 4, 1797	Unaffiliated
2	John Adams	1735	1826	March 4, 1797	March 4, 1801	Federalist
3	Thomas Jefferson	1743	1826	March 4, 1801	March 4, 1809	Democratic-Republican
4	James Madison	1751	1836	March 4, 1809	March 4, 1817	Democratic-Republican
5	James Monroe	1758	1831	March 4, 1817	March 4, 1825	Democratic-Republican
6	John Quincy Adams	1767	1848	March 4, 1825	March 4, 1829	Democratic-Republican
7	Andrew Jackson	1767	1845	March 4, 1829	March 4, 1837	Democratic
8	Martin Van Buren	1782	1862	March 4, 1837	March 4, 1841	Democratic
9	William Henry Harrison	1773	1841	March 4, 1841	April 4, 1841	Whig
10	John Tyler	1790	1862	April 4, 1841	March 4, 1845	Whig
11	James K. Polk	1795	1849	March 4, 1845	March 4, 1849	Democratic
12	Zachary Taylor	1784	1850	March 4, 1849	July 9, 1850	Whig

Loading this is simple enough, and you can easily create a dashboard:

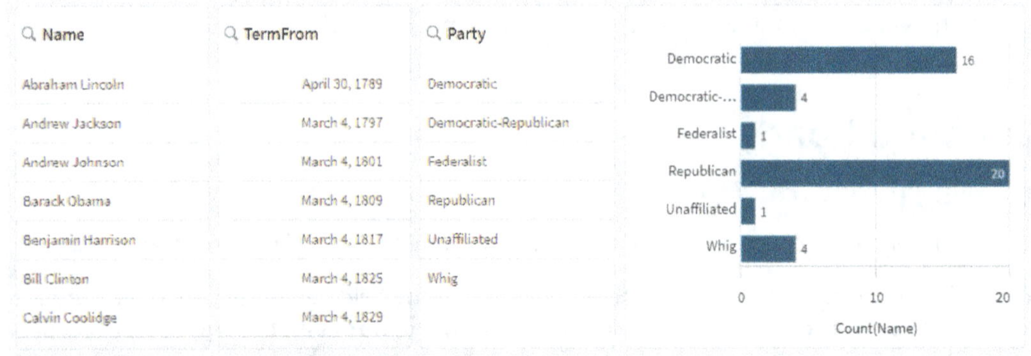

But navigating the data could be a challenge. Once you have a president selected, you may ask "Well, who was before him?"

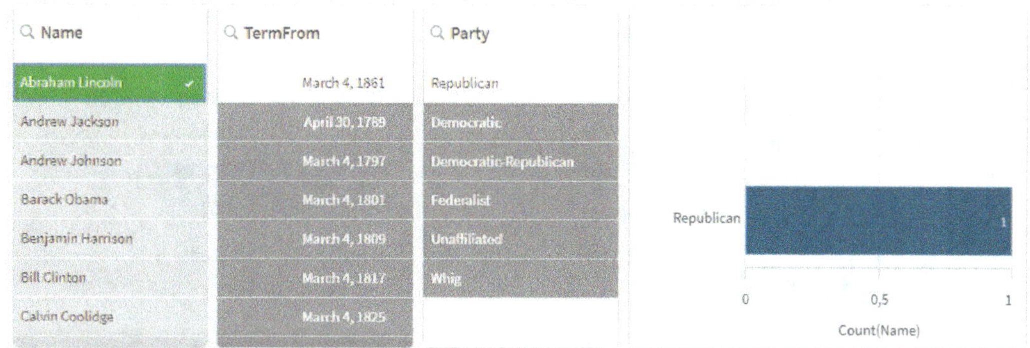

But this question is clunky to answer. You will need to look at the sequence numbers of the presidents and manually select the number before the possible one. Ideally, you should instead have some kind of navigational element that helps you select 'successor' or 'predecessor' directly.

Enter the *Semantic Links*.

The Semantic links are like fields but can never hold a selection – they can only *perform a selection in another field*. But that is exactly what you want! You want to click on 'Predecessor' and thereby select the person that was predecessor. So, if you have 'Abraham Lincoln' selected, and click on 'Predecessor', the engine will select 'James Buchanan':

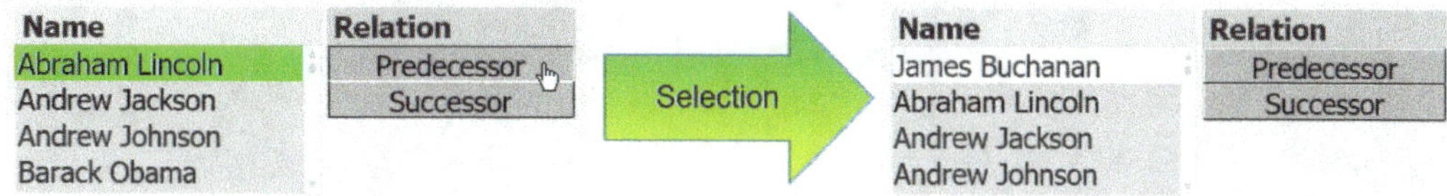

In QlikView, the Semantic links look like buttons in list boxes – they represent possible *actions.* In Qlik Sense they (erroneously) look like normal filter panes:

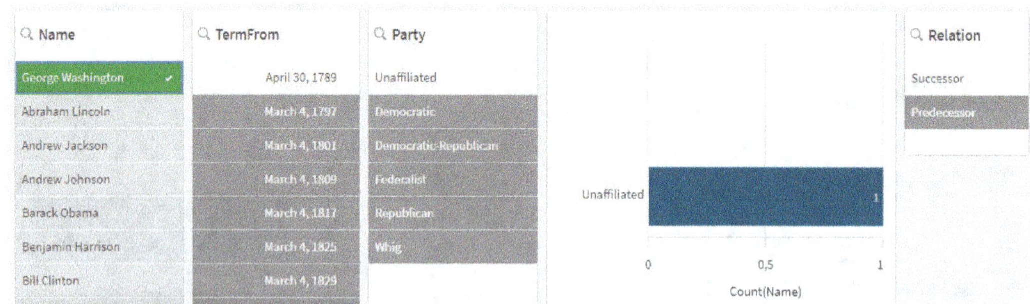

Note that 'Predecessor' is greyed out in the above picture, since George Washington didn't have a predecessor. *The action "select predecessor" isn't defined for 'George Washington'.* Hence, the logical inference works also for semantic links.

The semantic links need to be defined in the script: They are created by loading a semantic table containing the relations between the instances in a field – in addition to the data table itself.

The semantic table should contain exactly four columns. The load statement could be of the form

```
Semantic Load
    <Instance>                 as InstanceID,
    <RelationName>             as Relation,
    <RelatedInstance>          as InstanceID,
    <InverseRelationName>      as Relation
  Resident  <Table> ;
```

Note that field 1 and 3 are named the same and that field 2 and 4 are also named the same. Field 1 and 3 contain the IDs for the two records that have a relation, and they link to the data table. Field 2 and 4 contain the names of the relations and the names of the inverse relations, respectively.

The load statement in the "Presidents" app would be:

```
SemanticTable:
Semantic
Load
    No - 1          as No,
    'Successor'     as Relation,
    No              as No,
    'Predecessor'   as Relation
    Resident Presidents
    Where No > 1 Order By No;
```

This Load statement will produce the following table, where the first row defines the relations between president number 1 and president number 2, and the subsequent rows define the relations between the following presidents:

No	Relation	No	Relation
1	Successor	2	Predecessor
2	Successor	3	Predecessor
3	Successor	4	Predecessor
4	Successor	5	Predecessor
5	Successor	6	Predecessor
6	Successor	7	Predecessor
7	Successor	8	Predecessor
8	Successor	9	Predecessor
9	Successor	10	Predecessor
10	Successor	11	Predecessor

When this table is loaded with the "Semantic" prefix, the Qlik engine will use this information for the semantic links.

Alternatively, the Semantic load can have all four fields different. Field 1 and 3 are still links to the data table, and field 2 and 4 are still names of relations. But in this case the Semantic load produces two semantic fields instead of one. This enables you to use the names of the presidents as values in semantic fields.

```
SemanticTable:
Semantic
Load distinct
    No-1               as No,
    Name               as Successor,
    No                 as No2,
    Previous(Name)  as Predecessor
    Resident Presidents
    Where No > 1 Order By No;
```

This would result in the semantic fields "**Predecessor**" and "**Successor**":

Predecessor	Name	Successor
George W. Bush	Barack Obama	Donald Trump
Abraham Lincoln	Abraham Lincoln	Abraham Lincoln
Andrew Jackson	Andrew Jackson	Andrew Jackson
Andrew Johnson	Andrew Johnson	Andrew Johnson

Note that for this to work, you need to have an additional key field in the data table: "**No as No2**".

Semantic links are rarely used today, but for some data models they are an excellent way of creating navigational elements. They are especially useful when handling hierarchies. But more about that in a later article.

Incremental Load

Originally posted in HIC's Blog on Nov 3, 2023

When you have large data amounts, running the script run can often take quite a lot of time. In such cases, you might consider making an *Incremental Load*, to save time. I.e. just loading the records that have changed since the last script run.

This used to be quite tricky to achieve, since the Qlik engine is designed to load a fresh copy of the data every time the script is run. However, functionality to support incremental loads was added to the Qlik engine a couple of years ago.

The *Merge* prefix.

The principle is to define a *change set* – a set of changed records – and then merge these into a table that already exists in the Qlik data model.

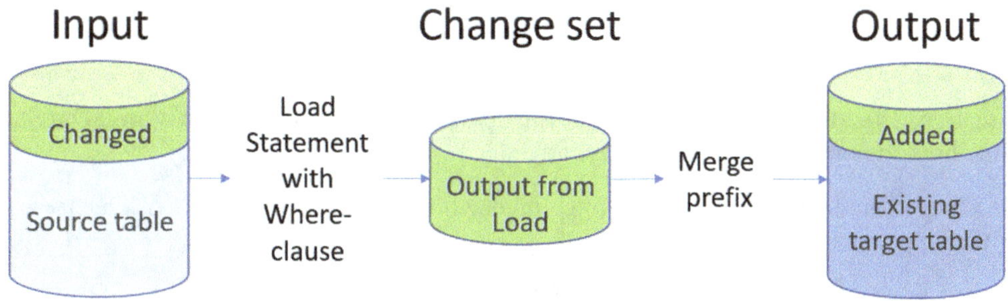

In its simplest form, the corresponding Load statement would look like the following:

```
Merge on Key Load Operation, Key, Attribute, ...
```

"**Merge**" means that a record can be inserted, updated or deleted in the existing table.

Two fields are mandatory: **Operation** and **Key**.

Operation
The first field in the Load statement needs to be a text field that defines what should be done: 'Insert', 'Update', or 'Delete'. This field will not be loaded into the target table.

Key
There must exist a field that identifies the record that should be changed – a primary key. This should be specified after the "**on**" clause. It is possible to use multiple keys.

Optionally, you may also want to include a timestamp or sequence number – here the field "**ChangeDate**":

```
Merge (ChangeDate) on Key
Load Operation, ChangeDate, Key, Attribute, ... From ...
```

ChangeDate
This field needs to be specified as the first parameter to the **Merge** prefix, i.e. put within the brackets after the prefix itself. It ensures that the operations are performed in the right order and that the last version of the record is the one that is kept. Without this sequence number, the engine uses the load order to determine which record is the last one. The sequence number does not need to be a date – it could be a timestamp or any number that defines the order of the changes.

To summarize: The **Merge** prefix will look at the fields **Operation**, **Key**, and **ChangeDate** to determine how the target table should be changed:

- The **Operation** determines the type of change: whether an Insert, Update or Delete should be performed.

- The **Key** determines which record is affected.

- The **ChangeDate** determines which record should be kept: Whether the record in the target table should be kept as it is, or the operation in the Merge Load should be performed. The Merge Load needs to have a sequence number higher (i.e. later) than the existing one.

The **Merge** prefix can be made much more complex, if needed. For example, if you want the **Merge** statement to be executed at partial reloads only, you can specify this with the "**Only**" clause. And if you need to specify several fields that together form a primary key, you can do that.

Further, if the change set and the target table have different sets of fields, you need to use the "**Concatenate**" prefix before the Load keyword.

And finally, if you want to store the last execution time in a variable, so that you can use this in a **Where** clause in the next script run, you can do this by using a second parameter for the **Merge** prefix.

In-app merge or QVD layer?

There are two principal approaches to incremental Loads: Either you make the changes directly in a Qlik app, or you use an incremental load to update a QVD layer.

In-app merge

If you choose the in-app approach, you need to use a *Partial reload* to run the script. In Qlik Sense you can do this by running script from the scheduler with "Partial reload" checked. If you do this, your incremental load should work properly.

A partial reload ensures that the existing tables in the app are *not* dropped at the beginning of the script run. This is different from a normal script run, that starts by dropping the entire existing data model. Further, a partial reload will *not* execute other Load statements, unless they are preceded by the prefix "**Add**", "**Replace**" or "**Merge**". So, if you have a script with several normal Load statements, and one single "**Merge Load**", only the "**Merge Load**" statement will be executed.

So, a best practice would be to do something similar to the following:

```
// === Load the entire table. Executed only at a full Load ===
Facts:
SQL Select
    ChangeDate, Key, Attribute, ...
    From ... ;

If not IsPartialReload() Then
    Let LastChangeDate = Now();
End If

// === Load the changed records only. Only at a partial Load ===
Merge Only (ChangeDate, LastChangeDate) on Key
Concatenate (Facts)
SQL Select Operation,
    ChangeDate, Key, Attribute, ...
    From ...
    Where ChangeDate >=#$(LastChangeDate)#;
```

In a normal reload, only the first Load/Select statement will be executed. In a partial reload, only the second Load/Select statement will be executed.

QVD layer

You can use the above approach also for a QVD layer, but here you also have a second option – one without the partial reload. Then you would create two QVD-generating apps: One that loads <u>all</u> data and one that makes an incremental load.

The script for the incremental load would be similar to the following:

```
// === Load the previous table from a local QVD file  ===
Facts:
Load
    ChangeDate, Key, Attribute, ...
    From LocalQVDFile.qvd (qvd);

// === Load changed records from the original source  ===
Merge (ChangeDate, LastChangeDate) on Key
Concatenate (Facts)
SQL Select Operation,
    ChangeDate, Key, Attribute, ...
    From ...
    Where ChangeDate >=#$(LastChangeDate)#;

// === Store the new table into a QVD  ===
Store Facts Into LocalQVDFile.QVD (qvd);
```

In both approaches, the variable **LastChangeDate** keeps track of when the last script run was made and makes sure that only new changes are loaded. The **Concatenate** prefix is, strictly speaking, not necessary. But it could still be good to have it there to ensure that the correct target table is used.

These scripts would both be proper ways of coding an incremental load of one single table. If you have several large tables, you need to repeat this process for each table.

A good practice would be to run a full reload regularly, perhaps once a week or month, and in addition run incremental loads every night.

With this I leave you to investigate the **Merge** prefix.

Subroutines

Subroutines are constructions where a set of statements are grouped together to form a coherent action that can be executed when needed. The concept exists in almost all programming languages, and Qlik scripting is no exception.

I the Qlik script, a subroutine needs to be defined *before* it is used, so this is usually done in the beginning of the script.

```
Sub NameOfSubroutine (Parameter)
    ...  ;
End Sub
```

Once defined, the subroutine can be called using the "**Call**" statement:

```
Call NameOfSubroutine(Variable) ;
```

There can be several parameters, and these are normally variables. The formal parameter – "**Parameter**" in the above subroutine definition – is local to the subroutine and cannot be accessed outside it. Other variables, also those created inside the subroutine, are global and are persisted after the execution of the subroutine.

The parameter is passed by reference, so it is possible to use the parameter also for output, e.g. you can use a subroutine to change the value of a variable. However, if the parameter is a static string enclosed in single quotes, it will be passed by value.

An example of a useful subroutine could be that you want to define a master calendar. Then you could define it the following way:

```
Sub  CreateMasterCalendar(Date,Prefix)
  Load // --- create all fields needed in the calendar ------------
    Year (Date)                             as [$(Prefix)Year],
    Dual('Q'&Ceil(Month(Date)/3),
        Ceil(Month(Date)/3))                as [$(Prefix)Quarter],
    Month(Date)                             as [$(Prefix)Month],
    Date (MonthStart(Date),'YYYY MMM')      as [$(Prefix)YearMonth],
    Date                                    as [$(Date)];
  Load // --- generate all dates --------------------------------
    Date(  CalendarBegin+Iterno()-1 )       as Date
    While  CalendarBegin+Iterno()-1<=CalendarEnd
  Load // --- find smallest and largest value in symbol table   ---
    YearStart(Min(Fieldvalue('$(Date)',RecNo())))) as CalendarBegin,
    YearEnd  (Max(Fieldvalue('$(Date)',RecNo())))) as CalendarEnd
    Autogenerate FieldValueCount('$(Date)');
End Sub
```

This subroutine can subsequently be used for several different date fields, generating one calendar per field:

```
Call CreateMasterCalendar('RequiredDate',   'Required');
Call CreateMasterCalendar('OrderDate',      'Order');
Call CreateMasterCalendar('ShippingDate',   'Shipping');
Call CreateMasterCalendar('InvoiceDate',    'Invoice');
Call CreateMasterCalendar('CanonicalDate',  '');
```

As soon as you have more complicated scripting challenges, the subroutine can help you structure your scripting.

4

Numbers, Dates, and Data Types

In a normal database, you have different data types: Dates, Timestamps, Numbers, Integers, Strings, Varchar, etc. Each field is a specific data type. This allows the users to handle different types of data in different ways.

In the Qlik engine, this challenge is handled in a different way – there are no data types. But the challenge of handling dates and other data types in a flexible way is still solved.

This chapter is about handling numbers, dates, and other data types. The core is the *Dual* data type. If you don't yet know what this is, you need to read this chapter.

Data Types in the Qlik engine

Posted in the Qlik Design Blog on Nov 13, 2012

There are no data types in the Qlik engine.

This is *not a limitation* – it is a *conscious design decision*.

One of the initial requirements of QlikView was that it should be possible to mix data from different sources: We wanted users to be able to have a data model with some data from a database, some from an Excel sheet, and some from a comma delimited text file. Some of these sources have proper data types, others don't. So, relying on the data types of the data source would be difficult. Further, we wanted the internal functions to be able to always return a relevant calculation – there must never be any type of conversion problems. We wanted *simplicity* for the user.

Enter the *Dual* type.

The dual format is a brilliantly simple solution to the above requirements: Its core is that every field value has two values – one string that is displayed, and one number that is used for sorting and calculations. The two values are inseparable; they are like the two sides of a single coin. They are both needed to describe the field value properly.

For example, months have the string values 'Jan', 'Feb' … 'Dec', which are displayed. At the same time, they have numeric values 1 to 12, which are used for sorting and arithmetic operations. Similarly, weekdays have the string values 'Mon', 'Tue' … 'Sun' and at the same time the numeric values 0 to 6.

Text(Month)	Num(Month)
Jan	1
Feb	2
Mar	3
Apr	4
May	5
Jun	6
Jul	7
Aug	8
Sep	9
Oct	10
Nov	11
Dec	12

Dates and times have string values that look like dates, e.g. '12/31/2011' or '06.06.1944 06:30' and at the same time they have numeric values corresponding to the number of days since Dec 30, 1899. As I write this, the (numeric) time is 41215.6971. How months, weekdays, dates and times should be displayed is defined in the environment variables in the beginning of the script.

Text(Date)	Num(Date)
8/24/75	27630
Dec 17 1981	29937
9/2/85	31292
11/16/99	36480
02.04.2001	36983
2009-05-13	39946
5/16/14	41775

This way the Qlik engine can sort months, days and dates numerically, or calculate the difference between two dates. Numbers can be formatted in arbitrary ways. As a result, the Qlik engine can have data that is much more complex than plain strings.

When dual values are used as parameters inside Qlik functions, the function always uses just one of the two representations. If a string is expected, as in the first parameter of Left(s,n), the string representation is used. And if a number is expected, as in the Month(date) function, the number representation is used.

Qlik functions all return dual values, when possible. Even the color functions do, see table below. However, string functions, e.g. Left(s,n), are the exception; because they dont have a number that can be associated with the string, they leave the number part of the dual empty.

Text(Color)	Num(Color)	Num(Color,'(HEX)')
ARGB(127,255,0,80)	2147418192	7FFF0050
RGB(0,0,0)	4278190080	FF000000
RGB(0,0,128)	4278190208	FF000080
RGB(0,128,0)	4278222848	FF008000
RGB(128,0,0)	4286578688	FF800000
RGB(255,255,0)	4294967040	FFFFFF00
RGB(255,255,255)	4294967295	FFFFFFFF

Finally, there is of course a function with which you can create your own dual values: Dual(s,n). With it you can create any combination of string and number. Use it if you want to assign a sort order to strings or if you want to assign text to numeric values.

The Document Locale

Posted in the Qlik Design Blog on Dec 2, 2022

The locale defines the regional settings. Here is how it is done in Qlik Sense and QlikView.

In the beginning of the load script, you will find a number of **Set** statements defining the environment variables. These determine the date format, the month names and several other things that pertain to the regional settings.

This is the ***Document Locale***.

In other products or situations, there is usually a locale per computer or per user, but for Qlik Sense and QlikView the locale is *per document*. The reason is that the locale affects selections and set expressions internally in the Qlik logic, so different locales for different users wouldn't work within one single app. Examples:

- The date format: Should the set expression {<Date={7/11/2022}>} refer to July 11th or to Nov 7th? The interpretation is different in different countries.

- The collation: Should the set expression {<Text={"*a*"}>} also match 'å', 'ä', 'â', or 'æ'? This is different in different countries.

Since we want a measure containing a set expression or a bookmark containing a search string to return the same value for different users, we *cannot* have different locales for different users. Everyone within the same app must use the same locale. The solution is to have a document locale.

If the set statements are organized a little, it becomes easier to see what they do. The following shows the locale I usually use:

```
// ========= Locale - Numbers =========
Set DecimalSep        =',';
Set ThousandSep       ='.';
Set MoneyDecimalSep  =',';
Set MoneyThousandSep='.';
Set MoneyFormat       ='#.##0 $';
Set NumericalAbbreviation='3:k;6:M;9:G;12:T;15:P;18:E;21:Z;24:Y;
                       -3:m;-6:µ;-9:n;-12:p;-15:f;-18:a;-21:z;-24:y';
// ========= Locale - Date and Time =========
Set DateFormat        ='YYYY-MM-DD';
Set TimeFormat        ='hh:mm:ss';
Set TimestampFormat  ='YYYY-MM-DD hh:mm:ss[.fff]';
Set TimeZone          ='+01:00';
Set TimeZoneName      ='Europe/Stockholm';


// ========= Locale - Calendar =========
Set FirstWeekDay      =0; // 0=Mon, 1=Tue, 2=Wed, ... , 6=Sun
Set BrokenWeeks       =0; // 0 means week number may span over Newyear
Set ReferenceDay      =4; // This day in Jan always belongs to week 1
Set FirstMonthOfYear=1;
Set MonthNames        ='Jan;Feb;Mar;Apr;May;Jun;Jul;Aug;Sep;Oct;Nov;Dec';
Set LongMonthNames    ='January;February;March;April;May;June;
                       July;August;September;October;November;December';
Set DayNames          ='Mon;Tue;Wed;Thu;Fri;Sat;Sun';
Set LongDayNames='Monday;Tuesday;Wednesday;Thursday;Friday;Saturday;Sunday';


// ========= Locale - Sort and Search =========
Set CollationLocale ='sv-SE';
Set CreateSearchIndexOnReload=1;
```

First, you have some variables that pertain to numbers, the decimal symbol, the thousand separator, etc. These will be used for interpreting text as numbers when loading data, as well as for formatting the values. Then you have some variables that pertain to date and time. Also, these are used for interpretation and formatting, but now of dates and timestamps.

Then you have some variables that pertain to calendars; names of months and weekdays, how the week numbers should be calculated etc.

All of the above variables are used internally by the Qlik functions, so if you change a variable, some functions will return a different value. For example, the WeekStart() function obviously uses the value of **FirstWeekDay**. Further, the month and day names are linked to format codes. For example, Date(Date,'MMMM') will always return one of the values in **LongMonthNames**.

Many functions have parameters that can override the environment variables, i.e. the variables define a default, but as a user you can change that by using an optional function parameter.

Example:

- Date(Date) will use the date format of the variable **DateFormat**
- Date(Date,'YYYY MMMM DD') will use the date format of the parameter

The week numbering is a chapter of its own: In some countries, the ISO week numbering is used: The week starts on a Monday, one week number may well span two years, and Jan 4th is always in week 1. This corresponds to

```
Set FirstWeekDay    =0; // 0=Monday
Set BrokenWeeks     =0; // Week 1 may start in Dec
Set ReferenceDay    =4; // Jan 4th is always in week 1
```

But in other countries, e.g. USA, a different system is used: The week starts on a Sunday, a week number never spans two years, and Jan 1st is always in week 1:

```
Set FirstWeekDay    =6; // 6=Sunday
Set BrokenWeeks     =1; // Dec 31 always belongs to week 53 or 54
Set ReferenceDay    =1; // Jan 1st is always in week 1
```

We recently had a bug that caused some problems: The MakeWeekDate() function ignored the environment variables and instead always returned the ISO 8601 values (the ISO standard assumes that Monday always is the first day of the week). This was an obvious error and was fixed, but unfortunately the fix caused negative effects for some customers, and we apologize for that. More info on the Qlik support blog.

Finally, the variable **CollationLocale** affects sort orders of text strings and searches: Which field values should be matched for a given search string.

Feel free to change these variables should you need to!

Get the Dates Right

Posted in the Qlik Design Blog on June 8, 2012

The Qlik engine has an intelligent algorithm to recognize dates independently of which region you are in. In most cases, you will have no problems loading them. It just works and you do not need to think about it. However, in some cases dates are not properly recognized and then you need to add some code in the script to make it work.

First of all – there are no data types in the Qlik engine. Instead, it uses a dual data storage for all field values; every field value is represented by a string and – if applicable – a number. The task of the developer is to make sure that the engine recognizes the date correctly so that both a textual and a numeric part of the date are created.

Dual dates – mixed formats	
MixDate.Text	**MixDate.Num**
31.03.1900	91
1956-02-28	20513
20111201	40878
31/1/2012	40939
4/4/2012 08:00 am	41003.333333333
13/13/2012	-

The numeric part of a date is a serial number (same as Excel), i.e. a number around 45000 for dates in the year 2023.

Here are some tips that will help you load dates correctly and hopefully help you better understand how the date handling works.

1) **Use the interpretation functions**
   If you have the date as text you may need to use an interpretation function, e.g. Date#() or Timestamp#().

2) **Nest functions**
   If you want to display the date a specific way, you may need to nest an interpretation function inside a formatting function, e.g. Date(Date#(DateField, 'YYYYMMDD'), 'M/D/YY').

3) **Use the MakeDate function**
   If you have Year, Month and Day as separate fields, use the MakeDate() function to create a date serial number.

4) **Use the rounding functions**
   If you have a timestamp and you want a date, you should probably use a rounding function, e.g. Date(Floor(Timestamp#(DateTimeField, 'YYYYMMDD hh:mm:ss')), 'M/D/YY').

5) **Use numeric variables**
   If you want to use the variable for comparisons, it is simpler to use the date serial number rather than the textual representation, e.g. Let vToday = Num(Today()).

6) **Use combination of entities as one field**
   It is often practical to display both year and month in one field, e.g. Date(MonthStart(DateField),'YYYY-MMM').

7) **Use the Dual function**
   If you want more complicated combinations of a string with an associated numeric value, you can do almost anything using the Dual() function.

8) **Use the Alt function for fields with mixed date formats**
   If you have a field with mixed date formats, you can resolve them using the Alt() function.

For a more elaborate description of these tips, see the next section "Qlik Date Fields".

Qlik Date Fields

Extract from the Technical brief "QlikView Date Fields" published on May 31, 2012

Many of the questions on QlikCommunity and other forums concern dates and how to use date functions in Qlik. Although the basics for dates are fairly simple, there are many misunderstandings. This chapter is an attempt to give some background and some suggestions. Those of you who are experienced Qlik users will maybe not find anything new here, but others most likely will.

Data types

There are no data types in the Qlik engine. Instead, it uses a dual data storage for all field values: every field value is represented by a string and – if applicable – a number. If a field value can be interpreted as a number (or a date) then a number is stored in the numeric part of the dual storage, while the display string is stored in the textual part of the dual storage.

The serial numbers used for dates are the same as in Excel: the number of days passed since the 30th of December 1899 using the Gregorian calendar. The integer part of the serial number is the date, and the fractional part is the time of the day. For example, if the 31st of January 2012 at 6 o'clock in the morning is loaded with US date format, then the number 40939.25 is stored together with the string '1/31/2012 6:00 am'.

Dual dates

Date.Text	Date.Num
3/31/1900	91
2/28/1956	20513
12/1/2011	40878
1/31/2012	40939
4/4/2012 8:00 am	41003.333333333
13/13/2012	-

This way, dates, weekdays, and month names can have textual names or arbitrary formats and still be numerically sorted. The fields can also be used in numerical calculations and comparisons and as continuous axes in graphs. Numerical functions always use the numeric part of the dual field and string functions always use the string part.

Dual Month values

Month.Text	Month.Num
Jan	1
Feb	2
Mar	3
Apr	4
Dec	12

Interpretation and formatting

There are two important types of Qlik functions that deal with time and dates: *Interpretation* functions and *Formatting* functions. The interpretation functions – e.g. Date#() and TimeStamp#() – are string-to-number conversions, i.e. the input is a string that contains a date and the function creates a correct date serial number. The output is a dual field, i.e. both string and number.

The formatting functions – e.g. Date() and TimeStamp() – are in a way the opposite: they are number-to-string conversions, i.e. the input is a date serial number and the function creates a string with the properly formatted date. Also here the output is a dual field, i.e. both string and number.

You rarely need to use the interpretation or formatting functions. Normally interpretation and formatting just work without you having to do anything. The reason for this, is that if there is no interpretation function explicitly used, the Qlik engine tries with the date format specified in the format variables, e.g. it uses what it finds in the "Set DateFormat = …" statement in the beginning of the script, which usually is just what you need.

But sometimes, the interpretation and formatting must be done using an explicit format. Here are some suggestions of how to work with dates and times if your fields aren't interpreted correctly:

Tip 1: Use interpretation functions

If the date isn't automatically recognized, you may need to use an interpretation function to interpret it:

```
Date#( DateField, 'M/D/YY') as Date,
```

Make sure you really use an interpretation function and not a formatting function – it should have a hash sign "#" in it.

Also, you should check that the Qlik engine really has interpreted the dates as numbers: Either implicitly by checking that the dates are right-aligned in the list box, or explicitly by formatting the dates as numbers (Properties – Numbers) and verifying that the numbers displayed have values around 40000 – 50000 for dates in present time.

The format code used is very similar to the one in Excel. Note, however, that the letters in it are case sensitive. "M" means months and "m" means minutes.

The string does not have to be a complete date. A partial date can also be interpreted. If you, for instance, have a field with only month names in it, you can convert the textual month names to dual months using:

```
Month( Date#( Month,'MMM') ) as Month,
```

Tip 2: Nest functions

It is often practical to nest an interpretation function inside a formatting function, e.g.

```
Date( Date#( DateField, 'M/D/YY'), 'YYYY-MM-DD') as Date,
```

The inner function ensures that the input text is interpreted correctly – so that a serial number representing the date is created. The outer function ensures that the serial number is displayed in a correct date format.

Example: You have a date field where the dates are stored as '20120131', i.e. no slashes or dashes between the day, month and year. The Qlik engine will incorrectly interpret this as an integer number with a value of slightly more than 20 million. I say 'incorrectly' since it assigns values that are other than the correct date serial numbers, making comparisons between dates impossible. If you for instance want to calculate the number of days between 20120131 and 20120201, you would get 70, when it obviously should be 1.

One correct way to load it could be

```
Date( Date#( DateField, 'YYYYMMDD'), 'M/D/YYYY') as Date,
```

where the inner function contains the actual date format, and the outer contains the preferred date format. Also, this way the dates get numeric values of around 40000 and can be correctly compared to other dates and used in calculations.

Nested functions		
Date	Date#(Date,'YYYYMMDD')	Date(Date#(Date,'YYYYMMDD'))
19000331	91	3/31/1900
19560228	20513	2/28/1956
20111201	40878	12/1/2011
20120131	40939	1/31/2012
20120404	41003	4/4/2012

Tip 3: Use the MakeDate function

If your date is stored in several fields, e.g. one field for year, a second for month and a third for day, you should use the MakeDate() function to create a proper date serial number for the specified day:

```
MakeDate( Year, Month, Day ) as Date,
```

Tip 4: Use the rounding functions

The date field in the source data is often not just a date, but instead a timestamp corresponding to a specific time during the day. The date serial number will then not be an integer. For instance, the time '6 pm 1/1/2012' corresponds to the date serial number 40909.75.

In such a case it is not enough to use the date function to remove hours and minutes from the formatting. Though formatting the timestamp as a date will hide the time from being displayed, the fractional part of the serial number will still be stored in the numeric part of the field and the field may hence give incorrect results in comparisons.

Instead, a rounding function must be used to make the additional 0.75 from the numeric value disappear, for example:

```
Date( Floor( Date ), 'YYYY-MM-DD') as Date,
```

Another case where a rounding function is good, is when the date is a key field linking two tables. If the field value is a timestamp where you have a time of the day other than midnight – 00:00:00 – then this value will not link to a date in another table even if you have formatted it as a date: The string part of the dual format is _not_ used as key, if there is a numeric value. The numeric value is always used as key. Hence it is not enough that two numeric values are formatted exactly the same. If you want to use a date as a key, you should use the integer part of the timestamp and omit the information about time of the day.

Example: You have a timestamp, e.g. '2012-01-28 08:32:45' in your transaction table and you want to link this to a master calendar table containing dates. One correct way to load this key could be

```
Date(
    Floor(TimeStamp#(Created,'YYYY-MM-DD hh:mm:ss')),
    'M/D/YYYY')                              as CreatedDate,
```

In addition to the key **CreatedDate**, other fields could also be created to show the fractional part of the timestamp

```
TimeStamp#(Created,'YYYY-MM-DD hh:mm:ss')    as CreatedTimeStamp,
Time(
    Frac(TimeStamp#(Created,'YYYY-MM-DD hh:mm:ss')),
    'hh:mm:ss')                              as CreatedDate,
```

Also note that the function Frac() is used to remove the integer part of the number for the field that only contains the time information.

Tip 5: Always use the numeric value in variables

Fields and variables are dual, but the dollar-expansion of variables is not. This means that whenever you want to store a date in a variable and use it later for e.g. a numeric comparison in a **Where** clause, it is easier if the variable is purely numeric instead of a string containing a date format. Hence, use the following construction:

```
Let Today        = Num(             Today()   ) ;
Let AMonthAgo    = Num(AddMonths(Today(),-1) ) ;
```

Subsequent use of the variable is then straightforward, for example:

```
… Where DeliveryDate>$(#AMonthAgo) and DeliveryDate<=$(#Today);
```

Note the hash sign in the dollar expansions: it forces an expansion using decimal point. This is helpful for users with decimal comma (as opposed to decimal *point*) in the regional settings.

Tip 6: Use combination fields, e.g. Year and Month as one field

Date numbers should be used for year-month fields and other similar situations:

```
Date(MonthStart(DateField),'YYYY-MMM') as YearMonth,
```

Here the MonthStart() function returns the date number of the beginning of the month and the Date() function is used to hide the day of the month. There are other similar useful functions like WeekStart, QuarterStart and YearStart.

Dual YearMonth values	
YearMonth.Text	**YearMonth.Num**
1900-Mar	61
1956-Feb	20486
2011-Dec	40878
2012-Jan	40909
2012-Apr	41000

Tip 7: Use the Dual function

The Dual function can often be used to solve trickier problems. The Dual function lets you specify both a numeric value as well as which text to associate with this value.

For instance, if you want to use the week number, but sorted correctly also over the change of the year, then you should use the date number as numeric value but display the week number, optionally together with the year:

```
Dual(
    Week(Date),
    WeekStart(Date)                         )    as YearWeek,
Dual(
    WeekYear(Date) & '-w' & Week(Date),
    WeekStart(Date)                         )    as YearWeek,
```

Or if you want to create fiscal months:

```
Dual(
    Month(Date),
    Mod(Month(Date)-$(vFirstMonthOfFiscalYear),12)+1
    )                                         as FiscalMonth,
```

Dual YearWeek values	
YearWeek.Text	**YearWeek.Num**
1900-w13	86
1956-w09	20512
2011-w48	40875
2012-w05	40938
2012-w14	41001

Tip 8: Use the Alt() function for fields with mixed date formats

If you have mixed date format in one field or you have data from different sources using different formats, you can use the Alt() function to define several possible date formats:

```
Alt(
    Timestamp#(MixDate,'M/D/YYYY h:mm tt'),
    Date#(     MixDate,'M/D/YYYY'),
    Date#(     MixDate,'D/M/YYYY'),
    Date#(     MixDate,'YYYYMMDD'),
    Date#(     MixDate,'DD.MM.YYYY'),
    Date#(     MixDate,'YYYY-MM-DD')
       )    as MixDate,
```

The order of the interpretation functions also defines the priority when the format of the date is ambiguous, e.g. 8/4/2012, which in the United States means 4th of August, but in the United Kingdom means 8th of April.

Summary

Always convert anything date- or time-like to a proper date serial number and use this as the number in the dual format. The text part of the dual format is a display topic; it is up to you to decide what to show. Good Luck!

The Date Function

Posted in the Qlik Design Blog on Dec 2, 2014

One Qlik function that occasionally causes confusion is the Date function. I have often seen errors caused by an incorrect usage of it, so today I will try to explain what the function does – and what it does not.

Interpretation vs Formatting

The first thing you should be aware of is that there are two different functions: Date#() and Date(). The first is an *Interpretation* function and the second is a *Formatting* function.

- Interpretation functions use the textual value of the input and convert this to a number.
- Formatting functions use the numeric value of the input and convert this to a text.

In both cases, the output is a dual, i.e. it has both a textual value and a numeric value. The textual value is displayed, whereas the numeric value is used for all numerical calculations and sorting.

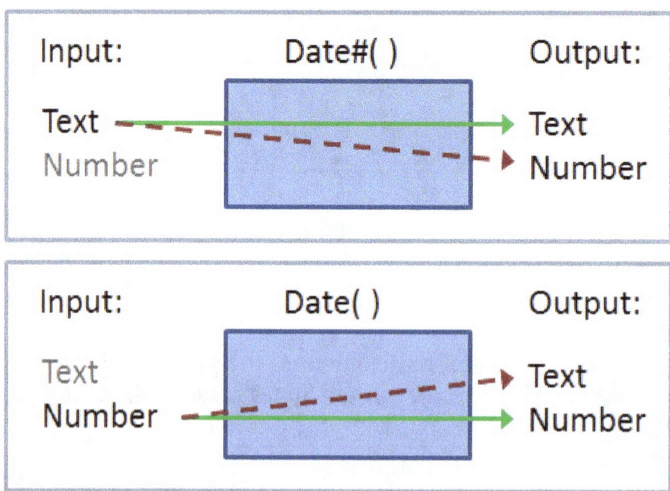

The table below shows how to use the interpretation function Date#(). Note that the format code must match the input parameter.

Function	Output.Text	Output.Num
Date#('20140831' , 'YYYYMMDD')	20140831	41882
Date#('8/31/14' , 'M/D/YY')	8/31/14	41882

This is very different from the formatting function Date(). Next table shows how to use this function. Note that the format code matches the format of the output text.

Function	Output.Text	Output.Num
Date(41882 , 'YYYY.MM.DD')	2014.08.31	41882
Date(41882 , 'M/D/YY')	8/31/14	41882
Date(41882 , 'YYYY-MMM')	2014-Aug	41882

In real life, it is often useful to nest an interpretation function inside a formatting function:

Function	Output.Text	Output.Num
Date(Date#('20140831' , 'YYYYMMDD') , 'YYYY.MM.DD')	2014.08.31	41882
Date(Date#('8/31/14' , 'M/D/YY') , 'YY-MM-DD')	14-08-31	41882

Formatting vs Rounding

The second thing you should be aware of is that the Date() function and other formatting functions *never* change the numeric value of the input value.

This means that you can format a timestamp as a date only, without the time information. This can sometimes be confusing since there is a "hidden" value. In the table below, you can see that the input value corresponds to 12:00 in the middle of the day, but the Date() function effectively hides this from the textual output – but it remains in the numeric value.

Function	Output.Text	Output.Num
Date(41882.5 , 'YY.MM.DD')	14.08.31	41882.5
TimeStamp(41882.5 , 'YY.MM.DD hh:mm')	14.08.31 12:00	41882.5

So, what should you do if you want to remove the time part of the field, and just keep the date part? Well, obviously you must use a function that changes the numeric value: You need a *Rounding* function, e.g. DayStart() or Floor().

In the table below, you can compare the output of the Date() function with a couple of different rounding and formatting options.

Function	Output.Text	Output.Num
Date(41882.5 , 'M/D/YY')	8/31/14	41882.5
DayStart(41882.5)	8/31/14 00:00:00	41882
TimeStamp(Floor(41882.5) , 'M/D/YY hh:mm')	8/31/14 00:00	41882
Date(Floor(41882.5) , 'M/D/YYYY')	8/31/14	41882

Summary

The above discussion is not relevant to dates only. It is just as relevant for Years, Weeks, hours, seconds and any other time interval. Further, it is relevant to a number of other functions:

- *Interpretation functions*: Date#(), TimeStamp#(), Time#(), Interval#(), etc.
- *Formatting functions*: Date(), TimeStamp(), Time(), Interval(), etc.
- *Rounding functions*: Round(), Floor(), Ceil(), DayStart(), WeekStart(), MonthStart(), etc.

Combine these functions sensibly, and you will be able to round or format any way you want.

Why don't my dates work?

Originally posted in the Qlik Design Blog on Feb 19, 2013

A common recurring question on the QlikCommunity forum is around dates that don't work. Here follows a help on fixing the three most common causes.

1. Incorrect Date Interpretation

When data is loaded into the Qlik engine, dates are often read as strings. The engine then tries to recognize a pattern in the string that looks like the date format specified in the **DateFormat** environment variable. This sometimes fails and then you need to use the Date#() function to help the engine understand that it is a date.

How do I know that a date is correctly interpreted? That's easy. Just look at whether it is right- or left-aligned. Numbers and dates are by default right aligned, and text is left aligned. Hence – if it is left-aligned, the dates have not been interpreted.

You can also format the date as a number and see what you get. If you have a number which is roughly 40000, then you are all set. But if you still have it formatted as a date or you have a blank, then you need to use the Date#() function in the script.

In Qlik Sense you can do this by wrapping the date in the Num() function. Then you will get a blank filter pane if the date hasn't been interpreted.

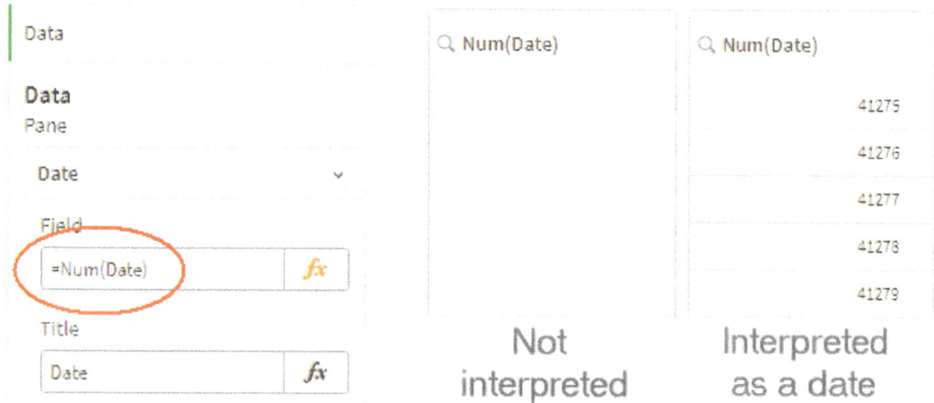

In QlikView, you have a display property under the "Number" tab.

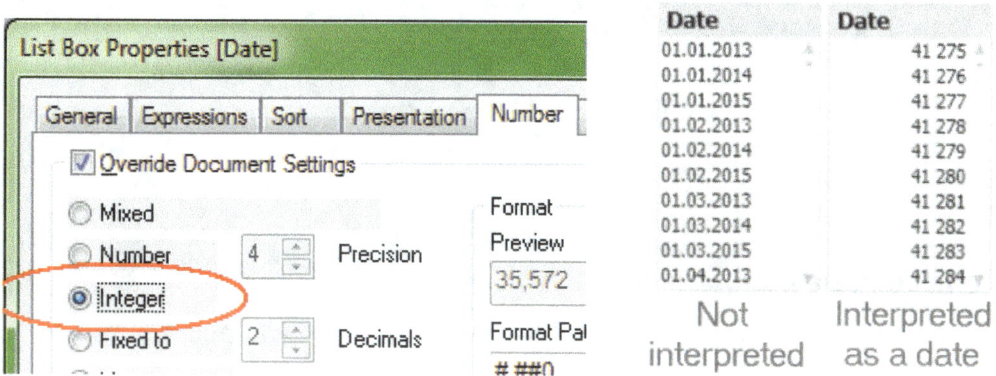

2. Linking integer dates with fractional dates

You have a date in two different tables, and you want to use this date as a key, but it doesn't seem to work. Then you should suspect that you have true dates (with integer values) in one table and timestamps (with fractional values) in the other, but the formatting of the dates hides this fact.

How do I know whether this is the case? That's easy. Just format it as a timestamp and see what you get. This is the same procedure as above, but you should use timestamp instead.

The question is now what your list box looks like. If you have timestamps where hours, minutes and seconds are all zero, then you are all set. But if you have numbers in these places, then you need to use the Floor() function in the script to get integer dates.

	QlikView			Qlik Sense	
	Date	**Date**		Timestamp(Date)	Timestamp(Date)
	01.01.2013 18:21:22	01.01.2013 0:00:00		01.01.2013 2:11:18	01.01.2013 0:00:00
	02.01.2013 3:34:44	02.01.2013 0:00:00		02.01.2013 3:25:43	02.01.2013 0:00:00
	03.01.2013 15:20:19	03.01.2013 0:00:00		03.01.2013 17:27:18	03.01.2013 0:00:00
	04.01.2013 20:50:58	04.01.2013 0:00:00		04.01.2013 4:20:51	04.01.2013 0:00:00
	05.01.2013 21:29:03	05.01.2013 0:00:00		05.01.2013 5:39:43	05.01.2013 0:00:00
	06.01.2013 9:27:12	06.01.2013 0:00:00			
	07.01.2013 11:28:47	07.01.2013 0:00:00			
	08.01.2013 4:05:52	08.01.2013 0:00:00			
	09.01.2013 21:16:26	09.01.2013 0:00:00			
	10.01.2013 10:34:26	10.01.2013 0:00:00			
	Non-integer dates	Integer dates		Non-integer dates	Integer dates

3. Incorrect date comparisons

The most subtle error is however the one with dates and timestamps in comparisons, e.g.

```
... Where Date = '2021-12-31' ;
```

Will this work? Yes, provided that the date format inside the string is recognized by the Qlik engine, i.e. that it corresponds to the date format specified in the environment variable **DateFormat** in the beginning of the script.

It becomes even more complex if you use variables. Then it is important to use quotes correctly. The following will work:

```
Let vToday = Today() ;

... Where Date = '$(vToday)' ;
```

But the following will **not**:

```
... Where Date = $(vToday) ;
```

The reason is that the $(**vToday**) will expand to a string containing the date, and then the comparison will be e.g.

```
... Where Date = 2/19/2013 ;
```

This means that the date (which is approximately 40000) will be compared to 2 divided by 19 divided by 2013, which of course is not what you want.

My recommendation is to always use numeric values in variables. They always work – quotes or no quotes:

```
Let vToday = Num(Today()) ;

... Where Date = '$(#vToday)' ;
```

Note the hash sign in the dollar expansion. It ensures that the number is expanded correctly: Decimal point and no thousand separators.

With this, I hope that you better understand how to avoid some errors when handling dates.

Automatic Number Interpretation

Posted in the Qlik Design Blog on July 8, 2013

I have in several previous blog posts written about the importance to interpret dates and numbers correctly e.g. in *Why don't my dates work?* These posts have emphasized the use of interpretation functions in the script, e.g. Date#().

But most of the time, you don't need any interpretation functions, since there is an automatic interpretation that kicks in before that.

So, how does that work?

In most cases when the Qlik engine encounters a string, it tries to interpret the string as a number. It happens in the script when field values are loaded; it happens when strings are used in **Where**-clauses, or in formulae in UI objects, or as function parameters. This is a good thing – the engine would otherwise not be able to interpret dates or decimal numbers.

The Qlik engine needs an interpretation algorithm since it can mix data from different sources, some typed, some not. For example, when you load a date from a text file, it is always a string: there are no data types in text files – all fields are strings. But when you want to link this field to date from a database, which usually is a typed field, you would run into problems unless you have a good interpretation algorithm.

	Text fields	Date and Number fields
Text files	Automatic interpretation	N/A
Database connections	Automatic interpretation	No interpretation. Stored as relevant data type
QVD / QVX files	No interpretation. Stored as text	No interpretation. Stored as relevant data type

For loaded fields, the Qlik engine uses the automatic interpretation when appropriate (See table: In a text file, all fields are text – also the ones with dates and timestamps.) The engine does not use any automatic interpretation for QVD or QVX files since the interpretation already is done. It was done when these files were created.

The logic for the interpretation is straightforward: The Qlik engine compares the encountered string with the information defined in the environment variables for numbers and dates in the beginning of the script. In addition, the Qlik engine will also test for a number with decimal point and for a date with the ISO date format.

If a match is found, the field value is stored in a dual format (see Data Types in the Qlik engine) using the string as format. If no match is found, the field value is stored as text.

An example: A where-clause in the script could look like this:

```
... Where Date > '2013-01-01'
```

The field **Date** is a dual that is compared to a string. The Qlik engine will automatically interpret the string on the right-hand side and make a correct numeric date comparison. The Qlik engine does not (at this stage) interpret the content of the field on the left-hand side of the comparison. The interpretation should already have been done.

A second example: The IsNum() function:

```
IsNum('2013-01-01')
IsNum('2013-01-32')
```

The first expression will evaluate as **True**, since the string can be interpreted as a valid date. The second expression, however, will evaluate as **False** since there is no 32:nd day of a month.

In both cases, strings are used as parameters. The first will be considered a number, since it can be interpreted as a date, but the second will not.

A third example: String concatenation:

```
Month(Year & '-' & Month & '-' & Day)
```

The expression inside the brackets will form a valid date, so the Qlik engine will recognize correct dates and the expression will return the corresponding dual month values.

Here the fields **Year**, **Month** and **Day** are concatenated with delimiters to form a valid date format. Since the Month() function expects a number (a date), the automatic number interpretation kicks in before the Month() function is evaluated, and the date is recognized.

A final example: The Dual() function:

```
Dual('Googol - A large number', '1E100')
```

This will evaluate to a very large number: 10^{100}.

Here the second parameter of Dual() is a string, but The Qlik engine expects a number. Hence: automatic interpretation. Here, you can see that scientific notation is automatically interpreted. This sometimes causes problems, since strings – that ought to be interpreted as strings – in some cases get interpreted as numbers. In such cases you need to wrap the field in a text function.

With this, I hope that the number handling in the Qlik engine is a little clearer.

On Format Codes for Numbers and Dates

Originally posted in the Qlik Design Blog on Dec 18, 2012

Numbers and dates are a never-ending source of concern when building any BI solution. But with the Qlik engine, there is always a way to solve a problem… First, the Qlik engine can interpret and format numbers and dates using functions in the script:

```
Date(                       // --- Formatting function
    Date#(                  // --- Interpretation function
        Field,
        'M/D/YY'            // --- Format code for input
    ),
    'YYYY-MM-DD'            // --- Format code for output
)                   as Date
```

Note the format codes that specify input and output format when loading this field.

Alternatively, the entity can be formatted the user interface, where each object, dimension or expression potentially can have its own number formatting:

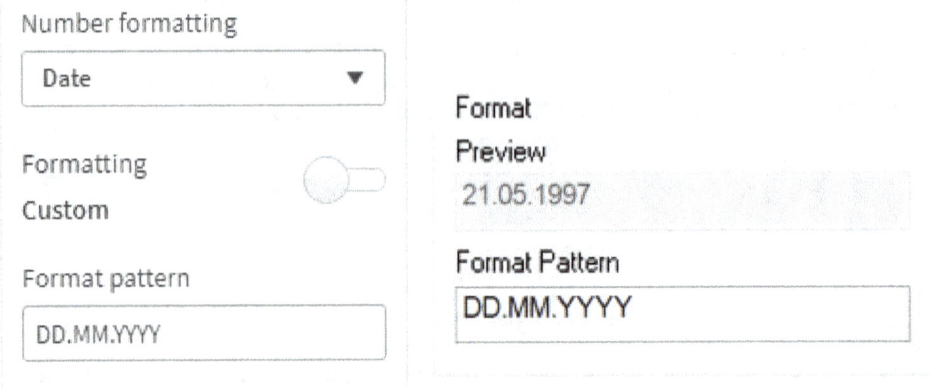

The common denominator for interpretation and formatting in the Qlik engine is the Format Code. The Qlik engine uses it as a parameter in many functions, and you can find it in the Format Pattern in the properties of the object.

The format code can contain several different characters to denote year, month, day, weekday, hour, minute, second, etc.

Some rules around the format codes:

- Unrecognized characters in the format code can prevent the Qlik engine from interpreting a number.

- The codes are case sensitive. For instance, M means month, whereas m means minutes. Some symbols can be written in either upper or lower case, e.g. AM/PM (or am/pm) and XIV (or xiv). For these, the format code must correspond to what you want: TT for AM/PM; tt for am/pm; (ROM) for XIV and (rom) for xiv.

- With the format code you can force a rounded display, e.g., by specifying two decimals on a multi-decimal number. You can also omit day when displaying a date, and just show year and month. Such a rounding will however only change the display and not the underlying number. To change the numeric value, you need to use a rounding function, e.g., Round(), Floor(), Ceil() or MonthStart().

Integers

You can specify integers to have leading zeros. You can also specify to display them as binary, octal, decimal and hexadecimal numbers. In fact, you can use any radix from 2 to 36. You can also format them as Roman numerals.

```
Num(Number, '000000') as Number // Always with at least 6 digits
Num(Number, '(R36)' ) as Number // Radix36
Num(Number, '(ROM)' ) as Number // Upper case Roman numerals
```

See picture below for the different cases. Each column denotes a specific format code. The rows are examples of input numbers and how the Qlik engine will format them.

Integers formatted using =Num(n,FormatCode)										
n FormatCode	##0	000	(bin)	(oct)	(hex)	(HEX)	(R04)	(R36)	(rom)	(ROM)
-64	-64	-064	-1000000	-100	-40	-40	-1000	-15	-lxiv	-LXIV
-1	-1	-001	-1	-1	-1	-1	-1	-1	-i	-I
0	0	000	0	0	0	0	0	0	0	0
1	1	001	1	1	1	1	1	1	i	I
7	7	007	111	7	7	7	13	7	vii	VII
29	29	029	11101	35	1d	1D	131	T	xxix	XXIX
89	89	089	1011001	131	59	59	1121	2H	lxxxix	LXXXIX

Floats

Real numbers are similar. If you need the Qlik engine to interpret a number that has a decimal symbol different from the one in the environment variables, be sure to use the third and fourth parameters of the Num#() function to specify decimal character and thousand separator. A correct format code is not enough.

```
Num#(Num,'0,0',',','.') as Num // decimal comma and thousand point
```

Floats formatted using	=Num(x,FormatCode)				
x FormatCode	##0	##0.00	(bin)	(HEX)	(HEX)##0.0
-63.14843750	-63	-63.15	-111111.0010011	-3F.26	-3F.2
-0.79296875	-1	-0.79	-0.11001011	-0.CB	-0.C
0.82421875	1	0.82	0.11010011	0.D3	0.D
1.94921875	2	1.95	1.11110011	1.F3	1.F
7.70312500	8	7.70	111.101101	7.B4	7.B
29.66406250	30	29.66	11101.1010101	1D.AA	1D.A
89.86718750	90	89.87	1011001.1101111	59.DE	59.D

Dates

The Qlik engine interprets the integer part of a date serial number as a *date* – the number of days from Dec 30, 1899 – same as Excel. But date formats are different from country to country, so you sometimes need to specify which format you want. Note that you can specify weekday also.

```
Date( MonthStart( Date ), 'YYYY MMM' ) as YearMonth
```

Integers formatted using	=Date(date,FormatCode)					
date FormatCode	YYYY-MM-DD	M/D/Y	DD/MM/YY	WWW DD MMM	MMM-YY	MMMM YYYY
-100000	1626-03-16	3/16/26	16/03/26	Mon 16 Mar	Mar-26	March 1626
-1	1899-12-29	12/29/99	29/12/99	Fri 29 Dec	Dec-99	December 1899
0	1899-12-30	12/30/99	30/12/99	Sat 30 Dec	Dec-99	December 1899
1	1899-12-31	12/31/99	31/12/99	Sun 31 Dec	Dec-99	December 1899
10000	1927-05-18	5/18/27	18/05/27	Wed 18 May	May-27	May 1927
41000	2012-04-01	4/1/12	01/04/12	Sun 01 Apr	Apr-12	April 2012
50000	2036-11-21	11/21/36	21/11/36	Fri 21 Nov	Nov-36	November 2036

Times

The Qlik engine interprets the fractional part of a date serial number as *time* of day. This can be specified in hours and minutes, etc. Note that the TT symbol denotes AM/PM. If this is not used, the Qlik engine will assume 24-hour notation.

```
Time(Floor(Time,1/24/4),'hh:mm') as Time // Truncated to quarter
```

Floats formatted using =Time(time,FormatCode)

time	FormatCode	h:mm	h:mm tt	h:mm TT	hh:mm:ss	hh:mm:ss:fff
0		0:00	12:00 am	12:00 AM	00:00:00	00:00:00:000
0.1111		2:39	2:39 am	2:39 AM	02:39:59	02:39:59:040
0.25		6:00	6:00 am	6:00 AM	06:00:00	06:00:00:000
0.3333		7:59	7:59 am	7:59 AM	07:59:57	07:59:57:120
0.5		12:00	12:00 pm	12:00 PM	12:00:00	12:00:00:000
0.75		18:00	6:00 pm	6:00 PM	18:00:00	18:00:00:000
0.9999		23:59	11:59 pm	11:59 PM	23:59:51	23:59:51:360

I recommend that you use interpretation, rounding, and formatting functions in the script to transform data into a form that you want.

On Boolean Fields and Functions

Originally posted in the Qlik Design Blog on Dec 7, 2012

The Qlik engine does not have any data types. Instead, there is the *Dual* format.

But it is still relevant to talk about data types, because Qlik functions and operators always return specific data types, albeit in the dual form. Further, the Qlik engine interprets dual parameters and operands differently depending on the expected data type.

And how does this work for Boolean functions?

All Boolean functions and operations, e.g. IsNull(), True() and comparisons such as **Date**=Today() return 0 for **FALSE** and -1 for **TRUE**. Why *minus* one? Because it is equivalent to setting all the bits in the byte to 1, which is how **TRUE** is represented in most software systems (as opposed to **FALSE**, where all bits are set to 0).

Further, in situations where the Qlik engine expects a Boolean, e.g. in the first parameter of the if() function or in a **Where**-clause, the Qlik engine will interpret 0 as **FALSE**, and _all other numbers_ as **TRUE**.

Number	if(Number,True(),False())	Num(if(Number,True(),False()))
-1	True	-1
0	False	0
1	True	-1
2.5	True	-1

This means that a number of functions can be used as either Boolean or numeric functions, e.g., Len(), Index(), Match(), Substringcount(), and FieldIndex(). For instance, the Match function compares an expression with a list of values and returns the position of the match. But when the Match() function is used in a Boolean position, the result will be interpreted as **TRUE** or **FALSE**.

Char	Match(Char,'A','B')	if(Match(Char,'A','B'),True(),False())
A	1	True
B	2	True
X	0	False

So when you use Match() in a where clause, you will have a condition that is very similar to the SQL "**IN**" operator. Further, with the WildMatch() function you can use wildcards, just like in the SQL "**LIKE**" operator. The two following statements do the same:

```
Load … Where Match(Char, 'A','B') or WildMatch(Name,'*son');

SQL SELECT … WHERE Char IN ('A','B') OR Name LIKE '%son';
```

But the real power of Booleans in the Qlik engine becomes obvious when you define flags in the dimensional tables. For instance, you can easily define a field in the master calendar that tells you if the date belongs to this year:

```
If(Year(Date)=Year(Today()), 1, 0) as IsThisYear
```

Then you can use this flag in expressions showing the numbers for this year only:

```
Sum(If(IsThisYear, Sales))
```

Or the same expression with Set Analysis:

```
Sum({<IsThisYear={1}>} Sales)
```

Similarly, you can create flags for almost anything: **IsLastYear**, **IsThisYearToDate**, **IsThisMonth**, **IsShipped**, **IsFirstClassCustomer**, etc.

One nice thing about flags is that they are stored in the dimensional tables, which are relatively small tables. Hence, the flags don't use much memory space. Secondly, The Qlik engine evaluates expressions with flags relatively fast. A third advantage is that it is an efficient way for a script developer to define complex concepts in a way that the business user easily understands.

Conclusions:

- Use the Match and Index functions as Boolean functions in **Where**-clauses and If-functions.
- Create flags in the dimensional tables and use these as Booleans in expressions.

Numbers, Dates, and Data Types

5

Data Modelling

The simplest apps only contain one single table. Then you don't need to know very much about the data model. A table is a table and there really isn't more to it.

But as soon as you load more than one table, you need to think. What does a record in a table represent? What is a primary key? How does this table link to other tables? Is the relation a many-to-one relationship, or is it a many-to-many relationship?

This chapter pertains to everything that relates to the data model.

Star schema and other data models

Normalized relational model

Most source databases are optimized for storing data, and not for analyzing data. They are almost always structured according to the third normal form. This means that data is normalized in a way so that redundant information is avoided: Every entity is stored in its own table; with a key that identifies the instance, together with all attributes of the entity.

> "Every attribute must provide a fact about the key,
> the whole key, and nothing but the key,
> so help me Codd." [1]

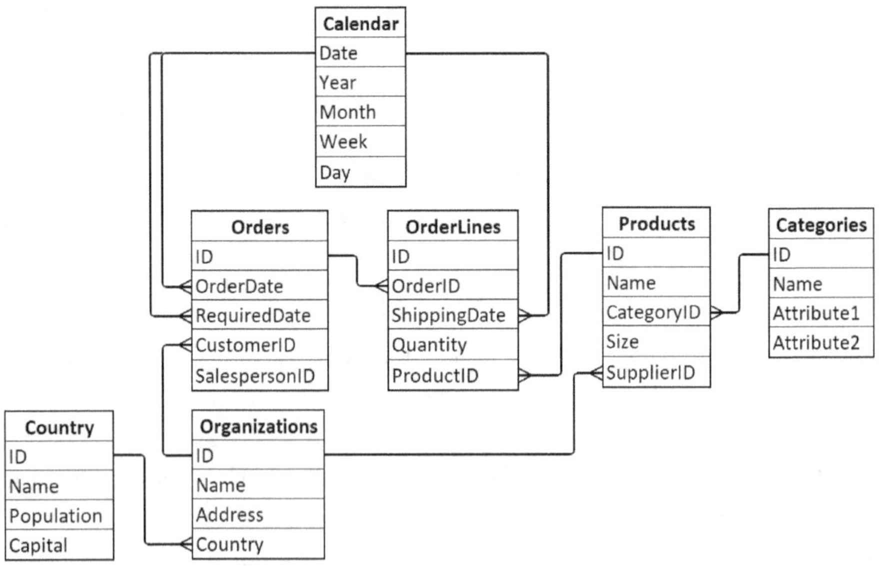

The tables are usually referred to as either *Transaction* tables or *Master* tables. Master tables, e.g. **Products, Calendar, Customers**, are rarely changed – they usually stay the same from day to day. The transaction tables, on the other hand, change all the time. This is where all the actions are registered, e.g. **Orders, Order lines, Invoices**, etc.

The above data model is a subset of an orders database and can serve as an example.

Note that one single primary key (e.g. the "ID" and "Date") can be used as foreign keys in multiple tables. This means that the entity can have different *roles*. For example, the entity "Organization" is used for both customers and suppliers. This is different from how data is organized for analysis: When analyzing data, different roles must be separated.

Note also that there are circular references. This must be avoided when analyzing data, since it will lead to ambiguities. But here it is not a problem, since any query will be made using a SELECT statement that can define a non-ambiguous join that resolves the circular reference.

Finally, note the field names: It is very common that field names like "ID", "Name" "Description", etc. are used in multiple tables and that they mean different things in the different tables. When analyzing data, such field must be qualified or renamed, so that a user understands what the presented field represents.

Hence, the above data model cannot be used as it is in a Qlik app.

Star Schema

When analyzing data, no matter which tool you use, a *Star Schema* is a common way to model the data. It is a multi-dimensional data model designed to make it easy to understand and analyze data. The idea is to put all metrics in a central, large *Fact* table, and surround this with the necessary *Dimension* tables. This way, the structure looks like a star. Hence the name.

The Fact table is based on the Transaction tables in the source database, and the Dimension tables are based on the Master tables in the source database.

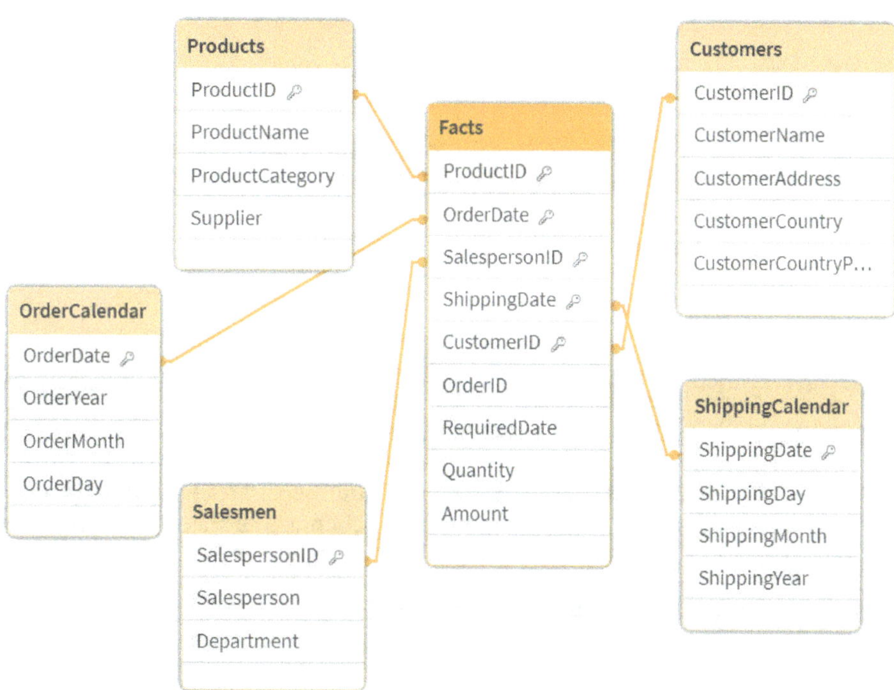

Note that the **Orders** table and the **OrderLines** tables have been joined into a single Fact table. Note also that the **Organizations** table is renamed **Customers** – because that is the role this data has here. Note finally that the **Calendar** has been loaded twice and has been linked to two different dates.

A Star Schema is very well suited for Qlik apps.

Snowflake schema

A *Snowflake Schema* is very similar to a Star Schema, but with the difference that it allows more than one layer of tables branching out from the Fact table.

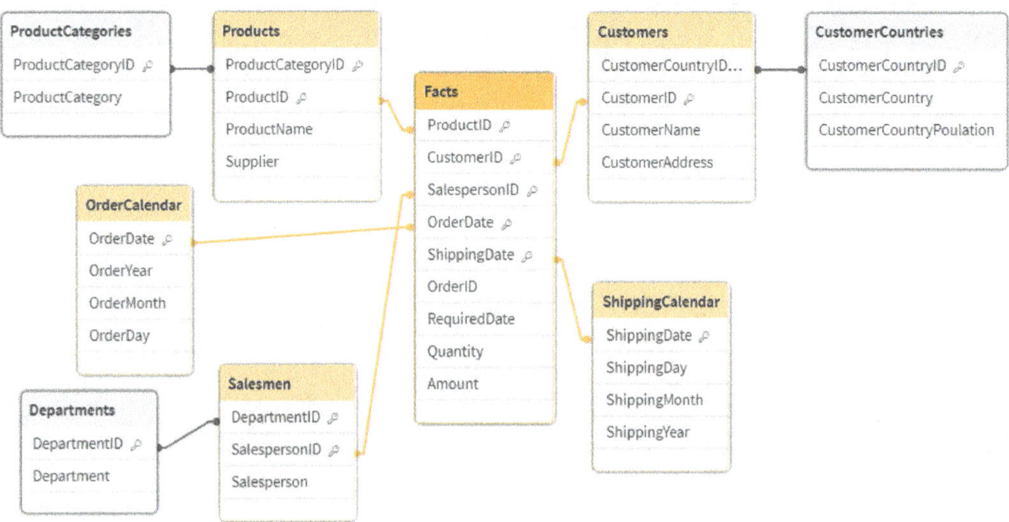

Note that here the **Product Categories**, the **Departments**, and the **Customer Countries** have been broken out into their own tables. Hence, a Snowflake Schema is more normalized than a Star Schema.

A Snowflake Schema is also very well suited for Qlik apps.

Link table

Both the Star Schema and the Snowflake Schema have a limitation: They can be difficult to implement if there is more than one Fact Table – especially if the Fact tables have different grain.

One example comes from the pharmaceutical industry:

- A sales representative makes visits to physicians presenting the different products of the pharma company. These sales calls are stored in a **Calls** table, where each row represents an individual product presented.
- Later, the physician prescribes the product to a patient, who buys it at a local pharmacy. This sales information is stored in a **Sales** table.
- The pharma company can also obtain information about the competitor products.

The three above bullets represent three different fact tables.

Further, the three fact tables have different keys. For example, information about the sales representative only exists in the **Calls** table.

Also, the three fact tables usually have different grain. For example, the **Calls** table could contain **Product** and **Date**, whereas the **Sales** table could contain **Package** (more detailed than **Product**) and **Month** (less detailed than **Date**).

So, linking the fact tables is not easy, but it can be done.

In the data model in the image, you have the fact tables to the right, and the dimension tables to the left. They are linked through a Link table in the middle. The L2 tables are second level link tables for the Generic keys used (See "Generic keys").

Link table solutions can solve very complex data modelling problems. But they come at a price: They are resource demanding, both when it comes to RAM and CPU. So, you can expect longer response times.

So, my recommendation is: Use them if you must. But avoid them if you can. In many cases a concatenated fact table can solve the problem just as well. And it is faster.

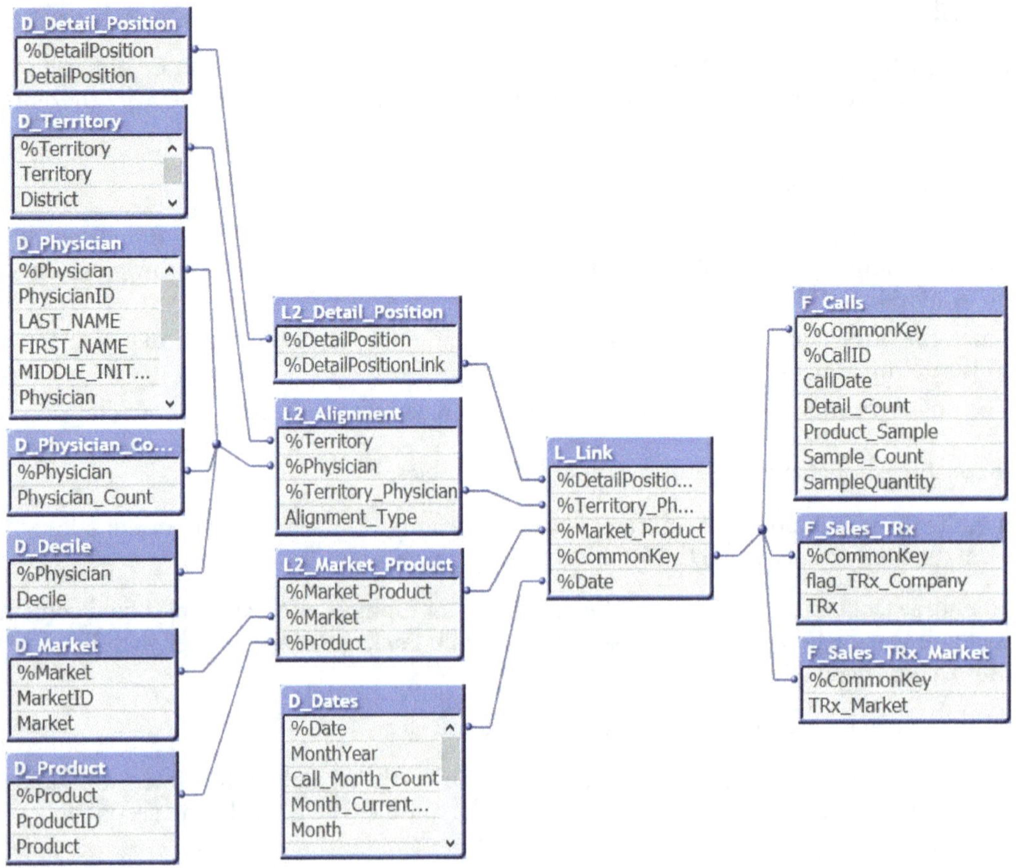

[1]   Kent, William. "A Simple Guide to Five Normal Forms in Relational Database Theory", Communications of the ACM 26 (2), Feb. 1983, pp. 120–125.

The Table Viewer

Originally posted in the Qlik Design Blog on Jun 18, 2013

The table viewer is a gem.

I use it for many things: to get an overview; to debug what I have done in the script; to check that all tables are linked; to check that I don't have any unwanted synthetic keys; to preview data. I can hardly remember what I did before QlikView had it.

In QlikView, you just hit <ctrl>-T and in Qlik Sense you choose "Data Model Viewer" in the top bar.

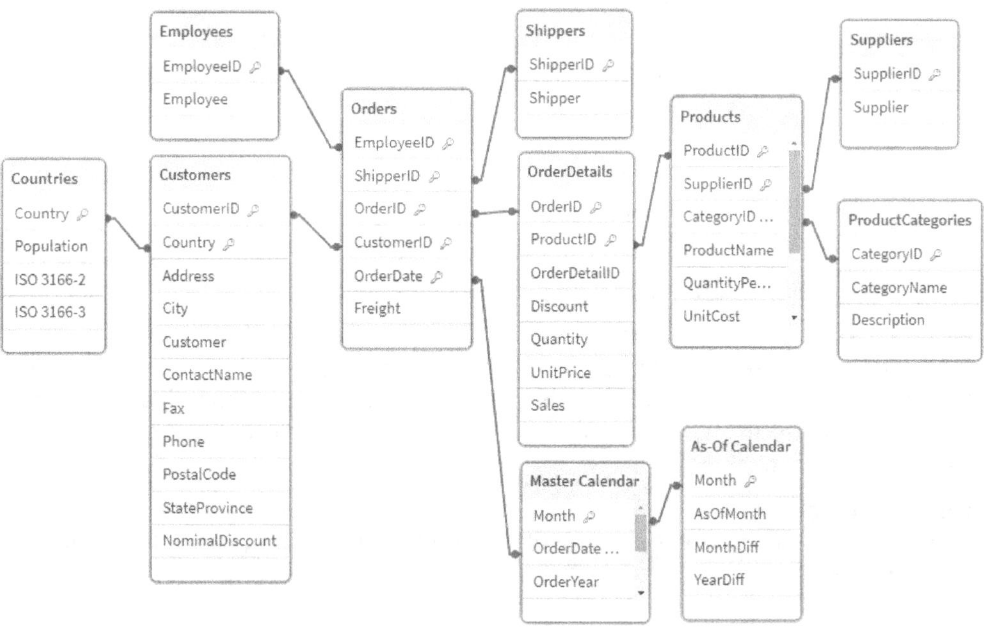

I move around the tables until the structure corresponds to the picture I have in my head. I tell new users developing applications to draw the wanted data model on a piece of paper, so they know what the goal is. If they can't draw it on a piece of paper, they need to sit down and think. Or play around with data in the app until they understand and can draw the data model. The structure seen in the table viewer then becomes an acknowledgement that the data model is correctly implemented. Or a warning that it isn't.

There are two modes of the table viewer: The Internal table view and the Source table view. The only difference is how the synthetic keys are displayed. During the script development, I always use the source table view, since it shows me exactly what I have done in the script.

If you mark a table header, you can see the number of rows and number of fields in the preview. If you hover above an individual field, you will get the data for this specific field: Whether it is a key, the information density, the subset ratio and – if applicable – the tags. In QlikView, you hover above it the table header or the field.

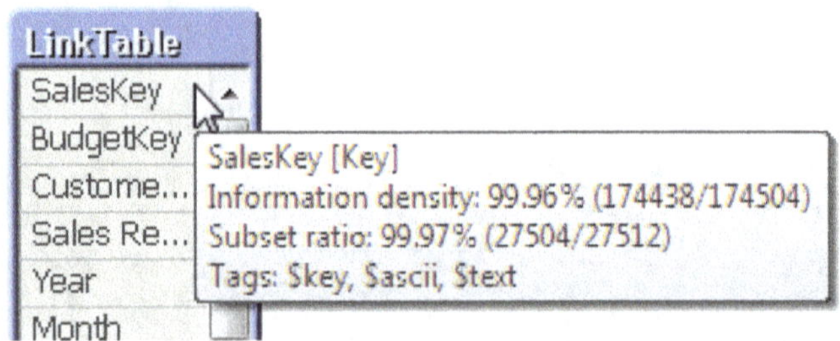

- **Key**
  Key fields are marked with "Key", "Primary key" or "Perfect key". "Perfect key" means that there are no duplicates in the table, and that the field has a complete set of values. "Primary key" means that there are no duplicates in the table, but additional values exist in other tables.

- **Information density**
  The information density is a measure of the number of NULL values. 100% means no NULL values.

- **Subset ratio**
  The subset ratio is a measure of the number of distinct values that exist in the table, compared to the number of distinct values of this field in all tables.

Many, when they see the table viewer, start thinking about a graphical tool to define which source data to load. But this is not what the table viewer is – it is a viewer only. So, take it for what it is: The best available tool to get an overview of the data model. And as one of the best debugging tools in the application development process.

*And **that** is not bad.*

Linking Tables

Extract from the Technical brief "Joins and Lookups" published on Sep 12, 2012

The data model defined in the Qlik script usually contains many tables that are linked with key fields. The links are implicit joins that are not yet made. In other words, they define where joins should be made when the user makes a selection. But since they are not yet evaluated, they are not called "joins". Instead, they are called "*associations*".

When the associations are evaluated, they are evaluated as *natural* joins, i.e. the Qlik engine requires the key field to have the same value in the two tables. It is hence <u>not</u> possible to use any other condition for the link, e.g. the following criterion cannot be used:

> TableA.key >= TableB.Key

In addition, the Qlik script can contain explicit joins. These are different and these are indeed called "*joins*". These are executed when the script runs, and the resulting table will constitute one table in the Qlik engine data model unless it is dropped. See more about these in the next section.

Hence, the main difference between the associations and joins is that the associations are evaluated at demand as the user makes selections. As opposed to the joins that are evaluated when the script runs.

A second difference is that a join is explicitly an inner join or an outer join (or a left or a right join) whereas the nature of an association depends on the situation. The association can be evaluated to a left join or a right join depending on where the user has made a selection. And with no selection, the association is always evaluated to a full outer join.

For example, if you have a table containing customers and a table containing orders, and you select some customers, then The Qlik engine will make a left join: All the selected customers (left table) will be possible, even though they are not represented in the order table. But only the orders (right table) that are represented in the customer table are possible.

So, when you make your data model in the Qlik script, you make the necessary data transformations, sometimes using explicit joins, and you make sure to name the keys so that the resulting tables are linked correctly. Also, you also make sure to name non-keys with unique names so that these do not link.

Circular References

Posted in the Qlik Design Blog June 25, 2013

There are two Swedish car brands, Volvo and SAAB. Or, at least, there used to be ... SAAB was made in Trollhättan and Volvo was – and still is – made in Gothenburg.

Two fictive friends – Albert and Herbert – live in Trollhättan and Gothenburg, respectively. Albert drives a Volvo and Herbert drives a SAAB.

If the above information is stored in a tabular form, you get the following three tables:

Car	City
Volvo	Gothenburg
SAAB	Trollhättan

Person	City
Albert	Trollhättan
Herbert	Gothenburg

Person	Car
Albert	Volvo
Herbert	SAAB

Logically, these tables form a circular reference: The first two tables are linked through City; the next two through Person; the last and the first through Car.

Further, the data forms an anomaly: Volvo implies Gothenburg; Gothenburg implies Herbert; and Herbert implies SAAB. Hence, Volvo implies SAAB – which doesn't make sense. This means that you have ambiguous results from the logical inference – different results depending on whether you evaluate clockwise or counterclockwise.

If you load these tables into Qlik, the circular reference will be identified, and you will get the following data model:

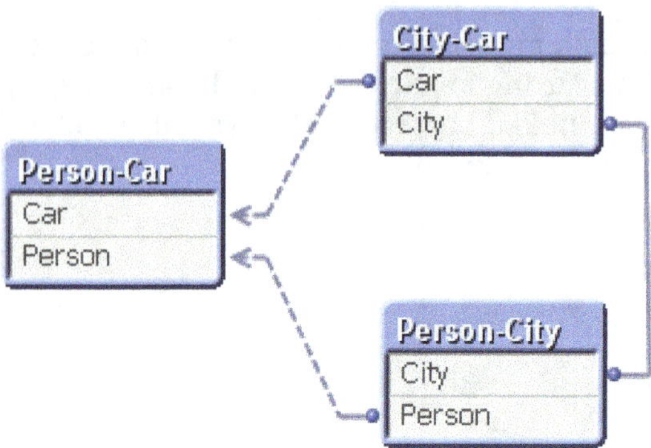

To avoid ambiguous results, the Qlik engine marks one of the tables as "loosely coupled", which means that the logical inference cannot propagate through this table. In the document properties you can decide which table to use as the loosely coupled table. You will get different results from the logical inference depending on which you choose.

So, what did I do wrong? Why did I get a circular reference?

It is not always obvious why they occur, but when I encounter circular references, I always look for fields that are used in several different *roles* at the same time. One obvious example is if you have a table listing external organizations and this table is used in several roles: as Customers, as Suppliers and as Shippers. If you load the table only once and link to all three foreign keys, you will most likely get a circular reference. You need to break the circular reference and the solution is of course to load the table several times, once for each role.

In the above data model, you have a similar case. You can think of Car as "Car produced in the city" or "Car that our friend drives". And you can think of City as "City where car is produced" or "City where our friend lives". Again, you should break the circular reference by loading a table twice. One possible solution is the following:

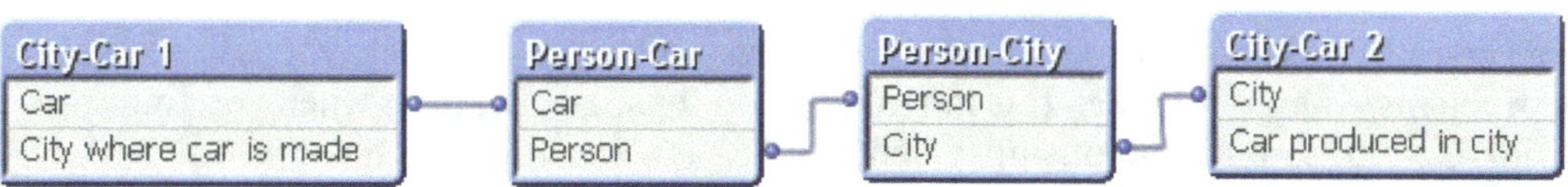

In real life circular references are not as obvious as this one. I once encountered a data model with many tables describing how different machines were configured. At first, I could not figure out what to do, but after some analysis, the problem boiled down to the interaction between three fields: **Customers**, **Machines** and **Devices**.

- A customer had bought one or several machines.
- A machine could have different optional devices connected to it – but not all devices were possible to connect.
- A customer had bought some devices.

Hence, the field "**Devices**" could have two roles: Devices that the customer actually had bought; and devices that would fit the machine that the customer had bought, i.e. devices that the customer potentially could buy. *Two roles.* The solution was to load the device table twice using different names.

Bottom line: Avoid circular references. But you probably already knew that …

Joins in the Script

Extract from the Technical brief "Joins and Lookups" published on Sep 12, 2012

Sometimes you need to join tables in the script, i.e. you use two or more tables as input, perform the join and get one table as output for the Qlik engine data model. It could be that you want to de-normalize the data model to improve performance or that you, for some other reason, choose to put fields from two tables into one.

When you join two tables, there is always a possibility that the number of records change. In most cases, this is not a problem – rather, it is exactly what you want.

One example could be that you have a table containing order headers and one containing order details. Each header can have several order lines in the order details table. When these two tables are joined, the resulting table should have the same number of records as the order details table: you have a one-to-many relationship so an order can have several order lines, but an order line cannot belong to several order headers. The only problem you encounter is that you can no longer sum a number that originally resides in the order header table.

If you join over a many-to-many relationship, the new number of records will possibly be larger than the number of records of any of the constituting tables.

In some cases, you get a change of number of records when you don't expect it, and this may cause problems. I have often seen this in real life, and it usually happens when you join what you think is a one-to-one relationship, when it in fact is a one-to-many relationship. An example is when you have product attributes in another table than the master product table. Then one product can potentially have several attributes, and a join may cause the Qlik engine to calculate some numbers incorrectly. Or rather – The Qlik engine calculates the numbers correctly, but the result is not what you expect.

There are two ways to perform joins in the Qlik script:

The external join – the SQL SELECT join

A join can be defined inside a **SELECT** statement, which in the script execution is sent as a string to the connector, usually a relational database management system (RDBMS) using the ODBC or OLE DB connection. Then the Qlik engine waits for an answer. In other words: the SQL join is performed on the DB system. This is sometimes more efficient and more robust than if you let the Qlik engine manage it. This is especially true if you have large tables; then you should make the join inside the **SELECT** statement.

A join inside a **SELECT** statement is often versatile: you can make any type of join that the database allows, e.g. also joins that are not natural:

```
Where TableA.key >= TableB.Key
```

One consequence of letting the DB system manage the join is that the syntax of the **SELECT** statement may differ from database to database. The Qlik engine does _not_ interpret the SELECT statement. Instead, it is evaluated by the database.

Examples of **SELECT** statements joining tables:

```
SELECT
    Customers.FirstName,
    Customers.LastName,
    SUM(Sales.SaleAmount) AS SalesPerCustomer
FROM Customers
    LEFT JOIN Sales
    ON Customers.CustomerID = Sales.CustomerID
GROUP BY Customers.FirstName, Customers.LastName;

SELECT
    Suppliers.SupplierID,
    Suppliers.SupplierName,
    Orders.OrderDate
FROM Suppliers, Orders
WHERE Suppliers.SupplierID = Orders.SupplierID;
```

The Qlik engine join – the Join prefix

The **Join** prefix in the Qlik script joins the loaded table with one that has been loaded previously in the script. It is performed by the Qlik engine itself. Just like the associations, the Qlik engine joins are natural joins based on fields with the same name. If there is no common key, the Cartesian product of the two tables will be generated.

The Qlik engine join is fast but will need a lot of primary memory. So, if the tables are large, the performance may become poor. For smaller tables it is, however, the best alternative.

The **Join** prefix can be put in front of a **Load** statement or in front of a **SELECT** statement. By default, an outer join is made. But it is also possible to make an inner, left or right join.

Examples of statements using the **Join** prefix:

```
Join Load … From … ;

Left Join (SomePreviousTable) Load … From … ;

Inner Join SQL SELECT … FROM … ;
```

The Keep prefix

Similar to the **Join** prefix is the **Keep** prefix. It works the same way as a join, but it does not *merge* the two tables. Instead, it keeps them as two separate tables. However, it performs the same type of comparison as a join and then removes the same records as it would have removed if it had been a join. An inner keep keeps only the records where a common key value exists in both tables. It is hence a very good way of removing unnecessary data.

The **Keep** prefix can be put in front of a **Load** statement or in front of a **SELECT** statement. The **Keep** prefix must be preceded by one of the keywords **Inner**, **Left** or **Right** to make sense.

Examples of statements using the **Keep** prefix:

```
Left Keep Load … From ;

Right Keep (SomePreviousTable) Load … From ;

Inner Keep SQL SELECT … FROM … ;
```

A common case where you want to use a **Keep** prefix is when you have used a **Where** clause to load a subset of the transactions, e.g. the orders for just one year or one region, and want to load only the corresponding data sets from the master tables:

```
OrderDetails:
Load * From OrderDetails
    Where <SomeCriterion>;


Products:
Left Keep (OrderDetails) Load * From Products;
```

This will reduce the number of records in the product table to fit with what has been loaded in the order details.

Lookup Functions

Extract from the Technical brief "Joins and Lookups" published on Sep 12, 2012

Similar to the joins are the lookup functions. These functions fetch information from another table or look up a specific value in another table and return this.

One case is a mapping or a translation: You could for instance have a product ID and you want to translate that into a specific product attribute. In other words – you never expect more than one value for the specific product ID. If there are several possible values in the lookup table, the lookup function will just take the first one found.

Another case is when you want to load all records from one table but exclude the records that have their IDs listed in another table.

If you want to solve these types of problems using SQL, you will most likely use joins. However, in the Qlik engine, you should avoid joins in these situations. Instead, you should use one of the lookup functions. Applymap() is usually the best choice. This way you get a faster script execution, and you ensure that the number of records do not change when they shouldn't.

If you *do* expect several values for each of the input values, you should not use a lookup function to solve the problem. Then a join is the appropriate solution.

The Lookup() function

The most obvious lookup function is the function with the same name. With it, you can look into another previously loaded table and retrieve a specific field value.

For example, you may, while loading a table containing order data want to retrieve the product category for the product found in the order data. You have the product ID in the order data table, but the product category is found in another table – in the product table.

Then you could solve this problem by using the Lookup() function:

```
Lookup('ProductCategory', 'ProductID', ProductID, 'ProductTable')
```

The Lookup() function will then return the value of the field **ProductCategory** (first parameter) in the table **ProductTable** (fourth parameter) from the record where the field **ProductID** (second parameter) has the same value as the field **ProductID** in the order data table (third parameter).

Note that references to fields in other tables must be enclosed by single quotes, whereas references to fields in the same table must *not* be enclosed by single quotes. In this hypothetical example, the Lookup() function is used inside the Load statement of the order data, so fields in the product table must be enclosed by single quotes.

The advantage with the Lookup() function is that it is flexible and can access any previously loaded table. The drawback is that it is slow compared to the Applymap() function.

The Applymap() function

My preferred lookup function is the Applymap() function. With it you can make any translation or mapping – but you need to define the translation in a mapping table before you can use it. Applymap() uses the mapping table as lookup table and returns the appropriate translation.

If we once again look at the case of getting the product category into the order data table, a solution using Applymap() would be the following:

```
Map_ProductID_2_Category:
Mapping Load ProductID, ProductCategory From ProductTable ;

OrderData:
Load *,
    Applymap('Map_ProductID_2_Category',ProductID,'ERROR')
                                        as ProductCategory
    From OrderData ;
```

The mapping table may only have two columns. How these are named is irrelevant: The first one is always the value from which to translate and the second one is always the value to translate into. The mapping table is discarded at the end of the script execution.

When you use the Applymap() function, you need to enclose the table name (first parameter) with single quotes. Also, I recommend that you use a third parameter to define what value the function should return when the product ID is not found in the mapping table. You may want to use the null() function or the string 'Missing'.

The advantage with the Applymap() function is that it is very fast compared to the Lookup() function. The drawback is that you need to prepare a dedicated mapping table before you can use it.

The Exists() function

The Exists() function is slightly different from other lookup functions, but can still be used for similar purposes. It doesn't return a specific value, but it can tell you whether a value has been previously loaded or not.

If you for instance want to load all products from the standard product table, but exclude some that are listed in another table, you can do it with the Exists() function:

```
DiscontinuedProducts:
Load
    ProductID as DiscontinuedProductID
    From DiscontinuedProducts;

Products:
Load * From Products
    Where not Exists (DiscontinuedProductID, ProductID);
```

Another case when you may want to use the Exists() function is when you have loaded a subset of the transactions, e.g. all orders for just one day or one region, and want to load only the corresponding data sets of the master tables:

```
OrderDetails:
Load * From OrderDetails
    Where <SomeCriterion>;

Products:
Load * From Products
    Where Exists (Products);
```

This will reduce the number of records in the Products table to fit with what has been loaded in the order details. The same reduction can be made using a Keep prefix.

The Peek() function

The Peek() function is similar to the Lookup() function, but instead of searching for a field value in other table, the peek function needs a row number. '-1' denotes the last record in the table.

```
Peek ('ProductCategory', -1, 'ProductTable')
```

Although the Peek() function is a lookup function, its use for solving similar problems is limited since you need the row number to get the desired value, and this is rarely the case.

To Join or not to Join

Originally posted in the Qlik Design Blog on Sep 12, 2012

The Qlik engine internal logic enables a data model with several associated tables. It not only allows – it encourages you to use several tables when building a data model.

This is very different from many other BI or query tools where, when several tables are used, they are all joined together into one table. The most obvious example of this difference is a simple **SELECT** statement. With it, you can use several tables as input and join them, but the output is *always* one single, de-normalized table.

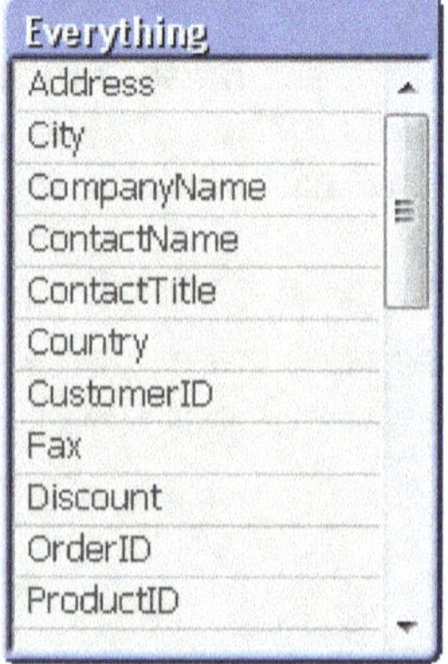

Completely denormalized. Everything in one table.

With Qlik, in contrast, you can have a multi-table relational data model that is evaluated in real-time. The associations are evaluated as joins at the moment when the user makes a selection in the application. After this, all objects, some with complex calculations based on these joins, are recalculated.

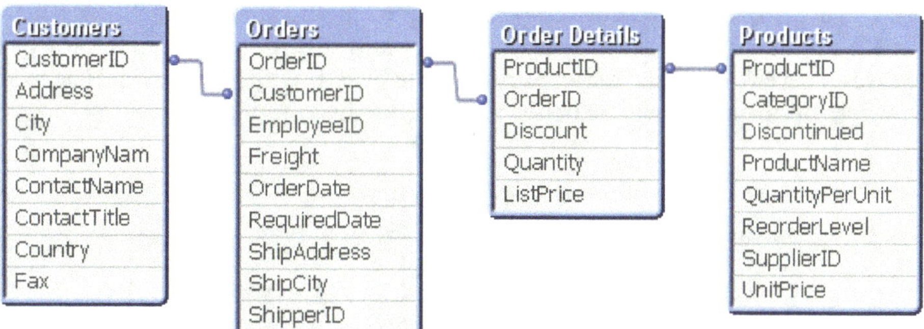

Normalized. Each entity type in its own table.

When creating a Qlik data model, you have a choice of loading the tables as several entities or joining some of them together. Joining in the script means that the result of the join is stored in the Qlik data model as one single table.

So, what should you do? Is it better to keep the data model normalized (many tables) or is it better to de-normalize (fewer tables)?

My view is that it usually is better to keep the data model as normalized as possible, although there are cases when it is better to join them in the script. This article will try to explain when you should do one or the other.

A normalized model has many advantages:

- **It is memory efficient**.
  A normalized solution is, by definition, the data model that uses least memory.
- **It is CPU efficient**.
  In most cases, calculations in a normalized model are as efficient – or only marginally slower – as in a denormalized model. However, with extremely large data amounts, de-normalized data model is faster.
- **It is easier to understand and manage**.
  It should be possible for other developers to read your script: A simple script – with as few transformations as possible – is often a script that is easy for other developers to understand and maintain. A script containing many joins is hard to read and understand.
- **It minimizes the risk for incorrect calculations**.
  Joins potentially change the number of records in the tables, which means that a normal Sum() or Count() function cannot always be used – they would sometimes return an incorrect result. You may counter that there is always a way to write a correct formula, but my point is that it should also be easy. Some expressions will be written by users that do not have special knowledge about the data model in the app.

But it is not a clear-cut case.

Often there is a trade-off between memory efficiency and CPU efficiency. In other words, there are cases where you can decrease response time by letting the data model use more memory; where performance will be better if you make the join in the script.

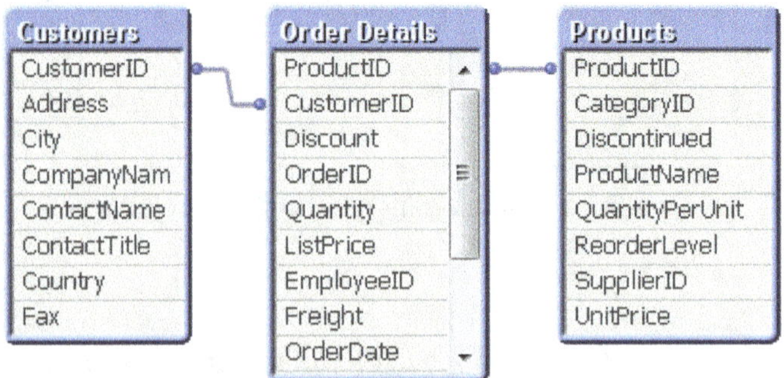

Slightly denormalized. Orders and Order Details are joined.

One such case is if you have two very large fact tables, like **Order Headers** and **Order Details**. Then you should usually join the two large tables.

Another is if you have chart expressions containing fields from different tables. For example

```
Sum( Quantity * UnitPrice )
```

where **Quantity** is in the transaction table and **UnitPrice** is in the Products table.

Then the Qlik engine has to perform the join in memory generating a virtual table over which the summation will be made. This can be both memory and CPU demanding, so you might get a better performance if you move a field so that both are in the same table. (See ApplyMap() for how to do this.) But the difference is sometimes only marginal. You need to test, to be sure.

Bottom line is that you'll have to weigh the pros and cons. *Don't join unless you have to.* If performance is important and you experience a noticeable improvement when you join, then you probably should join. But ask yourself what the implications are. Is the script still manageable? Can a user understand how the formula should be written?

The best join is often the one that never is made. Often – but not always.

Don't join – use Applymap instead

Originally posted in the Qlik Design Blog on Sep 18, 2012

My latest blog post was on joins in the Qlik engine (see To Join or not to Join). In it I claimed that you should avoid making joins in the Qlik script, if possible. This blog post is about a function that can help you avoid joins. It is about the function Applymap().

It is, in fact, one of my favorite functions and I do not seem to be alone in this choice. Several of the Qlik app developers who regularly write on QlikCommunity seem to share this preference and have written about this function.

So, what does the function do? Well, basically it is just a lookup function – it takes one value as input, checks if this value exists in a mapping table and returns the corresponding value from the second column in the mapping table. Think of it as a translation function where the translation is fetched from a pre-defined, two-column table. A simple translation function, but you can still do a lot with it ...

What has this got to do with joins?

Everything. A very common situation in data modeling is that you for a specific record need to get a single field value from a different table than the current one. Then the standard way to do this is to use a join. However, in a Qlik app you can – and should – use Applymap() instead. The only time that you cannot use Applymap() instead of a join is if you want to fetch more than one single corresponding value from the second table.

Let's look at an example of how to use Applymap(): In an ERP system, the customer table is the table where all information about the customer is stored, e.g. the name and country of the customer. Further, it could be that you need the customer's country when making a calculation in the order table. This is, however, a field that you don't have in the order table. In SQL you would join the two tables to get country into the order table.

In the Qlik script you would instead first define the mapping table that maps a customer ID to a customer country, and then use this information in a subsequent Load:

```
Customer2Country:
Mapping Load CustomerID, Country From Customers;

Orders:
Load *,
    ApplyMap('Customer2Country',CustomerID,Null()) as Country
    From Orders;
```

The second Load statement uses the ApplyMap() function to make a lookup in the mapping table.

The "Null()" as third parameter of the function defines what it should return when the customer ID isn't found in the mapping table.

And with this, you have joined the field **Country** with the **Orders** table – without using a join. And you have done it faster and with less chance of errors. Bottom line: Whenever you know that you just want to fetch one single value per record – don't join. Use Applymap() instead.

Synthetic Keys

Originally posted in the Qlik Design Blog on Apr 16, 2013

In a well visited post on the QlikCommunity forum, John Witherspoon some time ago asked, "Should We Stop Worrying and Love the Synthetic Key?" John's post begins:

> *"Synthetic keys have a bad reputation. The consensus seems to be that they cause performance and memory problems, and should usually or even always be removed. I believe that the consensus is wrong."*

Here's my view on this topic.

The creation of synthetic keys is simply Qlik engine's way of managing composite keys. There is nothing strange or magic around it.

A single key is easy to manage: Just list all unique values in a symbol table (see Symbol Tables and Bit-Stuffed Pointers), and then link the data tables using a natural join.

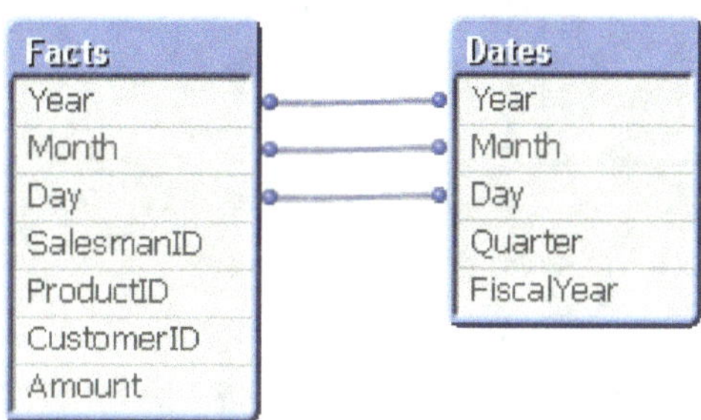

But a composite key is slightly different – there is no single symbol table that contains the relevant combinations of the multiple key fields. So QlikView needs to create such a table for all combinations: the **$Syn** table. In a way, you can say that the **$Syn** table is a symbol table for composite keys. In the data tables, the multiple keys are replaced by an identifier that uniquely identifies the combination of the values of the original keys: the **$Syn** key.

Hence, if you have the same set of multiple keys in two or more tables, the Qlik engine synthetic keys create a general, correct, compact and efficient solution. Synthetic keys **do not** per se cause performance or memory problems. They **do not** use a lot more memory than if you autonumber your own concatenated key. And they treat NULLs correctly, as opposed to an explicit concatenated key.

Hence: The synthetic key is in itself good, and we should all love it.

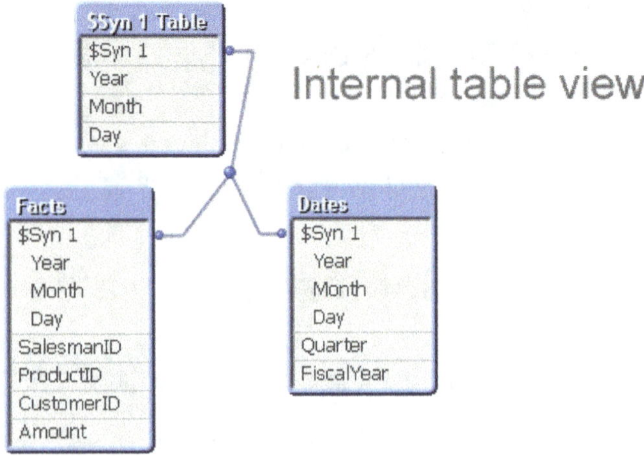

However… also I avoid synthetic keys. Why?

1. A synthetic key is in my experience often a sign of a *poorly designed data model*. I say that, given the number of times I have found a synthetic key in the table viewer only to realize that I made a mistake in the script. If you get a synthetic key and didn't expect it, I can only say: *Back to the drawing board! You should most likely change your data model.*

2. The Qlik engine creates an additional table (the *$Syn* table) that in many cases is superfluous: An additional table is the best solution if none of the data tables by itself completely spans the set of composite keys. But in real life, there is usually one table that contains all relevant combinations of the keys, and then this table can be used to store the clear text of the individual keys.

3. For clarity, I like to create my own concatenated keys. It forces me to think and create a data model that I believe in. Removing the synthetic keys becomes *a method* to ensure a good data model, rather than a goal in itself.

But in principle, I totally agree with John's initial conclusion: Any problem around synthetic keys is really a data modeling problem and not a problem with the synthetic key itself.

The short answer to John's question is **Yes and No**. Yes, we should love the synthetic key. But, no, we should not stop worrying. We should always be alert and ask ourselves: *"Do I want this synthetic key? Is the data model OK?"*

> *And so, because of the automated and irrevocable data-modeling process which rules out human meddling, the Synthetic Keys are scaring. But they are simple to understand. And completely credible and convincing.*

Dr StrangeHIC

Why You should Load the same Master Table several times

Originally posted in the Qlik Design Blog on Aug 30, 2012

How normalized should the Qlik data model be? To what extent should you have the data in several tables so that you avoid having the same information expressed on multiple rows?

Usually as much as possible. The more normalized, the better. A normalized data model is easier to manage and minimizes the risk of incorrect calculations.

This said, there are occasions where you need to de-normalize. A common case is when the source database contains a generic master table, i.e. a master table that is used for several purposes. For example: you have a common lookup table for customers, suppliers, and shippers. Or you have a master calendar table that is used for several different date fields, e.g. order date and shipping date (see image below).

A typical sign for this situation is that the primary key of the master table links to several foreign keys, sometimes in different parts of the data model. The **OrganizationID** links to both **CustomerID** and **ShipperID** and the **Date** field links to both **OrderDate** and **ShippingDate**.

The master table has several roles.

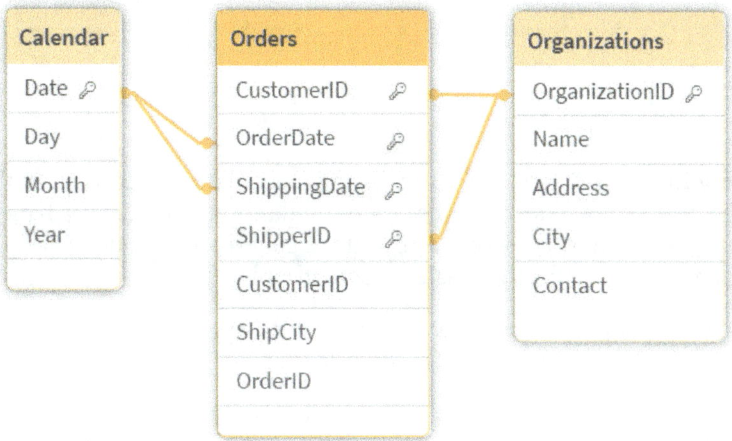

The necessary de-normalization in a Qlik data model is easy. You should simply load the master table several times using different field names, once for every role. (See image below).

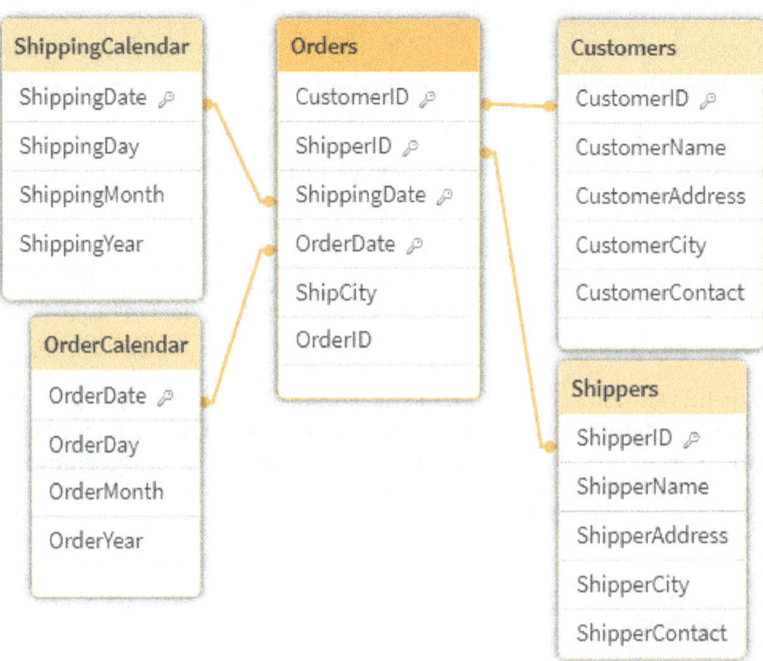

However, loading the same data twice is something many database professionals are reluctant to do; they think that it creates an unnecessary redundancy and hence is a bad solution. So, they sometimes seek a solution where they can use a generic master table also in the Qlik data model. This is especially true for the master calendar table.

If you belong to this group, I can tell you that loading the same table several times is _not_ a bad solution. *Au contraire* – in my opinion, it is *the best solution*. Here's why:

- From the user's perspective it can be confusing to have an unspecified "**Date**" field if there are several dates in the data model. For example, the user will not understand whether the date refers to order date or shipping date.

- Without loading the master calendar several times, it will not be possible for the user to make selections that place simultaneous restrictions on several date fields, e.g. "show transactions where the order was placed in September and the items were shipped in November".

In fact, loading the same table several times in a Qlik app is no stranger than doing it in SELECT statements using aliases. For example, if you want to have an answer to the above question, you should do the following:

```
SELECT OrderID
    FROM          Orders
    INNER JOIN    Calendar AS OrderCalendar
        ON        Orders.OrderDate    = OrderCalendar.Date
    INNER JOIN    Calendar AS ShippingCalendar
        ON        Orders.ShippingDate = ShippingCalendar.Date
    WHERE         OrderCalendar.Month = 9
        AND   ShippingCalendar.Month = 11
```

In other words – you should create a SELECT statement that loads the calendar twice. In SQL you would never try to solve such a problem without joining the master table twice. And you should do the same in Qlik.

So, if you have several dates in your data model – load the master calendar several times!

Finally, there *is* a way to have a common date that can cover several different dates. It is called "Canonical Date" – see next article. But you should still have one calendar for each date field.

Canonical Date

Originally posted in the Qlik Design Blog on Feb 17, 2014

A common situation when loading data into a Qlik document is that the data model contains several dates. For instance, in order data you often have one order date, one required date and one shipped date.

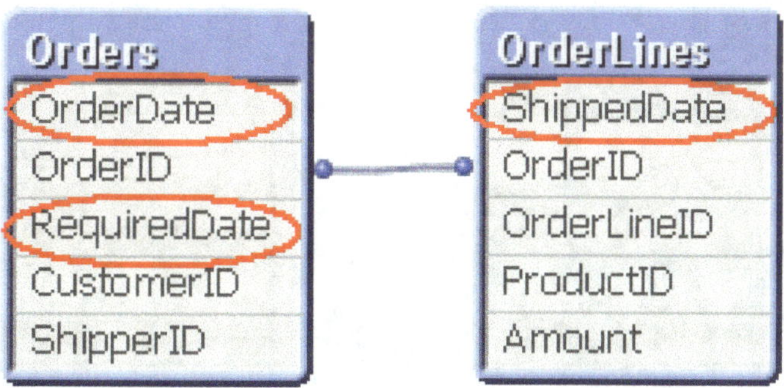

This means that one single order can have multiple dates; in this example one **OrderDate**, one **RequiredDate** and several **ShippedDates** – if the order is split into several shipments:

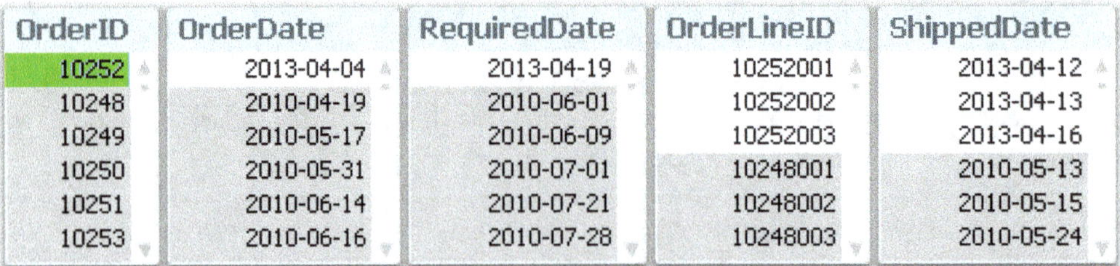

So, how would you link a master calendar to this?

Well, the question is incorrectly posed. You should not use one single master calendar for this. You should use *several*. You should create three master calendars.

The reason is that the different dates are indeed *different* attributes, and you don't want to treat them as the same date. By creating several master calendars, you will enable your users to make advanced selections like "*orders placed in April but delivered in June*". See more in the previous article "Why You should Load the same Master Table several times".

Your data model will then look like this:

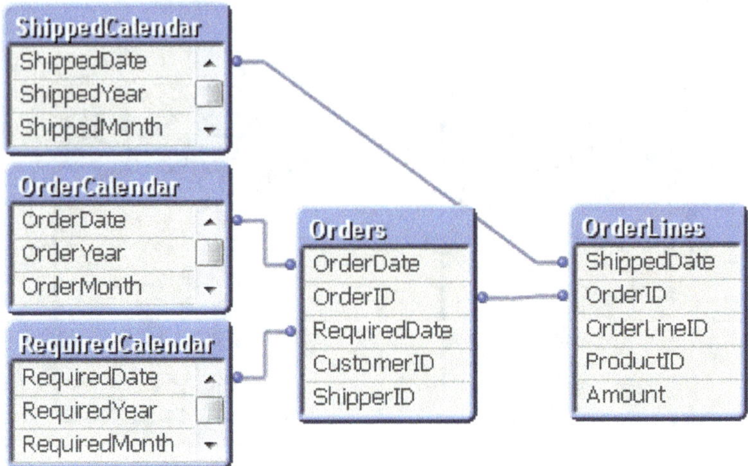

But several different master calendars will not solve all problems. You cannot for instance plot ordered amount and shipped amount in the same graph using a common time axis. For this you need a date that can represent all three dates – you need a *Canonical Date*. This is how you create it:

First, you must find a table with a grain fine enough; a table where each record only has one value of each date type associated. In my example this would be the **OrderLines** table, since a specific order line uniquely defines all three dates. Compare this with the **Orders** table, where a specific order uniquely defines **OrderDate** and **RequiredDate**, but still can have several values in **ShippedDate**:

*The **Orders** table does not have a grain fine enough.*

This table should link to a new table – a date bridge – that lists all possible dates for each key value, i.e. a specific **OrderLineID** has three different canonical dates associated with it. Finally, you create a master calendar for the canonical date field.

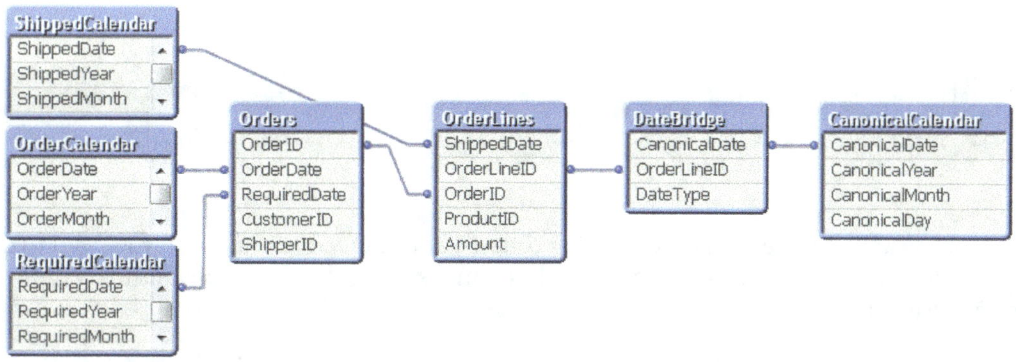

You may need to use ApplyMap() to create the date bridge. One way is to first create two mapping tables where you map the **OrderID** to the two dates found in the **Orders** table, and use the following script:

```
OrderID2OrderDate:
Mapping Load OrderID, OrderDate                    Resident Orders;

OrderID2ReqDate:
Mapping Load OrderID, RequiredDate                 Resident Orders;

DateBridge:
Load                              // --- Load all order dates
   OrderLineID,
   Applymap('OrderID2OrderDate',OrderID,Null()) as CanonicalDate,
   'Order'                                        as DateType
   Resident OrderLines;
Load                              // --- Load all required dates
   OrderLineID,
   Applymap('OrderID2ReqDate',OrderID,Null())   as CanonicalDate,
   'Required'                                     as DateType
   Resident OrderLines;
Load                              // --- Load all shipping dates
   OrderLineID,
   ShippedDate                                    as CanonicalDate,
   'Shipped'                                      as DateType
   Resident OrderLines;
```

If you now want to make a chart comparing ordered and shipped amounts, all you need to do is to create it using a canonical calendar field as dimension, and two expressions that contain Set Analysis expressions:

```
Sum( {<DateType={'Order'}>}     Amount )

Sum( {<DateType={'Shipped'}>}   Amount )
```

This chart will look similar to this:

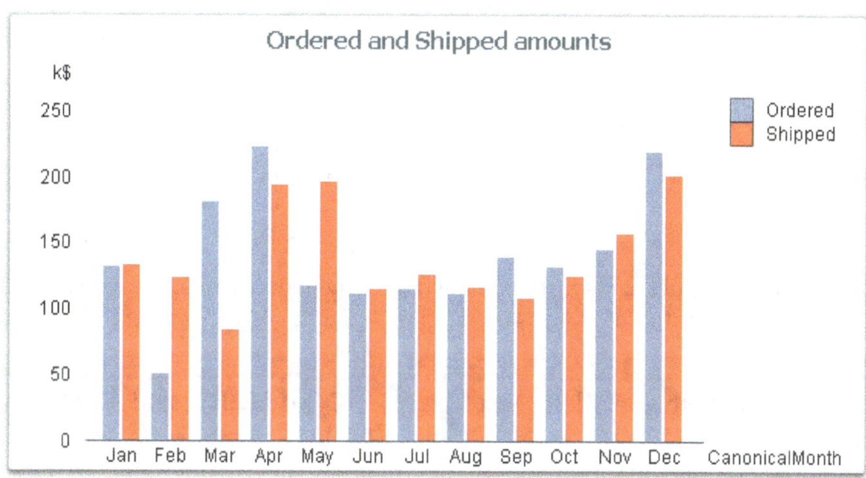

The canonical calendar fields are excellent to use as dimensions in charts but are somewhat confusing when used for selections. For this, the fields from the standard calendars are often better.

Summary:

- Create a master calendar for each date. Use these for list boxes and selections.
- Create a canonical date with a canonical calendar. Use these fields as dimensions in charts.
- Use the **DateType** field in a Set Expression in the charts.

Thank you, Rob W. for inspiration and good discussions.

A Myth About Count distinct

Originally posted in the Qlik Design Blog on Oct 22, 2013

Do you belong to the group of people who think that Count distinct in a chart is a slow, single-threaded operation that should be avoided?

If so, I can tell you that you are wrong.

Well – it used to be single-threaded and slow, but that was long ago. It was fixed already for QlikView version 8, but the rumor of the function's slowness lives on like an urban myth that refuses to die. Today the calculation is multi-threaded and optimized.

To prove that Count(distinct…) is faster than what many people think, I constructed a test which categorically shows that it is not slower – it is in fact *a lot faster* than the alternative solutions.

I created a data model with a very large fact table: 1M, 3M, 10M, 30M and 100M records. In it, I created a secondary key, with a large number of distinct values: 1%, 0.1% and 0.01% of the number of records in the fact table.

The goal was to count the number of distinct values of the secondary key when making a selection. There are several ways that this can be done:

- Use count distinct in the fact table: Count(distinct [Secondary ID])

- Use count on a second table that just contains the unique IDs: Count([Secondary ID Copy])

- Use sum on a field that just contains '1' in the second table: Sum([Secondary ID Count])

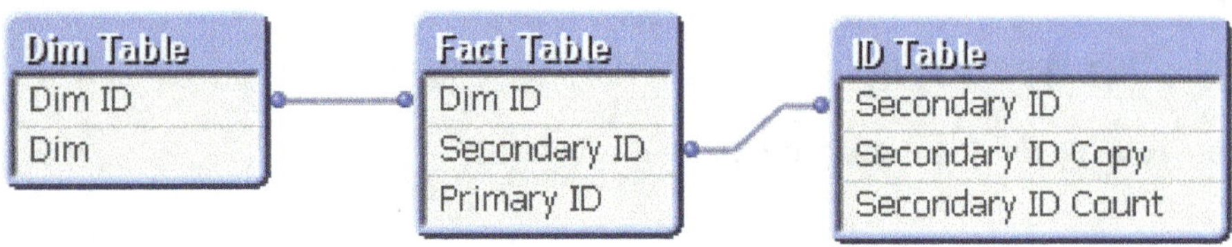

I also created a dimension ("Dim" in the "Dim Table") with 26 values, also randomly assigned to the data in the fact table. Then I recorded the response times for three charts, each using "Dim" as dimension and one of the three expressions above. I made this for four different selections.

This is what the three charts looked like in QlikView. Note the progress bar of the chart that calculates the Count distinct: It is almost done when the two others only are half-way.

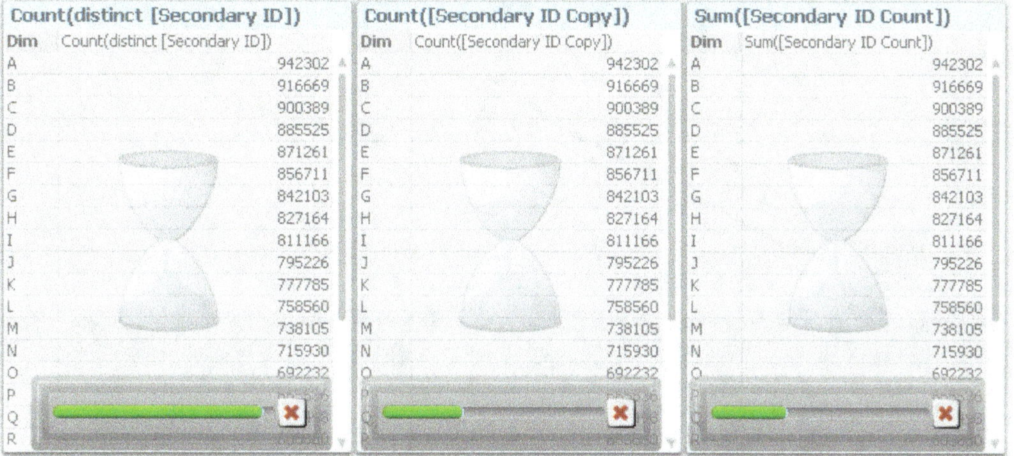

Then I remade all measurements using "Dim ID" as dimension, i.e. I moved also the dimension to the fact table. Finally, I loaded all the measured response times into QlikView and analyzed it.

The first obvious result is that the response time increases with the number of records in the fact table. This is hardly surprising …

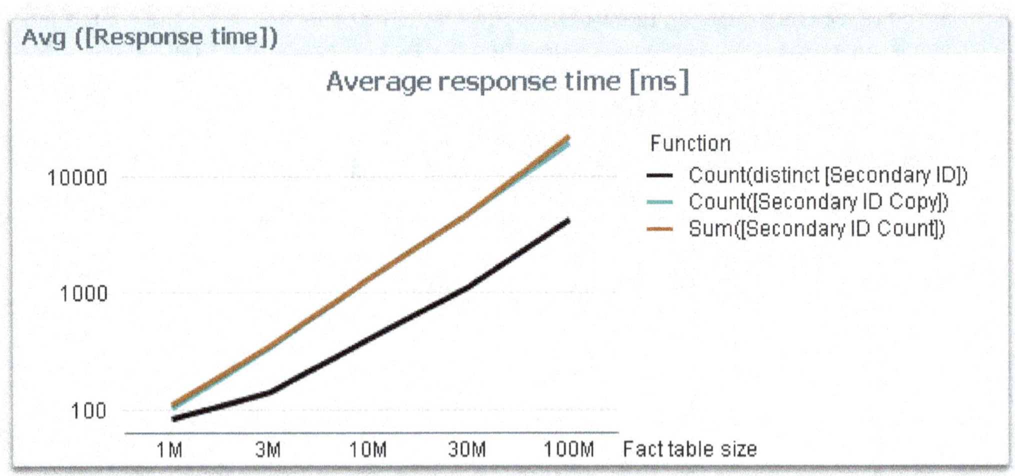

… so I need to compensate for this: I divided the response times with the number of fact table records and thus got a normalized response time in picoseconds. I.e. the CPU time needed per record in the fact table.

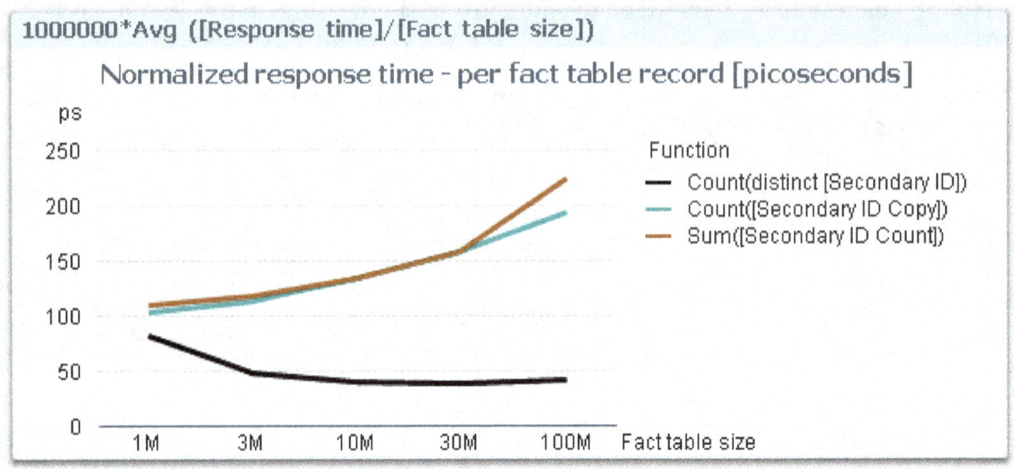

This graph is extremely interesting. It clearly shows that a Count(distinct…) performed in the fact table has a response time that is considerably smaller than a count or a sum in a dimensional table. The table below shows the numbers.

Normalized response time [ps]							
Dimension location	**Function**	**Fact table size**	1M	3M	10M	30M	100M
	Count(distinct [Secondary ID])		95	54	49	52	59
In dim table	Count([Secondary ID Copy])		111	120	140	164	196
	Sum([Secondary ID Count])		126	124	141	163	235
	Count(distinct [Secondary ID])		71	41	33	25	26
In fact table	Count([Secondary ID Copy])		97	107	128	154	192
	Sum([Secondary ID Count])		95	113	128	156	215

Finally, I calculated the ratios between the response times for having the dimension in the fact table vs. having it in a dimensional table, and the same ratio for making the aggregation in the fact table vs. in a dimensional table.

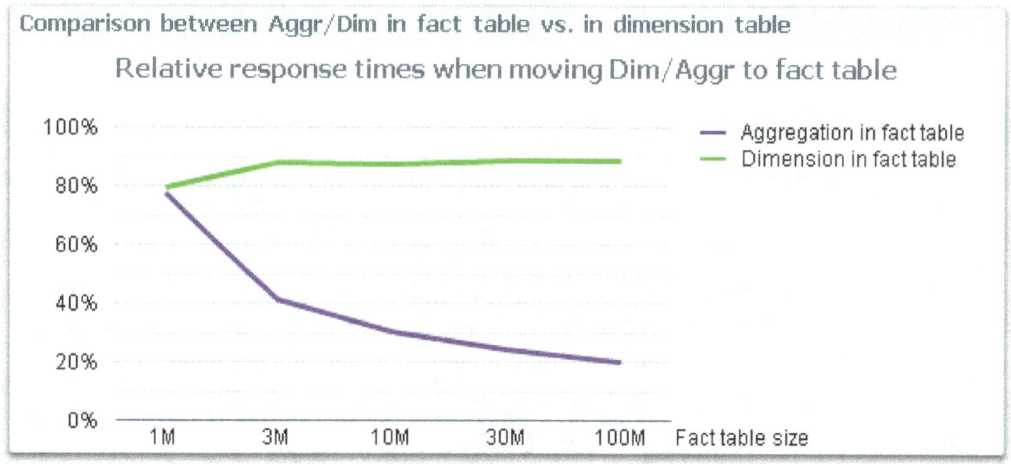

This graph shows the relative response time I get by moving the dimension or the aggregation into the fact table. For instance, at 100M records, the response time from a fact table aggregation (i.e. a Count(distinct…)) is only 20% of an aggregation that is made in a dimensional table.

This is the behavior on my mock-up data on my four-core laptop with 16GB RAM. If you do a similar test, you may get a slightly different result since the calculations depend very much on both hardware and the data model. But I still think it is safe to say that you should not spend time avoiding the use of Count(distinct…) on a field in the fact table.

In fact, you should consider moving your ID to the fact table if you need to improve the performance. *Especially* if you have a large fact table.

Data Modelling: Clarity vs. Speed

Originally posted in the Qlik Design Blog on Oct 29, 2013

Now that the waves from last week's post about Count distinct have settled, it is time for me to draw some conclusions.

First, I must say that it is astonishing that no one – including myself – sooner openly questioned the assertion that Count(distinct) is single-threaded and slow. We have all had plenty of time to do so: It is true that Count(distinct) was single-threaded and slow in QlikView version 7.52, but it was fixed already for version 8 (I double-checked it), which was released in 2007.

By the way, you can see what it looks like in 7.52 in the picture below. The two charts to the right are both finished, but the Count distinct to the left is still calculating, using only one of the four cores (CPU usage = 25%). Hence, slow, and single-threaded.

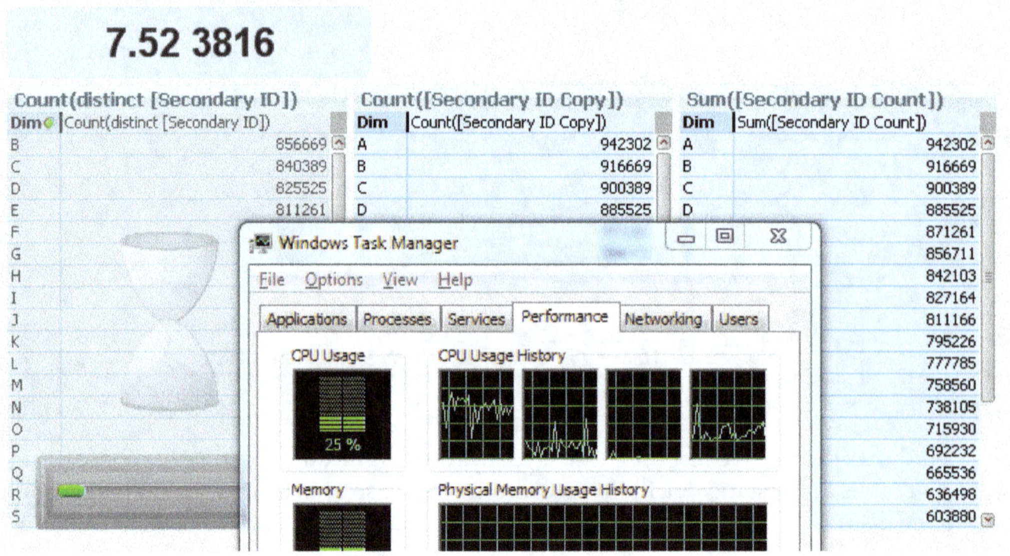

Compare this with the corresponding screen dump from 11.20 in the previous article, where it is obvious from the progress bars that Count distinct is faster than the alternative ways to calculate the same number.

My first conclusion is that we need to sometimes challenge "the truth". Because, in the software world, the truth changes. What was true yesterday is not necessarily true tomorrow. And if the map and reality conflict, one must never forget that the map is only an incomplete model of the real world …

Further, from a technical perspective, we can see that:

1. Charts are calculated faster if the fields used for the aggregation reside in the largest table, in the fact table. This becomes especially true when the fact table is large.

2. Charts are calculated slightly faster if also the dimension fields reside in the fact table.

3. The above conclusions are valid only if there is an "external" dimension involved, i.e. that the chart needs to make the calculation linking over the fact table. A single number in a text box, or chart where the fact table isn't involved, will not be affected the same way.

Does this mean that you should join everything together into one, single, de-normalized fact table? For extremely large fact tables, the answer is probably "Yes". In such cases, you will most likely need to optimize for speed, and then you should probably put everything in one table.

But when doing so, the app uses more RAM. Further, you lose clarity, and simplicity.

A normalized model usually has a simpler script and is easier to understand for the person that has to maintain the application or develop it further. It is simpler to make modifications, to add tables or calculations, and to create correct formulae, if the data model and the script are conceptually simple. So, for smaller data sets, where the chart response time already is acceptably low, I claim that you should _not_ optimize for speed.

Instead, you should optimize for clarity and maintainability, which means keeping things simple, i.e. keeping the data model normalized. See more in "*To Join or not to Join*".

Bottom line: Keep it as simple as possible, and don't make unnecessary optimizations.

"Premature optimization is the root of all evil." – Donald Knuth

A Myth about the Number of Hops

Originally posted in the Qlik Design Blog on Jan 20, 2015

In the QlikCommunity forum I have often seen people claim that you should minimize the number of hops in your Qlik data model in order to get the best performance.

I claim that this recommendation is not (always) correct.

In most cases, you do not need to minimize the number of hops since it affects performance only marginally. This post will try to explain when an additional table significantly will affect performance and when it will not. The question concerns which data model to choose:

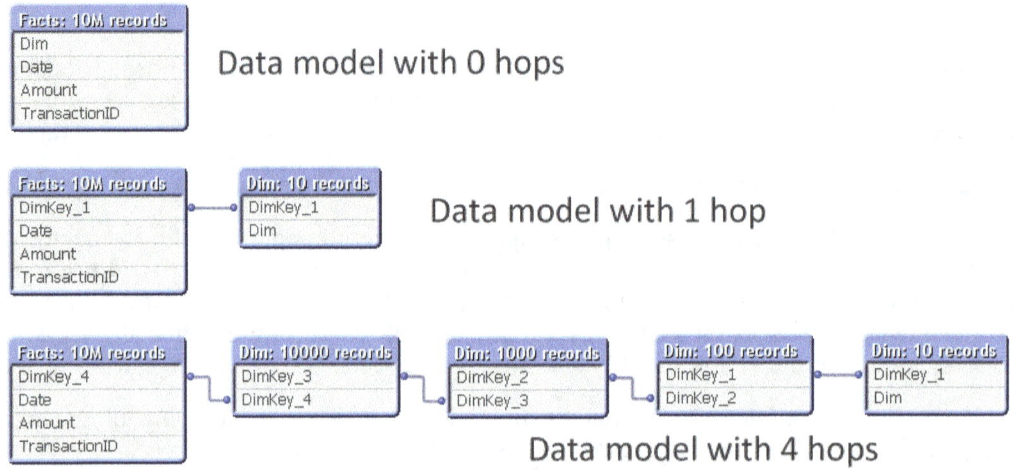

The question is: Should you normalize and have many tables, with several hops between the dimension table and the fact table? Or should you join the tables to remove hops?

So, I ran a test where I measured the calculation time of a pivot table calculating a simple sum in a large fact table and using a low-cardinality dimension, while *varying the number of hops between the two*. The graph below shows the result.

I ran two series of tests, one where the cardinality of the dimensional tables changed with a factor 10 for each table; and one where it changed with a factor 2.

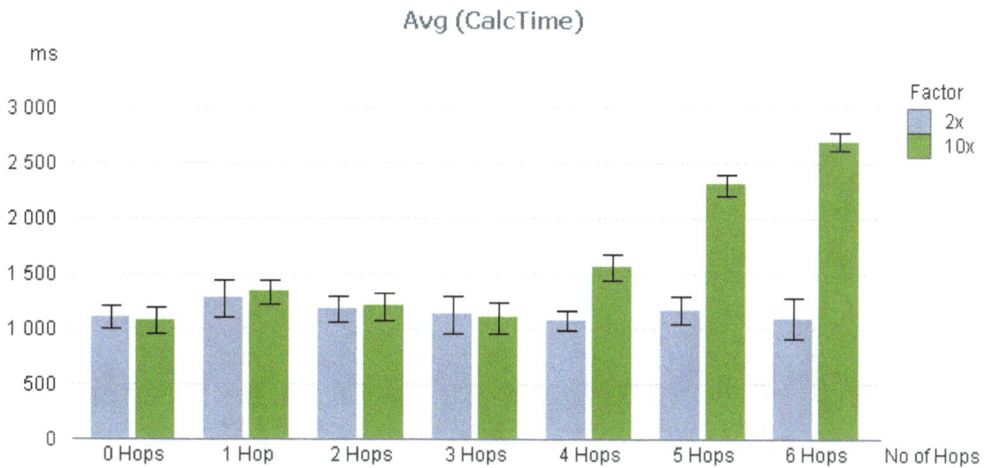

You can clearly see that the performance is not affected at all by the number of hops – at least not between 0 and 3 hops.

By 4 hops, the calculation time in the 10x series however starts to increase slightly and by 5 hops it has increased a lot. But this is _not_ due to the number of hops. Instead, it is the result of the primary dimension table (the dim table closest to the fact table) getting large: By 5 hops it has 100.000 records and can no longer be regarded as a small table.

To show this, I made a second test: I measured the calculation time of the same pivot table using a fix 3-table data model, varying the number of records in the intermediate table, but keeping the sizes of the other tables.

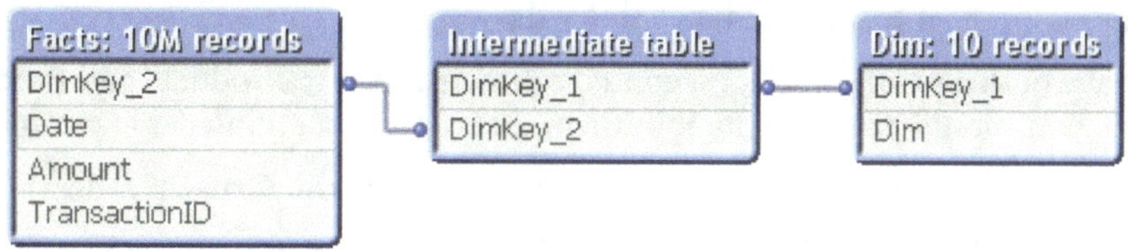

In real life, this structure would correspond to a part of a more complex data model, e.g.

- Facts - Products - Product Groups, or
- Order Lines - Order Headers - Customers

The result of my measurement can be seen in graph below. The red bars correspond to using the snowflake model with an intermediate table. The green and blue bars correspond to joining the intermediate table with the fact table or the dimension table, respectively.

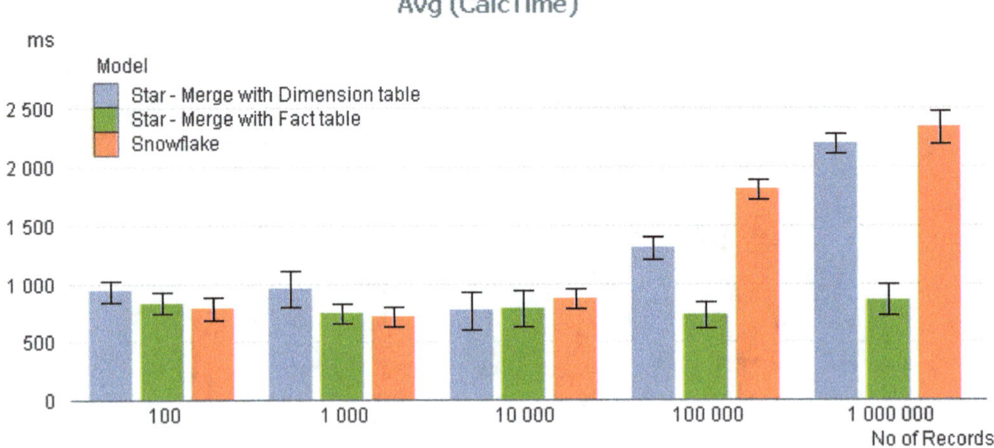

The graph confirms that the size of the intermediate table is a sensitive point: If it has 10.000 records or less, its existence hardly affects performance. But if it is larger, you get a performance hit. Just as you will if the dimension table is large.

I also measured the calculation times after joining the intermediate table, first to the left with the fact table, and then to the right with the dimension table, to see if the calculation times decreased (blue and green bars). You can see that joining tables with 10.000 records or less does not change the performance. But if you have larger tables, a join with the fact table may be a good idea.

Conclusions:

- The number of hops does _not_ always cause significant performance problems in the chart calculation. But a large intermediate table will.

- If you have both a primary and a secondary dimension (e.g. Products and Product Groups), you should probably _not_ join them. Leave the data model as a snowflake.

- If you have the facts in two large tables (e.g. Order Lines and Order Headers), you _should_ probably join them into one common transaction table.

A couple of disclaimers:

1. The above study only concerns the _chart calculation time_ – which usually is the main part of the response time.

2. If the expression inside your aggregation function contains fields from different tables, none of the above is true.

3. Your data is different than mine. You may get slightly different results.

Fan traps and Chasm traps

Originally posted in the Qlik Design Blog on Sep 8, 2015

In data modelling and in Business Intelligence there is something called connection traps. These are inconsistencies in the data model that sometimes cause problems. This blog post is about describing the fan trap and the chasm trap and how these should be handled in a Qlik data model.

When designing a data model, connection traps are sometimes built into the data model. It could be that the source data has been misinterpreted, or it could be that some relations are missing in the data. Usually, the traps should be avoided. However, this is not always possible. But as you will see, it is not a problem.

There are two main types of connection traps: The *fan trap* and the *chasm trap*.

Fan Trap

"Where a model represents a relationship between entity types, but pathway between certain entity occurrences is ambiguous".[1]

Example of a fan trap:

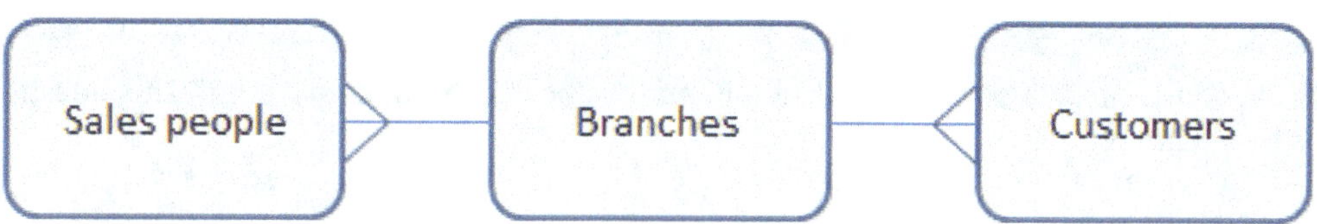

In this model of a sales organization, a branch has several salespeople. A branch also has several customers. But the above data model says nothing about which salesperson is responsible for which customer, although such an assignment may exist. Instead, the data model links all salespeople to all customers within the branch.

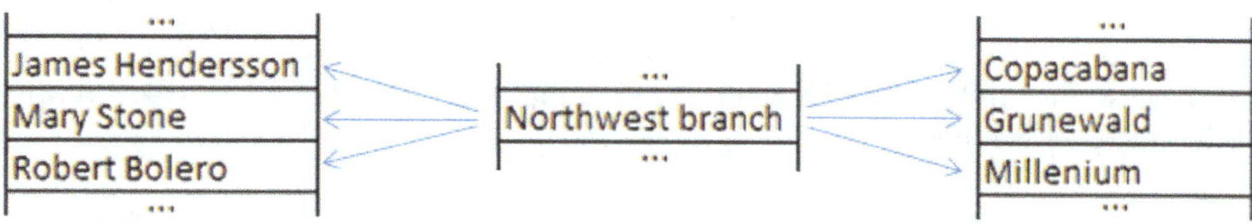

Joining the three tables is not a good solution since it will increase the number of records – every combination of salesperson and customer will get a record of its own – which means that aggregations will result in incorrect numbers. A single salesperson will be counted several times. This is a problem with SQL and many other database tools.

The Qlik engine is however different: Since the three tables are stored as three different tables, the Qlik engine is able to aggregate correctly anyway. A count of a non-key field from the Customers table will count just the records in the Customers table. As long as the aggregation function contains fields from only one table, the aggregation will be correct.

Hence, *a Fan trap is not a problem.* The Qlik engine will automatically handle the data correctly.

However, if you have information about assignments between customers and salespeople, you should of course change the data model and load this information, e.g.

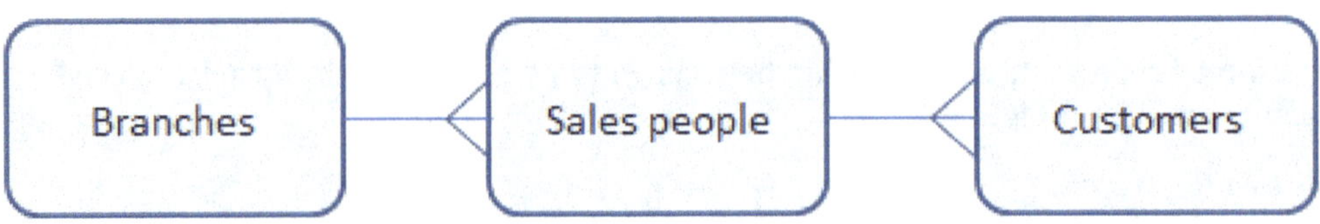

But what if a customer is assigned to a branch, but has not yet bought anything? This question takes us to the next trap.

Chasm Trap

"Where a model suggests the existence of a relationship between entity types, but pathway does not exist between certain entity occurrences".[1]

While a fan trap can be identified by looking at the data model only, a chasm trap can be more difficult to spot. The above data model (Branches - Sales people - Customers) may in fact contain a chasm trap. But the data model looks perfectly fine.

The chasm trap appears only if there is *missing data* in the middle table, e.g. if you have a customer who belongs to a branch but has not yet been assigned a salesperson. Then the link between the customer and the branch will be broken and it will not be possible to see to which branch the customer belongs.

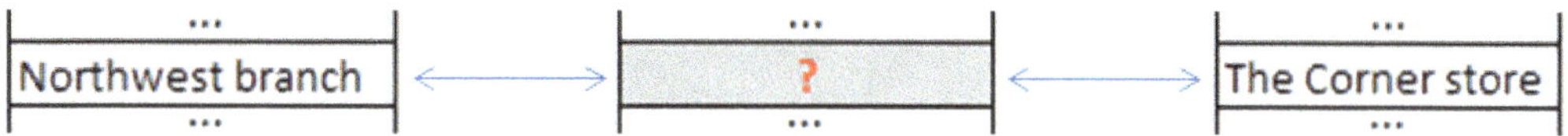

If you don't need this link, the data model will still work fine. However, if you want this link, you can create it by adding dummy records labelled 'No salesperson' to the **Salespeople** table – one record per branch – and link unassigned customers to these. An additional advantage is that these customers will then be easily selectable. If you click on 'No salesperson', you will immediately find all unassigned customers.

Hence, a Chasm trap can easily be handled.

Bottom line: Connection traps are not a problem in the Qlik engine.

Note: On the Internet you sometimes find incorrect descriptions of Fan trap and Chasm trap where the two are confused with each other. The definitions I use come from the original description of traps:

[7]   Thomas Connolly, Carolyn Begg: Database Systems: A Practical Approach to Design, Implementation and Management (Addison-Wesley, 1998).

6

Hierarchies

Hierarchies are an important part of many business intelligence solutions, used to describe dimensions that naturally contain different levels of granularity. Some are simple and intuitive whereas others are complex and demand a lot of thinking to be modelled correctly.

- How can a hierarchy be loaded into a Qlik app?
- Which data model should be used?
- What is the difference between a balanced and an unbalanced hierarchy?
- How do I create an authorization scheme using a hierarchy?
- How can I check for data integrity problems in the hierarchy data?

This document tries to answer the above questions and describe which types of hierarchies there are, define some basic attributes and explain how they should be modelled and loaded into a Qlik app.

Hierarchy Basics

Extract from the Technical brief "Hierarchies" published on Nov 11, 2013

A data hierarchy is a basic concept in database theory. It helps to show the relationships between different related entities, whether it is a question of larger/smaller, more/less important, or consists of/belongs to. It is used to give a better sense of understanding about how things are related.

From the top of a hierarchy to the bottom, the members are progressively more detailed. For example, in a dimension that has the levels Market, Country, State and City, the member Americas appears in the top level of the hierarchy, the member U.S.A. appears in the second level, the member California appears in the third level and San Francisco in the bottom level. California is more specific than U.S.A., and San Francisco is more specific than California.

Hierarchies

Examples in real life:

- **The time dimension**
  Year, month, day, hour, minute and second are entities that form a hierarchy.

- **The product dimension**
  A product can often be delivered in different packages, e.g. in different sizes. At the same time a product belongs to a product group, which in turn may belong to a product category. Hence, the product category, the product group, the product, and the package are entities that form a hierarchy. A product from the pharmaceutical industry can serve as example:
    - Product category: Pharmaceuticals
    - Product group: Pain killers
    - Product: Paracetamol
    - Package: Paracetamol package with 20 x 500 mg.

- **The geography / customer dimension**
  A customer is usually associated with a City, a State, a Country and a Market region. These fields form a hierarchy.

- **The employee dimension**
  An employee often belongs to a team, a department, and a unit. These fields form a hierarchy.

- **The wine districts of the world**
  A wine always has an origin. It could for instance come from Bordeaux, which is part of France, which in turn is part of Europe and the World. Bordeaux also has sub-levels such as Graves, Sauternes and Médoc, which in turn also have sub-levels such as Haut-Médoc and Barsac. These wine-districts form a hierarchy.

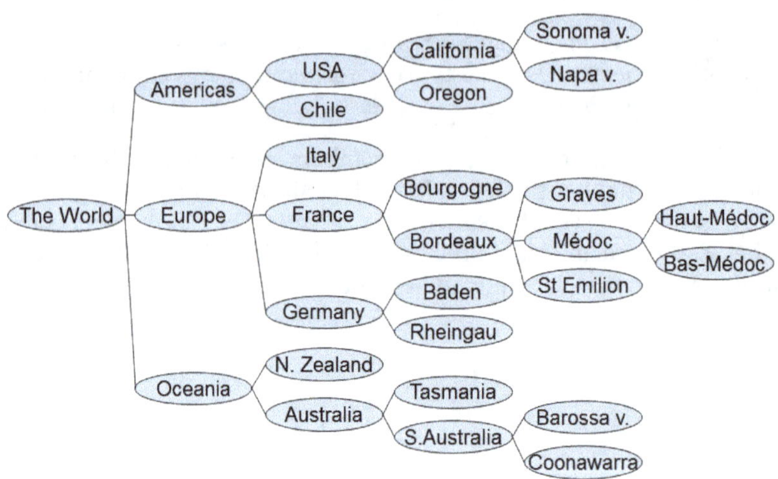

Different types of hierarchies

Extract from the Technical brief "Hierarchies" published on Nov 11, 2013

A hierarchy always consists of a number of members – nodes – that have one parent each. In the general case, each node can have any number of children. This way, a hierarchy often looks like a tree: A starting point – the root – and a structure of nodes that branches out from the root.

Sometimes you encounter "hierarchies" where some nodes have more than one parent. These are strictly speaking not hierarchies at all, but more general directed graphs.

Just like a real tree, a hierarchy can also have leaves. These are objects that usually are of a different type than the nodes, but still belong to a specific node.

In a database situation, the nodes in a hierarchy typically form the dimension whereas the leaves usually are the transactions in the fact table, associated to one specific node each.

Balanced or unbalanced?

One property of a hierarchy is whether it is balanced or unbalanced. "Balanced" means that all leaves belong to nodes of the same level.

One good example is the calendar dimension: In the common case, all branches go down to the bottom level, the dates, and all leaves, e.g. orders, invoices, or some other transaction type, have dates and are linked to this level.

The opposite case is if the hierarchy is unbalanced. In such a case you have consistent parent-child relationships but logically inconsistent levels. This means that all leaves are not connected to the same level: they can be found on different levels.

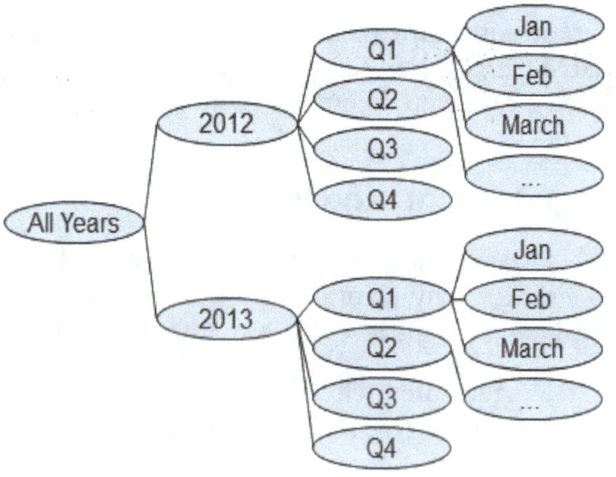

A good example is the wine districts of the world: A bottle of wine often has its origin written on the label – a specific wine district. But a district can belong to a bigger district, which in turn can belong to an even bigger district. Depending on whether the wine is specified to come from one specific vineyard or is a bulk wine from a larger area, origin can be more or less precise. So, in principle, a wine can be labelled to belong to any of the nodes in the tree. It can for instance be an unspecified table wine from Bordeaux or it can be a better wine that comes from a vineyard in one of the sub districts of Bordeaux, e.g. Bas-Médoc.

That the levels are "logically inconsistent" means that a wine district is not necessarily organized or named the same way as in another district. France has, for instance, a different system for denomination of wine districts than Germany.

Fix-level or n-level?

Closely related to balanced/unbalanced is the question of number of levels. An unbalanced hierarchy usually has an unknown, maybe even dynamic, number of levels, whereas a balanced hierarchy usually has a fix number of levels, well defined when you decide your data model.

But the two concepts – fix-level vs. balanced – are still not the same thing. There are fix-level, unbalanced hierarchies: An example is if you have a fact table with mixed granularity. Then you have a fix-level calendar hierarchy (Year, Quarter, Month, Day) while at the same time you have transactions that link to different levels in the hierarchy: It could be that the actual numbers are linked to dates, but the budget numbers are linked to months. Hence – an unbalanced hierarchy.

Named levels or non-named levels?

The main question, however, when loading data into a Qlik app, is whether the levels have specific names or not. If a level has a name, you most likely want to display that level in the app as a field with that name. But if you instead have unnamed levels, the situation is quite different. Again, the wine districts can serve as example: A wine district could be referred to as "**District**" irrespectively if it is a district on the third level or on the fifth level of the hierarchy. In such a case, you do not want the different levels in different list boxes.

Ragged or not ragged?

A special case of a hierarchy with named levels is the ragged hierarchy. In a normal, balanced, fix-level hierarchy, all branches of the hierarchy descend to the same level, and each member's logical parent is the level immediately above the member.

But in a ragged hierarchy, this need not be true. In a ragged hierarchy, there may be levels missing in some branches.

One good example is The U.S. states and cities: Cities always belong to a state – except Washington DC. This city does not belong to any state, but still belongs to the U.S. Hence, this is a ragged hierarchy where the state is missing for this node.

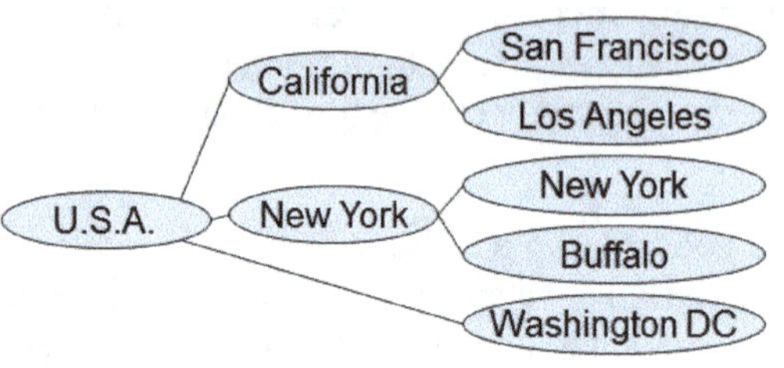

Unbalanced, n-level Hierarchies

Originally posted in the Qlik Design Blog on Nov 12, 2013

Hierarchies are very common in all database and business intelligence solutions. Usually, they are balanced and with a fix number of levels, and then they do not pose any problems. Just load the data, add a drill-down group, and you're done.

But there is one type of hierarchy that is somewhat tricky to get right – an unbalanced, n-level hierarchy. Typical for this type of hierarchy is that the levels are not named – all nodes are stored in the same field – and you really don't know on which level you need to search for a specific node.

The Adjacent nodes table – a compact storage method

Usually such a hierarchy is stored in an *Adjacent nodes* table, i.e., a table that has one record per node and each node has a reference to its parent. The table below shows an unbalanced hierarchy with some wine districts. Each district constitutes a node, and they are all stored with a reference to their respective parent district.

NodeID	ParentID	Name
1	-	The World
4	1	Europe
5	1	North America
6	1	Oceania
21	4	France
23	4	Germany
46	5	United States
48	6	New Zealand
99	21	Bordeaux
119	23	Rheingau
228	46	California
255	48	Marlborough
292	99	Médoc
495	228	Napa Valley
712	292	Haut-Médoc
921	712	Margaux

The Adjacent nodes table is easy to maintain and modify, so it is often the method of choice for storing a hierarchy.

The Expanded nodes table – for the analysis

The Adjacent Nodes table is, however, not suitable for analysis. It is possible to select a node, but you still wouldn't know anything about the sub-nodes, since the links to them aren't obvious.

But if the table is loaded into the app using the **Hierarchy** prefix, you will get a useful table – the *Expanded nodes* table:

```
Nodes:
Hierarchy (NodeID,ParentID,Name,ParentName,Name,Path,'/',Depth)
Load
    NodeID,
    ParentID,
    Name
    From Winedistricts.txt;
```

This prefix will transform the Adjacent Nodes table into an Expanded Nodes table that has additional fields that you can use in your app:

NodeID	ParentID	Name	Name1	Name2	Name3	Name4	Name5	Name6	Name7	Depth
1	-	The World	The World	-	-	-	-	-	-	1
4	1	Europe	The World	Europe	-	-	-	-	-	2
5	1	North America	The World	North America	-	-	-	-	-	2
6	1	Oceania	The World	Oceania	-	-	-	-	-	2
21	4	France	The World	Europe	France	-	-	-	-	3
23	4	Germany	The World	Europe	Germany	-	-	-	-	3
46	5	United States	The World	North America	United States	-	-	-	-	3
48	6	New Zealand	The World	Oceania	New Zealand	-	-	-	-	3
99	21	Bordeaux	The World	Europe	France	Bordeaux	-	-	-	4
119	23	Rheingau	The World	Europe	Germany	Rheingau	-	-	-	4
228	46	California	The World	North America	United States	California	-	-	-	4
255	48	Marlborough	The World	Oceania	New Zealand	Marlborough	-	-	-	4
292	99	Médoc	The World	Europe	France	Bordeaux	Médoc	-	-	5
495	228	Napa Valley	The World	North America	United States	California	Napa Valley	-	-	5
712	292	Haut-Médoc	The World	Europe	France	Bordeaux	Médoc	Haut-Médoc	-	6
921	712	Margaux	The World	Europe	France	Bordeaux	Médoc	Haut-Médoc	Margaux	7

In the data model below, the table "**Nodes**" is loaded with this prefix.

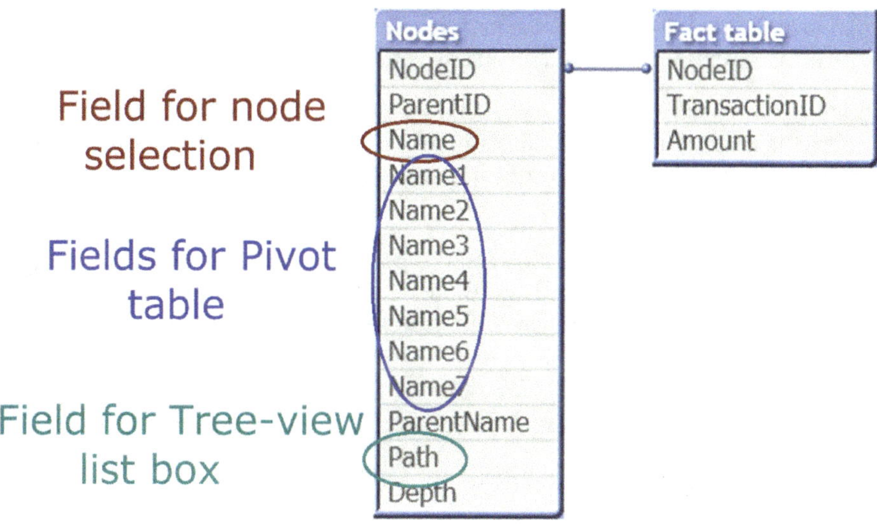

With the columns listing the different node levels (**Name1**...**Name7**), you will be able to create a pivot table showing the proper aggregations from the fact table. Further, the **Path** field can be used in a QlikView tree-view list box. Below you can see some wine districts displayed in both these object types:

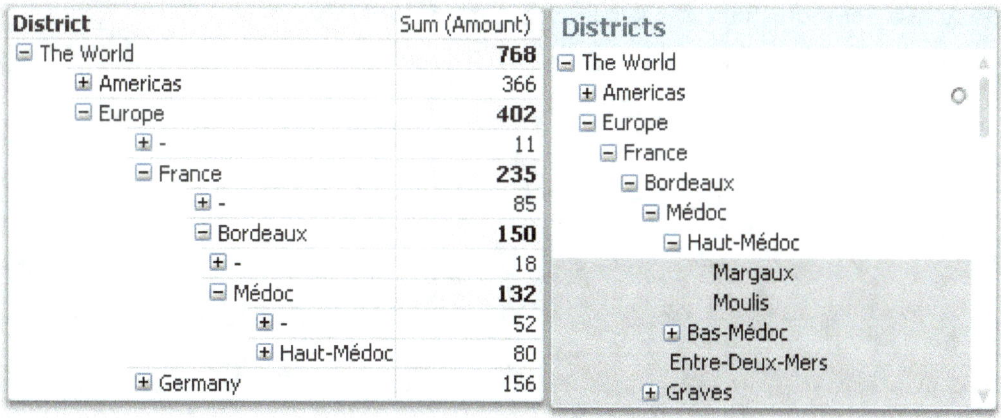

The Ancestor table

One challenge with hierarchies is that you can refer to a node in two different ways: Either to the node *including the entire sub-tree*, or to *the node only, excluding all sub-nodes*. In the example with the wine districts, the entire tree would mean any wine from Bordeaux (including all sub-nodes).

The alternative is to specify *the node only*. This would mean an *unspecified* Bordeaux where the sub-district is unknown or irrelevant (unspecified bulk wine). In the pivot table above, the difference is obvious: All wine from Bordeaux sums up to 150 units, and the unspecified Bordeaux sums up to 18 units.

A user usually wants to make selections referring to the entire sub-tree, but the above solution does not have any field for this. To create such a field, you need to use the second hierarchy-resolving prefix – the *HierarchyBelongsTo*:

```
Trees:
HierarchyBelongsTo (NodeID, ParentID, NodeNameCopy, TreeID, Tree)
Load
    NodeID,
    ParentID,
    Name as NodeNameCopy
    From Winedistricts.txt;
```

This prefix will also transform the adjacent nodes table. The result will be an *Ancestor table* (the "**Trees**" table in the picture below) containing one record per descendant-ancestor pair. In other words, the ancestor ("**TreeID**)") will link to all its descendants ("**NodeID**") as well as to itself and will thus link to entire sub-trees.

Further, the Ancestor table is also perfect for authorization purposes, e.g. as reducing field in Section Access. See more in the chapter about Security.

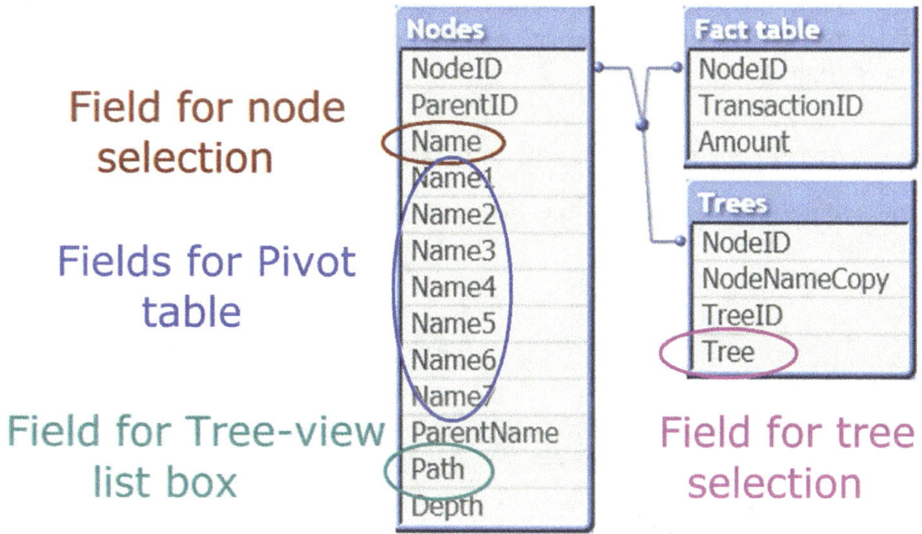

The name of the ancestor node is here called "**Tree**" so the user can understand the difference between a wine district as a node or as a tree. This field can be used for searches and selections of entire sub-trees.

The data model with the two hierarchy tables is the one I recommend: It generates all fields you need.

How a hierarchy is stored in a database

Extract from the Technical brief "Hierarchies" published on Nov 11, 2013

Storing hierarchies in a relational model is a common challenge, with multiple solutions. There are several approaches:

- The Horizontal hierarchy
- The Adjacency list model (Adjacent Nodes)
- The Path enumeration method
- The Nested sets model (Tree traversal)
- The Ancestor list (Reflexive Transitive Closure)

There is no general rule for how to load a hierarchy. It all depends on what type of hierarchy you have, and how this is stored. You will need to check your data to find out in which form the hierarchy is stored and use the appropriate loading algorithm. Below you will find descriptions for the most common cases.

The Horizontal hierarchy – Each level in its own field

The most common way to store a simple hierarchy is to have names on the levels and store each level in its own field.

ID	Customer	Country	Region
1	Eintrach GS	Germany	Europe
2	La Tienda de la Esquina	Mexico	Americas
3	La Ropa Vieja	Mexico	Americas
4	Dr Jims Trousers	UK	Europe
5	Urras Shop	Sweden	Europe
6	Man Kleider	Germany	Europe
7	Menàge à Trois	France	Europe
8	Las Corbatas	Spain	Europe
9	La Legion Mercenaire	France	Europe
10	Big Foot Shoes	Canada	Americas
11	Shoe Expert	UK	Europe

The hierarchy need not be in one table only, but can be split in several tables, e.g. one table for products and several ones for different levels of product groups.

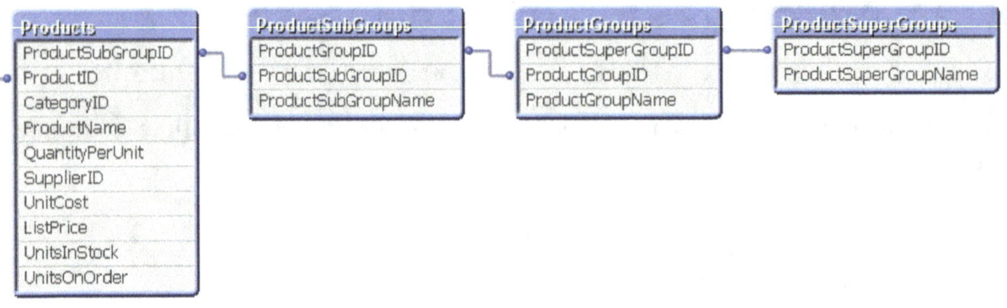

The most common case of a horizontal hierarchy is a balanced, fix-level hierarchy with named levels. This means that all the transactions link to the same level in the hierarchy, i.e. to one single field. Typically, this field is a date, a customer ID or a product ID. Examples of such hierarchies are:

- Year – Quarter – Month – Day
- Customer – State – Country – Market
- Product Group – Product – Package

Just load the table and create a drill-down group from the appropriate fields in the hierarchy. Then use a drill-down dimension as a field in charts, tables and list boxes.

However, sometimes you have an unbalanced, fix-level hierarchy with named levels.

You cannot see by looking at the dimensional table that you have an unbalanced, fix-level hierarchy. Instead, you must look at the facts and see whether the transactions always link to the same field or not.

One case where they don't, is when you have both budget and actual numbers in one single fact table. It could be that the budget numbers are per month and country whereas the actual numbers all have a timestamp and a customer ID.

The way you load this in a Qlik app is by using generic keys. See the chapter "Generic Keys" for more information.

The Adjacency list model

The adjacency list model, or *Adjacent nodes* table, is by far the most common way to store an unbalanced n-level hierarchy. The principle is that each node is stored in its own record, and that each record has a foreign key pointing out the parent. In other words, there is exactly one record per node.

The ID is the primary key that links the hierarchy to other data, typically transactions or inventory records.

The root is defined by the record that has NULL or blank as parent. Several roots are possible, although it often is preferable to have one common root node.

NodeID	ParentID	Name
1		The World
20	1	Americas
79	20	United States
85	79	California
178	1	Europe
281	178	France
283	281	Bordeaux
288	283	Médoc
294	288	Haut-Médoc
354	178	Germany

The main advantage of this model is that it is extremely easy to manage and maintain. If a node is to be added, it does not affect any other node. If an entire sub-tree needs to be moved, the **ParentID** of the root of the sub-tree is changed, and that is all.

The table completely defines the hierarchy, but since it doesn't explicitly store the information about daughters, it needs to be transformed to be usable in the Qlik script. This transformation can be made using one of the two hierarchy-resolving load prefixes in the Qlik script: *Hierarchy* and *HierarchyBelongsTo*. See more below about these.

Path Enumeration

Similar to the adjacency list, is the *Path Enumeration*. It is also a general way to store an unbalanced n-level hierarchy.

However, instead of storing the parent ID explicitly, a path to the node is stored. It has the advantage that some SQL queries are easier to perform. The disadvantage is manageability. It is not as easy to change the structure or to move a tree.

Also this table completely defines the hierarchy, and also here the table needs to be transformed to be usable in a Qlik app.

NodeID	Path	Name
1	1	The World
20	1/20	Americas
79	1/20/79	United States
85	1/20/79/85	California
90	1/20/79/85/90	Napa Valley
178	1/178	Europe
281	1/178/281	France
283	1/178/281/283	Bordeaux
288	1/178/281/283/288	Médoc
294	1/178/281/283/288/294	Haut-Médoc
354	1/178/354	Germany
368	1/178/354/368	Rheingau

The Nested sets model

The *Nested sets* model is an additional, general way to store an unbalanced n-level hierarchy.

Instead of having a key to the parent, each node is associated with a numeric range; a lower bound and an upper bound. All descendants have ranges that are completely enclosed by all ancestors. So, by looking at whether a number of a node is enclosed by the bounds of another node, the parent-child relationship can be determined.

Also this table completely defines the hierarchy, and also here the table needs to be transformed to be usable in a Qlik app.

LBound	RBound	Name
1	1382	The World
38	313	Americas
155	308	United States
166	189	California
175	176	Napa Valley
354	1195	Europe
559	702	France
562	613	Bordeaux
571	588	Médoc
582	587	Haut-Médoc
705	750	Germany
732	737	Rheingau

The nested sets model is not as commonly used as the adjacency list model, since it is not as easy to make changes. However, the nested sets model is usually faster to query on a SQL database than the adjacency list model.

The Ancestor table

The *Ancestor list*, or the Reflexive Transitive Closure table, is not commonly used to store the source data. But it is very common that a database view is defined this way, and called "Bridge table", since it presents the hierarchy in a form that is directly usable in a query.

In this table, every combination of an ancestor and a descendant is listed as a separate record. Hence, it is very easy to find all ancestors or all descendants of a specific node.

NodeID	Name	BelongsToID	BelongsTo
1	The World	1	The World
20	Americas	1	The World
20	Americas	20	Americas
178	Europe	1	The World
178	Europe	178	Europe
79	United States	1	The World
79	United States	20	Americas
79	United States	79	United States
281	France	1	The World
281	France	178	Europe
281	France	281	France
354	Germany	1	The World

Sometimes it includes records that are self-references, where a node belongs to itself, e.g. 'France' belongs to 'France', sometimes not.

In the Qlik script, this table can be created using the ***HierarchyBelongsTo*** prefix.

Hierarchy Tools in Qlik

Extract from the Technical brief "Hierarchies" published on Nov 11, 2013

There are several tools in Qlik Sense and QlikView that you can use when you analyze data containing hierarchies.

The Drill down dimension

If your hierarchy has named levels, so that the levels are stored in different fields, you should create a drill-down dimension. This is possible in both Qlik Sense and in QlikView.

In Qlik Sense, you do this by adding a Master Dimension.

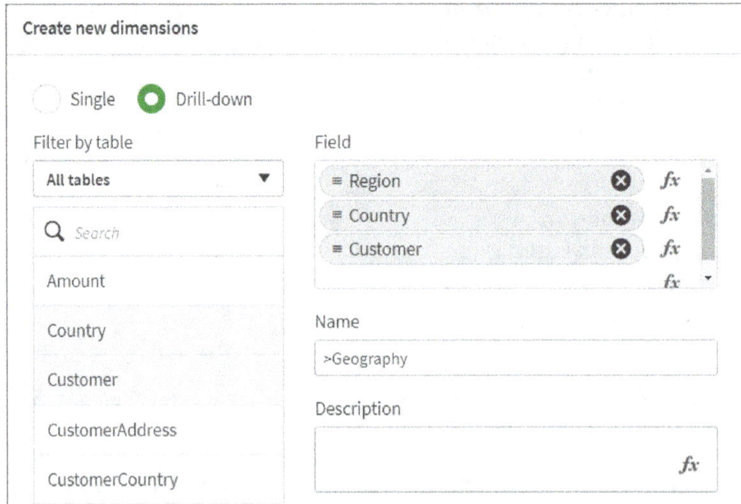

In QlikView, you do this under *Document Properties → Groups*.

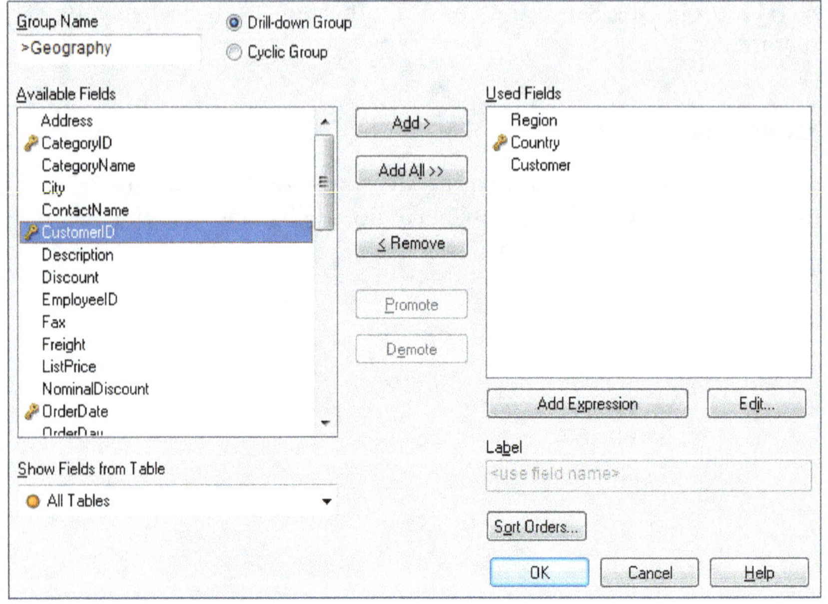

This means that you can use the group instead of the separate fields in charts and list-boxes. If there is only one value possible in the top field, it will automatically display the field of the next level instead.

The Hierarchy prefix

If your hierarchy is stored in an adjacent nodes table, you can load this using a Hierarchy prefix. It is a script command that you put in front of a Load or SELECT statement that loads the adjacent nodes table:

NodeID	ParentID	Name
1		The World
20	1	Americas
79	20	United States
85	79	California
178	1	Europe
281	178	France
283	281	Bordeaux
288	283	Médoc
294	288	Haut-Médoc
354	178	Germany

The Load statement needs to have at least three fields: An ID that is a unique key for the node, a reference to the parent node and a name for the node itself.

```
Hierarchy (NodeID, ParentID, Name)
Load NodeID, ParentID, Name From Winedistricts.txt;
```

The reference to the parent should have a match among the node IDs. If it doesn't, or if it is NULL, the node will be considered a root node. The node name has to be there – if your source table lacks node name, you need to create a name using "**NodeID as Name**".

It is possible to have additional fields in the Load statement.

The prefix will transform the loaded table into an Expanded Nodes table; a table that has a number of additional columns; one for each level of the hierarchy:

NodeID	ParentID	Name	Name1	Name2	Name3	Name4	Name5	Name6
1		The World	The World	-	-	-	-	-
20	1	Americas	The World	Americas	-	-	-	-
79	20	United States	The World	Americas	United States	-	-	-
85	79	California	The World	Americas	United States	California	-	-
90	85	Napa Valley	The World	Americas	United States	California	Napa Valley	-
178	1	Europe	The World	Europe	-	-	-	-
281	178	France	The World	Europe	France	-	-	-
283	281	Bordeaux	The World	Europe	France	Bordeaux	-	-
288	283	Médoc	The World	Europe	France	Bordeaux	Médoc	-
294	288	Haut-Médoc	The World	Europe	France	Bordeaux	Médoc	Haut-Médoc
354	178	Germany	The World	Europe	Germany	-	-	-
368	354	Rheingau	The World	Europe	Germany	Rheingau	-	-

Note that the resulting Expanded Nodes table has the same number of records as its source table: One per node. This will be true in all well-formed hierarchies. There are however some exceptions, see below under "Data Integrity".

The prefix needs at least the three first parameters, but there are additional ones that are useful:

```
Hierarchy (NodeID, ParentID, Name, ParentName, Name, Path, '/', Depth)
```

The Expanded Nodes table is very practical since it fulfills several requirements for analyzing a hierarchy in a relational model:

- All the node names exist in one and the same column, so that this can be used for searches.

- In addition, the different node levels have been expanded into one field each; fields that can be used in drill-down groups or as dimensions in pivot tables.

- It can be made to contain a path unique for the node, listing all ancestors in the right order.

- It can be made to contain the depth of the node, i.e. the distance from the root.

The HierarchyBelongsTo prefix

Just as the Hierarchy prefix, the **HierarchyBelongsTo** is a script command that you put in front of a Load or SELECT statement that loads an adjacent nodes table:

```
HierarchyBelongsTo (NodeID, ParentID, Name, BelongsToID, BelongsTo)
Load
    NodeID,
    ParentID,
    Name
    From Winedistricts.txt ;
```

Also here, the Load statement needs to have at least three fields: An ID that is a unique key for the node, a reference to the parent and a name.

The prefix will transform the loaded table into an Ancestor table – a reflexive transitive closure table – a table that has every combination of an ancestor and a descendant listed as a separate record. Hence, it is very easy to find all ancestors or all descendants of a specific node.

NodeID	Name	BelongsToID	BelongsTo
1	The World	1	The World
20	Americas	1	The World
20	Americas	20	Americas
178	Europe	1	The World
178	Europe	178	Europe
79	United States	1	The World
79	United States	20	Americas
79	United States	79	United States
281	France	1	The World
281	France	178	Europe
281	France	281	France
354	Germany	1	The World

The Ancestor table is very practical since it fulfills a number of requirements for analyzing a hierarchy in a relational model:

- If the node ID represents the single nodes, the ancestor ID represents the entire trees and sub-trees of the hierarchy.

- All the node names exist both in the role as nodes and in the role as trees, and both can be used for searches.

- It can be made to contain the depth difference between the node depth, and the ancestor depth, i.e. the distance from the root of the sub-tree.

The Tree-view list box

In QlikView, there is a special list box designed for hierarchies: The Tree-view list box.

If you have a path to the node, it is possible to display this as a tree by using a list box in Tree-view mode (*List box properties → General → Show as Tree view*). This simplifies navigation and allows you to collapse entire sub-trees.

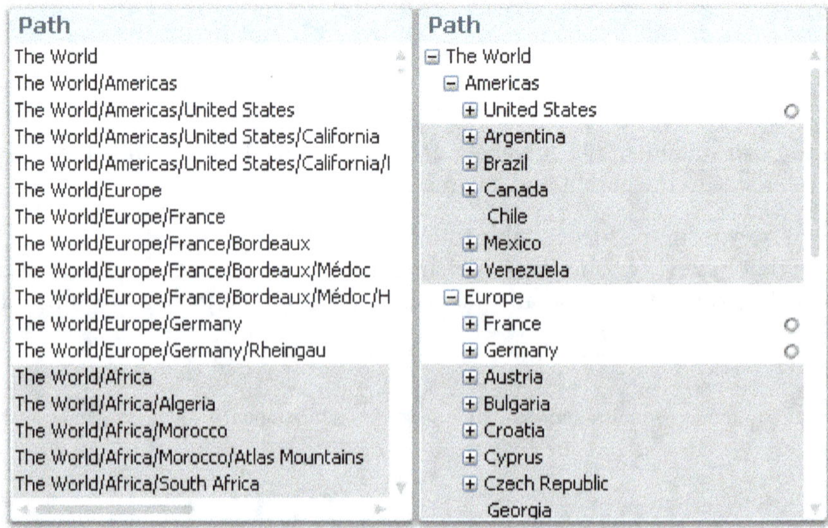

In the left list box, you can see what the field "**Path**" looks like originally, and in the right one you can see how the tree-view displays this information.

The Pivot table

The pivot table is excellent to display hierarchies. But to do this, you need to use all the different hierarchy levels as pivot table dimensions.

Name1	Name2	Name3	Name4	Sum (Amount)
	⊟ Americas ⊞			145
		⊟ France	⊟ Bordeaux ⊞	157
			- ⊞	24
The World	Europe	Germany ⊞		173
		-	⊞	97
		Total		**451**
	Total			**596**

To make this table look better, you need to turn on "*Indent mode*". In Qlik Sense, it is on, by default, and in QlikView you can find it on the *Style* tab.

	Sum(Amount)
⊖ The World	38
⊕ Americas	5
⊖ Europe	33
⊖ France	13
⊕ -	1
⊕ Bordeaux	3
⊕ Bourgogne	9
⊖ Germany	20
⊕ -	6
⊕ Baden	8
⊕ Rheingau	6

District	Sum (Amount)
⊟ The World	**596**
⊞ Americas	145
⊟ Europe	**451**
⊞ -	97
⊟ France	**181**
⊞ -	24
⊞ Bordeaux	157
⊞ Germany	173

Data integrity in an unbalanced Hierarchy

Extract from the Technical brief "Hierarchies" published on Nov 11, 2013

A common problem with unbalanced n-level hierarchies is data integrity. The data may be inconsistent, and it could be a good idea to check that the source table contains what you expect it to contain. And maybe correct the source…

Duplicates or Multiple parents

Source data may contain duplicate records for single nodes, e.g. that a node is described in two records with different names or that a node has multiple parents.

You need to determine whether you think this is OK. The Qlik engine can load this type of data, but it often looks inconsistent in the eyes of the user. I would recommend not having duplicates.

Also, it could imply performance problems. Loading such a table will mean duplicate rows in the resulting Expanded Nodes table, so that a daughter node may get not only two records, but four or eight or more, depending on how many of its ancestors have multiple parents.

The following script may help you find the duplicates:

```
Load
    NodeID,
    Count(NodeID)              as NoOfInstances,
    Count(distinct ParentID)   as NoOfParents
    From Source
        Group By NodeID;
```

Unlisted parent nodes

Each node needs a record of its own in the Adjacent Nodes table, but it is not uncommon that some parent nodes, especially the root node, are missing from this list.

You need to determine whether you think this is OK. The Qlik engine can load this type of data, but this may lead to the hierarchy having several root nodes and that root nodes aren't selectable.

The following script may help you find the unlisted nodes:

```
ExistingNodes:
Load distinct NodeID
    From Source ;


CheckIfParentExists:
Load distinct NodeID,
    ParentID,
    If(Exists(NodeID,ParentID), 'Existing',
        'ParentIsNotListed')    as ParentExistence
    From Source ;
```

Circular references

If the source table contains a circular reference, e.g. node A has node B as parent, node B has node C as parent, and node C has node A as parent, the hierarchy resolution will break up the loop and remove one of the parent IDs. In more complex situations it may result in that some nodes are excluded. My recommendation is to always avoid such structures.

The following script may help you find the circular references:

```
Tree:
Load
    NodeID        as Level_1
    From Source ;

For nLevel = 0 to 20
    Let nLevelBelow = nLevel + 1 ;
    Left Join (Tree)
    Load
        ParentID    as Level_$(nLevel),
        NodeID      as Level_$(nLevelBelow)
        From Source ;


    CountAddedNodes:
    Load Count(Level_$(nLevelBelow)) as NoOfAddedNodes
        Resident Tree;

    For nAncestorLevel = 0 to nLevel
        AncestorScan:
        Load
            Level_$(nLevelBelow) as NodeIDThatAlreadyExists
            Resident Tree
                Where Level_$(nAncestorLevel) = Level_$(nLevelBelow);
    Next nAncestorLevel


    Let vExitCriterion1 =
        Peek('NoOfAddedNodes',-1,'CountAddedNodes') = 0 ;
    Let vExitCriterion2 =
        not IsNull(Peek('NodeIDThatAlreadyExists',-1,'AncestorScan'));
    exit for when vExitCriterion1 or vExitCriterion2
Next nLevel
```

Semantic Links in Hierarchies

Originally posted in HIC's blog on Nov 22, 2023

Previously, I have written about the challenge that *Hierarchies* can constitute. See "Unbalanced, n-level Hierarchies". I have also written about *Semantic Links* as a useful way to navigate data. But they are especially useful to navigate hierarchies.

A good example of hierarchies is that of the wine districts of the world, where you can see some in this picture:

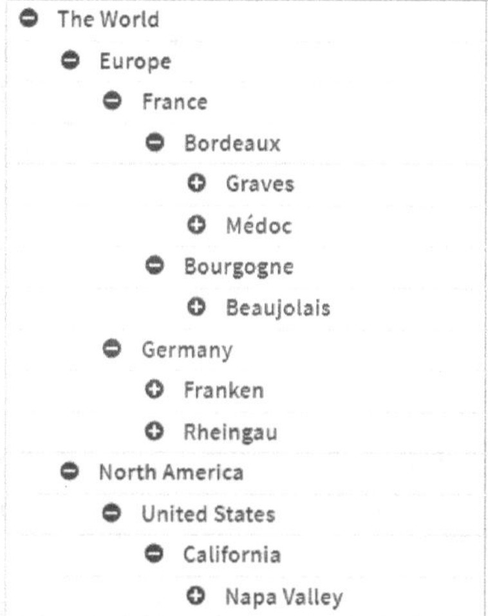

The benefit of using Semantic links with hierarchies is that it is possible to create list boxes showing the daughters, ancestors, or all sub-nodes of the selected wine district, thus giving a better overview and enabling a simple navigation of the data.

In the image below you can see what it looks like in QlikView:

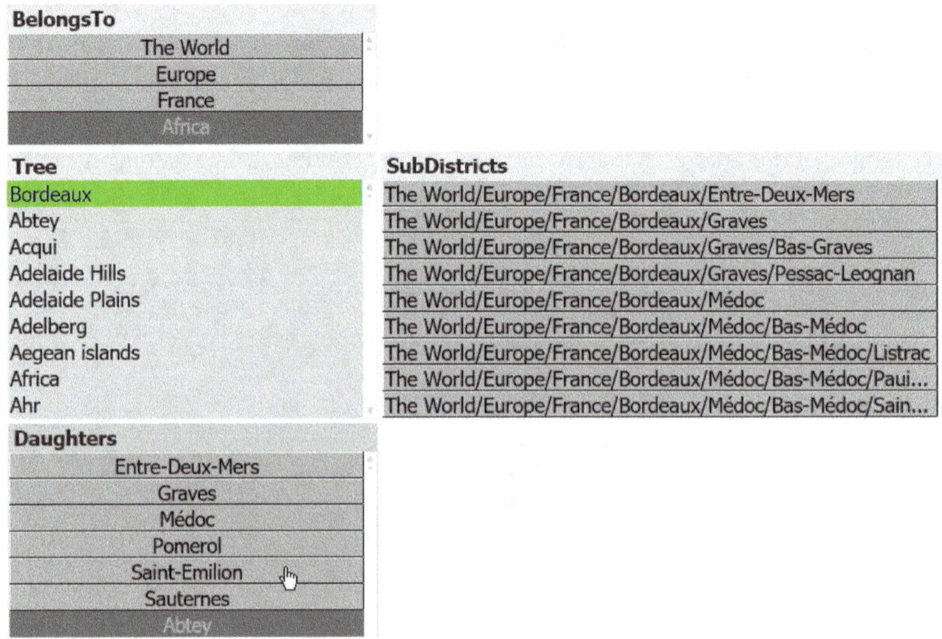

In the middle, there is a standard list box with 'Bordeaux' selected. The three semantic links surrounding this list box show how Bordeaux relates to other wine districts: The ancestors (above) show that Bordeaux belongs not only to 'France', but also to 'Europe' and 'The World'. The list box below shows the immediate daughters: 'Entre-Deux-Mers', 'Graves', etc.

And finally, to the right, all sub-districts of Bordeaux are listed using the path of the wine district.

The overview you can get of a hierarchy this way is excellent.

But that's not all. The semantic links of course also allow selections. All links are clickable, so if the user now clicks on 'Saint-Emilion', this will become selected instead of Bordeaux:

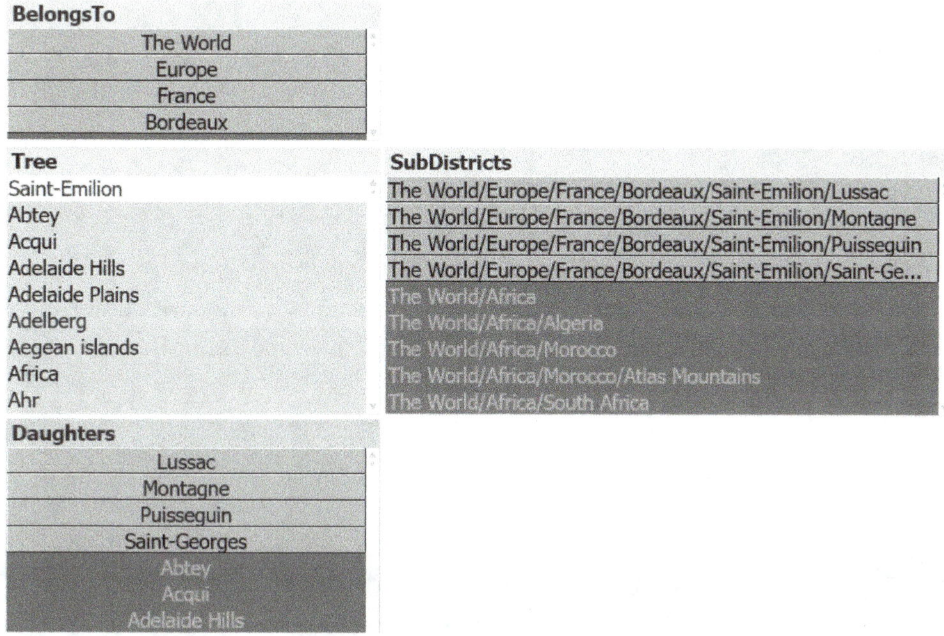

This way a user can walk through the hierarchy and navigate the data.

To create such semantic links, you first need to create the relations in the script using the **Hierarchy** and **HierarchyBelongsTo** prefixes. Then you need to load these relations in the script using the **Semantic** prefix.

Here is how I have done it. First a **Directory** statement to enable relative paths, and then a mock-up transaction table:

```
// ===================== Relative paths ==========================
// To simplify the script, relative paths are defined through a
// 'Directory' statement. Comment the one you don't need.
// ===============================================================
Directory C:\PathToFiles\ ;      // QlikView
Directory lib://DataFiles/ ;     // Qlik Sense
```

```
// ===================== Transaction tabe =========================
// This is just a mock-up for the example. In real life, you need
// to remove this and load the real fact table.
// ================================================================
Transactions:
Load
    NodeID,
    Round(10*rand())                 as Production
FROM [Winedistricts.txt]
    (txt, utf8, embedded labels, delimiter is ',', msq);
```

After these statements, there are two hierarchy-defining statements in line with how a hierarchy should be loaded:

```
// ===================== Nodes ====================================
// Generate Expanded Nodes view of the Wine district, i.e. keep
// original table, but add one field per level in the hierarchy
// ================================================================
WineDistricts:
Hierarchy (NodeID, ParentID, District, ParentDistrict, District,
    Path, '/', Depth)
LOAD
    NodeID                           as NodeID,
    If(Len(ParentID),ParentID)       as ParentID,
    Name                             as District
FROM [Winedistricts.txt]
    (txt, utf8, embedded labels, delimiter is ',', msq);
```

```
// ===================== Trees ===================================
// An Ancestor table, i.e. a table with one record per Ancestor-
// Descendant relation. Each ancestor will have ALL its sub-nodes
// represented.
// ===============================================================
WineDistrictsSubNodes:
HierarchyBelongsTo (NodeID, ParentID, DistrictCopy, TreeID, Tree)
Load
    NodeID                          as NodeID,
    ParentID                        as ParentID,
    District                        as DistrictCopy,
    Path                            as PathCopy,
    Depth                           as DepthCopy
Resident WineDistricts ;
```

Once the hierarchy has been loaded, we can proceed to the semantic load statements. The first one loads from the **WineDistricts** table to establish the parent-child relationship, and the second one loads from the **WineDistrictsSubNodes** table to establish the ancestor-descendant relationship.

Each semantic load links to the data using **TreeID** and **TreeIDCopy**.

Each semantic load also creates two semantic fields, i.e four fields all in all. However, only three of these fields are used: The **Parents** field really adds no value, so it is not used. But it needs to be there for syntactical reasons. However, the other three fields are very useful: **Daughters**, **BelongsTo**, and **SubDistricts**.

The **BelongsTo** field is special: In the UI it needs to be sorted not alphabetically, but rather *top-down*. This is achieved by ordering the Load statement according to the **Depth** field and displaying the list box using the load order.

```
// ====================== Semantic Parents  ========================
// Semantic table with links to direct parents and direct children
// ================================================================
[SemanticParents]:
Semantic
Load distinct
    NodeID                      as TreeID,
    ParentDistrict              as Parents,
    ParentID                    as TreeIDCopy,
    District                    as Daughters
Resident WineDistricts
    Where   Len(Trim(NodeID)) > 0
        and Len(Trim(ParentID)) > 0
        and NodeID <> ParentID
    Order By Depth;


// ====================== Semantic Ancestors ======================
// Semantic table with links to all ancestors and all descendents
// ================================================================
[SemanticAncestors]:
Semantic
Load distinct
    NodeID                      as TreeID,
    Tree                        as BelongsTo,
    TreeID                      as TreeIDCopy,
    PathCopy                    as SubDistricts
Resident WineDistrictsSubNodes
    Where   Len(Trim(NodeID)) > 0
        and Len(Trim(TreeID)) > 0
        and NodeID <> TreeID
    Order By DepthCopy;
```

A copy of the **TreeID** is created since the semantic loads need this. Finally, unnecessary fields are dropped:

```
// ====================== Copy of TreeID ==========================
// Add a copy of the tree ID in the Ancestors table.
// (Needed for the Semantic Loads)
// ===============================================================
Inner Join (WineDistrictsSubNodes)
Load distinct
    TreeID,
    TreeID                              as TreeIDCopy
Resident WineDistrictsSubNodes ;



// ==================== Clean Up ==============================
Drop Field PathCopy, DepthCopy, DistrictCopy ;
```

The illustrations are from QlikView, but this works just as well also in Qlik Sense. Good luck with your semantic links!

Bill of Materials

Originally posted in the Qlik Design Blog on Sep 1, 2015

Most hierarchies are *dimensional hierarchies*. This implies several things: First, you have a many-to-one relationship between the levels: a day belongs to one (and only one) month, a month to one (and only one) quarter, etc. Strictly speaking, it is not a hierarchy unless this condition is fulfilled.

Secondly, the hierarchy contains no measures. Instead, numbers are stored in a transactional table that is linked to the dimensional hierarchy.

But there is another hierarchy-like structure, the *Bill of Materials*, the "BoM". This is a list of items, assemblies and sub-assemblies representing the design of a product or device. Many products are planned and documented with BoMs.

A multi-level BoM depicts parent-child relationships and shows the hierarchical structure of the assemblies and their related subcomponents. A multi-level BoM is essentially a nested list whose items are listed to illustrate multiple assemblies within a product.

LineNo	Level	Quantity	Item	Part No	UnitCost
1	1	1	Trailer	10420-1001	
2	2	1	Chassis	10112-1001	
3	3	1	Wooden board,15mm, 2400x1200	10409-1001	1,5
4	3	1	Paint	10111-1009	1
5	3	4	Labor	10430-1000	10
6	2	4	Wheel assembly	10410-1001	
7	3	2	Side Piece	10410-1003	
8	4	2	Steel profile 180x8	10107-1001	2
9	4	1	Surface coating	10111-1001	0,5
10	4	1	Labor	10430-1000	10
11	3	1	Top Piece	10410-1002	
12	4	1	Steel profile 180x8	10107-1001	0,1
13	4	1	Surface coating	10111-1001	0,5
14	4	0,5	Labor	10430-1000	10
15	3	1	Wheel, 120mm	10404-1108	5
16	3	2	Ball bearing	10404-1110	2
17	3	2	Bolt, M10x70, Stainless	10400-1001	0,2
18	3	2	Washer, M10, Stainless	10400-1002	0,01
19	3	2	Nut, M10, Stainless	10400-1003	0,05
20	3	1	Bolt, M10x30, Stainless	10400-1004	0,05

But a BoM is very different from a dimensional hierarchy. It does not have to have a strict many-to-one relationship between the levels. For instance, a specific bearing type can be used in several places. For the BoM, this means that the bearing can have several parents in the hierarchy.

Further, each line in the BoM has numbers in it, typically **Quantity** and **Cost**. These are measures that should be summed. In a sense, a BoM is more similar to a transaction table than a dimensional table.

A BoM can easily be loaded and analyzed with Qlik Sense or QlikView, but there are some challenges: First, the list often lacks a parent reference. Instead, the parent-child relationship is implied by the order of the rows and the **Level** field and visualized by indentations.

Secondly, aggregating the measures is not straightforward. When summing the costs, the multiplicities of all the nodes above must be taken into account. In the example in the above table, the wheel assembly uses two bearings, and the trailer uses four wheel assemblies. Then the trailer obviously needs eight bearings. In other words: The row for the wheel assembly – *and all rows belonging to it* – must be looped four times when summing the cost.

Luckily, both these challenges can be handled in the Qlik script. One possible solution is the following:

```
Hierarchy (PartNo, Parent, Description)
Load *,
   Subfield(Path, '/', Level)                 as Parent;
Load *,
   Left(Peek(Path), Index(Peek(Path)&'/', '/',Level)-1)&'/'&PartNo
                                    as Path
   While IterNo() <= Units;
Load *,
   If( Frac(Quantity)=0, Quantity, 1 )  as Units,
   If( Frac(Quantity)=0, 1, Quantity )  as Amount
   From BoM ;
```

The reference to the parent is created in two steps: First a **Path** is built using the **Level** and the **Path** of the above row. Having the path, it is straightforward to extract the parent id using Subfield().

Further, each row is loaded several times using a while loop. Hence, row 16 (the ball bearings) is loaded twice since its **Quantity** is 2. But it should be loaded 8 times since the **Quantity** of its parent (row 6, Wheel assembly) is 4. This multiplication is achieved using the **Hierarchy** prefix.

Finally, the above multiplication algorithm only works for integer quantities. For this reason, the bottom Load splits the **Quantity** into two fields: a field **Units** that is used in the **While** loop, and an **Amount** that is used in the aggregation:

```
Sum( Amount * UnitCost )
```

However, this means that nodes that have non-integer quantities cannot have any children. If they do, the above algorithm cannot be used, and the cost roll-up must be made a different way. Luckily, this is rarely – or never – the case in real life.

Good luck with your Bill of Materials!

Hierarchies

7

Intervals

Intervals of dates or other numeric fields often occur in data. A common use case is when you have a list of numbers or dates in one table – below called events – and a list of intervals in a second table. The goal is to link the two tables.

In the general case, this is a many-to-many relationship, i.e. an interval can have many dates belonging to it and a date can belong to many intervals. To model this correctly, you need to create a bridge table between the two original tables.

There are several ways to do this. This chapter describes how to do this and answers other questions pertaining to the same topic:

- What techniques are there to match a number with an interval?
- How does the **IntervalMatch** prefix work?
- Should I join the interval match table with the event table?
- How do I generate an interval from a single change date?
- What is a Slowly Changing Dimension?
- How do I model a multi-level Slowly Changing Dimension?

These questions and others are answered in this Chapter.

Thank you, Barry H., for good discussions.

Creating a date interval from a single date

Originally posted in the Qlik Design Blog on Feb 25, 2013

Sometimes when you load data into a Qlik app you have validity ranges, but the range is only implied by one field – a single change date.

It could be like in the table to the right where you have currency rates for multiple currencies: Each currency rate change is on its own row; each with a new conversion rate. Also, the table could contain rows with empty dates corresponding to the initial conversion rate, before the first change was made.

Currency	Change Date	Rate
EUR		8.59
EUR	1/28/2013	8.69
EUR	2/15/2013	8.45
USD		6.50
USD	1/10/2013	6.56
USD	2/3/2013	6.30

This problem is very similar to the one in another blog post "How to populate a sparsely populated field", but this time I will approach the problem in a different way.

Instead of inserting records and populating these with the correct field values, I will instead maintain the number of rows and create a new column **"To Date"**, so that the new table will become a list of intervals.

Here's how you do it:

1. Determine which time range you want to work with. The beginning of the range must be before the first date in the data and the end of the range must be after the last.

2. Load the source data but change empty dates to the beginning of the range defined in the previous bullet. The change date should be loaded as **"From Date"**.

3. Sort the table first according to **Currency**, then according to the **"From Date"** descending so that you have the latest dates on top.

4. Run a second pass through data where you calculate the **"To Date"**. If the current record has a different currency from the previous record, then it is the first record of a new currency (but its last interval), so you should use the end of the range defined in bullet 1. If it is the same **Currency**, you should take the **"From Date"** from the previous record, subtract a small amount of time, and use this value as **"To Date"** in the current record.

Currency	From Date	To Date	Rate
EUR	2/15/2013	vEndTime	8.45
EUR	1/28/2013	2/14/2013 23:59:59	8.69
EUR	vBeginTime	1/27/2013 23:59:59	8.59
USD	2/3/2013	vEndTime	6.30
USD	1/10/2013	2/2/2013 23:59:59	6.56
USD	vBeginTime	1/9/2013 23:59:59	6.50

In the Qlik script, it could look like this:

```
Let vBeginTime   = Num('1/1/2013');
Let vEndTime     = Num(Now());


Tmp_Rates:
Load Currency, Rate,
    Date(
        If(IsNum([Change Date]), [Change Date],
            $(#vBeginTime))
        )                           as FromDate
    From Rates ;

Rates:
Load Currency, Rate, FromDate,
    Date(
        If(Currency=Peek(Currency),Peek(FromDate)-0.00000001,
        $(#vEndTime))
        )                           as ToDate
    Resident Tmp_Rates
    Order By Currency, FromDate Desc;
Drop Table Tmp_Rates;
```

When this is done, you will have a table listing the intervals correctly.

Currency	FromDate	ToDate	Rate
USD	1/1/2013	1/9/2013	6.50
USD	1/10/2013	2/2/2013	6.56
USD	2/3/2013	2/22/2013	6.30
EUR	1/1/2013	1/27/2013	8.59
EUR	1/28/2013	2/14/2013	8.69
EUR	2/15/2013	2/22/2013	8.45

This table can then be used in a **While** loop to generate all dates in the intervals (See "Creating Reference Dates for Intervals") or with an **IntervalMatch** to compare with an existing date.

In this example, I subtract 0.00000001 from the date in the previous record. This corresponds to roughly a millisecond. This means that the "**ToDate**" will have a value of one millisecond before midnight but formatted to show the date only. The reason I do it this way, is for the **IntervalMatch** to work: No point in time will belong to two intervals.

IntervalMatch

Originally posted in the Qlik Design Blog on Apr 4, 2013

A common problem in business intelligence is when you want to link a number to a numeric range. It could be that you have a date in one table and an interval – a "**From**" date and a "**To**" date – in another table, and you want to link the two tables. In SQL, you would probably join them using a **BETWEEN** clause in the comparison.

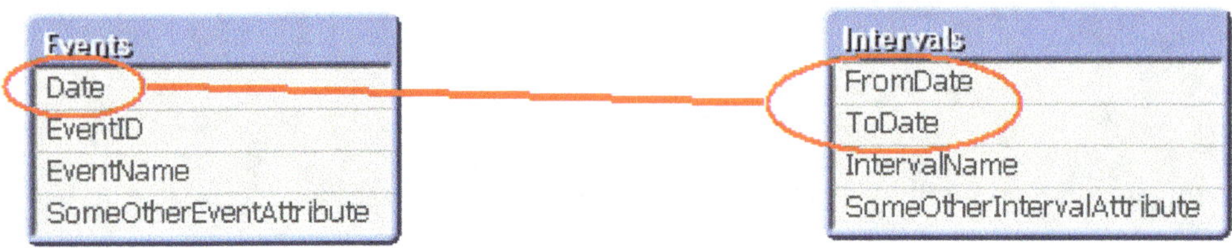

But how do you solve this in a Qlik app, where you should avoid joins in the data model?

The answer is to use **IntervalMatch**.

IntervalMatch is a prefix that can be put in front of either a Load or a SELECT statement. The Load or SELECT statement needs to contain two fields only: the "**From**" and the "**To**" fields defining the intervals. The **IntervalMatch** will generate all the combinations between the loaded intervals and a previously loaded numeric field.

Typically, you would first load the table with the individual numbers (the **Events**), then the table with the **Intervals**, and finally an interval match that creates a third table that bridges the two first tables.

```
Events:
Load Date, ...                          From Events;

Intervals:
Load FromDate, ToDate, ...              From Intervals;

IntervalMatch:
IntervalMatch (Date)
Load distinct FromDate, ToDate  Resident Intervals;
```

The resulting data model contains three tables:

1. The **Events** table – that contains exactly one record per event.
2. The **Intervals** table – that contains exactly one record per interval.
3. The **IntervalMatch** table – that contains exactly one record per combination of event and interval, and that links the two previous tables.

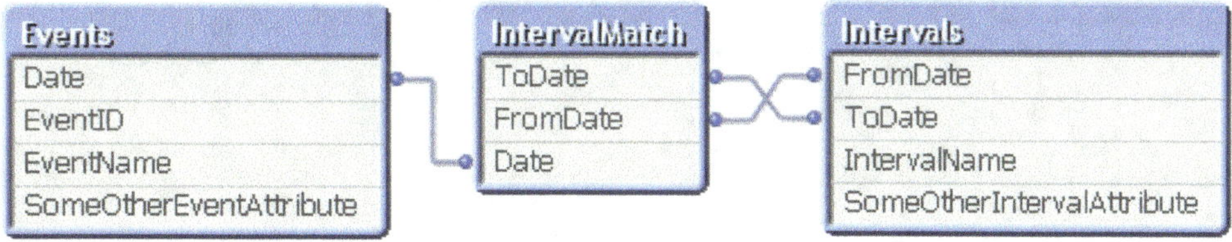

Note that this means that an event may belong to several intervals if the intervals are overlapping. And an interval can of course have several events belonging to it.

This data model is optimal, in the sense that it is normalized and compact. All Qlik calculations operating on these tables e.g. Count(**EventID**) will work and will be evaluated correctly. This means that it is *not* necessary to join the **IntervalMatch** table onto one of the original tables. Joining it onto another table may even cause the Qlik engine to calculate aggregations incorrectly, since the join can change the number of records in a table.

Further, the data model contains a composite key (the **FromDate** and **ToDate** fields) which will manifest itself as a Qlik synthetic key. But have no fear. This synthetic key *should* be there; not only is it correct, but it is also optimal given the data model. You do *not* need to remove it.

IntervalMatch can also be used with an additional key between the tables – i.e. when you have *Slowly Changing Dimensions*. But more about that in a later post.

Using a While loop

Extract from the Technical brief "IntervalMatch and Slowly Changing Dimensions" published on Jun 03, 2013

A different way to solve the problem with intervals is to use a **While** loop. With it, you can often achieve almost the same bridge table that creates enumerable values between the lower and upper bounds of the interval.

If you have a primary key for the intervals – the **IntervalID** – the only difference in the script will be how the bridge table is created:

```
BridgeTable:
Load distinct * Where Exists(EventDate);
Load
    IntervalBegin + IterNo() - 1 as EventDate,
    IntervalID
    Resident Intervals
    While IntervalBegin + IterNo() - 1 <= IntervalEnd ;
```

If you don't have a primary key in the interval table, you can create one using the following definition:

```
    RecNo() as IntervalID,
```

This solution has the advantage that other fields can be included in the bridge table, e.g. the primary key from the interval table, so that you can use this instead of the composite key in the above example.

It, however, has the drawback that it can only handle enumerable values, e.g. integers and dates.

Using a Join

Extract from the Technical brief "IntervalMatch and Slowly Changing Dimensions" published on Jun 03, 2013

A third way to create the bridge table is to use the join prefix to create all combinations of the number and the intervals and then, in a second pass, filter out the relevant ones:

```
tmpBridgeTable:
Load distinct EventDate                    Resident Events ;
Join (tmpBridgeTable)
Load IntervalID, IntervalBegin, IntervalEnd
                                      Resident Intervals ;


BridgeTable:
Load distinct EventDate, IntervalID    Resident tmpBridgeTable
    Where   IntervalBegin <= EventDate
        and EventDate < IntervalEnd ;


Drop Table tmpBridgeTable ;
```

This solution has the advantage that other fields can be included in the bridge table, e.g. the primary keys from both the event table and the interval table, so that you can use these for the links to the initial tables. Further, the method can handle both open and closed intervals (see the relational operators in the where clause).

However, it does have one major drawback: The join is memory consuming, so this method should not be used for large data amounts. In fact, the method below with a **While** loop is often a better solution. It has all the mentioned advantages but uses less memory.

Bottom line: Don't use this method unless you have very small tables, or you have an additional key between the tables (i.e. a slowly changing dimension. See further below.)

A variant on the join method is to use a while loop with a Peek() function to create the bridge table. The idea is to make a join "manually" by making a lookup in each loop of the while clause.

The first (bottom) load statement loads data from the interval table and has a while loop that loads all records from the Events table. Effectively it creates the Cartesian product between the two tables. The preceding load then filters out the relevant records:

```
BridgeTable:
Load distinct
    IntervalID, EventDate
    Where   IntervalBegin <= EventDate
        and EventDate < IntervalEnd;
Load
    IntervalID, IntervalBegin, IntervalEnd,
    Peek('EventDate', IterNo()-1, 'Events') as EventDate
    Resident Intervals
        While IterNo() <= NoOfRows('Events') ;
```

Just as the method using the Join prefix, this solution has the advantage that other fields can be included in the bridge table. Also, the method can handle both open and closed intervals.

It, however, has the drawback that it is slower than the two initial methods.

Simplifying the data model

Extract from the Technical brief "IntervalMatch and Slowly Changing Dimensions" published on Jun 03, 2013

Removing the bridge table

In the general case, the solution with three tables is the best one, because it allows for a many-to-many relationship between intervals and events. But a very common situation is that you know that an event can only belong to one single interval. In such a case, the bridge table is really not necessary: The **IntervalID** can be stored directly in the event table. There are several ways to achieve this, but the most common is to join the bridge table with the event table.

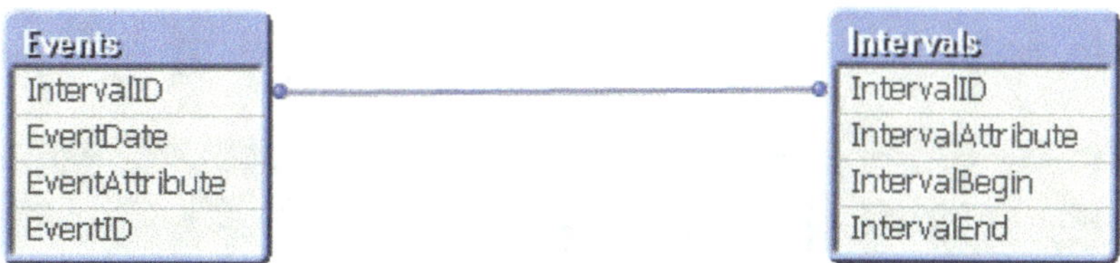

A word of caution: If you join the bridge table with the event table in a situation where an event belongs to several intervals, you will change the number of records in the event table and the Qlik engine may make incorrect calculations: Some events will be counted twice.

Bottom line: Double check that you *really* have a many-to-one relationship and not a many-to-many relationship.

Removing the synthetic key

The synthetic key may look like a wart on an otherwise beautiful data model. But I can only reiterate that a synthetic key like the one you get from using **IntervalMatch** is harmless, and that you do not need to remove it. Synthetic keys need to be removed only if one of the constituent fields shouldn't be a key, or if you have a synthetic key created from another synthetic key.

On the other hand, it is fairly straightforward to remove the synthetic key: Just create a composite key manually from the constituent fields and use this instead:

```
IntervalBegin & '|' & IntervalEnd                        as IntervalID
```

or slightly more advanced:

```
Autonumber(Num(IntervalBegin)&'|'& Num(IntervalEnd)) as IntervalID
```

The Num() functions format the dates to integers, which means that the created strings are independent of the date format. If this is of no concern, the Num() function calls are not needed.

The Autonumber() function converts the string to an integer that takes a lot less memory space. If this is of no concern, the Autonumber() function call is not needed.

You may need to run through the bridge table a second pass to achieve this solution, but since it normally is a fairly small table, this should be no problem.

The script

The script will then look like the following:

```
Events:
Load EventDate, … From Events;

Intervals:
Load
    IntervalBegin, IntervalEnd, …,
    Autonumber(
        Num(IntervalBegin) & '|' & Num(IntervalEnd)
        )                                   as IntervalID
    From Intervals;

tmpBridgeTable:
IntervalMatch (EventDate)
Load distinct IntervalBegin, IntervalEnd Resident Intervals;


Join (Events)
Load
    EventDate,
    Autonumber(
        Num(IntervalBegin) & '|' & Num(IntervalEnd)
        )                                   as IntervalID
    Resident tmpBridgeTable;

Drop Table tmpBridgeTable;
```

Finally, I have seen cases where the developer joins the bridge table onto the interval table, instead of the events table, to get rid of the synthetic key. This is not a good idea: Since there usually are many more events than intervals, the new interval table grows dramatically in size and the whole point of having the data in two tables is lost.

Bottom line: In a simple interval match where you don't have additional keys, you do not need to remove the synthetic key. However, if you know that an event only belongs to one interval, you can remove both the bridge table and the synthetic key by moving the **IntervalID** into the events table.

Open and closed intervals

Extract from the Technical brief "IntervalMatch and Slowly Changing Dimensions" published on Jun 03, 2013

Intervals can be defined in different ways: They can be open, closed or half-open. Whether an interval is open or closed is determined by the endpoints – whether these are included in the interval or not.

- If the endpoints are included, it is a closed interval; $[a,b] = \{x \in \mathbb{R} \mid a \le x \le b\}$
- If the endpoints are not included, it is an open interval; $]a,b[= \{x \in \mathbb{R} \mid a < x < b\}$
- If one endpoint is included, it is a half-open interval; $[a,b[= \{x \in \mathbb{R} \mid a \le x < b\}$

If you have a case where the intervals are overlapping, and a number can belong to more than one interval, you usually want to use closed intervals.

However, in some cases you do not want overlapping intervals – you want a number to belong to *one interval only*. Hence, you will get a problem if one and the same point is the end of one interval and at the same time the beginning of next. A number with exactly this value will be attributed to both intervals. Hence, you want half-open intervals.

In the Qlik engine, open intervals cannot be represented. A practical solution to this problem is, however, to subtract a very small amount from the end value of all intervals, thus creating closed, but non-overlapping intervals. If your numbers are dates, one simple way to do this is to use the function DayEnd() which returns the last millisecond of the day:

```
DayEnd(IntervalEnd-1)                          as IntervalEnd
```

But you can also subtract a small amount manually. If you do, make sure the subtracted amount isn't too small since the operation will be rounded to 52 significant binary digits (14 decimal digits). If you use an amount too small, the difference will not be significant, and you will be back using the original number.

If your numbers are dates, you can subtract an amount as small as 2^{-37} which is slightly less than a microsecond. Here the small amount is created in the variable **Epsilon**:

```
Let Epsilon = Pow(2,-37) ;    //   = 7E-12 = 0.000 000 000 007
Intervals:
Load … ,
    Date(IntervalEnd-$(#Epsilon))              as IntervalEnd
    From Intervals;
```

If the subtracted amount is smaller than 2^{-27}, the time difference will not be visible in the date and timestamp formats. The reason is that the date and time functions display the formatted date or time for the nearest millisecond while keeping a numeric value that has higher precision. I.e. the Date() function will display the original date. If you want the time difference to be visible, you can at most subtract 2^{-27}.

It is also possible to use the Dual() function to create the desired display value:

```
Dual(IntervalEnd, IntervalEnd-$(#Epsilon))  as IntervalEnd
```


Slowly changing dimensions

Originally posted in the Qlik Design Blog on Jun 03, 2013

As one creates Qlik applications one sometimes encounters a data modeling problem where a dimensional attribute varies over time. It could be that a salesperson changes department or a product is reclassified to belong to another class of products.

This problem is called *Slowly Changing Dimensions* and is a challenge for any Business Intelligence tool. Creating an application with static dimensions is simple enough, but when a salesperson is transferred from one department to another, you will have to ask yourself how you want this change to be reflected in your application. Should you use the current department for all transactions? Or should you try to attribute each transaction to the proper department depending on *when* the transaction was made?

First of all, a changed attribute must be recorded in a way that the historical information is preserved. If the old value is overwritten by the new attribute value, there is of course nothing Qlik or any other tool can do to save the situation. Below, you can see an example where Cynthia has changed department, and there is no information about previous department in the "After" table.

Before

SPID	Name	Department
1	Bob	Dept B
2	Cynthia	Dept C

After: Original Department is lost

SPID	Name	Department
1	Bob	Dept B
2	Cynthia	Dept D

In such a case, the new attribute value will also be used for the old transactions and sales numbers will in some cases be attributed to the wrong department.

However, if the changes have been recorded in a way so that historical data persists, then Qlik can show the changes very well. Normally, historical data are stored by adding a new record in the database for each new situation, with a change date that defines the beginning of the validity period.

It is not uncommon that there are two tables for each dimension, one with the history containing fields that may change and one with static data, similar to the following:

Dynamic dimension data

SPID	FromDate	Department
1		Dept B
2		Dept C
2	12/31/2011	Dept D

Static dimension data

SPID	Name
1	Bob
2	Cynthia

In such a case, we will have four tables that need to be linked correctly: A transaction table, a dynamic salesperson dimension, a static salesperson dimension and a department dimension. The transaction date needs to be matched against the intervals defined in the dynamic salesperson dimension.

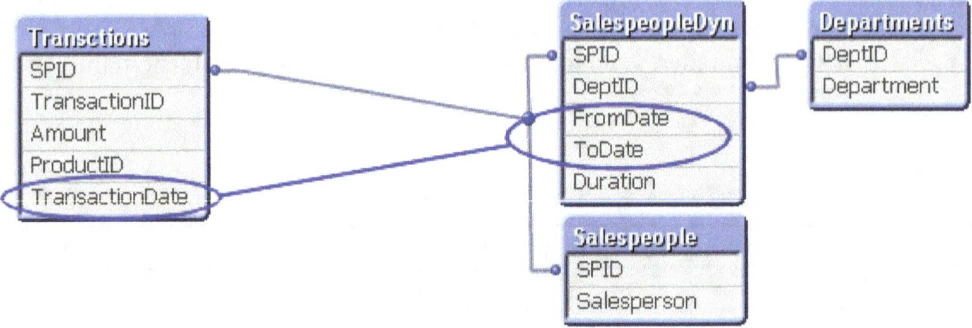

This is an interval match, but with a constraint of an additional key. The solution is to create a bridge table between the transaction table and the dimension tables. And this should be *the only link* between them. This means that the link from the transaction table to the bridge table should be a composite key consisting of the salesperson ID (in the picture called **SPID**) and the transaction date.

It also means that the second link, the one from the bridge table to the dimension tables, should be a key that points to a specific salesperson interval, e.g. a composite key consisting of the salesperson ID and the beginning and end of the interval. Finally, the salesperson ID should only exist in the dimension tables and must hence be removed from the transaction table.

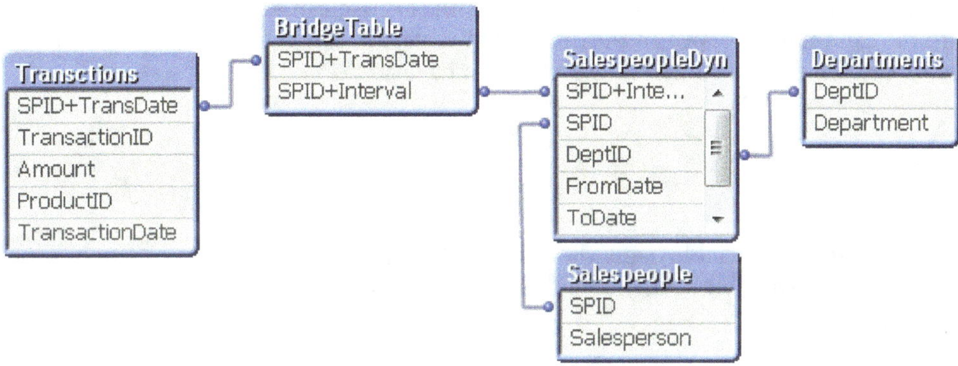

In most cases of slowly changing dimensions, a salesperson (or product, customer, etc.) can only belong to one department (or product group, region, etc.) at a time. In other words, the relationship between salesperson and interval is a many-to-one relationship. If so, you can store the interval key directly in the transaction table to simplify the data model, e.g. by joining the bridge table onto the transaction table.

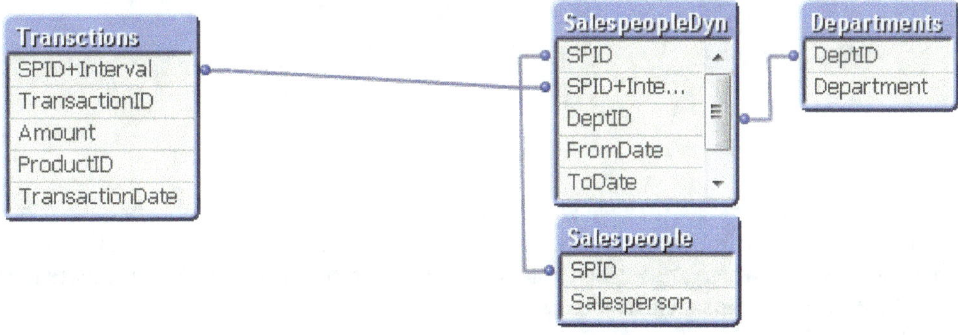

A word of caution: If a salesperson belongs to several departments at the same time, such a join may cause the Qlik engine to make incorrect calculations. Bottom line: Double-check before you join.

Creating the bridge table

Hence, we first need to create the bridge table that links the salesman-date in the transaction table with the salesman-intervals in the dimension table. For this, I use the **IntervalMatch** prefix, in its extended syntax where it is possible to have additional keys:

```
IntervalMatch (TransactionDate, SPID)
Load distinct FromDate, ToDate, SPID Resident SalespeopleDyn;
```

But just creating the bridge table using the above statement and joining it together with the three other tables will not work, since too many links are created:

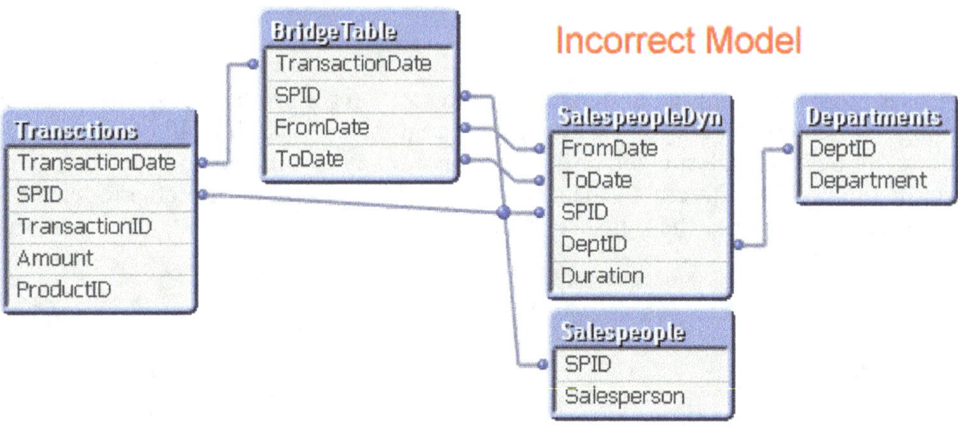

Instead, we must *create* the structure we want: We need to create a bridge table between the transaction table and the dimension tables. And it should be *the only link* between them. This means that the link from the transaction table to the bridge table should be a composite key consisting of **SPID** and **TransactionDate**.

It also means that the next link, the one from the bridge table to the dimension tables, should also be a composite key, but now consisting of **SPID**, **FromDate** and **ToDate**. Finally, the field **SPID** may only exist in the dimension tables and must hence be removed from the transaction table.

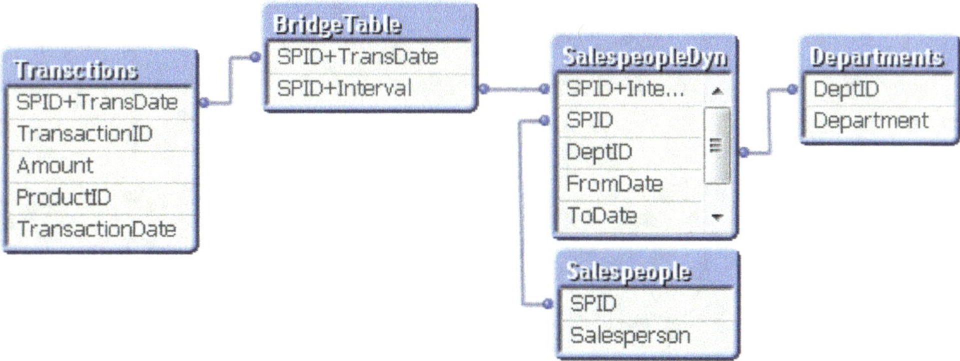

To achieve this, the bridge table is created in the following steps:

1) The dimension tables are loaded. In the dynamic salesperson dimension, a composite key is created from the salesperson ID and the interval dates.

2) The transaction table is loaded. In addition, a composite key is created from the salesperson ID and the date.

3) The interval match is made, assigning an interval to each combination of salesperson and transaction date. The resulting table is a temporary table: the first version of the bridge table and it will have four fields: **TransactionDate**, **FromDate**, **ToDate** and **SPID**.

4) In a second pass over the temporary bridge table, these four fields are used to create two new fields that are composite keys: First the key that links to the transaction table and then the key that links to the dimension tables. The definitions of the composite keys must be the same in the bridge table as in the two tables in bullet 1 and 2.

5) Finally, the temporary bridge table is dropped, as well as **SPID** from the **Transaction** table.

Intervals

In the Qlik script, the main part of the script could be implemented like this:

```
// ========================= Sales People =========================
// Load all fields. Create a new key from SPID and interval data.
// ================================================================
SalespeopleDyn:
Load *,
    SPID & '|' & FromDate & '|' & ToDate    as [SPID+Interval]
From SalespeopleDyn;


// ========================= Transactions =========================
// Load all fields. Create a new key from SPID and the event date.
// ================================================================
Transactions:
Load *,
    SPID & '|' & TransactionDate            as [SPID+TransDate]
From Transactions;


// ========================= temp Bridge table =====================
// Create a Bridge table using IntervalMatch, with SPID as
// additional key.
// ================================================================
tmpBridgeTable:
IntervalMatch (TransactionDate,SPID)
Load distinct FromDate, ToDate, SPID    Resident SalespeopleDyn ;


// ========================= Bridge table =========================
// Create the final Bridge table by generating the new keys from
// the temporary Bridge table.
// ================================================================
BridgeTable:
Load
    SPID & '|' & TransactionDate            as [SPID+TransDate],
    SPID & '|' & FromDate & '|' & ToDate    as [SPID+Interval]
    Resident tmpBridgeTable;
```

```
// ========================== Clean Up ===============================
// Drop SPID from the Trancaction table, and drop the temporary
// bridge table
// ===================================================================
Drop Field SPID From Transactions;
Drop Table tmpBridgeTable;
```

Using the above method to link a dynamic dimension to the transaction table, the problem with a Slowly Changing Dimension can be solved. All transactions will be connected to the appropriate department and the Qlik engine will always show the correct numbers.

Joining the bridge table onto the transaction table

In most cases of slowly changing dimensions, a salesperson (or product, customer, etc.) can only belong to one department (or product group, region, etc.) at a time. In other words, the salesperson – interval relationship is a many-to-one relationship. If so, you should join the bridge table onto the transaction table. This join will not change the number of records in the transaction table.

A word of caution: I have more than once been in a situation where the application developer with great confidence says that it is a many-to-one relationship, e.g. that there can only be one product group per product. So, we make the join – only to find out that the number of records in the transaction table changes. I.e. the application developer was wrong: in the data a product could in fact belong to more than one product group. Such a join may cause the Qlik engine to make incorrect calculations. Bottom line: Double-check before you join.

With a join, the script changes only marginally: Most statements are identical, with the small difference that the composite key with salesperson ID and date is no longer necessary.

However, the bridge table should not be loaded as a separate table, but this Load is instead preceded by a **Join** prefix. The salesman ID and the date are loaded instead of the composite key, so the join with the transaction table has the correct keys.

In the Qlik script, the bridge table Load statement could be implemented like this:

```
// ========================= Bridge table =========================
// Create the new key [SPID+Interval] from the temporary Bridge
// table, and join this onto the Transaction table.
// ================================================================
Left Join (Transactions)
Load SPID, TransactionDate,
    SPID & '|' & FromDate & '|' & ToDate      as [SPID+Interval]
    Resident tmpBridgeTable;
```

Multiple interval tables

Extract from the Technical brief "IntervalMatch and Slowly Changing Dimensions" published on Jun 03, 2013

In more advanced data models, you may encounter situations where you have several interval tables that need to be matched against each other or against a common date. In this section I will elaborate a little around these cases.

Interval Partitioning

In some cases, you will need to transform a set of overlapping intervals into its most basic components: the unique sub-intervals. This is called partitioning.

The pictures below show an example. The upper graph shows five intervals that are partly overlapping. If you compare these intervals to a set of events, you will get a data model where each event can belong to several intervals.

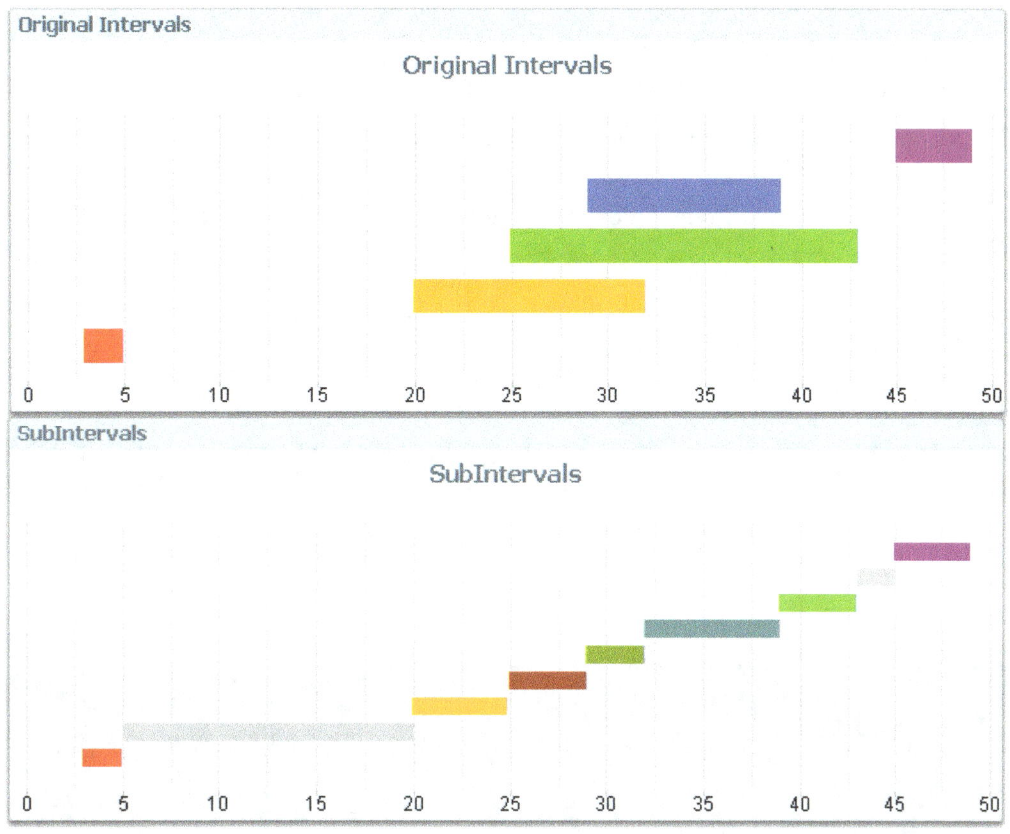

The lower graph shows the sub-intervals for the same data. If you instead compare these sub-intervals to the same set of events, you will have a situation where you know that each event can only belong to one interval.

By finding the sub-intervals, you can in some situations simplify your data model.

Note that in the picture above, you don't have any additional dimensions. But in real life, you usually have an additional dimensional key, e.g. salesperson ID, which makes it a slowly changing dimension. In such a case, the intervals should only be compared within each salesperson and not between different salespeople.

If you have one table with overlapping intervals, you can do it this way:

1. Create a table containing all beginnings and ends of the original intervals, stored in one field. In addition, the table needs the dimensional key.

2. Convert this table to intervals as described in the section "Creating a Date Interval from a Single Date".

The script will look similar to the following, assuming that the dimensional key is **SPID** (salesperson ID).

```
// ========================= Breakpoints =========================
// Find all beginnings and ends of the intervals.
// ===============================================================
tmpBreakPoints:
Load distinct SPID, Begin   as SubFromDate  Resident Intervals;
Load distinct SPID, End     as SubFromDate  Resident Intervals;


// ========================= SubIntervals =========================
// Create intervals from single dates
// ===============================================================
Let Epsilon = Pow(2,-37) ;


SubIntervals:
Load SPID, SubFromDate,
    RecNo()                                    as SubIntervalID,
    Dual(SubToDate, SubToDate - $(#Epsilon))    as SubToDate
    Where not IsNull(SubToDate) ;
Load SPID, SubFromDate,
    If(SPID=Previous(SPID), Previous(SubFromDate))  as SubToDate
    Resident tmpBreakPoints
    Order By SPID, SubFromDate Desc;


// ========================= Clean Up =========================
Drop Table tmpBreakPoints;
```

With this script, you have created a new set of intervals that you can use as a replacement for the original intervals. Each subinterval can belong to several original intervals and each original interval can have several subintervals, so you may need to use an interval match to connect the new and old intervals.

Two interval tables with common dimension and common time line

A case where you could use partitioning is when you have two tables with different entities, and both with intervals. An example could be that you have one table with incidents – events that have both a start time and an end time – and another table with the shift schedule of the working staff. Both tables should be mapped against the same timeline and both tables also contain the ID of the production machine where the incident took place.

And the question is: which work shift managed which incident?

To solve this, you need to partition the intervals and map both original tables against a common sub-interval table.

One simple partition is to use discrete minutes as the common timeline – it solves the problem. However, you will probably get too many combinations of minutes and machine IDs, so that the data amount will be too large. Further, it is only roughly right: The beginnings and the ends of the events and shifts need to be rounded to discrete minutes, so you lose the information about seconds.

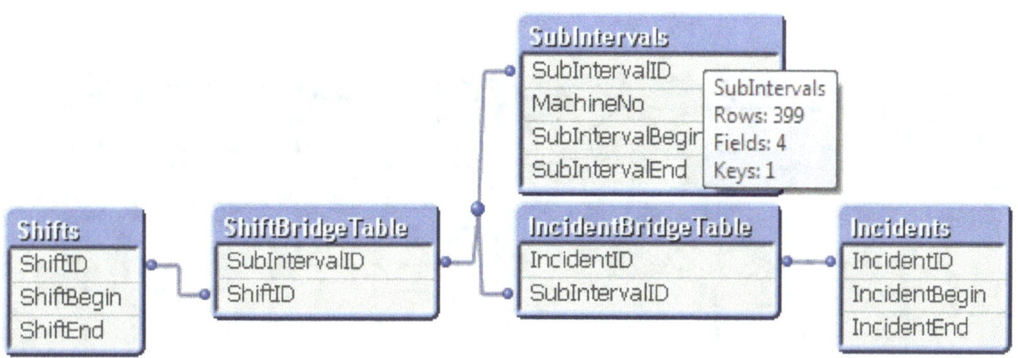

Then it might be better to make the partitioning properly and reduce the number of records in the sub-interval table.

Two-level slowly changing dimensions

A second case where you could use partitioning is when you have a slowly changing dimension in two levels. Example:

- The salesperson can change department. Which department he/she belongs to is described in the dynamic salesperson table, which contains the department ID and the intervals for when the department was relevant.

- The department can change unit. Which unit it belongs to is described in the dynamic department table, which contains the unit ID and the intervals for when the unit was relevant.

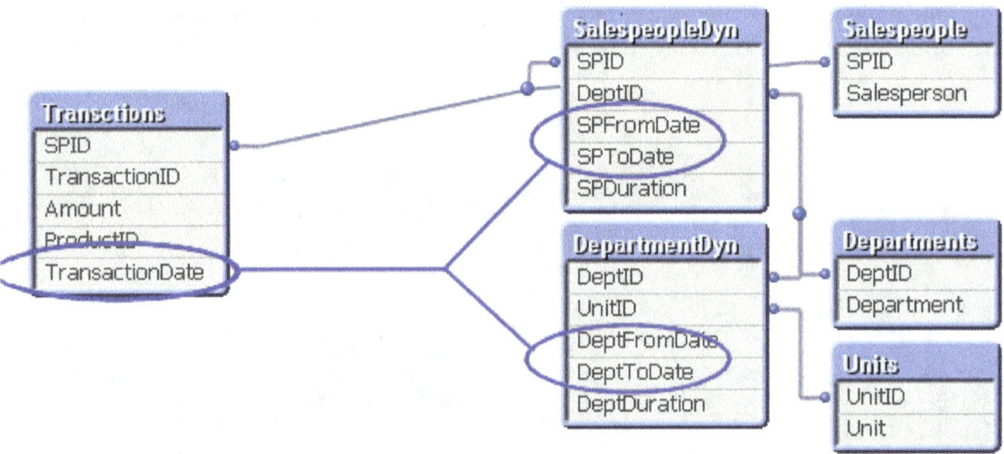

In such a situation, you will need the date from the transaction table to determine not only the relevant department, but also the relevant unit. Partitioning the intervals the way it is described previously could be one way to solve this problem. But since the salesperson ID is missing in one of the two interval tables, we have to use another algorithm for the partitioning: Joining, using an algorithm which is very similar to the method described previously in this chapter.

Intervals

By joining the two interval tables on department ID into a temporary table, and in a second step check where the two interval tables have overlaps, it is possible to create the relevant set of subintervals. The script for creating the subintervals will look similar to the following:

```
// ========================== Sales People dynamic data ============
// Load all fields. Create a new key from SPID and interval data.
// ================================================================
SalespeopleDyn:
Load *,
    SPID & '|' & SPFromDate & '|' & SPToDate     as SPIntervalID
    From SalespeopleDyn;


// ========================== Departments dynamic data ============
// Load all fields. Create a new key from DeptID + interval data.
// ================================================================
DepartmentDyn:
Load *, DeptID & '|' & DeptFromDate & '|' & DeptToDate
                                            as DeptIntervalID
    From DepartmentDyn;


// ========================== tmp SubIntervals ====================
// Join the two interval tables into a temporary table to generate
// all possible combinations of the intervals. DeptID is the key.
// ================================================================
tmpSubIntervals:
NoConcatenate
Load distinct
    DeptIntervalID, DeptID, UnitID, DeptFromDate, DeptToDate
    Resident DepartmentDyn;
Inner Join
Load distinct SPIntervalID, SPID, DeptID, SPFromDate, SPToDate
    Resident SalespeopleDyn;
```

```
// ============================ SubIntervals ============================
// Select only the combinations where the two intervals overlap.
// Calculate beginning and end for the overlapping sub-intervals.
// ======================================================================
SubIntervals:
Load *,
   SPID &'|'& SubFromDate &'|'& SubToDate    as SPSubIntervalID;
Load
   DeptIntervalID, SPIntervalID, SPID,
   Date(RangeMax(SPFromDate,DeptFromDate))  as SubFromDate,
   Date(RangeMin(SPToDate,DeptToDate))      as SubToDate
   Resident tmpSubIntervals
   Where SPFromDate <= DeptToDate and DeptFromDate <= SPToDate ;


// ======================= Clean up =============================
// Drop DeptID from the Sales people table, and drop the
// sub-intervals table
// ==============================================================
Drop Field DeptID   From SalespeopleDyn;
Drop Table tmpSubIntervals;
```

The **Where** clause in the **SubIntervals** table picks out the combinations where the two interval types have overlaps. The RangeMax() and RangeMin() functions determine the beginning and the end of the overlap.

Once the subintervals table has been created, it is straightforward to connect this new table to the transaction table using the method for slowly changing dimensions described previously:

```
// ======================= Transactions =========================
// Load the Transactions table as it is. Make sure it contains the
// necessary keys, here SPID and TransactionDate
// ==============================================================
Transactions:
Load * From Transactions;
```

```
// ======================= temp Bridge table ====================
// Create a Bridge table using IntervalMatch, using SPID as
// additional key.
// ==============================================================
tmpBridgeTable:
IntervalMatch (TransactionDate,SPID)
Load distinct SubFromDate, SubToDate, SPID Resident SubIntervals;


// ======================= Bridge table =========================
// Create the new key SPSubIntervalID from the temporary Bridge
// table, and join this onto the Transaction table.
// ==============================================================
Left Join (Transactions)
Load SPID, TransactionDate,
    SPID & '|' & SubFromDate & '|' & SubToDate   as SPSubIntervalID
    Resident tmpBridgeTable;


// ======================== Clean up ============================
// Drop SPID from the Transactions and SubIntervals table, and
// drop the temporary Bridge table
// ==============================================================
Drop Field SPID     From Transactions;
Drop Fiéld SPID     From SubIntervals;
Drop Table tmpBridgeTable;
```

You will then get a data model similar to the following:

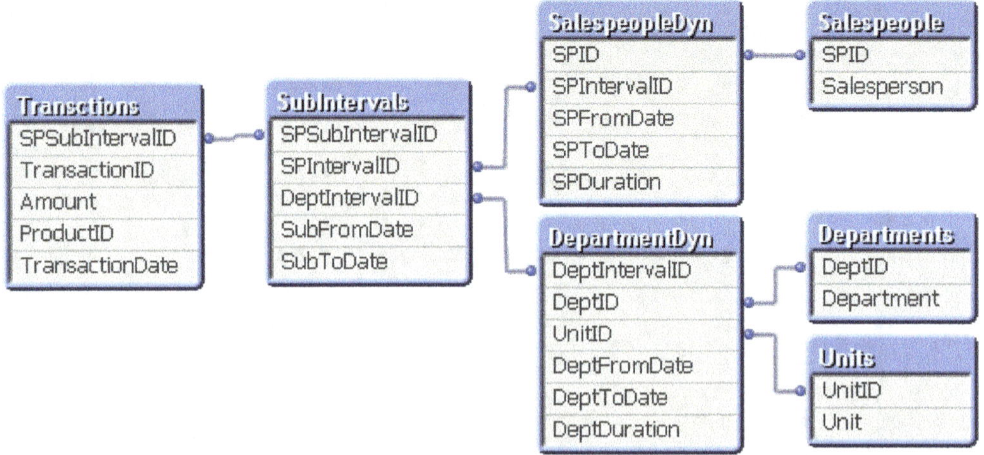

8

Generic Keys

Generic keys are a way to define keys between tables in a more general way, so that their values can represent other things than individual key values: They can be made to represent groups of key values or any key value. As an example, you can create a key that represents a specific product, or a product group, or *all* products.

You can use generic keys to solve many data modelling problems:

- **Authorization table with OR-logic between fields**
  If you have an authorization table you sometimes want to have a slightly more complex access restriction than a simple logical AND between fields. It could be e.g., that a user is allowed to see sales for all regions for a specific product and at the same time the European sales for all products. Generic keys can be used here.

- **Mixed dimensional granularity in a single fact table**
  Often you want to compare actual numbers with budget numbers. The standard method is to concatenate these two tables into one common fact table. However, this new fact table could have mixed granularity in many of the dimensions. Generic keys can be used here.

- **Multiple fact tables linked using a master link table**
  Sometimes you have fact tables that are so different that you don't want to concatenate them. To solve this problem, you can make a data model that has a central link table and uses generic keys.

Generic keys should not be confused with composite keys, which is a different concept. Composite keys are keys that contain information from several individual keys, e.g. by a simple concatenation of the two individual keys, whereas generic keys are keys, often from a single field, that contain symbolic key values that represent several or all individual key values.

An example: In many data models, there is a product table where each product has a unique product ID. If you create a generic key for such a dimension, the generic key could contain not only the individual product IDs, but also generic symbols for product categories and a symbol representing all products.

In most apps, generic keys are not necessary and should not be used. But there are cases where it can solve real problems and then you should not hesitate to use them.

Thank you, Phil B. for the idea and good discussions.

Basics

Extract from the Technical brief "Generic keys" published on Oct 02, 2012

In a normal app, a dimensional table is typically linked directly to a fact table, or to an authorization table, or to a link table, using the appropriate key. For a product dimension this would be the **ProductID**:

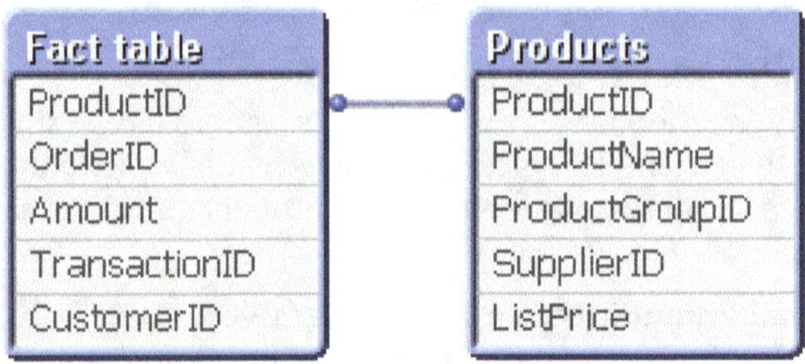

If the same product table would be linked to the fact table, but now using a generic key, the solution would instead look like this:

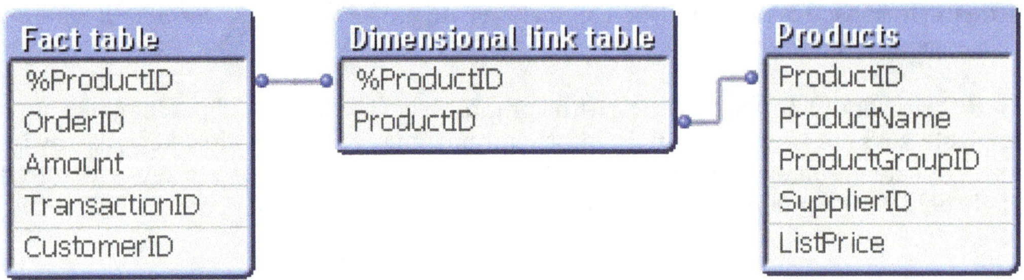

The dimensional link table allows all products to link to the proper records in the fact table, but also to records that use a generic symbol – the <ANY> symbol. The table could look like this:

Dimensional link table	
%ProductID	ProductID
2	2
1	1
<ANY>	1
<ANY>	2

So, basically the **Products** table is linked to the fact table using a bridge, a dimensional link table. The key between the link table and the unmodified dimensional table is the original dimensional key, **ProductID**. The key between the link table and the fact table is the generic key, **%ProductID**. The only difference between the generic product key and the original product key is that the symbol '<ANY>' has been introduced as a generic symbol; a key value that links to all products.

The dimensional link table is created by loading the product ID from the product table twice, using two Load statements:

```
[Dimensional link table]:
Load ProductID, ProductID as %ProductID From Products;
Load ProductID, '<ANY>'   as %ProductID From Products;
```

With this new data model, we can allow records in the fact table that use '<ANY>' as product id and link to all products. This is useful in some data modeling situations e.g. when you want to load budget and actual in the same fact table or if you have a complex security model involving access restrictions in a matrix of several dimensions.

This is a very simple example, but it shows quite well the basic principles: the dimensional link table as a bridge and the generic key that contains symbols for groups of field values. In real life, however, the model becomes more complex than this. But more about that later.

Groups in the dimension

Extract from the Technical brief "Generic keys" published on Oct 02, 2012

In most databases, some dimensional values are categorized into groups, e.g. products are categorized into product groups. Also these can be represented in a generic key. Hence, just as the generic key can contain a symbolic value such as '<ANY>', it can also contain generic symbols representing entire product groups, e.g. '<Group:1>', '<Group:2>', etc.

Data model

In a standard solution, you would link the product group table to the product table in a snowflake scheme. (It is called snowflake since this is what it looks like when you have linked all dimensions to the fact table this way; customers/countries, dates/periods, departments/business units, etc.).

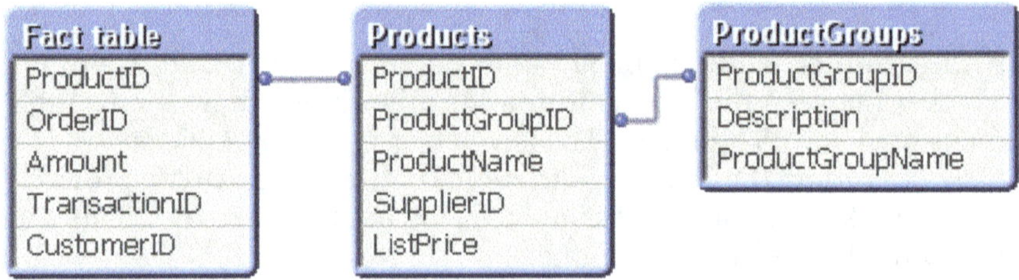

But if you use generic keys, it will not work to link product group information to the fact table indirectly via the product table: there may exist records in the fact table that pertain to a product group – and products groups are not found in the product table. So, the attributes in the product group table would not link to these records.

Instead, the product group table should link to the dimensional link table. Only this way can you ensure that selections are propagated correctly through the data model.

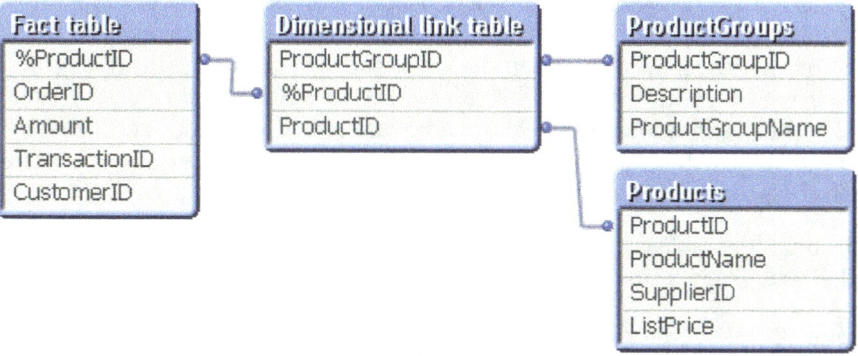

Dimensional link table

The dimensional link table would in this situation have three groups of records – one where the original product IDs link to product IDs; a second where the product groups link to the correct product IDs; and a third where the <ANY> symbol links to all product IDs.

The dimensional link table would have three columns: the generic product key, the original product key and the product group key. It could then look like this:

Dimensional link table		
%ProductID	ProductGroupID	ProductID
<Product:1>	1	1
<Product:2>	1	2
<Product:3>	2	3
<Product:4>	2	4
<Productgroup:1>	1	1
<Productgroup:1>	1	2
<Productgroup:2>	2	3
<Productgroup:2>	2	4
<ANY>	1	1
<ANY>	1	2
<ANY>	2	3
<ANY>	2	4

Note that all products link to themselves, and – in addition – the <ANY> symbol and the product groups link to the relevant products.

Here the generic key has been created by a concatenation of the field label and the field value. But the generic symbols do not have to look exactly like these. However, they do have to include not only the field value – e.g. the ID of the product or the product group – but also the information about which field it refers to. This way, a product group record cannot by mistake get the same value as another record that refers to a product. In other words, the product group ID which is a number cannot be stored as a number only since it then would collide with the product IDs which also are numbers.

The dimensional link table is created using three consecutive Load or SELECT statements, one for the individual products, one for the product groups, and one for the <ANY> symbol:

```
[Dimensional link table]:
Load ProductID, ProductGroupID,
    '<Product:' & ProductID & '>'              as %ProductID
    From Products;
Load ProductID, ProductGroupID,
    '<Productgroup:' & ProductGroupID & '>' as %ProductID
    From Products;
Load ProductID, ProductGroupID,
    '<ANY>'                                    as %ProductID
    From Products;
```

An alternative approach to achieve the same goal is to concatenate the product group ID with the product ID using a known delimiter, e.g:

Dimensional link table		
%ProductID	ProductGroupID	ProductID
1|1	1	1
1|2	1	2
2|3	2	3
2|4	2	4
1|<ANY>	1	1
1|<ANY>	1	2
2|<ANY>	2	3
2|<ANY>	2	4
<ANY>|<ANY>	1	1
<ANY>|<ANY>	1	2
<ANY>|<ANY>	2	3
<ANY>|<ANY>	2	4

Here, the product group ID and product ID are concatenated using the piping character, and the <ANY> symbol is used to denote multiple values.

Whether to choose this or the one above is just a matter of taste. Both work.

Inclusive and exclusive generic symbols

A generic symbol can be inclusive or exclusive. "Inclusive" means that the symbol includes all IDs within the group, e.g. <Productgroup:1> does indeed link to all the products within this product group. Hence, the example above uses inclusive generic symbols.

In contrast, an exclusive generic symbol would not link to the individual IDs within the group, but it would only link to the group itself. In principle, the <ANY> symbol has been replaced by a <N/A> symbol (Not Applicable). Instead of an <N/A> symbol, you can also use Null().

Another way to express it is to say that an inclusive generic symbol links to *all* relevant elements in the group, whereas an exclusive generic symbol links to *no* elements. It links to the group only. This means that all products link to themselves, and in addition, the product groups link to the respective product groups but not to the individual products.

Dimensional link table		
%ProductID	ProductGroupID	ProductID
1|1	1	1
1|2	1	2
2|3	2	3
2|4	2	4
1|<N/A>	1	-
2|<N/A>	2	-
<N/A>|<N/A>	-	-

Whether to use inclusive or exclusive generic symbols is up to you. In some situations, it is better to use inclusive generic symbols; in other situations, it is better to use the exclusive generic symbols.

For example, if you have an authorization table where a specific user is allowed to see a specific region in combination with any product, you obviously want the <ANY> symbol to link to all individual products. Otherwise, the reduction would exclude the relevant records. Hence, you should use inclusive generic symbols.

However, if you have a comparison between actual numbers and budget numbers and you have a mixed granularity, e.g. the actual numbers are per product, but the budget is per product group, then the budget is unspecified (N/A) for the individual products. In such a situation, you probably want the budget numbers to disappear when the user selects a specific product but have them visible when no such selection is made. The budget number would otherwise be misleading. In such a case, you should use exclusive generic symbols.

Just as before, the dimensional link table is created using several consecutive Load or SELECT statements, one for the individual products, one for the product groups, and one for the top <N/A> symbol. The third load statement is really not necessary, since it does not link any generic symbols to real values. But here I use it just to show the analogy with the inclusive generic symbols.

```
[Dimensional link table]:
Load
    ProductGroupID & '|' & ProductID  as %ProductID,
    ProductGroupID                    as ProductGroupID,
    ProductID                         as ProductID
    From Products;
Load distinct
    ProductGroupID & '|' & '<N/A>'    as %ProductID,
    ProductGroupID                    as ProductGroupID,
    Null()                            as ProductID
    From Products;
Load distinct
    '<N/A>' & '|' & '<N/A>'           as %ProductID,
    Null()                            as ProductGroupID,
    Null()                            as ProductID
    From Products;
```

Composite generic keys

Extract from the Technical brief "Generic keys" published on Oct 02, 2012

In some cases, you want IDs from several dimensions in the same generic key. As always when you create composite keys, it is just a matter of concatenating the different keys with a proper delimiter. The table below is an example of a master link table, where the individual keys are concatenated into a master generic key.

Link table		
%MasterKey	ProductID	CustomerID
<ANY>|<ANY>	1	BERGS
<ANY>|<ANY>	1	BLONP
<ANY>|<ANY>	2	BERGS
<ANY>|BERGS	1	BERGS
<ANY>|BERGS	2	BERGS
<ANY>|BLONP	1	BLONP
1|<ANY>	1	BERGS
1|<ANY>	1	BLONP
1|BERGS	1	BERGS
1|BLONP	1	BLONP
2|<ANY>	2	BERGS
2|BERGS	2	BERGS

Just as before, the link table is created using several consecutive Load or SELECT statements, one for each combination of the different cases:

```
[Link table]:
Load ProductID, CustomerID,
    ProductID & '|' & CustomerID          as %MasterKey
    From FactTable;
Load ProductID, CustomerID,
    ProductID & '|' & '<ANY>'             as %MasterKey
    From FactTable;
Load ProductID, CustomerID,
    '<ANY>' & '|' & CustomerID            as %MasterKey
    From FactTable;
Load ProductID, CustomerID,
    '<ANY>' & '|' & '<ANY>'               as %MasterKey
    From FactTable;
```

One minor complication when creating composite keys is that you can no longer create the keys by loading records from the dimensional tables: There is rarely one single dimensional table that contains keys from several dimensions. Instead, you must create the link table loading from the fact table(s).

This sometimes leads to the next complication: You may not have all the necessary keys in your fact table. For example, you probably do not have the key for product group. Should you need a key that does not exist there, then the best way to get that information is to use the Applymap() function. With this, you can make a lookup and get the information you need.

Authorization bridge table

Extract from the Technical brief "Generic keys" published on Oct 02, 2012

Generic keys are useful for *Authorization*, i.e. access restriction where a user is allowed to see some, but not all data. Here we assume that the process of authentication (user identification) has been made, so that the Qlik engine "knows" which user it is that holds the session. The step of authorization is then a matter of determining which data the user is allowed to see.

The Qlik engine can reduce the data so that the user can only see that which has been approved for that specific user. Such a reduction can be made either using Section Access within the Qlik load script or using a distribution within the QlikView Publisher. In both cases, you need one or several reducing fields that are connected to the user IDs. I.e., you need an authorization table listing field values approved for each user. QlikView or QlikView Publisher will then make the selection as defined by the listed field values and purge all excluded data from the session or from the file.

If you want to make a reduction in a single field, you do not need generic keys.

Also, if you want to limit data to the *intersection* of filters set in two or more fields, e.g. a user is allowed to see records that pertain to product X and customer A – *but nothing else* – then you can just link the two reducing fields to your data model. You do not need generic keys.

However, if you want to limit data to the *union* of multiple filters set in two or more fields, e.g. product X OR customer A, then you will need generic keys. Such an authorization table could look like the following one.

The user "DAVID" is allowed to see all products, but just for customer 5 and 7. In addition, he is also allowed to see all customers, but just for product 6 or 7.

ACCESS	NTNAME	PRODUCT_ID	CUSTOMER_ID
ADMIN	ADMIN	ANY	ANY
USER	ALAN	ANY	1;2;3
USER	BETTY	2;3;4	ANY
USER	CHRISTA	3;4	5;6
USER	DAVID	ANY	5;7
USER	DAVID	6;7	ANY

In other words: David is allowed to see the union of rows 5 and 6.

This authorization table already contains symbols for groups of products or groups of customers. To load this into the Qlik engine, you will need to interpret the generic keys in an authorization bridge table. The authorization bridge table (second table from the right in the data model below) will link your authorization table with your transaction table using **AuthID** and **%AuthID**, which both are composite keys with information on both product ID and customer ID. In addition, **%AuthID** is a generic key.

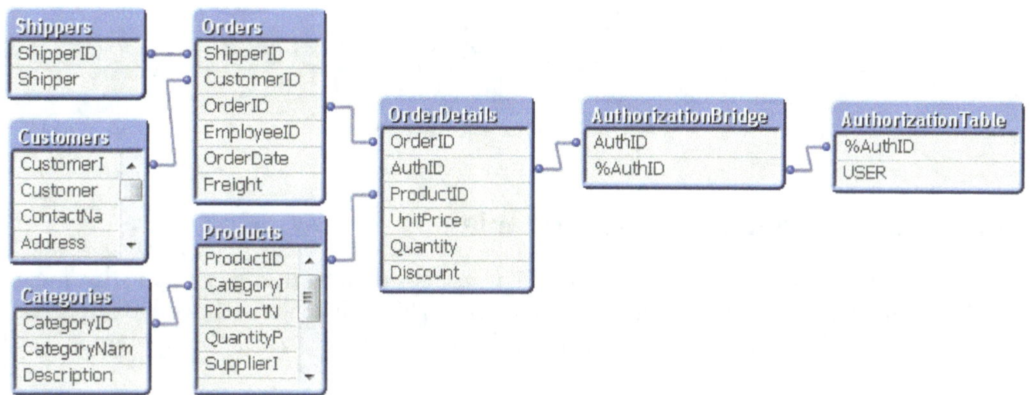

Authorization table in the Qlik data model

The first step is to load the authorization table (rightmost table in the data model above). To do this, I expand the individual rows into their components, using the subfield function. The subfield function will make the Load statement loop over the individual records so that each subfield ends up in its own record. But I do not want to map the <ANY> symbols to individual products and individual customers yet. Instead, I will load this as a generic key.

Further, I will in this example use a copy of the user ID (NTNAME) as reducing field. Hence:

```
AuthorizationTable:
Load
   Upper(NTNAME)                                    as USER,
   Subfield(PRODUCT_ID, ';') & '|' & Subfield(CUSTOMER_ID, ';')
                                        as %AUTH_ID
   From AuthorizationTable ;
```

The expanded authorization table will look like the following:

Authorization table	
USER	**%AuthID**
ADMIN	\<ANY\>|\<ANY\>
ALAN	\<ANY\>|1
ALAN	\<ANY\>|2
ALAN	\<ANY\>|3
BETTY	2|\<ANY\>
BETTY	3|\<ANY\>
BETTY	4|\<ANY\>
CHRISTA	3|5
CHRISTA	3|6
CHRISTA	4|5
CHRISTA	4|6
DAVID	\<ANY\>|5
DAVID	\<ANY\>|7
DAVID	6|\<ANY\>
DAVID	7|\<ANY\>

Authorization ID in the transaction table

I also need to define the authorization ID in the transaction table. In my example, this means the order details table. However, there is no customer ID in this table, so I need to fetch this from the order header table. But rather than joining the two tables, I use the Applymap() function.

```
OrderID_2_CustID:
Mapping Load OrderID, CustomerID                 From Orders;

OrderDetails:
Load *,
   ProductID &'|'& Applymap('OrderID_2_CustID', OrderID, 'NONE')
                                        as AuthID
   From OrderDetails ;
```

Authorization bridge table

The next step is to create the authorization bridge table, which is the table that will link the generic symbols to their real values. It could look like this:

AuthID	%AuthID
1|1	<ANY>|1
2|3	<ANY>|3
4|24	4|<ANY>
11|2	<ANY>|2
11|3	<ANY>|3

This is a table that potentially can become very large: If I would generate all combinations of product ID and customer ID, with the possibility of generic keys, I would face a very large number of records. So, instead of generating all possible combinations, I load only the combinations that exist in the transaction table and at the same time in the authorization table. But to do this I need four Load statements, each with a preceding load. Hence:

```
AuthorizationBridge:
Load distinct * Where Exists(%AuthID);
Load AuthID,
    AuthID                                          as %AuthID
    Resident OrderDetails ;

Load distinct * Where Exists(%AuthID);
Load AuthID,
    '<ANY>' &'|'& Applymap('OrderID_2_CustID', OrderID, 'NONE')
                                          as %AuthID
    Resident OrderDetails;

Load distinct * Where Exists(%AuthID);
Load AuthID,
    ProductID & '|' & '<ANY>'             as %AuthID
    Resident OrderDetails;
```

```
Load distinct * Where Exists(%AuthID);
Load AuthID,
    '<ANY>' & '|' & '<ANY>'                  as %AuthID
    Resident OrderDetails;
```

In other words: I load from the order details, so I only get the combinations that really exist in the transactional data. In addition, I pipe the result into a preceding load to filter it further; I only save the records where the corresponding generic key exists in the authorization table.

Finally, I need to create the Section Access table with the usernames. The reduction will then be made in the USER field.

```
Section Access;
Load ACCESS, NTNAME,
    Upper(NTNAME)                            as USER
    From AuthorizationTable;


Section Application;
```

An alternative to the section access table is to distribute the app using the QlikView Publisher. All you need to do then is to reduce and distribute on the field USER.

And with this the problem is solved.

See also the article "Basics for complex authorization" under "Security and Section Access".

Fact table with mixed granularity

Originally posted in the Qlik Design Blog on Oct 26, 2012

A common situation when modeling the data for a Qlik application is that you have several fact tables, and the fact tables have different grain. An example is budget vs. actual numbers, where the budget typically is made on a higher level than the actual numbers, e.g. the budget has regions instead of specific customers and months or quarters instead of specific dates.

It could also be that you want to have different grains in a mixture, e.g. you want full details for the numbers for the current year, but – due to the amounts of data – you want to compare these to aggregated numbers from previous years.

In a Qlik data model, it is possible and not very difficult to use a fact table with mixed granularity. Say for instance that you have a detailed fact table with the numbers for current year:

CustomerID	ProductID	OrderDate	Amount
32	12	2012-04-18	28890
32	2	2012-05-11	16160
32	7	2012-05-21	75024
89	18	2012-05-25	47660
32	1	2012-06-02	17552
32	19	2012-07-09	2018
32	1	2012-07-30	86000

Detailed fact table. One row per transaction.

Country	CategoryID	OrderMonth	Amount
USA	1	2009-05	6696
USA	5	2009-05	6910
USA	7	2009-05	57450
USA	2	2009-10	208530
USA	5	2009-11	70956
USA	6	2009-11	235560
USA	2	2009-12	274280

Aggregated fact table. Fewer records.

In addition, you have an aggregated fact table for previous years: Instead of **CustomerID**, **ProductID** and **OrderDate**, you have **Country**, **CategoryID** and **OrderMonth** as foreign keys.

The solution is to concatenate these two tables into one common fact table and use generic keys for the three dimensions.

%CustomerID	%ProductID	%OrderDate	Amount
USA|	8|	Month:40817	114516
USA|	8|	Month:40848	14448
USA|	8|	Month:40878	3858
USA|32	1|1	Date:41062	17552
USA|32	1|1	Date:41120	86000
USA|32	1|2	Date:41040	16160
USA|32	1|11	Date:41120	29950

Concatenated fact table.

The generic keys contain information about both the higher and lower levels of the dimensional hierarchy and can be used for either the higher level only or for both levels. This way, the detailed records of the fact table link to customer, product, and date, while the records with aggregated numbers link to country, but not to customer; to product category but not to individual products; and to order month but not to individual dates.

It can sometimes be tricky to create the generic keys because the detailed fact table lacks direct information about the higher levels in the dimensional hierarchies, e.g. country and product category. But this can be solved using the function Applymap().

If you define mapping tables that translate **CustomerID** to **Country**, and **ProductID** to **CategoryID**, you can define the generic keys in the detailed part of the fact table as:

```
Applymap('MapCustomerToCountry', CustomerID)
         & '|' & CustomerID                          as %CustomerID,
Applymap('MapProductToCategory', ProductID)
         & '|' & ProductID                           as %ProductID,
'Date:'     & '|' & Num(OrderDate)                   as %OrderDate,
```

And in the aggregated part of the fact table, the corresponding definitions could be:

```
Country     & '|' & Null()                           as %CustomerID,
CategoryID  & '|' & Null()                           as %ProductID,
'Month:'    & '|' & Num(MonthStart(OrderMonth)) as %OrderDate
```

The generic keys must be mapped to the real keys using several dimensional link tables, but once this is done the application will work like a normal Qlik app.

%CustomerID	Country	CustomerID
France|	France	-
France|7	France	7
France|26	France	26
USA|	USA	-
USA|32	USA	32
USA|89	USA	89

Dimensional link table.

This method can be used in a number of cases where you want to define keys that link to several values simultaneously, the most common one being comparison of actual numbers with budget.

Actual vs Budget

Extract from the Technical brief "Generic keys" published on Oct 02, 2012

One special case of mixed granularity is when you want to compare actual numbers with budget or forecast numbers. The best way to do this is in my opinion to concatenate the two fact tables into a common fact table.

When doing so you need to solve the problem of different granularity: The actual numbers have a finer grain. The grain could e.g. be customer, salesman, product, date and shipper.

Actual numbers						
OrderID	**CustomerID**	**SalesRepID**	**ProductID**	**OrderDate**	**ShipperID**	**Amount**
10248	4	2	11	2004-06-29	2	34.344 $
10253	34	3	31	2004-07-05	2	16.560 $
10254	19	2	24	2003-01-06	2	6.780 $
10258	17	7	2	2004-07-12	2	100.100 $
10258	17	7	5	2004-07-12	2	39.845 $

The corresponding snowflake data model would have dimensional tables for these five foreign keys:

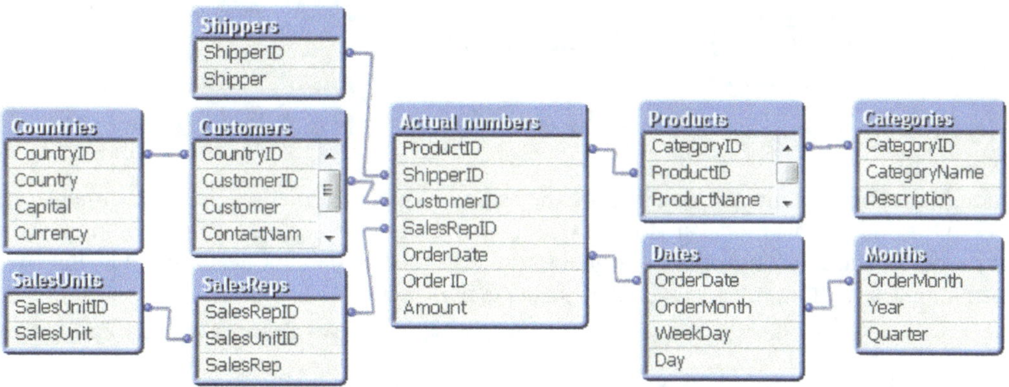

In addition, it would have secondary dimensions, such as product categories, countries, sales units, etc.

The budget numbers would however not have the same foreign keys: It would have a different grain. The grain could e.g. be customer countries, sales units, product groups and months. Note that the shippers' dimension is missing, as well as the detailed level of the four existing dimensions.

Budget numbers				
CountryID	**SalesUnitID**	**CategoryID**	**Month**	**Amount**
France	2	1	2012-01	2.523.000 $
France	3	1	2012-01	3.928.000 $
Brazil	6	1	2012-01	3.615.000 $
Germany	6	1	2012-01	455.000 $
Ireland	6	1	2012-01	4.567.000 $

The corresponding snowflake data model would have dimensional tables for the four foreign keys:

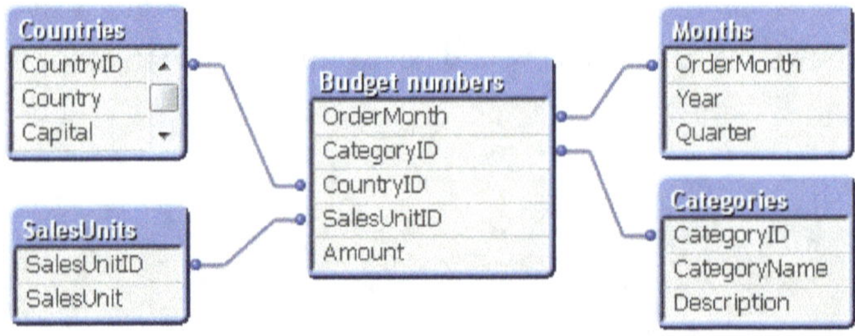

Although the two data models are different, they share a lot of information. The four dimensional tables in the budget data model are identical to the corresponding secondary dimensions in the data model for the actual numbers. The goal is to merge the two data models without losing any information, something which can be done using generic keys.

Loading the actual numbers

First, I load the actual numbers. However, instead of the normal keys for the four common dimensions, I use generic keys. But these cannot be created without knowledge about the dimensional groups, e.g. which product group a specific product belongs to.

This is information that can be fetched from the dimensional tables using the Applymap() function. Hence:

```
CustomerID_to_CountryID:
Mapping Load    CustomerID, CountryID              From Customers;
SalesRepID_to_SalesUnitID:
Mapping Load    SalesRepID, SalesUnitID            From SalesReps;
ProductID_to_CategoryID:
Mapping Load    ProductID,  CategoryID             From Products;


Facts:
Load
   Amount, OrderID, ShipperID,
   Applymap('CustomerID_to_CountryID', CustomerID,  Null())
            & '|' &      CustomerID           as %CustomerID,
   Applymap('SalesRepID_to_SalesUnitID',SalesRepID, Null())
            & '|' &      SalesRepID           as %SalesRepID,
   Applymap('ProductID_to_CategoryID', ProductID,   Null())
            & '|' &      ProductID            as %ProductID,
   Num(MonthStart(OrderDate))
            & '|' & Num(Floor(OrderDate))     as %OrderDate,
   'Actual'                                   as Type
   From ActualNumbers ;
```

In other words: The **CountryID** is fetched from the customer table; the **SalesUnitID** is fetched from the salesman table; and the **CategoryID** is fetched from the product table. All three are stored in the corresponding generic keys. For the fourth generic key, I use the date serial number as integers; first for the month, then for the date.

Loading the budget numbers

Next step is to append the budget numbers onto this table using the concatenate prefix. Also here I use generic keys, but this time I use the <N/A> symbol for the detailed level:

```
Concatenate (Facts) Load
    Amount,
    CountryID    & '|' &        '<N/A>'              as %CustomerID,
    SalesUnitID  & '|' &        '<N/A>'              as %SalesRepID,
    CategoryID   & '|' &        '<N/A>'              as %ProductID,
    Num(MakeDate(Year, Month))
                 & '|' &        '<N/A>'              as %OrderDate,
    'Budget'                                         as Type
    From Budget ;
```

The fields **OrderID** and **ShipperID** are missing so they will get NULL values in the budget part of the fact table, which is OK since these fields are irrelevant for the budget numbers. The field **Type** finally, is a created field with just two values: 'Actual' and 'Budget'. It can be used as dimension in charts and as flag in expressions.

Dimensions and dimensional link tables

Further, I create the dimensional link tables, just as described above in the section "Groups in the dimensions". The group symbols should be exclusive, since I do not want the individual dimensional values to link to budget numbers.

```
[%Products]:
Load
    CategoryID   & '|' &        ProductID            as %ProductID,
    CategoryID,
    ProductID
    From Products;
Load distinct
    CategoryID   & '|' &        '<N/A>'              as %ProductID,
    CategoryID,
    Null()                                           as ProductID
    From Products;
```

The other dimensional link tables are created in a similar way.

Finally, when loading the dimensions like the product table, these must not contain the key to the dimensional group like the product group. The obtained data model now looks like in the data model below. All information is there and all links work correctly.

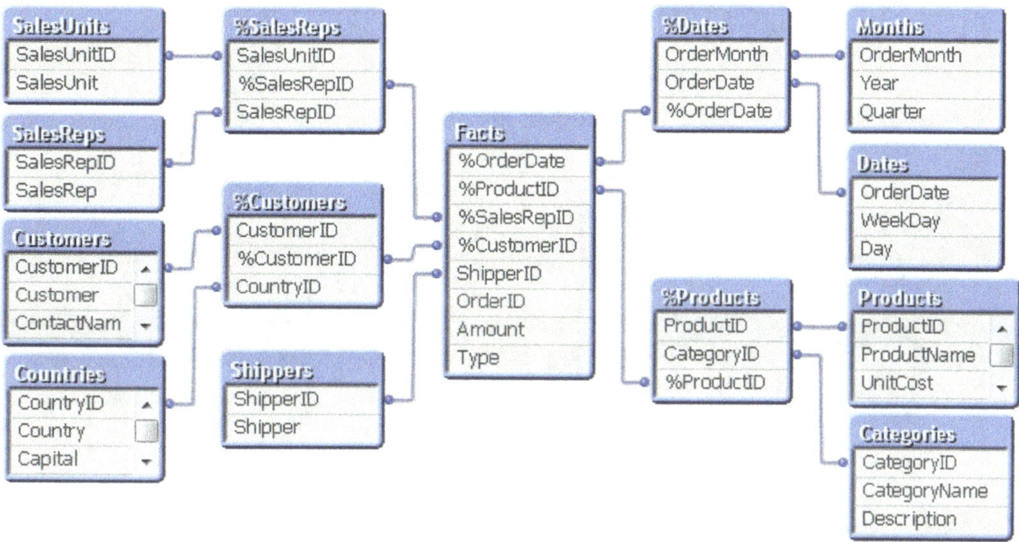

Link table and multiple fact tables

Extract from the Technical brief "Generic keys" published on Oct 02, 2012

In some cases, the fact tables are so different that you do not want to concatenate them. Then you can create a solution using generic keys in combination with a master link table.

My example comes from the pharmaceutical industry where the situation often is that you want to compare sales numbers from pharmacies with the sales calls that your sales representatives have made to physicians. The problem is similar to the previous example, however much more complex.

The sales numbers are per product package, i.e. a sub-group in the product dimension. Geographically the sales numbers are reported per physician, per pharmacy or per territory (depending on country), which only indirectly is connected to the sales representtative.

The sales calls are found in two tables: **Visits** and **VisitDetails**. These describe how a sales representative visits a physician and shows products. Several products can be shown in a sales call.

Finally, the sales representatives have targets on how many calls they should make and how many products they should show. These are stored in the Targets table.

If the tables were loaded as they are, we would get the following data model. Dimensions to the left; fact tables to the right.

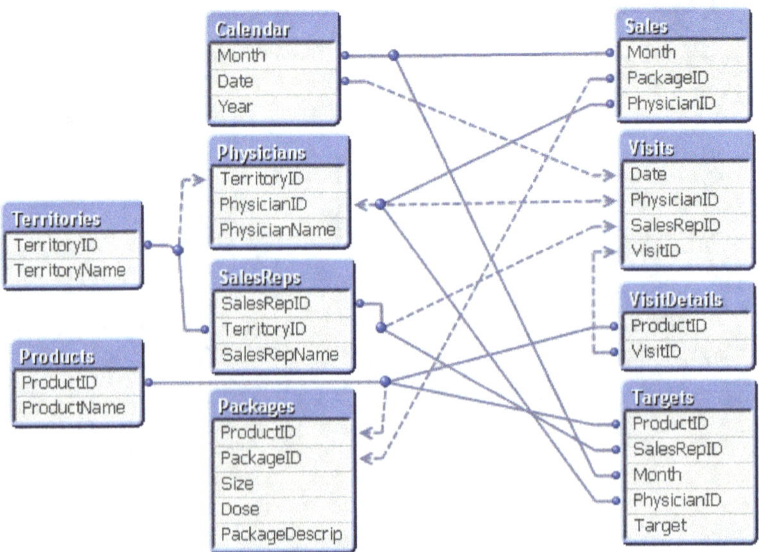

Obviously, this is not a good data model. There are circular references and too many keys.

An additional complication is the forked territorial dimension: Both physicians and sales representatives belong to territories, but there is no direct connection between a specific sales representative and a specific physician.

The details of the challenge differ from country to country and from company to company, but the example still describes the general problem well.

Loading these tables into a Qlik app as they are will not work. There are far too many links that create circular dependencies. Instead, the data must be remodeled into a snowflake scheme. For this, generic keys in combination with a master link table can be a great help.

There are four table types in this solution: Dimensions, Dimensional link tables, Fact tables and the Master link table. For each type there are some things to be aware of:

Dimensions

First there are the dimensional tables. These should be loaded in a standard way, however without the keys to the groups. For instance, the product table should not contain a key to product groups. The dimensional groups should still be loaded as individual dimensional tables. In this case it means that products, months, and territories should be loaded as separate tables.

All fields that the user will use to make selections should exist in the dimensional tables.

Dimensional link tables

Then there are the dimensional link tables. These should be loaded as described above in the section "Groups in the dimension", i.e. with several consecutive Load statements so that also the <ANY> symbol links to all individual dimensional elements.

The question is which generic keys you should have. In my example I choose to have territories as a separate independent dimension, but I combine date and month into one generic key and package and product into another. All in all, I get five generic keys: **%TerritoryID, %ProductID, %SalesRepID, %PhysicianID** and **%Date**.

Fact tables

The third group of tables is the fact tables. These should be loaded in such a way that they only contain a master key and numbers that should be used in aggregations. They may not contain any fields used for selections. The master key should contain information from all keys used as generic keys. If the key is not relevant for the specific table, this part of the master key should have the <ANY> symbol. The master key should be defined in the same way in all fact tables.

In this case it means that the master key should consist of the information that constitutes the five generic keys:

%TerritoryID + %ProductID + %SalesRepID + %PhysicianID + %Date

But this is just half the truth: **%Product** and **%Date** have groups within the generic key, so in practice the master key will be a concatenation of seven keys:

TerritoryID + ProductID + PackageID + SalesRepID + PhysicianID + Month + Date

Some of the keys are not directly available and need to be fetched from other tables using Applymap().

The data model we are trying to achieve is the following:

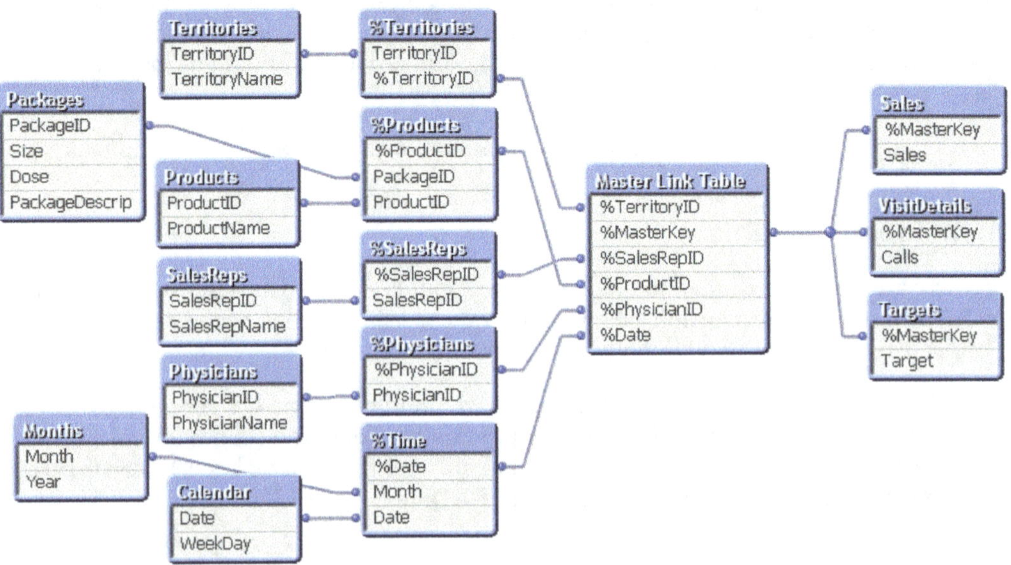

The structure is a snowflake, but with the link table in the center instead of the fact table. Tables are loaded using generic keys and dimensional link tables are used. All dimensions are to the left and all fact tables to the far right.

First, I look at the sales table: It has keys for month, package, and physician. The territory and the product can be deduced from these keys using Applymap(). However, the sales representative and date are not applicable, so these should be replaced with the <ANY> symbol. Hence, the corresponding Load statement will be:

```
Sales:
Load
   Sales                                      as Sales,
   Applymap('Physician_to_Territory',PhysicianID, Null())
                                     &'|'&    // TerritoryID
   Applymap('Package_to_Product',    PackageID,   Null())
                                     &'|'&    // ProductID
   PackageID                         &'|'&    // PackageID
   '<ANY>'                           &'|'&    // SalesrepID
   PhysicianID                       &'|'&    // PhysicianID
   Num(Month)                        &'|'&    // Month
   '<ANY>'                                    // Date
                                              as %MasterKey

   From Sales ;
```

Visits and **VisitDetails** are joined, and this new table has date, physician, sales representative and product as keys. Hence, the corresponding Load statement will be:

```
Visits:
Load
   1                                          as Calls,
   Applymap('Physician_to_Territory',PhysicianID, Null())
                                     &'|'&    // TerritoryID
   ProductID                         &'|'&    // ProductID
   '<ANY>'                           &'|'&    // PackageID
   SalesRepID                        &'|'&    // SalesrepID
   PhysicianID                       &'|'&    // PhysicianID
   Num(MonthStart(Date))             &'|'&    // Month
   Num(Floor(Date))                          // Date
                                              as %MasterKey

   From Visits ;
```

The third fact table is the table with the target numbers. This table has month, physician, sales representative and product as keys. Hence, the corresponding Load statement will be:

```
Targets:
Load
    Target                                     as Target,
    Applymap('Physician_to_Territory',PhysicianID, Null())
                                        &'|'&   // TerritoryID
    ProductID                           &'|'&   // ProductID
    '<ANY>'                             &'|'&   // PackageID
    SalesRepID                          &'|'&   // SalesrepID
    PhysicianID                         &'|'&   // PhysicianID
    Num(Month)                          &'|'&   // Month
    '<ANY>'                                     // Date
                                        as %MasterKey

    From Targets ;
```

Master link table

Finally, there is the master link table. It should contain only the keys that link it to the dimensional link tables and the master key that links it to the fact tables. No other fields should be loaded in this table.

Potentially this table can become very large, so it is important that is loaded in a way so that the number of records is minimized. Therefore, I load only the master keys that exist in the fact tables. But as a consequence, three consecutive Load statements are needed to create the link table, one for each fact table.

Further, the link table should be loaded with the distinct clause.

The Load statement loading the records from the sales table hence becomes:

```
[Master Link Table]:
Load distinct
    // ------------------------------------------- dimensional keys
    Applymap('Physician_to_Territory',PhysicianID, Null())
                                        as %TerritoryID,
    Applymap('Package_to_Product',   PackageID,  Null())
                     &'|'&   PackageID   as %ProductID,
    '<ANY>'                              as %SalesRepID,
    PhysicianID                          as %PhysicianID,
    Num(Month)               &'|'&   '<ANY>'   as %Date,
    // ------------------------------------------- master key
    Applymap('Physician_to_Territory',PhysicianID, Null())
                            &'|'&   // TerritoryID
    Applymap('Package_to_Product',    PackageID,  Null())
                            &'|'&   // ProductID
    PackageID               &'|'&   // PackageID
    '<ANY>'                 &'|'&   // SalesrepID
    PhysicianID             &'|'&   // PhysicianID
    Num(Month)              &'|'&   // Month
    '<ANY>'                         // Date
                                    as %MasterKey

    From Sales ;
```

There are three things to note here:

1. The definition of the master key is identical to the definition used when loading the sales fact table.

2. The Load statement has two parts; one where the dimensional generic keys are defined and one where the master key is defined.

3. The definitions of the dimensional generic keys (first part of the load) are identical to the sub-parts of master key (second part of the load).

Similar load statements must also be created for the other two fact tables. Once this is done, you will get a correct link table data model with generic keys.

Some practical tips

Hide the generic keys

If you name all your generic keys with e.g. a percent sign as the first character, and then set this character as the "HidePrefix", the generic keys will be hidden for the users.

```
Set HidePrefix = % ;
```

Use variables for the generic symbols

To ensure that you only store the actual text representing the <ANY> symbol in one place, you could store it in a variable that you can access in your load statements. You can do the same with the <N/A> symbol:

```
Set ANY = "'<ANY>'" ;
Set NA  = "'<N/A>'" ;
```

The load statement then becomes more compact, for example:

```
Load
    ProductID &'|'& $(ANY)                 as %MasterKey,
    ProductID,
    CustomerID
    From …;
```

Use Autonumber()

The generic keys may become long since they are concatenated strings. One way to make them shorter and less memory consuming is to use Autonumber(), a function which assigns an integer instead of the long string. No information is lost.

```
Load
   Autonumber( ProductID &'|'& $(ANY) ) as %MasterKey,
   ProductID,
   CustomerID
   From …;
```

Use Applymap()

If you do not have a key that you need, you can use Applymap() as a lookup function. The below load statement uses the order ID as key to make a lookup for the correct customer ID.

```
OrderID_To_CustomerID:
Mapping Load OrderID, CustomerID From Orders ;

OrderDetails:
Load *,
   ProductID &'|'&
   ApplyMap('OrderID_To_CustomerID',OrderID,'NONE') as AuthID
   From OrderDetails ;
```

9

Generating Missing Data

Extract from the Technical brief "Generating Missing Data" published on Feb 4, 2013

When you create a Qlik data model, you often need to *create* data in the script. It could e.g. be that

- An entire table is missing but it can be inferred from other data.

- Some records are missing, but that common sense tells you that they should be there. Then you probably want to generate them, so the corresponding values become clickable in the Qlik app. One situation is that you want to create several records from one single existing record.

- The records exist, but a field value is missing or incorrect, so you want to propagate the value from the record immediately above.

In all these cases, you need to generate data in the Qlik script. This chapter is about different methods to do this. Some cases from real life:

Conversion rates

The source data is a table that lists currency conversion rates. However, this table only contains dates where the conversion rate changed, not the dates between the changes. Then you need to generate the dates between the changes as individual records and use the value from the previous date.

Warehouse balance

Just as in the example above, only the changes are stored in the source data, and you need to generate the records that correspond to the days between the changes and in these new records use the balance of the last change. But in this example, you need to do this for each product in the warehouse, so that you have a balance for each combination of product and date.

Contracts with a limited validity in time

The source data has a table which is a list of contracts; one contract per record. Each record contains a "Begin" date and an "End" date that defines the validity time of the contract. The user will want to ask questions like "How many valid contracts do I have a given day?" To answer this, you need to generate all dates between the beginning and the end of the validity interval – you need to loop over the existing record – so that it is possible to click on the date in order to make this selection.

Master calendar table

The most common case is however the Master Calendar: In almost all Qlik applications there is a date and from this date you can infer year, month, weekday, etc. This is best done as a separate table with date as a key linking to the original data. This table needs to be generated in the Qlik script and in it you can have many columns for the different calendar entities.

Date	Rate
2013-01-01	1.01
2013-01-04	1.08
2013-01-08	1.07

Basic table generation

Extract from the Technical brief "Generating Missing Data" published on Feb 4, 2013

Generate a table using Resident Load

One common way to generate a new table is to load one or several fields from an already loaded table – typically the transaction table – using a distinct or group by clause.

One drawback with this method is that the already loaded table might not have all the values of the field in question. If you want all values, you should generate the table using autogenerate instead.

Example: Master Calendar using Load Resident

The master calendar is a table that often does not exist in the source database, but is needed to hold all fields that can be inferred from date: Month, week no, weekday, etc. It can be created in many different ways. The simplest way is to use a Load resident with a distinct clause that picks out all distinct values of a date that exists in a transaction table:

```
MasterCalendar:
Load distinct
   Date,
   Year (Date)   as Year,
   Month(Date)   as Month,
   Day (Date)    as Day
   Resident TransactionTable;
```

The basic load statement creates a table with the distinct values of **Date**. The **Date** is then in turn used to create fields for year, month, and day. Of course, other fields like **YearMonth**, **FiscalYear**, etc. can be created.

Generate a table using Autogenerate

Another common way to generate data in Qlik is to autogenerate records:

```
Load
    RecNo()      as RecordNumber,
    Rand ()      as RandomNumber
    Autogenerate 100;
```

This construction is very similar to the other possibilities of Load. You can feed the Load statement in different ways:

```
Load … From         <File>           ; // From file
Load … Resident     <Table>          ; // An already loaded table
Load … Inline       <InlineTable>    ; // A table inside the script
Load … Autogenerate <Number>         ; // No source
Load … From_field   <Field>          ; // Parts inside a field
Load … Extension    <ExtensionCall>; // An external program
```

But with autogenerate there is no source – the records are generated and all field values must be derived from functions like Rand() or RecNo(). The number of records is specified in the number after the Autogenerate keyword.

Example: Autogenerated Master Calendar using Min and Max from transaction table

Another way to create the master calendar is to use autogenerate to generate all dates in a range. To do this, you need to first define the range. One way is to look for the smallest and largest dates in the date field and then generate all the dates in between the two:

```
MinMaxDate:
Load Min(Date) as MinDate, Max(Date) as MaxDate
   Resident TransactionTable;
Let vMinDate = Peek('MinDate',-1,'MinMaxDate') - 1;
Let vMaxDate = Peek('MaxDate',-1,'MinMaxDate')     ;
Drop Table MinMaxDate;

MasterCalendar:
Load
   Year (Date)  as Year,
   Month(Date)  as Month,
   Day  (Date)  as Day ,
   *;
Load Date(RecNo()+$(vMinDate)) as Date
   Autogenerate vMaxDate - vMinDate;

Drop Table MinMaxDate ;
```

First the **MinMaxDate** table is created. It has one line only and contains the largest and smallest dates in the data. These values are stored in two separate variables using Let statements and the Peek() function.

The variables are then used in a following Load statement to generate all dates in the range. Note that a preceding load is used to define all calendar fields, except the primary key **Date**.

The range can be created in other ways, for instance this full year and last full year only:

```
Let vMinDate = Floor(YearStart(Today(),-1)) - 1 ;
Let vMaxDate = Floor(YearEnd (Today()   ))      ;
```

Example: Autogenerated Master Calendar using Min and Max from symbol table

Finally, if you want a super-fast definition of the Master Calendar, try the below script. The result is the same as in the above script, but this algorithm skips the step with the temporary table and uses the FieldValue() function that operates on the symbol table instead.

```
MasterCalendar:
Load // ----------- generate additional fields -----------
   Year (Date)                                     as Year,
   Month(Date)                                     as Month,
   Day  (Date)                                     as Day,
   *;
Load // ------ dates between smallest and largest date ------
   Date (CalendarBegin + Iterno()-1 )         as Date
   While CalendarBegin + Iterno()-1 <= CalendarEnd;
Load // ------ establish begin and end of calendar ------
   YearStart(Min(FieldValue('Date',RecNo()))) as CalendarBegin,
   YearEnd  (Max(FieldValue('Date',RecNo()))) as CalendarEnd
   Autogenerate FieldValueCount('Date');
```

The Peek function

Extract from the Technical brief "Generating Missing Data" published on Feb 4, 2013

In all cases where you want to propagate values downward in a loaded table, the Peek() function is my preferred solution. This function returns the value of the preceding record. It can be used to fetch any record from any table, but here we are only interested in fetching the record immediately above, which is also the default behavior of Peek().

Example: Replace NULL with the value above

You want to replace NULL values with the value from the above record. Then you should use

```
If( IsNull( Field ), Peek( Field ), Field ) as Field
```

In this example, the condition is a simple "IsNull(Field)" but you can of course have other, much more complex logic here.

Example: Grouped data

In some cases, you want to propagate values downward in the loaded table, but just within some sort of group definition. It could be that you have the group names as "labels" inside the data, in this case the Country names:

Name	Population
United States	
California	39 029 342
Texas	30 029 572
Florida	22 244 823
New York	19 677 151
Pennsylvania	12 972 008
Canada	
Ontario	14 223 942
Quebec	8 501 833
British Columbia	5 000 879
Alberta	4 262 635
Manitoba	1 342 153

Then you want 'United States' and 'Canada' to be propagated down to the relevant records. The above data can be loaded using the following script:

```
tmpData:
Load *,
    If(IsLabelRow,      Name, Peek(Country))    as Country,
    If(not IsLabelRow,  Name)                    as State;
Load *,
    If(IsNull(Population),1,0)                    as IsLabelRow
    From Populations;

Data:
Load Country, Population, State
    Resident tmpData Where not IsLabelRow;

Drop Table tmpData;
```

Two passes are made over the data: In the first the **Country** name is propagated downwards, and in the second rows are filtered – only the relevant ones are kept.

Example: Accumulate a number

You have a number, and you want to accumulate this amount over time, but only within the same product. In the following example, an additional field with the accumulated amount is created:

```
tmpData:
Load Product, Date, Amount                      From DataTable ;

Data:
Load Product, Date, Amount,
   If(Product=Peek(Product),  // If the same as in previous row
       RangeSum(Amount, Peek(AccumulatedAmount)),
       RangeSum(Amount))                    as AccumulatedAmount
   Resident tmpData
       Order By Product, Date ;   // By Date within each Product

Drop Table tmpData ;
```

Also in this example, two passes are made over the data. The reason is that you need the "order by" and this is only possible within a resident load, i.e. in the second pass.

The Peek() function is used first to check that the record pertains to the same product as the previous record, then a second time to fetch the "**AccumulatedAmount**" value from the previous record.

Product	Date	Amount	AccumulatedAmount
A	2013-01-20	20	20
A	2013-01-21	NULL	20
A	2013-01-22	40	60
B	2013-01-20	NULL	0
B	2013-01-21	10	10
B	2013-01-22	NULL	10

The RangeSum() function is used to add the two numbers. The reason you need to use this function is that normal addition does not work for NULL values, whereas RangeSum() considers NULL as a zero.

Finally, the temporary data table is dropped.

For an example of using Peek() together with a **Join**, see the next article "How to populate a sparsely populated field".

How to populate a sparsely populated field

Originally posted in the Qlik Design Blog on Feb 5, 2013

Sometimes when you load data into a Qlik app you find that a field is sparsely populated, i.e. it has discrete enumerable values where some values are missing.

It could be like in the table above where you have three dates, each with some kind of conversion rate. The table only contains the dates where the conversion rate changed, not the dates between the changes.

However, the user will want to ask the question: "What was the status on this specific day?" In other words, the user wants to be able to click on a reference date to see the number that is associated with this date – but the date might not exist in the source data.

In such a situation, you need to generate the missing dates between the changes as individual records and use the "**Rate**" value from the previous date.

There are several ways to do this when the data is loaded, and all of them involve some script programming, using temporary tables. One algorithm is

1. Load the source table containing the rates (below called "**Rates**").
2. Find largest and smallest date in the "**Rates**" table.
3. Generate all dates between the largest and smallest dates (below called "**Dates**").
4. Join the "**Dates**" table (outer join) onto the "**Rates**" table.
5. Sort the resulting table according to date.
6. Propagate the value of "**Rate**" downwards to all records that have NULL in the "**Rate**" field, using the Peek() function.

Visually, the join and peek steps of the algorithm look like this:

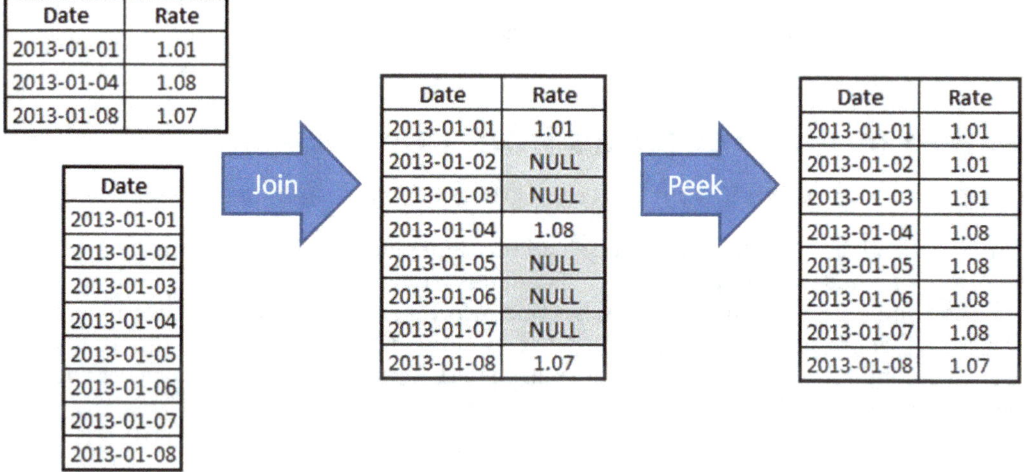

In the Qlik script, the algorithm would look like the following:

```
tmpRates:
Load Date, Rate From Rates ;

MinMaxDate:
Load Min(Date) as MinDate , Max(Date)        as MaxDate
    Resident tmpRates;
Let vMinDate = Num(Peek('MinDate',-1,'MinMaxDate') - 1);
Let vMaxDate = Num(Peek('MaxDate',-1,'MinMaxDate'))   ;

Join (tmpRates)
Load Date(RecNo()+$(#vMinDate))              as Date
    Autogenerate vMaxDate - vMinDate;

Rates:
NoConcatenate
Load Date,
   If( IsNull( Rate ), Peek( Rate ), Rate ) as Rate
   Resident tmpRates
   Order By Date ; // Previous values are propagated downwards

Drop Table MinMaxDate, tmpRates;
```

Problem solved!

This method can be adapted for most situations when you need to insert additional records in existing data: Warehouse balances, Exchange rates, etc.

Creating multiple records from one

Extract from the Technical brief "Generating Missing Data" published on Feb 4, 2013

Sometimes when loading data, you want to load the same record (with some small variation) several times. It could be that the source data contains a range – an upper bound and a lower bound – and you want a second table that has one record per discrete value in the range. It could also be that one record in the source data contains a list of possible discrete values and you want a second table with record per value in the list. You can do such loops either with a **While** loop or using the Subfield() function.

While and IterNo()

A loop inside the Load statement can be created using the **While** clause:

```
Load Date, IterNo() as Iteration From … While IterNo() <= 4 ;
```

Such a Load statement will loop over each input record and load this over and over as long as the expression in the **While** clause is true. The IterNo() function returns "1" in the first iteration, "2" in the second, etc.

The **While** clause can be combined with any of the source possibilities, e.g.

```
Load … From          File            While Expression ;
Load … Resident      Table           While Expression ;
Load … Inline        [InlineTable]   While Expression ;
Load … Autogenerate  Number          While Expression ;
Load …                               While Expression ; Load … ;
```

A Load statement with a **While** clause *cannot* at the same time have a **Where** clause. The reason is that it would be unclear which of the two clauses should be evaluated first. If you want to combine them, you should use a preceding Load, so the original Load contains one of the clauses, and the preceding Load contains the other.

I.e., if you want to loop over only the records that fulfil the **Where** condition, you should use the following construction:

```
Load …                                    While Expression ;
Load … From File                          Where Expression ;
```

And if you want to loop over *all* records, but just keep the ones that fulfil the **Where** condition, you should use the following construction:

```
Load …                                    Where Expression ;
Load … From File                          While Expression ;
```

The **While** clause in the second of the two Loads will be evaluated first and the result will be piped into the first Load.

Which one to choose depends on which precedence you want: Should the filter of the **Where** clause be applied before or after the loop?

A good example of how to generate multiple records with a **While** clause is explained in the next article "Creating Reference Dates for Intervals".

The Subfield function

A second way of looping over one record is to use the SubField() function: If you have list of values in one field and you want to split the record into several records (have one record per value in the list) you should instead use this function.

```
Load RecordID, Subfield( ListOfValues, ',') as Value Resident … ;
```

Such a Load statement will loop over each input record and load it several times, once for each value in the list of values. The return value of the Subfield() function will be the n:th value in the list.

The second parameter of the Subfield() function defines the separator of the list. It is possible to have a third parameter in the Subfield() function, but then the function will lose its looping functionality.

For example, in the following table the employees have different skills. If you want to list all individual skills in a single field, you need to use the SubField() function.

Emp No	Skills
159	Economics,Pharmacology
163	Marketing,Sociology
174	Bookkeeping,Particle physics
210	Economics,Marketing
215	Economics,Law,Marketing
279	Law,Marketing
286	Finance,Marketing
300	Bookkeeping,Finance

A good example of how to generate multiple records with the SubField() function from this table can be found in the article "Loops in the Script" in the Scripting chapter.

Creating Reference Dates for Intervals

Originally posted in the Qlik Design Blog on Feb 12, 2013

Previously, in "How to populate a sparsely populated field" I wrote about how to create reference dates for exchange rates and warehouse balances.

There is, however, also a second case where you want to create reference dates, but the data model is quite different. It is when you have contracts with validity periods, i.e. a start date and an end date. Examples: Rental contracts, Insurance policies, Healthcare commitments, etc.

Each contract has a beginning and an end. The analysts of an insurance company would probably want to ask the question: "How many valid insurance policies did we have on this specific day?" In other words, they want to click on a reference date to see the count of policies that are associated with this date – even though this date doesn't exist in the source data.

The solution is to first load all policies into one table. Then load a second table that has one record per combination of policy and date (**Policies_x_Dates**). This second table can in turn link to a master calendar.

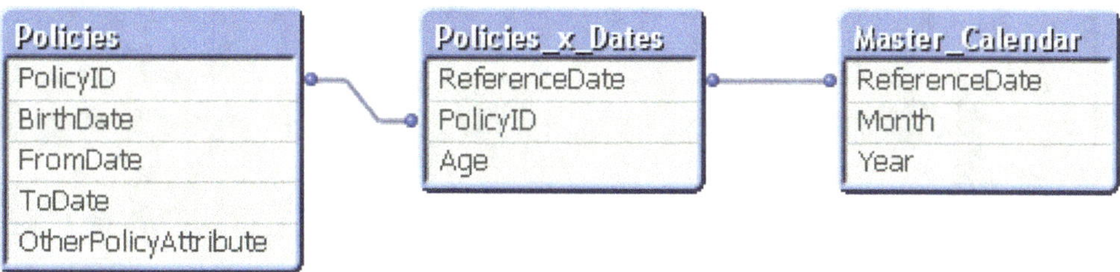

But the middle table does not exist in the source database. Instead, you must generate it using a While loop that loops over each record in the **Policies** table, i.e. each source record will be loaded several times. This way, you can load not only the "From" date and the "To" date, but also all dates in between:

```
Policies:
Load PolicyID, BirthDate, PolicyAmount, FromDate, ToDate,
    OtherPolicyAttribute
    From Policies;

Policies_x_Dates:
Load PolicyID,
    Age( FromDate + IterNo() - 1, BirthDate )    as Age,
    PolicyAmount / (ToDate - FromDate + 1)        as DailyAmount,
    Date( FromDate + IterNo() - 1 )               as ReferenceDate
    Resident Policies
    While IterNo() <= ToDate - FromDate + 1 ;
```

Note that the **Policies** table has exactly one record per insurance policy, and the newly created **Policies_x_Dates** table has exactly one record per combination of policy and date. Note also that there are other fields that should be put in the **Policies_x_Dates** table, e.g., the age of the insured person, since this depends on the reference date. Further, it is possible to break up a cost or an income into daily amounts, which is useful when you want to show the correct amount distributed over the year.

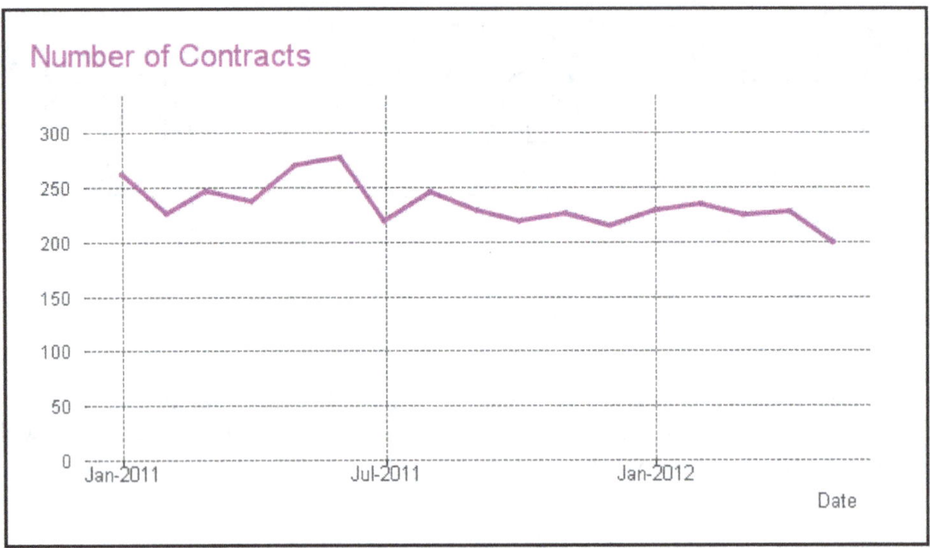

The While loop is a very useful tool whenever you need to create additional tables in the data model. It is often a better option than the **IntervalMatch**.

Generating all combinations of two or more fields

Cartesian product using Join

Sometimes you need to compare two or more fields and generate all possible combinations between them. In SQL, you can easily do this using a Cartesian product:

```
SQL SELECT Table1.A, Table2.B FROM Table1, Table2;
```

It is basically a join, but without joining condition.

This will create all combinations of the two fields, without any limitation from other relationships, and you will get a table that most likely has many more records than any of the two individual tables.

Using Load statements, you can do the same:

```
Load A From Table1.csv ;
Join
Load B From Table2.csv ;
```

Once you have made the join, you have a new table that you can process further, e.g. only select some records that fulfil specific demands or generate new fields based on the initial ones. However, further processing must be done in a second pass using a resident Load. Finally, the initial table must be dropped.

Example: Populating a table with warehouse balances

In this example, the source data is a table that lists the balances of a number of products in a warehouse over a number of dates. However, only records where the balance has changed exist. This means that for a specific product, there may be dates missing. For these dates, the latest balance should be used.

The example is similar to the previous example on conversion rates, but with the difference that there exist several products and each product has its own series of dates and balances. Hence, we now have a two-dimensional problem: Each combination of product and date should exist in the table.

In such a case you should first load all existing product balances (step "A" below). The second step is to generate all combinations of product and date using a join ("B" below).

The third step is to run through all these combinations picking out the missing ones (using "Where Not Exists()") and appending these to the initial product balance table ("C" below). Then you need make an additional pass in the ordered product balance table, so that you can propagate the appropriate values downwards ("D" below).

And finally, you need to drop the temporary tables.

```
// ----   A: Load all existing product balances
TempProductBalances:
Load ProductID, Date, Balance,
    ProductID & '|' & Num( Date )    as Product_x_DateID
    From ProductBalances;
```

```
// ----    B: Create all combinations of product and date
TempProduct_x_Dates:
Load distinct ProductID Resident TempProductBalances;
Join (TempProduct_x_Dates)
Load Date(recno()+$(vMinDate))      as Date
    Autogenerate vMaxDate - vMinDate;


// ----    C: Append missing records onto the product balance table
Concatenate (TempProductBalances)
Load * Where not Exists( Product_x_DateID );
Load ProductID, Date,
    ProductID & '|' & Num( Date )   as Product_x_DateID
    Resident TempProduct_x_Dates ;


// ----    D: Create final product balance table.
//             Propagate value from above record.
ProductBalances:
NoConcatenate
Load ProductID, Date,
    If( ProductID=Peek( ProductID ) and IsNull( Balance ),
        Peek( Balance ),
        RangeSum( Balance ))       as Balance
    Resident TempProductBalances
    Order By ProductID, Date; // Values are propagated downwards


// ----    E: Drop all temporary tables
Drop Table TempProduct_x_Dates, TempProductBalances;
```

IntervalMatch

A special case is when you need to generate all combinations between a numeric field, e.g. the date of an event or a transaction and numeric intervals defined in another table. In SQL, you would solve this by joining the two tables and use a BETWEEN condition:

```
SQL SELECT Events.Date, Intervals.BeginDate, Intervals.EndDate
    FROM Events, Intervals
    WHERE Events.Date
        BETWEEN Intervals.BeginDate AND Intervals.EndDate;
```

In a Qlik app you would normally use the **IntervalMatch** prefix to solve this problem. The general structure of the script would be to first load the events table and the intervals table as they are, and then generate a third table defining a bridge between the two.

```
Events:
Load TransactionID, Date, OtherEventFields    From Events;

Intervals:
Load IntervalName, BeginDate, EndDate, OtherIntervalFields
                                              From Intervals;
IntervalMatchBridge:
IntervalMatch (Date)
Load distinct BeginDate, EndDate              Resident Intervals;
```

The interval match will compare the intervals defined by **BeginDate** and **EndDate** with the discrete values of Date and generate all combinations.

Note that with **IntervalMatch** you will get a synthetic key in your data model. This is nothing you need to worry about. **Intervalmatch** is one of the cases where a synthetic key is the most efficient way of modeling the data. In fact, **BeginDate** and **EndDate** together form a primary key for the intervals, so it is quite natural to have them form a synthetic key.

Monte Carlo Methods

Originally posted in the Qlik Design Blog on Aug 27, 2013

In some situations in business intelligence you need to make simulations, sometimes referred to as "Monte Carlo methods". These are algorithms that use repeated random number sampling to obtain approximate numerical results. In other words – using a random number as input many times, the methods calculate probabilities just like actually playing and logging your results in a real casino situation: hence the name.

These methods are used mainly to model phenomena with significant uncertainty in inputs, e.g. the calculation of financial risks, the forecast of insurance claims, the prices of stock options, etc.

The Qlik engine is *very well suited* for Monte Carlo simulations.

The basic idea is to generate data in the Qlik script using the random number generator Rand() in combination with a Load ... Autogenerate, which generates a number of records without using an explicit input table.

To describe your simulation model properly, you need to do some programming in the Qlik script. Sometimes a lot ... However, this is straightforward if you are used to writing formulae and programming code, e.g. Visual Basic scripts.

The Rand() function creates a uniformly distributed random number in the interval [0,1], which probably isn't good enough for your needs: You most likely need to generate numbers that are distributed according to some specific probability density function. Luckily, it is in many cases not difficult to convert the result of Rand() to a random number with a different distribution.

The method used for this is called *Inverse Transform Sampling*: Basically, you use the Rand() function as input into the inverse cumulative probability function of the distribution. The output will then have the desired distribution. See figure below.

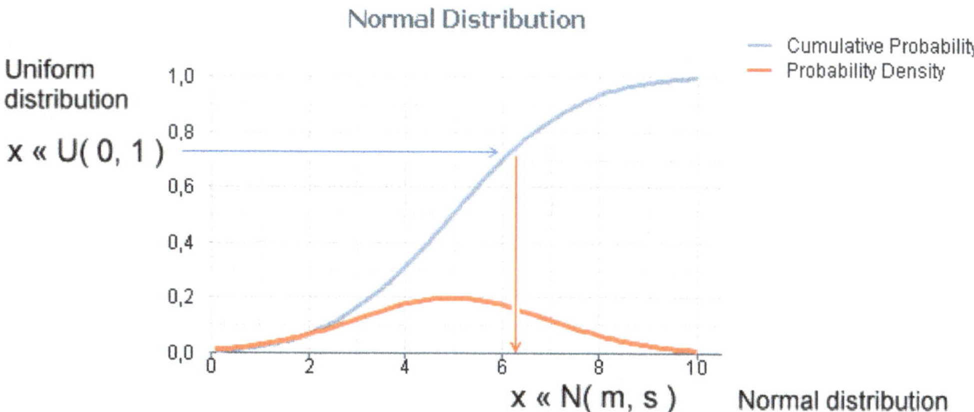

The y-axis corresponds to the input – the uniformly distributed random number- and the blue line corresponds to the cumulative probability function, so the result of the transformation can be found on the x-axis.

The most common probability distributions already exist in the Qlik engine as inverse cumulative functions; Normal T, F and Chi-squared. Additional functions can be created with some math knowledge. The following definitions can be used for the most common distributions:

- Normal distribution: NormInv(Rand(), m, s)
- Log-Normal distribution: Exp(NormInv(Rand(), m, s))
- Student's T-distribution: TInv(Rand(), d)
- F-distribution: FInv(Rand(), d1, d2)
- Chi-squared distribution: ChiInv(Rand(), d)
- Exponential distribution: -m * Log(Rand())
- Cauchy distribution: Tan(Pi() * (Rand()-0.5))

Finally, an example that shows the principles around Monte Carlo methods: You want to es1timate π (pi) using a Monte Carlo method. Then you could generate an arbitrary position x,y where both x and y are between 0 and 1, and calculate the distance to the origin. The script would e.g. be:

```
Load
    Sqrt(x*x + y*y)        as r,
    * ;
Load
    Rand()                 as x,
    Rand()                 as y,
    RecNo()                as ID
    Autogenerate 1000;
```

The ratio between the number of instances that are within one unit of distance from the origin and the total number of instances should be π/4. Hence π can be estimated through

```
4 * Count( {< r ={"<=1"}>} ID ) / Count( ID )
```

I have plotted the result in the image below. The points that are within a radius of 1 are black and the others are gray.

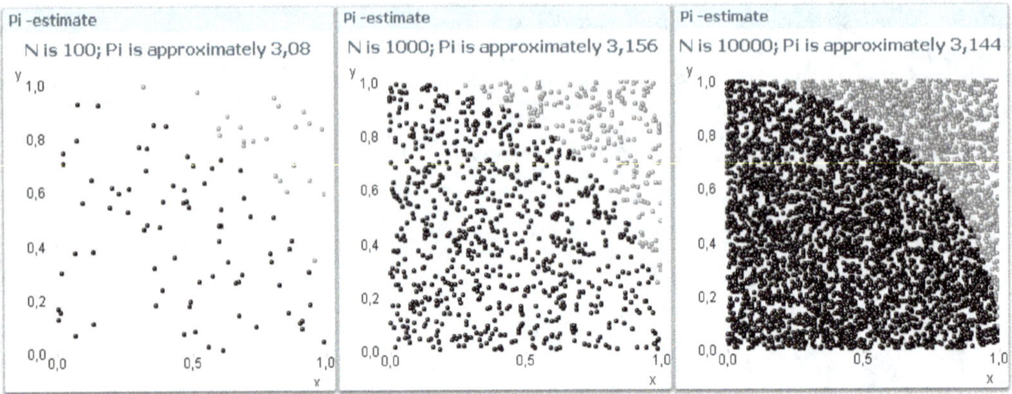

Bottom line: Should you need to make Monte Carlo simulations – don't hesitate to use a Qlik app. You will be able to do quite a lot.

More on simulations

Extract from the Technical brief "Generating Missing Data" published on Feb 4, 2013

Using the techniques described in this chapter, it is fairly straightforward to make simulations in a Qlik app. You can combine autogenerate and while loops to create data sets on which you make statistical analysis.

When doing so, there are some functions that are very useful:

- RecNo()   – the row number of the input table
- RowNo()   – the row number of the output table
- Rand()   – random numbers, uniformly distributed between 0 and 1
- Ceil()   – round upwards to nearest integer
- Pick()   – pick a specific value in a list of values

A small note of warning: If you use the result of the simulation for anything relevant, you need to be aware of the uncertainties (statistical errors) of the result, which can be calculated using standard statistical methods.

The statistical error decreases as the sample size increases. A good rule of thumb is that the relative error is approximately:

```
= 1 / Sqrt(SampleSize)
```

For example, if you have a sample of 100 events (which is a a fairly small sample), the square root will be 10, and the relative error approximately 10%.

If you want to use an empirical approach to get a feeling for how large the uncertainties are, just run the script several times to see how much a value changes from time to time.

Example: Monte-Carlo simulation of throwing two dice

What is the chance of getting a sum higher than a specific number when throwing two dice?
To simulate this, you need to generate a large number of throws and randomly create the
result of throwing two dice:

```
DiceThrowing:
Load
    Dice1 + Dice2              as SumOfDice,
    *;
Load
    RecNo( )                   as ThrowNo,
    Ceil( Rand( ) * 6 )        as Dice1,
    Ceil( Rand( ) * 6 )        as Dice2
    Autogenerate 100000;
```

This script will autogenerate 100000 throws and store the result of each throw in the field
SumOfDice. The result can then be analyzed in a normal Qlik chart. Below I have a bar chart
and a straight table sorted descending showing the result. As formulae, I have used

```
Count ( ThrowNo ) / Count ( total ThrowNo ) // Percentage
RangeSum( Above( Accumulated ), Percentage ) // Accumulated
```

From these, you can deduce that the chance of getting two sixes (the "12" bar) is around 3%.

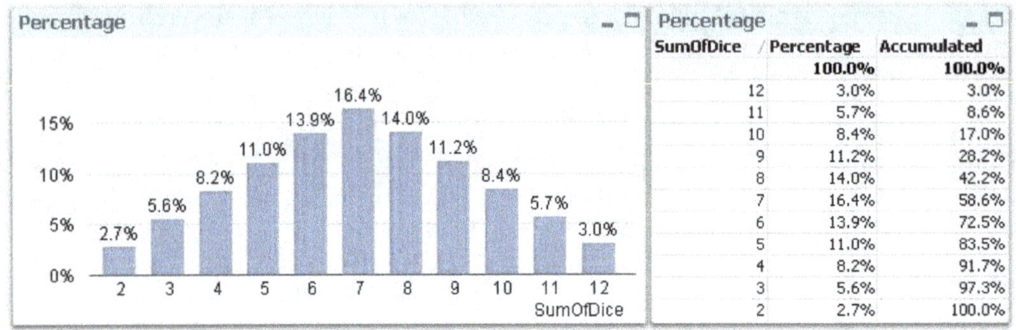

SumOfDice	Percentage	Accumulated
	100.0%	100.0%
12	3.0%	3.0%
11	5.7%	8.6%
10	8.4%	17.0%
9	11.2%	28.2%
8	14.0%	42.2%
7	16.4%	58.6%
6	13.9%	72.5%
5	11.0%	83.5%
4	8.2%	91.7%
3	5.6%	97.3%
2	2.7%	100.0%

Example: Monte-Carlo simulation of initial poker hand

What is the chance of getting a full house in the initial hand? To simulate this, you need to create the set of cards and randomly generate a large number of hands.

In the below solution, I generate a random number "**ShuffleSeed**" and order the deck by this number to get a shuffled deck. Then I deal ten hands with five cards each from the shuffled deck. The field "**HandNo**" is the ID for which hand it is.

This, I repeat 10000 times in a For – Next loop.

Finally, I analyze the result by additional Load statements using Group By, looking for pairs, three of a kind, full house etc:

```
// ---- Create a Deck of cards
DeckOfCards:
Load
    CardValue & ' of ' & Suit                       as CardName,
    *;
Load
    Pick(RecNo(),'Spades','Hearts','Diamonds','Clubs') as Suit,
    Pick(IterNo(),'2','3','4','5','6','7','8','9','10',
        'Jack','Queen','King','Ace')                as CardValue
    Autogenerate 4  While IterNo() <= 13;


// ---- Shuffle and deal the deck many times
For vHandNo = 1 to 10000   // ---- ---- begin For-Next loop ----
    // -- Load the deck and assign a random number to each card
    LoadDeck:
    Load
        Rand()                                  as ShuffleSeed,
        *
        Resident DeckOfCards;
```

```
    // -- Order randomly and deal. Five cards form a hand.
    // -- Each loop produces 10 hands, each with a unique HandNo
    PokerHands:
    Load
        CardName,
        Suit,
        CardValue,
        10*$(vHandNo) + Mod(RecNO(),10) as HandNo
        resident LoadDeck
            Where RecNo() <= 50
            Order By ShuffleSeed;

    Drop Table LoadDeck;
 Next vHandNo    // ---- ---- ---- ---- end For-Next loop ---- ----
 Drop Table DeckOfCards;


// ---- Check each hand for Flush
GroupByHandNo:
Load
    HandNo,
    If(Count(distinct Suit)=1,1,0)        as HandHasAFlush
    Resident PokerHands
        Group By HandNo;


// ---- Check each card value in the hand for a pair, three of
//      a kind, and four of a kind
GroupByHandNoAndCardValue:
Load
    HandNo,
    CardValue                      as CardInCombo,
    If(Count(CardName)=2,1,0)      as ComboIsPair,
    If(Count(CardName)=3,1,0)      as ComboIsThreeOfAKind,
    If(Count(CardName)=4,1,0)      as ComboIsFourOfAKind
    Resident PokerHands
        Group By HandNo, CardValue;
```

```
// ---- Check each hand in the above table for two pairs
//      and a full house
GroupByHandNo2:
Load
    If(HandHasAPair and HandHasThreeOfAKind, 1,0)
                                            as HandHasAFullHouse,
    *;
Load
    HandNo,
    If(Sum(ComboIsPair)=1,1,0)              as HandHasAPair,
    If(Sum(ComboIsPair)=2,1,0)              as HandHasTwoPairs,
    Max(ComboIsThreeOfAKind)                as HandHasThreeOfAKind,
    Max(ComboIsFourOfAKind)                 as HandHasFourOfAKind
    Resident GroupByHandNoAndCardValue
        Group By HandNo;
```

The result is displayed in a pivot table with six expressions:

```
// Pair =
Count({1<HandHasAPair={1}>} distinct HandNo)         /
                                  Count({1} distinct HandNo)
// Three of a Kind =
Count({1<HandHasThreeOfAKind={1}>} distinct HandNo) /
                                  Count({1} distinct HandNo)
// Four of a Kind =
Count({1<HandHasFourOfAKind={1}>} distinct HandNo)  /
                                  Count({1} distinct HandNo)
// Two Pairs =
Count({1<HandHasTwoPairs={1}>} distinct HandNo)      /
                                  Count({1} distinct HandNo)
// Full House =
Count({1<HandHasAFullHouse={1}>} distinct HandNo)   /
                                  Count({1} distinct HandNo)
// Flush =
Count({1<HandHasAFlush={1}>} distinct HandNo)        /
                                  Count({1} distinct HandNo)
```

Probabilities	
Pair	42.0%
Three of a Kind	2.4%
Four of a Kind	0.01%
Two Pairs	4.8%
Full House	0.14%
Flush	0.22%

10
Calendars and Time

Almost all reports and business intelligence solutions contain one or several time and date components. Calculations over periods are an essential part of every analysis. The analysis over periods is quite independent from other analyses regardless of if it is sales, finance, human resources or production data. Without time and date components it is impossible to discuss trends and changes.

So, you need a calendar in the script.

Once you have that, you will ask yourself questions like

- How can a date be transformed to other fields: Year, Quarter, Month?
- How can fiscal calendars be included?
- How can several dates be linked to one Master Calendar?

This chapter tries to answer some of these topics and will give examples of best practices.

The Auto-Calendar

During the development of Qlik Sense, we had a requirement to make the handling of dates simpler. In QlikView, it wasn't very difficult if you knew some scripting, but since we now had our focus on non-technical users and self-service, it was impossible to use the approach of having the user code a master calendar in the script.

It had to be *automatic, out of the box*.

So, an algorithm to recognize dates already at the script generation was introduced, as well as script commands to define a calendar template and apply it to fields that were identified as dates. The result is what we now have in Qlik Sense. If you let the data manager generate the script using data that contains dates you will get a script with an auto calendar.

Go to the script editor (the Data Load Editor), click on the "Auto-generated section" and scroll down. Then you will find a "**Declare**" statement that defines the calendar:

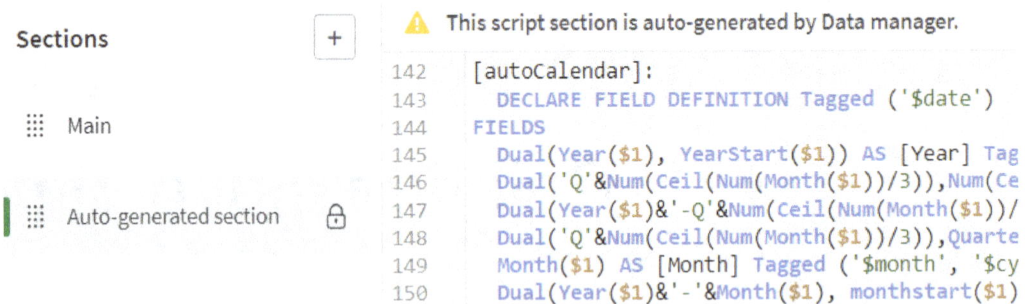

And right after this, you will find a "**Derive**" statement that applies the calendar to several date fields.

It is possible to edit this calendar and add new fields. It is also possible to have several calendar templates, e.g if you want both a Gregorian calendar and a financial calendar. Here's how you do it:

First, you need to unlock the auto-generated section. This is not dangerous – it only means that the data manager no longer can make automatic changes to it. But instead, *you* can make changes. So, now you can make the changes you want.

The logic is simple: Each line in the "**Fields**" section is a function call that defines a derived field. These fields will appear among the other fields in the asset panel and can be used as any other field in e.g. in set analysis. They have names like "**OrderDate.autoCalendar.Year**".

The "**$1**" denotes the formal parameter, i.e. the date that is used as input to the function.

All fields are tagged, so that the software "knows" how to use the fields. For example, the time-aware line chart needs to know which fields to use when the user zooms in on a smaller time scale. It uses the tags for this.

With this knowledge you can start adding or changing fields. For example, I always change the definition of **Year**, which I think Qlik Sense defines incorrectly. In the automatically generated calendar, it is:

```
Dual(Year($1), YearStart($1)) AS [Year] Tagged ('$axis', '$year'),
```

Hence, it uses the YearStart() function, which returns the day serial number. I.e. the numeric value is not the same as the year. This causes problems as soon as you use year in arithmetic operations, e.g. when you subtract 1 to get previous year. It should instead have a numeric value that corresponds to the year. But the time-aware line chart still needs to have a year field that contains a date. So, I add this in a second field "**%Year**":

```
Year($1)                            as Year  Tagged('$year'),
Date(YearStart($1),'YYYY') as %Year Tagged('$axis','$year','$hidden')
```

I also rename the sections as well as the calendar and clean up the structure, so that it is easier to see what goes on:

```
StandardCalendar:
Declare Field Definition Tagged ('$date')
    Fields
    // ----------------------- Year fields ------------------------
    Year($1)                                                          as [Year]
    Date(YearStart($1),'YYYY')                                        as [%Year]
    Year(Today())-Year($1)                                            as [YearsAgo]
    If($1-YearStart($1) <= Today()-YearStart(Today()), 1, 0)          as [InYTD] ,
    // ---------------------- Quarter fields ----------------------
    Dual('Q'&Ceil(Month($1)/3), Ceil(Month($1)/3))                    as [Quarter]
    Dual(Year($1)&'-Q'&Ceil(Month($1)/3), 4*Year($1)+Ceil(Month($1)/3)) as [YearQuarter]
    Dual(Year($1)&'-Q'&Ceil(Month($1)/3), QuarterStart($1))           as [%YearQuarterQ]
    Dual('Q'&Ceil(Month($1)/3), QuarterStart($1))                     as [%YearQuarterS]
    4*Year(Today())+Ceil(Month(Today())/3)-4*Year($1)-Ceil(Month($1)/3) as [QuartersAgo]
    Mod(Ceil(Month(Today())/3)-Ceil(Month($1)/3),4)                   as [QuarterIndex]
    If($1-QuarterStart($1) <= Today()-QuarterStart(Today()),1,0)      as [InQTD] ,
    // ---------------------- Month fields ------------------------
    Month($1)                                                         as [Month]
```

If you add a second calendar, make sure that it is named differently from the first one. For example, if you add a calendar for the financial year, you should name this accordingly. Then you can use the two calendars in two **Derive** statements, e.g:

```
Derive Fields From Fields OrderDate     Using FiscalCalendar ;
Derive Fields From Fields VacationDate  Using StandardCalendar ;
```

The auto-calendar helps a non-technical user to get a good calendar. But it comes at a price: The fields in the auto-calendar are *Fields-On-The-Fly* and they have performance problems. See "Calculated Fields" in the "Expressions" chapter.

So, if you know how to make an old-fashioned master calendar in the script, I can only recommend you do this. It is a better solution. See below for how to make this.

The Master Calendar

Originally posted in the Qlik Design Blog on Oct 16, 2012

One of the most common problems to solve in data modeling is that of time. How to assign month name and other time attributes to a date. The solution is called a master calendar.

A master calendar table is a dimensional table that links to a date in the data, e.g. **OrderDate**. The table usually does not exist in the database but is nevertheless needed in the Qlik application for a proper analysis. In the master calendar table, you can create all time and date fields that you think the user needs, e.g. **Month**, **Year**, **Quarter**, **RollingMonth**, **FiscalMonth** or flags like **IsCurrentYear**, etc.

A typical master calendar table contains one record per date for the time period used in the Qlik app, perhaps a two-year period, i.e. 730 records. It is in other words a very small (short) table. Since it is small, you can allow yourself to have many fields in it – it will not affect performance in any significant way.

There are in principle three ways you can generate the records (with an infinite number of variations in the details):

- Load from the fact table, e.g.

```
Load distinct Date, Month(Date) as Month, Year(Date) as Year
    Resident TransactionTable ;
```

- Generate all dates within a range, using autogenerate or while, e.g.

```
Load Date, Month(Date) as Month, Year(Date) as Year ;
Load Date('$(vStart)' + RecNo()) as Date
    Autogenerate '$(vEnd)' - '$(vStart)' ;
```

- Generate all dates within a range, using a while loop, e.g.

```
Load Date, Month(Date) as Month, Year(Date) as Year ;
Load Date(MinDate+IterNo()-1) as Date
    While IterNo() <= MaxDate - MinDate + 1 ;
Load Min(Date) as MinDate, Max(Date) as MaxDate
    Resident TransactionTable ;
```

In the first case you use the table to which you are going to link the master calendar. This way you will get exactly those values that really exist in the database. Meaning that you will also miss some dates – e.g. Saturdays and Sundays most likely – since they often do not exist in the transaction table.

In the second case, you generate a range of dates, based on the values of two variables. This is a good solution, but it means that you will need to define the range beforehand. There are several ways to do this, e.g. find the largest and smallest value in the data; or hard code the days for the relevant year.

In the third solution, you generate all dates between the first and last date of your transaction table. This is my preferred solution.
Optionally you can use YearStart(Min(Date)) and YearEnd(Max(Date)) to define the range.

Further, you can speed up the process by reading the dates from the symbol table instead of from a potentially large transaction table: If you use the FieldValue() function instead of a resident Load, this will fetch the correct value from the symbol table:

```
Load Date, Month(Date) as Month, Year(Date) as Year ;
Load Date(MinDate+IterNo()-1) as Date
    While IterNo() <= MaxDate - MinDate + 1 ;
Load
    YearStart(Min(Fieldvalue('Date',RecNo())))) as MinDate,
    YearEnd(  Max(Fieldvalue('Date',RecNo())))) as MaxDate
    Autogenerate FieldValueCount('Date');
```

The word "Master" for the calendar table is really misleading. There is no reason to have only one calendar table. If you have several dates, you should in my opinion use several calendar tables in the same data model. The alternative – to have the same calendar for all dates – is possible using a link table but complicates the data model and limits how the user can make selections. For example, the user will not be able to select **OrderMonth**='Sep' and at the same time **ShipperMonth**='Nov'.

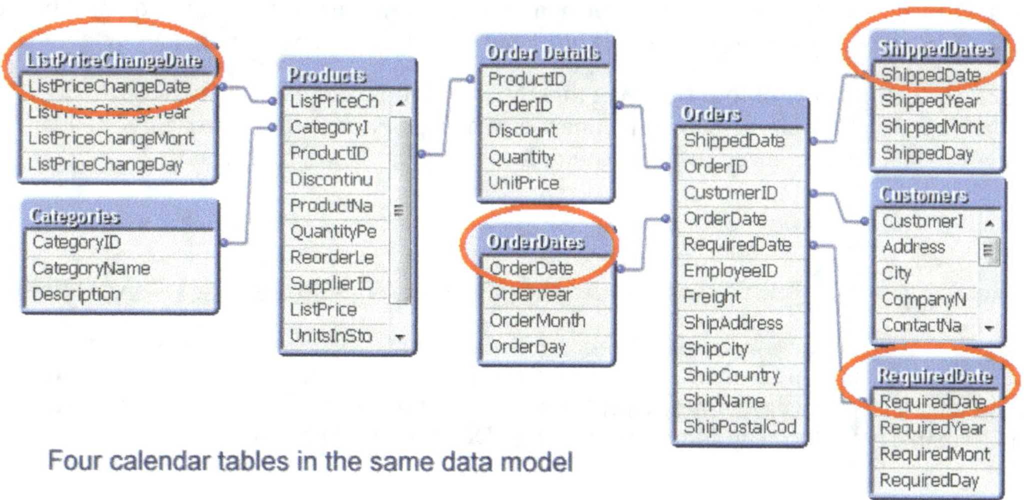

Four calendar tables in the same data model

Bottom line: Use a calendar table whenever you have a date in your database. Use several if you have several dates.

See more under "Canonical Date" about how to build a data model with several date fields.

Ancient Gods and Modern Days

Originally posted in the Qlik Design Blog on Oct 23, 2012

The use of the seven-day week is ancient. Signs are found in the old Greek, Indian, Persian, Babylonian, Jewish, Akkadian, and Sumerian cultures. Most likely it was invented by the Sumerians around 4500 years ago.

The Sumerians named the weekdays after the celestial bodies: The sun, the moon and the five known planets. Since the planets had names after gods, some days were thus also named after gods. These names were then translated into Babylonian, then into ancient Greek. In both translations the corresponding local gods were used.

```
// ---- Sumerian, Babylonian, and two different Greek definitions
Set LongDayNames='Nanna;Gugalanna;Enki;Enlil;Inanna;Ninurta;Utu';
Set LongDayNames='Sin;Nergal;Nabû;Marduk;Ishtar;Ninurta;Shamash';
Set LongDayNames='Moon;Ares;Hermes;Zeus;Aphrodite;Cronos;Sun';
//             'Σελήνης;Ἄρεως;Ἑρμοῦ;Διός;Ἀφροδίτης;Κρόνου; Ἡλίου';
```

The Romans, however, did not initially use a seven-day week. But a decision by Emperor Constantine in AD 321 eventually established the seven-day week also for the Roman Empire. Once again, the names of the gods were translated to their local counterparts.

Hence, the Latin names of the gods were mostly translations of the Greek names, which in turn were translations of the Babylonian names, which go back to the Sumerians. The Latin names can still be recognized in most Romanic languages, e.g. in French.

```
// ---- Latin and French
Set DayNames='Lunae;Martis;Mercurii;Iovis;Veneris;Saturni;Solis';
Set DayNames='Lundi;Mardi;Mercredi;Jeudi;Vendredi;Samedi;Dimanche'
```

The Germanic tribes in northern Europe used the seven-day week long before they converted to Christianity. So, the day names, except sun day and moon day, often have the names of the old Germanic gods: Tyr/Tiw, Odin/Wotan, Thor/Donar and Freyja/Frige.

```
// ---- English and Swedish
... ='Monday;Tuesday;Wednesday;Thursday;Friday;Saturday;Sunday';
... ='måndag;tisdag;onsdag;torsdag;fredag;lördag;söndag';
```

But for Saturday, the day was not translated. It is still "Saturn's" day in e.g. both Dutch and English. And in all Nordic languages it is the "Washing day". Because that is what you were supposed to do on Saturdays.

Nabû   Tyr   Venus

Picture 2: *Ancient Gods.*

In the Qlik script, you can customize the short day names by changing the variable **DayNames** as I have done above. These values will then be used by the WeekDay() function and by the 'WWW' format code in the Date() function.

There is also a second variable called **LongDayNames** that is used by the the 'WWWW' format code in the Date() function.

Alternatively, you can create a new variable, e.g. vDays, and use this in the following field definition:

```
Dual( Subfield('$(vDays)',';',WeekDay(Date)+1),
      WeekDay(Date)                                ) as WeekDay
```

But on which weekday does the week start? And which week is the first week of the year? The ISO 8601 defines these things clearly:

- The week starts on a Monday.
- Week no 1 is the first week of the year with four days or more.

This means that if Jan 1st is a Friday, then week no 1 starts Monday Jan 4th, and the first three days of the year belong to the last week of the previous year. It also means that if Jan 1st is a Thursday, week 1 starts Dec 29th. The ISO 8601 is used in many countries, among them most European ones.

But in North America and in the Middle East, different conventions are used. Often Sunday is considered the first day of the week. And Jan 1st is in some countries always part of week 1. As a consequence, the first and last week of the year are often broken.

Up until a few years ago, all Qlik week functions used ISO 8601. Now, the software will instead look at the regional settings of the user or the computer, and define environment variables that are used for the week functions:

```
Set FirstWeekDay = 0; // 0=Mon, 1=Tue, 2=Wed, ... , 6=Sun
Set BrokenWeeks  = 0; // Broken weeks allowed? 0=No, 1=Yes
Set ReferenceDay = 4; // This day in Jan is always in week 1
```

Bottom line: Define fields for weekday and week number in your master calendar. And don't hesitate to change the environment variables if you want long day names or different day names.

Roman emperors and the Month names

Posted in the Qlik Design Blog on Nov 5, 2012

Our current month names come from the Roman calendar. The original Roman calendar had ten months: Martius, Aprilis, Maius, Junius, Quintillis, Sextilis, September, October, November and December. The first four months were named after gods: Mars, Venus (Aphrodite in Greek and Apre in Etruscan), Maia and Juno. The origin of Aprilis is debated, but we know that the month was sacred to Venus because the *Festum Veneris et Fortunae Virilis* was held on its first day. The last six months are based on the latin words for five, six, seven, etc.

Each year started in March and ended in December, 304 days later. It was then followed by a period of festival between the years.

Picture 3: Numa Pompilius and Julius Caesar.

But the calendar was soon changed by the king Numa Pompilius around 700 BC, who added Januarius (after the god Janus) and Februarius (after the purification festival Februa). He also moved the beginning of the year to Januarius.

However, the year was still too short so the Pontifices – the highest-ranking priests – occasionally had to add an extra intercalary month to keep the calendar in sync with the seasons. This decision was political and was sometimes made just to extend the term of a particular public official. Or it wasn't done at all if the official was an opponent.

By the 1st century BC, the calendar had become hopelessly confused, so in 46 BC, Julius Caesar initiated a reform that resulted in the establishment of a new calendar, the Julian, which was a vast improvement: Leap years were introduced and the year in the Julian calendar was on the average 365.25 days, so no extra intercalary month was needed. After Julius' death, the month of Quintilis was renamed Julius in his honor, hence July.

Julius Caesar was succeeded by Augustus, and after his death the senate renamed Sextilis after him. At the same time, the senate also suggested that September be renamed after the reigning Caesar Tiberius. But Tiberius refused with the words: "And what will you do if there be thirteen Caesars?"

Today most countries use the Gregorian calendar, which is based on the Julian and still has the Roman month names from 2000 years ago.

In QlikView and in Qlik Sense, the abbreviated month names are defined in the environment variable **MonthNames**.

```
Set MonthNames='Jan;Feb;Mar;Apr;May;Jun;Jul;Aug;Sep;Oct;Nov;Dec';
```

This variable is used by several functions, e.g. Month() and Date(). The format code 'MMM' is always mapped against the content of this variable.

You can also create an environment variable for the long month names, corresponding to the format code 'MMMM':

```
Set LongMonthNames='January;February;March;April;May;June;July;
                    August;September;October;November;December';
```

If you have these variables, you can use the long format codes not only for formatting of date fields, but also for interpretation of fields, for example:

```
// --- Creation and formatting of a sequential month:
Date(MonthStart(Date),'MMMM  YYYY')                  as YearMonth,
// --- Interpretation of a long date, e.g. 'October 9, 2012'
Date#(Date,'MMMM DD, YYYY')                          as Date,
// --- Conversion of a string, e.g. 'Oct', into a numeric month
Dual(TextMonth, Month(Date#(TextMonth,'MMM')))       as Month,
```

Bottom line: You should define fields for months in your master calendar and make sure you have an environment variable for long month names.

Cyclic or Sequential?

Originally posted in the Qlik Design Blog on Jan 4, 2013

Calendar fields and time fields can be either cyclic or sequential. The sequential fields have values that are consecutive, never repeat themselves and have an open range. Here are some examples of sequential fields:

Year	[.., 2011, 2012, ..],
YearMonth	[.., 2011-Dec, 2012-Jan, ..]
Date	[.., 2011-12-31, 2012-01-01, ..].

This is in contrast to the cyclic fields that have a limited number of values in a closed range, where the values are repeated after a time:

Month   [Jan..Dec]
WeekDay   [Mon..Sun]
WeekNumber   [1..53]

This may seem obvious. Why do I write a blog post about this?

Because I think that we often are caught in the conventional. As Qlik app developers, we tend to use the existing functions as they are, without questioning what we really want to show. However, we can create any fields we want. It's all about how data is best visualized and how the user can best interact with data. Your role as a Qlik app developer is to create a user interface that supports a good user experience and enables the user. How the field values are constructed is a very important part of the user experience.

This post is about encouraging you to use your imagination to create customized calendar fields.

First of all, the same field can be created in two versions: as a cyclic field and as a sequential field. Think of the difference between **Month** and **YearMonth**, for example. The first contains cyclic months, and the next two contain sequential months:

```
Month(Date)                           as Month,          // Cyclic
MonthName(Date)                       as YearMonth,      // Sequential
Date(MonthStart(Date), 'YYYY-MM') as YearMonth_Alt2,// Sequential
```

Month	YearMonth	YearMonth_Alt2
Jan	Jun 2005	2005-06
Feb	Jul 2005	2005-07
Mar	Aug 2005	2005-08
Apr	Sep 2005	2005-09
May	Oct 2005	2005-10
Jun	Nov 2005	2005-11
Jul	Dec 2005	2005-12
Aug	Jan 2006	2006-01
Sep	Feb 2006	2006-02

The above is true for most calendar and time fields: they can be created in pairs – one cyclic and one sequential. For example

Quarters:

```
Dual('Q' & Ceil(Month(Date)/3),
     Ceil(Month(Date)/3)              ) as Quarter,        // Cyclic
QuarterName(Date)                      as YearQuarter,     // Sequential
```

... or Week numbers:

```
Week(Date)                              as WeekNumber,      // Cyclic
Dual(WeekYear(Date) & '-W' & Week(Date),
     WeekStart(Date)                    ) as YearWeek,       // Sequential
```

... or Hours:

```
Hour(Date)                              as Hour,            // Cyclic
Timestamp(Round(Date,1/24),
      'MMM DD, hh:mm'                   ) as DateHour,       // Sequential
```

Quarter	YearQuarter		WeekNumber	YearWeek
Q1	Apr-Jun 2005		1	2005-W22
Q2	Jul-Sep 2005		2	2005-W23
Q3	Oct-Dec 2005		3	2005-W24
Q4	Jan-Mar 2006		4	2005-W25
	Apr-Jun 2006		5	2005-W26
	Jul-Sep 2006		6	2005-W27
	Oct-Dec 2006		7	2005-W28
	Jan-Mar 2007		8	2005-W29
	Apr-Jun 2007		9	2005-W30

Secondly, you can use the Dual function to create fields that are cyclic and sequential at the same time, i.e. they have a cyclic textual (display) value, but an underlying sequential numeric value. This means that the same cyclic value, e.g. 'Q1', will be shown several times in the sequence.

```
Dual(Month(Date), MonthStart(Date))                    as SeqMonth,
Dual('W' & Week(Date), WeekStart(Date))                as SeqWeek,
Dual('Q' & Ceil(Month(Date)/3), QuarterStart(Date)) as SeqQuarter,
```

Such fields are very useful in charts. The chart below uses such a field – **SeqQuarter** – as first dimension and **Year** as second dimension. This way the color coding and the **Year** legend are created automatically.

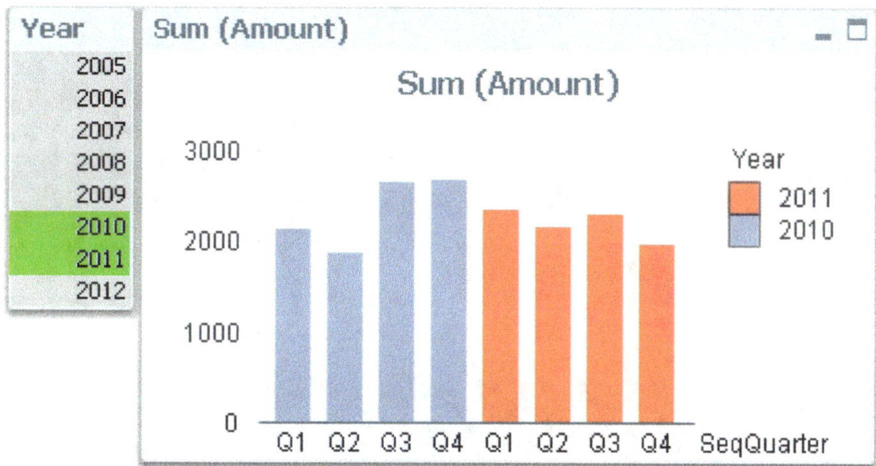

Recommendations:

- Create many fields in your master calendar. A few extra fields in the calendar table don't cost very much – neither in terms of script execution time, nor in terms of memory usage.

- Create both cyclic and sequential fields in your master calendar.

- Use cyclic fields in list boxes.

- If you have a chart with a single dimension, a sequential field is often preferable.

- If you have a chart with several dimensions, cyclic fields are often preferable.

Month-based financial calendar

Originally posted in the Qlik Design Blog on May 28, 2013

A common situation in Business Intelligence is that an organization uses a financial year (fiscal year) different from the calendar year. Which financial year to use varies between businesses and countries. But how would you solve that in a Qlik app?

A financial year other than the calendar year implies a number of additional requirements in the Qlik app: The most obvious is that the year used in all charts and reports must correspond to the financial year which runs over a different set of dates than the calendar year.

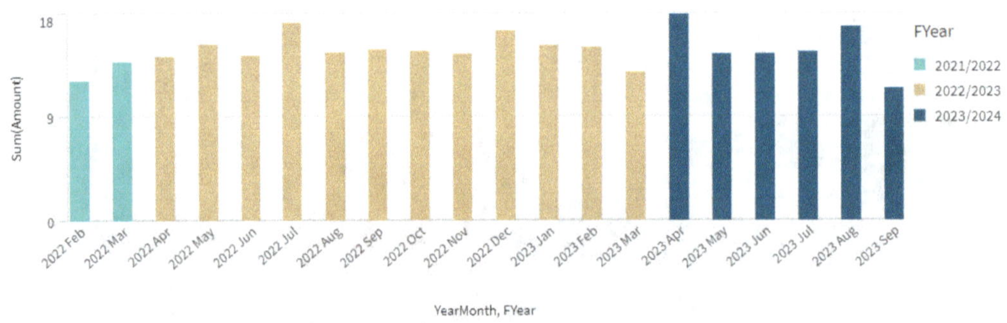

Further, the notation sometimes changes: You probably want to display years as '2022/2023' instead of just the year number.

Also, other fields, e.g. **Month** and **Week** must be assigned to the financial year as well as the calendar year.

Finally, the sort order of field values changes in some cases. E.g. you want to sort the months using the first financial month as the first month, e.g. [Apr..Mar] instead of [Jan..Dec]. Note the month order in the list box below.

There is a very simple way to achieve a month-based financial calendar in a Qlik app: Just add the necessary fields in the master calendar and use these in all situations where you need a calendar field. There are many ways that this can be done, but my suggested solution is the following:

1. Create a variable that contains the month number of the first month of the financial year. Assuming that April is the first month of your financial year, this variable should get the value '4'.

2. Create numeric values of the necessary fields. Usually, the number of the financial year is defined by its end, so (again using April as the first month) April 2023 belongs to the financial year '2024'.

3. Create dual values of the necessary fields.

The script for creating financial year and financial month then becomes:

```
Set vFM = 4 ;                          // First month of fiscal year

Calendar:
Load
    Dual((fYear-1) &'/'& fYear,
        fYear)              as FYear,   // Dual fiscal year
    Dual(Month, fMonth)     as FMonth,  // Dual fiscal month
    *;
Load
    Year+If(Month>=$(vFM),1,0) as fYear,// Numeric fiscal year
    Mod(Month-$(vFM),12)+1  as fMonth,  // Numeric fiscal month
    *;
Load    // ----- Your standard master calendar -----
    Year(Date)              as Year,
    Month(Date)             as Month,

    ...
```

YearMonth	fYear	fMonth	FYear	FMonth
2022 Jan	2022	10	2021/2022	Jan
2022 Feb	2022	11	2021/2022	Feb
2022 Mar	2022	12	2021/2022	Mar
2022 Apr	2023	1	2022/2023	Apr
2022 May	2023	2	2022/2023	May
2022 Jun	2023	3	2022/2023	Jun
2022 Jul	2023	4	2022/2023	Jul
2022 Aug	2023	5	2022/2023	Aug
2022 Sep	2023	6	2022/2023	Sep
2022 Oct	2023	7	2022/2023	Oct
2022 Nov	2023	8	2022/2023	Nov
2022 Dec	2023	9	2022/2023	Dec

Other fields, like week, day, etc. can also be created in a similar way.

A comment on the field naming: In this script I use lowercase 'f' as prefix for the numeric values and uppercase 'F' for the dual values. In real life you may want to just have the dual fields (no numeric duplicates) and name these differently, e.g. just **Year** and **Month**. If you do, you must also rename the original Gregorian calendar year and calendar month accordingly.

The bottom line is anyway that you can solve the challenge of a fiscal calendar just by adding a couple of lines in your master calendar. No set analysis is needed. And no complex chart expressions are needed.

Year-over-Year Comparisons

Originally posted in the Qlik Design Blog on Mar 4, 2014

A number alone doesn't tell you very much – you need to compare it with something. And very often you want to compare this year's number with last year's.

It is called Year-over-Year (YoY).

In such a comparison, you can for example compare the sales of the current month with the sales for the same month last year. Or – if you want to avoid fluctuations due to good or bad months, you instead look at the accumulated sales in the current year compared the same period last year. Then you look at the Year-to-Date (YTD) number.

But how do you calculate it? How do you write a simple formula that picks out a subset of transactions from last year and compares them to the corresponding transactions from the current year?

If you have Month as dimension and show accumulated numbers in the chart, you don't need to do anything. The numbers are directly comparable as they are.

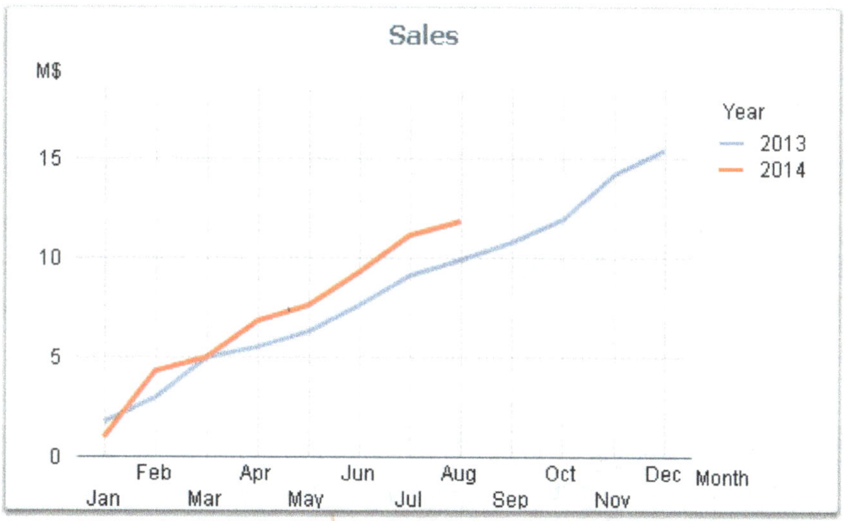

However, if you don't use Month as dimension, the numbers will no longer be comparable since last year contains transactions from a longer period. You still may want to make the comparison, but with another first dimension and Year as the second.

There are several ways to do this, and they differ in how the reference date is defined. One way is to let the user define an arbitrary reference date – either through a selection or through a variable – and then use this in an advanced Set Analysis expression.

Another, much simpler way is to use the date of the script run as reference date. If your application is refreshed every night, this would mean that the Year-to-Date calculation always is up until today's date.

Here's how you do it:

In your Master Calendar you should define flags – Boolean fields – that define whether a specific date should be included in the calculation:

```
If(DayNumberOfYear(Date) <= DayNumberOfYear(Today()),
    1,0)                                        as IsInYTD,
```

The above formula tests whether the date falls before today's date or not. Note that this flag will be useful also for dates belonging to other years than the current. The value of the flag will be 1 for dates in the beginning of the year irrespective of which year it is.

Then you can use this flag in a simple Set Analysis expression:

```
Sum( {<IsInYTD={1}>} Sales )
```

The Set Analysis expression will pick out the correct dates and thus the correct transactions for the comparison. Further, this expression can be combined with any dimensions.

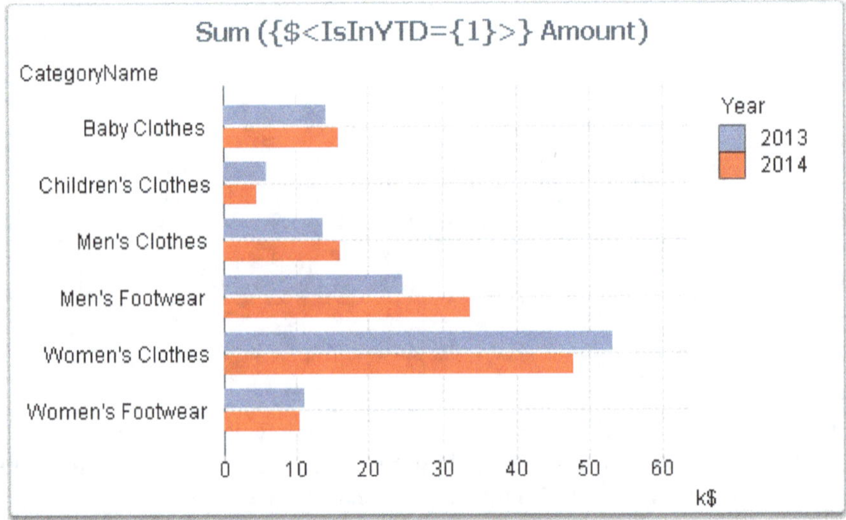

Flags for a number of different time periods can be created like this, not just Year-to-Date, but also Quarter-to-Date, Month-to-Date, Current Month, Last Month, etc.

```
If(DayNumberOfQuarter(Date) <= DayNumberOfQuarter(Today()),
    1,0)                                        as IsInQTD,
If(Day(Date) <= Day(Today()),
    1,0)                                        as IsInMTD,
If(Month(Date) = Month(Today()),
    1,0)                                        as IsCurrentMonth,
If(Month(AddMonths(Date,1)) = Month(Today()),
    1,0)                                        as IsLastMonth,
```

Summary: Create the necessary flags in your Master Calendar. It will simplify your Set Analysis expressions tremendously.

However, the above method will always use the date of the script run as reference date. But what if the user wants to make a comparison using another date? For example, the user clicks on the last day of March and wants to see what the situation was then.

This is a little more complicated, but it can still be achieved: If you create a field **DayOfYear** in the script, it is straightforward. Use one of the following:

```
DayNumberOfYear(Date)        as DayOfYear,
Date - YearStart(Date) + 1   as DayOfYear,
```

Once that is done, you need a Set expression in your measure that will pick out the correct values of this this field:

```
Sum ({<DayOfYear={"<=$(=Max(DayOfYear))"}>} Amount)
```

This expression will effectively select the beginning of all years and exclude the end. How large part of the year that is considered "beginning" is determined by Max(DayOfYear), i.e. the user selection. However, the user may make the selection in another calendar field, e.g. **Month** or **Week**, so these selections must be cancelled in the set expression. Hence:

```
Sum ({<Month=,Week=,DayOfYear={"<=$(=Max(DayOfYear))"}>} Amount)
```

Or better yet – use a variable that contains a reset of *all* calendar fields:

```
Sum({<$(vClearCalendar),DayOfYear={"<=$(=Max(DayOfYear))"}>}Amount)
```

For an explanation of the variable **vClearCalendar**, see "The Magic of Dollar Expansions".

Relative Calendar Fields

Originally posted in the Qlik Design Blog on Jun 10, 2013

A common question in the QlikCommunity forum is how to show only the last N months. The suggested answers are most of the time relatively complex set analysis expressions including dollar expansions with aggregation functions, e.g.

```
Sum({<Date={">=$(=MonthStart(AddMonths(Max(Date),-12)))
           <$(=MonthEnd  (            Max(Date)))"}>}  Amount)
```

Such an expression may work fine. However, it is *not* simple. When seen by someone who didn't write it, it is almost incomprehensible. So instead of such an expression, I would like to suggest a slightly different method: *Relative calendar fields.*

The idea is to define relative calendar fields in the master calendar. By doing this, it will be a lot simpler to define chart expressions. For example, you can in your master calendar define fields calculating how many days or months ago a specific date was. You can also number the months using zero for current month and -1 for last month, etc:

```
Today() - Date                                           as DaysAgo,
12*(Year(Today())-Year(Date)) + Month(Today())-Month(Date)
                                                         as MonthsAgo,
Dual(Month(Date),
    12*(Year(Date)-Year(Today())) + Month(Date)-Month(Today())
    )                                                    as RMonth,
```

Then you will be able to have much simpler chart expressions, e.g:

```
Sum({<MonthsAgo={">=0<12"}>} Amount)
```

This expression is almost the same as the initial expression. But it is much easier to read and understand. Below, you have a chart using **RMonth** as dimension and the above measure showing the last 12 months.

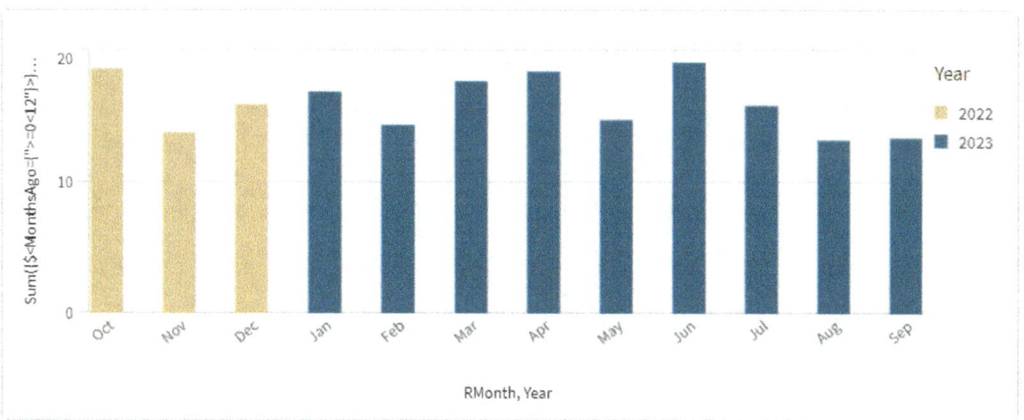

The **RMonth** field is a sequential field (see the article "Cyclic or Sequential?") but you may need a cyclic field also. And you may want it in a financial calendar. Then you should define the relative day and month numbers within the financial year, that you can use for a year-on-year comparison, e.g:

```
(Today()- YearStart(Today(),0,$(vFM))) -
(Date    - YearStart(Date,   0,$(vFM)))            as DaysAgoYTD,
Mod(Month(Today()) -$(vFM),12) -
Mod(Month(Date)      -$(vFM),12)                   as MonthsAgoYTD,
```

The variable **vFM** is the first month of the financial year, see more in the article Financial Year. If you use April as first month of the financial year, you will get the following table in September 2023:

April is first month of the financial year

YearMonth	FYear	MonthsAgo	MonthsAgoYTD
2022 Nov	2022/2023	10	-2
2022 Dec	2022/2023	9	-3
2023 Jan	2022/2023	8	-4
2023 Feb	2022/2023	7	-5
2023 Mar	2022/2023	6	-6
2023 Apr	2023/2024	5	5
2023 May	2023/2024	4	4
2023 Jun	2023/2024	3	3
2023 Jul	2023/2024	2	2
2023 Aug	2023/2024	1	1
2023 Sep	2023/2024	0	0

Note that future months will have negative numbers in **MonthsAgoYTD**.

If you have these fields defined, you can easily make a year-to-date chart comparing the different years. The expression will be almost the same as before, but with **MonthsAgo** changed to **MonthsAgoYTD**:

```
Sum({<MonthsAgoYTD={">=0"}>} Amount)
```

Below you have a chart of a year-over-year comparison (using the built-in accumulation):

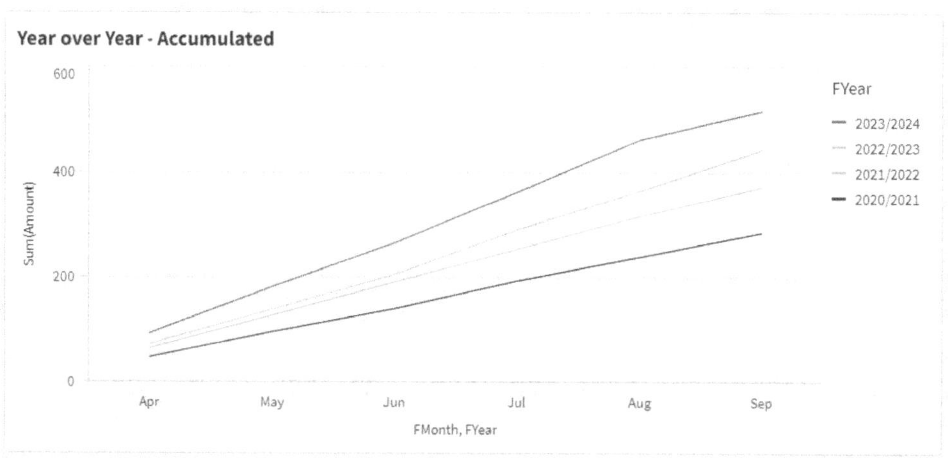

Bottom line: By defining relative dates and months in your master calendar, you can significantly simplify your set analysis expressions. Also, such fields will help your users create new charts. And your charts may even evaluate faster …

The As-Of Calendar

Originally posted in the Qlik Design Blog on Nov 3, 2015

Last week I wrote about how the Above() function can be used for calculating rolling averages and other accumulations. There is however also an alternative method for doing the same thing:

The *As-Of table*.

When you use the Above() function in a chart, all operations are performed inside the chart: you fetch one or several values from other rows in the chart. The As-Of table is slightly different in this respect: It is not a transient table created by an object or an expression – instead it is a real table in the data model.

The idea is to create a secondary month field – the **AsOfMonth** – that links to multiple real months.

In the example above, the field **Month** is a standard field in the calendar. You can see that '2015 Oct' in the **AsOfMonth** links to several preceding months, and each **Month** in turn links to several rows in a fact table. This means that a specific transaction will be linked to several **AsOfMonths**.

In the data model, the As-Of table should appear as a separate calendar table that links to the existing primary calendar table:

One way to create this table is the following:

First, make sure that you in your master calendar have a field "**Month**" with a numeric value corresponding to the first date of the month, e.g.

```
Date(MonthStart(Date),'YYYY MMM') as Month,
```

Then add the following lines at the end of the script:

```
// ========= Create a list of distinct Months ========
tmpAsOfCalendar:
Load distinct Month                Resident [Master Calendar] ;

// ======== Cartesian product with itself ========
Join (tmpAsOfCalendar)
Load Month as AsOfMonth        Resident tmpAsOfCalendar ;

// ======== Reload, filter and calculate additional fields =======
[As-Of Calendar]:
Load
    Month,
    AsOfMonth,
    Round((AsOfMonth-Month)*12/365.2425)    as MonthDiff,
    Year(AsOfMonth)-Year(Month)             as YearDiff
    Resident tmpAsOfCalendar Where AsOfMonth >= Month;

Drop Table tmpAsOfCalendar;
```

Once this table has been created, you can use the **AsOfMonth** as dimension in charts where you want rolling averages and accumulations.

If you as measure use

```
Sum({<YearDiff={0}>} Amount)
```

you will get a yearly accumulation – year-to-date up until the day of the script run.

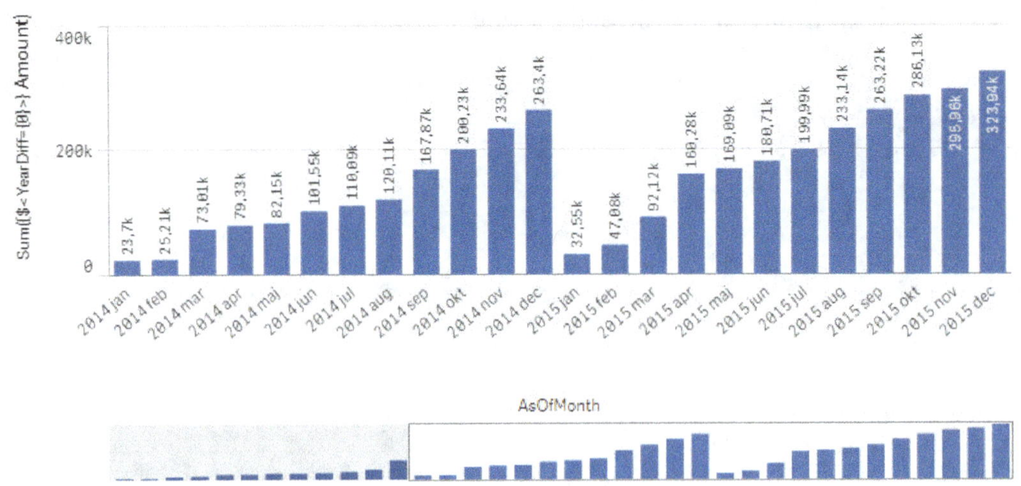

If you instead use

```
Sum({<MonthDiff={"<6"}>} Amount) /
    Count(distinct {<MonthDiff={"<6"}>} Month)
```

you will get a 6-month rolling average:

And finally, if you use:

```
Sum({<MonthDiff={0}>} Amount)
```

You will get the real, non-accumulated numbers.

I have made the Set Analysis expressions based on two fields: **YearDiff** and **MonthDiff**. However, for clarity it could be a good idea to add flags in the As-Of table, so that the Set Analysis expressions become even simpler, e.g.

```
If(MonthDiff=0, 1,0)     as IsSameMonth,
If(YearDiff =0, 1,0)     as IsSameYear,
If(MonthDiff<6, 1,0)     as IsRolling6,
```

Summary: The As-Of table is a good way to calculate rolling averages and accumulations.

Redefining the Week Start

Originally posted in the Qlik Design Blog on Jan 21, 2014

Six days thou shalt work, but on the seventh day thou shalt rest.

[Exodus 34:21]

The idea that you should rest on the seventh day is a central concept in both Christianity and Judaism. But which weekday is the seventh day of the week? *And which day is the first?*

The old texts of the Abrahamic religions clearly consider the Sabbath – Saturday – as the seventh day of the week. This day is also still today the resting day for Jews around the world. The same texts also describe how Adam was created on the sixth day, which is one of the reasons why Friday is the day of congregation and prayers for Muslims.

Hence, these two religions agree on the numbering of weekdays: Friday is the sixth day of the week and Saturday is the seventh.

However, in the rest of the world, the situation is more confusing: Although Sunday is observed as resting day in most countries, there is a disagreement on whether Sunday is the first or the seventh day of the week. In North America, Sunday is the first day of the week, but in many European countries it is the last day of the week. According to the International Organization for Standardization (ISO 8601), the week starts on a Monday, and Sunday is thus the seventh and last day of the week.

How weekdays are ordered makes a difference in all Business Intelligence applications, most notably in how list boxes and charts are sorted. Note the order of the weekdays in the list boxes below. In the left one, Sunday is on top of the list and in the right one it is Monday.

This difference can also be seen in calendar displays, used in many types of software and on many sites on the web. Again, note the first day of the week.

Su	Mo	Tu	We	Th	Fr	Sa
						1
2	3	4	5	6	7	8
9	10	11	12	13	14	15
16	17	18	19	20	21	22
23	24	25	26	27	28	

February 2014

Mo	Tu	We	Th	Fr	Sa	Su
					1	2
3	4	5	6	7	8	9
10	11	12	13	14	15	16
17	18	19	20	21	22	23
24	25	26	27	28		

Originally, QlikView used ISO 8601 to define the weekdays and the week start. Now, the Qlik engine uses the regional settings of either the user or the computer.

The function WeekDay() returns the name of the weekday (as defined in the variable **DayNames**) and a number from 0 to 6. If ISO 8601 is used, Monday is day number 0, and WeekStart() returns the date of the Monday immediately before the date supplied as parameter.

If you want to redefine this, e.g. if you want QlikView to show Sunday as the first day of the week, you need to change the user preferences.

But you can also do it the old-fashioned way – by recalculating everything in the script. Here's how you do it:

Start by creating a variable that defines the beginning of the week:

```
Set FirstWeekDay = 6; // 0=Mon, 1=Tue, ... , 6=Sun
```

The WeekStart() function has an offset parameter, and if you use your variable here, you can redefine how the function works and get the week start on the correct day. The WeekDay() function, however, cannot take any offset parameter, so you need to define the week day using the Dual() function:

```
WeekStart( Date, 0, $(FirstWeekDay) )               as WeekStart,
Dual(WeekDay(Date),
     Mod(WeekDay(Date-$(FirstWeekDay)),7)+1)        as WeekDay,
```

Using these two expressions in your Master Calendar instead of the standard function calls, you can redefine the week start to any of the weekdays.

Note:

The Qlik engine has been improved since this article originally was written. Today, it doesn't always use ISO 8601 – it is sensitive to the user settings. So, you don't need to create an expression for the weekdays. Just make sure the variable **FirstWeekDay** is what you want, and the functions will automatically return the correct values.

Redefining the Week Numbers

Originally posted in the Qlik Design Blog on Jan 27, 2014

Week numbers are often used in calendars, although not as commonly in some countries as in others. In northern Europe, it is very common to refer to a week by its number, but in many other countries it is not used at all. Just as with the week start, week numbers are defined differently depending on country, so you may need to add code in the Qlik script to generate your own week numbers.

So, how do you count the weeks? Is Jan 1st always part of week one? *Not necessarily.*

If week 53 starts as late as Dec 28th, does Jan 1st also belong to week 53? *Sometimes, yes.*

There is a definition made by the International Organization for Standardization (ISO 8601) that QlikView uses to calculate week numbers. It states that

1. The week starts on a Monday.

2. A week is always unbroken.
    I.e. some years week 1 starts already in December, and in other years week 52 or 53 continues into January.

3. Week 1 always contains Jan 4th.
    Or, differently put: Week 1 always has at least 4 days in January. A third way to say the same thing is: The first Thursday of the year always lies in week 1.

These three bullets define the three parameters you need to define general week numbers. Define them in the script according to:

```
Set FirstWeekDay = 0; // 0=Mon, 1=Tue, 2=Wed, ... , 6=Sun
Set BrokenWeeks  = 0; // Broken weeks allowed? 0=No, 1=Yes
Set ReferenceDay = 4; // This day in Jan is always in week 1
```

How the week start – the first parameter – influences the week number can be seen in the following table. It shows how the week number will change for the days around New Year 2013 for different week starts. To the left you have the weekday on which the week starts: "**First Day**". The other parameters are kept constant at 0 and 4 respectively.

Week Numbers for an "x/0/4" calendar																	
	Year	2012						2013									
	Month	Dec						Jan									
	Day	25	26	27	28	29	30	31	1	2	3	4	5	6	7	8	9
First Day	WeekDay	Tue	Wed	Thu	Fri	Sat	Sun	Mon	Tue	Wed	Thu	Fri	Sat	Sun	Mon	Tue	Wed
Mon		52	52	52	52	52	52	1	1	1	1	1	1	1	2	2	2
Tue		52	52	52	52	52	52	52	1	1	1	1	1	1	1	2	2
Wed		51	52	52	52	52	52	52	52	1	1	1	1	1	1	1	2
Thu		52	52	53	53	53	53	53	53	53	1	1	1	1	1	1	1
Fri		52	52	52	53	53	53	53	53	53	53	1	1	1	1	1	1
Sat		52	52	52	52	1	1	1	1	1	1	1	2	2	2	2	2
Sun		52	52	52	52	52	1	1	1	1	1	1	1	2	2	2	2

The second parameter concerns whether broken weeks should be used. If broken weeks are used, a new week number will always be used on Jan 1st, and consequently the first and last weeks of the year can have less than 7 days. The other parameters are kept constant at 6 and 4 respectively.

Week Numbers for a "6/x/4" calendar

Broken Weeks	Year	2013							2014								
	Month	Dec							Jan								
	Day	25	26	27	28	29	30	31	1	2	3	4	5	6	7	8	9
	WeekDay	Wed	Thu	Fri	Sat	Sun	Mon	Tue	Wed	Thu	Fri	Sat	Sun	Mon	Tue	Wed	Thu
Broken weeks possible		52	52	52	52	53	53	53	1	1	1	1	2	2	2	2	2
No broken weeks		52	52	52	52	1	1	1	1	1	1	1	2	2	2	2	2

And finally, the third parameter, the reference day. It defines which day that always belongs to week 1. In the table below, you can see how the week number will change if the reference day is changed. The other parameters are kept constant at 6 and 0 respectively.

Week Numbers for a "6/0/x" calendar

Reference Day	Year	2010							2011								
	Month	Dec							Jan								
	Day	25	26	27	28	29	30	31	1	2	3	4	5	6	7	8	9
	WeekDay	Sat	Sun	Mon	Tue	Wed	Thu	Fri	Sat	Sun	Mon	Tue	Wed	Thu	Fri	Sat	Sun
1		52	1	1	1	1	1	1	1	2	2	2	2	2	2	2	3
2		52	53	53	53	53	53	53	53	1	1	1	1	1	1	1	2
3		51	52	52	52	52	52	52	52	1	1	1	1	1	1	1	2
4		51	52	52	52	52	52	52	52	1	1	1	1	1	1	1	2
5		51	52	52	52	52	52	52	52	1	1	1	1	1	1	1	2
6		51	52	52	52	52	52	52	52	1	1	1	1	1	1	1	2
7		51	52	52	52	52	52	52	52	1	1	1	1	1	1	1	2

For example, if the reference day is set to 1, Jan 1 will belong to week 1, which then will start on Sunday Dec 26th. But if the reference day instead is set to 2, Jan 2 will belong to week 1, which means that it will start on Sunday Jan 2nd.

The ISO standard is thus a "0/0/4" week numbering. In the US, a "6/1/1" is usually used. But there are also other variants, e.g. "6/0/3" and "6/0/4".

If you copy the above parameters to your Qlik script and the following lines to your Master Calendar definition, you can redefine the week numbers any way you want:

```
Load *,
   Div(Date-WeekStart(WeekYearRefDate,0,$(FirstWeekDay))+7,7)
                                          as WeekNumber,
   Year(WeekYearRefDate)                  as WeekYear;
Load *,
   Date(YearStart(If($(BrokenWeeks),Date,WeekRefDate)) +
      $(ReferenceDay) - 1)                as WeekYearRefDate ;
Load *,
   Date(WeekStart(Date,1,$(FirstWeekDay))-$(ReferenceDay))
                                          as WeekRefDate ;
```

The fields **WeekYearRefDate** (Jan 4th in the ISO definition) and **WeekRefDate** (the Thursday of the week in the ISO definition) are really not necessary, but the expressions become somewhat simpler if these intermediate calculations are used.

Until we get a general week numbering functionality built into the QlikView standard functions (and, yes, we are looking into this) you will have to redefine the week numbers using the above script. Good luck!

Note:

The Qlik engine has been improved since this article was written. Today, it doesn't always use ISO 8601 – it is sensitive to the user settings. Just make sure the three mentioned variables have the values you want, and everything will work automatically.

Calendar settings in the Locale

Originally posted in the Qlik Design Blog on Mar 31, 2015

Last year I wrote a blog post on how to set Sunday as the first day of the week, instead of using the ISO 8601 default. This is fairly straight-forward – all you need to do is to write some formulas in the script. See "Redefining the Week Start".

However, now it has become even simpler. You don't need any custom formulas and usually it just works – without you doing anything.

When you create your Qlik app, a number of environment variables are created in the beginning of the script. These variables are based on your user profile or on the regional settings of your computer, so usually you don't need to change any of them.

```
Set FirstWeekDay = 0; // 0=Mon, 1=Tue, 2=Wed, ... , 6=Sun
Set BrokenWeeks  = 0; // Broken weeks allowed? 0=No, 1=Yes
Set ReferenceDay = 4; // This day in Jan is always in week 1
```

One of the variables is **FirstWeekDay** and this defines which day of the week you want to use as your first day.

If you want Monday, then you should use

```
Set FirstWeekDay = 0; // Monday is the first day of the week
```

And if you want Sunday, you should use

```
Set FirstWeekDay = 6; // Sunday is the first day of the week
```

Change it if you need to!

This variable is used as default for several functions, most notably WeekDay() and WeekStart(). So when you call these functions, you will automatically get the correct week start and the correct order of the week days.

Q WeekDay

Sun
Mon
Tue
Wed
Thu
Fri
Sat

Dates and Week Starts

Measures

Date	WeekDay	WeekStart	Day of WeekStart
3/28/2015	Sat	3/22/2015	Sun
3/29/2015	Sun	3/29/2015	Sun
3/30/2015	Mon	3/29/2015	Sun
3/31/2015	Tue	3/29/2015	Sun
4/1/2015	Wed	3/29/2015	Sun
4/2/2015	Thu	3/29/2015	Sun
4/3/2015	Fri	3/29/2015	Sun
4/4/2015	Sat	3/29/2015	Sun
4/5/2015	Sun	4/5/2015	Sun
4/6/2015	Mon	4/5/2015	Sun

If you use **FirstWeekDay**=6, you will get a result like in the picture above. You can clearly see that both the order of the weekdays (in the filter pane to the left) and the week starts (in the pivot table) are correctly defined. I have used US settings and the following expressions to define these fields:

```
WeekDay  ( Date )                    as WeekDay,
WeekStart( Date )                    as WeekStart,
WeekDay  ( WeekStart( Date ) )       as [Day of WeekStart],
```

The environment variable changes the defaults of these functions, but you can of course also override the default by using an explicit parameter in the function call:

```
WeekDay  ( Date, $(MyFirstWeekDay) )     as MyWeekDay,
WeekStart( Date, 0, $(MyFirstWeekDay) ) as MyWeekStart,
```

The other two variables **BrokenWeeks** and **ReferenceDay** define how week numbers are calculated:

The ISO definition states that weeks cannot be broken – one week number can span over two different years. Further, Jan 4th always belongs to week 1, i.e. week 1 is the first week with 4 days in the new year.

```
Set FirstWeekDay = 0; // Monday is the first day of the week
Set BrokenWeeks  = 0; // One week number may span over Newyear
Set ReferenceDay = 4; // Jan 4th always belongs to week 1
```

The US practice is to have broken weeks – one week number can never span two years. Which means that Jan 1st always belongs to week 1.

```
Set FirstWeekDay = 6; // Sunday is the first day of the week
Set BrokenWeeks  = 1; // A week number can never span over Newyear
Set ReferenceDay = 1; // Jan 1st always belongs to week 1
```

Bottom line: Date and time management has now become a lot easier.

Recipe for a 4-4-5 Calendar

Originally posted in the Qlik Design Blog on Jul 5, 2016

Calendars are used in most Qlik apps. In most cases, a standard Gregorian calendar is used, but in some cases a more complex calendar is needed. This post is about how to create a week-based financial calendar of a 4-4-5 type.

The 4-4-5 calendar is a week-based calendar, where the year is divided into 4 quarters, each with 3 months. The first month has 4 weeks, the second has 4 weeks, and the last has 5 weeks. Occasionally the 12th month has an additional week.

However, these quarters and months have nothing in common with the standard calendar months. First, they are not in sync with the Gregorian calendar. The 4-4-5 year can for example start in the last week of August. Further, the 4-4-5 months do not have the same lengths as the Gregorian months.

Below, you can see what such a calendar looks like.

- FQ1 to FQ4 are the financial quarters.
- FP1 to FP3 are the financial months. In this example the renumbering starts every quarter.
- FW1 to FW5 are the financial weeks within a financial month.

4-4-5 Calendar 2015/2016

Quarter	Week In Month	FP1 From	FP1 To	FP2 From	FP2 To	FP3 From	FP3 To
	Month In Quarter						
FQ1	FW1	Sun 08-31	Sat 09-10	Sun 09-28	Sat 10-08	Sun 10-26	Sat 11-05
	FW2	Sun 09-07	Sat 09-17	Sun 10-05	Sat 10-15	Sun 11-02	Sat 11-12
	FW3	Sun 09-14	Sat 09-24	Sun 10-12	Sat 10-22	Sun 11-09	Sat 11-19
	FW4	Sun 09-21	Sat 10-01	Sun 10-19	Sat 10-29	Sun 11-16	Sat 11-26
	FW5	-	-	-	-	Sun 11-23	Sat 12-03
FQ2	FW1	Sun 11-30	Sat 12-10	Sun 12-28	Sat 01-07	Sun 01-25	Sat 02-04
	FW2	Sun 12-07	Sat 12-17	Sun 01-04	Sat 01-14	Sun 02-01	Sat 02-11
	FW3	Sun 12-14	Sat 12-24	Sun 01-11	Sat 01-21	Sun 02-08	Sat 02-18
	FW4	Sun 12-21	Sat 12-31	Sun 01-18	Sat 01-28	Sun 02-15	Sat 02-25
	FW5	-	-	-	-	Sun 02-22	Sat 03-04
FQ3	FW1	Sun 03-01	Sat 03-11	Sun 03-29	Sat 04-08	Sun 04-26	Sat 05-06
	FW2	Sun 03-08	Sat 03-18	Sun 04-05	Sat 04-15	Sun 05-03	Sat 05-13
	FW3	Sun 03-15	Sat 03-25	Sun 04-12	Sat 04-22	Sun 05-10	Sat 05-20
	FW4	Sun 03-22	Sat 04-01	Sun 04-19	Sat 04-29	Sun 05-17	Sat 05-27
	FW5	-	-	-	-	Sun 05-24	Sat 06-03
FQ4	FW1	Sun 05-31	Sat 06-10	Sun 06-28	Sat 07-08	Sun 07-26	Sat 08-05
	FW2	Sun 06-07	Sat 06-17	Sun 07-05	Sat 07-15	Sun 08-02	Sat 08-12
	FW3	Sun 06-14	Sat 06-24	Sun 07-12	Sat 07-22	Sun 08-09	Sat 08-19
	FW4	Sun 06-21	Sat 07-01	Sun 07-19	Sat 07-29	Sun 08-16	Sat 08-26
	FW5	-	-	-	-	Sun 08-23	Sat 09-02

One major advantage over a regular calendar is that the end date of the period is always the same day of the week, which is useful in planning. Similarly, the beginning of the year, the quarters and the months are all on the same day of the week. This means that different years start on different dates. In the table below this is clearly visible. The end of the year is blue, and the beginning of the new year is green.

Year ends last Saturday in August

	Month											Aug							Sep
Year	Day	20	21	22	23	24	25	26	27	28	30	31	1	2	3	4	5	6	7
2014		Wed	Thu	Fri	Sat	Sun	Mon	Tue	Wed	Thu	Sat	Sun	Mon	Tue	Wed	Thu	Fri	Sat	Sun
2015		Thu	Fri	Sat	Sun	Mon	Tue	Wed	Thu	Fri	Sun	Mon	Tue	Wed	Thu	Fri	Sat	Sun	Mon
2016		Sat	Sun	Mon	Tue	Wed	Thu	Fri	Sat	Sun	Tue	Wed	Thu	Fri	Sat	Sun	Mon	Tue	Wed
2017		Sun	Mon	Tue	Wed	Thu	Fri	Sat	Sun	Mon	Wed	Thu	Fri	Sat	Sun	Mon	Tue	Wed	Thu
2018		Mon	Tue	Wed	Thu	Fri	Sat	Sun	Mon	Tue	Thu	Fri	Sat	Sun	Mon	Tue	Wed	Thu	Fri
2019		Tue	Wed	Thu	Fri	Sat	Sun	Mon	Tue	Wed	Fri	Sat	Sun	Mon	Tue	Wed	Thu	Fri	Sat
2020		Thu	Fri	Sat	Sun	Mon	Tue	Wed	Thu	Fri	Sun	Mon	Tue	Wed	Thu	Fri	Sat	Sun	Mon
2021		Fri	Sat	Sun	Mon	Tue	Wed	Thu	Fri	Sat	Mon	Tue	Wed	Thu	Fri	Sat	Sun	Mon	Tue
2022		Sat	Sun	Mon	Tue	Wed	Thu	Fri	Sat	Sun	Tue	Wed	Thu	Fri	Sat	Sun	Mon	Tue	Wed
2023		Sun	Mon	Tue	Wed	Thu	Fri	Sat	Sun	Mon	Wed	Thu	Fri	Sat	Sun	Mon	Tue	Wed	Thu

The definition of when the year starts is often described in a phrase like "the year ends on the last Saturday of August". But this is the same as saying that

- All weeks start on Sundays.
- September 1st always belongs to week 1. This is the Reference Date.

These two bullets can be expressed as integer parameters, which can be used when generating the calendar in the Qlik script. For the first day of the week, 0 is used to denote Monday and 6 is used to denote Sunday. Further, the number of days between the reference date and the Dec 31st is used to define the beginning of the year.

Finding the reference day may sometimes take some thinking. To help you, I have compiled some examples:

Description	First day of week	Reference date	Reference day
ISO week numbers: Week 1 may have a few days in December, but has at least 4 days in January	0	2016-01-04	4
4-4-5 year that ends the last Saturday in December	6	2016-01-01	1
4-4-5 year that ends the last Saturday in August	6	2016-09-01	-121
4-4-5 year that ends the second last Friday in August	5	2016-08-25	-128
4-4-5 year that begins the last Monday in August	0	2016-08-31	-122
4-4-5 year that begins the Sunday closest to September 1st	6	2016-09-04	-118

Once the two parameters have been defined, a calendar can be created using e.g. the script that is found on Calendars. This script also creates some other calendars, e.g. 4-5-4, 5-4-4 and Broadcast calendars.

The logic in the script has many steps but is still fairly straightforward. For each date, the script needs to

- Find the week start of the date.
- Use the week start to find the reference date of the input date. Note that the relevant reference date sometimes is after the date itself.
- Use the reference date to find which fiscal year the date belongs to. The start date of the year is also calculated.
- Use the start of the year to calculate the day number within the year.
- Finally, the day number of the year can be used to calculate the remaining fields.

Summary: It is possible to create a script that generates a correct 4-4-5 calendar. Don't hesitate to download the script example from www.qhic.se and modify it if you need a 4-4-5 calendar.

Week-based financial calendars

Originally posted in the Qlik Knowledge Base on Jul 4, 2016

A calendar is very useful when you want to link your data to different time periods, e.g. when you want to display your KPIs over different years or months. Often you just want to use a standard Gregorian calendar. Then it is straightforward: Just add a Master Calendar and define your fields.

But if you want to use a non-standard calendar, like a financial calendar or a week-based 4-4-5 calendar, the challenge becomes more difficult. Below you can see how the year shifts look for a 4-4-5 calendar where the year ends on the last Saturday in August.

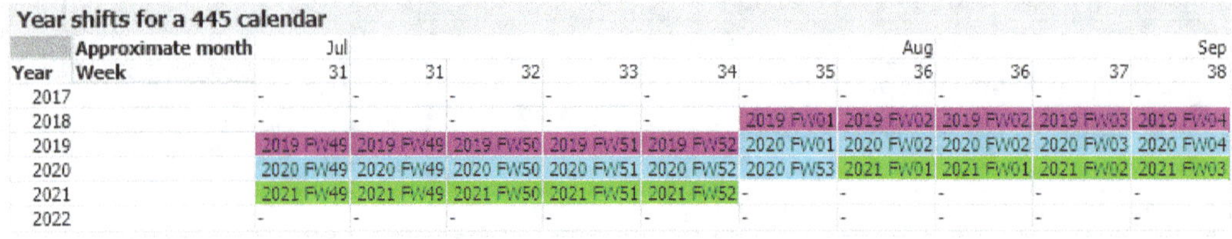

Year shifts for a 445 calendar

	Approximate month	Jul						Aug			Sep
Year	Week	31	31	32	33	34	35	36	36	37	38
2017		-	-	-	-	-	-	-	-	-	-
2018		-	-	-	-	-	2019 FW01	2019 FW02	2019 FW02	2019 FW03	2019 FW04
2019		2019 FW49	2019 FW49	2019 FW50	2019 FW51	2019 FW52	2020 FW01	2020 FW02	2020 FW02	2020 FW03	2020 FW04
2020		2020 FW49	2020 FW49	2020 FW50	2020 FW51	2020 FW52	2020 FW53	2021 FW01	2021 FW01	2021 FW02	2021 FW03
2021		2021 FW49	2021 FW49	2021 FW50	2021 FW51	2021 FW52	-	-	-	-	-
2022		-	-	-	-	-	-	-	-	-	-

For that purpose, I have created a number of scripts that create the wanted calendars. The script will help you create a more complicated calendar. It has parametrized examples for the following calendars:

- **Month-based financial calendar**
  The Gregorian months are used as financial months, but January is not necessarily the first month of the financial year.

- **Week-based 4-4-4 calendar**
  The financial year is divided into 13 months with 4 weeks each. Occasionally there is a 14th month with one week.

- **Week-based 4-4-5 calendar**
  The financial year is divided into 4 quarters, each with 3 months. The first month of the quarter has 4 weeks, the second has 4 weeks, and the last has 5 weeks. Occasionally the last month of the year has an additional week.

- **Week-based 4-5-4 calendar**
  The financial year is divided into 4 quarters, each with 3 months. The first month of the quarter has 4 weeks, the second has 5 weeks, and the last has 4 weeks. Occasionally the last month of the year has an additional week.

- **Week-based 5-4-4 calendar**
  The financial year is divided into 4 quarters, each with 3 months. The first month of the quarter has 5 weeks, the second has 4 weeks, and the last has 4 weeks. Occasionally the last month of the year has an additional week.

- **Broadcast calendar**
  The months are week-based and start on the first day of the week that contains the first day of the Gregorian month.

There are several parameters that you can use to configure your calendar: The first month of the year, the first day of the week and the first week of the week-based year.

The scripts are commented, so hopefully you can read them and understand them. You can paste a script straight into an empty app and run it to evaluate how it works. If you want to use parts of it inside one of your own apps, you may need to rename some fields. Also, you must remove the mock-up fact table.

The scripts can be downloaded from www.qhic.se and should work in both Qlik Sense and QlikView

Good Luck!

Inter Gravissimas – The Gregorian calendar

Excerpt from the Technical brief "QlikView Date Fields" published on May 31, 2012

… or some interesting but useless facts.

The dates in the Qlik engine are stored as serial numbers, the same as those of Excel. Qlik serial numbers are well defined and behaving correctly according to a generalized Gregorian calendar from Jan 1st, year 0 and roughly 2 billion years forward. As a comparison, you can note that the Excel date functions are defined from March 1, 1900. If you enter dates before this, Excel will incorrectly assume that 1900 was a leap year.

If you are a calendar aficionado, you might argue that there is no year 0 in the proleptic calendar; that the year 1 AD was preceded by the year 1 BCE without an intervening year 0. This is correct – at least how it was defined initially, since historians never included a year zero. This system was designed by the monk Dionysius Exiguus in the 6th century, when the existence of zero as a number was not known in Europe and the Julian calendar was used.

The Gregorian calendar was introduced much later, in 1582 by Pope Gregory XIII.

The papal bull did not say anything about how the new calendar should be applied backwards in time. As a consequence, when the new calendar was extended backwards, the old logic from the 6th century was used. This is today called the proleptic Gregorian calendar. It has no year zero and the common AD/CE or BC/BCE notation is used.

But there is a second generalization of the Gregorian calendar: the astronomical year numbering, with a separate year zero. Very early, astronomers used a separate year for year 0 (Christi) in the astronomical tables, as opposed to the years before (Ante Christum) and after (Post Christum), e.g. Johannes Kepler (1627, the Rudolphine Tables) and Philippe de la Hire (1702, *Tabulæ Astronomicæ*). However, it was not until 1740 that Jacques Cassini introduced the number 0 to mark this year in his *Tables Astronomiques*.

The astronomical year numbering is now an ISO standard (ISO8601) and is used worldwide in all scientific contexts. Hence, year -0001 (ISO 8601) is the same as year 2 BCE (proleptic Gregorian). The Qlik engine follows the ISO 8601 standard. Unfortunately, many Qlik date

CALENDARIVM
GREGORIANVM
PERPETVVM.

Orbi Christiano vniuerso à GREGORIO XIII. P. M. propositum. Anno M. D. LXXXII.

GREGORIVS EPISCOPVS
SERVVS SERVORVM DEI
AD PERPETVAM REI MEMORIAM.

functions do not work properly for the years before 1 AD. However, it is still possible to use Qlik serial numbers for this period. The things to be aware of are:

- Some functions do not work properly, e.g. Date(), Date#() and MakeDate(). Hence, formatting the date will produce something incorrect.

- If you want to use the proleptic Gregorian calendar, you can use the following as year function:

```
Num(
    If(Year(Date)>0, Year(Date), Year(Date)-1),
    '#0 AD;#0 BCE')                              as ProlepticYear,
```

- You can create the dates using something similar to e.g.

```
Dual(
    Num(Year(Date),'0000') &'-'& Date(Date,'MM-DD'),
    Date)                                       as Date
```

Non-Gregorian calendars

Originally posted in the Qlik Design Blog on Jul 19, 2016

The most common way to group days, months and years in the world today is the Gregorian calendar. However, there are also other types of calendars used around the globe. This post is about how to create a non-Gregorian calendar in Qlik Sense or QlikView.

The Gregorian calendar was introduced by pope Gregorius XIII in 1582. It is by far the most common calendar in the world today. Before this, the Julian calendar was used.

The Julian calendar with the Anno Domini era was used from around 500 AD, and is still today used by the Christian orthodox churches. The basic rules are well known: 365 days in a year, and a leap year with an additional day every fourth year.

But this results in *too many leap years*, so the calendar year slowly drifts off from the tropical year. Eventually we will have midsummer in May or even April. By 1582 the difference between the tropical year and the calendar year was 10 days. This problem was fixed by the introduction of the Gregorian calendar.

Julian Calendar

Gregorian Date	Julian Date
1900-03-11	1900 Feb 27
1900-03-12	1900 Feb 28
1900-03-13	1900 Feb 29
1900-03-14	1900 Mar 1
1900-03-15	1900 Mar 2

The Gregorian calendar has leap years every fourth year, just as the Julian, but not always: It doesn't have leap years every change of a century, even though these years fulfil the rule of every 4th year. Further, only every 4th century change is a leap year, the other ones are not. Hence, the year 1900 was _not_ a leap year in the Gregorian calendar, but it was in the Julian.

The Julian calendar is easy to recreate in a master calendar in a Qlik app. All you need to do is to generate all days in a four-year cycle and assign the appropriate months and day numbers.

But there are also other calendars, and to create these you need help tables; tables that list when the month or year starts, and tables with the names of the months or the weekdays.

The Hijri calendar – or Islamic calendar – is used by Muslims all over the world to determine the proper days for the annual fasting and to celebrate other Islamic holidays and festivals. The first year in the calendar was 622 AD during which the emigration of Muhammad from Mecca to Medina took place. This journey is known as the Hijra.

Hijri Calendar

Gregorian Date	Hijri Date
2016-07-04	Ramaḍān 29, 1437 A.H.
2016-07-05	Ramaḍān 30, 1437 A.H.
2016-07-06	Shawwāl 1, 1437 A.H.
2016-07-07	Shawwāl 2, 1437 A.H.
2016-07-08	Shawwāl 3, 1437 A.H.

It is a purely lunar calendar, containing 12 months based on the motion of the moon. This means that the Hijri year is always shorter than the tropical year, and therefore it shifts with respect to the Gregorian calendar.

To create a Hijri calendar, you need a table containing the month starts expressed as Gregorian dates. From this, you can generate a Hijri master calendar for your data model. It is however important to understand that this calendar, like any other Hijri calendar based on calculation, only gives estimated dates. The calendar is not based on the actual sighting of the moon, which is required for the beginning of some of the months. To get a proper calendar for religious purposes you should contact your local Muslim scholar.

The Hebrew calendar is used today predominantly for Jewish religious observances. It is a lunisolar calendar with 12 months based on the motion of the moon. However, to prevent it from shifting with respect to the seasons, a leap month is inserted approximately every third year.

Hebrew Calendar

Gregorian Date	Hebrew Date
2016-07-04	Sivan 28, 5776
2016-07-05	Sivan 29, 5776
2016-07-06	Sivan 30, 5776
2016-07-07	Tammuz 1, 5776
2016-07-08	Tammuz 2, 5776

To create a Hebrew calendar, you need a table containing the month starts expressed as Gregorian dates. From this, you can generate a Hebrew master calendar for your data model.

The Shamsi calendar, also known as Persian calendar or the Jalaali Calendar, is the official calendar in Iran. It is a purely solar calendar, containing 12 months originally based on the zodiac constellations. The year always starts at the vernal equinox as seen from the Tehran horizon. This means that the Shamsi calendar never shifts with respect to the tropical year.

Shamsi Calendar

Gregorian Date	Shamsi Date
2016-07-19	Tir 29, 1395
2016-07-20	Tir 30, 1395
2016-07-21	Tir 31, 1395
2016-07-22	Mordad 1, 1395
2016-07-23	Mordad 2, 1395

Further, no rules for leap years are needed: Depending on when the vernal equinoxes occur, some years automatically become leap years, others not.

To create a Shamsi calendar, you need a table containing the vernal equinoxes expressed as Gregorian dates. From this, you can generate a Shamsi master calendar for your data model.

The French Republican calendar is a purely solar calendar, containing 12 months, each with 30 days. At the end of the year, there are 5 or 6 additional days. Each month was divided into three ten-day weeks, called "decades".

French Republican Calendar

Gregorian Date	French Date
2016-07-16	28. Messidor CCXXIV
2016-07-17	29. Messidor CCXXIV
2016-07-18	30. Messidor CCXXIV
2016-07-19	1. Thermidor CCXXIV
2016-07-20	2. Thermidor CCXXIV

It originally started at the autumnal equinox as seen from the Paris horizon, but it is not clear whether the intent was to have the year always start at the autumnal equinox, and thereby solving the leap year question, or the intent was to use Gregorian-like leap year rules. However, it is possible to use the autumnal equinox to recreate this calendar also for our time.

So, to create a French Republican calendar, you need a table containing the autumnal equinoxes expressed as Gregorian dates. From this, you can generate a French Republican master calendar for your data model. Its practical use can be questioned, perhaps, but the poetic month names can make it worthwhile.

Scripts for all the above calendars can be found on www.qhic.se. The scripts all generate non-Gregorian dates and assign these to existing Gregorian dates.

You should see these scripts as templates and examples of how to include a non-Gregorian calendar in your app, but don't trust the content too much – there may still be errors. Change the input data, if needed, and use scripts as models for additional calendars.

The Master Time Table

Originally posted in the Qlik Design Blog on Jul 23, 2013

The Master Calendar table is a central component in many Qlik applications: It is a dimension table listing different calendar attributes such as Year, Month, Day, etc.

But what about time attributes, such as hours, minutes and seconds? How should these be handled? Should these also be included in the Master Calendar? Or should you create a *Master Time table*?

Often you *should* create a separate table for the Time dimension. To understand why, we need to look at the cardinality of the field used as key, i.e. the number of possible values. If a date is used as key, there can be at most 366 unique values per year. Hence, *the Master Calendar will have at most 366 records per year*. This makes the Master Calendar a small, efficient dimension table.

Unit	Values in a Year	No of bits for one Year	Values in a Day	No of bits for one Day
Dates	366	9	1	0
Hours	8 784	14	24	5
Quarter hours	35 136	16	96	7
Minutes	527 040	20	1 440	11
10-sec intervals	3 162 240	22	8 640	14
Seconds	31 622 400	25	86 400	17
Milliseconds	31 622 400 000	35	86 400 000	27

But if we instead use a timestamp as key, we have a different situation. A timestamp rounded to the nearest second will have over 30 million possible values per year. And if it has milliseconds too, it becomes even worse… *A timestamp usually has almost the same number of unique values as the transaction table has records*. It goes without saying that such a timestamp is inappropriate as primary key for a dimension. The dimension table would in many cases become just as big as the transaction table and nothing would be gained.

So, what should we instead do?

One good way is to convert the timestamp to *two* keys: **Date** and **Time**. The **Date** key needs to be truncated to the nearest integer so that no time information remains. For the **Time** key, it's the other way around: The integer part of the number needs to be removed so that no date information remains. In addition, it should be truncated – preferably to the nearest minute or 10-second interval – to keep the cardinality down.

These keys can be created through:

```
Date(Floor(      Timestamp))                        as Date,
Time(Floor(Frac(Timestamp),1/24/60),'hh:mm')    as Time,
```

This way you will be able to have two master tables, one with 366 records per year, and one with perhaps 1440 records – both tables small and efficient. The Master Time table can have fields for hours, minutes and e.g. work shifts and can easily be created from the above key.

However, you lose information when you remove the information about seconds and milliseconds. So, you need to ask yourself whether you need this information or not. If you do, the best option is often to keep the original timestamp in the transaction table, in addition to the created keys, so that it can be used to calculate different measures. If not, just don't load the original timestamp.

Summary:

- Think of the cardinality when you create dimensions.

- Make sure that the key to the Master Calendar table is an integer (formatted as a date): Use the Floor() function to remove the time component.

- If you need hour and minute as fields, create a Master Time table.

- Make sure that the key to the Master Time table is the fractional part of the timestamp, truncated to e.g. the nearest minute: Use a combination of the Floor() and the Frac() functions to create it.

11

The Qlik Engine

The Qlik engine is the back end of both QlikView and Qlik Sense. It evaluates the users' selections and returns both the colors – the green-white-gray – and the numbers presented in all visualizations.

This chapter describes how it works internally.

A Forgiving Engine

Originally posted in the Qlik Design Blog on Mar 15, 2016

Databases are usually not very forgiving.

Strict rules apply, defining what's allowed and what's not. For example, you are not allowed to enter data unless it has the right data type and is formatted the right way. Further, you are often not allowed to enter a value for a foreign key unless this value already exists in the master table. And you are not allowed to enter the same value twice if the field is a primary key.

The reason is of course to ensure data integrity. Without such rules, the database would soon be cluttered with bad quality data and contain a large number of errors.

The fact is that a good system is one that has many rules, but at the same time is easy to use: Equipped with a user interface designed in a way so that the user doesn't notice the rules – or at least isn't disturbed by them.

But with the Qlik engine it is a very different situation.

QlikView and Qlik Sense should <u>not</u> make sure that the data is free from errors. Instead, they should do exactly the opposite: *Display the source data along with all its errors.* This requirement is totally different from the demands you have on a database, and as a result the Qlik engine is built in a different way.

Data Types

There are no data types in the Qlik engine. The reason is simple: You may have data from different tables or even from different data sources in one single field. Then there is a potential risk that you have different data types in the different sources.

When loaded, all fields are converted into duals (number and text, or just text), and so one field can contain data that originally had different types.

Formatting

A single field can have a mixed data format. Also here, the reason is simple: Different sources may have different formats. As a result, it doesn't matter if a date is formatted as 3/31/16, 2016-03-31 or 42460. They will all three represent March 31, 2016.

Each distinct field value has its own format, and a single field may thus be displayed with different formats.

Referential integrity

The Qlik engine does not enforce referential integrity. For example: You may have a customer ID in your fact table that does not exist in the customer table (which would be an error in the data integrity of the database). But the Qlik engine will accept this and show NULL as customer name.

Relationship type

Often you know if you have a many-to-one or a many-to-many relationship between two entities. But this information is not loaded from the database. Instead, the Qlik engine assumes the worst case and is always prepared for a many-to-many relationship.

Links between tables don't carry information about relationship type. And all calculations involve aggregations since there is a possibility for multiple values of the referenced field.

The bottom line is that the Qlik engine is a very forgiving engine. It handles errors in all the above cases gracefully. No matter how many such errors you have in the data, the Qlik engine will always make a best-effort attempt in evaluating and showing the loaded data.

Symbol Tables and Bit-Stuffed Pointers

Originally posted in the Qlik Design Blog on Nov 20, 2012

Today I have a blog post for the Geeks[1]. For the hard-core techies who love bits and bytes. The rest of you can stop reading now. For you, there are other interesting posts in the QlikCommunity Blog.

Now to the bit-stuffed pointers:

During the Qlik script run, after each load statement, the Qlik engine transforms the data loaded into two table types: one data table and several symbol tables. The engine creates one symbol table per field:

Symbol table CompanyName

Pointer	Value
1101	Berglund's store
1110	Centro comercial Montezuma
...	...

Symbol table ProductName

Pointer	Value
100	Cajun Seasoning
101	Escargots de Bourgogne
...	...

Symbol table SalesAmount

Pointer	Value
10001	3300,04
10010	79,50
...	...

The symbol tables contain one row per distinct value of the field. Each row contains a pointer and the value of the field, both the numeric value and the textual component. Basically, the symbol tables are look-up tables for the field values.

In addition to the symbol tables, one data table per load statement is created. These are the same tables as you can see in the data model viewer when you have chosen the "Internal table view" – the same number of rows, the same number of columns. However, the tables do not contain the data itself – they contain the pointers only. But since the pointers can be used to look up the real value in the symbol tables, no information has been lost.

Data table

CompanyName	ProductName	SalesAmount
1101	100	10001
1101	101	10010
1110	100	10011
1110	101	10100
...	...	...

The pointers are not ordinary pointers. Rather, they are bit-stuffed indices, meaning – they only have the needed number of bits, as many as it takes to represent the field, never more. So, if a field contains four distinct values, the index is only two bits long, because that is the number of bits it takes to represent four values. Hence, the data table becomes *much* smaller than it would have been otherwise.

The bit-stuffed pointers and the symbol tables are the reasons why the Qlik engine can compress data the way it can.

Understanding this will help you optimize your document. It's obvious that the number of records and number of columns in a table will affect the amount of memory used, but there are also other factors:

- **The length of the symbols** will affect the size of the symbol table.
- **The number of distinct values** in a field will affect the number of rows in the symbol table as well as the length of the pointers.

When creating Qlik scripts, always ask yourself if there is any way to reduce these numbers, to minimize the memory usage. Here are a couple of common cases:

- You have a long, concatenated, composite key that you don't need to display. Use Autonumber() and the symbols will take no space in the symbol table. The integer values will instead be calculated implicitly.
- You have a field with many unique timestamps. Then you are sometimes better off if you first split it into two fields – Date and Time – and round the Time downwards to closest 15-seconds interval or to nearest full minute, for example:

```
Date(Floor(      Timestamp              ))      as Date,
Time(Floor(Frac(Timestamp),1/24/60))     as Time,
```

These expressions will give you at most 24*60=1440 distinct time values (11 bits) and typically 365 distinct dates (9 bits). In other words, as soon as you have a timestamp field with more than 1 million (20 bits) distinct values, the pointer for the timestamp field takes more space than the pointers for the two individual fields. And for the number of rows in the symbol tables you hit the break-even much sooner. So, you should consider splitting it into two fields sooner, maybe when you have around 100k distinct values.

If you find this post interesting, I greet you welcome to the *QlikGeeks*. 

[1] Geeks, see pictures:

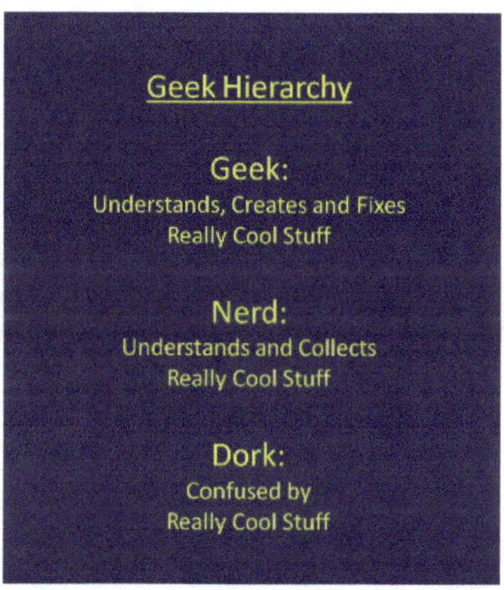

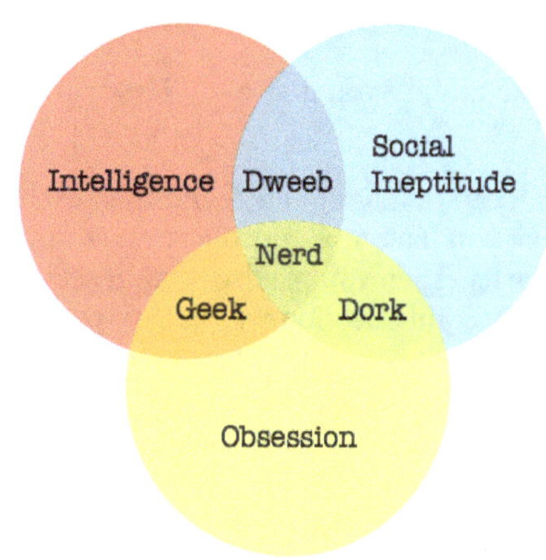

Colors, States and State vectors

Originally posted in the Qlik Design Blog on Jan 15, 2013

The color coding – Green, White, and Gray – is the hallmark of the Qlik user interface. These are the colors that convey information to the user about which field values are selected, which are possible, and which are not possible.

These are *the states*.

If you think about it for a while, you will realize that there are two different states for each field value: One is the input state; the selection that the user has made – whether the field value is selected or not; and the other is the output state: whether the field value is possible or not, given the logical inference of the selection.

Two statuses, each with two possibilities. This makes four combinations: Selected possible, Selected excluded, Optional and Excluded. Hence: There are not just three states – there are four.

	Possible	Not possible
Selected	Selected	Selected excluded
Not selected	Optional	Excluded

"Selected excluded?" you may ask. "How can a value be selected and excluded at the same time?"

It's simple. It can first be selected, and then excluded by a selection in *another* field. An example: Let's say that you have a sales application, and you select Jan, Feb and Mar to get the sales for the first quarter. Then you make a second selection – a product that incidentally was sold just in March. This second selection will then of course exclude Jan and Feb from the possible Month values. Jan and Feb will be selected excluded.

The field states are stored in vectors; binary arrays that have the same number of bits as the symbol tables excluding NULL values; the same number of bits as the number of distinct values of a field. There is in fact also a third field state vector that keeps track of alternative field values: the field values that would be possible, had there not been a selection in the same field.

The blue color is sometimes used in QlikView to show whether a field is locked or not. But note that *this is not a state* – it is a flag for the entire field and has thus nothing to do with the individual field values.

Finally, there are state vectors for the binary data tables also – vectors that keep track of which records in the data that are possible, and which are excluded.

All these vectors are referred to as *the state space*. The vectors are updated at every selection and used every time the Qlik engine evaluates which symbols to show in an object and which record to include in the calculation. One state space per user and alternate state is created. In addition, there is also one state space per set expression.

This way, the state space vectors keep track of which data is relevant right now – they "remember" the user selection.

Logical Inference and Aggregations

Originally posted in the Qlik Design Blog on Jul 15, 2013

Every time you click, the Qlik engine recalculates everything.

Everything.

A new selection implies a new situation: Other field values than before are possible; other summations need to be made; the charts and the KPIs get other values than before. *The state vectors and the objects are invalidated.* Everything needs to be recalculated since this is what the user demands.

Well, there is of course a cache also – so that the Qlik engine doesn't have to recalculate something which has been calculated before. So, it isn't quite true that everything is recalculated: If a calculation has been made before, the result is simply fetched from the cache. But it is true that nothing needs to be pre-calculated. Everything can be done in real-time.

The Qlik engine is an on-demand calculation engine.

From a principal point, there are two steps in the recalculation of data: The *logical inference* in the data model, and the *calculations of all objects*, including sheet labels and alerts.

The logical inference is done first. The goal is to figure out which field values in the symbol tables are possible and which records in the data tables are possible, given the new selection. There is no number crunching involved – it is a purely logical process. The result is stored in the state vectors.

Think of it as if the selection propagates from one table in the data model to all other tables. Table after table is evaluated and the Qlik engine figures out which values and records are possible, and which are excluded.

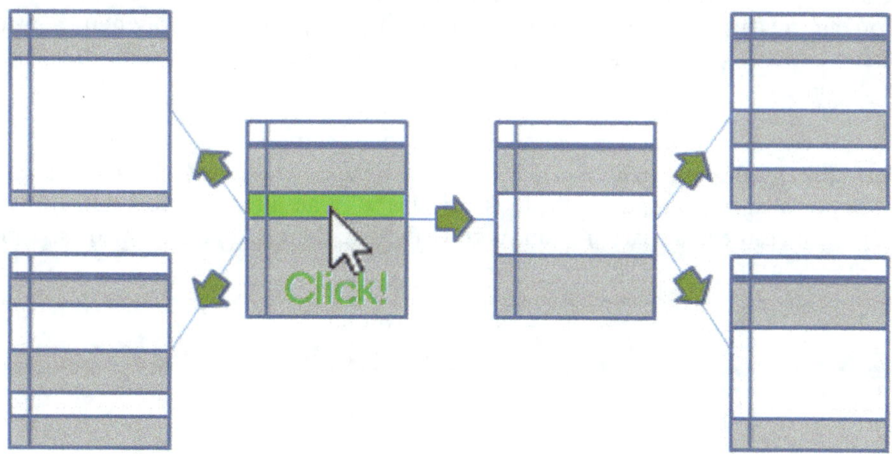

When the logical inference is done, the Qlik engine starts to evaluate all exposed objects. List boxes and dimensions in charts must be populated and sorted. All expressions – in charts, in text boxes, in labels, in alerts – must be calculated. Objects that are on other sheets, minimized or hidden, are however not calculated.

The calculations are always aggregations based on the data records that have been marked as possible by the logical inference engine. I.e., the objects do not persist any data on their own.

The calculation phase is usually the phase that takes time – often over 90% of the response time is due to calculations. The calculations are asynchronous and multi-threaded on several levels: First of all, every object is calculated in its own thread. Secondly, in the 64-bit version, many aggregations e.g. Sum() are calculated using several threads, so that a sum in one single object can be calculated quickly using several CPUs.

When an object has been calculated, it is rendered. Since the calculation is asynchronous and multi-threaded, some objects are rendered long before other objects are ready.

And when an object has been rendered, you can click again. And everything is repeated.

The Calculation Engine

Originally posted in the Qlik Design Blog on Aug 20, 2013

In a previous blog post, I wrote about Logical Inference and Aggregations, explaining that two different evaluation steps are executed every time you click in the Qlik user interface. This post will focus on the second evaluation step – The calculation of all objects.

This is *The Calculation Engine.*

The Calculation Engine (sometimes called the Chart Engine) is used in all places where you have aggregations. And since you have aggregations in almost every expression, the calculation engine can be invoked from any object: Usually it is invoked when calculating the measure in a chart, but it is also used for labels, for calculated colors, for text boxes, for show conditions, and for advanced search strings.

The calculation engine runs through two steps: First it finds combinations of the values of the fields used in the aggregation function, and, if necessary, builds a temporary look-up table. Then, it performs the actual aggregation using the look-up table to create all relevant combinations. If the aggregation is a measure in a chart or in an Aggr() function, the aggregation is made separately for every dimensional value, using the appropriate scopes.

So, to summarize, the order of events is

1) The Logical Inference

2) The Calculation Engine (once for every object or aggregation)
   a. Find all combinations (create the necessary look-up tables)
   b. Aggregate

The different phases can be seen in the picture. The text "Chart" here represents any object with an aggregation, and the text "List box" represents a standard Filter pane or List box without aggregation.

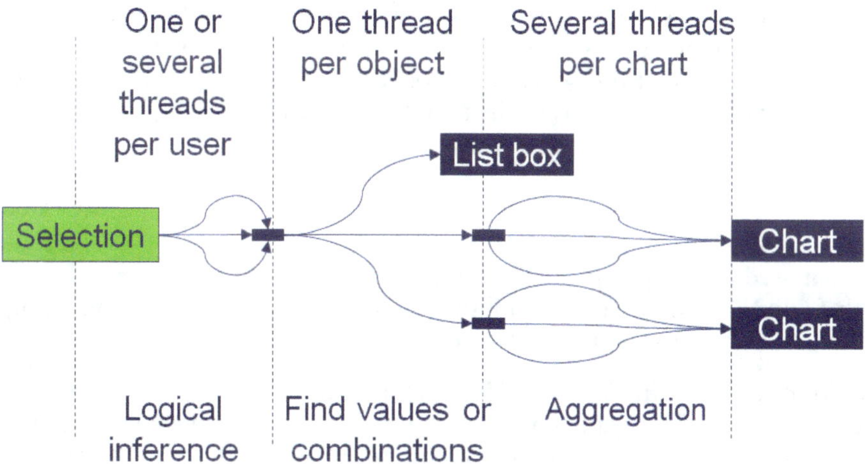

Examples:

```
Sum( Amount )
```

In this case, the summation is made in the data table where the field **Amount** is found: The summation loops over the records in this table. Hence, "finding the combinations" is reduced to looking in this table.

```
Sum( NoOfUnits * UnitCost )
```

In this case, there are several fields inside the aggregation function. If the fields reside in different data tables, the Qlik engine first generates the look-up table for **UnitCost** using the appropriate key, e.g. **ProductID**. Then it generates all combinations of the relevant field values using the look-up table – basically a join – and makes the summation on the fly.

```
Sum( NoOfUnits * UnitCost ) / Count( distinct OrderID )
```

The numerator is the same as before (and treated the same) but now there is an additional aggregation in the denominator. So, the Qlik engine will need to generate a help table for this aggregation too, listing the distinct order IDs. For each dimensional value, two aggregations are made, whereupon the ratio between the two is calculated.

```
Sum( If( IsThisYear, Amount ) )
```

Flags are often used inside aggregation functions, and usually this is not a problem. However, be aware that QlikView will create all combinations of the two fields before summing, and that this could in odd cases cause duplication of records.

The aggregation step is multi-threaded. However, finding the relevant combinations of field values is currently a single threaded operation, and may occasionally be the bottleneck when calculating a chart. So be aware of this when you use fields from different tables in the same aggregation function. You might want to consider moving a field to the "correct" table to minimize the impact of this step.

The Qlik Engine Cache

Originally posted in the Qlik Design Blog on Apr 15, 2014

The Qlik engine has a very efficient, patented (US8244741) caching algorithm that effectively eliminates the calculation time for calculations that have been made before. In other words, if you use the "back" button in the toolbar, or if you happen to make a selection that you have made before, you usually get the result immediately. No calculation is necessary.

But how does it work? What is used as lookup ID?

For each combination of selection, expression and data set, the Qlik engine calculates a digital fingerprint that identifies the context. This is used as lookup ID and stored in the cache together with the result of the calculation.

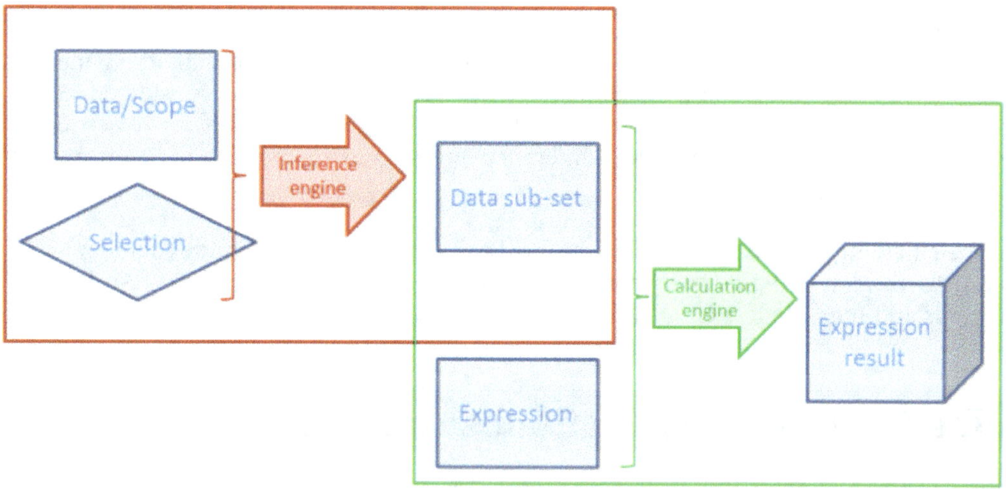

Here "calculation" means both the logical inference and chart calculation – or in fact, any expression anywhere. This means that both intermediate and final results of a selection are stored.

There are some peculiarities you need to know about the cache …

- **The cache is global**
  The cache is used for all users and all documents. A cache entry does not belong to one specific document or one user only. So, if a user makes a selection that another user already has made, the cache is used. And if you have the same data in two different apps, one single cache entry can be used for both documents.

- **Memory is not returned**
  Allocated memory is not returned when the document is unloaded. Cache entries will usually not be purged until the RAM usage is close to – or has reached – the lower working set limit. The Qlik engine will then purge some entries and re-use the memory for other cache entries. This behavior sometimes makes people believe there is a memory leak in the product. But have no fear – it should be this way. So, you do not need to restart the service to clear the cache.

- **The oldest cache entries are not always purged first**
  Instead, several factors are used to calculate a priority for each cache entry; factors like RAM usage, cost to calculate it again and time since the most recent usage. Entries with a combined low priority will be purged when needed. Hence, an entry that is cheap to calculate again will easily be purged, also if it recently was used. And another value that is expensive to recalculate or just uses a small amount of RAM will be kept for a much longer time.

- **The cache is not cleared when running macros**
  which I have seen some people claim.

- **You need to write your expression exactly right**.
  If the same expression is used in several places, it should be written exactly the same way – capitalization, same number of spaces, etc. – otherwise it will not be considered to be the same expression. If you do, there should be no big performance difference between repeating the formula, referring to a different expression using the label of the expression or using the Column() function.

The cache efficiently speeds up the Qlik engine. Basically, it is a way to trade memory against CPU-time: If you put more memory in your server, you will be able to re-use more calculations and thus use less CPU-time.

Recipe for a Memory Statistics Analysis

Originally posted in the Qlik Design Blog on Jan 29, 2013

In a previous blog post I described the internal data tables and the symbol tables. (See "Symbol Tables and Bit-Stuffed Pointers"). These tables constitute the Qlik internal data model. Then there are the state space vectors that keep track of the user's selections (See "Colors, states and state vectors").

In addition to these, there are other structures used to calculate expressions in sheet objects. Sometimes a sheet object can use quite a lot of memory, e.g., a chart with many dimensions.

Often you need to ask yourself – "What in this application uses a lot of memory? What can I improve or optimize?" Is it the data model itself or is it the symbol tables? Or is there a chart that uses a lot of memory?"

To get an answer to these questions, you can use the memory statistics tool in QlikView. Here follows a basic recipe for a memory analysis:

1) Create a memory statistics file from the application you want to analyze (Document Properties -> General -> Memory Statistics).
   This will export some memory statistics data to a tab separated file.

2) Create a new QlikView document in which you load the created file.

3) Create list boxes for the fields Class, Type, and Subtype.

To understand what these fields display, see the table below.

Class	Type	SubType
Database	Field	Symbols
	Table	Records
	Graph	Internal
Sheetobject	ListBox	Internal
	MultiBox	Internal
	PivotTableBox	Internal
	StraightTableBox	Internal
	TableBox	Internal
State Space	Field State	Selection State
	Table State	Internal
Variable	Variable	Internal

The **Class** field tells you whether the memory used is part of the internal database (data tables and symbol tables), the state space (the selections), the sheet objects (volatile structures to calculate the sheet objects), or a variable. The **Type** and **SubType** fields give you additional information about where memory is used.

- Create a drill-down group of the fields **Class**, **Type**, and **Subtype** named ">Type".

- Create a stacked bar chart with **Id** as first dimension, >**Type** as second dimension, and Sum(Bytes) as expression.

- Sort the chart descending according to y-value.

- Restrict the chart to show only the first 10 bars.

- You should now have a graph similar to the one below.

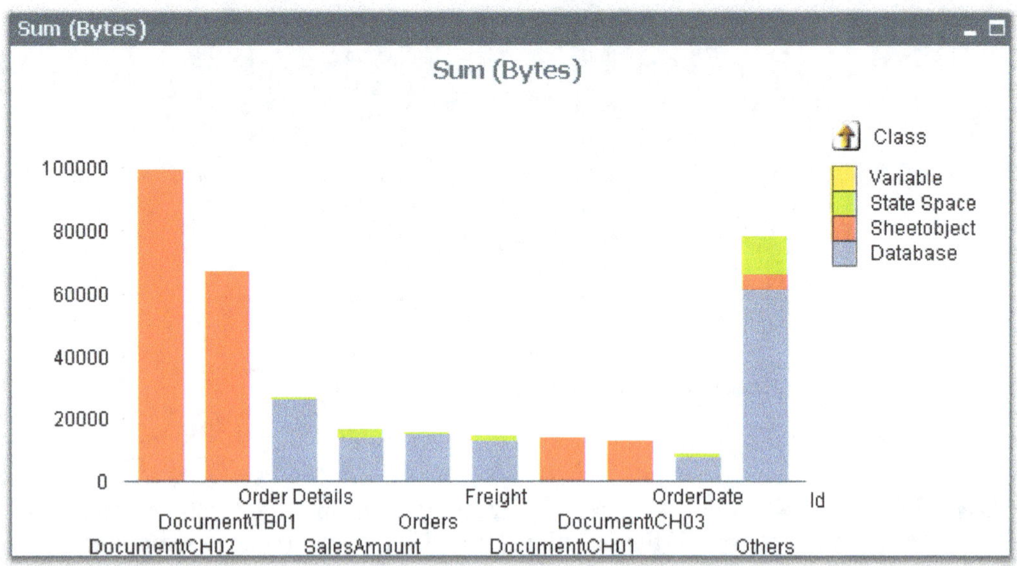

In this you can see which objects, tables, or fields are consuming memory in your application. The bars to the left are the ones that use a lot.

Now you can start to optimize!

If most of your memory consumption is made by sheet objects, look at them and see if there is anything you can do. Does this chart have too many dimensions? Is the expression too complex? Do I really need to sort this list box with a very large number of distinct values? Do I need to show it at all?

If most of your memory consumption is due to database symbols, look at whether you can use the autonumber function to make these symbol tables use less memory.

If most of your memory consumption is made by database tables, you might want to remove columns, or aggregate data. Or maybe realize that optimization isn't worth wile…

One small word of warning: The numbers in the memory statistics analysis should not be trusted too literally – they do not always describe the situation completely. For instance, if a calculation is cached, it will not show up in the memory usage. Further, if an object has not been opened yet, its memory consumption is unknown and will display as zero. But in spite of these shortcomings, the memory statistics function will most of the time help you find where memory is used.

In Qlik Sense, some of the corresponding functionality is found under the hub command "Evaluate performance":

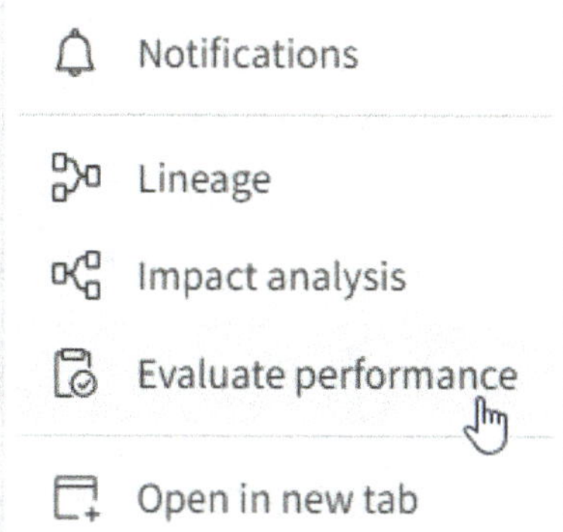

Totals in Charts

Originally posted in the Qlik Design Blog on Jun 24, 2014

The total in a chart is *not* the sum of the individual rows of the chart.

Instead, the total and the subtotals are calculated using the expression – but on a larger subset of the data than for the individual row.

Usually, the two methods result in the same numbers, but sometimes there is a huge difference. One example of this is if you use a non-linear function, e.g. Count(distinct …) as expression. The example below clearly shows this.

Source data

Country	State
Canada	Manitoba
Canada	Ontario
USA	Massachussetts
USA	New Jersey

Number of countries

State	Count(distinct Country)
Totals	2
Manitoba	1
Massachussetts	1
New Jersey	1
Ontario	1

The source data to the left assigns a country to each state, and if you count the number of countries per state using a Count(distinct Country), you will get the chart to the right. Note the "Totals" row: Each state belongs to one country only, and the total number of countries is 2, also if the chart has four rows.

A second example is if you have a many-to-many relationship in the data. In the example below, you have three products, each with a sales amount. But since each product can belong to several product groups, the sales amounts per product group will not add up: The total will be smaller than the sum of the individual rows, since there is an overlap between the product groups. The summation will be made correctly in the fact table, and not in the table in the user interface.

Source data: Dimensions

ProductGroup	Product
Dairy products	Ecological Milk
Dairy products	Standard Milk
Ecological products	Ecological Milk
Ecological products	Ecological Wine

Source data: Facts

Product	Amount
Ecological Milk	100
Ecological Wine	200
Standard Milk	200

Sum of sales amount

ProductGroup	Sum(Amount)
Totals	500
Dairy products	300
Ecological products	300

Another way to describe it would be to say that a specific dollar belongs to both product groups and would be counted twice if you just summed the rows.

In both cases, the Qlik engine will show the correct number, given the data. To sum the rows would be incorrect.

So, how does this affect you as an application developer?

Normally not very much. But it is good to be aware of it, and I would suggest the following:

- When you write your expression, you should have the total line in mind. Usually, the expression will automatically be right also for the individual rows.

- Always use an aggregation function. This will ensure that the Qlik engine is able to calculate the total correctly.

- If you want an average on the total line, you should most likely divide your expression with Count(distinct <Dim>). Then it will work both for the individual rows (where the count is 1) and the total lines. Example:

```
Sum( Amount ) / Count( distinct Customer )
```

- For cases where you want to show something completely different in the total line, you should consider the Dimensionality() function, that returns 0, 1, 2, … depending on whether the evaluation takes place in a total, subtotal or row. Example:

```
If(Dimensionality()=0, TotalExpression, RowExpression)
```

But If I *want* to show the sum of the individual rows? I don't want the expression to be calculated over a larger data set. What do I do then?

There are two ways to do this. First, you can use an Aggr() function as expression, where the outer aggregation is the function you want:

```
Sum( Aggr( OriginalExpression , Dimension ) )
```

This will work in all objects. Further, if you have a straight table, you have a setting in the object properties tab where you can specify the Total mode.

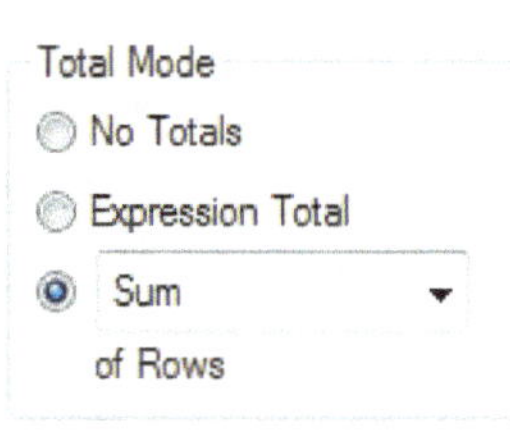

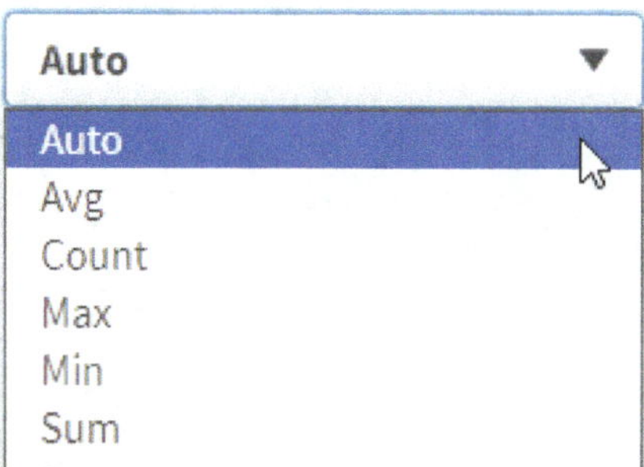

To the left, the QlikView setting, and to the right, the Qlik Sense setting.

Setting this to Sum will change the chart behavior to show exactly this: The sum of the rows.

12

Hypercubes and Aggregations

In all Business Intelligence tools there is a need to visualize the data. This is often done using a concept that is called a 'Multidimensional Cube' or a 'Hypercube'. This is a data-structure that calculates metrics along predefined dimensions.

In QlikView and Qlik Sense, most sheet objects are hypercubes: Bar charts, Pie charts, Pivot tables etc. Hence, 'hypercube', 'visualization', 'chart' and 'object' are usually different words for the same thing.

This chapter explains the properties and limitations of such objects.

Dimensions and Measures

Originally posted in the Qlik Design Blog on Mar 25, 2013

To make a chart in Qlik – or in any Business Intelligence tool, for that matter – you need to know what Dimensions and Measures are. But not all people have a clear picture of the difference between the two. So, this week's post will try to straighten out what's what.

When you make a chart, you should start by asking yourself "*What do I want to show?*" The answer is usually Sales, Quantity, or some other number. ***This is your Measure.*** In QlikView we have traditionally called this an "Expression", but "Measure" or "Metric" is really the correct word. (There are also expressions that are not measures, e.g. expressions used as labels, or as sort order definitions).

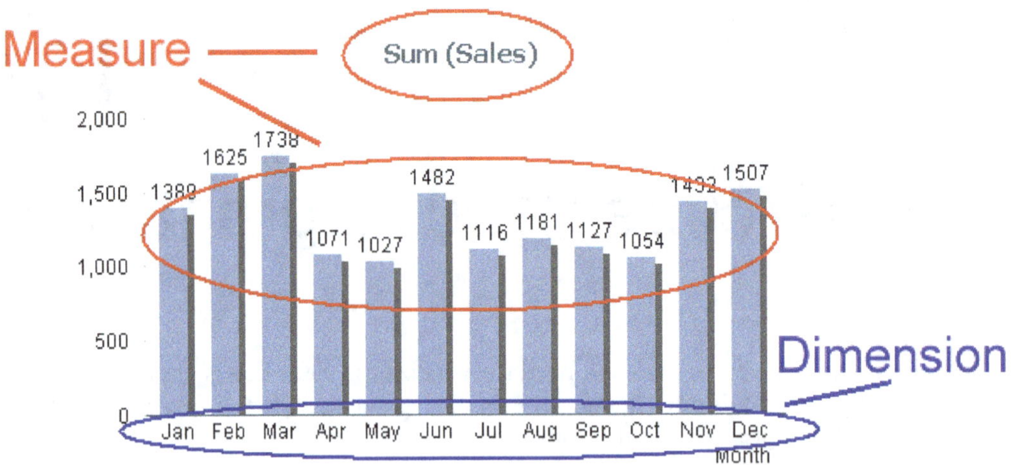

The second question you should ask yourself is *"How many times should this be calculated? Or: Per what do I want to show this measure?"* The answer could be once per month, once per customer, once per supplier or something similar. **This is your Dimension.**

In the bar chart, you have one bar per month, and a general rule is that you always have one data point per distinct dimensional value: But depending on which visualization form you have chosen, it can be a row (in a table), a point (in a scatter chart) or a slice (in a pie chart).

Measures

A database or a Qlik app can consist of thousands or millions of records that each contains a small piece of information. A Measure is simply a calculation that can be made over multiple records in this data set. The calculation always returns one single value that summarizes all relevant records. This type of calculation is called *aggregation*. There are several aggregation functions: Sum(), Count(), Min(), Max(), etc.

Examples:

- Each record contains a sales number. Then Sum(Sales) is a relevant measure that calculates the total sales value.

- Each record represents an order and **"OrderID"** is the key. Then Count(OrderID) is a relevant measure that calculates the number of orders.

A Measure can be used almost anywhere in a Qlik app: In charts, in text boxes, as label for objects, in gauges, etc. Typical measures are all KPIs, Revenue, Number of orders, Performance, Cost, Quantity, Gross Margin, etc.

Once again: A Measure is *always* based on an aggregation. Always!

Dimensions

Contrary to Measures, dimensions are descriptive attributes – typically textual fields or discrete numbers. A dimension is always an array of distinct values, and the measure will be calculated once per element in the array.

Examples:

- In a sales database, each transaction belongs to a specific customer. If the field "**Customer**" is used as dimension, the individual customers will be listed, and the measure will be calculated once per customer.
- The field "**Month**" is also an attribute that can be used as dimension. The possible months will then be listed, and the measure will be aggregates per month.

Typical dimensions are Customer, Product, Location, Supplier, Activity, Time, Color, Size, etc.

Like a For-Next loop

You can regard a chart like a For-Next loop: The Dimension is the loop variable; the calculations will be made once per dimensional value. So, the Dimension determines how many rows, bars, points, or slices the chart will have. The Measure is what is calculated in each loop.

Several Dimensions

If you have two or three dimensions in a chart, the dimensional values no longer form an array, but instead a matrix or a cube, where the measures are calculated once per cell in the cube.

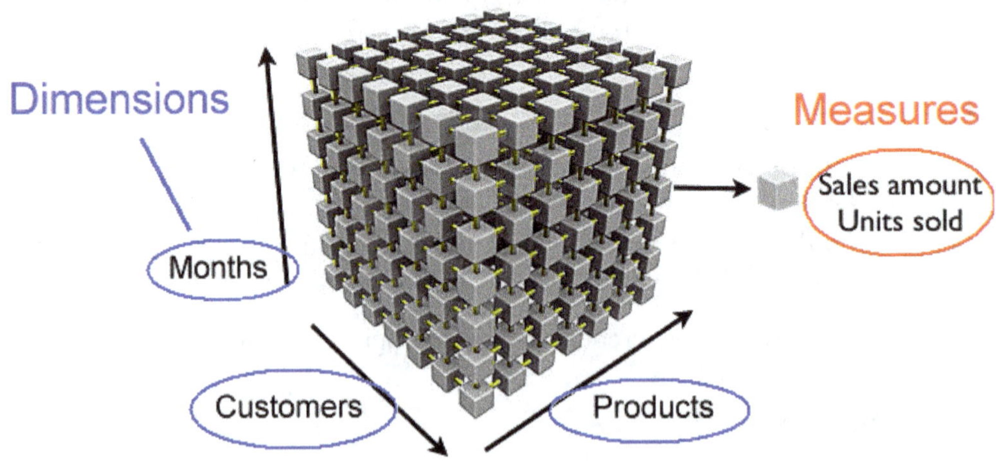

SQL

You can also compare a chart with an SQL SELECT statement. The GROUP BY symbols are the dimensions and the aggregations are the Measures.

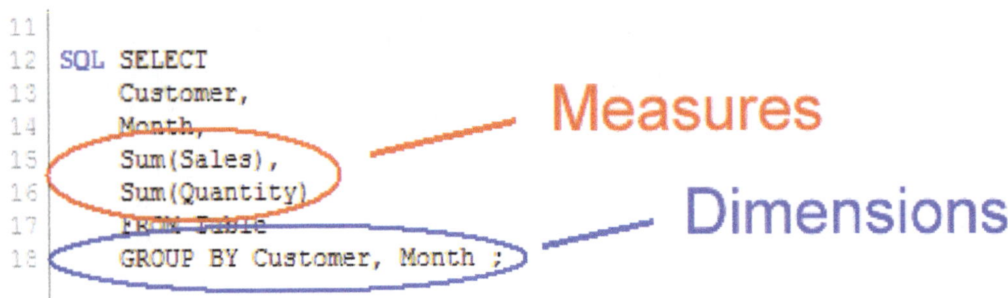

```
11
12  SQL SELECT
13      Customer,
14      Month,
15      Sum(Sales),
16      Sum(Quantity)
17      FROM Table
18      GROUP BY Customer, Month ;
```


With this, I hope that the difference between Dimensions and Measures is a little clearer.

The Only Function

Originally posted in the Qlik Design Blog on Aug 3, 2012

There is a little-known function in the Qlik engine that hardly anyone uses and that doesn't do very much, but still has a tremendous impact on many of the calculations made in many Qlik apps.

It is the *Only()* function.

It returns the value of a field – but only if there is just one possible value. Hence, if you have a one-to-one relationship between the chart dimension and the parameter, the Only() function returns the only possible value back. But if there are several values, it returns NULL.

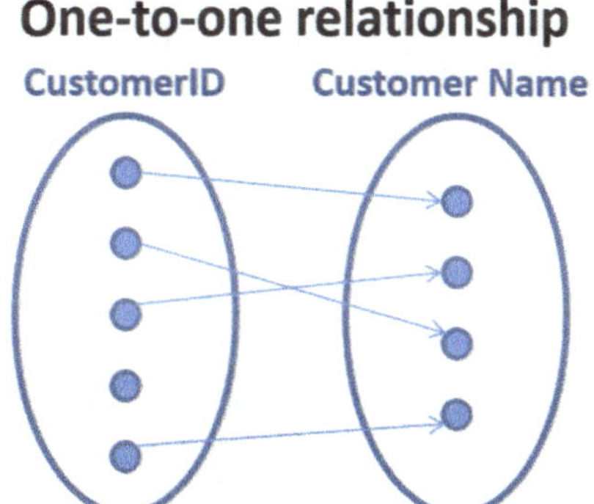

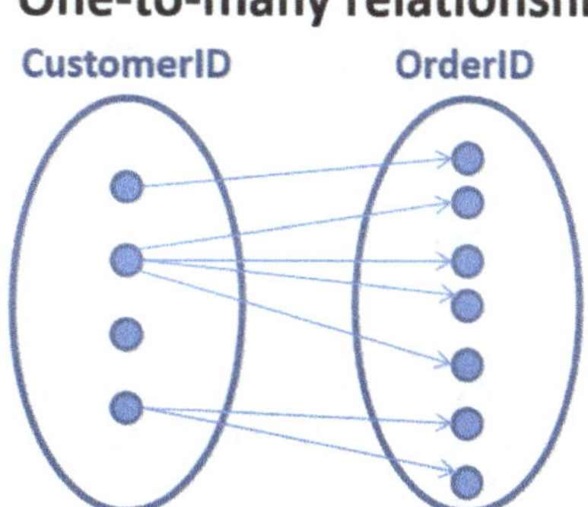

The Only() function is an aggregation function, which means that it uses many records as input and returns one value only. The Sum() and Count() functions are examples of other aggregation functions. Aggregations are used whenever you have a group of records and need to show only one value representing all records.

If you think about it, the Qlik engine uses aggregations in virtually *all* calculations: The expression in a chart, in a sort order, in a text box, in an advanced search and in a calculated label are all aggregations and *cannot be calculated* without involving an aggregation function.

But what if the user enters an expression that lacks an explicit aggregation function? What does the Qlik engine do then? For example, if the sort expression is set to "**Date**"? Or if there is an advanced search for customers using the expression "=Product='Shoe' " (the intent is to find customers that have bought this product)?

This is where the Only() function affects the calculation without the user knowing it; *if there is no explicit aggregation function in the expression, the Qlik engine uses the Only() function implicitly*. Hence, in the above cases, "Only(Date)" is used as sort expression and "=Only(Product)='Shoe' " is used as search criterion.

Sometimes the new expression returns a result that the user does not expect. Both the above examples will work fine for cases when there is only one possible value of **Date** or **Product**, but neither of them will work for cases when there is more than one value.

Therefore, when you write expressions you should always ask yourself which aggregation you want to use, or: *Which value do you want to use if there are several values?* If the answer is that you want to use NULL to represent several values, then you indeed want to use the Only() function and you can leave the expression as it is.

But if you do not know the answer, then you should probably think again. For numbers, you probably want to use Sum(), Avg() or Min() instead, and for strings you may want to use Only() or MinString().

For debugging you can always use something like, "Concat(distinct <Field>, ',')" and analyze the result.

But you should not leave your expression without an aggregation function.

It's all Aggregations

Originally posted in the Qlik Design Blog on Aug 6, 2013

I often see incorrect expressions being used in the QlikCommunity forum. Expressions that seem to work correctly – but really don't …

So, let me make this clear: *Calculations in the Qlik engine are aggregations.*

It doesn't matter if it is a measure in a chart, or a calculated object label, or a show condition for an object, or a calculated color, or an expression search – *all expressions in the user interface are evaluated as aggregations.* (Except calculated dimensions, and some search strings.)

This means that it is correct to use the Sum() function in an expression, since this is an aggregation function – a function that uses several records as input. But if you omit the aggregation function or use a scalar function only, e.g. RangeSum(), you can get an unexpected behavior.

Amount	Cost
7836	-1751
7900	-908
8646	-1093
9968	-569
1396	-304
335	-358
5130	-94

RangeSum(Amount, Cost)

Sum(Amount)

Basically, *all field references should be wrapped in an aggregation function*. The Aggr() function and some constructions using the total qualifier can even have several layers of aggregations.

But if the created expression does not contain an aggregation function, and uses naked field references, the expression is ill-formed and potentially incorrect.

Examples:

```
Sum  ( Amount  )
Count( OrderID )
```

These are both correct aggregations. **Amount** is wrapped in the Sum() function which will sum several records of the field Amount. **OrderID** is wrapped in the Count() function, which will count the records where **OrderID** has a value.

```
Only( OrderID )
```

This is also a correct aggregation. **OrderID** is wrapped in the Only() function, which will return the **OrderID** if there is only one value, otherwise NULL.

```
OrderID
```

A single field reference is not an aggregation, so this is an ill-formed expression. But the Qlik engine will not throw an error. Instead it will use the Only() function to interpret the field reference. I.e., if there is only one value, this value will be used. But if there are several possible values, NULL will be used. So, it depends on the circumstances whether an expression without aggregation function is correct or not.

```
If(Year=Year(Today()), Sum(Amount), -1*Sum(Amount))
```

Here, the **Amount** is correctly wrapped in the Sum() function. But the field reference "**Year**" in the first parameter of the if() function, the condition, is not. Hence, this is an ill-formed expression. If it is used in a place where there are several possible **Years**, the naked field reference will evaluate to NULL and the condition will be evaluated as FALSE, which is not what you want. Instead, you probably want to wrap the **Year** in the Min() or Max() function.

```
ProductGroup= 'Shoes'
IsNull(ProductGroup)
```

These expressions can both be used as show conditions or as advanced searches. However, since there are no aggregation functions, the expressions are ill-formed. If you want to test whether there exists Shoes or NULL values among the field values, you probably want to use one of the following instead:

```
Count({<ProductGroup={'Shoes'}>} ProductGroup)) > 0
NullCount(ProductGroup) > 0
```

Conclusions:

- An aggregation function is a function that returns a single value describing some property of several records in the data.

- All UI expressions, except calculated dimensions and most search strings, are evaluated as aggregations.

- All field references in expressions must be wrapped in an aggregation function. If they are not, the Qlik engine will use the Only() function.

The Aggregation Scope

Originally posted in the Qlik Design Blog on Sep 9, 2013

When a calculation is made in a Qlik app session, it always involves an aggregation over the relevant data records. But which records are relevant? What is *the scope of the aggregation*?

This seems like a simple question, but there are in fact quite a few things that could be said about it.

Normally, there are two different restrictions that together determine which records are relevant: *The Selection*, and – if the formula is found in a chart – *the Dimensional value*. The aggregation scope is what remains after both these restrictions have been taken into consideration.

But not always…

There are ways to define your own aggregation scope: This is needed in advanced calculations where you want the aggregation to disregard one of the two restrictions. A very common case is when you want to calculate a ratio between a chosen number and the corresponding total number, i.e. a relative share of something.

```
Sum( Amount ) / Sum( total Amount )
```

In other words: If you use the total qualifier inside your aggregation function, you have redefined the aggregation scope. The denominator will disregard the dimensional value and calculate the sum of all possible values. So, the above formula will sum up to 100% in the chart.

Dim	Sum(Number)	Sum(total Number)	Sum(Number) / Sum(total Number)
A	66	826	8%
B	264	826	32%
C	496	826	60%
Total	**826**	**826**	**100%**

However, there is a second way to calculate percentages. Instead, you may want to disregard the selection in order to make a comparison with all data before any selection. Then you should not use the total qualifier; you should instead use Set analysis:

```
Sum( Amount ) / Sum( {1} Amount )
```

Using Set analysis, you will redefine the Selection scope. The set definition {1} denotes the set of all records in the document; hence the calculated percentages will be the ratio between the current selection and all data in the document, split up for the different dimensional values.

Dim	Sum(Number)	Sum({1} Number)	Sum(Number) / Sum({1} Number)
A	66	240	28%
B	264	776	34%
C	496	1457	34%
Total	**826**	**2473**	**33%**

In other words: by using the total qualifier and set analysis inside an aggregation function, you can re-define the aggregation scope.

- To disregard the dimensional grouping – Use the Total qualifier
- To disregard the selection – Use Set Analysis

The above cases are just the basic examples. The total qualifier can be qualified further to define a subset based on any combination of existing dimensions, and the Set analysis can be extended to specify not just "Current selection" and "All data", but any possible selection.

And of course, the total qualifier can be combined with Set analysis.

```
Sum( {SetExpression} total Amount )
```

A final comment: If an aggregation is made in a place where there is no dimension (a gauge, text box, show condition, etc.), only the restriction by selection is made. But if it is made inside a chart or an Aggr() function, both restrictions are made. So, in these places it could be relevant to use the total qualifier.

Use Aggregation Functions!

Originally posted in the Qlik Design Blog on Jun 17, 2014

On the discussion forum, I often see people posting questions around expressions that don't work. When looking at the descriptions, I usually find that the reason is that the expressions lack aggregation functions. So, here is a suggestion …

Always use an aggregation function in your expression.

The reason is that a field reference in an expression always means an array of values. Which in turn means that you must enclose it in an aggregation function to make it collapse into one value:

```
OrderDate            // An array of values
Max(OrderDate)       // A single value
```

If you don't use an aggregation function, the Qlik engine will use the Only() function. Hence, if the field reference returns several values, the Qlik engine will interpret it as NULL, and the expression will not be evaluated the way you want it to.

Example 1: Use of the If() function:

If() functions are often used for conditional aggregations:

```
If( OrderDate >= vReferenceDate, Sum(Amount) )
```

At first glance, this expression may look correct: For dates after a reference date, the field **Amount** should be summed. Right?

Wrong.

OrderDate is a naked field reference: It does not have an aggregation function. Hence, it is an array, possibly with several values, and if so, evaluates to NULL. If you are lucky, there is only one date per dimensional value in your chart, and the expression will calculate fine. However, the Qlik engine will probably not be able to calculate the expression for the subtotals in the chart, since there for those exists several dates.

A correct expression that always works should use a Min() or some other aggregation function in the first parameter of the If() function:

```
If( Min(OrderDate) >= vReferenceDate, Sum(Amount) )
```

Or, alternatively, the If() function could be put inside the Sum() function:

```
Sum( If(OrderDate >= vReferenceDate, Amount) )
```

In the first of the two expressions, the If() function will be evaluated once per dimensional value; in the second once per row in the raw data. The results are slightly different, but both return an answer, as opposed to the original expression. The picture below shows the difference between the expressions, using 2013-02-01 as reference date.

Sum(Amount)

Quarter	Sum(Amount)	If(OrderDate>=vReferenceDate, Sum(Amount))	If(Min(OrderDate)>=vReferenceDate, Sum(Amount))	Sum(If(OrderDate>=vReferenceDate, Amount))
Q4 2012	23758	-	-	0
Q1 2013	21528	-	-	15353
Q2 2013	23422	-	23422	23422
Q3 2013	21908	-	21908	21908

Example 2: Sort by expression:

The expression used to sort the dimensional values in a chart is also an aggregation. Often you don't think about this since you choose an expression that returns just one value per dimensional value, and then a naked field reference works fine.

But sometimes this still doesn't work…

For example, say that you want to show support cases in a CRM system. You create a chart with the support case as dimension and some measure as expression. Of course, you want to sort the support cases chronologically, so you use "Sort by Expression" and as expression you choose

```
[Opening Date]
```

This will work in most cases. However, some CRM systems allow you to re-open a support case, hence assigning two opening dates to one single support case. For these cases, the above expression will not work.

Instead, you should always ask yourself which function to use, should there be two values. The answer is usually Sum(), Avg(), Min() or Max(). In the above case, you should probably use one of the two following

```
Min( [Opening Date] )
Max( [Opening Date] )
```

depending on whether you want to use the first or last date.

Bottom line: Use aggregation functions, not just in your chart measures, but also in sort expressions, labels, show conditions, calculation conditions, text boxes, sheet names and searches.

Conditional Aggregations

Originally posted in the Qlik Design Blog on Jul 1, 2014

Often you need to create conditional aggregations in the Qlik app, e.g. when you want to create a graph that shows this year's numbers only, also if there are several years possible.

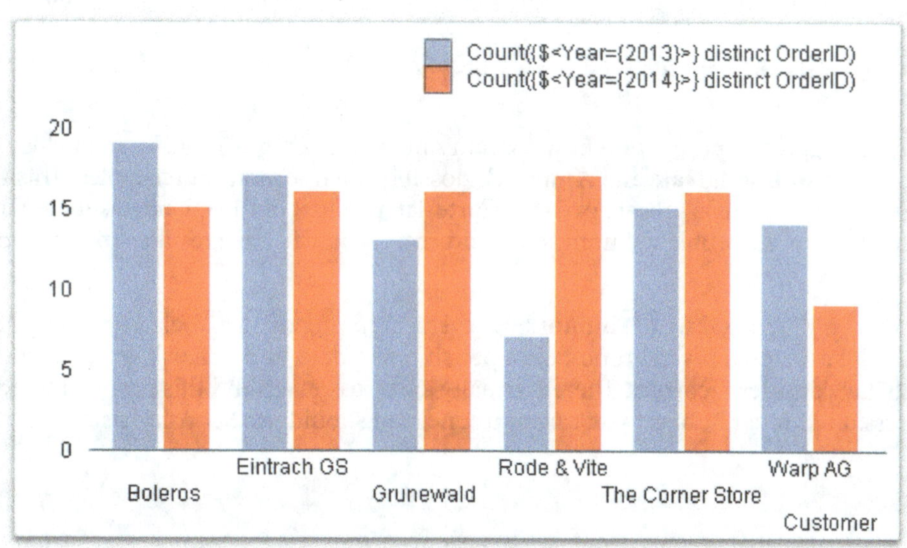

Hypercubes and Aggregations

There are basically three ways to do this:

- A conditional expression outside the aggregation function, e.g.

```
If( <Condition> , Sum( <Expression> ))
```

- A conditional expression inside the aggregation function, e.g.

```
Sum(If( <Condition> , <Expression> ))
```

- Set Analysis, e.g.

```
Sum( {SetExpression} <Expression> )
```

If you choose a conditional expression outside the aggregation function, you will have a condition that is evaluated once per dimensional value. Further, all three parameters of the If() function are aggregations, so you need to use aggregation functions, also in the condition, otherwise the expression will not be evaluated the way you want to.

So – don't use naked field references!

```
If(    ShippingDate >= vReferenceDate, Sum(Amount)) // Incorrect !
If(Min(ShippingDate)>= vReferenceDate, Sum(Amount)) // Correct
```

If you instead put the conditional expression inside the aggregation function, you will have a very different situation: First, the condition will be evaluated on the record level of the source data. In other words: You may get performance problems if you have large data amounts.

```
Sum(If(ShippingDate >= vReferenceDate, Amount)) // Correct, but slow
```

Secondly, the aggregation function now contains an expression based on several fields (in the above example, **ShippingDate** and **Amount**), possibly from several source tables. This means that the Qlik engine will aggregate over the Cartesian product of the included source tables. Normally this is not a problem, but in some odd cases, you will have results different from what you expect.

For instance, if the record with **Amount** has several shipping dates associated with it, the amount will be counted several times, once per shipping date, and you will get a result that you probably consider incorrect. There is usually a way to get around this problem by writing the expression differently, but if you can't find one, you should use Set Analysis instead.

The conditional expression can be written in several ways:

```
Sum(If( Field = 'string', Amount ))      // String comparison
Sum(If( Field = number,   Amount ))      // Numeric comparison
Sum(If( Flag,             Amount ))      // Boolean condition
Sum(    Flag           * Amount  )       // Multiplication
```

The two first examples contain comparisons, whereas the two last contain flags – Boolean fields created in the script, e.g. **IsThisYear**, that have either 0 or 1 as value. All four ways work fine, but I would recommend avoiding comparisons altogether. Use flags instead. See e.g. Year-over-Year Comparisons for more on flags.

Finally, you can choose to use Set Analysis. This is slightly different from other conditional expressions in that it uses the Qlik selection metaphor for the analysis: First, the Set Expression is interpreted as a selection, whereupon the aggregation is evaluated given this selection.

```
Sum( {$<ShippingDate = {">='$(vReferenceDate)'"}>} Amount )
Sum( {$<IsThisYear   = {1}>}                        Amount )
```

This means that Set Analysis often is faster than using a conditional expression inside the aggregation. It also means that it calculates what you expect, as opposed to a case where an inside condition creates an unwanted Cartesian product.

However, a drawback with the Set Analysis is that it needs to be performed *before* the Qlik engine performs the aggregation – you cannot have a Set Expression that evaluates to different values for different rows. The work-around is to calculate the condition in the script and store it in a flag.

Bottom line: Define flags in the script. And use Set Analysis.

Performance of Conditional Aggregations

Originally posted in the Qlik Design Blog on Jul 8, 2014

In my previous post I compared different methods for making Conditional Aggregations. In it, I claimed that Set Analysis often is faster than other methods, like an If()-function or a multiplication with a flag.

Also, in a recent discussion on the forum performance benefits of the different methods are discussed, and the multiplication method is favored by some.

So, I decided to make my own test.

The main conclusion from my test is that Set Analysis is by far the most performant way to make a conditional aggregation – in the cases when you have a lot of data and *need the performance*. The chart below shows the average chart calculation time for the five different ways to make a conditional aggregation in a situation where you have a large amount of data.

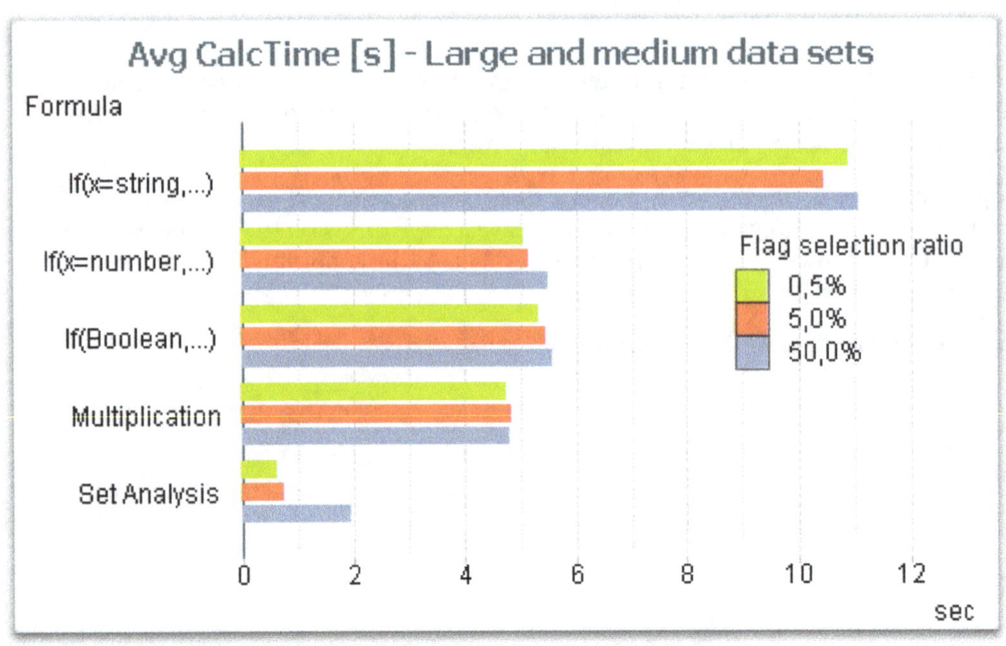

From this chart, you can draw several conclusions:

- Set Analysis is the fastest alternative for large data sets.

- Set Analysis is better if the selection ratio is small (the sub-set of data that the condition picks out), since the following aggregation runs over a much smaller number of rows. This is in sharp contrast to the other methods where the selection ratio hardly affects the result.

- The three methods in the middle (numeric comparison as condition, Boolean flag as condition and multiplication) are roughly the same from a performance perspective.

- An If()-function with a string comparison is by far the worst choice.

But it is not a clear-cut case: If you instead make the same measurements with a smaller data set, Set Analysis is *not* the most efficient method. The chart below shows the result for a smaller data amount. Note that even though the data amount still is considerable (1M records), it is small enough for all response times to be under a second, whereas they in most cases are an order of magnitude larger in the above graph.

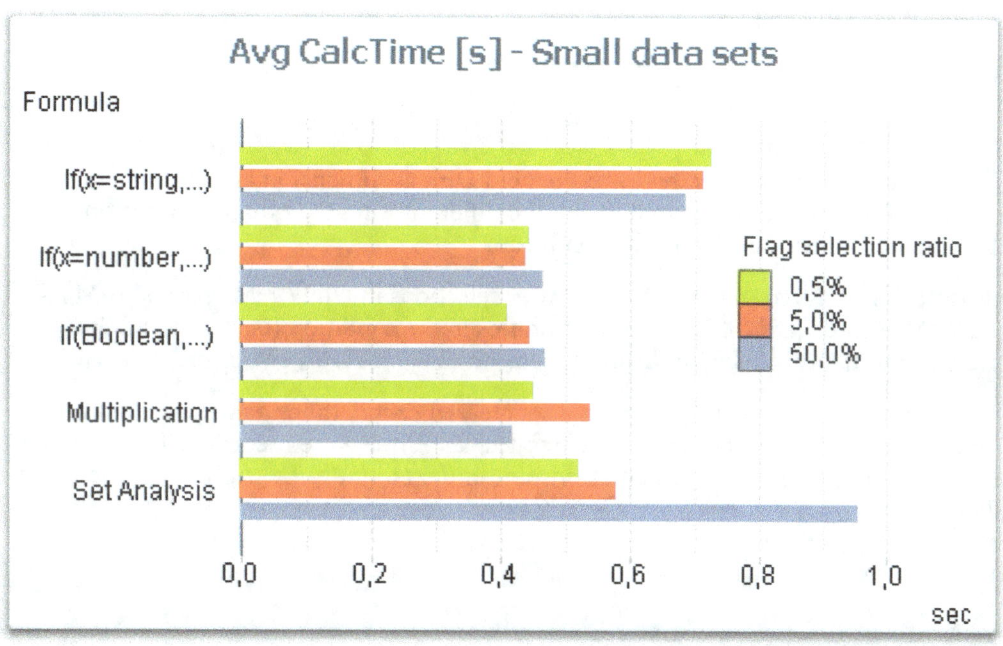

The reason is that there is an overhead in Set Analysis, that has to be performed independently of whether the data amount is large or not. So, for small data amounts, the performance gain in the aggregation is not large enough to cover the overhead.

The bottom line is that Set Analysis is the method you should use for large data amounts. For smaller data amounts, it doesn't really matter which method you choose: They are all fast enough.

About the test:

The test was made on my dual-core laptop with 16GB of memory. The data model consisted of three tables: one fact table and two dimension tables. The fact table contained 100 million records.

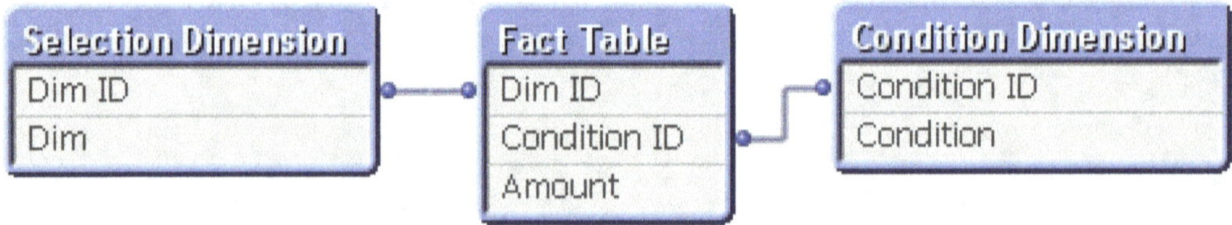

The calculation time of a pivot table with the field **Dim** as dimension and the sum of **Amount** as expression was measured, using the different ways to code the condition. The field **Condition** was used as flag in the condition.

The measurement was repeated for different user selections in Dim (99M records, 10M records and 1M records), for different selection ratios in the condition (0.5%, 5% and 50%), and for different cardinality in the **Condition** dimension (1000 records, 1M records).

The measurements were made starting with a cleared cache, then making a series of different selections in the field **Dim** of which the last three were recorded. This way the cache was populated with basic calculations and indexes, but not with the specific chart calculation.

13
Expressions

Calculations can be made in many places: As measures, as calculated colors, as show conditions, and as sort parameters. This chapter is about how to write such expressions.

Aggregations and Function Classes

Originally posted in the Qlik Design Blog on May 20, 2014

A typical Qlik application may have one million records in the data, one hundred rows in a pivot table and a single number, a KPI, in a gauge or text box. Although different in magnitudes, all three numbers may still represent *all data*, i.e. data without any filter applied. The numbers are just different aggregation levels.

There are many functions in the Qlik engine that can help you write the necessary formulae to calculate aggregated metrics. Some will collapse many records into one value, others will not. Today I will write about the different function classes, and how you can combine them.

- The *Scalar Functions* constitute the first class. Typical for these is that they are one-to-one functions, i.e. they take a single value as parameter and return a single value (of the dual data type). The input may still be an array of values, and if so, the output is an array of the same cardinality. Examples: Left(), If(), Num(), Date(), Year(), Subfield(), etc.

  $$1 \rightarrow 1$$

- The *Aggregation Functions* constitute the second class. These are many-to-one functions, i.e. they use the values from many records as input and collapse these into one single value that summarizes all records. Examples: Sum(), Count(), Avg(), Min(), Only(), Concat(), etc.

  $$N \rightarrow 1$$

Aggregation functions are special: You *must* use one if you want to collapse several records into one number – which means that you need them in pretty much *any* formula in a Qlik app: In Chart expressions, in Text boxes, in Labels, etc. If you don't write an aggregation function in your expression, the Qlik engine will assign one for you: It will use the Only() function.

Scalar functions can be used both inside and outside the aggregation function:

```
Date( Min( Date )
Money( Sum( If( Group='A', Amount ) ) )
```

- Scalar function
- Aggregation function

There is one restriction: You can normally not use an aggregation function inside another aggregation function. Hence, you usually need every field reference to be wrapped in *exactly* one aggregation function.

- The ***Array Functions*** constitute the third class. Both ValueList() and ValueLoop() are array functions, but the most important function in the group is the Aggr() function. It is – despite its name – not an aggregation function. It is a many-to-many function, rather like a tensor or a matrix in mathematics. It converts a table with N records to a table with M records. In other words: It returns an array of values. Regard it as a virtual straight table with one measure and one or several dimensions.

$$N \longrightarrow M$$

Syntactically, the Array functions are similar to field references: They are all arrays of values; they can be used as dimensions; and they can be used as measures, when wrapped in an aggregation function.

Most expressions in a Qlik app are like measures, and demand that you write your expression so that it returns one single value. This means that you must wrap the Aggr() function in an aggregation function to get a meaningful result. This means that you have two aggregation steps: one nested in the other. The only exception is if you use the Aggr() function to define a calculated dimension or field.

```
Avg( Aggr( Sum( Amount ), Month ) )
Aggr( Only( {SetExpression} Customer ), Customer ) )
```

- Aggregation function
- Field or Aggr function

Charts complicate the matters slightly: A chart is like a For-Next loop where the number of distinct dimension values determines the number of loops. In each loop, the expression must return one value only, and this is the value used for the bar/slice/pivot table row.

However, sometimes you need values from other rows in the chart, and it could even be that you need values from several rows. To solve this, there are two additional classes of functions that should be used together:

- The ***Range Creation Functions*** are chart inter-record functions that return values fetched from specific other rows in the chart. These can be made to return several values, i.e. an array of values. Hence, for a specific row, the function can return an array of values. These functions are only meaningful inside a chart or Aggr() function. Examples: Above(), Below(), Top(), etc.

$$1(N) \rightarrow N$$

- The ***Range Aggregation Functions*** are functions that can collapse a range function array into one single value. Examples: RangeSum(), RangeMin(), RangeMax(), etc.

$$N \rightarrow 1$$

Example of a twelve-month accumulation:

RangeSum(Above(Sum(Amount), 0, 12))

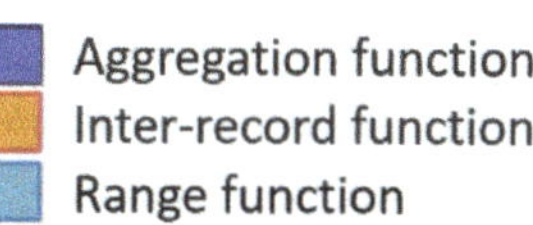

Finally, there is another class of functions where other rows in the chart are needed for the calculation:

- The ***Relational Functions*** are chart inter record functions that use *all* records in the chart to calculate a property that is specific to the current row in the chart. A typical example is the rank, something that is specific to the current row, but cannot be calculated without knowledge of how this row relates to all other rows in the chart. Examples: Rank(), KMeans2D(), STL_Trend(), etc.

$$1(N) \rightarrow 1$$

Bottom line: Know your functions. It will help you write correct expressions.

Calculated Dimensions

Originally posted in the Qlik Design Blog on Apr 8, 2014

To make a chart in a Qlik app – or in any Business Intelligence tool, for that matter – you need to have one or several dimensions; entities with discrete values that you use as grouping symbols. But where should you define these dimensions: In the script or in the object where the dimension is used?

In most cases, you will use an existing field as dimension, i.e. an attribute that exists in the source data. In such a case, the answer to the above question is easy: Just make sure to load the field in the script, and you're done.

But in some cases, you want to use derived attributes: Attributes that do not exist in the source data but one way or another can be calculated from existing fields.

One example is the fields of the Master Calendar: Year, Month, etc. These can all be derived from a date found in the source data:

```
Month(Date) as Month,
Year (Date) as Year,
```

A more advanced example is if you want to classify or rank a field. The following expression returns 'A' for the 10 best customers and a 'B' for the rest:

```
=If(Aggr(Rank(Sum(Amount)),Customer)<=10,'A','B')
```

For such fields, the above question is very relevant: Should they be calculated in the script and saved as fields, or should they be calculated on the fly in a sheet object?

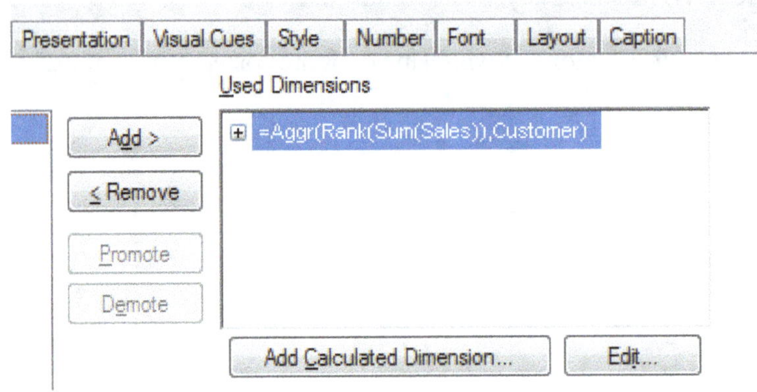

There are pros and cons with both approaches: A field calculated in the script is calculated once and for all, so it does not need to be re-calculated every time the user clicks. Hence, response times will be slightly shorter if the field is calculated in the script.

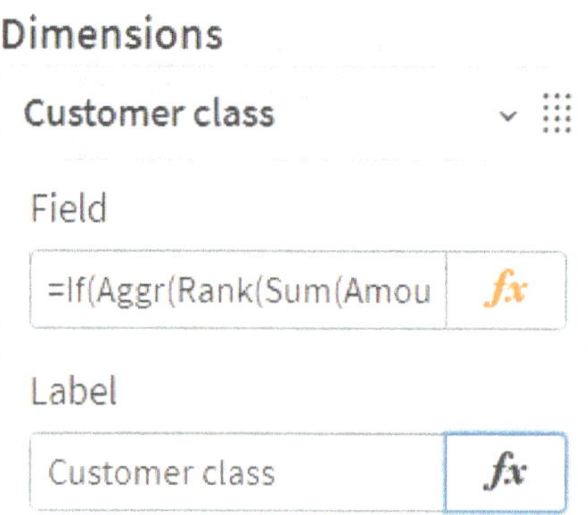

On the other hand, in some cases you *want* the field to be re-calculated every time the user clicks. A good example is the classification using Rank() above. Most likely you want this field to depend on the selection made: If you have selected a product, you want to see the classification of the customers given this selection. Such a number is in its nature dynamic and should be calculated every time the user clicks.

The key is whether the calculated field should be static or dynamic. The field **Month** is static: A specific date always belongs to the same month, irrespective of what the user has selected. As opposed to a classification or a rank where the calculation usually should be dynamic since the result potentially could change every time the user clicks.

Bottom line is that dynamic fields must be calculated in the chart or the list box. But for static fields it is better if they are calculated in the script, since precious CPU-time otherwise will be unnecessarily spent every time the user clicks.

Calculated Fields

Originally posted in the Qlik Design Blog on Apr 21, 2020

Calculated fields are often created in the script and stored under new aliases. But you can also create them in the user interface. What are the pros and cons of the two methods? And how are the user interface fields calculated?

Normally, new fields are created in the script and stored as additional columns in the data model. Just write your expression inside a Load statement and you're done:

```
Year    (Date) as Year    ,
Month   (Date) as Month   ,
Week    (Date) as Week    ,
WeekDay(Date) as WeekDay,
```

But you can also do the same thing in the user interface, and then it could look like this:

So, which way should you do it?

Generally, I would say that you should put as much as possible in the script. In most cases, it is far better to have these calculations pre-made, so that they do not have to be calculated at run-time, i.e. when the user clicks.

The Qlik engine has two fundamentally different ways to calculate such expressions: As "Calculated dimension" or as "Field-on-the-fly". The engine automatically decides how a specific calculation should be made, depending on the expression.

Fields-on-the-fly

This method was introduced in one of the early versions of Qlik Sense. As the expression is evaluated, the engine creates an additional column *in the data model*, with a corresponding symbol table. Just as for a real field, the selection is stored in state vectors linked to this column.

In the picture below you can see a table dimension defined as "=Year(Date)", which results in four rows.

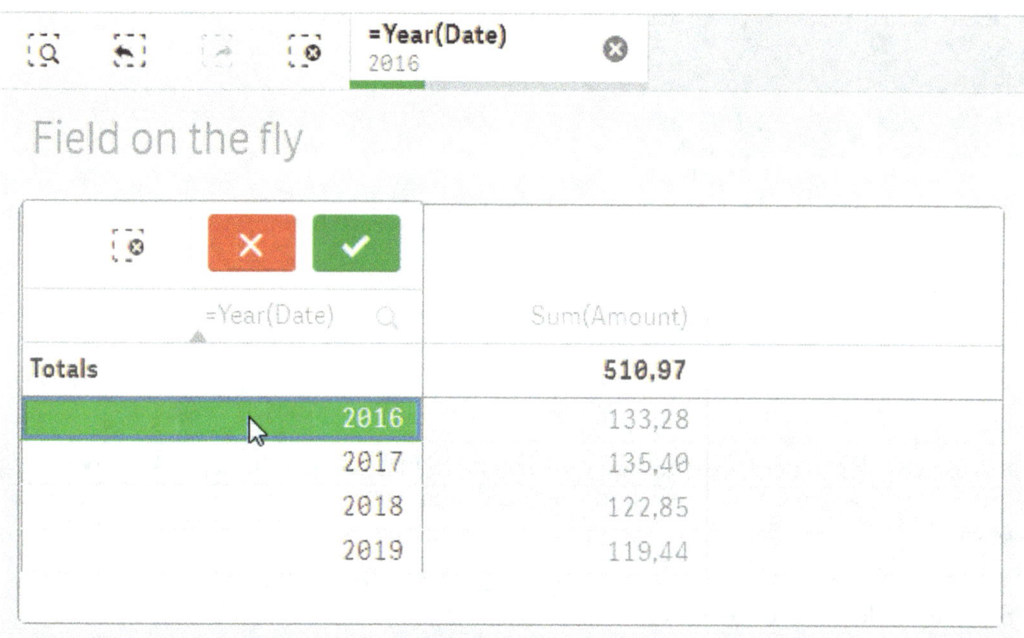

Now look at the selection bar: When a selection is made, the corresponding year is selected in the Field-on-the-fly called "**=Year(Date)**" – a field that does not exist in the original data model. And in the selection bar you can see that the selection is indeed stored in this "virtual" field, and not in the Date field.

Calculated dimensions

This is the old-fashioned way, and this is how QlikView still today does it. In the example below, the table dimension is "**=Aggr(Year(Date),Date)**" and it also results in four rows. Logically, this expression is equivalent to the above one.

But here the selection is instead made in the underlying field: in the **Date** field.

Calculated dimension

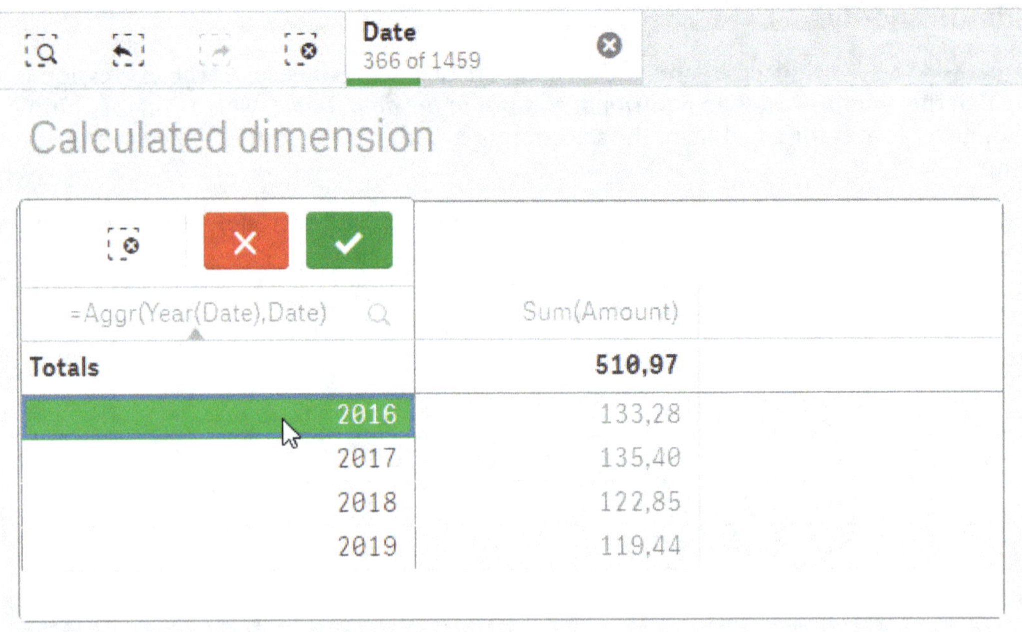

It is always possible to create a Calculated dimension, no matter what the expression looks like. But the same is not true for Fields-on-the-fly. There are limitations to when they can be generated:

- The expression must be based on one single field only, or on multiple non-key fields from the same table in the data model

- The expression cannot depend on the selection state, e.g. through the GetSelectedCount() function

- The expression cannot contain an Aggr() function

If a Field-on-the-fly cannot be generated, the expression will be evaluated as a Calculated dimension instead.

Performance

Both Calculated dimensions and Fields-on-the-fly can cause performance problems, so it is a good idea to consider moving them to the script instead. Fields-on-the-fly can always be moved to the script.

For Fields-on-the-fly, the performance problems become especially severe if the underlying field has many distinct values. A common example is when calendar functions like Year() and Month() are used on a timestamp with millions of distinct values, rather than on a date with fewer values. Further, since Fields-on-the-fly are added to the data model, and the hash of the data model is used in the ID of the cache entry, Fields-on-the-fly can prevent the cache from being re-used properly.

To improve the performance, Master dimensions containing Fields-on-the-fly are now (since Nov 2019) calculated already when the first user opens the app, something which can increase the time it takes to open a document. On the other hand, this will improve the response time considerably in the analysis phase, as well as mitigate some cache problems, so we are confident that this is the correct decision. Hence, put your Fields-on-the-fly in the Master dimensions!

Should you want to tweak the behavior of the engine, you can always try the following:

- Using "UseAutoFieldOnTheFly=0" in Settings.ini will disable Fields-on-the-fly for all documents served by the engine
- Using "Set QlikInternalDisableFotfMode=1;" in the script will disable Fields-on-fly in the app
- Using "Set QlikInternalDisableFotfPregen =1;" in the script will prevent Fields-on-fly from being pre-calculated when the app is opened
- Wrapping the expression in "=CalcDim(…)" will force it to be a Calculated dimension

But most importantly – don't use a timestamp to create your calendar! Use a date instead:

```
Date(Floor( TimeStamp )) as Date,
```

Good luck!

Count or Count distinct?

Originally posted in the Qlik Design Blog on May 13, 2014

When counting something in a Qlik app, you should use the Count() aggregation function. But – should you use Count or Count distinct?

Although very similar, the two constructions return completely different results. And often the wrong one is used …

So, let me start by clarifying what the two constructions really count:

- **Count(<expression>)** counts the number of records in the data.
- **Count(distinct <expression>)** counts the number of distinct values of the expression.

Only instances where the expression isn't NULL are included. Further, if the expression contains references to more than one field, an n-tuple (a temporary table) is created from the cross product of the constituent fields, and the count is performed in the n-tuple instead of in the data table.

This means that in the common case – when the <expression> is a simple field reference – the Count(…) is equivalent to the number of rows in the data table, whereas the Count(distinct …) is equivalent to the number of distinct values in the field or number of rows in the symbol table. Read more about data tables and symbol tables in "Symbol Tables and Bit-Stuffed Pointers".

An example: You have a fact table and you want to count the number of orders. Then Count(OrderID) will return the number of records in the fact table, which often is a number larger than the number of orders, since one order usually has several order lines. In this case you probably want to count the number of unique Order IDs, and should most likely choose Count(distinct OrderID) instead.

So, Count(OrderID) does not count the orders!

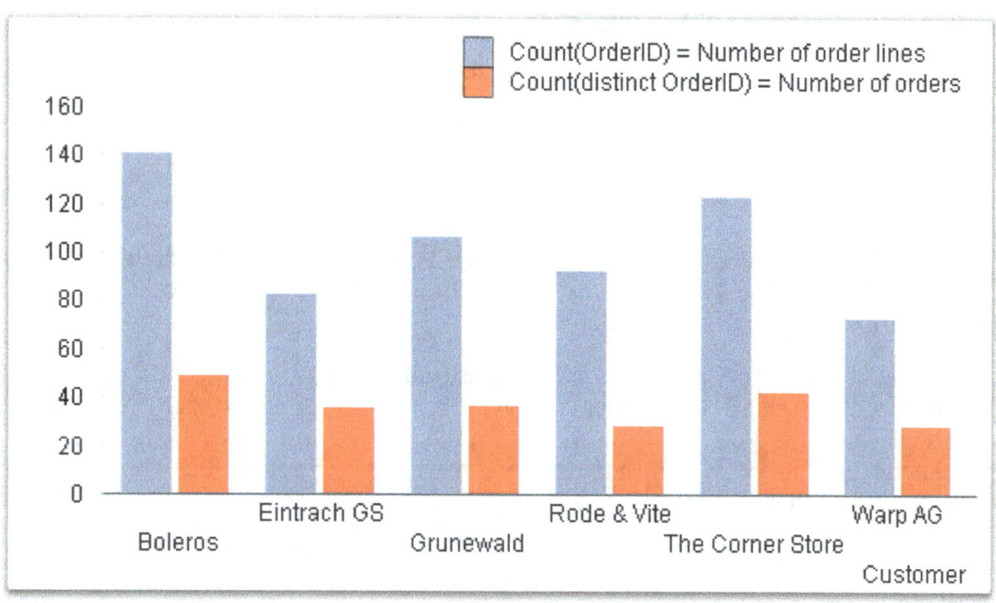

Another trap I have seen people fall into, is when a *key field* is used as parameter in the Count() function. If the distinct clause is used, there is no problem: The number of distinct values is well defined also for key fields. But if you omit the distinct clause, the number is ***not*** well defined: In which data table should the Qlik engine count the number of records? There are several possible source tables since the field is a key.

The Count(Key) will however return a number, but this number is not always the number you want. Sometimes it will be the count from the "wrong" table. So I would recommend that you never use a Count() function on a key field, unless you use the distinct clause.

Otherwise, the work-around for using the Count() function (without the distinct clause) on a key field, is the create a copy of this field (in the load script) in the table where you want to count the records, and use this field inside the Count() instead of the key field.

Bottom line: For key fields, either use the distinct clause, or the above work-around.

Average – Which average?

Originally posted in the Qlik Design Blog on Jul 30, 2013

If you want to display an average number of something in a Qlik app, you should use the Avg() function, right?

Wrong.

Yes, there is an Avg() function that returns the average value, but – this is usually not the value that you are looking for. The Avg() function returns the average *transactional* value, whereas you probably are looking for a larger amount.

For example, let's say that you have an orders database where the grain – the most atomic level – of the data is the *Order Line*. Each order can have several order lines and each order line has an amount. Then, the Avg() function will return the average order line amount, which is utterly uninteresting. No, you are most likely more interested in questions like "How much do we sell *per month*, on the average?"

In other words – a calculation of an average has an implicit internal grouping entity; the average per month, per day, per order, per delivery or something else. You can look at it as a two-step aggregation:

1) Sum all the amounts – per each value of the internal grouping entity (e.g. month, day, order or delivery)

2) Calculate the average of the sums from previous bullet

In a Qlik app, you would calculate the average monthly sales value in one of the two following ways:

```
Sum( Amount ) / Count( distinct Month )
Avg( Aggr( Sum(Amount), Month ) )
```

… and similarly for orders, days or deliveries. Use of the Aggr() function will work, but it is not as fast as the first option, and should therefore be avoided.

Sometimes there are several internal grouping entities. You may for instance want to show the average monthly sales value per customer, i.e. you want to use both month and customer as grouping entity. Then you should use one of the following expressions:

```
Sum( Amount ) / Count( distinct Month & '|' & Customer )
Avg( Aggr( Sum(Amount), Month, Customer ) )
```

The Count() aggregation with a string concatenation will find every unique combination of month and customer.

Note that the internal grouping entity has nothing to do with the dimension you choose to use when you display it. It would make perfect sense to show the above number using Product as the only dimension, as shown in the graph below. Hence, the internal grouping entity is not necessarily visible in the end result.

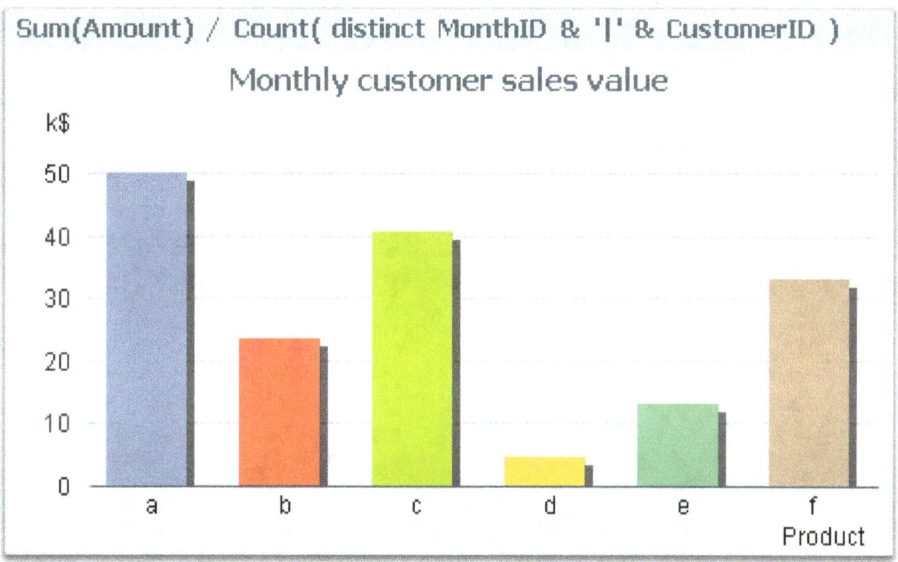

So, you need to figure out which internal grouping entity you want and then use this in a smart way in your expression.

And by the way – an internal grouping entity can be used also for other aggregation functions: Smallest, largest, most common: Min(), Max(), Mode(). But for these, you will need to use the Aggr() function.

Buckets

Originally posted in the Qlik Design Blog on Jul 15, 2014

Often when creating a Qlik application, you want to add some grouping of a number, and then use this as a dimension in a chart or as a field where you make selections.

Usually, the number is in itself not interesting, but the rough value is interesting as an attribute. It could be that you group people into age groups: Children, Adults and Seniors. Or you want to classify shipments to or from your company by how delayed they are: **Too early**, **Just in time** or **Delayed**.

These groups are often called buckets.

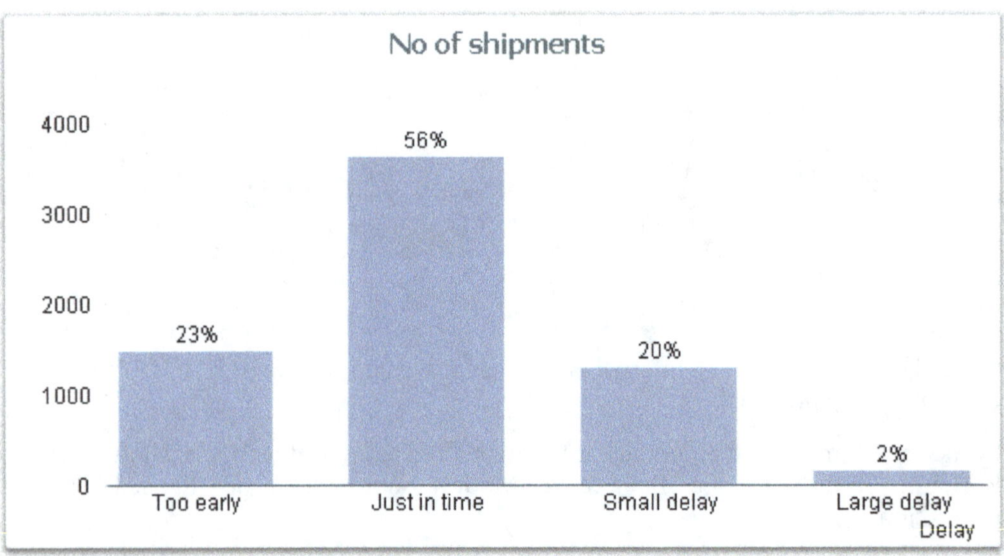

The most straightforward way to create buckets, is to use multiple nested if() functions, e.g.:

```
If( ShippedDate - RequiredDate <= -5,    'Too early',
If( ShippedDate - RequiredDate <=  0,    'Just in time',
If( ShippedDate - RequiredDate <=  5,    'Small delay',
                                         'Large delay'
    )))                                                 as Delay,
```

Or if you use dual values:

```
If( ShippedDate - RequiredDate <= -5, Dual( 'Too early'    , -5 ),
If( ShippedDate - RequiredDate <=  0, Dual( 'Just in time',  0 ),
If( ShippedDate - RequiredDate <=  5, Dual( 'Small delay' ,  5 ),
                                      Dual( 'Large delay' , 10 )
    )))                                                 as Delay,
```

However, if you have many classes, the above statements are neither pretty, nor manageable. Then it might be better to use a rounding function or the Class() function:

```
Round( ShippedDate - RequiredDate , 5 )                 as Delay,
Class( ShippedDate - RequiredDate , 5 )                 as Delay,
```

A third option is to use **IntervalMatch**:

```
DelayClasses:
Load Lower, Upper, Delay Inline
[Lower, Upper,  Delay
   -E99,     -5,  Too early
    -4,      0,  Just in time
     1,      5,  Small delay
     6,    E99,  Large delay];

IntervalMatch (DelayInDays)
Load Lower, Upper Resident DelayClasses;
```

All the above three methods create a field **Delay** already in the script, and this is what you should do if you have a static definition of the grouping.

However, there are cases where you may want a dynamic definition, and then you need to create a calculated dimension using the Aggr() function. Say, for example, that you want to assess the reliability of your suppliers – but since this is something that varies over time and location, you want to make the classification *after* you have made the appropriate selections. This you cannot make in the script.

But you should still calculate the necessary static fields in the script, i.e. in this case the delay of a shipment, e.g. by

```
ShippedDate - RequiredDate                          as DelayInDays,
```

One way to define reliability is to measure how many percent of the deliveries were on time, classified into percent intervals.

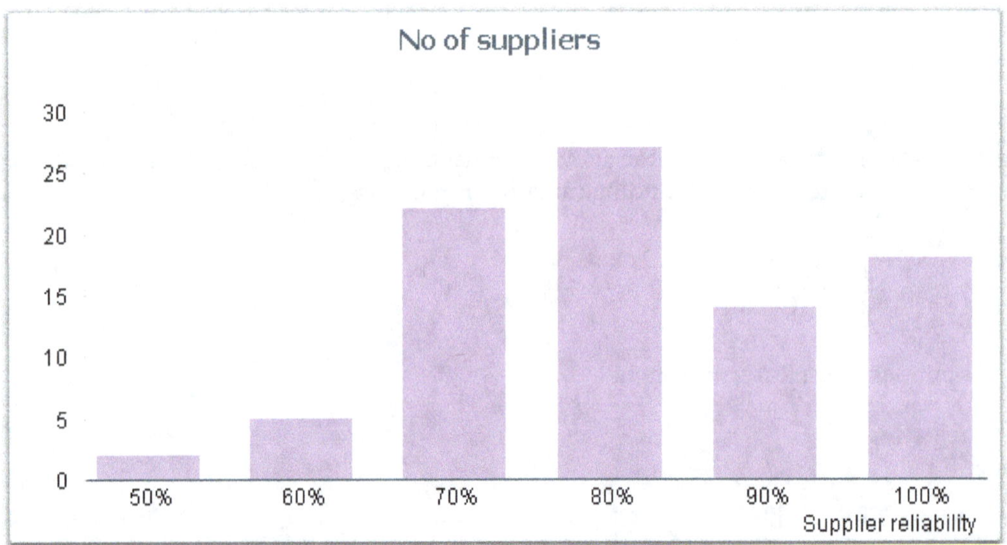

In the above chart, the following expression was used as dimension:

```
Aggr(
   Num(
      Round(
         Count(If(DelayInDays<=0,ShipmentID))/Count(ShipmentID),
         0.1),
      '0%'),
   Supplier)
```

The Aggr() function creates an array of values – one value per supplier: For each supplier, the number of "good" shipments is counted and divided by the total number of shipments. The number is rounded to nearest 10% to create the buckets and finally the Num() function formats the number as a percentage.

You can also rank the suppliers, bucket them in quartiles, and show the total amount per bucket:

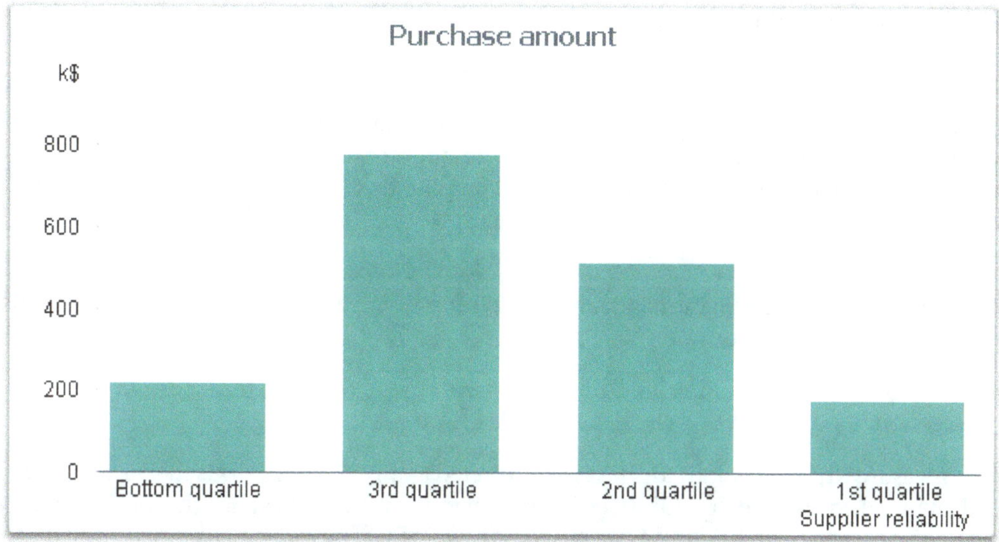

In the above chart, the following expression was used as dimension:

```
Aggr(
  Pick(
    Ceil(
      4*Rank(
        Count(If(DelayInDays<=0, ShipmentID))/Count(ShipmentID),
        4
        )
      /
      Count(distinct total Supplier)
      ),
    '1st quartile',
    '2nd quartile',
    '3rd quartile',
    'Bottom quartile'
    ),
  Supplier
  )
```

By clicking on a bar in either of these charts, you will select the corresponding suppliers.

Bottom line: Create buckets in all cases where a classification helps the user to get a better overview of data.

The Little Equals Sign

Originally posted in the Qlik Design Blog on Nov 25, 2014

In QlikView, as well as in Qlik Sense, there are numerous places where you can enter texts or expressions: In text objects, as measures in charts, as labels of objects, in variables, etc. If you start the text with an equals sign, this tells the Qlik engine that "here comes a formula". So, the Qlik engine evaluates the string and calculates the expression instead of just treating it as a text constant.

Sometimes you *must* use an equals sign, and sometimes not. But how can you know whether you must use an equals sign or not?

Basically, the Qlik engine can interpret the text in two ways; either as a text (i.e. as a value) or as an expression. And what it does by default varies from place to place.

In a chart measure (the expression), the text is interpreted as an expression. This means that you do not need an initial equals sign. It is OK to enter one anyway – it will not change the interpretation. This is an *assignment by expression*. This means that the value will be recalculated every time the user clicks. If you instead want to show the text as text, and not evaluate it, you need to enclose it in single quotes. There are many places in QlikView that behave this way: Measures, background colors, show conditions, calculation conditions, etc.

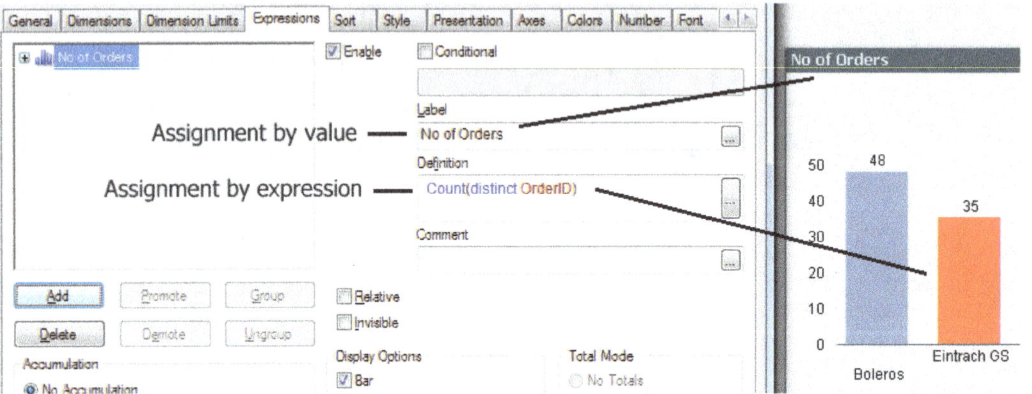

This is very different from e.g. object labels. Here, the text is interpreted as text. This is an assignment by value. This means that if you write an expression, it will not be evaluated unless it starts with an equals sign. Many places in Qlik apps behave this way: Text boxes, labels, Set statements, dollar expansions, etc. All places where it makes sense to use a plain text, or a simple value, behave this way.

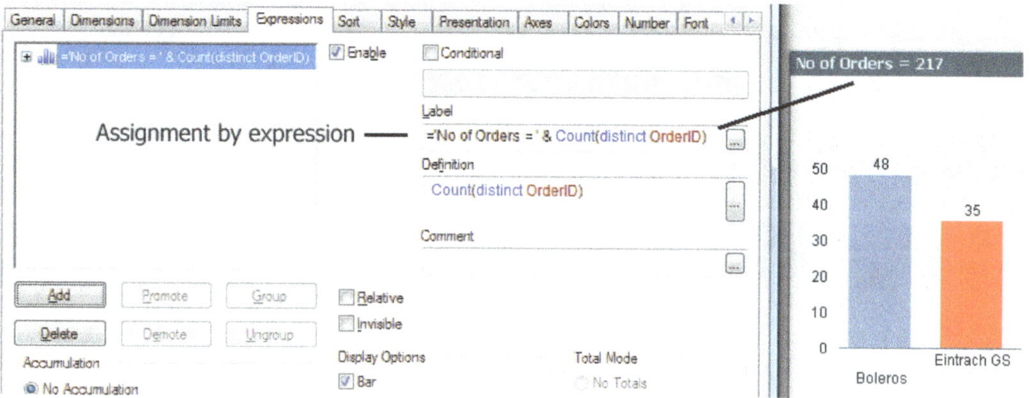

The same difference exists in Qlik Sense, but there an additional difference is that an equals sign is added when you open the expression editor. For example, if you add a label to your chart, you will see it in the chart properties without an equals sign. But if you subsequently open the expression editor, you will have an expression with a leading equals sign instead:

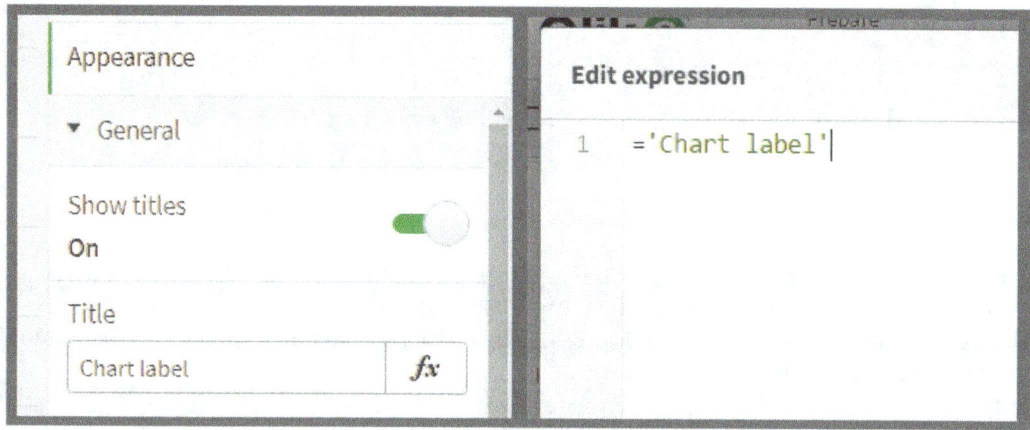

Variables need a couple of extra words. Normally, you assign a variable by value; either in the script using a Set or Let statement, or in the user interface through an Input box or in document properties.

```
12
13   Set vStartYear = 2012 ;
14   Let vEndYear = Year(Today()) ;
15
```

Value

6.75

An alternative is to use an assignment by expression. Then the value of the variable will be recalculated every time the user clicks, before it is used in other formulas. Just make sure that the little equals sign is there, and it will work.

```
12
13   Set vStartYear = '=Min(Year)' ;
14   Set vEndYear   = '=Max(Year)' ;
15
```

Value

=Avg(UnitCost)

Dollar expansions use a similar logic. If you have a dollar expansion without an equals sign, the enclosed text will be read as-is and used as a variable name. But if you instead use an equals sign, the enclosed text will be evaluated before it is expanded.

For example, assume that the variable **vEndYear** has the value of '2023'. Then

```
$(vEndYear)
```

will be expanded as '2023', whereas the following will be expanded as '2022'.

```
$(=vEndYear-1)
```

Finally, a small word of warning: The initial equals sign means an extra calculation every time the user clicks. And every small calculation uses some CPU time and carries a small performance penalty. Hence, you should not use too many calculated expressions. Use them only in the cases where you really need them.

The little equals sign is your friend. Use it wisely.

The Above Function

Originally posted in the Qlik Design Blog on Oct 27, 2015

The Above() function is a very special function. It is neither an aggregation function, nor a scalar function. Together with some other functions, e.g. Top(), Bottom() and Below(), it forms a separate group of functions: Chart inter-record functions. These functions have only one purpose: To get values from other rows within the same chart.

The basic construction is to use a measure as input, like the following:

```
Above(Sum(Amount))
```

This will calculate the sum of **Amount**, but for the row above.

The most common use case is when you want to compare the value of a specific row with the value of the previous row, e.g. this month's sales compared to last month's sales.

Sum(Sales)		
YearMonth	Sum(Sales)	Sum(Sales)-Above(Sum(Sales))
2014-Jun	909	3
2014-Jul	986	77
2014-Aug	1,111	125
2014-Sep	1,063	-48
2014-Oct	1,128	65
2014-Nov	1,233	105
2014-Dec	1,166	-67
2015-Jan	993	-173
2015-Feb	788	-205
2015-Mar	831	43
2015-Apr	773	-58
2015-May	894	121
2015-Jun	1,028	134
2015-Jul	921	-107
2015-Aug	1,140	219
2015-Sep	1,137	-3
2015-Oct	1,156	19

Another use case is when you want to calculate accumulations or rolling averages. Then you need to use the second and third parameter, the offset and the number of cells. Below, I use

```
Above(Sum(Amount),0,12)
```

The function will return 12 rows: the value for current row and the 11 rows above. This means that you need to wrap it in a range function in order to merge all values to one value. In this case, I use RangeAvg() to calculate the average of the 12 rows.

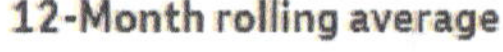

YearMonth	Sum(Sales)	RangeAvg(Above(Sum(Sales),0,12))
2014-Jun	909	944
2014-Jul	986	962
2014-Aug	1,111	965
2014-Sep	1,063	971
2014-Oct	1,128	978
2014-Nov	1,233	990
2014-Dec	1,166	996
2015-Jan	993	1,000
2015-Feb	788	989
2015-Mar	831	986
2015-Apr	773	991
2015-May	894	990
2015-Jun	1,028	1,000
2015-Jul	921	994
2015-Aug	1,140	997
2015-Sep	1,137	1,003
2015-Oct	1,156	1,005

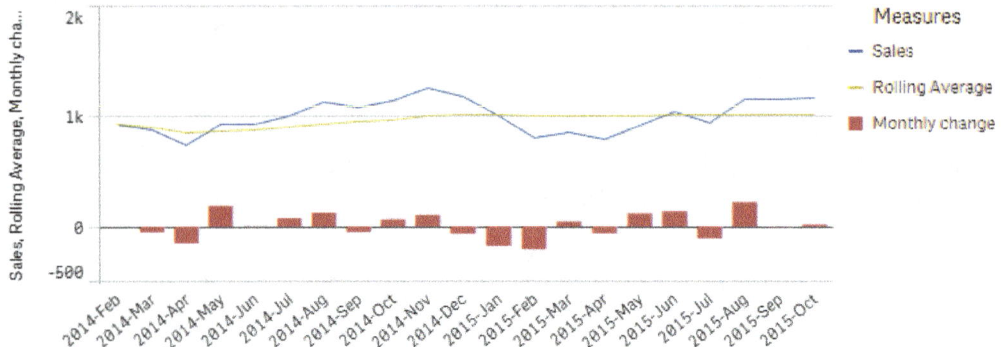

However, both the above solutions have a flaw: They don't take excluded dimensional values into account. For example, if April is excluded due to a selection, March will be considered as the month preceding May, which probably isn't what you want.

To correct this, you need to make the chart show all months, also the excluded ones. In QlikView, you have a chart option "Show all values" that you can use. A method that works also in Qlik Sense, is to add zero to all values, also for the excluded dimensional values:

```
Sum(Sales) + Sum({1} 0)
```

Make sure to enable "Show zero values".

You can also use the Above() function inside an Aggr() function. Remember that the Aggr() produces a virtual table, and the Above() function can of course operate in this table instead. This opens tremendous new possibilities.

First, you can make the same calculations as above by using either of the two following expressions:

```
Only(Aggr(           Above(Sum({1} Sales)        ) , YearMonth))
Only(Aggr(RangeAvg(Above(Sum({1} Sales),0,12)), YearMonth))
```

Note the Set Analysis expression in the inner aggregation function. The {1} ensures that all values in the virtual table are calculated, so that the Above() function can fetch also the excluded ones. Using {1} is sometimes too drastic – it is often better to use a Set expression that clears only *some* fields, e.g.

```
{<Year=,Month=,YearMonth=>}
```

Further, you can have a virtual table that is sorted differently from the chart where the expression is displayed. For example, the expression

```
Aggr(Above(Sum(Sales)),Year,Month)
```

displays the value from the previous month from the same year. But if you change the order of the dimensions, as in

```
Aggr(Above(Sum(Sales)),Month,Year)
```

the expression will display the value from the same month from the previous year. The only difference is the order of the dimensions. The latter expression is sorted first by **Month**, then by **Year**.

The result can be seen below:

Sum(Sales)

Year	Month	Sum(Sales)	Only(Aggr(Above(total Sum({$<Year=,Month=>}Sales)), Year,Month))	Only(Aggr(Above(Sum({$<Year=,Month=>}Sales)), Month,Year))
2012	Jan	783	-	-
2012	Feb	676	783	-
2012	Mar	547	676	-
2012	Apr	753	547	-
2012	May	587	753	-
2012	Jun	786	587	-
2012	Jul	915	786	-
2012	Aug	992	915	-
2012	Sep	954	992	-
2012	Oct	1018	954	-
2012	Nov	969	1018	-
2012	Dec	1087	969	-
2013	Jan	878	1087	783
2013	Feb	785	878	676
2013	Mar	788	785	547
2013	Apr	828	788	753
2013	May	770	828	587

An Aggr() table is by default sorted by the load order of the dimensions, one by one. This means that you can change the meaning of Above() by changing the order of the dimensions.

Finally, in Qlik Sense you can get much of this functionality automatically generated by using the measure modifiers.

With this, I hope that you understand the Above() function better.

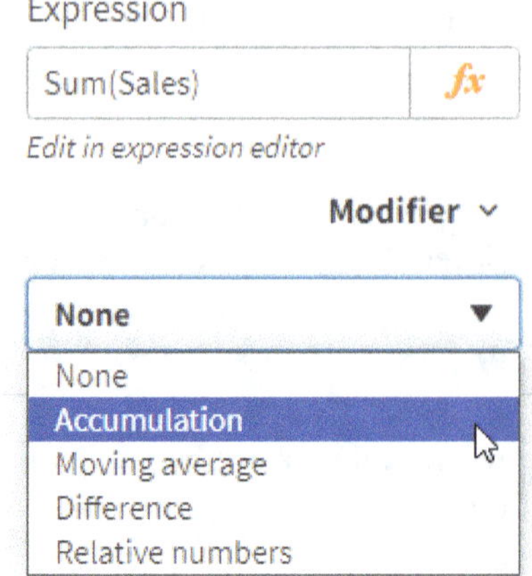

Accumulations

Originally posted in the Qlik Design Blog on Nov 10, 2015

When building analytical applications, you very often encounter cases where you want to accumulate numbers inside a chart. It could be that you want to calculate a Year-to-date number, or a rolling 6-month average, or a moving annual total.

When creating an accumulation, there are two fundamental challenges:

- Missing value in dimension
- Multiple dimensions

The first challenge is the question of how to treat dimensional values with no data. The tables below illustrate the problem:

Amount

Month	Amount	Rolling 3 Total
2014 Dec	9	9
2015 Jan	15	24
2015 Feb	11	35
2015 Apr	9	35

Amount

Month	Amount	Rolling 3 Total
2014 Dec	9	9
2015 Jan	15	24
2015 Feb	11	35
2015 Mar	0	26
2015 Apr	9	20

In this example, there is no data for the month of March. The default behavior is that this row then is omitted, see left table. This leads to an incorrect accumulation – the rolling 3-month total for April includes January, which it shouldn't. The table to the right, however, treats missing months correctly.

The second challenge is the question of how to treat the first dimension when there are several dimensions. The tables below illustrate the problem:

Amount

Product	Month	Amount	Rolling 12 Total
	2015 Jul	6	93
A	2015 Aug	9	95
	2015 Sep	6	91
	2014 Jan	8	8
	2014 Feb	4	12
B	2014 Mar	7	19
	2014 Apr	10	29

Amount

Year	Month	Amount	Rolling 12 Total
	2014 Oct	25	209
2014	2014 Nov	13	222
	2014 Dec	25	247
	2015 Jan	23	248
	2015 Feb	15	241
2015	2015 Mar	16	239
	2015 Apr	19	235

In the left table, you want the accumulation to re-start for each new product. You do not want the accumulation to continue from the previous product. Note that for '2014 Jan', the accumulation is reset.

But in the right table, it is the other way around: A moving annual total *should* span over two calendar years, so here you want the accumulation to continue over into a new value of the first dimension.

In QlikView and Qlik Sense there are several ways to create accumulations, each with its own pros and cons.

1. Using the control in QlikView charts

In a QlikView chart, you can easily create an accumulation just by selecting the right chart setting:

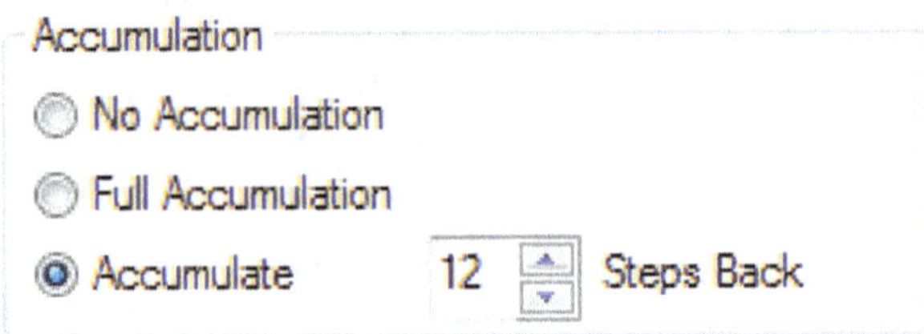

This method will however fail both the above challenges. Also, an accumulation can only be made over the first dimension, and the accumulation will always be reset for a new value in the second dimension.

Further, you cannot use it to calculate moving averages. It only works for calculations of sums.

So, this is not a good solution.

2. Using the Above() function

If you use the Above() function in a chart table like

```
RangeSum(Above(total Sum(Amount),0,12))
```

or in an Aggr() function call – which creates a table – like

```
Only(Aggr(RangeSum(Above(total Sum(Amount),0,12)), YearMonth))
```

you will get a 12-month moving total. It will pass the "multiple dimensions" challenge: By using – or not using – the total specifier in the Above() function you can decide which behavior you want.

But it will fail the "no data" challenge. There is a however a way to make an accumulation in an Aggr() table work also for this problem: Trick the Qlik engine to show all rows by adding a zero term for all dimensional values:

```
Only(Aggr(
    RangeSum(Above(total Sum(Amount) + Sum({1} 0),0,12)),
    YearMonth
    ))
```

and enable the display of zero values. Then you will get the right numbers also when some dimensional values are excluded.

This is a good method, and in Qlik Sense you can get expressions like this automatically generated by using the measure modifiers.

3. Using an As-Of table in the data model

The As-Of table is an excellent solution that will pass both challenges. See more in the "Calendars and Time" chapter.

Here you must set the condition using Set Analysis:

```
Sum({$<MonthDiff={"<12"}>} Amount)
```

However, it has one drawback: When a user clicks in the chart, a selection will be made in the **AsOfMonth**. But you don't want the user to make selections here: You want month selections to be made in the real month field. So, I usually make my charts read-only if they use the **AsOfMonth** as dimension.

With this, I hope that you understand accumulations better.

The Magic of Variables

Originally posted in the Qlik Design Blog on Nov 5, 2013

Variables can be used in many ways in a Qlik app. They can have static values, or they can be calculated. But when are they calculated? Should they be calculated at script run-time or when the user clicks? And how should they be used? With or without dollar expansion?

One basic way to assign a value to a variable is to use a Let statement in the script:

```
Let vToday  =  Num(Today()) ;
```

This will calculate the expression and assign it to the variable when the script is run. This is exactly what you want if you want to use a variable as a numeric parameter in your expressions.

But if you want the expression to be evaluated at a later stage, e.g. every time the user clicks, what should you do then? You can store the expression as a string in the variable, using either the Set or the Let statement:

```
Set vSales  =  Sum(Sales) ;
Let vSales  =  'Sum(Sales)' ;
```

You can also define variables in the document properties:

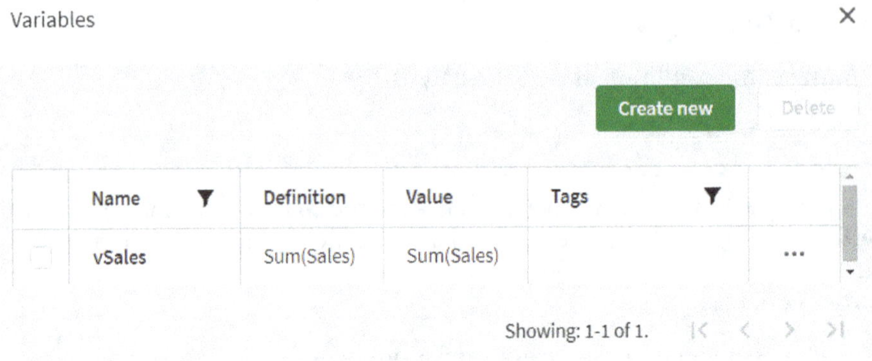

But in neither case, the expression will be calculated. The variable will only contain the string with the expression. Note the "Value" column in the image, where you can see that the value of the variable is the string 'Sum(Sales)'.

However, this string can subsequently be used in an expression using a dollar expansion – $(vSales) – and then it will be evaluated.

With a dollar expansion, the Qlik engine will substitute the '$(vSales)' with 'Sum(Sales)' before the expression is evaluated. Some of you will recognize this as an old-style assembler macro expansion. The expansion can be seen in the preview in the bottom of the Qlik Sense expression editor:

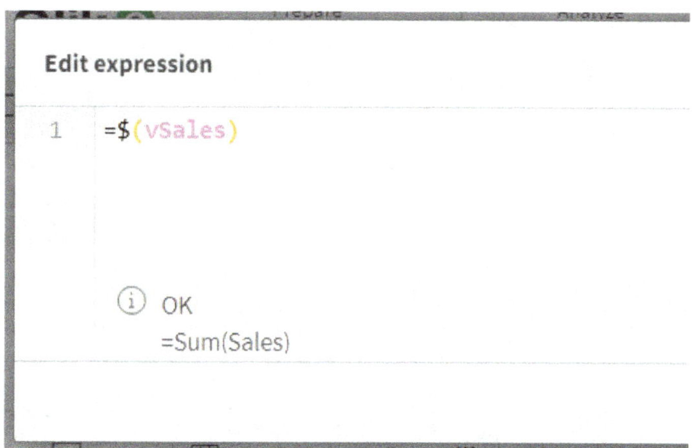

The subsequent calculation will be made based on the evaluation of the resulting expression. Note the two steps: (1) Variable expansion; and (2) Expression evaluation.

Dim	=vSales	=$(vSales)
Totals	**Sum(Sales)**	**19581**
A	Sum(Sales)	4242
B	Sum(Sales)	4462
C	Sum(Sales)	7478
D	Sum(Sales)	3399

In the chart above, you can see the result of using a normal variable reference (the first expression) or using a dollar expansion (the second expression). In the second expression the variable is expanded, whereupon the numbers are calculated correctly.

But this is just the beginning…

It is also possible to *calculate* the variable value, i.e. determine how it should be expanded, by using an initial equals sign in the variable definition.

```
Let vSales2 = '=Sum(Sales)';
```

Or in the variables UI (note the "Value" column):

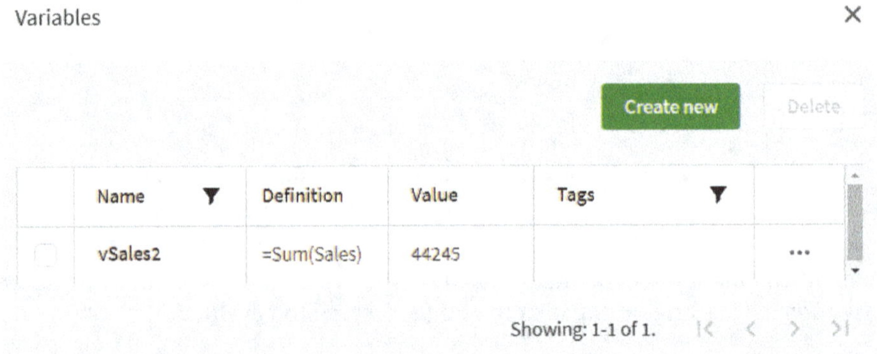

In this case, the variable value is calculated after each click, whereupon the dollar expansion in the chart expression is made, and finally the expression is evaluated. This means that the evaluation of 'Sum(Sales)' is done *before* the variable expansion. Note the three steps:

1. Variable calculation
2. Variable expansion
3. Expression evaluation.

The table below summarizes the three methods.

Expressions

	Alt 1	Alt 2	Alt 3
Variable definition	Sum(Sales)	Sum(Sales)	=Sum(Sales)
What you write (What you see in the expression editor)	*vSales*	*$(vSales)*	*$(vSales2)*
Number of steps	One-step evaluation	Two-step evaluation	Three-step evaluation
Variable value	Sum(Sales)	Sum(Sales)	257810
Expression after the $-expansion (What the Qlik engine sees)	*vSales*	Sum(Sales)	257810
Result of the expression evaluation (What the user sees)	Sum(Sales)	152051	257810
Comment on the result	I.e. The *string* = 'Sum(Sales)'	I.e. the correct number = Sum(Sales)	I.e. the correct number = Sum(total Sales)
Good for	Static value (a parameter)	Static expression	Dynamic expression

With the above, you can do almost magical things. You can for instance make conditional calculations that depend on e.g. selections, client platform or user.

Example:

- Create a field [Field to Aggregate] containing the names of two other numeric fields: 'Quantity' and 'Sales'
- Create a variable vConditionalAggregationField = '=Only([Field to Aggregate])'
- Create a chart with an expression = Sum($(vConditionalAggregationField))

The calculation in a chart will now toggle between Sum(Quantity) and Sum(Sales) depending on your selection.

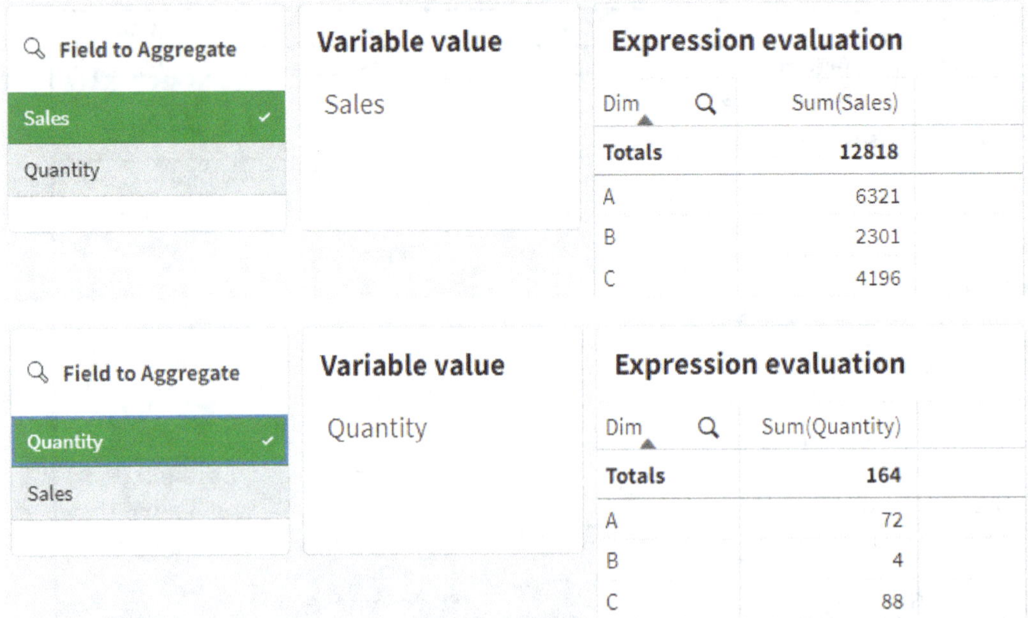

The use of variables is an extremely powerful tool that you can use to create flexible applications. Use it – but with caution. Too much magic behind the curtains can be confusing for the user.

The Magic of Dollar Expansions

Originally posted in the Qlik Design Blog on Nov 19, 2013

A couple of weeks ago I wrote about the Magic of variables and showed how you can use these in advanced expressions. Today's post will continue this topic, but now with a focus on the dollar expansions.

First of all, it is important to understand that variables and dollar expansions are – although intimately connected – still not the same things. You can use variables without dollar expansions, and you can use dollar expansions without variables.

One common example is Set analysis, where a dollar expansion with an expression often is used instead of one with a variable, e.g:

```
Sum({<YearMonth = {"<=$(=Max(YearMonth))"}>} Amount )
```

Note that there are _no variables_ used here.

Secondly, a dollar expansion is something that is done _before_ the expression (or statement) is evaluated. An example is an include directive in the script:

```
$(Include=some_script_file.qvs)
```

This is also a dollar expansion, and obviously it is expanded before the resulting script is parsed and executed. Otherwise, the _Include_ directive wouldn't work ... 😊

Further, in a chart the dollar expansion is made _before_ the cube is expanded, so it cannot expand to different expressions for different dimensional values. Since the expansion is done before the parsing, you can use dollar expansions to create tokens for the expression. In other words – the dollar expansion is not just a value used for the calculation; rather it is something you can use to build your expression.

One use-case is if you want to load a large number of similar files: Then you would need a **For – Next** loop that loops over the files and concatenates them into one table. This is easy if all files have identical sets of fields.

But what if the files have slightly different sets of fields? Then the auto-concatenate will not work, so you will need to use the **Concatenate** prefix. But you must not use this on the first iteration, only on the second and subsequent iterations.

One solution is to use a dollar expansion:

```
Set vConcatenate = ;
For each vFile in FileList('.\*.txt')
   Data:
   $(vConcatenate)
   Load * From [$(vFile)];
   Set vConcatenate = Concatenate ;
Next vFile
```

Here the variable **vConcatenate** is initiated to an empty string, so the first time it is expanded in front of the Load, it is expanded to nothing. But in the second iteration it will produce a correct **Concatenate** prefix, i.e. a script keyword. The syntax color coding assumes that this is an error, but it isn't. The result can easily be seen in the script debugger.

First iteration:

```
23
24    Set vConcatenate = ;
25    For each vFile in FileList('*.txt')
26        Data:
27          $(vConcatenate)
28          Load * From [$(vFile)];
```

```
   Data:

       Load * From [lib://DataFiles/Document1.txt]
```

Note that there is no "Concatenate" executed in the script. But there is in the second iteration:

```
23
24    Set vConcatenate = ;
25    For each vFile in FileList('*.txt')
26        Data:
27          $(vConcatenate)
28          Load * From [$(vFile)];
```

```
   Data:
       Concatenate
       Load * From [lib://DataFiles/Document2.txt]
```

You can use dollar expansions to generate tokens also in the user interface. One use-case is that you want to define a set analysis definition in which all selections in an entire table are cleared, e.g. you want to clear all fields in the Master Calendar without having to explicitly list them all.

Expressions

One good solution is to define a variable that can be used as Set modifier:

```
Set vClearCalendar =
     "= '['                                                     &
     Concat({1<$Table={'Calendar'}>} $Field, ']=,[') &
     ']=' ";
```

and then use this in a chart expression:

```
Sum ({<$(vClearCalendar)>} Amount)
```

This expression uses the system fields **$Table** and **$Field** to find the possible fields of the table "**Calendar**". The Concat() function lists these fields with the appropriate delimiters so that the Set modifier contains the relevant list of fields. Note the expression preview at the bottom of the expression editor:

Edit expression

```
1  Sum ({<$(vClearCalendar)>} Amount)
```

ⓘ OK

Sum ({<[IsThisYear]=,[Month]=,[OrderDate]=,[Year]=,[YearMonth]=>} Amount)

This effectively removes all selections in the **Calendar** table.

Dollar expansions are extremely powerful in many situations where you want to simplify for the user by hiding the difficult parts in a formula. Use them wisely.

Thank you, Oleg T. for the inspiration and examples.

Expressions

14
Set Analysis

Set Analysis is a way to programmatically redefine the scope for a calculation. Internally, it is very similar to a selection, and conceptually, it is similar to a SQL where-clause.

This chapter is about its syntax and all its intricacies.

A Primer on Set Analysis

Originally posted in the Qlik Design Blog on Feb 17, 2015

Set analysis is one of the more complex things you can use in a Qlik app. Its syntax is often perceived as complicated and there are some misunderstandings around it. So here is my short explanation.

Set analysis is a way to define an aggregation scope *different from current selection*. Think of it as a way to define a condition in an aggregation. The condition, however, is in itself like a selection that is evaluated *before* the cube (the chart) is expanded. Hence, it is *not* possible to have a condition that is evaluated row by row.

The set analysis is used inside an aggregation function, e.g. in an expression like

```
Sum( Amount )
```

The first step is to add the markers for the set analysis – the curly brackets:

```
Sum( {…} Amount )
```

What is written inside the curly brackets defines the record set over which the new aggregation should be made. You can use different identifiers and operators, e.g. '$' for records implied by current selection, '1' for all records, '1-$' for all excluded records, etc. Hence, the following expression normally doesn't change anything – the result is usually the same as not having a set expression.

```
Sum( {$} Amount )
```

A set of records that you can define by a simple selection is called a natural set. Not all record sets are natural; for instance, {1-$} cannot always be defined through a selection.

The next step is often to add a set modifier, which is defined by angle brackets. The set modifier adds or changes a selection. It can be used on any natural set and consists of a list of fields, where each field can have a new selection:

```
Sum( {$<…>} Amount )
```

The next step is to specify a field and define the element set for this field; the set of field values that defines the selection. The element set is usually an explicit list of field values or a search, and then you need the curly brackets to define the element set. The element set could also be a set function, P() or E(), or a field reference.

```
Sum( {$<Date={…}>} Amount )   or   Sum( {$<Date=P(…)>} Amount )
```

A search can be defined through double quotes. This way, field values that match the search string will be selected:

```
Sum( {$<Date={"…"}>} Amount )
```

Do not use single quotes to initiate a search here! Single quotes denote literals, i.e. explicit field values. (Yes, single quotes work as a search in older apps, but this was a bug that now has been fixed…)

Often a numeric search is made, defined by a leading relational operator. Then, field values will be selected based on a comparison:

```
Sum( {$<Date={"<=…"}>} Amount )
```

To make it worse, the value to which the field values are compared is often a calculated one. And in order to get a calculated value into the expression, a dollar expansion is needed:

```
Sum( {$<Date={"<=$(…)"}>} Amount )
```

Inside the dollar expansion, you need an expression that starts with an equals sign and contains an aggregation function, for example:

```
Sum( {$<Date={"<=$(=Max(Date))"}>} Amount )
```

The aggregation function inside the dollar expansion is evaluated globally, before the cube is expanded, i.e. **not** once per dimensional value.

As you can see, there are many levels of a set expression, and many pairs of brackets and delimiters that need to match. When you write set expressions, you should always write both brackets directly, and then continue with the expression between them. This way you will avoid simple syntax errors.

Good luck with your set analysis expressions!

Why is it called Set Analysis?

Originally posted in the Qlik Design Blog on Oct 13, 2015

Set Analysis is a commonly used tool when creating advanced formulas in Qlik Sense or QlikView. But why is it called "Set Analysis"? And why are there so many curly brackets?

Set Analysis is really a simple and straightforward tool, but with advanced syntax. "Simple" since its only purpose is to allow you to define a calculation scope different from the current selection. The basics are very much like defining a SQL Where clause.

A different term for *the scope* is the "record set". With this, we mean the set of records in the data over which the aggregations should be calculated.

```
Sum({$<OrderYear={2015}>} Sales)
```

The above Set analysis expression is equivalent to selecting 2015 from **OrderYear**. It is also equivalent to a SQL condition "Where OrderYear=2015".

The Set analysis syntax is advanced because there are so many different ways to define a record set; you can use a selection, a bookmark, or an alternate state. Further, just as in any set algebra, you can define intersections, unions and other set operations, e.g. the difference between two sets:

```
Sum({$-State2} Sales)
```

This expression describes the Set difference between current selection in the default state $ and selection in the alternate state State2: I.e. records that are included by the default state, but not included in State2.

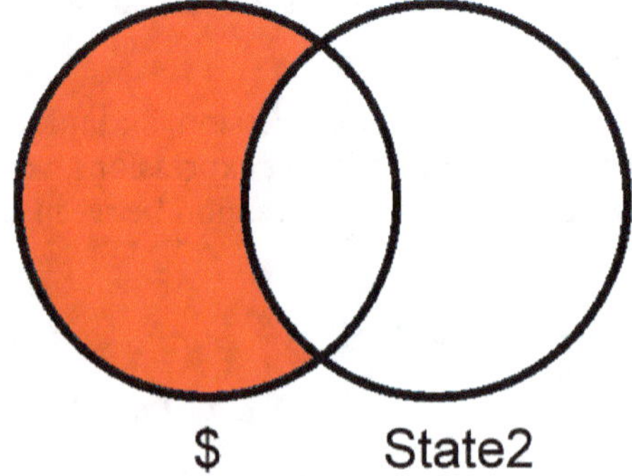

Another set expression is the following:

```
Sum({$<Date={"<=$(=Date(Max(Date)))"}>} Sales)
```

This defines the records belonging to any date that occurs before the latest date in the current selection. The dollar expansion is needed since the parser expects field values in clear text in the search string.

Note that this Set expression contains two pairs of curly brackets. Set analysis expressions with many curly brackets look complicated, but there is in fact method in the madness …

- **The outer brackets**: Sum({ … } Sales)
  These define the record set; i.e. the records in the data over which the aggregation should be made.

- **The inner brackets**: Sum({$<Field= { … } >} Sales)
  These define the element set; i.e. the set of individual field values that define the selection in this field.

For those of you who have read about *Symbol Tables and Bit-Stuffed Pointers* in the engine chapter, it may be interesting to know that the element set operates on the symbol tables, whereas the record set is defined on the data tables.

The element set can be a list of values or a search string. It can also be described by field references or by the P() and E() functions, e.g.

```
{$<Country=Country+P({1<OrderYear={2015}>})>}
```

Summary:

- There are two different sets in a Set expression: The Record Set and the Element Set.

- The record set (the outer curly brackets) defines the records in the data tables. Use 1, $, a bookmark or an alternate state as Set identifier.

- The element set (the inner curly brackets) defines the selection that modifies a record set. Use one or several of the following to define your element set:
    - A list of values, e.g: {2013,2014,2015}
    - A search, e.g: {">=2015-01-06<=2015-02-05"}
    - A field reference
    - A set function, i.e: P() or E()
- Set operators can be used to define both the record set and the element set.

With this, I hope that you understand Set Analysis somewhat better.

Dates in Set Analysis

Originally posted in the Qlik Design Blog on Sep 29, 2015

Several aspects of the Qlik search mechanism have been described in previous posts. There is however one that has not been covered: Searches in dual fields, e.g. dates. This post will try to explain the basics.

When making searches in text fields, you can search either by using a normal search or by using a wildcard search, and when you search in numeric fields you can use a numeric search. But what about dual fields, like dates, where you have both a textual and a numeric representation?

The answer is displayed in the picture below.

Normal search	Wildcard search	Numeric search	
ISO Date	US Date	ISO Date	US Date
2023	*/4/*	<=2023-01-04	>2/27/2023<3/4/2023
2023-01-01	1/4/2023	2023-01-01	2/28/2023
2023-01-02	2/4/2023	2023-01-02	3/1/2023
2023-01-03	3/4/2023	2023-01-03	3/2/2023
2023-01-04	4/4/2023	2023-01-04	3/3/2023
2023-01-05	5/4/2023		

Normal searches and wildcard searches are straightforward. See the chapter about searches for an explanation. Numeric searches are also possible and do pretty much what you expect them to.

You should however note that the search string of a numeric search in a date field must contain *the correct formatted date*. It is in most cases not possible to use the numeric value of the date. E.g. you cannot search for 45284 when you want Dec 24th, 2023, even though this is the value of the date.

The same logic is used in Set Analysis, which means that a correct Set Analysis expression with a date could look like one of these:

```
Sum({<[ISO Date]={"<=2023-02-28"}>} Amount)
Sum({<[US Date] ={"<=2/28/2023"}>}  Amount)
```

Note that the search string format corresponds to the format of the field.

Often you want the Set Analysis expression to be dynamic, and then you need to put a dollar expansion with an aggregation function inside it. Again, you need to use the correct format.

Let's look at what happens if you don't: One case is that you want to compare the selected month with the preceding month. In principle, the solution is something like the following:

```
Sum({<Month={"$(=Max(Month))"}>}   Amount) // Last possible month
Sum({<Month={"$(=Max(Month)-1)"}>} Amount) // 2nd Last month
```

The Max(Month) will calculate the last possible month, and the dollar expansion will enter this value into the expression before the expression is parsed.

How the expression looks after the dollar expansion can be seen in the column header of a QlikView table. The above formulas have been used in the table below. Note that the dollar expansions with Max(Month) have been replaced with numbers.

Product	Sum(Amount)	Sum({<Month={"12"}>} Amount)	Sum({<Month={"11"}>} Amount)
A	514,33	0,00	0,00
B	496,47	0,00	0,00
C	498,72	0,00	0,00

So far, so good.

However, the above expressions do not work. You can see that both expressions return zero amounts.

First, if you have created the **Month** using the Month() function, the field is cyclic which means that December of one year has a higher numeric value than January the following year, although it comes before January. Hence, the Max() function will not respect the order of months belonging to different years.

Secondly, the **Month** field has a dual value. This means that the Max(**Month**) will return a numeric when you need the textual value ('Dec') in the Set analysis expression.

One solution is to use a sequential month instead, and format it the same way everywhere:

Script:

```
Date(MonthStart(Date),'MMM-YY') as Month,
```

Expressions:

```
Sum({<Month={"$(=Date(Max(Month),                'MMM-YY'))"}>}Amnt)
Sum({<Month={"$(=Date(AddMonths(Max(Month),-1),'MMM-YY'))"}>}Amnt)
```

Here the field **Month** is a date – the first day of the month – but formatted with just month and year. In other words: A number that equals roughly 45000 and is formatted as 'Jan-23'. The same formatting is applied inside the dollar expansion. Note the column headers below.

Product	Sum(Amount)	Sum({<Month={"Sep-23"}>} Amount)	Sum({<Month={"Aug-23"}>} Amount)
A	502,41	13,41	14,04
B	502,96	14,82	15,50
C	494,88	11,84	14,18

Often it is practical to put the calculation of the Set analysis condition in variables. This way, the formula is kept in one place only and the Set analysis expressions become simpler and easier to read:

Script:

```
Set vLastMonth    =    "=Date(Max(Month),'MMM-YY')";
Set v2ndLastMonth = "=Date(AddMonths(Max(Month),-1),'MMM-YY')";
```

Expressions:

```
Sum({<Month={"$(vLastMonth)"}>}    Amount )
Sum({<Month={"$(v2ndLastMonth)"}>} Amount )
```

Note that the variable definitions start with equals signs. This way they will be recalculated at every click.

Summary: Format the dates used inside Set analysis expressions and use variables to simplify the expressions.

Quotes in Set Analysis

Originally posted in the Qlik Design Blog on Sep 12, 2017

Today, (Sep 2017) the Qlik engine has some bugs in the area of a search and a subsequent select. These affect both interactive searches and searches in Set Analysis expressions. We are working on fixing them. However, one of these coming bug fixes may cause some backward incompatibility. This post explains what the bug fix will mean, and what you can do to avoid future problems.

When you use Set analysis, you can choose to have a condition in the form of a list of values in the Set expression, or you can choose to have a rule-based definition – a search for field values.

Examples of hard coded lists:

```
Sum({<Year     = {2013,2014,2015}>}                    Amount)
Sum({<Country = {'Australia','Canada','France'}>}    Amount)
```

Examples of searches:

```
Sum({<Year     = {">=2013"}>}                          Amount)
Sum({<Country = {"Austr*"}>}                           Amount)
Sum({<Customer= {"=Sum(Amount)>100000"}>}             Amount)
```

All the above constructions work today, and they will work correctly also after the bug fix.

Note the double quotes in the search expressions. These define the search strings, and between them you can write any search string – the same way as you would in a list box search.

*However, you should **_not_** use single quotes to define a search string.*

Single quotes are reserved for literals, i.e. exact matches. Hence, they should be used when you want to make a list of valid field values, like the above list of explicit countries. But they should not be used for searches. Single quotes imply a case sensitive match with a single field value.

This difference between single and double quotes has been correctly described in the reference manual that states that searches are "always defined by the use of double quotes". Also, all examples with literal field values in the documentation use single quotes.

Now to the bug: QlikView and Qlik Sense currently do not respect the above difference between single and double quotes. Instead, strings enclosed in single quotes are interpreted as search strings. As a consequence, it is not possible to make case sensitive matches with field values, something which you sometimes want to do.

This bug will be fixed in the coming November releases of Qlik Sense and QlikView. Then, *wildcards in strings enclosed by single quotes will no longer be considered as wildcards.* Instead, the strings will be interpreted as literals, i.e. the engine will try to match the string with a field value containing the '*' character. The same logic will apply also to relational operators and equals signs.

Unfortunately, this bug has been incorrectly utilized by some developers: I have seen Set Analysis expressions with correct search strings, but erroneously enclosed in single quotes; for example:

```
Sum({<Country = {'Austr*'}>} Amount) // Incorrect!
```

This search should instead have been written:

```
Sum({<Country = {"Austr*"}>} Amount) // Correct
```

Hence, there are documents with expressions that will not work in the corrected algorithm. However, the bug fix will be implemented in such a way that old documents will use the old logic, and new documents will use the new logic. In addition, it will be possible to force the new logic for all documents by using a parameter in Settings.ini.

You can of course also change the single quotes in existing search strings to double quotes, and the expression will continue to do what it always has done.

This post is mainly to give you a heads-up on a coming change and give you a chance to make a quality control of your own documents. We will publish more information as we get closer to the release.

Implicit Set Operators

Originally posted in the Qlik Design Blog on Feb 16, 2016

In Set expressions, an equals sign can be used to assign a selection to a field. But this is not the only assignment symbol that can be used. There are a couple of others. This post is about the alternative assignments symbols that can be used, and their respective use cases.

Strictly speaking, the equals sign in set expressions is *not* an equals sign. Rather, it is a lexical assignment symbol. This is the reason why you cannot use relational operators in its place. The equals sign defines an element set used to assign a selection state to a field e.g.

```
{<Country = {'Sweden', 'Germany', 'United States'}>}
```

In this case, the element set 'Sweden', 'Germany', 'United States' is assigned as selection to the field "Country".

But what if the set identifier already has a selection in the field "Country"?

In such a case, the old selection will be replaced by the new one. It will be like first clearing the old selection of the field, then applying a new selection.

However, this is not the only way to assign a set as selection in a field. You can also use assignments with implicit set operators. These will use the existing selection in the field to define a new selection:

Implicit Union:

```
{<Country += {'United States'}>}
```

Note the plus sign.

This expression will use the union between the existing selection and 'United States' as new selection in the field, i.e. add the listed values to the previously select ones. The use case is not a common one, but it happens sometimes that you always want to show a specific country (or product or customer) as a comparison to the existing selection. Then the implicit union can be used.

Implicit Intersection:

```
{<Country *= {"=Continent='Europe' "}>}
```

Note the asterisk.

This will use the intersection between the existing selection of countries and the countries in Europe as new selection in the field. (The search is an expression search that picks out European countries.) The set expression will not remove any part of the existing condition – instead it will just be an additional limitation.

This construction can in many cases be used instead of a normal assignment. In fact, it is often a much better solution than the standard assignment, since it respects the existing user selection and thus is easier for the user to understand.

The implicit intersection should be used more.

Implicit Exclusion:

```
{<Country -= {'United States'}>}
```

Note the minus sign.

This expression will use the existing selection but exclude 'United States' from the selected values. The use case for an implicit exclusion is exactly this – you want to exclude a value. Hence, this construction is very useful.

Implicit Symmetric Difference:

```
{<Country /= {'United States'}>}
```

Note the slash.

The above expression will select values that belong either to existing selection, or to the values in the set expression, but not to both. It's like an XOR. I have never used this, and I would like to challenge the readers to come up with a relevant use case.

Bottom line: Assignments with implicit set operators are sometimes very useful. You should definitely consider using the implicit intersection and the implicit exclusion.

Excluding values in Set Analysis

Originally posted in the Qlik Design Blog on Oct 20, 2015

Set Analysis is a commonly used tool when creating static or dynamic filters inside aggregations in Qlik Sense or QlikView. But sometimes you need the opposite to selecting – you need to exclude values. How can this be done?

In Set Analysis, it is straightforward to make selections; to define the criteria for inclusion. But it is not as straightforward to define an exclusion. But there are in fact several ways to do this.

First of all, an inclusion can be defined the following way:

```
Sum({<Field = {X}>} Amount)
```

This expression is equivalent to saying, "Sum the Amounts where Field equals X".

But if you want to say the opposite – "where field does *not* equal X" – it becomes more complicated. The relation "not equal to" is not a Set operation. However, one way to do this is to use the implicit exclusion operator:

```
Sum({<Field -= {X}>} Amount)
```

Note the minus sign in front of the equals sign. This will create an element set based on the existing selected values, but with the value X removed.

A second way to do this is to use the unary exclusion operator:

```
Sum({<Field = - {X}>} Amount)
```

This will return the complement set of X and use this as element set in the set expression.

In many situations the two methods return identical sets. But there are cases when they are different. In the table below you can see that it makes a difference if there already is a selection in the field.

Field	Q	Sum({1} Amount)	Sum({<Field -= {X}>} Amount)	Sum({<Field = - {X}>} Amount)
Totals		19	3	6
A		1	1	1
B		2	2	2
C		3	0	3
X		5	0	0
-		8	0	0

Note the difference on the 'C' row in the table. Since the implicit operator (the 2nd expression) is based on the current selection, the value C is excluded from the calculation. This is in contrast to the unary operator (the 3rd expression) that creates a completely new element set, not based on current selection.

We can also see that both the above expressions exclude records where the field is NULL (the line where Field has a dash only). The reason is simple: As soon as there is a selection in the field, the logical inference will exclude NULL in the same field.

So, what should you do if you want to exclude X but not NULL?

The answer is simple: *Use another field for your selection.* Typically, you should use the primary key for the table where you find the **Amount**.

```
Sum({1<ID = E({<Field={X}>} ID)>} Amount)
```

Here you need to use the element function E(), that returns excluded values. Hence, the above Set expression says: "Select the IDs that get excluded when selecting X."

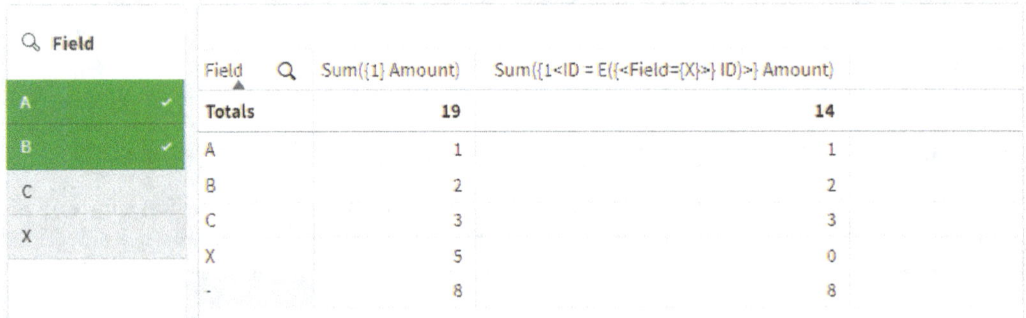

The table confirms that we get the records we want: X is excluded but NULL is still included.

With this, I hope that you understand Set Analysis somewhat better.

Natural Sets

Originally posted in the Qlik Design Blog on Apr 12, 2016

Set Analysis is a commonly used tool when creating advanced formulas in Qlik Sense or QlikView. The basics are fairly simple, but it's clear that some aspects of it are very complex. In this post, I will try to answer some simple questions that touch the core of the complexity, such as: Can all sets have set modifiers? Are some sets more fundamental than others?

All sets are <u>not</u> equal. Some sets are indeed more fundamental than others.

Apart from the two trivial sets {0} (nothing) and {1} (everything), the most fundamental group of sets are the Natural Sets. These are the sets that can be defined as a selection or through a Set modifier, e.g.

```
{$}
{$<Country={France}>}
{State2<Product=>}
```

Compare these to the non-natural sets, where set operators are used for the record set definitions:

```
{1-$}
{BookMark01*$}
```

To understand the difference between the two, you need to know the difference between element sets (lists of distinct field values) and record sets (lists of records in the internal database). See "Why is it called Set Analysis?".

Internally, all sets are stored as element sets and record sets in state vectors. For Natural sets, both the element sets and the record sets can be stored, but for the non-natural sets only the record sets can be stored. The reason is that *there are no well-defined element sets for non-natural sets.*

Consider for instance the following table, where you want to sum numbers that are *not* assigned to a customer:

Customer	Amount
ACME Inc.	1
Coyote Ltd.	2
<NULL>	2

With Set analysis, this is straightforward. The second expression in the chart calculates exactly this, using a non-natural set:

Customer Q	Sum(Amount)	Sum({1-1<Customer={"*"}>} Amount)
Totals	**5**	**2**
ACME Inc.	1	0
Coyote Ltd.	2	0
-	2	2

But if you try to create the same filter using a selection in the list boxes, you will find that it is not possible – NULL is not selectable.

Q **Customer**	Q **Amount**
ACME Inc.	1
Coyote Ltd.	2

No matter how you select from the two list boxes, you cannot recreate this filter. Hence, a non-natural set cannot always be defined through a selection, and thus cannot be stored as element sets.

From a logical perspective, you could say that Natural sets are always defined by the element sets (the state vectors of the symbol tables), while the record set (the state vector of the data table) is just the result of the logical inference. For non-natural sets, it is the other way around: These are defined by the record set.

This has a number of consequences. First, it is not possible to modify a non-natural set: A set expression like the following cannot be used:

```
{ (BookMark01 * BookMark02) <Field={x,y}> }
```

where the normal (round) brackets imply that the intersection between **BookMark01** and **BookMark02** should be evaluated before the set modifier is applied. The reason is of course that there is no element set that can be modified once the intersection is created.

Further, you cannot use non-natural sets inside the P() and E() functions. The reason is that these functions should return an element set, but it is not possible to deduce that from the record set of a non-natural set.

Finally, a measure cannot always be attributed to the correct dimensional value if a non-natural set is used. For example, in the QlikView chart below, you can see that some excluded sales numbers are 1attributed to the correct **ProductCategories**, whereas others have NULL.

ProductCategory
Baby Clothes
Children's Clothes
Men's Clothes
Men's Footwear
Sportswear
Swimwear
Women's Clothes
Women's Footwear

Sales per Category

ProductCategory	Country	Sum ({$} Sales)	Sum ({1-$} Sales)
Baby Clothes		56,223 $	0 $
Children's Clothes		0 $	81,682 $
Men's Clothes		0 $	140,987 $
Men's Footwear		0 $	232,747 $
Sportswear		0 $	270,273 $
Swimwear		0 $	29,549 $
Women's Clothes		0 $	649,349 $
Women's Footwear		0 $	140,654 $
	Argentina	0 $	151 $
-	Austria	0 $	2,410 $
	Brazil	0 $	3,403 $

Whether the assignment is correctly made or not, depends on the data model. In this specific case, the number cannot be assigned if it pertains to a country that is excluded by the selection.

Summary:

- Only natural sets can be re-created as interactive selections and stored in bookmarks

- Only natural sets can be modified

- Only natural sets can be used inside the P() and E() functions

- A measure cannot always be attributed to the correct dimensional value if a non-natural set is used

New Set Analysis syntax

Originally posted in the Qlik Design Blog on Sep 26, 2022

Set analysis is one of the more powerful tools you can use in Qlik Sense and QlikView. Its syntax is sometimes perceived as complicated, but once you learn it, you can achieve fantastic things. There is now an additional way of writing the Set expression, that may simplify your code.

Set analysis is a way to define an aggregation scope different from current selection. Think of it as a way to define a conditional aggregation. The condition – or filter – is written inside the aggregation function. For example, the following will sum the amounts pertaining to 2021:

```
Sum({<Year={2021}>} Amount)
```

This syntax, however, has a couple of drawbacks: First, it is not easy to combine a master measure with different set expressions, since the set expression is hard coded inside the master measure. Secondly, if you have an expression with multiple aggregations, you need to write the same set expression in every aggregation function.

Therefore, we introduce an additional position for set expressions: They can now be written outside the aggregation function and will then affect all subsequent aggregations. This means that the below expression is allowed:

```
{<Year={2021}>} Sum(Amount) / Count(distinct Customer)
```

For master measures, this change will allow a very powerful re-usability: You can now add set expressions to tweak existing master measures:

```
{<Year={2021}>} [Master measure]
```

Lexical scoping

The outer set expression will affect the entire expression, unless it is enclosed in round brackets. If so, the brackets define the lexical scope. For example, in the following expression, the set expression will only affect the aggregations inside the brackets – the Avg() calculation will not be affected.

```
({<Year={2021}>} Sum(Amount)/Count(Customer)) - Avg(Sales)
```

Position

The set expression must be placed in the beginning of the lexical scope.

Context and inheritance

Aggregation functions that lack a set expression will inherit the context from the outside: In earlier versions the context was always defined by the current selection. Now we have added the possibility of having the context defined by a set expression. So, now "context" means *current selection* or an *outer set expression.*

Inner set expression

If an aggregation function already contains a set expression, this will be merged with the context. The same merging rules as today will apply:

- An inner set expression with a set identifier will *not* inherit from the context. It will inherit the selection from the set identifier instead.
- An inner set expression that lacks set identifier – it has only a set modifier – will inherit from the context.
- How the merge is made depends on the set assignment for the field; whether it is made with an equals sign "=" or with an implicit set operator, e.g. "+=". The logic is identical to how current selection is merged with a set expression.

Examples:

```
{<OuterSet>} Sum( {<InnerSet>} Field )
```

The OuterSet will be inherited into the InnerSet, since the inner set lacks set identifier.

```
{<OuterSet>} Sum( {$<InnerSet>} Field )
```

The OuterSet will not be inherited into the InnerSet, since the inner set expression contains a set identifier.

Aggr()

The set expression of the outer aggregation will never be inherited into the inner aggregation. But a set expression outside the outer aggregation will be inherited into both.

Examples:

```
Sum({<Set1>} Aggr(Count({<Set2>} Field )))
```

The Set1 will not be inherited into Set2.

```
{<OuterSet>} Sum({<Set1>} Aggr(Count({<Set2>} Field )))
```

The OuterSet will be inherited into both Set1 and Set2.

Summary

Nothing changes for existing set expressions – they will continue to work. But with this additional syntax we hope to simplify your work and your expressions and allow you to re-use your master measures more effectively.

This change affects all Qlik Sense editions from the August 2022 release. It will also be included in the next major QlikView release, planned for late spring 2023.

15

Aggr() and Nested Aggregations

Aggr() is one of the most powerful functions in the Qlik engine. It allows a user to define arbitrary nested aggregations. But it is also one of the most complicated functions, and so it merits a chapter of its own.

This chapter is about its syntax and all its intricacies.

A primer on the Aggr() function

The Aggr() function was introduced because there was a need for nested aggregations, and the Qlik engine couldn't at the time handle such calculations. For example, if you want to calculate the largest order value in a sales database, you need to do it in two steps:

1) Calculate the value for all orders. (An order can have multiple order lines, so this value is in itself an aggregation.)

2) Among the order values created in bullet 1, find the largest one.

The first bullet will aggregate the order lines using Sum(), and the second bullet will aggregate the orders using Max(). Hence, two aggregations.

The Aggr() function was designed to solve this problem. Its structure allows aggregations in two steps – an inner and an outer aggregation.

In fact, this is the *only* thing the function does: It allows you to define a for-next loop where an aggregation is made in each loop, that produces an array of values that you subsequently can aggregate in a second step.

The syntactical structure of the function is:

```
Aggr( InnerMeasure, GroupBySymbol )
```

The **InnerMeasure** defines what should be calculated in each step, and the **GroupBySymbol** is the iterator. Normally, when you use it, you would use aggregation functions both inside and outside the Aggr() call. In the case of the largest order value, the expression would look like the following:

```
Max( Aggr( Sum(Amount), OrderID ))
```

This means that the Aggr() function creates an intermediate temporary table that can be used for further calculations:

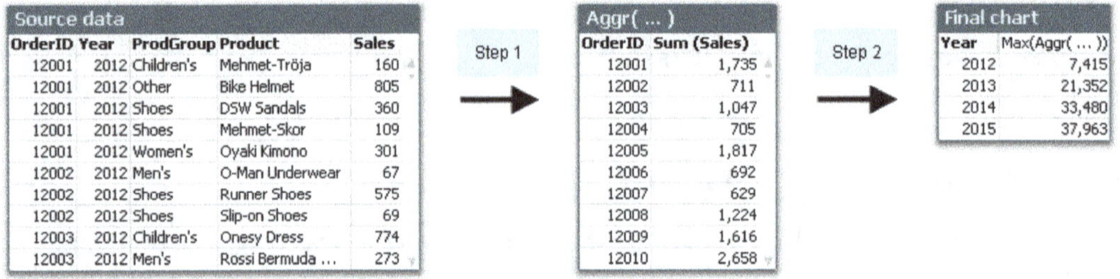

This intermediate table is not visible in your Qlik app, and this can sometimes be confusing. So, if you have a problem with your expression, you may need to create this table manually, just to be able to debug.

The Aggr() function can also be used to create new dimensions and new fields. Say, for example, that you have a sales database, and want to make a bar chart with the number of customers that have placed 1, 2, 3, etc. orders – one bar for how many orders they have placed. Then you can do this by using the following expression as *dimension*:

```
Aggr( Count(distinct OrderID), Customer )
```

As measure in your bar chart, you can use anything you want, but one of the two following would make sense:

```
Count(distinct Customer)
Sum(Amount)
```

The Aggr() function is an extremely powerful tool that can solve very complicated problems. The only drawback is that it is fairly CPU-demanding. So, be careful when you have a lot of data.

When should Aggr() NOT be used?

Originally posted in the Qlik Design Blog on Mar 11, 2013

I have noticed in the discussion forum on QlikCommunity that Aggr() often is used when it isn't necessary. And since you get a performance penalty when you use the function, today's post is about *discouraging* you from using it when you don't need to.

So, when should you *not* use it?

1. Standard Aggregations

Standard, non-nested aggregations, e.g. "Sum(**Sales**)" or "Count(distinct **OrderID**)" can be used almost anywhere in a Qlik app, in charts, in text boxes and as labels in any object. They will work directly as they are. *Here you do not need any Aggr() function.*

If you want to calculate the aggregation several times, e.g. once per customer, just use the aggregation function in a chart and use **Customer** as dimension. Nothing else.

This seems obvious, but I have on multiple occasions seen developers use the Aggr() function in such situations. Totally unnecessary – and it will just increase response times.

Bottom line: You should not use Aggr() for standard non-nested aggregations.

2. Calculation of a subtotal within the same chart

In some cases, you need to use a subtotal from the same chart in your calculation. Then you should use the total qualifier inside your Sum() function (or other aggregation function). It will perform the given calculation disregarding one or several dimensions of the chart. It will however respect the selection.

For instance, the sales in percent can be calculated using

```
Sum( Sales ) / Sum( total Sales )
```

This expression will return the sum of sales for each possible dimensional value, as a fraction of all possible sales. In other words; "Sum(total **Sales**)" disregards all dimensions of the chart.

Sum (Number)						
Dim1	Dim2	Dim3	X	Y	Z	Total
	⊟ a		2	1	1	4
A	b		6	4	6	16
	Total		8	5	7	20
	⊟ c		4	7	4	15
B	d		14	12	9	35
	Total		18	19	13	50
	⊟ e		6	16	24	46
C	f		22	18	20	60
	Total		28	34	44	106
Total			54	58	64	176

Annotations (pointing to circled values):
- Sum(total <Dim2> Number) → 16
- Sum(total <Dim1,Dim3> Number) → 5
- Sum(total <Dim1> Number) → 50
- Sum(total Number) → 176
- Sum(total <Dim3> Number) → 58

Bottom line: You should not use Aggr() for calculating subtotals that you can calculate with the total qualifier.

3. Calculation of an Average

If you can avoid the Aggr() function by writing your expression smarter, you should. One specific case is a standard average.

For example, say that you want to calculate the average order value. This is a nested aggregation: First you need to sum the sales value per order (an order can have several order lines), and then you need to average over the resulting set of sales values per order. In other words: You can calculate it using:

```
Avg( Aggr( Sum( Sales ), OrderID ) )
```

But since it is a linear calculation, you can also calculate the same number just by dividing with the number of orders:

```
Sum( Sales ) / Count( distinct OrderID )
```

… which in most cases is evaluated faster. Also, the latter expression is easier to understand for the person responsible for the application maintenance.

Bottom line: You should usually not use Aggr() for calculating an average that is a ratio of two separate aggregations.

4. Static aggregations

Sometimes you want to classify a dimensional value (customers, products, suppliers, etc.) using static aggregations, e.g. "Customers that only placed one order" or "Customers that bought goods at a total value higher than X". "Static" meaning that you do not want the classification to change as you make a selection.

In such a case, the aggregation should not be made in the UI, but rather when creating the data model and stored as a separate field.

Bottom line: Aggregations for classification of dimensional values should often be made by creating an attribute field in the script using a "Group By".

Pitfalls of the Aggr() function

Originally posted in the Qlik Design Blog on Oct 6, 2015

The Aggr() functions is one of the most advanced functions in the Qlik engine, and it is not always easy to use. This blog post is about its most common pitfalls.

This is a function that enables the app developer to create nested aggregations, i.e. aggregations in two steps. Essentially the Aggr() is a For-Next loop where each loop contains a measure calculation. When all loops have been performed, a final aggregation based on the array of calculated measures can be made.

If we, for instance, want to calculate the monthly product sales, we could do it by using

```
Aggr( Sum(Sales), ProductName, OrderMonth )
```

This will produce a virtual table that looks like

InnerMeasure	ProductName	OrderMonth
7 060	Davenport Shoes	2022 Dec
6 030	Davenport Shoes	2022 Sep
5 982	Davenport Shoes	2022 Jun
1 496	Davenport Shoes	2022 Oct
45 442	Halter Dress	2022 Mar
36 813	Halter Dress	2022 Sep
16 143	Halter Dress	2022 Nov
8 106	Halter Dress	2022 Dec
7 725	Jack Flash Dress	2022 Oct
1 640	Jack Flash Dress	2022 Jun
1 558	Jack Flash Dress	2022 Sep
1 265	Jack Flash Dress	2022 Apr
…	…	…

Note that there is exactly one row per distinct combination of the two dimensions.

So, the Aggr() function creates a virtual table; an array of values that need to be aggregated in a second step. Hence you should wrap the Aggr() in an outer aggregation function. For instance, if you want to use the above table to calculate the average monthly sales, you should use

```
Avg( Aggr( Sum(Sales), ProductName, OrderMonth ))
```

Average monthly sales

ProductName	Avg(Aggr(Sum(Sales),ProductName,OrderMonth))
Totals	**5 542**
Davenport Shoes	4 030
Halter Dress	16 910
Le Baby Dress	1 620
Slip-on Shoes	3 221
Summit Hiking Boots	3 459
Terence Top	969

With this mental picture of how the function works, we can start looking at the pitfalls.

1. Missing inner aggregation function

The first parameter of the Aggr() is the inner measure, and as such it is *always* an aggregation. Hence, you should use an aggregation function. If you don't, the calculation will use Only() and the virtual table may inadvertently get NULLs in the measure column. See more in the chapter on "Hypercubes and Aggregations".

2. Missing outer aggregation function

The outer aggregation function is needed whenever Aggr() returns more than one value. If no aggregation function is specified, Only() will be used, which may cause your chart measure to contain NULLs.

Note the totals line in the chart above: It shows the average over both products and months. Generally, totals will be NULL if the outer aggregation is omitted.

3. Missing Set Analysis expression

So, there are both inner and outer aggregation functions. Where do I put my Set Analysis expression?

The answer is often "In both". It may not be enough to have it in only one of the levels.

The current selection (or the relevant selection state) will always affect the aggregation scope of an aggregation function, unless you specify otherwise using Set Analysis. So, if you need Set Analysis you should in most cases have similar or identical Set Analysis expressions in both the inner and outer aggregation function. See the next article for a more detailed description of the problem.

4. Grain mismatch

When an Aggr() is used in a chart, you have inner dimensions in the Aggr() and outer dimensions in the chart. Then it is important that these match.

The grain of the Aggr() dimensions must be identical or finer than that of the chart dimensions.

For example, an Aggr() with **OrderMonth** as dimension can be put in a chart that has **Year** as dimension, provided that **OrderMonth** contains both year and month. In the following table, the average monthly sales numbers are correctly calculated, and displayed as an average per year and product.

Avg(Aggr(Sum(Sales),ProductName,OrderMonth))					
ProductName	**OrderYear**	2020	2021	2022	2023
Davenport Shoes		1 780	4 030	4 620	4 892
Halter Dress		-	16 910	25 789	18 057
Le Baby Dress		1 524	1 620	2 325	4 273
Slip-on Shoes		420	3 221	2 571	1 052
Summit Hiking B…		1 204	3 459	4 331	4 073
Terence Top		2 188	969	1 944	3 413

But the opposite isn't necessarily possible. If you put an Aggr() with **Year** as dimension in a chart with **OrderMonth** as dimension, you will get problems. You may get a table that looks like this:

Avg(Aggr(Sum(Sales),ProductName,OrderYear))					
ProductName	**OrderMonth**	2022 Jan	2022 Jul	2022 Aug	2022 Nov
Davenport Shoes		-	-	53 810	-
Halter Dress		162 512	-	-	-
Le Baby Dress		-	-	-	34 188
Slip-on Shoes		-	-	9 470	-
Summit Hiking B…		-	36 653	-	-
Terence Top		-	27 305	-	-

Here, the Aggr() function has produced one number per product and year, and this number has been assigned to one single month while the other months contain NULL. This is a result of the grain mismatch and most likely not what you want.

With this, I hope that you have a better understanding of Aggr().

Set Analysis in the Aggr() function

Originally posted in the Qlik Design Blog on Mar 8, 2016

The Aggr() function is one of the most advanced functions in the Qlik engine, and it is not always easy to use. It does not get easier when you put set analysis expressions in it.

In one of my previous posts (Pitfalls of the Aggr function) I recommended having the set analysis expression in both the inner and the outer aggregation function when using set analysis in the Aggr() function. This is a good rule of thumb, because in most cases doing so will generate the result that you want.

But this is not always correct.

In more complex calculations you often need to use the condition *in one place only* – sometimes in the inner aggregation, sometimes in the outer. It depends on how the condition is formulated. Then it is important to understand the difference between the two positions.

The evaluation of the Aggr() function is a two-step process: In the first step, an intermediary virtual table is created using the inner aggregation and the dimension of the Aggr(). In the second step, this virtual table is aggregated using the outer aggregation.

For example, say that you want to find the largest order value per year. Then you would need to first calculate the sales value per order, and in a second step find the largest of these values:

```
Max( Aggr( Sum( Amount ), OrderID ) )
```

The first step aggregates the source data: The Sum(Amount) is calculated over multiple records per **OrderID** into a virtual table with one record per **OrderID**. The second step – the Max() function – finds the largest values in the virtual table.

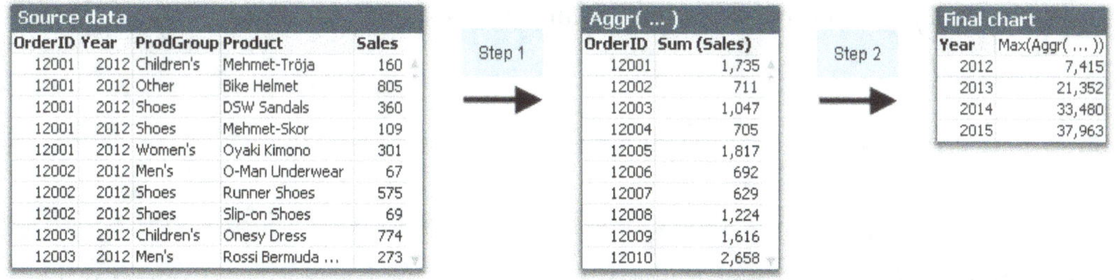

However, there is not yet any set analysis in the expression. So, let us use the following requirement instead:

1. Show the largest order value per year
2. Include only products from the product group "Shoes" in the order value
3. Calculate these numbers only for 2014 and 2015

The two conditions correspond to the following set analysis expression:

```
{<ProdGroup={Shoes}, Year={2014,2015}>}
```

But where should this expression be written? In the outer or in the inner aggregation?

To answer this question, we must ask ourselves *in which step* the conditions should be used. Then it becomes obvious that the condition on the product group *must* be used in step one – in the inner aggregation. If it is used in the outer aggregation only, the order values will be incorrect – they will be calculated from *all* products.

The condition in year, however, can be put in either place. Hence, the following expression will work fine:

```
Max(Aggr(
    Sum({<ProdGroup={Shoes}, Year={2014,2015}>} Amount),
    OrderID
))
```

From the above example one might draw the conclusion that you always should put the condition in the inner aggregation. But this is *not* the case. Sometimes you have a condition that cannot be put in the inner aggregation. The following requirement can serve as example:

1. Per year, show the bestselling product within the product group "**Shoes**"
2. Show how this product ranks compared to all products, also non-shoes

The goal is the following table:

Best ranking product within "Shoes"		
Year	Product	Rank
2012	Davenport Shoes	2
2013	Summit Hiking Boots	4
2014	Summit Hiking Boots	2
2015	Davenport Shoes	2

Since the rank should be calculated over all products, you cannot have the condition on product group already in step one – it must be in step two. The inner aggregation must calculate the rank, and the outer must pick out the best product.

So, the expressions used for Product and Rank, respectively, are:

```
FirstSortedValue({<ProdGroup={Shoes}>}
    Product,
    Aggr(Rank(Sum({1} Amount)), Year, Product)
    )

Min({<ProdGroup={Shoes}>}
    Aggr(Rank(Sum({1} Amount)), Year, Product)
    )
```

Bottom lines are:

- You need to figure out if your condition should be evaluated in step one (in the inner aggregation) or in step two (in the outer aggregation). This will determine where to put the set analysis expression. You may need to use The Feynman Problem Solving Algorithm. (See the last chapter).

- If you can't figure out where to put your set analysis expression – try putting it in both the outer and the inner aggregation function, and keep your fingers crossed. Afterwards you should however verify that the numbers are what you want.

Aggr() and Nested Aggregations

16

NULL and Missing Values

Nothing is a concept that can take many forms.

- What is the difference between a NULL and a missing value?
- How are NULLs propagated in expressions?
- How does a Qlik app display NULLs?
- How do I make NULLs selectable?
- How do I search for NULLs?
- Can NULLs be used in key fields to link tables?
- What is Ternary Logic?

These questions and others are answered in this chapter.

The Importance of Nothing

Originally posted in the Qlik Design Blog on Jun 29, 2012

Few things are as important to understand as the concept of nothingness. Or, rather, the fact that there are always many levels of nothingness.

In physics, **vacuum** is the word used for nothingness. But whereas the best vacuum on earth contains billions of molecules per cubic meter, vacuum in outer space contains fewer than a dozen. So, these two vacua are completely different. And neither is really empty.

What if we find some space completely void of molecules? Would that represent nothingness? No, because the space would still be traversed by force fields, e.g., gravitation from distant stars. But space void of force fields, then? No, you would still have vacuum fluctuations, a quantum mechanical effect that can create particles from nothing. True nothingness may perhaps not exist. But one thing we know for sure is that there are levels of nothingness; one vacuum is not the same as the other.

In Lund there is a statue of Nothingness (Swedish: "Intighet"). There is nothing there, except the void of statue. But the statue's existence is shown by a small plaque in the ground.

To complicate matters, there is a second plaque some distance away that announces that the statue of Nothingness has been stolen. The two plaques illustrate both the sense of humor in the student city of Lund and the universal existence of different levels of nothingness.

Picture 4: *The statue of Nothingness.*

In databases and in the Qlik engine, NULL is the word used for nothingness. But this is not the only type of nothingness. Also here you have different levels:

- The simplest representation of nothingness is the numeric 0 (zero). But this is not true nothingness since there is a numeric value in the field. The value will be used for calculations, e.g., it will affect both Count() and Avg(). So, it is certainly not NULL.

- Another level of nothingness is the empty string. This may not be as obvious, but also this is a field value that affects the calculation of Count(). Hence still not NULL.

- The next level is the true NULL. This is when you have a record in the database, but there is no value for the specific field. This cell in the table is marked as NULL, meaning that "a value is missing here."

- The final level is when the entire record is missing. An example is if you have a **Customers** table and an **Orders** table and a specific customer has not placed any orders. Then the customer is not represented in the order table and there is no table cell that can be marked as NULL. These are called Missing values and are treated the same as NULL values – when possible.

If you want to present data in a correct way and at the same time enable the user to search for missing values, e.g., customers that have not bought a specific product, you need to understand the different cases of nothingness. Nothing could be more important.

NULL – The Invisible Nothing

Originally posted in the Qlik Design Blog on Apr 30, 2013

NULL is not a value. It is a *lack of value.* It is a placeholder that marks nothingness.

So, how does the Qlik engine show the concept of nothing – when this is the relevant answer to the user's click? To investigate this, I will use a hypothetical database with two tables: **Customers** and **Orders**. The **Customers** table is a list of customers, and the **Orders** table is a list of orders that these customers have placed.

List boxes

In the picture below, you have a selection of two customers that haven't placed any orders, i.e. they exist in the **Customers** table but there are no corresponding records in the **Orders** table. As a result, all values in the **OrderID** list box are gray.

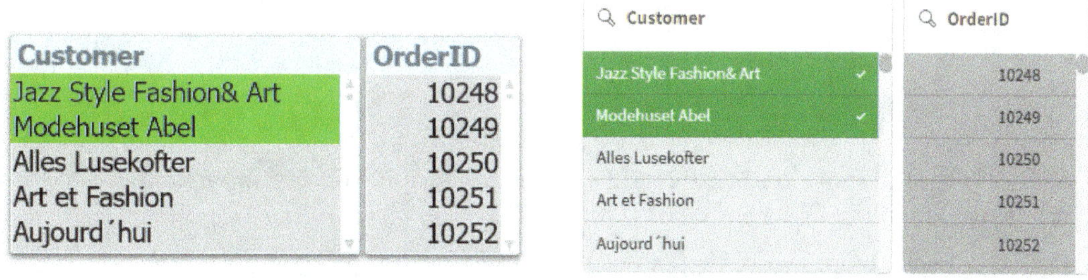

In other words, for a list box, it is simple: NULL is not visible as an explicit list box entry. If all entries are marked as gray, then the empty set is the answer to the click. I.e. NULL is the answer.

If you have a list box where you have a visible entry that is blank; that you can click on and that can be selected, then it is not a NULL. NULLs are *never* visible in list boxes and can never be selected. Instead, you have an empty string or some kind of white space.

Chart dimensions

For a chart, it becomes more complicated. First of all, a NULL can occur either as a dimensional value or in the measure – the expression. These are two very different cases and should not be confused. Further, the two cases are managed in two different places in the chart properties.

With the above data, it would be reasonable to make a chart that shows sales per customer. If there are orders that are not attributed to any customer (an error in the database), then you will get a NULL in the dimension of the chart – a NULL which is displayed as a dash. Below you can see that order nr 10874 has no customer associated:

Customer	OrderID	Sum(Amount)
Alles Lusekofter	10639	193,36
For The Dark Night	10545	263,70
TTT-The Ticky Tie	11081	1 057,50
-	10874	66,00
Total		**1 580,56**

If you don't want to show lines with NULLs in the dimension, you can suppress these on the **Dimensions** tab in the QlikView chart properties.

In Qlik Sense it looks almost the same:

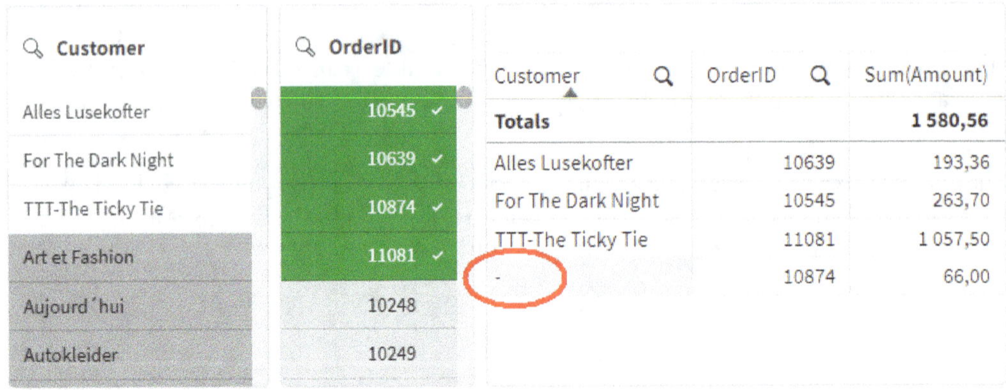

Customer	OrderID	Sum(Amount)
Totals		**1 580,56**
Alles Lusekofter	10639	193,36
For The Dark Night	10545	263,70
TTT-The Ticky Tie	11081	1 057,50
-	10874	66,00

Also here you can suppress NULL values. Just uncheck "Include NULL values" in the dimension.

Chart measures

If your data is the other way around, so that you have NULLs in the measure, it will be different. For example, if you have customers that are not attributed to any orders, you will get NULLs in **OrderID** and **Amount**. However, the Sum() and Count() functions still return zero, which is correct, since Sum(NULL) is zero. Other aggregation functions such as Only() may return NULL, though, and this will be displayed as a dash.

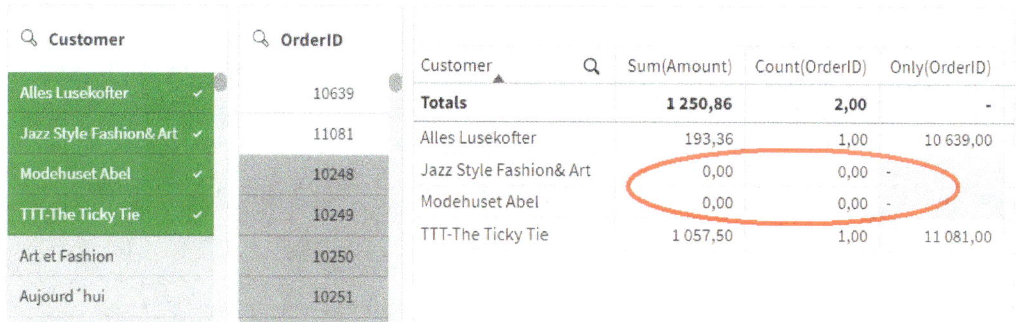

If you don't want to show lines with zeros or NULLs as expression value, you can suppress these in the chart properties: In QlikView, on the Presentations tab, and in Qlik Sense under Add-ons, "Include zero values".

Labels and Text boxes

In other places where a NULL can occur, e.g. labels, text boxes, buttons, etc., NULLs are displayed as dashes. In these places, NULL is visible but not selectable.

So, the bottom line is that NULLs are sometimes visible, sometimes not. Sometimes they are displayed as dashes, and when aggregated, usually as zeros. But they are never selectable.

And with this, I hope that the mystery around NULLs is somewhat less of a mystery.

Finding Missing Values

Originally posted in the Qlik Design Blog on May 02, 2013

There are different cases for missing values in a data model. Either there are NULLs or there are entire records missing. But how can you find them?

So how do you search for NULLs? How do you find the customers that didn't buy product X? Or, how do you find the users that didn't log on this month? There is no search string that matches NULL and even if there were, you can't select NULL.

NULLs cannot be selected explicitly, so to find the records with NULLs, the selection must always be made in *another field*. In the example of customers not having bought product X, it means that the **Product** field for some customers is NULL. Hence, you need to select the customers for which the **Product** is NULL.

In other words – you need to make the selection in a field other than where you have the NULL. And here's how you do it:

1. Set your selection criteria the normal way.
2. Use Select Excluded on the field where you want to negate the selection.

For example, if you want to find customers that have not bought Basket Shoes, then you should first select Basket Shoes from the Product list box. Then you will in your **Customer** list box have the customers that indeed bought Basket Shoes. But the grey customers are the ones you are looking for. So, click the magnifying glass on the **Customer** list box, then the three dots, and then **Select Excluded**. Voilà!

In QlikView, you right click, and then **Select Excluded**.

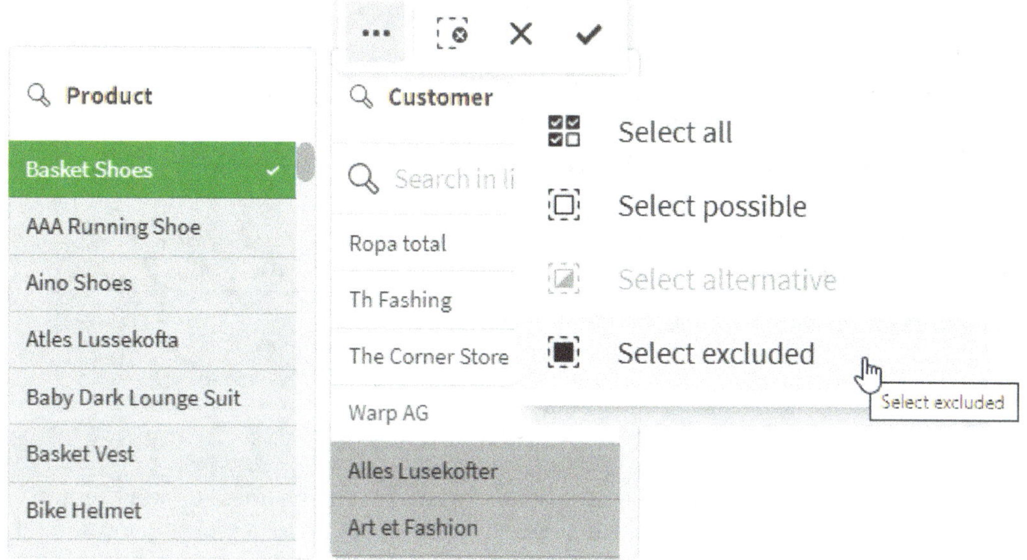

A second example was how to find users that have not logged on this month. Analogously, you first select the month and then you negate the selection by using **Select Excluded** on the **User** list box.

A third example could be that you want to find the customers that have not bought any product at all. Then you should first right-click the products and **Select All**. This will maybe not change very much, but it will exclude the customers that never placed any orders. In other words: These are now gray and can be selected using **Select Excluded**.

A final example could be that you have a combination of criteria, e.g. you want to find customers that have not bought any shoes in the last few months. The method is still the same: Select relevant products and select relevant time range. The possible customers are the ones that have bought of the products in the time range, and the excluded customers are the interesting ones. **Select Excluded**!

However, when you have a combination of selections, the Qlik engine doesn't always remove both of the initial selections when you select the excluded values, so to get it right you should combine it with a **Clear Other Fields**.

A good, user-friendly solution in QlikView is to put both commands in a button that you label **Select Excluded Customers**.

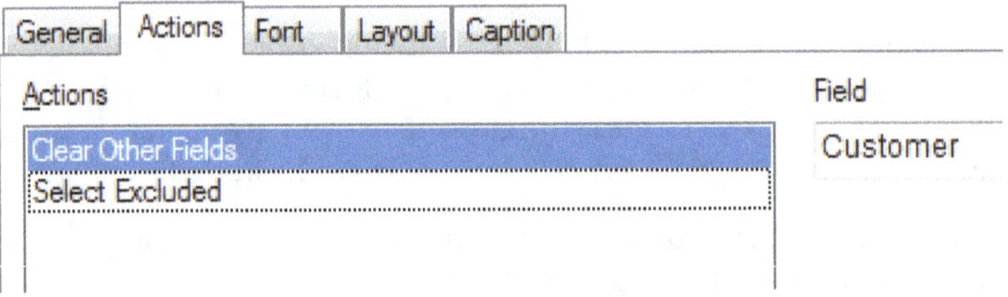

NULL – A Deep Dive

Extract from the Technical brief "NULL and Nothing" published on Apr 26, 2013

In databases as well as in the Qlik engine, nothingness is represented by the concept of NULL, i.e. a field "value" to show that there is no value assigned to the field in this record. Strictly speaking, NULL is not a value – it is a lack of value. Although I know this well, I sometimes call it "NULL value" anyway.

NULLs have certain basic properties:

- All Qlik fields and all data types in a SQL database are NULL-able.

- In SQL, NULL does not have a data type. In the Qlik engine, this corresponds to the fact that NULLs are not dual, i.e. they do not have both a string representation and a numeric representation.

- NULLs propagate. If you use a NULL in an expression, it will *not* cause an error. Rather, it will propagate through the expression and yield a result which often – but not always – is NULL.

- NULLs cannot be used as key value to join or link tables.

- NULLs are neither visible nor clickable in Qlik list boxes and charts, unless you make them visible and clickable using a method described below. This means that NULLs are not selectable in the Qlik engine.

A consequence of the above is that if you select all values in list box, you will get a different result in other list boxes than if you select no values.

The reason for this is that the first case excludes records with NULLs, which could mean that you exclude real values in other fields that potentially are used in calculations.

But there are also other types of nothingness …

Different types of Nothingness

NULL is not the only way to describe nothingness in a Qlik app. There are many other cases of nothingness, some which should not be confused with NULL:

Numerical zero

If a field has a numerical zero in it – 0 – then this of course represents a numerical nothingness, but it is certainly not the same as NULL. The field *has* a value and is hence not NULL. The IsNull() function will return FALSE and the record will be included in the calculation of both Avg() and Count().

Empty strings and white space

A string that looks empty is another candidate for nothingness, but also this is different from NULL. It could be an empty string, i.e. a string with the length zero, or it could be a string containing white space. In any case, such a string *is a string* and not a NULL. For these, the IsNull() function will return FALSE and the record will be included in the calculation of Count() but not in Sum() and Avg() since it is not numeric.

Note that there are several type of characters for white space: soft blanks, hard blanks, the tab character, and ideographic space. (Character 32, 160, 09, and 12288, respectively). If you use the trim functions, you should be aware that these only remove soft blanks and no other characters.

True NULLs

True NULLs are cases when an existing record in the data model has a field where the value is missing and it hence is marked as NULL. These NULLs have all the properties described in the introduction.

There are several ways that true NULLs can get into the Qlik data model:

- Databases often contain NULLs and if you use a database connector to load data into a Qlik app, you may well get NULLs in your application.

- If you have joins or concatenations in the Qlik script, the missing values will be converted to NULLs. This is true both for the external SQL commands (“**JOIN**” and “**UNION**”) and for the internal Qlik prefixes (“**Join**” and “**Concatenate**”).

- Some functions, e.g. an If() with only two parameters, Only(), and most notably Null(), may return NULL and if these functions are used in the Qlik script, you will most likely get NULLs in your application.

A text file does not contain any NULLs in itself, so unless you load it using functions that can generate NULLs, or the table is part of a concatenate or a join operation, the data model will not have any NULLs in the table.

The IsNull() function will return TRUE for NULLs and the record will not be included in the calculation of any aggregation function, except NullCount().

Missing values – Type one: Different cardinality of key field

In Qlik there is also the concept of missing values. These are cases where the entire record is missing for a specific field value or combination of field values. Hence, there is no specific cell in the table that can be marked as NULL.

The first type of missing value is the case when a record is missing in one table in the data model, for a specific field value existing in another table. This happens when the key field has different sets of distinct values – different cardinality – in two different data tables. To get this type of missing value, you must thus have at least two data tables.

For example, if you have a customer table and an order table, it could happen that a specific customer has not placed any orders yet. I.e., the customer is represented in the customer table but not in the order table. So, there are no records in the order table for this customer.

Customers			Orders		
CompanyName	**CustomerID**		**CustomerID**	**OrderID**	**OrderDate**
Bólido Comidas preparadas	BOLID		BOLID	10326	10/7/1993
GROSELLA-Restaurante	GROSR		BOLID	10801	12/26/1994
Paris spécialités	PARIS		BOLID	10970	3/21/1995
			GROSR	10268	7/27/1993
			GROSR	10785	12/15/1994

In the example in the picture, the customer with the **CustomerID** 'PARIS' is not represented in the **Orders** table and values for **OrderID** and **OrderDate** are missing for this specific customer.

If you in such a situation create a chart that uses fields from both tables, the chart will for calculation purposes generate an internal virtual table – the combination of the two data tables. In this virtual table, a missing field value will be treated as NULL and the IsNull() function will return TRUE. The record will not be included in the calculation of any aggregation function using this field, except NullCount().

CustomerID	Count (OrderID)	NullCount (OrderID)
BOLID	6	0
GROSR	4	0
PARIS	0	1

Missing values – Type two: Cross table with incomplete Cartesian product

The second type of missing value occurs if you have a Qlik chart with two or more dimensions. The best example is a cross table, i.e. a pivot table with at least one vertical dimension and at least one horizontal dimension. Then you might get a situation where a specific combination of dimensional values is not represented in the data but still has a cell in the pivot table.

Both dimensional fields may even exist in the same data model table. Hence, you can potentially get this type of missing values with just one data model table and two dimensions.

Data

Year	Quarter	Amount
2011	Q1	120000
2011	Q2	110000
2011	Q3	130000
2011	Q4	190000
2012	Q1	125000
2012	Q2	140000

Sum(Amount)

Year	Quarter Q1	Q2	Q3	Q4
2011	120000	110000	130000	190000
2012	125000	140000	-	-

IsNull(Amount)

Year	Quarter Q1	Q2	Q3	Q4
2011	False	False	False	False
2012	False	False	-	-

This type of missing value is also treated as a NULL when possible. It is, however, not always calculated. An example of this situation is if you have a data table with amounts per quarter and the table also holds a field Year.

In the example shown in the picture, there are amounts for all quarters in 2011 but not for Q3 and Q4 2012. When the pivot table is calculated, an algorithm loops over all records in the database. Since there are no data records for the last two quarters, the consequence is that the expression is never calculated for these cells (middle and rightmost tables). So basically it looks as if IsNull() has returned NULL, when it in fact has not been calculated at all.

Kleenean logic

Before we look at how NULLs propagate through expressions, we need to look at Kleenean logic. (From Stephen Cole Kleene, a US mathematician.)

Most people know well what Boolean logic is: It is the algebra you use when you want to deal with concepts that are TRUE or FALSE. Using Boolean logic, you can set up truth tables to define how to propagate values through an expression. Below you see the Boolean truth tables for the OR and AND operators.

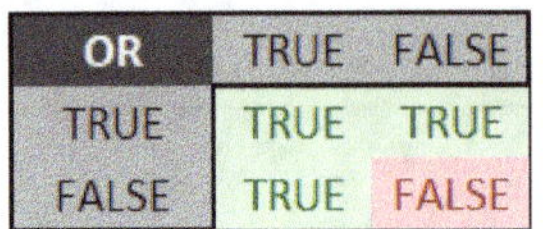

OR	TRUE	FALSE
TRUE	TRUE	TRUE
FALSE	TRUE	FALSE

AND	TRUE	FALSE
TRUE	TRUE	FALSE
FALSE	FALSE	FALSE

However, neither SQL databases nor the Qlik engine use Boolean logic internally. Instead, they use Kleenean logic, also called three-valued logic or ternary logic. The reason for this is that although Boolean fields are defined as having two possible values, they have in reality *three* possible states: TRUE, FALSE or NULL. As a consequence, you need to define how to propagate a NULL just as well as propagating a TRUE or a FALSE. Below you find the truth tables for the OR and AND operators, but using Kleenean logic.

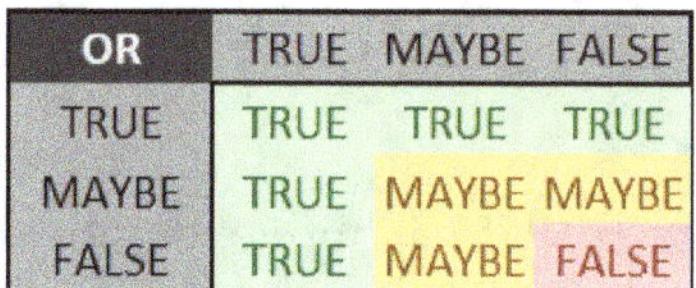

OR	TRUE	MAYBE	FALSE
TRUE	TRUE	TRUE	TRUE
MAYBE	TRUE	MAYBE	MAYBE
FALSE	TRUE	MAYBE	FALSE

AND	TRUE	MAYBE	FALSE
TRUE	TRUE	MAYBE	FALSE
MAYBE	MAYBE	MAYBE	FALSE
FALSE	FALSE	FALSE	FALSE

In the above tables, the third value is referred to as MAYBE, but it could just as well be denoted as "Undefined", "Unknown", "Indeterminate" or NULL.

Kleenean logic is a tool that helps us define how NULL should be propagated through different operators and functions. The two truth tables above (MAYBE replaced with NULL) define how the OR and AND operators work in the Qlik engine.

The tables above show that [NULL OR TRUE] evaluates to TRUE, whereas [NULL AND TRUE] evaluates to NULL.

NULL propagation

NULL propagates in all expressions. This means that the calculation will be made although some operands or function parameters are NULL. The result is often NULL, but sometimes not. Here follow the main rules for how NULL propagates.

- The NOT operator will return NULL only if the operand is NULL.

- If the condition (the first parameter) of an If() function evaluates to NULL, the ELSE expression (the third parameter) will be returned. I.e. the If() function does not necessarily return NULL just because the condition is NULL.

X	X	If(X,True(),False())	NOT X
TRUE	TRUE	TRUE	FALSE
NULL	NULL	FALSE	NULL
FALSE	FALSE	FALSE	TRUE

- Boolean operators return NULL when appropriate. For the AND operator it is enough that one of the operands is FALSE for the operation to return FALSE, and for the OR operator it is enough that one of the operands is TRUE for the operation to return TRUE. See below.

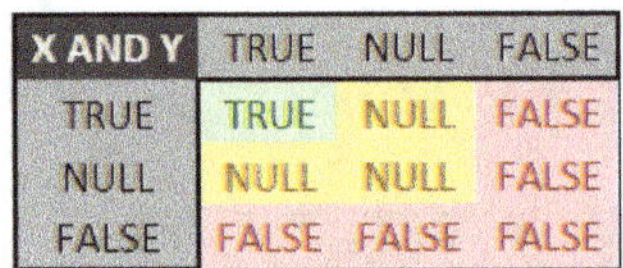

X AND Y	TRUE	NULL	FALSE
TRUE	TRUE	NULL	FALSE
NULL	NULL	NULL	FALSE
FALSE	FALSE	FALSE	FALSE

X OR Y	TRUE	NULL	FALSE
TRUE	TRUE	TRUE	TRUE
NULL	TRUE	NULL	NULL
FALSE	TRUE	NULL	FALSE

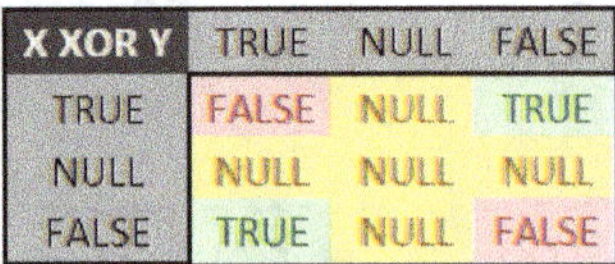

X XOR Y	TRUE	NULL	FALSE
TRUE	FALSE	NULL	TRUE
NULL	NULL	NULL	NULL
FALSE	TRUE	NULL	FALSE

- The equality and inequality operators will return NULL if both operands are NULL. But if only one of the operands is NULL, the comparison will always *deny equality*, i.e. the equality operator will return FALSE and the inequality operator will return TRUE. So, in principle, equality operators should be avoided when testing for NULL. Equality operators will *never* confirm the existence of NULL. Use the function IsNull(Field) instead. Examples:
  - Field = Null() evaluates to FALSE or NULL. It will never evaluate to TRUE.
  - IsNull(Field) evaluates to TRUE or FALSE depending on the field value.

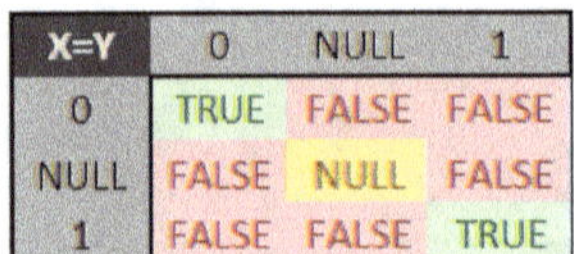

X=Y	0	NULL	1
0	TRUE	FALSE	FALSE
NULL	FALSE	NULL	FALSE
1	FALSE	FALSE	TRUE

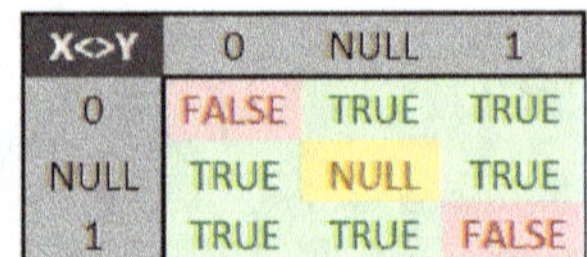

X<>Y	0	NULL	1
0	FALSE	TRUE	TRUE
NULL	TRUE	NULL	TRUE
1	TRUE	TRUE	FALSE

- Other relational operators will always return NULL if any of the operands is NULL.

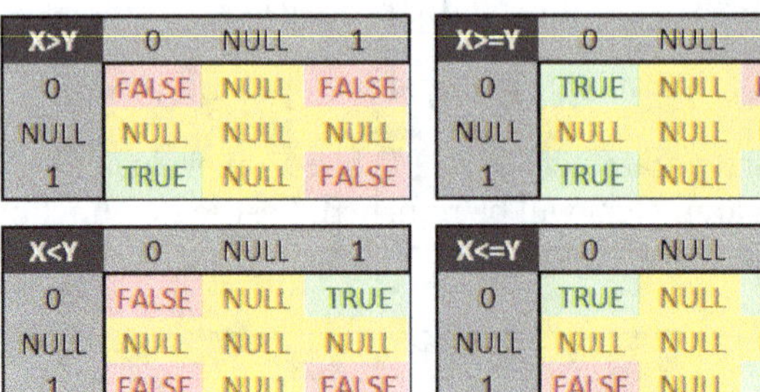

X>Y	0	NULL	1
0	FALSE	NULL	FALSE
NULL	NULL	NULL	NULL
1	TRUE	NULL	FALSE

X>=Y	0	NULL	1
0	TRUE	NULL	FALSE
NULL	NULL	NULL	NULL
1	TRUE	NULL	TRUE

X<Y	0	NULL	1
0	FALSE	NULL	TRUE
NULL	NULL	NULL	NULL
1	FALSE	NULL	FALSE

X<=Y	0	NULL	1
0	TRUE	NULL	TRUE
NULL	NULL	NULL	NULL
1	FALSE	NULL	TRUE

- The LIKE operator is special. It is not a symmetric comparison – it is a test of the first operand only to see whether this resembles the second operand. It returns NULL if the second operand is NULL, and only then.

X LIKE Y	0	NULL	1
0	TRUE	NULL	FALSE
NULL	FALSE	NULL	FALSE
1	FALSE	NULL	TRUE

- The string concatenation operator returns NULL only if both operands are NULL. This means that string concatenation works fine and returns a string if one of the operands is a string. Examples:
  - Null() & Null()　　　　evaluates to NULL.
  - 'xyz' & Null()　　　　evaluates to 'xyz'.
  - '' & Null()　　　　evaluates to an empty string and not to NULL

X & Y	C	NULL	D
A	AC	A	AD
NULL	C	NULL	D
B	BC	B	BD

- Any arithmetic operation having NULL on one side will evaluate to NULL. However, if you use the Range functions instead, you can get an expression that interprets NULL as zero. Examples:
  - Null() + 5　　　　evaluates to NULL
  - RangeSum(Null(), 5) evaluates to 5

X + Y	1	NULL	2
4	5	NULL	6
NULL	NULL	NULL	NULL
8	9	NULL	10

X - Y	1	NULL	2
4	3	NULL	2
NULL	NULL	NULL	NULL
8	7	NULL	6

X * Y	1	NULL	2
4	4	NULL	8
NULL	NULL	NULL	NULL
8	8	NULL	16

X / Y	1	NULL	2
4	4	NULL	2
NULL	NULL	NULL	NULL
8	8	NULL	4

- Most numeric functions return NULL if the parameter is NULL. The Range functions are an exception. Examples:
    - Sqrt(Null())   returns NULL
    - Sqrt(RangeSum(Null()))   returns 0
- Most string functions return NULL if the parameter is NULL. If you want an empty string instead, you can use a string concatenation inside the string function. Examples:
    - Left(Null(), 1)   evaluates to NULL
    - Left('' & Null(), 1)   evaluates to an empty string
    - Len(Null())   evaluates to 0: NULL has zero length
    - Index(Null(), 'x')   evaluates to 0: 'x' cannot be found in NULL
- An If() function where only two parameters are used will use Null() as ELSE expression.

- Aggregation functions are normally not affected by NULLs, i.e. they do not use the record with the NULL in the calculation. Except NullCount() which counts the records having NULL.

- The Only() aggregation function returns NULL if there are multiple possible values of the parameter, or if there are no possible values. It returns the parameter value if there is only one possible value. This includes the case when there are several records with only one possible value, but at the same time there are some records with NULL.

- The NullCount() aggregation function returns the number of records with NULLs. When used in charts, it returns 1 also for missing values of type one (although there are no records in data) and 0 for missing values of type two.

Some tips

How to convert empty fields or blank strings to NULL?

If you have blanks or a specific symbol in a text file and you want to convert these to NULLs, you can use the Qlik variable **NullInterpret**:

```
Set NullInterpret = '';
```

This will convert all blank fields in a text file to NULLs.

You can also set a specific field to NULL using the following construction in the Load script. If the condition is not fulfilled, the If() function will return NULL.

```
If( Len(Trim(Field))>0, Field ) as Field
```

How to display NULLs?

NULLs are normally not displayed. However, there are a couple of ways that you can assign values to NULLs to make these visible.

First, if you load data from ODBC and want to display these, you can use the Qlik variable **NullDisplay** to define a string that replaces NULLs:

```
Set NullDisplay = '<NULL>';
```

But if your data comes from another source, e.g. text files, you can use the statement **NullAsValue** together with a definition of a string that should replace the NULLs. Subsequent Load statements will convert the NULLs to this string.

```
NullAsValue *;
Set NullValue = '<NULL>';
```

Instead of the wild card, you can specify in which fields this should be done.

There are however several things to be careful of when using **NullAsValue**. The first one is when you load tables using optimized QVD loads. An optimized load will not change the data within the QVD and will hence not convert the NULLs. You will need to force the Qlik engine to load the data unoptimized. A simple where-clause will do the trick, but I prefer to write code that is more explicit, so I remember why I did it when I look at the script a year later.

My suggestion is hence:

```
If( Len(Trim(Field))>0, Field, '$(NullValue)' ) as Field,
```

Another problem is that NULLs created through the **Join** and **Concatenate** prefixes will only be partially converted. The only way to make these values visible is to run a second pass through the table, using Load resident after the join or the concatenate has been performed. Example:

```
// --------- Temporary table ---------
Temp:
Load * From A;
Concatenate
Load * From B;

// --------- Final table ---------
Data:
NoConcatenate
Load * Resident Temp;
Drop Table Temp;
```

How to test for NULLs and missing values?

You cannot use the equal sign to test if a field value is NULL. You need to use the IsNull() function:

```
IsNull(Field)
```

However, this function will return FALSE for empty strings and often you want to treat empty strings and strings only containing spaces (soft blanks, Chr(32)) the same way as you treat NULLs. Then you could instead use the test

```
Len(Trim(Field)) = 0
```

This expression first removes leading and trailing soft blanks, then calculates its length. Soft blanks, empty strings, NULLs and missing values will all have zero length in this test.

Sometimes you want to extend the test to include also field values with any type of whitespace, i.e. also hard blanks (Chr(160)), tabs (Chr(09)) and ideographic space (Chr(12288)). Then you should use the following test:

```
Len(Purgechar(Field, Chr(09)&Chr(32)&Chr(160)&Chr(12288)))=0
```

A test for missing values is almost the same. All the above functions work for these also. In addition, when you test for missing values in the script, you can use the Exists() function and compare the content of the current table with what you previously have loaded. If you do not have a proper field to compare with, you can always create a temporary field that is used for this comparison only.

How to search and select NULLs or missing values?

NULLs cannot be selected explicitly, so to find the records with NULLs, the selection must always be made in another field. For example, if you have a list of people and you know that some of the records lack phone numbers, i.e. the phone field is sometimes NULL, you need to select the unique person identifiers for which the phone number is NULL.

Using "Select Excluded"

The easiest way to find values that lack an attribute is to make a selection in two steps:

1) First select all phone numbers (right-click the phone numbers and choose **Select All**, or search using a star as a wildcard: "*").
2) Then look for the excluded person identifiers, and select these (right-click the person identifiers and choose **Select Excluded**).

This method works for both NULLs and missing values of type one. It can also be used for similar questions like "Which customers have not bought a certain product?" Just select the product and then select the excluded customers.

See more in the article "Finding Missing Values".

Using advanced search

Another approach is to make an advanced search. Then the user can explicitly search for a person having records that lack phone numbers. Mark the list box with the person identifier and enter the following search expression:

This will explicitly find people that have one or several records with NULL in the phone field. This method works for both NULLs and missing values of type one.

Create a field in the data model that allows selecting excluded values

A third possibility is to prepare logic for selecting NULLs and missing values in the script, i.e. by creating fields that hold the information necessary.

For the missing phone numbers (true NULLs), you could add a Boolean field that indicates whether the record has a phone number of not:

```
People:
LOAD
    PersonID,
    If( Len(Trim(Phone))>0, 'Yes', 'No') as [Has phone],
    ...
    FROM People;
```

For the customers that have not placed any orders (missing values type one), you could add a Boolean field that indicates whether the customers have placed any orders or not (whether the key is represented in another table):

```
Orders:
LOAD CustomerID,
    ...
    FROM Orders;

Customers:
LOAD CustomerID,
    If(Exists(CustomerID),
        Dual('Yes',True()),
        Dual('No',False())
        ) as [Has orders],
    ...
    FROM Customers;
```

The Exists() function compares the value of **CustomerID** in the **Customers** table with all previously loaded values of this field. If the value has been loaded before, the Exists() function returns TRUE; if not, it returns FALSE. Note that in order for this to work, the **Orders** table must be loaded first.

The Dual() functions are not necessary, but by using them the created field can be used directly as a Boolean flag in conditions.

This approach has the advantage that it is obvious for the user how to find the missing values and at the same time all other search possibilities are maintained.

NULLs and missing values in Set analysis

Most of the above is applicable also in set analysis.

In set analysis, searches are made using double quotes. Also advanced searches can be made, and a search for NULLs can be made using the logic described above. Hence:

```
Concat({<PersonID={"=NullCount(Phone)>0"}>} distinct PersonID)
```

will work the same way as the example above in the paragraph "Using advanced search": The expression will count the people that do not have a phone number.

Empty element sets, either explicitly e.g. <Product = {}> or implicitly by a search with no hits <Product = {"Perpetuum Mobile"}>, mean no product, i.e. they will result in a set of records that are not associated with any product.

Note that the set modifier <Product = > is not the same as <Product = {} >. The former merely removes the existing selection in the field, whereas the latter returns an empty set.

Set operators

In set analysis, set operators can be used to find the complement to a selection, i.e. the excluded records. For example, the set expression

```
{$<OrderID={"*"}>}
```

will pick out all possible **OrderIDs** – but not the NULLs – and consequently,

```
{1-$<OrderID={"*"}>}
```

will return the complement: it will pick out records from all customers that have an empty **OrderID** set, i.e. that have not placed any orders.

Implicit field value definitions

Finally, in set analysis it is also possible to use the implicit field value definitions P() and E(), which returns the set of possible values and excluded values, respectively. The E() set function is especially useful. Example:

```
{<Customer = E({1<Product={"*"}>})>}
```

This expression will pick out the customers that are excluded when all products are selected, i.e. the customers that have not bought anything.

Further:

```
{<Customer = E({1<Product={'Shoe'}>})>}
```

This specific expression will pick out the customers that are excluded when the product "Shoe" is selected, i.e. the customers that have not bought any shoes.

17

Security and Section Access

Data security refers to a range of tools, controls, and measures designed to establish and preserve data confidentiality, integrity, and availability. This chapter will focus on how to preserve the confidentiality of data in a Qlik app.

A security mechanism in Qlik can be set up in several different ways: It can either be built into the Qlik app script, or it can be set up using rules in the Qlik Management Console, or it can be set up using the QlikView Publisher.

Authentication and Authorization

When dealing with security, there are two central concepts you need to understand: *Authentication* and *Authorization*.

Authentication is the process of verifying that the users really are who they claim themselves to be.

Authorization is the process of granting the authenticated user access to data or tools and features, based on who the user is and what groups he belongs to.

Although the two terms sound alike, they play separate roles in securing applications and data. Understanding the difference is crucial. Combined, they determine the security of a system. You cannot have a secure solution unless you have configured both authentication and authorization correctly.

The authentication process is always performed *outside* the Qlik infrastructure. It can be performed using Passwords, PIN codes, Authentication apps or biometrics. For cloud solutions, there are different identity providers that can be used. Often a log-on is made on a web site, that produces a token that is sent to the Qlik server. For on-premise solutions, the Windows log-on is the most common authentication method.

The authorization is however handled by the Qlik infrastructure. Access to apps can be defined e.g. in the Qlik Management Console.

Further, access to specific rows inside an app can be defined in Section Access in the load script.

How Section Access can be configured is described in the following articles.

A Primer on Section Access

Originally posted in the Qlik Design Blog on May 27, 2014

Section Access is a feature that is used to control the security of an application. It is basically a part of the load script where you can define an authorization table, i.e. a table where you define who gets to see what. The Qlik engine uses this information to reduce data to the appropriate scope when the user opens the application.

This function is sometimes referred to as *Dynamic Data Reduction*, as opposed to the loop-and-reduce of the QlikView Publisher, which is referred to as *Static Data Reduction*.

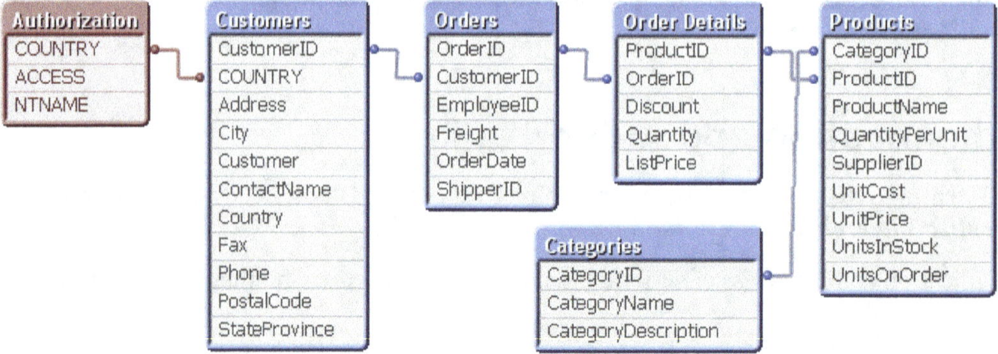

For example, above you have the authorization table in Section Access to the left, linking to the field **COUNTRY**. (In a real application, the authorization table is not visible in the data model.) This means that when a user opens the application, the Qlik engine uses the username (in QlikView "**NTNAME**" and in Qlik Sense "**USERID**") to establish which countries this user is allowed to see, and then makes the corresponding selection in the **Customers** table.

The selection propagates to all the other tables in the standard Qlik manner, so that the appropriate records in all tables are excluded, whereupon the Qlik engine reduces the scope for this user to only the possible records. This way, the user will only see data pertaining to the countries to which he is associated.

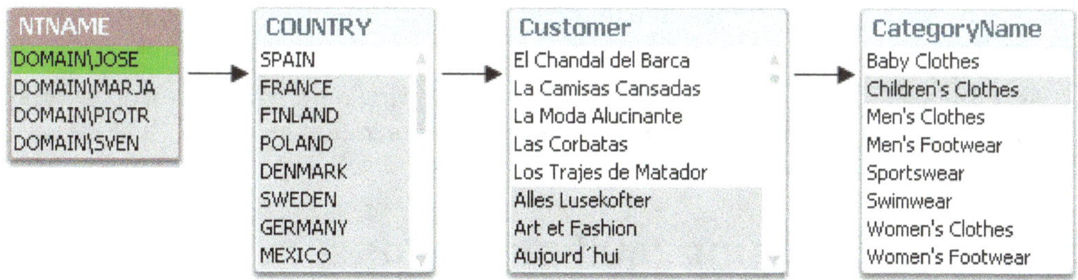

A good way to debug your Section Access is to temporarily remove the Section Access statement and run the script. The authorization table will then be visible in the data model, and you can make selections in **NTNAME**.

Within Section Access you should define at least three fields: **ACCESS**, **USERID/NTNAME** and a third reducing field that links the authorization table with the real data. You may have additional fields also, like user roles or departments.

Some points to note around Section Access:

- All fields in Section Access must be upper case. Hence, the reducing field must be in upper case also in the data. Use the Upper() function and name the fields in upper case.

- In QlikView, don't use the fields **USERID** and **PASSWORD**, unless it is for testing or debugging. Proper authentication is achieved through **NTNAME**.

- **USERID/NTNAME** is the field used to match an authenticated user – also if you set up ticketing using other authentication mechanisms than Windows integrated security.

- **NTNAME** may contain names of groups as well as individual users.

- In QlikView, make sure "Initial Data Reduction … " and "Strict Exclusion" are checked (Document properties - Opening). If the field value of the reducing field in Section Access doesn't exist in the real data, there will be no data reduction unless Strict Exclusion is used.

- If your QlikView users work off-line, i.e. download the physical qvw file, the security offered by Section Access has limited value: It does keep honest people honest, but it will not prevent a malicious user from seeing data which he shouldn't have access to. So, for off-line usage I instead recommend the static data reduction offered by the QlikView Publisher, so that no files contain data the user isn't allowed to see.

- In most of the examples in the online help, an inline Load is used in Section Access. But it is of course not a good place to keep an authorization table in the load script. Store it in a database and load it using a SELECT statement instead!

And finally

- Always save a backup copy when making changes to Section Access. It is easy to lock yourself out ...

Section Access is a good, manageable and flexible way of allowing different access scopes within one document. And when used on a server, it is a secure authorization method.

Data Reduction Using Multiple Fields

Originally posted in the Qlik Design Blog on Jun 3, 2014

Last week I wrote about authorization using Section Access and data reduction. In the example, a user was associated with a country and this entry point in the data model determined whether a record was visible or not: Only records associated with the country were visible. **COUNTRY** was the reducing field.

But if you want several reducing fields? You may have a user that should see one product group in one country, and another product group in another country. Then both **COUNTRY** and **PRODUCTGROUP** should be reducing fields. Is that possible?

Yes and No.

Yes, it is possible. But *No*, you cannot just add a second reducing field. In simple cases, just adding a second reducing field will work fine, but as soon as the logic is slightly more complex, it will not work. Below I'll explain why.

Let's use the following example: A user named Markus should see the machines in Germany and food in France – but not the other way around. Then the obvious approach would be to create an authorization table like the following:

ACCESS	NTNAME	COUNTRY	PRODUCTGROUP
USER	MARKUS	GERMANY	MACHINES
USER	MARKUS	FRANCE	FOOD
USER	MARJA	FINLAND	<ALL>
USER	...	...	...

I.e. the table has two reducing fields – **COUNTRY** and **PRODUCTGROUP** – defining the following logic for Markus:

('GERMANY' AND 'MACHINES') OR ('FRANCE' AND 'FOOD')

However, *this will not work in the Qlik engine.*

If you do the above, you will get a data model like the following (where the red table is the Section Access table).

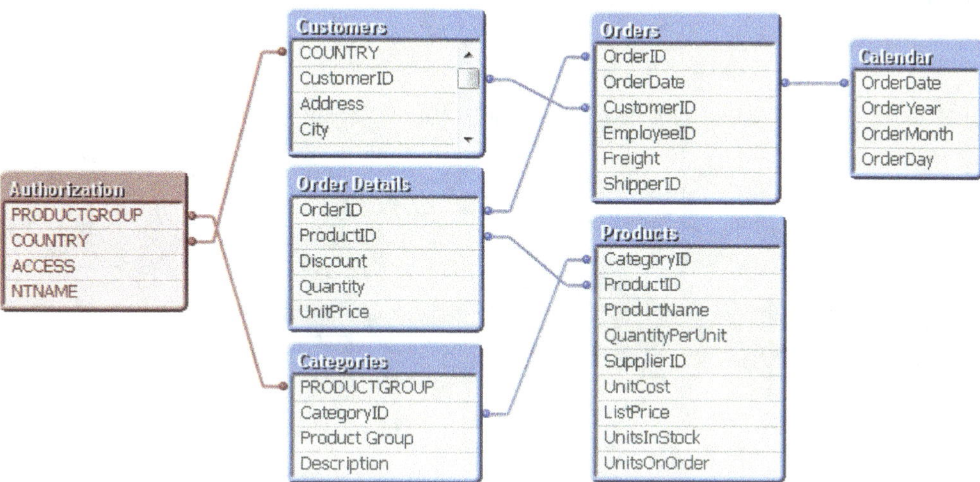

This means that the Section Access selections will be made in **COUNTRY** and in **PRODUCT-GROUP**. But remember that the Qlik engine always uses OR-logic between values of the same field and AND-logic between fields. This means that the Qlik engine will interpret the selection in these two fields as

('GERMANY' OR 'FRANCE') AND ('MACHINES' OR 'FOOD')

which is not the same as the initial requirement. The selection made will include Machines in France and Food in Germany, which is against the initial requirement. In fact, it is impossible to make a selection that corresponds to the initial requirement using only these two fields.

So, what should you do?

The solution is to create a new, single reducing field based on **COUNTRY** and **PRODUCT-GROUP**, e.g. through

```
COUNTRY & '|' & PRODUCTGROUP as AUTHORIZATIONKEY,
```

The first challenge is to find the table where this key should be created. It must be in a table with a grain fine enough that both country and product group are uniquely defined on each record. In the above data model this is the **Order Details** table: Each order line has only one product and one customer – thus one product group and one country – associated with it. So, the authorization key should be created here.

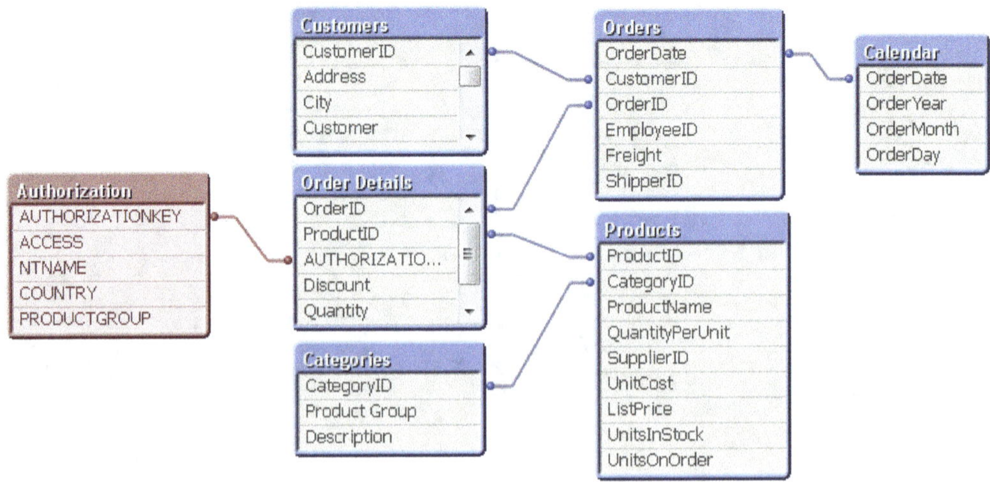

There are other challenges also, e.g. how to get the country and product group information into the load of the **Order Details** table (Solution: ApplyMap) and how to handle the concept of *Any Value* (Solution: Generic Keys), but these can all be solved. For details, see the blog post about Complex Authorization.

Bottom line: You can use multiple reducing fields in Section Access, but only if each user has only one record in the authorization table. If a user has several records, you need to create one single authorization key.

Also, the above example clearly shows that authorization is part of the data modelling and should be thought of at an early stage in the development process.

Basics for complex authorization

Originally posted in the Qlik Design Blog on Oct 03, 2012

Authorization is about determining which data a user is allowed to see. QlikView has several different ways by which you can reduce the data so that the user only gets to see the data he is allowed to see.

In the simplest case, the authorization table defining who-gets-to-see-what is just a two-column table linking usernames to e.g. regions. But sometimes you need a more complicated logic. It could be that you have users that are allowed to see all products but just within one region, and at the same time all regions but just for one product. In other words, you want to make the reduction in several fields with the possibility of OR-logic.

The Qlik engine can do this and here's how you do it:

1) Create an authorization table using a special symbol like '<Any>' to denote any value in this field. See the left table in the image below.

2) Load this authorization data into the Qlik app after concatenating the reducing fields into one single generic authorization key:

```
Section Access;
[Qlik Authorization Table]:
Load
    Upper('USER')                  as ACCESS,
    Upper(User)                    as USERID,
    Upper(Region &'|'& Product) as %AUTHID
    From AuthorizationTable;
Section Application;
```

The resulting table should look like the right one below:

Source Authorization Table			Qlik Authorization Table	
User	**Region**	**Product**	**USERID**	**%AUTHID**
Adam	<Any>	A	ADAM	<ANY>|A
Adam	USA	<Any>	ADAM	USA|<ANY>
Bruce	<Any>	C	BRUCE	<ANY>|C
Bruce	Australia	B	BRUCE	AUSTRALIA|B

3) Create an authorization key in the table with the most detailed transactions:

```
FactTable:
Load *,
    Region &'|'& Product as AuthID From OrderDetails;
```

If you don't have all the necessary keys in the table, you can fetch fields from other tables using Applymap(). See more about Applymap() in the chapter "Data modelling".

4) Create an authorization bridge table linking the two above tables. Since the %AUTHID field can contain generic symbols such as '<ANY>', several load statements are needed to create the bridge table:

```
AuthorizationBridge:
Load distinct
    Region        &'|'& Product  as AuthID,
    Upper(Region &'|'& Product) as %AUTHID From OrderDetails;
Load distinct
    Region        &'|'& Product  as AuthID,
    Upper(Region &'|'& '<Any>') as %AUTHID From OrderDetails;
Load distinct
    Region        &'|'& Product  as AuthID,
    Upper('<Any>'&'|'& Product) as %AUTHID From OrderDetails;
Load distinct
    Region        &'|'& Product  as AuthID,
    Upper('<Any>'&'|'& '<Any>') as %AUTHID From OrderDetails;

Right Join (AuthorizationBridge)
Load distinct
    Upper(Region &'|'& Product) as %AUTHID
    From AuthorizationTable;
```

The last load statement (with the **Right Join**) is there to reduce the number of records: Only the necessary records are kept. The resulting table should look like the following one:

Authorization Bridge Table	
AuthID	**%AUTHID**
Australia|A	<ANY>|A
Australia|B	AUSTRALIA|B
Australia|C	<ANY>|C
Germany|C	<ANY>|C
USA|A	<ANY>|A
USA|A	USA|<ANY>
USA|B	USA|<ANY>
USA|C	<ANY>|C

5) Reduce the file on the USERID field using either Section Access or QlikView Publisher.

Using the above method, you can create quite complex security models. For instance, you can use generic symbols also for product groups. Read more about generic keys in the chapter with the same name.

Authorization using a Hierarchy

Originally posted in the Qlik Design Blog on Nov 26, 2013

Hierarchies are very common in all database and business intelligence solutions. Often, they are used for authorization purposes, i.e. the permissions to see data follows a hierarchy.

One example is an organizational hierarchy. Each manager should obviously have the right to see everything pertaining to their own department, including all its sub-departments. But they should not necessarily have the right to see other departments.

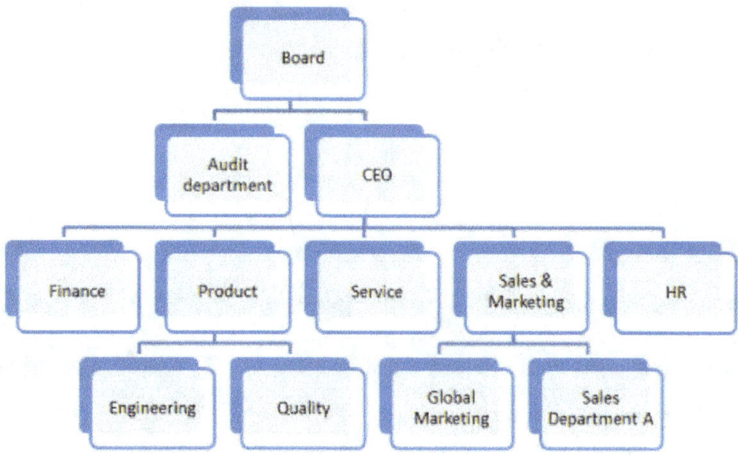

This means that different people will be allowed to see different parts of the organization. The authorization table may look like the following:

ACCESS	NTNAME	Person	Position	Permissions
USER	ACME\BKO	Bill	CPO	HR
USER	ACME\DKN	Diane	CEO	CEO
USER	ACME\DPT	Debbie	Director Engineering	Engineering
USER	ACME\JOO	John	CFO	Finance
USER	ACME\LBY	Les	COO	Sales & Marketing
USER	ACME\SDN	Steve	CTO	Product

In this case, Diane is allowed to see everything pertaining to the CEO and below; Steve is allowed to see the Product organization; and Debbie is allowed to see the Engineering organization only. Hence, this table needs to be matched against *sub-trees* in the above hierarchy.

Often the hierarchy is stored in an Adjacent Nodes table, and if so, the above problem is easy to solve: Just load the Adjacent nodes table using a **HierarchyBelongsTo** and name the ancestor field **Tree**. See the blog post "Unbalanced, n-level hierarchies" how this is done.

If you want to use Section Access, you need to load an upper-case copy of **Tree** and call this new field **PERMISSIONS**. Finally, you need to load the authorization table. These two last steps can be done using the following script lines: (The **TempTrees** table is the table created by the **HierarchyBelongsTo**.)

```
Trees:
Load *,
    Upper(Tree) as PERMISSIONS
    Resident TempTrees;
Drop Table TempTrees;

Section Access;
Authorization:
Load ACCESS,
    NTNAME,
    Upper(Permissions) as PERMISSIONS
    From Organization;
Section Application;
```

When you have done this, you should have a data model that looks like the following:

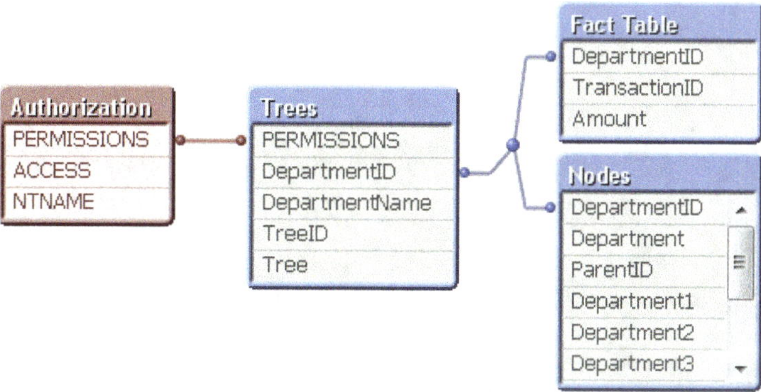

The red table is in Section Access and is invisible in a real application. Should you want to use the QlikView Publisher for the reduction, you can reduce right away on the **Tree** field, without loading the Section Access. In either case, this solution will effectively limit the permissions to only the sub-tree as defined in the authorization table.

But what if the hierarchy is stored as a horizontal hierarchy? Then you cannot use the **HierarchyBelongsTo**.

DepartmentID	Department	Board level	Director level	Department	Unit
1	Board	Board	-	-	-
2	Audit department	Board	Audit department	-	-
4	CEO	Board	CEO	-	-
5	Finance	Board	CEO	Finance	-
13	Engineering	Board	CEO	Product	Engineering
14	Quality	Board	CEO	Product	Quality
16	Global Marketing	Board	CEO	Sales & Marketing	Global Marketing
17	Sales Department A	Board	CEO	Sales & Marketing	Sales Department A
18	Sales Department B	Board	CEO	Sales & Marketing	Sales Department B
23	Logistics Group	Board	CEO	Service	Logistics Group
26	Salary Group	Board	CEO	HR	Salary Group

A horizontal hierarchy

The solution is not very different from the above one. The only difference is that you need to create the bridging table manually, e.g. by using a loop:

```
For each vAncestor in 'Director level','Department','Unit'
    Trees:
    Load distinct
        Upper([$(vAncestor)]) as PERMISSIONS,
        DepartmentID
        Resident [Horizontal Hierarchy]
            Where Len([$(vAncestor)]) > 0;
Next vAncestor
```

Having done this, you will have the following data model:

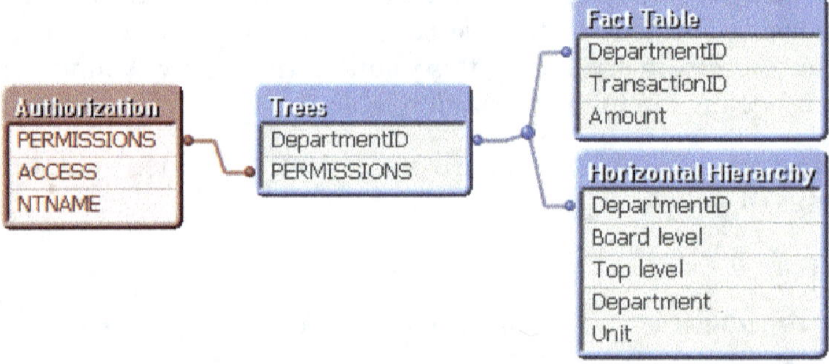

Bottom line is that it is fairly straightforward to implement a hierarchical authorization scheme. See more about Hierarchies in the chapter with this name.

Data Reduction – Yes, but How?

Originally posted in the Qlik Design Blog on Jun 9, 2014

I recently wrote a blog post about authorization using Section Access and data reduction. In the example, a person was associated with a country and this entry point in the data model determined whether a record was visible or not: Records associated with the country were visible. "**Country**" was the reducing field.

The data reduction was made using row-level security. But there are other ways of limiting access to data. This post is about how you limit access to the data:

- **Row-level access**
  You have a reducing field that determines whether a user can see a specific piece of data. If you use **Country** as reducing field and the user is allowed to see 'Spain', this will mean that only rows associated with Spain will be visible: E.g. sales transactions to customers in other countries will not be visible.

- **Aggregation-level access**
  This is similar to the above, however with the difference that all data are in principle visible but the aggregation level changes depending on country: A user that is allowed to see 'Spain' will see the detailed information about Spain, but only high-level aggregated information about other countries. For other countries detailed information will be hidden.

- **Column based access**
  Instead of limiting per row, you can limit per column. Here you can define that only some users are allowed to see specific fields, typically fields like **Salary** or **Bonus**.

- **Object based access**
  You can also limit access to a specific sheet, graph or pivot table depending on which user it is.

An application can use a combination of the four different methods.

Both Section Access and the loop-and-reduce in the QlikView Publisher use row-level access to allow one single (master) file to be used in different security scopes. It is *by far* the best way to limit access to data and should be the one you normally aim for.

It is difficult to achieve aggregation-level access within one single application, so it is better to solve this problem using multiple applications: One with detailed data that you reduce using a reducing field, and a second unreduced with aggregated data for all countries.

The column-based access can be achieved using two applications, one that includes the sensitive fields and the other that doesn't. It can also be achieved in one single application using the **OMIT** field in Section Access.

Finally, the object-based access: This method has in my mind very little to do with security: If a chart is hidden for a specific user, he can still see the same data through other objects. Or even worse – if you allow collaboration, he can create a private object that shows the same thing. A show condition could be convenient to use for document objects, but it is a poor tool for security.

Bottom line: If you want security, you should use Section Access or the loop-and-reduce of the QlikView Publisher. You should also consider having your data in several applications. But you should *not* use show conditions for security purposes.

Row-level security in Qlik Cloud

Originally posted in the Qlik Design Blog on Nov 4, 2020

Implementing Section Access in Qlik Coud can be challenging. There are several hurdles: The username could be different in the cloud than in an on-premise installation, and the logic in Section Access is different between Qlik Sense and QlikView. This blog post will help you set up a secure solution.

Security in a Qlik app is often achieved using a feature called "Section Access". It is an extremely flexible and useful feature that permits row-level security inside an app. It also allows data-driven security definitions instead of manually defined static rules. See more on "A Primer on Section Access".

The basic idea is to load an authorization table that defines what different users are allowed to see:

NTNAME	COUNTRY
ACME\JOE	USA
ACME\URSULA	GERMANY
ACME\STEFAN	SWEDEN

When the app is opened, the Qlik engine makes an invisible selection corresponding to the proper user scope (**COUNTRY**) and removes all excluded data, also in other tables. This way, each user will only see what he or she is authorized to see.

First, is the question of username: In QlikView and Qlik Sense on Windows, the username needs to be in the NetBIOS format:

ACME\jsmith

But this username cannot always be found among the claims of the identity provider used in the cloud. To see the claims of your identity provider, you need to log on to Qlik Cloud and append "/api/v1/diagnose-claims" to the URL:

You will then get something that, when formatted, is similar to the following:

```
{
"subType":"user",
"internalClaims":{
    "userId":"ivhM0mwD_a3TjQYbgndDwVWrTaEwfIAy",
    "name":"Henric Cronström",
    "preferred_username":"hic@qlik.com",
    "email":"henric.cronstrom@qlik.com",
    "groups":[
        "AP-QlikTech All",
        "AP-Licenses",
        "AP-RnD"
```

Here you can see the attributes sent by your identity provider to Qlik Cloud. In this example, there is no attribute among the claims that corresponds to the NetBIOS username.

Solution 1

When you set up your Qlik Cloud tenant, you should make sure that the NetBIOS username (also called sAMAccountName) is mapped to the "sub" claim. This will be compared to NTNAME and USERID in Section Access.

```
{
"subType":"user",
"internalClaims":{
    "userId":"ixbM0mwD_a3TjQYb
    "sub":"QLIK\\HIC"
    "name":"Henric Cronström",
```

If you do this, your on-premise Section Access will work in Qlik Cloud. No other changes are needed. You can use an authorization table like the one below, both on premise and in the cloud, since the field NTNAME now works in all Qlik platforms.

ACCESS	NTNAME	COUNTRY
USER	ACME\JOE	USA
USER	ACME\URSULA	GERMANY
USER	ACME\STEFAN	SWEDEN

Solution 2

Without the NetBIOS username, you need to authenticate the user in a different way, e.g. through the e-mail address. But this means that you need to modify your authorization table slightly. The new table could look like this:

ACCESS	NTNAME	USER.EMAIL	SERIAL	Comment	COUNTRY
USER	ACME\JOE	*	*	Access on-prem	USA
USER	*	joe.smith@acme.com	QLIKCLOUD	Access in cloud	USA
USER	ACME\URSULA	*	*	Access on-prem	GERMANY
USER	*	ursula.schultz@acme.com	QLIKCLOUD	Access in cloud	GERMANY
USER	ACME\STEFAN	*	*	Access on-prem	SWEDEN
USER	*	stefan.svensson@acme.com	QLIKCLOUD	Access in cloud	SWEDEN

Note that each user now has two records: One for on-premise access, one for cloud access. The wildcards ensure that only the relevant authenticating fields are used.

The simplest way to create the duplicate records is to add a second Load statement in the script:

```
LOAD ACCESS,
    NTNAME,
    '*'              as USER.EMAIL,
    '*'              as SERIAL,
    COUNTRY
FROM "AuthorizationTable.xlsx" ... ;

LOAD ACCESS,
    '*'              as NTNAME,
    EMAIL            as USER.EMAIL,
    'QLIKCLOUD'  as SERIAL,
    COUNTRY
FROM "AuthorizationTable.xlsx" ... ;
```

The SERIAL field is used for an environment test. Without it, the records pertaining to cloud would give access to all users in an on-premise QlikView environment: Existing QlikView installations ignore the field USER.EMAIL. But with the SERIAL field, QlikView will deny access for all records where SERIAL doesn't have a wildcard.

Solution 3

Use groups in NTNAME or GROUP to identify users. These fields will be compared to the "groups" claim. By using groups, you don't need to identify individual users.

Summary

- NTNAME can be used in all environments. On-premise it is checked against the name of the authenticated user. In Qlik Cloud it is checked against the "sub" claim and the "groups" claim.

- USERID can be used in Qlik Cloud. It is checked against the "sub" claim.

- GROUP can be used in Qlik Cloud. It is checked against the "groups" claim.

- USER.EMAIL can be used in Qlik Cloud where it is checked against the "email" claim. It does not yet work in other platforms.

- SERIAL can be used in Qlik Cloud as an environment test. It passes the test if it contains the string 'QLIKCLOUD'. The corresponding check does not yet work in QlikView.

- The prefix 'USER.' is reserved for new Section Access fields.

Finally – we will continue our work to improve Section Access so that customers can create one single authorization table that works across all platforms.

Good luck with your cloud deployment!

18
Searches

Searches can be made in many places in the Qlik products: In the catalog, in the hub, and in the app – both in fields and inside set expressions.

This chapter covers only the searches that can be made in fields, i.e. searches that aim to pick out individual field values and select them. It is applicable to both interactive searches and searches in set expressions.

The Search String

Originally posted in the Qlik Design Blog on Mar 3, 2015

One of the strengths of the Qlik engine is its search function. With it, you can find pieces of information in a fraction of a second and select the found field values. But how is the search defined? And where can the search be used?

Obviously, a search is defined by the search string that you enter when you search for something. But there are several different ways a search string can be interpreted. See for instance the picture below: In the normal search to the left, you have a different result set from what you get in the wildcard search.

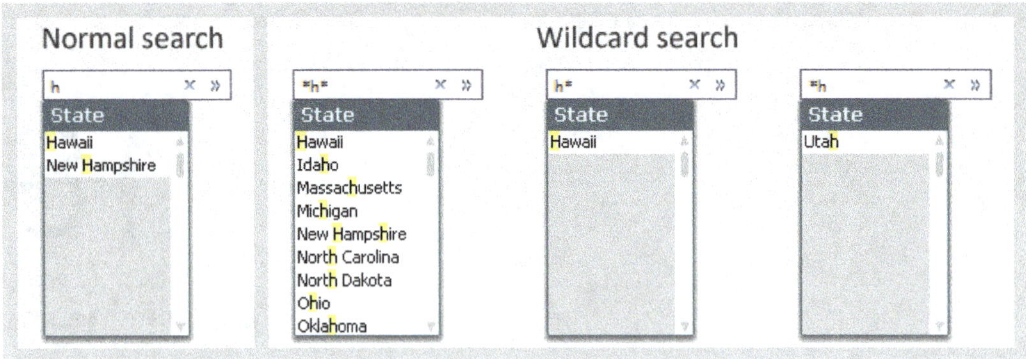

The logic is the following:

- **Normal search**
  The search string is matched against the *beginning of every word* in the field value. Normal search is used only in interactive searches.

- **Wildcard search**
  If the search string contains a wild card or the search string is used in a programmatic search (e.g. in a Set Analysis expression), a wildcard search is made instead of a normal search. This means *a strict, case insensitive, match between the search string and the field values*, where the only way of representing unknown characters is explicit use of wild cards.

- **Numeric search**
  If the search string begins with '<' or '>', *a numeric comparison* is made. E.g. '>=1000'. Only values that fulfill the numeric requirement will be matched.

- **Expression search**
  If the search string begins with an equals sign '=', an expression search is made. E.g. '=Sum(Sales)>1000'. Then *an aggregation* is made for each value in the field, and a match is found if the expression is true. This means that you can make a search in one field based on an aggregation in another field.

- **Fuzzy search**
  If the search string begins with '~', a fuzzy search is made. This means that all field values are ranked according to similarity and the top one will be selected when you hit return.

- **Compound search**
  Using a compound search, you can express more complicated search conditions with logical operators. Use brackets and '&' or '|', e.g. '(California|Nevada)'.

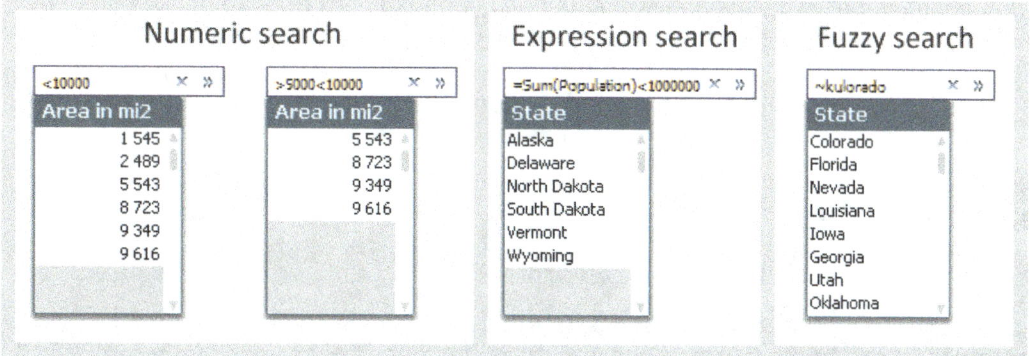

Hence, how the search string is interpreted depends only on which characters it contains. The settings in the list box properties do _not_ affect the evaluation. The "Default Search Mode" only affects how the initial search string is created.

Further, you can use the search string in a number of different places, not just in the search area in the user interface: You can also use it in Set analysis, in actions, in bookmarks, in API calls, etc.

In principle, you can combine any search string with any search place. There are however some anomalies and exceptions. For example, you cannot use normal search or fuzzy search in programmatic searches, and you cannot use the advanced search modes in the Qlik Sense global search.

Search type	Example
Normal search	ca
Wildcard search	*ca*
Numeric search	>200
Expression search	=Sum(Sales)>200
Fuzzy search	~burbon
Compound search	(Cal*|Ala*)

Place where search string can be used		
Interactive	Global search / Search object	
	Filter pane / List box	
	Multi box	
	Table box	
	Bookmark	
Programmatic	Set analysis	
	Inside Compound search	
	Action	
	Advanced search dialog	
	API calls	

The bookmark deserves a special mention. If a search is made and the resulting selection is stored in a bookmark, the bookmark *remembers the search string* and not the result from the search, i.e. the selection. This means that if new values appear when the script is run, they may be selected by the bookmark, even though they didn't exist when the bookmark was created.

Text searches

Originally posted in the Qlik Design Blog on Oct 16, 2013

One of the strengths of the Qlik engine is its search engine. With it, you can find pieces of information in a fraction of a second and select the found field values. The response is immediate, which is necessary for the user experience. Without it, you would easily get an empty result set without understanding why.

Search strings can be made in many different ways, and the Qlik engine will respond differently depending on how the search string is defined. Normally you just enter a text, and the search engine will match this against the beginning of the words in the field values. If several strings are entered, the engine will return the union of the matches of each of the strings.

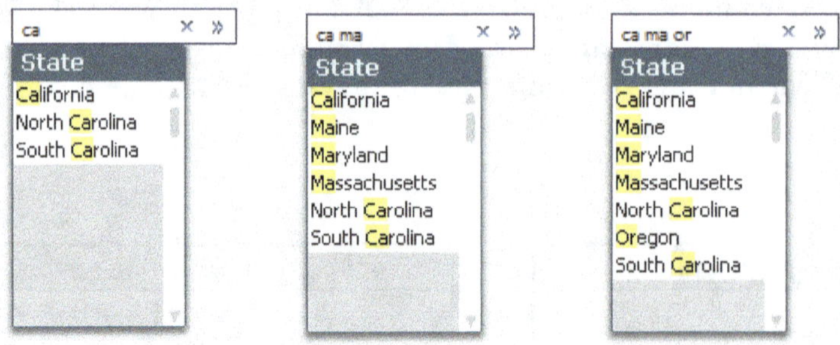

But if you instead use a wildcard in your search string, the evaluation of the search string will be made in a different way: The entire search string with the wild card will be matched against the entire field value, sometimes yielding more matches, sometimes fewer.

If you want to create more complex search strings (and e.g. store them in actions or bookmarks) you can do this too. Just use (, |, & and double quotes to define the syntax.

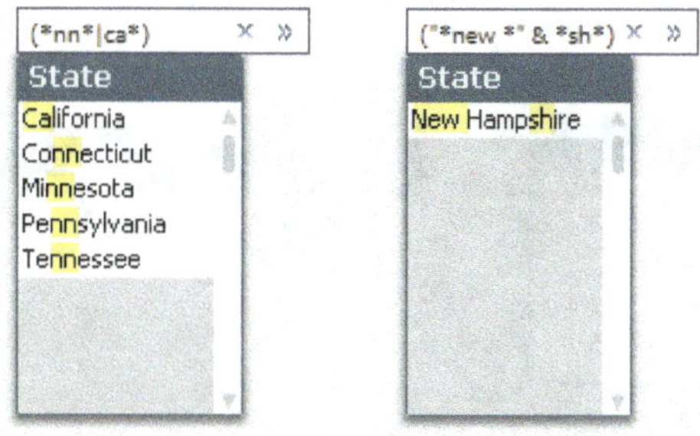

In all the above cases, the search and the selection are made in one and the same field. But sometimes you want to make the search in one field but make the selection in another. In QlikView, this can be done using the associated search, which is an indirect search method. Start with the field where you want to make the selection, enter the search string, and click on the small chevron to the right. You will then get a list of other fields containing this search string. By clicking the desired match, you will narrow down the number of matches in the primary list to show just the relevant values. You can then make your selection by hitting Enter.

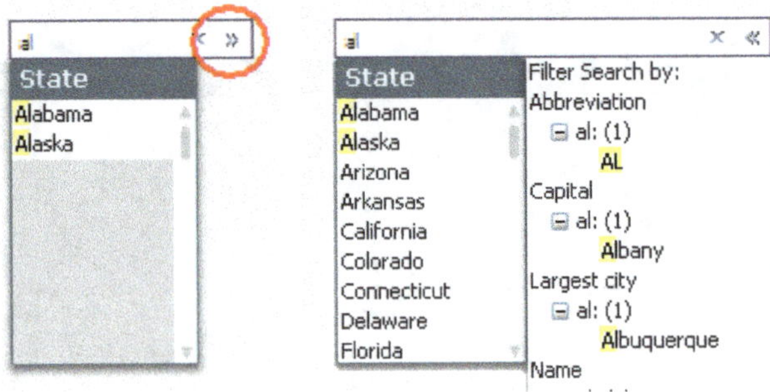

Further, did you know that

- Both in QlikView and in Qlik Sense, you can define how a default search string should be created, but this does not affect how it is evaluated – only how it is created. Once created, you can add or remove wild cards as you please.

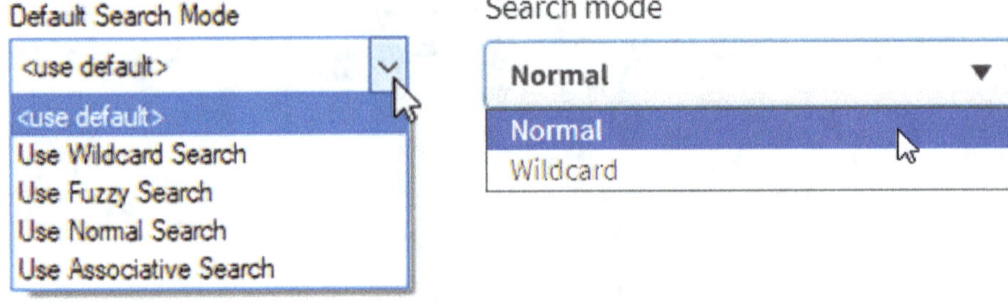

- When you make a search and save the resulting selection in a bookmark, the bookmark will contain the search string and not the list of selected values. When the bookmark is applied, it will perform the search and select the found values. If data has changed, this may imply a different search result than before.

- You can use the same search string in many places: In list boxes, in Set analysis, in the Advanced search dialog, in actions and in bookmarks.

Bottom line: The search string is a powerful tool that helps you find the values you want. Use it.

The Expression Search

Originally posted in the Qlik Design Blog on Mar 17, 2015

In my last blog post I wrote about the overall logic in the search string. Today I will dive into one specific search method: the Expression search.

Any search string beginning with an equals sign will be interpreted as an expression search, for example:

=Sum(**Sales**)>80000

If you use this search string in a field listing customers, it will pick out customers for which the total sales number is more than 80000. This means that the Qlik engine will create a hypercube – the same as what you have in a chart – with **Customer** as dimension and Sum(**Sales**)>80000 as measure, and use this to determine the search result.

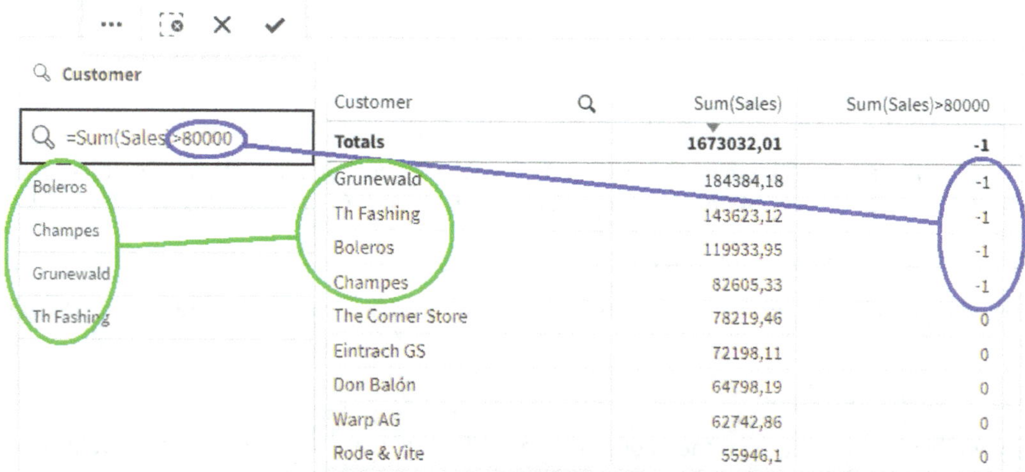

You can of course use the same search string in any field, e.g. **Products** or **Months**. But the results will be different, just as the different charts would show different numbers.

There are many implications of the above; implications you need to be aware of in order to make correct use of an expression search.

Searches

First of all: A hypercube is normally *based on the current selection,* which means that the search will not include excluded values. This is different from the wildcard search and the numeric search where the search is made in the symbol tables that hold all values, also excluded ones. If you want to include excluded values in your search, you need to use Set Analysis in your search string, for example:

=Sum({1} Sales)>80000

Further, the search string is a *Boolean expression.* This means that you can have several criteria, for example:

=Sum(Sales)>80000 or Count(distinct OrderID)>100

But it also means that you can simplify your expression, using the fact that all non-zero numbers are interpreted as TRUE. As an example, the two following expressions are equal:

=Count(If(**Product**='Trousers', **OrderID**))>0
=Count(If(**Product**='Trousers', **OrderID**))

Finally, the expression search implies an *aggregation.* This means that you must use an aggregation function. If you don't, the Only() function will be used. For example, if you want to search for customers from a specific country, you perhaps write

=**Country**='Germany'

This will work fine if each customer is associated with one country only. However, it will not work if there are several possible values per customer, since the search string is interpreted as

=Only(**Country**)='Germany'

Further, if you want to search for customers that have bought a specific product, you perhaps try:

=**Product**='Trousers'

Then you will find some customers, but probably not all you are looking for. You will find those that have bought *only* trousers and nothing else, since it is interpreted as

=Only(**Product**)='Trousers'.

If you want to find all customers that have bought trousers and perhaps also other products, you should instead try one of the following

=Count (If(**Product**='Trousers', **OrderID**))>0
=Count ({<**Product**={'Trousers'}>} **OrderID**)
=Index (Concat(distinct **Product**, ','), 'Trousers')
=Sum   (**Product**='Trousers')

I admit that neither of the above expressions is very user-friendly, but it is nevertheless how it works.

If you want a simpler way to find these customers, you will just have to do it the manual way: Click on 'Trousers' in the Product list box, then look at the list of customers. 😎

Search – But what shall you find?

Originally posted in the Qlik Design Blog on Dec 3, 2013

The search functionality is central to the Qlik engine. You enter a string, and it immediately searches in the active list box and displays the matches. But what really defines a match? For example, should you find strings containing 'Š' when your search string contains an 'S'? Or 'Ä' when you search for 'A'?

These may be odd questions for people with English as first language, but for the rest of us who use "strange" characters daily, these questions are important as the answers affect not just search results, but also sort orders.

It is called *Collation*.

A collation algorithm defines a process of how to compare two given character strings and decide if they match and also which string should come before the other. So, the collation affects everything from which search result you get in a query, to how the phone directory is sorted.

Basically, the collation is defined differently in different languages. Examples:

- The English collation considers A, Å and Ä to be variants of the same letter (matching in searches and sorted together), but the Swedish collation does the opposite: it considers them to be different letters. They can change the meaning of a word. For example, Åra (oar in a rowing boat) and Ära (honor) are very different things.

- The English collation considers V and W to be different letters (not matching, and not sorted together), but the Swedish collation does the opposite: it considers them to be variants of the same letter.

- Most Slavic languages consider S and Š to be different letters, whereas most other languages consider them to be variants of the same letter.

- In German, Ö is considered to be a variant of O, but in Nordic and Turkish languages it is considered a separate letter.

- In most western languages I is the upper case version of i, but in Turkish languages, I is the upper case of dotless ı, and İ (dotted) is the upper case of dotted i.

An example of how these differences affect sort orders and search results can be seen in the picture below:

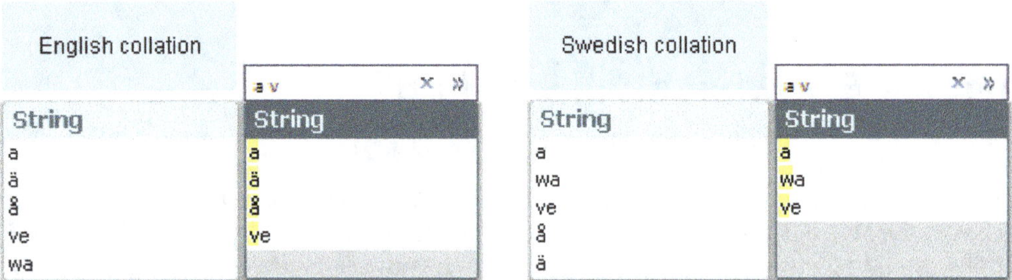

The search string is the same in both cases and should match all field values that have words beginning with 'a' or 'v'. Note that sort orders as well as search results differ.

Hence: A number of differences exist between languages that have special characters or characters with diacritic marks, e.g. Å, Ä Ö, Æ, Ø, Þ, Š, Ł, Î, Č. Sometimes these characters are considered as separate letters, sometimes not. Some languages even have collation rules for letter combinations and for where in the word an accent is found. An overview can be found on Wikipedia.

So, how does the Qlik engine handle this?

For Qlik Cloud, the preferred Region is stored in the user profile. For QlikView, the regional settings of the operating system are used. In both cases, the regional settings are used for the environment variables when the app is created. These variables are subsequently used for collation in the app.

Usually, you don't need to think about this, but should you want to test it yourself, just change the relevant regional settings, create a new app, and investigate the environment variables.

19
Visualizations

In all Business Intelligence tools there is a need to visualize the data. This is often done using a concept that is called a 'Multidimensional Cube' or a 'Hypercube'. This is a data-structure that calculates metrics along predefined dimensions.

The hypercube is described in the chapter "Hypercubes and Aggregations". But the graphical considerations – with some tips and tricks – merits its own chapter.

Several of the recipes below pertain to QlikView, simply because they were written when there were no or very few Qlik Sense users. Today, it is easier to create good visualizations since Qlik Sense has much better tools than QlikView ever had. But the articles can still be useful for Qlik Sense users, in that they present ideas of how to visualize data.

Chart Dimensionality

Originally posted in the Qlik Design Blog on Jan 27, 2015

A chart in QlikView or in Qlik Sense has Dimensions and Measures. What these are is described in the previous post "Dimensions and Measures". This post is about charts with multiple dimensions and/or multiple measures and your options when designing such charts.

In a simple chart with one dimension and one measure, the number of data points is determined by the number of possible values in the dimension. For example, a bar chart with **Month** as dimension typically has twelve bars – one per month.

If you want to add complexity to your chart, you can choose between adding a dimension and adding a measure. Whichever you do, the chart will increase its rank – or *dimensionality* – and change its appearance.

Below you have two bar charts: The left chart has two dimensions and one measure, while the right chart has one dimension and three measures. Yet, they are almost identical.

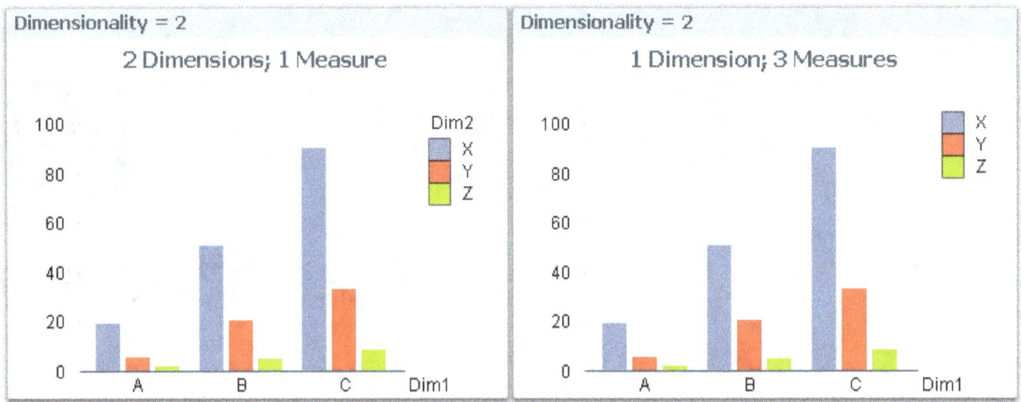

The left chart has Sum(Amount) as measure, while the right has Sum({<Dim2={X}>} Amount) as first measure, and similar expressions for the additional two measures.

The reason why they look identical is that they have the same dimensionality: An array of measures can be regarded as a virtual dimension, and if so, both charts have two "dimensions", i.e. a dimensionality of two.

This property is not unique for bar charts. Most charts can be altered this way, e.g. pie charts:

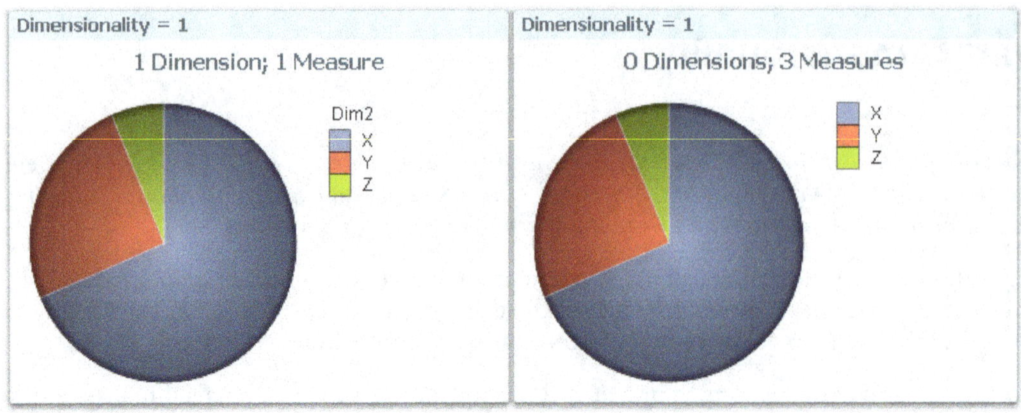

Note that the pie chart to the right has zero dimensions. It is a *dimensionless* chart with several measures.

Several chart types can display relevant information without having a dimension: e.g. the Pie chart, the Bar chart, the Funnel chart, the Radar chart, the Pivot table and the Straight table. Try it, and you'll see.

There are some charts that don't fit the above description though. First of all, the *Gauge* is a dimensionless chart that always has zero as dimensionality.

Secondly, the *Trellis chart* is just a container for multiples of another chart type. By using a Trellis, you effectively can add one or two dimensions. For example, you can add a dimension to a Gauge using a Trellis chart:

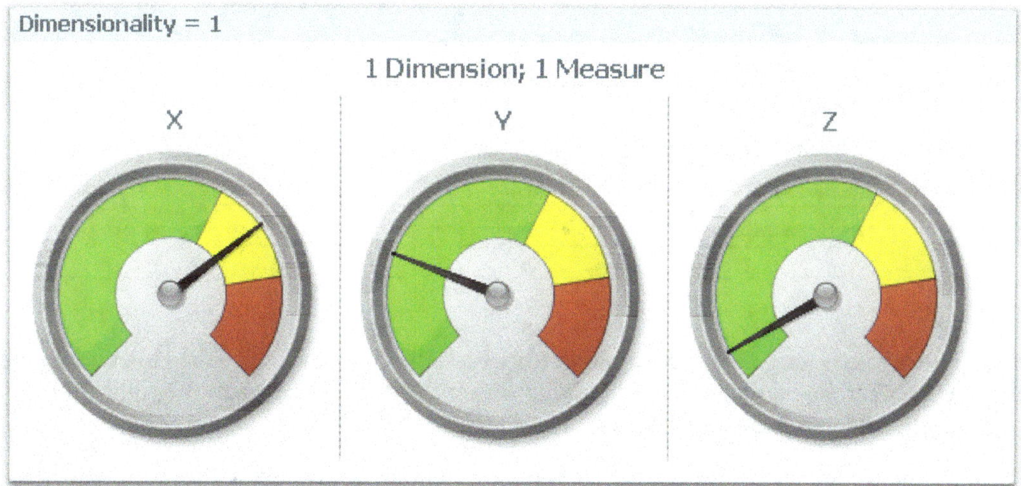

Further, the *Scatter chart* is different from other charts in that it always needs one dimension to define the number of data points, and two measures to define the coordinates. The dimension cannot be replaced by an array of measures.

With the above knowledge, it is easier to describe the limits of different chart types:

	Largest sensible dimensionality	Largest dimensionality
Gauge	0	0
Pie chart	1	2
Funnel chart	1	1
Bar chart	2	3
Line chart	2	2
Radar chart	2	2
Mekko chart	2	2
Grid chart	2	3
Tree map	3	3

The first number is the largest dimensionality for which the chart makes sense. However, some QlikView charts can be made to display a higher dimensionality (number to the right), but it is rarely easy to understand such a chart, so I don't recommend it.

Finally, the conclusion from the above is that you have a choice of displaying the last dimension either as dimension or as an array of measures. If you choose a dimension, then you have the advantage that the user can select in this dimension by clicking in the chart. But if you instead choose an array of measures, you have a greater flexibility for customizing the measures. You can for instance add a measure which is different than the first ones; e.g. in addition to 'Sales 2014' and 'Sales 2015' you can display the relative change.

With this, I hope that you have some new ideas for visualizations.

Colors in charts

Originally posted in the Qlik Design Blog on Dec 4, 2012

It is not uncommon that users want specific products or customers to be displayed in specific colors. The most obvious way to do this is to change the colors in the chart properties. In QlikView, this is in fact quite easy if you use the copy and paste functions found when you right-click a color button. Just copy one button and paste on another, and you have moved the color.

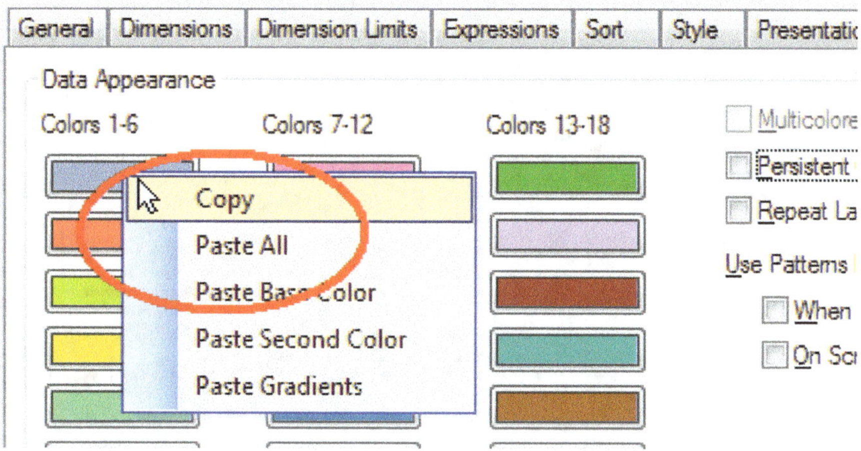

This way you can assign which color is to be used for the different values of the field. However, a prerequisite for this to work is that the order of the field values doesn't change.

A more robust way is to use color functions. Usually, you want to set the color of a bar, line or bubble, and this can be done in the object properties. In Qlik Sense, this can be done under "Appearance":

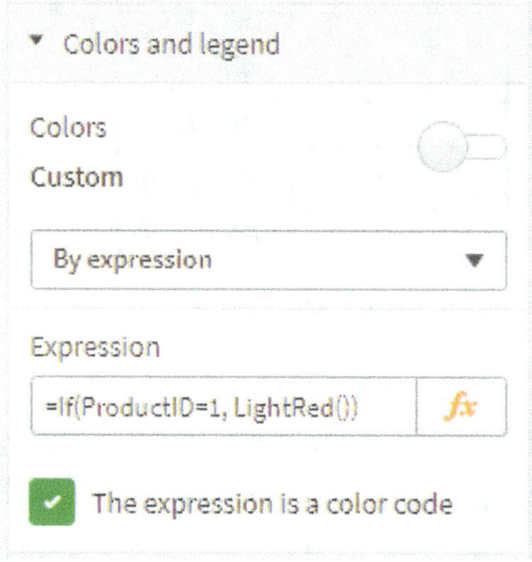

In QlikView, this is done by using the "Background Color" on the Expression tab:

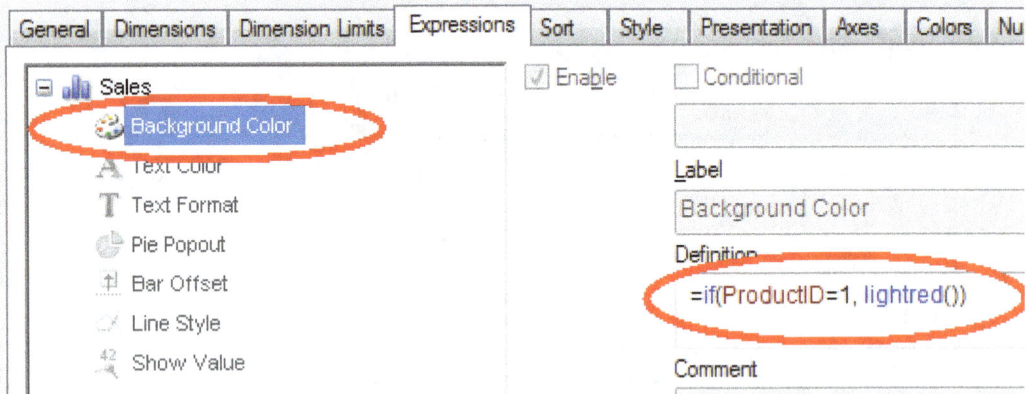

In the pictures above, both the product ID and the color are hard-coded in the expression. However, if you want to define colors for many products, the if-function will not be manageable. Then it is better to store this information in a table – either in the database or in an Excel sheet or as an inline statement in the script. Hence,

1. Create your color definition table and store it in an appropriate place. The Red, Green and Blue columns hold the different color components and define the color uniquely.

ProductID	Red	Green	Blue
1	255	0	0
2	0	255	0
3	0	0	255
4	127	40	40
5	0	186	186
6	25	127	25

2. Load the color definitions into a mapping table:

```
ProductColors:
Mapping Load ProductID, Rgb(Red,Green,Blue)        as ProductColor
    From ProductColors;
```

3. Use this mapping table when loading the products table, creating a new field for the product color:

```
Applymap('ProductColors', ProductID, LightGray()) as ProductColor
```

The third parameter, here LightGray(), defines which color the unlisted products should get. If you instead use Null(), the unlisted products will be multicolored according to the color settings in the chart properties.

4. Finally, use this field as product color in the charts:

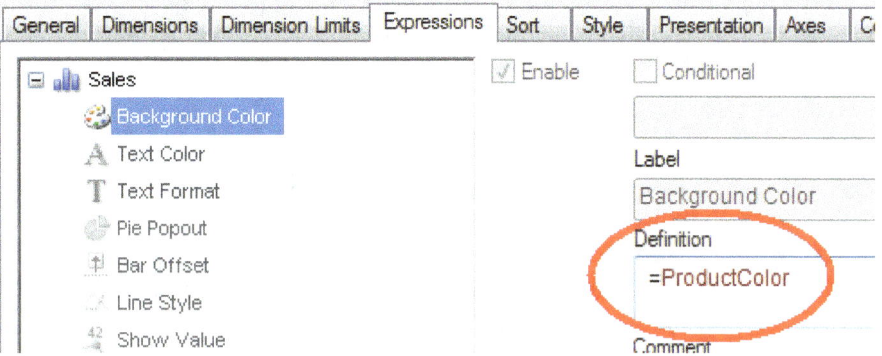

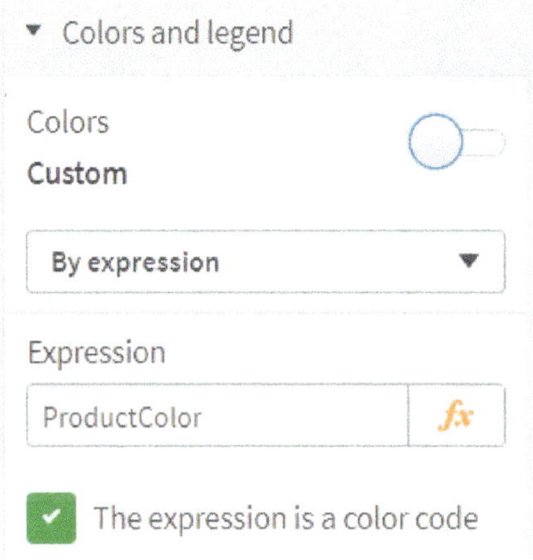

This way it is easy to define which color specific products, customers, or other dimensions should get.

Which colors to use? Oh, that is a completely different topic. You can find a lot about that on the net, so I will not go into that. However, I will say one thing:

Don't use color as a decoration. The color should carry information.

Recipe for a QlikView Scatter Chart

Originally posted in the Qlik Design Blog on Mar 18, 2013

A scatter chart or a bubble chart is easy to make in QlikView – if you know how to… There are however a couple of things that may be confusing when you make the chart.

The first thing is the Dimension. Many think that this is identical to one of the axes of the chart, and for most chart types it is. *But not for a scatter chart*. Here, the logical dimension is *not* the same as the graphical.

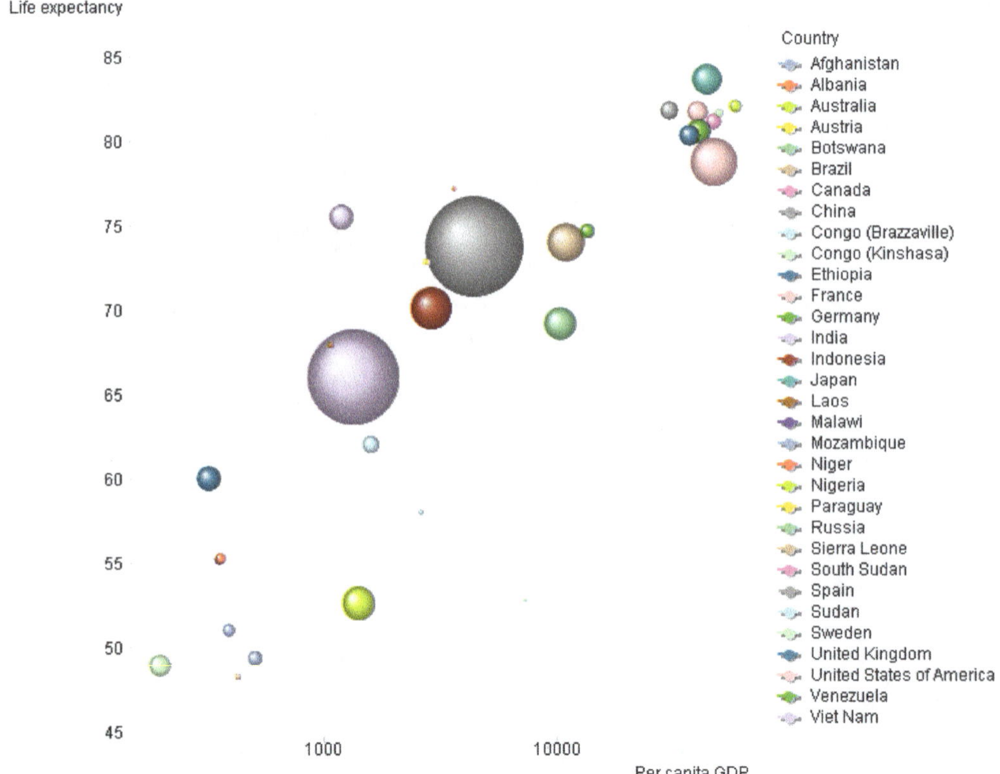

Instead, you should visualize your graph and ask yourself: "*What should each dot or bubble represent?*"

In the graph above, each bubble represents a country. In your case, it could perhaps be one bubble per customer, supplier or product. *This* is your dimension.

The next question is: "*Where should the bubble be positioned?*" In the graph above, the x-coordinate is per capita GDP and the y-coordinate is the life expectancy. You may want to use e.g. the total order value, gross margin, net cost or some other numbers. *These* are your measures. These are used for the axes in the graph.

You need at least two measures. Optionally, you can have a third expression that will be used for the size of the bubbles. In the chart above, the country population is used as third expression.

When defining the measures, you encounter the next confusing thing: A country has only *one* GDP, but the Qlik engine still wants you to use an aggregation function, e.g. Sum() or Avg(). The reason is that the Qlik engine cannot "know" if your data has one or several records for each dimensional value. So, you need to use an aggregation function to tell it what to do, should there be more than one record. If there really is only one record per dimensional value, then it doesn't matter if you use Sum() or Avg(). Any will work fine.

But if you have several records per dimensional value, then you need to stop and think. Do you want to sum the records? Or do you want the average?

Once you know which dimension and measures to use, it is straightforward in QlikView:

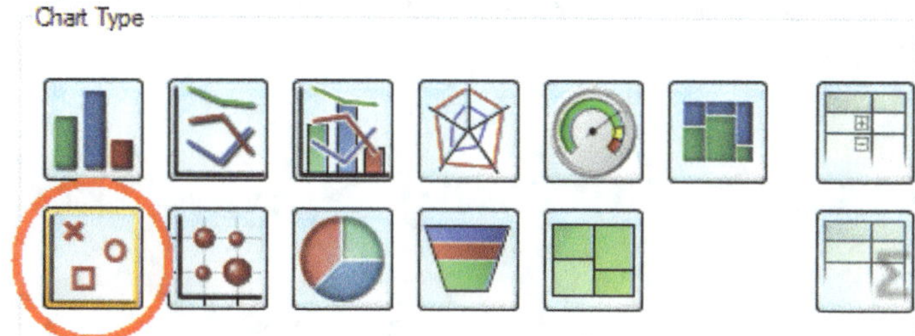

1. Create a chart and choose Scatter Chart. Click Next.
2. Add your dimension. Click Next.
3. Add the fields that you want to use for your two measures in the "X" and "Y" controls.
4. If you want a bubble chart, you need to add the third expression that determines the size of the bubbles.

5. Check "Advanced mode" to the lower left. QlikView 11 unfortunately jumps to the "Sort" page here, so you need to click "Back" to verify that the right aggregation functions for your expressions are used. You may need to change the functions.
6. Click Finish.

Now you will have made a scatter chart. To make it more beautiful, you should also consider the following:

- Choose a style [Style – Look]

- Increase the Bubble size [Presentation – Max bubble Size]

- Change the scale of one or both axes. [Axes]
    - Remove the "Force 0" option.
    - Use a logarithmic scale.

And in Qlik Sense it is even easier to create a scatter chart. The basic principles are, however, the same.

Recipe for a QlikView Histogram

Originally posted in the Qlik Design Blog on Aug 13, 2014

In quality control, you often want to look at the distribution of a measurement, to understand how the output of a process or a machine relates to expectations; to targets and specifications. In such a case, a histogram (or frequency plot) is one possibility.

It could be that you want to examine some physical property of the output of a machine and want to see how close to the target the produced units are. Then you could plot the measurements in a chart like the following:

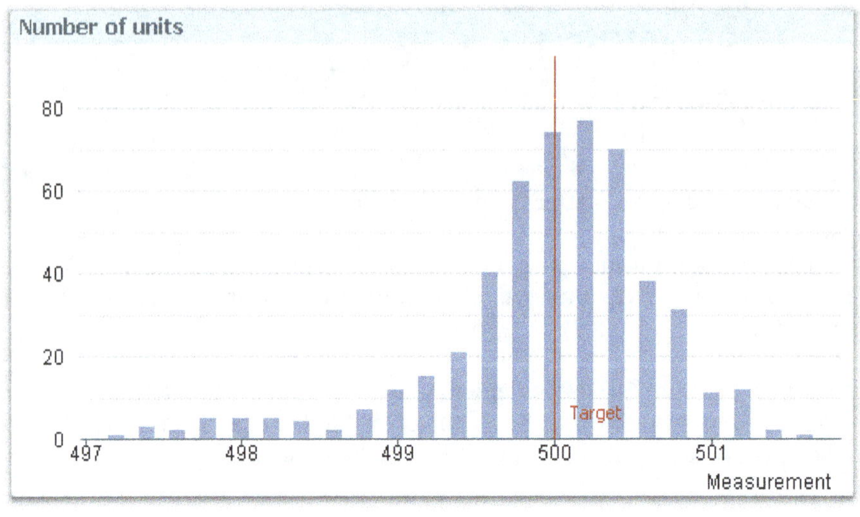

The above graph clearly shows you the distribution of the output of the machine: Most measurements are around target and the peak of the distribution is in fact slightly above target. But the histogram also raises questions: *Is the variation small enough? And why is there such a long tail towards lower values? Could it be that we have a problem with a machine?*

Finding such questions and their answers is central in all quality work, and the histogram is a good tool in helping you find them.

A histogram is a special type of bar chart and is easy to create in QlikView. A peculiarity is that it uses only one field, not several: As dimension, it uses the measurement in grouped form: Each measurement is assigned to an interval or *bin*, and this way the dimension gets discrete values.

As expression it uses the count of the measurement, and so the graph shows the distribution of one single field.

One small challenge is to determine how many bins the histogram should have: Having too many bins will exaggerate the variation, whereas too few will obscure it. It depends on the number of measurements you have, but a simple rule of thumb is to have 15-25 bins.

This is how you create a histogram in QlikView:

1. Create an Input Box. In its properties, create a new variable called **BinWidth**. Click OK.
2. Set **BinWidth** to 1 in the Input Box.
3. Create a Bar Chart with a calculated dimension, using =Round(**Value**, **BinWidth**)
4. Set the label for the calculated dimension to "**Measurement**". Click Next.
5. Use Count(**Value**) as expression. Click Next.
6. Sort the calculated dimension numerically. Click Next three times.
7. On the "Axes" page, enable "Continuous" on the Dimension Axis. Click Next.
8. On the "Colors" page, disable the "Multicolored" under Data appearance. Click Finish.

You should now have a histogram.

If you have too few bars, you need to make the bin width smaller. If you have too many, you should make it bigger.

In order to make the histogram more elaborate you can also do the following:

- Add error bars to the bins. The error (uncertainty) of a bar is in this case the square root of the bar content, i.e. Sqrt(Count(Value))

- Add a second expression containing a Gaussian curve (bell curve):
    - Convert the chart to a Combo chart
    - Use the following as expression for the bell curve:

```
BinWidth * Count(total Measurement)*
Only(Normdist(
    Round(Measurement,BinWidth),
    Avg(total Measurement),
    Stdev(total Measurement),
    0
    ))
```

    - Use bars for the measurement and line for the curve.

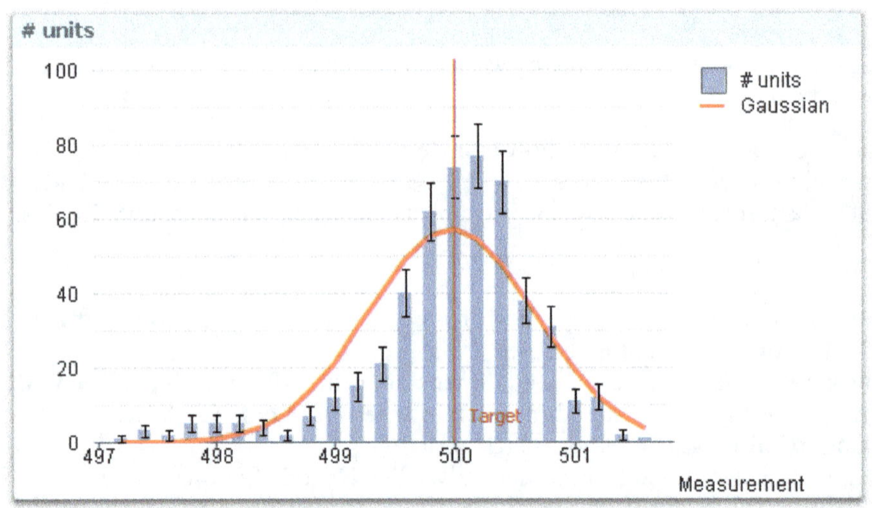

With these changes, you can quickly assess whether the measurements are normally distributed or whether there are some anomalies.

Good luck!

Recipe for a QlikView Box Plot

Originally posted in the Qlik Design Blog on Aug 19, 2014

When you want to look at the distribution of a measurement, a histogram is one possibility. However, if you want to show the distribution split over several dimensional values, a Box Plot may be a better choice.

You may, for instance, want to evaluate the quality of units produced in different machines, or delivered by different suppliers. Then, a Box Plot is an excellent choice to display the characteristic that you want to examine:

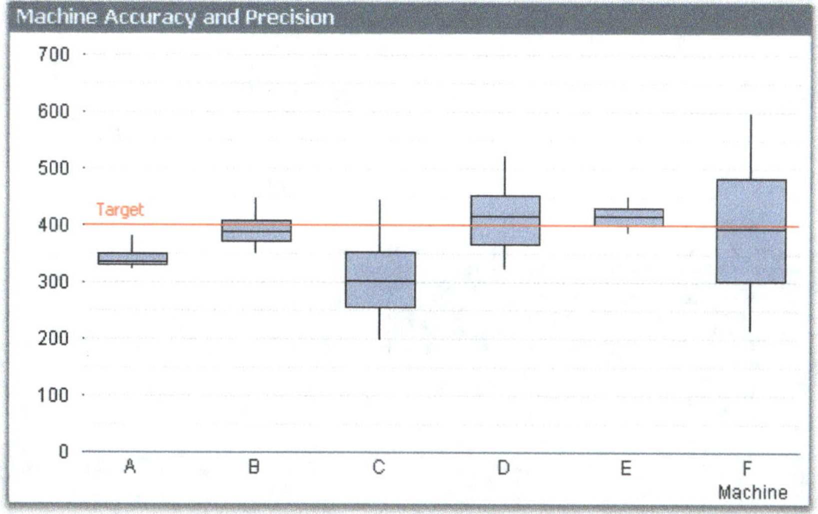

The graph clearly shows you the performance of the different machines compared to target: Machine A has the precision, but not the accuracy. Machine F has the accuracy, but not the precision.

The Box Plot provides an intuitive graphical representation of several properties of the data set. The box itself represents the main group of measurements, with a center line representing the middle of the data. Usually, the median and the upper and lower quartile levels are used to define the box, but it is also possible to use the average plus/ minus one standard deviation.

The whiskers are used to show the spread of the data, e.g. the largest and smallest measurements can be used. Usually, however, the definition is slightly more intricate. Below I will use the definition used in *Six Sigma* implementations.

There, the whiskers are often used to depict the largest and smallest values within an acceptable range, whereas values outside this range are outliers.

The concept of the Inter Quartile Range (IQR) – the difference between the upper and lower quartile level – is used to calculate the acceptance range. Hence:

- Inter Quartile Range (IQR) = Upper Quartile Line (UQL) – Lower Quartile Line (LQL)
- Upper Acceptance Limit (UAL) = UQL + 1.5 * IQR
- Lower Acceptance Limit (LAL) = LQL - 1.5 * IQR

The picture below summarizes the box plot.

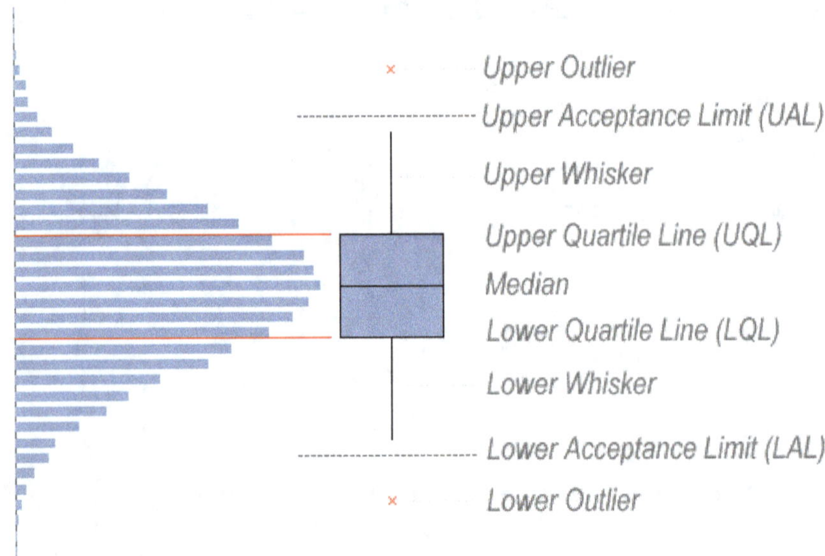

And here is how you implement this in QlikView…

1. Go to the Tools menu and choose "Box Plot Wizard".
2. On the "Step 1 - Define data" page, you choose your dimension. In my example, this was **Machine**, but it could be **Supplier** or **Batch** or something similar.
3. Use the same dimension once more in the "Aggregator" control.
4. Use the average of your measurement in the "Expression" control – Avg(**Measurement**).
5. Click "Next".
6. On the "Step 2 - Presentation" page, you should choose "Median mode".
7. Check "Include Whiskers" and "Use Outliers".
8. Click "Finish".

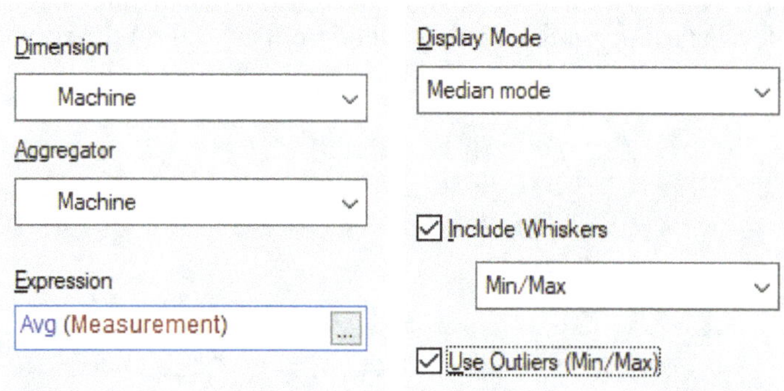

QlikView has now created a Box Plot with general expressions that almost always display a meaningful result and allows for an intermediate aggregator.

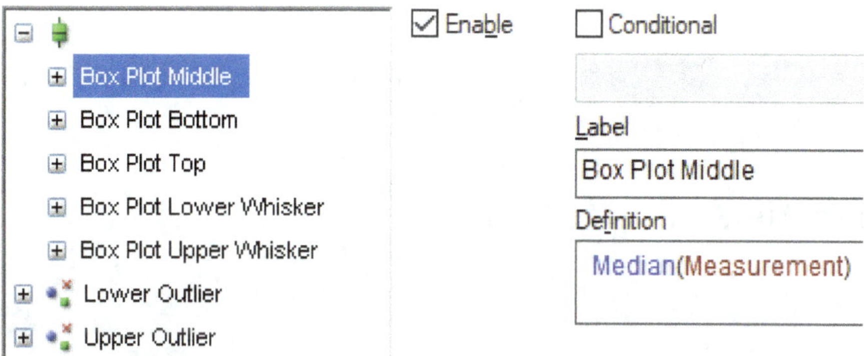

However, the expressions are not what we want for a *Six Sigma* box plot, so we need to change them to the following: (Below, the dimension is called **Dim**, and the measurement is called **Meas**.)

```
/* Box Plot Middle */     Median  (Meas)
/* Box Plot Bottom */     Fractile(Meas,0.25)
/* Box Plot Top */        Fractile(Meas,0.75)
```

The whiskers and the outliers all need a nested aggregation – each value needs to be compared to the acceptance levels *for the group* – so they all contain an Aggr() function that calculates the relevant acceptance limit:

```
// ============= Box Plot Lower Whisker: =============
Min(If( Meas>= Aggr(2.5*Fractile(total <Dim> Meas,0.25)-
                    1.5*Fractile(total <Dim> Meas,0.75),
                    Dim, Meas),
        Meas))
// ============= Box Plot Upper Whisker: =============
Max(If( Meas<= Aggr(2.5*Fractile(total <Dim> Meas,0.75)-
                    1.5*Fractile(total <Dim> Meas,0.25),
                    Dim, Meas),
        Meas))
// ============= Lower Outlier: =====================
Min(If( Meas< Aggr( 2.5*Fractile(total <Dim> Meas,0.25)-
                    1.5*Fractile(total <Dim> Meas,0.75),
                    Dim, Meas),
        Meas))
//============= Upper Outlier: =====================
Max(If( Meas> Aggr( 2.5*Fractile(total <Dim> Meas,0.75)-
                    1.5*Fractile(total <Dim> Meas,0.25),
                    Dim, Meas),
        Meas))
```

And with this, I leave you to create your own box plots.

Recipe for a Pareto Analysis

Originally posted in the Qlik Design Blog on Dec 10, 2013

"Which products contribute to the first 80% of our turnover?"

This type of question is common in all types of business intelligence. I say "type of question" since it appears in many different forms: Sometimes it concerns products, but it can just as well concern customers, suppliers or salespeople. It can really be *any* dimension. Further, here the question was about turnover, but it can just as well be number of support cases, or number of defect deliveries, etc. It can in principle be any additive measure.

It is called Pareto analysis. Sometimes also known as 80/20 analysis or ABC analysis.

The logic is that you first sort the products according to size, then accumulate the numbers, and finally calculate the accumulated measure as a percentage of the total. The products contributing to the first 80% are your best products; your "A" products. The next 10% are your "B" products, and the last 10% are your "C" products.

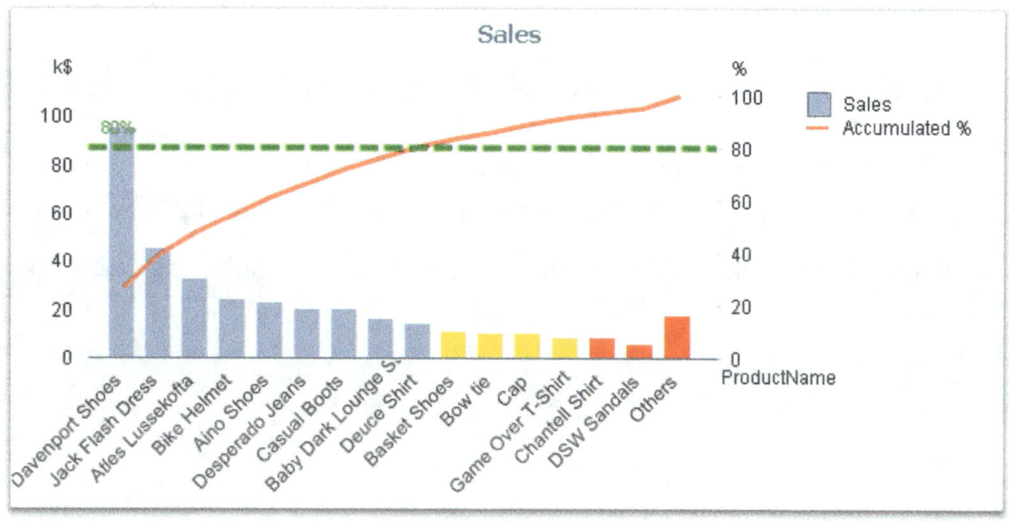

And here's how you do it in QlikView:

1) Create a pivot table and choose your dimension and your basic measure. In my example, I use **Product** and Sum(**Sales**).

2) Sort the chart descending by using the measure Sum(**Sales**) as sort expression. It is not enough just to check "Sort by Y-value".

3) Add a second expression to calculate the accumulated sales value:

    RangeSum(Above(Sum(Sales), 0, RowNo()))

    Call this expression **Accumulated Sales**. The Above() function will return an array of values – all above values in the chart – and the RangeSum() function will sum these numbers.

4) Create a third expression from the previous one; one that calculates the relative accumulated sales in percent:

    RangeSum(Above(Sum(Sales), 0, RowNo())) / Sum(total Sales)

    Format it as a percentage and call it **Inclusive Percentage**.

5) Create a fourth expression from the previous one; one that calculates the accumulated sales in percent, but this time excluding the current row: Note the "1" as the second parameter of Above().

    RangeSum(Above(Sum(Sales), 1, RowNo())) / Sum(total Sales)

    Format it as a percentage and call it **Exclusive Percentage**.

6) Create a fifth expression for the ABC classification:

    If([Exclusive Percentage]<= 0.8, 'A', If([Exclusive Percentage]<= 0.9, 'B', 'C'))

    Call this expression **Pareto Class**. The reason why the **Exclusive Percentage** is used is that the classification should be determined by the *lower bound* of a product's segment, not the upper.

7) Create a conditional background color, e.g.

    If([Pareto Class]='C', Lightred(), If([Pareto Class]='B', Yellow()))

You should now have a table similar to the following. In it you can clearly see the classification of different products.

<h1 style="text-align:center">Visualizations</h1>

ProductName	Sales	Accumulated Sales	Inclusive Percentage	Exclusive Percentage	Pareto Class
Davenport Shoes	94 933	94 933	27%	0%	A
Jack Flash Dress	44 593	139 526	39%	27%	A
Atles Lussekofta	32 088	171 614	48%	39%	A
Bike Helmet	23 667	195 281	55%	48%	A
Aino Shoes	22 707	217 988	61%	55%	A
Desperado Jeans	19 656	237 644	67%	61%	A
Casual Boots	19 514	257 158	72%	67%	A
Baby Dark Lounge Suit	15 860	273 018	77%	72%	A
Deuce Shirt	14 055	287 073	81%	77%	A
Basket Shoes	10 287	297 360	84%	81%	B
Bow tie	10 118	307 478	86%	84%	B
Cap	10 016	317 494	89%	86%	B
Game Over T-Shirt	8 026	325 520	92%	89%	B
Chantell Shirt	7 661	333 181	94%	92%	C
DSW Sandals	5 373	338 554	95%	94%	C

In this table, there are five different expressions that you can use for Pareto analysis. The graph in the beginning of this post uses **Sales** and **Inclusive Percentage** for the bars and the line, respectively, and **Pareto Class** for the coloring of the bars.

Finally, you may want to put the entire calculation in the definition of the **Pareto Class**:

```
If(RangeSum(Above(Sum(Sales),1,RowNo())) / Sum(total Sales) <= 0.8, 'A',
If(RangeSum(Above(Sum(Sales),1,RowNo())) / Sum(total Sales) <= 0.9, 'B',
    'C'))
```

All the above expressions can be used also in Qlik Sense.

Good luck in creating your Pareto chart!

Recipe for an alternative ABC Analysis

Originally posted in the Qlik Design Blog on Sep 16, 2014

An ABC analysis is a dynamic bucket classification of e.g. products, based on some property, usually the sales number. The best products are your "A" products and the worst are your "C" products.

It is used in all types of business intelligence applications and can appear in many different forms: It can concern any dimension, e.g. customer, supplier, sales person, etc. and be based on any measure. The sales number is one example, but it can just as well be e.g. number of support cases, or number of defect deliveries, etc.

One way to make an ABC analysis is to use a Pareto analysis where the classification is based on the accumulated number after the entities have been sorted according to their numbers. The products contributing to the first 80% are usually the A products.

However, the Pareto analysis, as described in the above blog post, is sometimes limiting: It is for instance not easy to use several dimensions, and it is (at this point) not possible to define the ABC classes as a dimension. Hence, it is sometimes better to use an alternative classification function:

The *Rank*.

The Qlik engine has a Rank() function that is well suited for this purpose. With it, you can rank any dimension according to any expression. You can use several dimensions and you can define your ABC classes as dimensions. The logic is that you calculate a relative rank, i.e. you divide the rank of the product with the total number of products:

```
(Rank(Sum(Sales),1)-1) / Count(distinct total Product)
```

If this number is lower than 0.5 the product belongs to the better 50% and thus to the "A" products. Similarly you can use 0.75 as a limit for belonging to group "B". The result will be similar to a Pareto analysis.

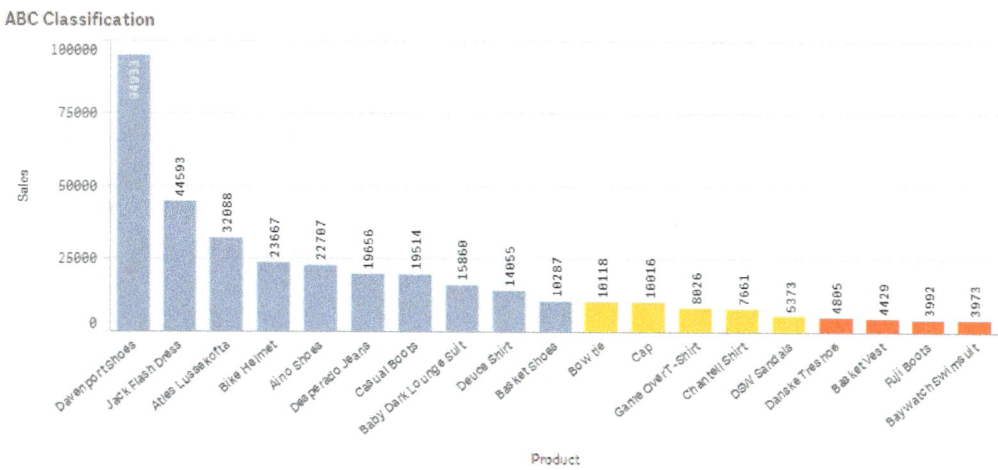

One possibility is to use colors to display the classification:

1. Create a bar chart and choose your dimension and your basic measure. In the example below, I use **Product** and Sum(**Sales**) labeled as "**Sales**".

2. Set the color of the bars to

```
If( (Rank(Sum(Sales),1)-1) /                  // --- Case 1 ---
       Count(distinct total Product) < 0.50,
    RGB(140,170,200),
If( (Rank(Sum(Sales),1)-1) /                  // --- Case 2 ---
       Count(distinct total Product) < 0.75,
    RGB(255,200,0),
    LightRed()                                // --- Else ---
))
```

In QlikView you do this under the expression "Background color" and in Qlik Sense you do it under "Appearance" – "Colors and Legend" for the object.

But you can also use this method to create a field or a calculated dimension, which means that you can make the ABC classes selectable:

```
Aggr(
    If((Rank(Sum(Sales),1)-1)/Count(distinct total Product)<0.50,
        'A',                            // --- Case 1 ---
    If((Rank(Sum(Sales),1)-1)/Count(distinct total Product)<0.75,
        'B',                            // --- Case 2 ---
        'C'                             // --- Else ---
    )),
    Product
)
```

ABC	Product		Sales
A	Slip-on Shoes	⊟	11286
	Jack Flash Dress		8631
	Le Baby Dress		3289
	Serve-Shirt		3249
B	AAA Running Shoe	⊟	2626
	Deuce Shirt		1835
C	Bow tie	⊟	1437
	Wimbledon T-Shirt		1027

Finally, if you want to use ranking in a two-dimensional chart, you can use the same logic. However, you must first decide how the rank should be calculated. Normally you would want the ranking to be done within each group defined by the second dimension, i.e. per column in a pivot table:

Rank within column: Rank(…) and Count(distinct total <Dim2> Dim1)

Customer	Bond Ltd			Don Balón			Nirvana Stores			Th Fashing		
Product	Sales	Rank	Count	Sales	Rank	Count	Sales	Rank	Count	Sales	Rank	Count
Slip-on Shoes	6305	1	6	2603	2	8	735	2	8	1643	2	7
Jack Flash Dress	3874	2	6	3116	1	8	623	4	8	1018	4	7
Le Baby Dress	-	-	-	1150	3	8	2139	1	8	-	-	-
Serve-Shirt	434	4	6	715	5	8	453	6	8	1647	1	7
AAA Running Shoe	-	-	-	669	6	8	650	3	8	1307	3	7
Deuce Shirt	99	6	6	1018	4	8	477	5	8	241	7	7
Bow tie	535	3	6	46	8	8	224	8	8	632	5	7
Wimbledon T-Shirt	192	5	6	131	7	8	363	7	8	341	6	7

The above chart shows sales per product and customer. The colors define the classes and the rank, and the count is done within each column, i.e. the products are classified within each customer. The following expression was used:

```
If( (Rank(Sum(Sales),1)-1) /                   // --- Case 1 ---
      Count(distinct total <Customer> Product)< 0.50,
    RGB(140,170,200),
If( (Rank(Sum(Sales),1)-1) /                   // --- Case 2 ---
      Count(distinct total <Customer> Product)< 0.75,
    RGB(255,200,0),
    LightRed()                                 // --- Else ---
    ))
```

But you may also want to do the ranking within each group defined by the first dimension, i.e. classify the customers within each product. Then you need to swap place of **Customer** and **Product** in the formula, and you need to use HRank() instead:

```
If( (HRank(Sum(Sales),1)-1) /                  // --- Case 1 ---
      Count(distinct total <Product> Customer)< 0.50,
    RGB(140,170,200),
If( (HRank(Sum(Sales),1)-1) /                  // --- Case 2 ---
      Count(distinct total <Product> Customer)< 0.75,
    RGB(255,200,0),
    LightRed()                                 // --- Else ---
    ))
```

Rank within row: HRank(…) and Count(distinct total <Dim1> Dim2)

Customer	Bond Ltd			Don Balón			Nirvana Stores			Th Fashing		
Product	Sales	Rank	Count	Sales	Rank	Count	Sales	Rank	Count	Sales	Rank	Count
Slip-on Shoes	6305	1	4	2603	2	4	735	4	4	1643	3	4
Jack Flash Dress	3874	1	4	3116	2	4	623	4	4	1018	3	4
Le Baby Dress	-	-	-	1150	2	2	2139	1	2	-	-	-
Serve-Shirt	434	4	4	715	2	4	453	3	4	1647	1	4
AAA Running Shoe	-	-	-	669	2	3	650	3	3	1307	1	3
Deuce Shirt	99	4	4	1018	1	4	477	2	4	241	3	4
Bow tie	535	2	4	46	4	4	224	3	4	632	1	4
Wimbledon T-Shirt	192	3	4	131	4	4	363	1	4	341	2	4

Good luck in creating your ABC analysis!

Recipe for a Pareto Analysis – Revisited

Originally posted in the Qlik Design Blog on Dec 13, 2016

"Which products contribute to the first 80% of our turnover?"

This type of question is common in all types of business intelligence. I say "type of question" since it appears in many different forms: Sometimes it concerns products, but it can just as well concern any dimension, e.g. customer, supplier, salesperson, etc. Further, here the question was about turnover, but it can just as well be e.g. the number of support cases, or number of defect deliveries, etc.

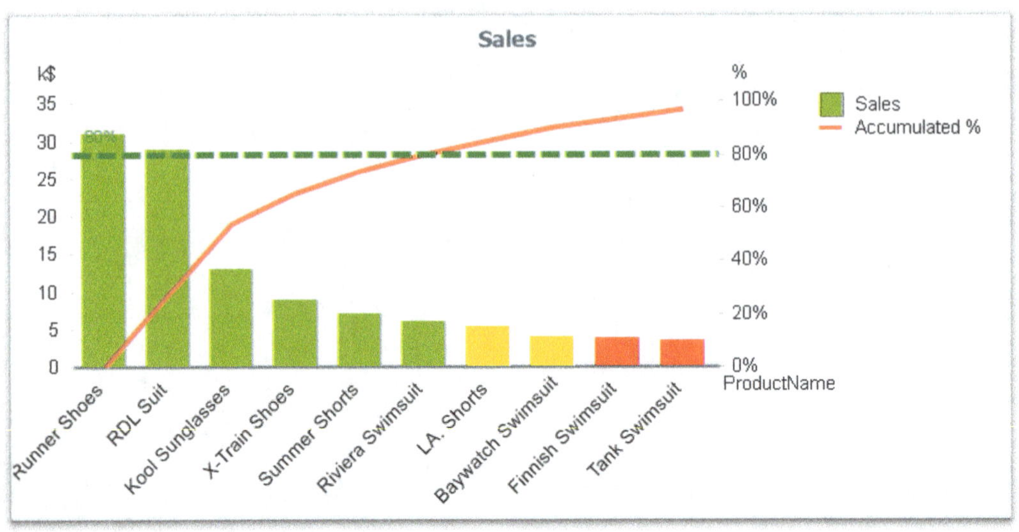

It is called Pareto analysis or ABC analysis and I have already written a blog post on this topic. However, in the previous post I only explained how to create a measure which showed the Pareto class. I never showed how to create a dimension based on a Pareto classification – simply because it wasn't possible.

But now it is.

But first things first. The logic for a Pareto analysis is that you first sort the products according to their sales numbers, then accumulate the numbers, and finally calculate the accumulated measure as a percentage of the total. The products contributing to the first 80% are your best, your "A" products. The next 10% are your "B" products, and the last 10% are your "C" products. In the above graph, these classes are shown as colors on the bars.

The previous post shows how this can be done in a chart measure using the Above() function. However, if you use the same logic, but instead inside a sorted Aggr() function, you can achieve the same thing without relying on the chart sort order. The sorted Aggr() function is a fairly recent innovation, and this is why it hasn't been possible to have a Pareto dimension before.

The sorting is needed to calculate the proper accumulated percentages, which will give you the Pareto classes. So, if you want to classify your products, the new expression to use is

```
Aggr(
    If(Rangesum(
            Above(Sum({1} Sales)/Sum({1} total Sales),1,RowNo())
            )<0.8,  'A',
    If(Rangesum(
            Above(Sum({1} Sales)/Sum({1} total Sales),1,RowNo())
            )<0.9,  'B',
                    'C'
    )),
    (Product,(=Sum({1} Sales),Desc))
)
```

The first parameter of the Aggr() – the nested If()-functions – is in principle the same as the measure in the previous post. Look there for an explanation.

The second parameter of the Aggr(), the inner dimension, contains the magic of the sorted Aggr():

```
(Product,(=Sum({1} Sales),Desc))
```

This structured parameter specifies that the field **Product** should be used as dimension, and its values should be sorted descending according to Sum({1} **Sales**). Note the equals sign. This is necessary if you want to sort by expression.

So the Products inside the Aggr() will be sorted descending, and for each Product the accumulated relative sales in percent will be calculated, which in turn is used to determine the Pareto classes.

The set analysis {1} is necessary if you want the classification to be independent of the made selection. Without it, the classification will change every time the selection changes.

But perhaps a better alternative is to use {$<Product=>}. Then a selection in Product (or in the Pareto class itself) will not affect the classification, but all other selections will.

The expression can be used either as dimension in a chart, or in a list box. Below I have used the Pareto class as first dimension in a pivot table.

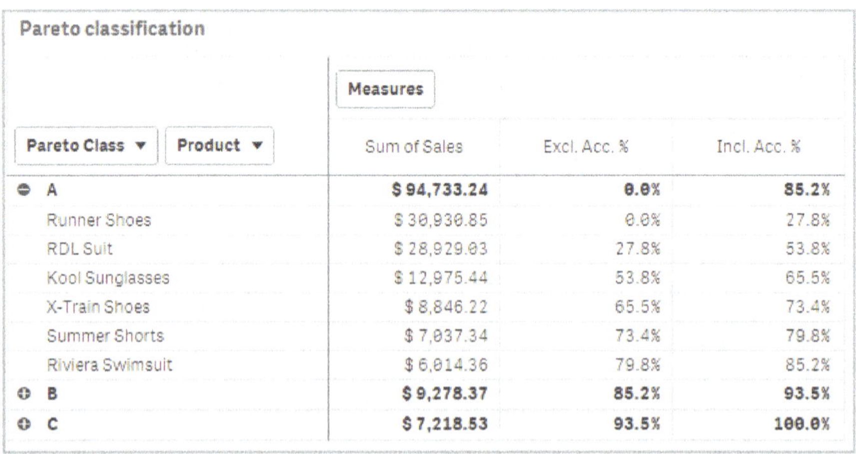

Pareto classification

	Measures		
Pareto Class ▾ Product ▾	Sum of Sales	Excl. Acc. %	Incl. Acc. %
⊖ A	$ 94,733.24	0.0%	85.2%
Runner Shoes	$ 30,930.85	0.0%	27.8%
RDL Suit	$ 28,929.03	27.8%	53.8%
Kool Sunglasses	$ 12,975.44	53.8%	65.5%
X-Train Shoes	$ 8,846.22	65.5%	73.4%
Summer Shorts	$ 7,037.34	73.4%	79.8%
Riviera Swimsuit	$ 6,014.36	79.8%	85.2%
⊕ B	$ 9,278.37	85.2%	93.5%
⊕ C	$ 7,218.53	93.5%	100.0%

If you use this expression in a list box, you can directly select the Pareto class you want to look at.

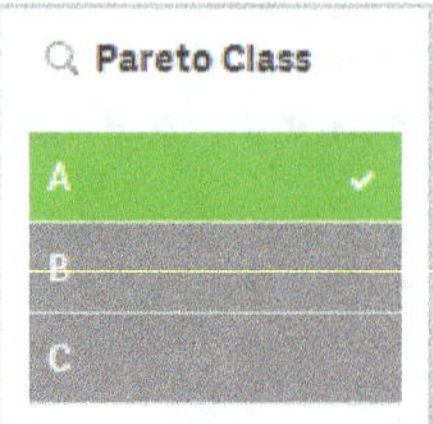

The other measures in the pivot table are the exclusive and inclusive accumulated relative sales, respectively. I.e. the lower and upper bounds of the product sales share.

Exclusive accumulated relative sales (lower bound):

```
Min(Aggr(
    Rangesum(
        Above(Sum({1} Sales)/Sum({1} total Sales),1,RowNo())
        ),
    (Product,(=Sum({1} Sales),Desc))
))
```

Inclusive accumulated relative sales (upper bound):

```
Max(Aggr(
    Rangesum(
        Above(Sum({1} Sales)/Sum({1} total Sales),0,RowNo())
        ),
    (Product,(=Sum({1} Sales),Desc))
))
```

Good luck in creating your Pareto dimension!

Recipe for a QlikView Gantt chart

Originally posted in the Qlik Design Blog on June 1, 2012

Have you ever wanted to create a Gantt chart in QlikView, only to find out that this chart type is not one of the pre-defined charts? Then you should be happy to learn that it _is_ possible to create a Gantt chart and that it is not very difficult.

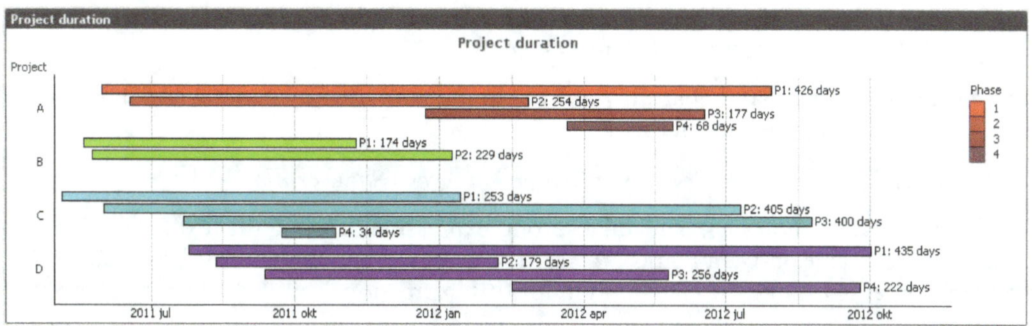

To be able to create this chart, you need some type of event in the data model, where each event has a start date – or time – and an end date. Further, an event should belong to some grouping, typically a project or a phase in time.

Given the above, we can now start making the graph:

1. Create a bar chart with the appropriate event grouping as dimension (e.g., project, phase, or other group of events)

2. Add the duration of the project as an expression: Max(**EndDate**)-Min(**StartDate**). If you only have one date per event, you just replace both **StartDate** and **EndDate** with the date that you have. The duration will then be the time between the first event and the last event in the group.

3. Add the start of the project as an offset to the bars: Min(StartDate). *[Chart Properties - Expressions - The plus sign to the left of the Expression - Bar Offset]*

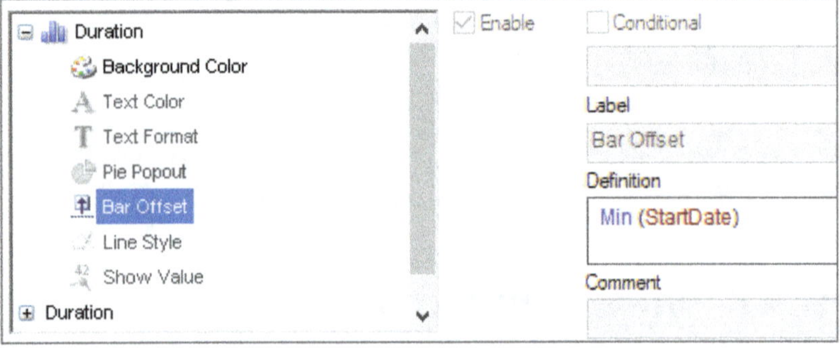

4. Set the graph orientation to horizontal bars. *[Chart Properties - Style-Orientation]*

5. Remove the "Force 0" option. Enabling this option will force the start of the time axis to be Dec 30th, 1899, and we don't want that. *[Chart Properties - Axes - Expression Axes - Force 0]*

6. Format the expression axis labels as dates or as months (e.g. M/D/YY or YYYY MMM). *[Chart Properties - Number-Date]*

Now you should have a Gantt chart. If you want to improve the way it looks, you may want to consider the following suggestions:

-   Add a grid. *[Chart Properties - Axes-Expression Axes - Show grid]*

-   If you want a label on each bar, add a second expression defining the text for the label and use this as "Value on Data Points." *[Chart Properties - Expressions - Display Options]* Don't forget to disable the "Bar" option for this expression. This is the first check box in the Display Options group.

- If the chart shows a range which is too large, add static min and static max to define the display range of the expression, e.g. Min(**StartDate**)-5 and Max(**EndDate**)+40, respectively. The additional distance on the upper limit is to leave space for the text. The unit is number of days. *[Chart Properties - Axes-Scale]*

- If you have a second dimension, you can add this too. But if you do, make sure you use the "Grouped" option and not "Stacked." The latter does not work well with bar offsets. *[Chart Properties - Style-Subtype]*

- You may want to use the same color within each value of the first dimension, e.g., one color per project. One good way to define the color (e.g. RGB values) is to do it already in the dimension table in the script and use this color in a color function in the bar background color, e.g. RGB (ProjR,ProjG,ProjB). *[Chart Properties - Expressions - The plus sign to the left of the Expression - Background Color]*

This Gantt chart solves most cases where you need to display the duration of a group of events. Should you need a more complex Gantt chart, you may need to make it as an extension object instead.

Visualizations

20

A Historical Odyssey

The history of Qlik is long and spans thirty years. In this chapter you will find my description of what happened.

Foundation

Originally presented at Qonnections in Dallas, May 2015

Qlik – or rather QuikTech – was founded in the autumn of 1993 by Björn Berg and Staffan Gestrelius.

They had both worked together previously with different software systems and knew well how computers could aid both knowledge management and product quality in large enterprises. Now they wanted to run their own company.

Picture 5: *Staffan and Björn at an office celebration.*

I was one of the very first employees, starting in January 1994. Initially, it wasn't clear what I was supposed to do: It was a typical startup company, and the two founders had many different ideas of what to do. Consulting around multimedia, SGML, or perhaps some knowledge management system? As a result, my business card didn't really say what my function was.

Picture 6: *My first business card.*

All employees were assigned a trigram – an identifier that was used both for computer log-on and as mail address. Mine was 'HIC' since these are my initials. I have been called 'HIC' ever since.

One day, Björn came into my office and put a shrink-wrapped FoxPro database on my desk. He started to describe an idea he had about how to color-code information based on whether an entity was possible or not, given the user's input. I.e., today's well-known Green-White-Gray paradigm. Then he asked me to develop this as a database application.

Björn had previously worked for Tetra Pak, a large Swedish company that makes solutions for packaging milk and other liquids. He had there identified a problem in communicating information with customers: For example, when a food producer wanted to invest in a packaging machine for its products, it wasn't immediately clear *which* packaging machine they should choose. It wasn't just a question about capacity – it was also about capabilities: Different machines had different limitations: Which sizes they could handle – metric or imperial? Which paper qualities they could handle – packaging for milk or for fruit juices? There were different opening systems, different straw applicators, different pallet sizes, different pallet patterns, shrink-wrapped or not, etc. And all these parameters had implications on the possible machine types.

There were just too many parameters, so it was difficult to get an overview. Björn's idea was that the user should be allowed any starting point in this jungle of different capabilities: If the food producer knew that the main requirements were "fruit juices" and "a straw on the side", they should be allowed to click on exactly this, and nothing else, and immediately see which machines were possible.

So Björn asked me to develop this. He also asked two other people in the company to do the same thing, but with other tools.

But neither of us really succeeded. Well, we created apps that worked – sort of – but the apps were too slow or kludgy to become sellable products.

We concluded that in order for this to work, we need to develop this as a specific piece of software. So, we contracted an excellent software developer that we knew from university: Håkan Wolgé.

He developed a prototype for this, using C++. However, he changed the color coding slightly:

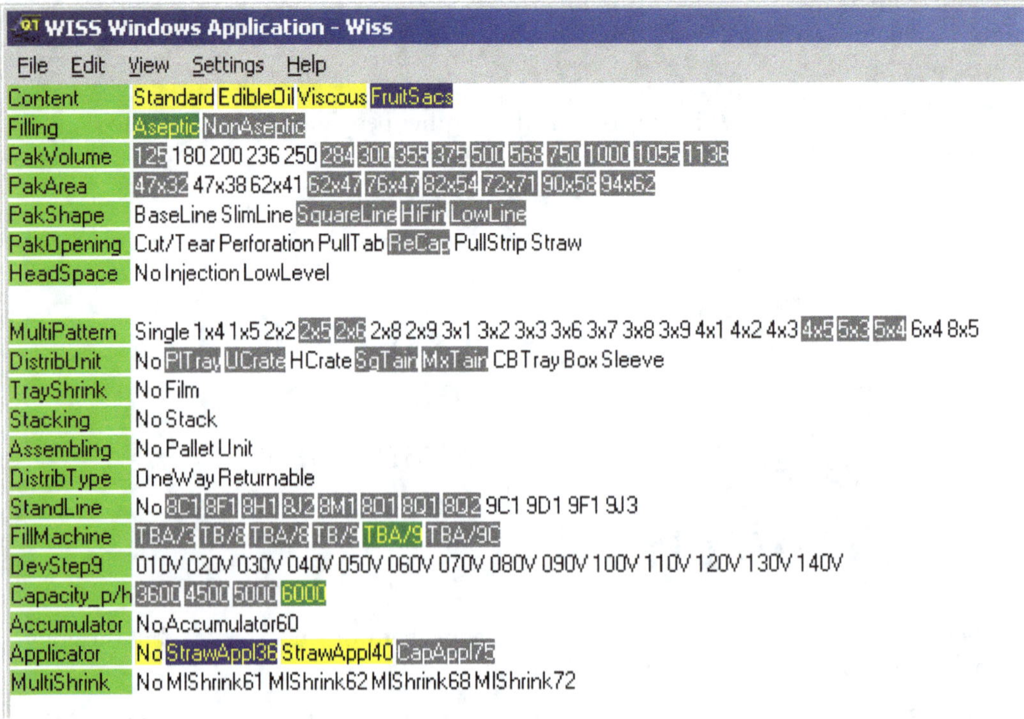

In the prototype, blue meant 'selected', green meant 'only possible value', and yellow meant 'alternative'. White and gray were used in their original meanings: 'possible' and 'excluded'. With this tool, a user could easily get the overview he so badly needed.

It was just a prototype with many limitations, but it was the first step. The next step was to generalize it, so that *any* tabular data could be used. And that led to the first version of QlikView.

Three Friends

Originally presented at Qonnections in Dallas, May 2015

Contracting Håkan for the development turned out to be an excellent move. We already knew that he was a very good C++ developer, but he also proved to have other qualities: He had a passion for data, and he had an extraordinary understanding of what users needed to get an overview of data.

Picture *7: The inventor – Håkan Wolgé.*

Håkan always sought the general solution. He also sought simplicity. And he was stubborn. He rarely did what he was told. He was always convinced that there was a better, more general way to solve the problem. And he was usually right. As a result, the Qlik engine contains a number of general tools that can be used to solve problems we hadn't thought of when they were introduced.

A Historical Odyssey

Set Analysis is a good example of this: The initial requirement was merely to find a way to be able to compare the result of the selection with a number that was *outside* the selection, e.g. the amount of a specific country or a specific product. Instead of solving this specific problem, Håkan designed a general syntax to formally describe a selection, a syntax that could be used inside any expression.

So, Håkan's stubbornness was in fact one of the reasons why the product became so good.

I was the Product Manager for the first two and a half years, which meant that I did everything from writing the documentation, presenting the product for prospects, building solutions for customers, to specifying the requirements for the next version. Customer contacts gave me an invaluable insight into what problems users were trying to solve.

Explaining user challenges to Håkan and persuading him to make necessary changes in the product was the core of product management at the time. However, Håkan rarely did what I asked for. Instead, he listened, thought about it for a day or two, and then made something that was better. This process was efficient: My suggested solution made Håkan understand the problem, and Håkan generalized the problem and created the solution.

Hence, Håkan is *The Inventor* of the Qlik engine. The rest of us were wing men.

As time passed, the company grew, and we hired more developers. So, in the autumn of 1996 we reorganized the development department. Jonas Nachmanson started as R&D Manager, and I moved into pre-sales, consulting and training.

Picture 8: *Henric Cronström and Jonas Nachmanson.*

Hiring Jonas was another good move: Jonas had a very good understanding of the problem space and the technology, and in addition he had excellent organizational skills. With Jonas, the R&D department got a clear leadership. With this change, Jonas took over many of my tasks, such as the documentation and the requirement specification. But the teamwork between the three of us continued and developed.

These three friends were the core of the development of QlikView, at least initially. But as time passed, more and more people got involved in the development as well as the testing, and the requirement specification. It became to a very large extent a teamwork, with many other significant contributors.

Picture 9: *The development team 2015.*

Quality - Learning - Interaction - Knowledge

Posted in the Business Discovery Blog on June 12, 2012

The first couple of years in QlikTech's history, the company was called QuikTech and the product was called QuikView. It was a game with words: The product name insinuated that you could view things quickly and at the same time the letters Q-U-I-K were an abbreviation for what we believed in: Quality, Understanding, Information and Knowledge.

We believed that a business could improve its processes and product quality by empowering employees and encouraging them to engage in lifelong learning. And we meant _all_ people – we saw everyone as a decision maker. Getting information from data was an important part of creating the understanding, the knowledge and the quality. We were inspired by the management trends of the time, especially by employee empowerment as described in the book "Moments of Truth" (Swedish: "Riv pyramiderna") by Jan Carlzon, president and CEO of Scandinavian Airlines.

Thus, the abbreviation was an early attempt to make a values statement and it was there long before the genesis of the product. What the abbreviation stood for was really the ideological base when founding the company.

Another, less glamorous reason for the strange spelling was the old DOS file name restriction. File names could not have more than 8+3 characters. There was just no room for a "C". Hence QuikView.exe.

And why did we change from Quik to Qlik?

Well, we tried to register "QuikView" as a trademark, but our application was rejected. There were already too many software products with the prefix Quick, Qwick, Qvick, or Quik. But we still wanted to protect the product name! However, at this time, we had started to realize that a defining characteristic of the product was that you clicked and viewed. The fact that it was quick was not the first thing that came to mind. So, the step to rename the product to "Qlik" + "View" was not very big – in fact, it was even an improvement of our values statement: We just replaced the words "Understanding" and "Information" with "Learning" and "Interaction".

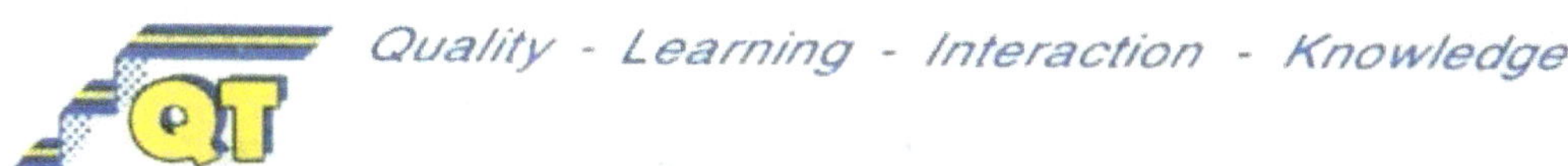

Today (2012) our mission statement is "***Simplifying Decisions for Everyone, Everywhere***". The words we use to describe our mission have changed slightly: From the general "Knowledge" and "Quality" to the more specific "Decisions" – which is the main step in transforming knowledge into quality. As I see it, the current mission statement is even more to the point than our original values statement. Further, it includes the idea that _all_ people are included, which is something we took for granted but failed to express in our initial values statement. In all aspects, the current mission statement is a very good description of what we stood for already 18 years ago and what we still stand for today.

We are still true to our initial values. We just express them differently.

What is QlikView?

Originally posted in the Business Discovery Blog on Nov 16, 2012

In the early days of QlikView, there was a big challenge in describing what QlikView is. A word processor is a word processor, and a spreadsheet is a spreadsheet. But what is QlikView? How do you describe QlikView to a person that hasn't experienced QlikView?

Technically, it is a logical inference engine with a visual user interface that utilizes color coding and group theory to display the possible combinations of field values. But that description doesn't help a lot – does it?

Our first attempt to describe what the product does is in fact found in the original product logo. It was the shape of an aperture that symbolized that the user could focus in on specific pieces of information.

We soon started to describe QlikView in terms of "associative" and "works like you think." We recognized that the human train of thought is not linear and predictable, and we started to market QlikView as a tool that supports the way the brain works. The brain associates and contemplates. It turns questions around and looks for the opposite, the excluded. We felt that there was a gap between man and machine and that QlikView was the tool to bridge this gap.

At one point there was much buzz about data warehouses and data marts. We of course wanted to position QlikView in this discussion, so for QlikView 3 we started to call it "the associative info mart program." "Mart" because it positioned QlikView as a tool with a subset of the data (compared to the data warehouse) dedicated for one specific purpose. Today we would instead use the term "app." "Info" because QlikView was more than just a data mart.

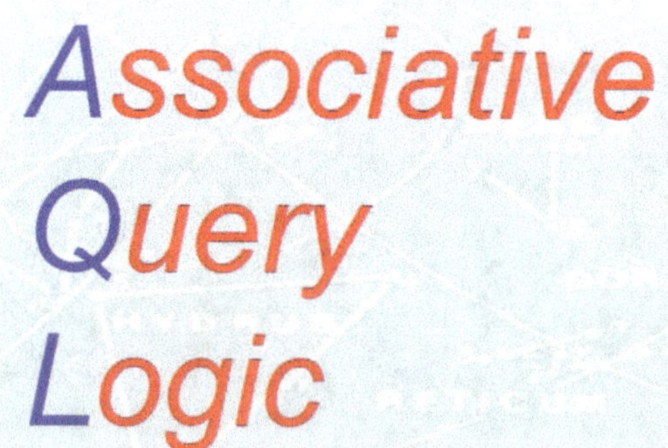

In 1996 at CeBIT, the big yearly IT exhibition in Hannover, I and a couple of colleagues found ourselves in the Münchner Halle late one evening. After a few drinks we were discussing with potential partners ways we could license our technology to other software vendors. At the same time, Alfredo – a local opera singer – was performing on the stage in his red tuxedo singing "Granada" and "O, sole mio." He did this every year. To make a long story short: We brainstormed possible trademarks for the technology and came up with AQL – Associative Query Logic. This abbreviation survived many years and is still used by some partners and users.

Since then, we have used many other descriptions of what QlikView is: intuitive data exploration, general purpose multi-dimensional query tool, a revolution in business intelligence, in-memory BI, and Business Discovery. All of these descriptions are correct. They describe different aspects of QlikView.

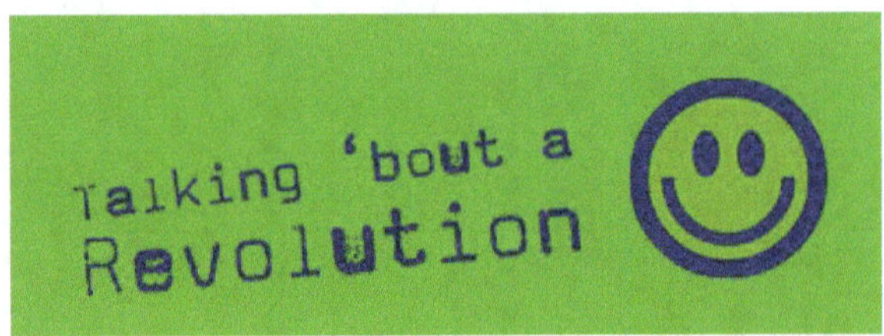

To me, the main difference between QlikView and more old-fashioned query tools is that QlikView supports the entire process – the process of coming from a blank mind, not knowing what you are looking for, all the way to attaining knowledge and taking action. It involves exploring the data. It involves discovering new facts. It involves playing with data, turning it around, scrutinizing the facts and formulating relevant questions. It involves conducting analysis to get an answer to the questions.

And, finally, it involves presenting the answers to the questions to other people as a basis for a decision or an action. It supports the entire process of going from ignorance to insight.

And how do you describe that in just a couple of words? Business Discovery is in fact quite good.

QuikView 1

Originally posted in the Qlik Design Blog on Jun 22, 2012

1994 was the year when the Swedish soccer team took bronze in the world championships. It was also the year the channel tunnel between France and Great Britain opened. Boris Yeltsin was the Russian president and Bill Clinton was one year into his first term. 1994 was also the year when the first version of QlikView – or QuikView – was released.

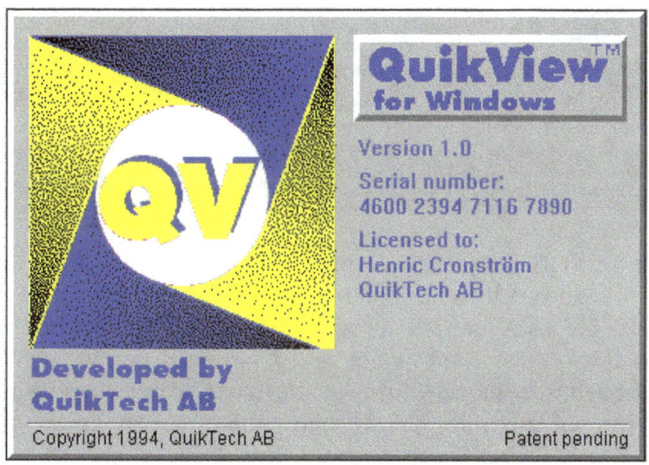

Version 1.0 had only the logical inference between fields – it had no graphics capabilities, and no calculations were possible. But during the lifetime of QlikView 1 graphics and numeric calculations were added and by the release of version 1.42, QlikView had the same basic structure as we still have today: a multi-table relational data model, a logical inference engine, and graphs that hold no data of their own but instead are calculated on the fly based on the result of the logical inference.

Further, the conceptual idea of an "app" came with QlikView 1: *the holy document*. A QlikView document is in its basic form still today a self-contained file that holds all necessary information: a snapshot of data, layout information, and information on how the data should be refreshed. A user can have several documents, each corresponding to a specific area of the data. The document can be mailed to other users and no installation is necessary. This approach ensured portability and has been key to simplifying backward and forward compatibility as well as compatibility between QlikView Desktop and QlikView Server.

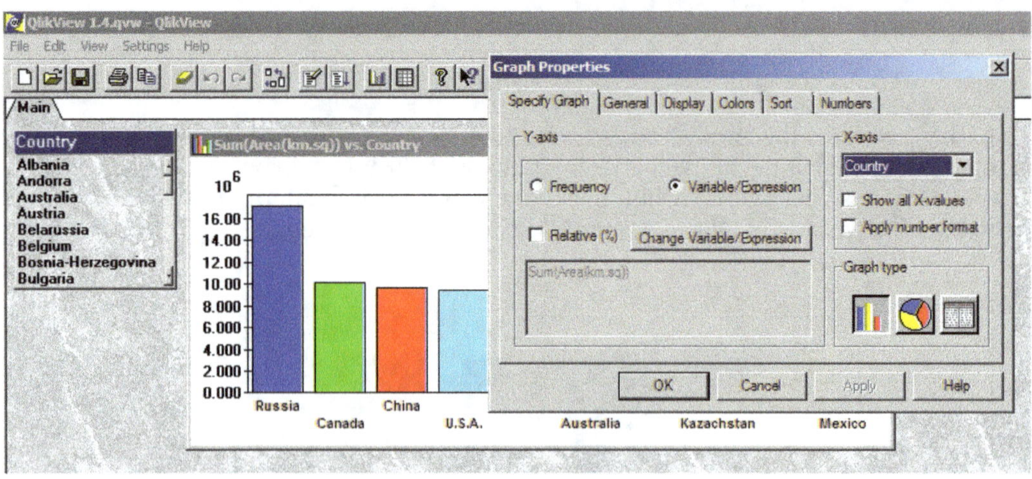

The mid-nineties were also the time when 32-bit Windows software started to emerge. Most programs, as well as Windows 3.1 itself, were only 16-bit, but if you installed the Microsoft Win32s module, you could also run 32-bit programs. Consequently, several of the QlikView 1 releases were produced in both a 16-bit version and a 32-bit version. In 1995 Microsoft released Windows 95 and although we today are not very impressed by this operating system, it was at the time a big leap forward. After that, 32-bit programs became standard.

With the 16-bit QlikView you could only have 16,000 distinct values in a field and 65,000 records in a table. These limits were, however, not a huge problem because most of the analysis in those days was made on data sets with few distinct values and often with pre-aggregated data. By the introduction of the 32-bit QlikView, these limits were removed, and this opened up the field for transactional analysis. It would take many years before the new limit of 2GB memory would become a problem.

Much of what was invented in QlikView 1 is still there today, in QlikView 11. In fact, the principal features from QlikView 1 are the core of the modern QlikView; they are the foundation of how QlikView still works today.

However, there is one thing from QlikView 1 that I miss – the marble background …

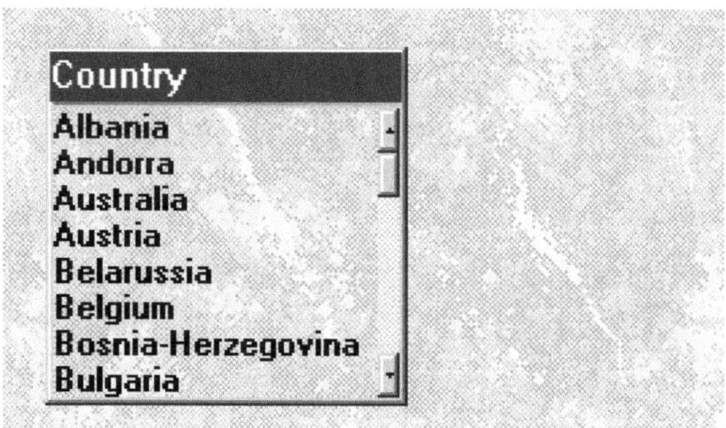

QlikView 2

Originally posted in the Qlik Design Blog on Jul 4, 2012

Software development is a learning process. In the development you sometimes reach a point when you realize how you should have done it in the first place. As a consequence, you want to re-write all or parts of the code from scratch.

In 1996, when starting the development for QlikView 2, we were in such a situation. We had learned a lot from coding 32-bit Windows code (which was still fairly new) and we had seen that the older Single Document Instance (SDI) paradigm was not what we wanted to have in the future: SDI programs could only hold one document open at a time. We wanted the Multiple Document Instance (MDI) paradigm instead.

To make a long story short: We re-wrote large parts of the code and as a consequence, we had problems with the product stability. We had to postpone many of the planned features and spend time bug fixing instead.

The features included in version 2.0 were hence few, the major ones being MDI interface, the introduction of the button object and the possibility to have several dimensions and several expressions in charts. With the button object you could e.g. export data to Excel.

And, yes, we discontinued the 16-bit version of QlikView. We saw that the future lay in 32-bit code. Also, and more specifically for QlikView, we saw that memory was getting cheaper and started realizing that it was possible to perform analysis down to the transactional level even for fairly large data sets – but for this we needed 32-bit code to be able to load the larger amounts of data.

After the release of version 2.0, we started working on the postponed features – and they were many! When we got closer to the release of 2.1, we noted that the new version would have little in common with the 2.0 version. So, someone (from marketing) suggested we'd number the new version "2.5" instead.

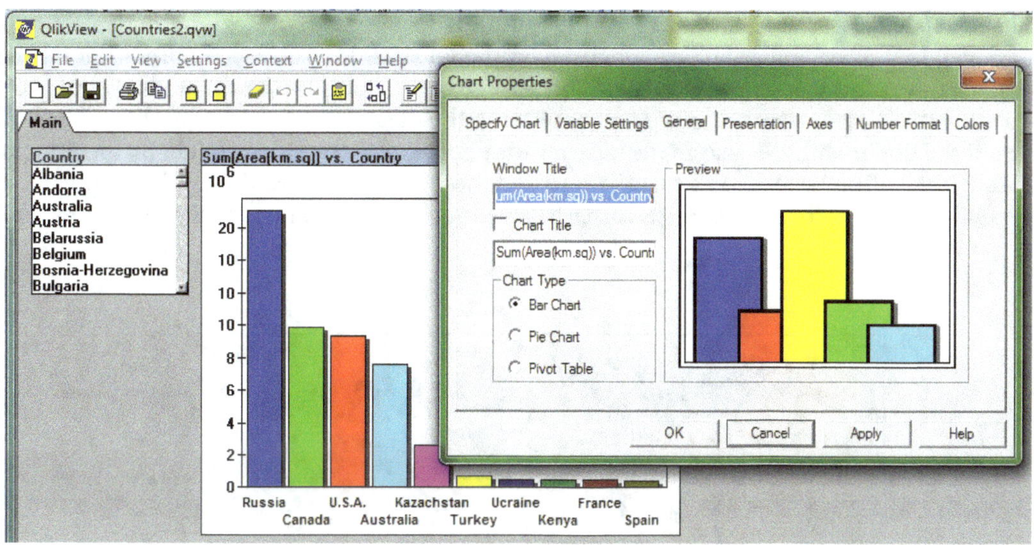

Here you must understand that the QlikTech company culture contains a large element of frankness. If you don't agree, you speak up; you say your meaning. So, at the suggested jump from 2.0 to 2.5, there were people – techies including myself – that expressed their dissatisfaction over the inconsistent version numbering. An animated argument followed where no side got the upper hand. The people in favor of jumping to 2.5 were just as stubborn as we.

In these early days, such decisions were always made in consensus. But now we were in a deadlock. The compromise was to release neither a version 2.1 nor a version 2.5. Instead, we labeled the new version "3.0", which in retrospect was a good decision. But more about that in a later blog.

Bottom line is, that QlikView 2 had a very short lifetime and did not have a big impact at all. But it did pave the road for versions to come: We had re-written the code and the new 32-bit architecture was sound and allowed to be built further upon.

QlikView 3

Originally posted in the Qlik Design Blog on Sep 4, 2012

Oh, glorious were the days! Businesswise we were perhaps not yet so successful, but product maturity made giant leaps forward. QlikView 3 was a very good product packed with new features that made life easier. Both developers and users loved it. It was easier for prospects to evaluate it and it was easier for us to sell than previous versions.

QlikView 3 was released in the spring of 1997, in time for the yearly IT exhibition CeBIT in Hannover. In version 1 and 2 we had focused on the UI (user interface) – on presenting data in such a way that a user could explore it and learn from it. For QlikView 3, we had changed focus slightly. We now worked more on simplifying the data loading process and the development of the document. We also made it easier for people to try out the product by introducing a 15-day evaluation license. As a result, more and more people started developing applications with QlikView. And it became much easier to convince prospects and partners to join us on our journey.

One major change in QlikView 3 was the *Automatic Outer Join*. Already in QlikView 1 and 2, you could have a data model with several tables. But the associations between the tables were like inner joins and no analysis was possible for values that lacked corresponding records in a neighboring table. For instance, customers that had no orders in the **Orders** table were *always* grayed out. But with QlikView 3 it became possible to select such customers. This is a feature that we today take for granted, but it was not there in the beginning.

Another change in QlikView 3 was that the scripting language developed immensely. We introduced a number of new script constructs. **Join**, **Concatenate**, **Crosstable**, **Intervalmatch**, resident load, preceding load, **Group by**, Peek, Previous, and variables the way we know them today, all arrived in QlikView 3 – as did the text file wizard and the possibility to load files over the internet. You could now make fairly complex data transformations right in the QlikView script.

We also introduced several new sheet objects in QlikView 3 (line chart, scatter chart, multi box, straight table and table box) as well as new property dialogs – one for user preferences, one for the sheet, and one for the document itself. And you could right-click on the sheet and get a float menu. It became a whole lot easier to navigate around all the product settings.

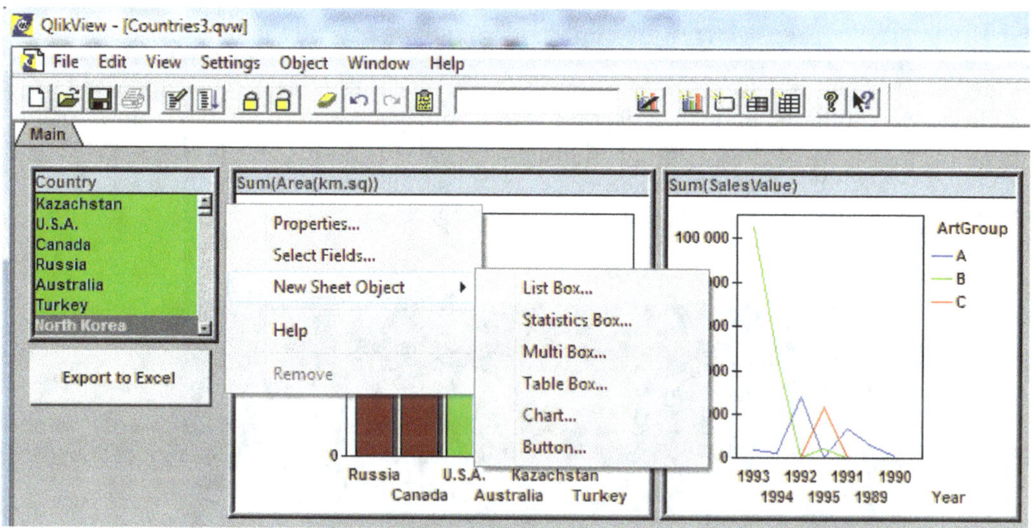

On top of all this, we released French and German language versions of QlikView, as well as a Macintosh edition. Yes, we had a Mac version of QlikView! However, we didn't sell much of it and since it meant a lot of extra work for R&D, both in terms of development and test, we discontinued it one release later.

And – most importantly of all – QlikView 3 was extremely stable.

As a curiosity, QlikView 3 also had one of the best error messages ever: "Time Travel is not allowed!" Anyone can figure out when this was used?

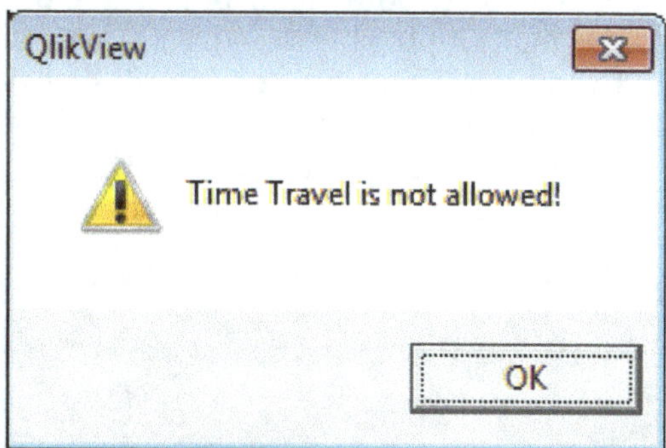

QlikView 4 and the first Server

Originally posted in the Qlik Design Blog on Oct 10, 2012

QlikView 3 was a giant leap forward. More and more people started developing applications with QlikView and it became much easier to convince prospects and partners to join us on our journey. As a result, we faced more and more demands from the real world: tools with which you can customize a document, tools for security, tools to save and re-use a selection, client/server, etc. Much of this didn't exist in QlikView 3.

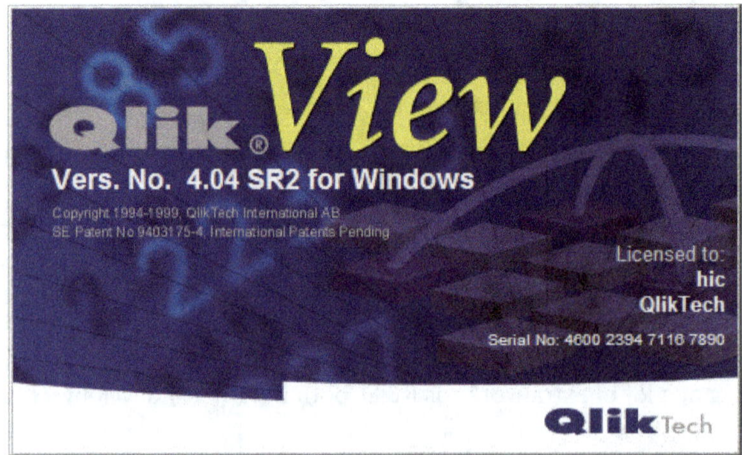

So, for QlikView 4 we started to develop features based heavily on customer requirements.

We had already experimented a little with macros in QlikView 3 but in QlikView 4 we did it properly. We introduced the first color coding in pivot tables so that our customers could mark negative numbers red. We made it possible to activate several objects and align them. We made it possible to load Excel files. We introduced control structures such as For-Next loops in the script language. We introduced Section Access to address security demands. We introduced bookmarks. We introduced a proper NULL value handling and we introduced the text object, so that customers could show also static information.

We also had a new logo and a new icon.

But there are two features that, more than any others should be noted as the principal features in QlikView 4:

- **The chart engine**
  With QlikView 4, you could write any expression as an aggregation and QlikView would be able to evaluate it on the fly. This is true still today; you can have an expression with several arbitrary fields, where the fields reside in different tables, and then aggregate this expression. The aggregate can in turn be used in a new expression that uses other aggregations with fields from yet other tables, e.g., $Sum(x*y)/Count(z)$. The Qlik engine evaluates this expression correctly. This feature is unique to the Qlik engine and is the core of one of QlikTech's patents.

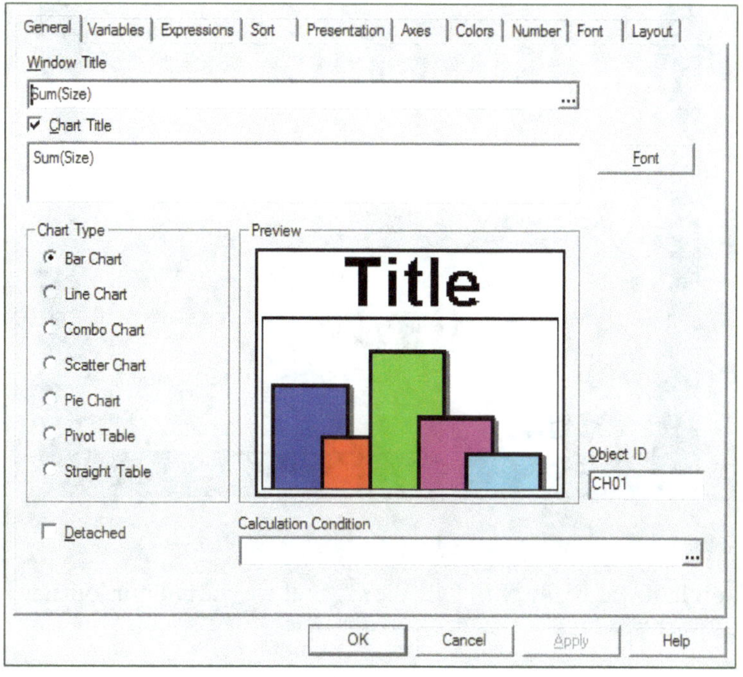

- **The Server**
  The second major advancement in QlikView 4 was the client-server capability. It was then called QlikView Web Solution. Compared to the QlikView Server of today, it was rudimentary. But it was a first step and some of the structure is still the same. Application development, then, was done just as it is today: on a standalone QlikView. The file could then be copied to the server. The only client that existed then was a Java client talking directly to the server. The server had to have Microsoft IIS (Internet Information Server) installed and the client had to have Microsoft Java installed. This meant that in practice we only supported Microsoft environments, both on the client and on the server side.

As I think back on it, it was really with QlikView 4 that we started our journey toward being an enterprise software product.

The Doctors' Special

Originally posted in the Qlik Design Blog on May 21, 2013

Already when we were selling QlikView 3, we received a fairly advanced customer demand from pharmaceutical companies. We solved it. And here's how we did it. But first some background:

In the pharmaceutical industry, the sales reps are not the ones that sell the products. Instead, they visit physicians and *demonstrate* one or several products. Days, weeks or months later, the physician prescribe the demonstrated medicine to a patient, and the actual sale takes place when the patient buys the drug at a pharmacy.

The demand on QlikView was to show pharmacy sales data, not only per physician, but also per physician visited once, twice, three times, etc. In other words, the physicians should be grouped by number of visits, and this number should be used as dimension in a QlikView chart. A nested aggregation that today easily can be solved using Aggr() in the dimension. But in QlikView 3, we didn't have Aggr().

We, however, made a solution for this in QlikView 4. Well, *solution* is perhaps not the right word… There was a kludgy, hidden feature with which you could use a count of a field as dimension. Internally it was called the Doctor Controls.

First you had to enable this feature in the list of hidden settings.

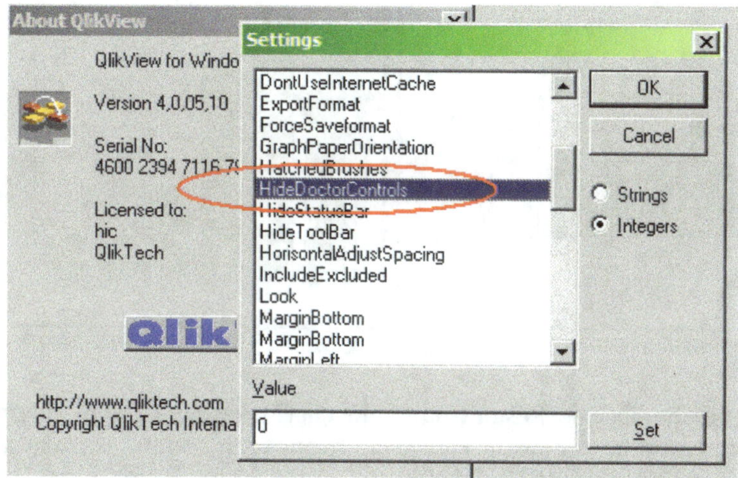

Then you could create your chart: Count(Visit) per **Physician**. After that, you needed to enable the "Display Result Count" in the chart:

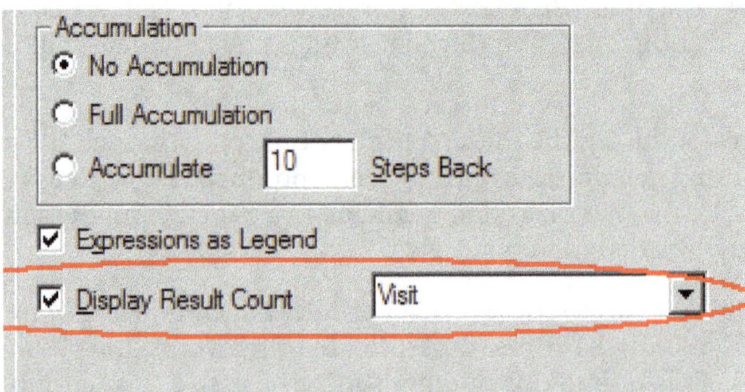

The left graph shows graph as-is – without the "Display Result Count" enabled. It shows the distinct count of visits per physician, just as the dimension and expression of the chart are defined.

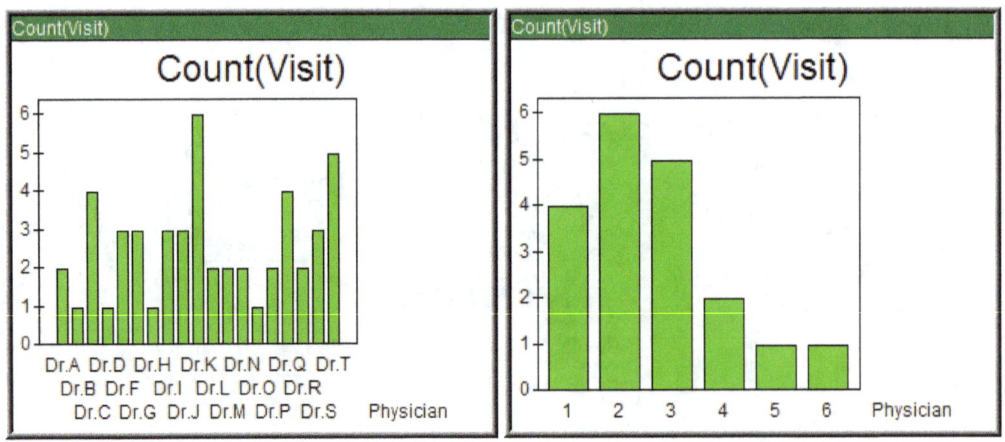

But, by turning on the "Display Result Count", the chart transformed into the right graph: The displayed dimension was now the equivalent to an Aggr(Count(Visit),Physician) and the displayed expression was Count(Physician).

We solved the customer's problem at the time, but this was not a good, long-term solution. And it was nothing we wanted to support. Instead, we wanted a general solution for nested aggregations. Six years later – after much thinking – Håkan (the Inventor) came up with the Aggr() function for QlikView 7. It is a general function for nested aggregations that made the Doctors' Special redundant.

But like a relic from the past, the Doctor Controls setting can still today be found in the QlikView's list of hidden settings. It doesn't affect anything – I hope.

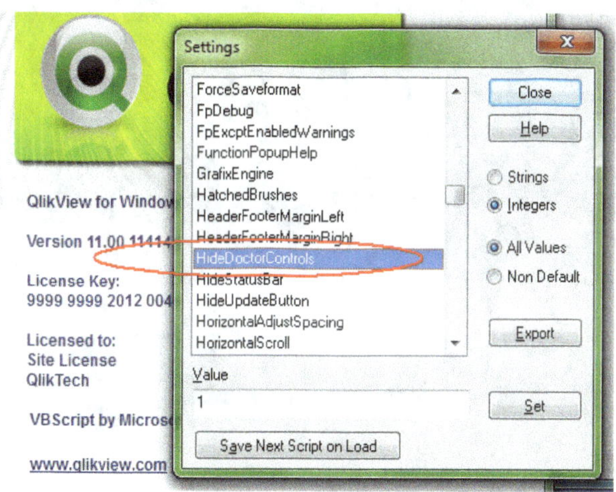

QlikView 5 and the Rainbow Border

Originally posted in the Qlik Design Blog on Nov 23, 2012

Product wise, QlikView 5 was about consolidation. We did not change very much from QlikView 4. We already had a feature-rich product – now it was about improving the details and making it more stable.

So, we improved the functions in the UI – made it look nicer, introduced a layout menu and a layout undo, made it possible to copy and paste objects, introduced the current selections box, an input box, fast type change in charts, windows selection style and fuzzy search. And we made it possible to export data to Excel.

We also improved the data loading capabilities. Now it became possible to load Unicode characters and HTML tables as well as XML files. It also became possible to load from SQL stored procedures. And the script editor was equipped with a debugger.

We developed the server further and made it more stable, but we really didn't change much in the basic architecture.

None of the above was incredibly exciting or ground-breaking. Instead, QlikView 5 could perhaps be remembered for one less impressive feature: the rainbow border. This was probably one of the less useful features we have introduced. Whether it was beautiful, I leave to you to decide ....

During the lifetime of QlikView 5, Intel introduced a new, promising processor architecture: the Itanium, a 64-bit RISC processor for PCs. This was the future! With such a processor QlikView would no longer be limited by the 3GB restriction on the amount of data it could handle. This opened up fantastic new opportunities! QlikView would be able to load much larger data amounts than before!

We immediately started to develop an Itanium edition of QlikView. As a consequence, the later releases of QlikView 5 were all compiled into both a 32-bit and a 64-bit edition. QlikView 5 therefore goes down in history as the first 64-bit version of the product (even though QlikView 6 was the first version where there was an official 64-bit version.)

As we developed QlikView 5 during the year 2000, QlikTech got new investors which led to a change of management. When we released QlikView 5 in the spring of 2001, Måns Hultman had been appointed CEO.

Måns had a very clear picture of what the company needed: A refined sales strategy and a bigger sales force. The new sales strategy was simple: Focus. Rather than selling QlikView as a tool that could do anything, we would focus on financial applications on top of ERP systems, especially Movex and JD Edwards (which were common systems in Sweden and USA at that time). The target prospects were controllers and CFOs.

And it worked. With Måns' new strategy and a good, stable QlikView 5, the company started growing faster than ever before. The course was set for becoming a public company.

QlikView 6 and Multi-threading

Originally posted in the Qlik Design Blog on Jan 9, 2013

Although QlikView 5 was a stable, good version with lots of functionality, it wasn't good enough for the new hardware that came along. We had already seen the arrival of the 64-bit Itanium processor, and we had responded by developing an Itanium edition. So far, so good. But when we experimented with large data amounts, we realized that although QlikView now could load and address very large amounts of data, QlikView couldn't process the data fast enough. QlikView needed more processor power. The amount of memory was no longer the limiting factor – instead it was the limited power of a single processor.

About this time, Intel had just launched its first dual core processors. There were already multi-processor motherboards, but the dual core processors were cheaper and could in addition share cache. The introduction of the dual core processors and QlikView's need for more processor power forced us to look at how we better could utilize parallel processing.

Hence: Time for a re-write! Multi-threading – here we come.

Already in the QlikView 5 server, there was some basic multi-threading: Each session was evaluated in its own thread. But now, we needed to take multi-threading several steps further; we needed to make the evaluation of every click multi-threaded.

Multi-threading is not easy. The software process needs to have mechanisms that can determine that one thread should be split into several, and other mechanisms that merge several threads into one. The threads are asynchronous and sometimes a thread needs to stop and wait for the result of another thread. This means that you can get situations where two threads wait for each other. So, you also need mechanisms to avoid such deadlocks.

Anyway, we re-wrote large parts of the code and when we released QlikView 6 in the spring of 2003, it was multi-threaded.

In the solution, the logical inference for a single click is multi-threaded and the evaluation of several threads are merged together to form the final result. After the logical inference, the sheet objects need to be calculated. Each object is then a thread of its own that subscribe to all changes in the data model. "Subscribe" means that it is re-evaluated every time there is a change in the selection state. In addition, the chart engine is multi-threaded, so that if an aggregation is made over a table with a large number of records, different parts of the table are aggregated in different threads.

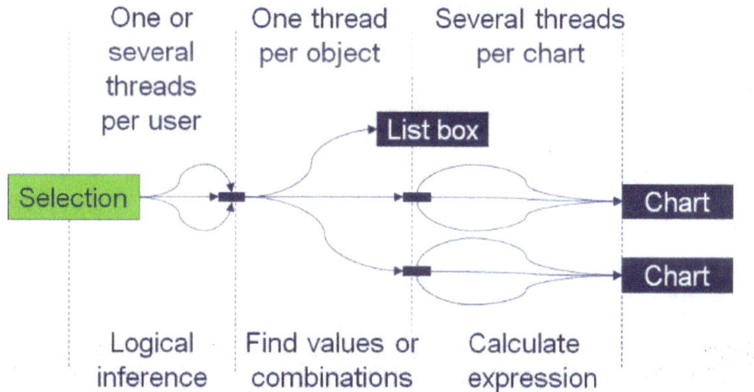

QlikView 6 also brought the LEF files, which enabled Client Access Licenses (CALs) for the server. It also brought the qvp protocol, the plug-in client, the OCX, the table viewer, copy and paste objects, the layout themes, semi transparency (GDI+), the color functions, variables in the layout, the grid chart, the gauge chart, the radar chart, the slider object and the language dlls.

We also introduced different license levels for the stand-alone version of QlikView 6: Enterprise, Professional and Analyzer, so that a customer could have different capabilities for developers, power users and standard users.

QlikView 6 should be remembered for bringing the multi-threading that we use still today. This is the core of the modern Qlik engine that can use the power of today's multi-core hardware.

The Early Days of QlikView Publisher

Originally posted in the Qlik Design Blog on Apr 22, 2013

With QlikView 4 and QlikView 5 we reached a much larger audience than before. We now had large enterprise customers that had demands on the product that we didn't quite satisfactory fulfill: The demands were around Security, Distribution and Workflow.

As a result, one large Swedish customer developed their own system to administrate QlikView: They developed software that used the QlikView COM Automation interface to update and distribute QlikView documents. They showed it to us and we were impressed – so impressed that we bought the code to develop it further. As a result, we could in 2001 release the *QlikView Administrator*.

The Administrator had three basic components:

- The Factory – which later became *The Distribution service*
- The User Access Portal – which later became *The Access Point*
- The Administration Panel – which later became *The Management Console*

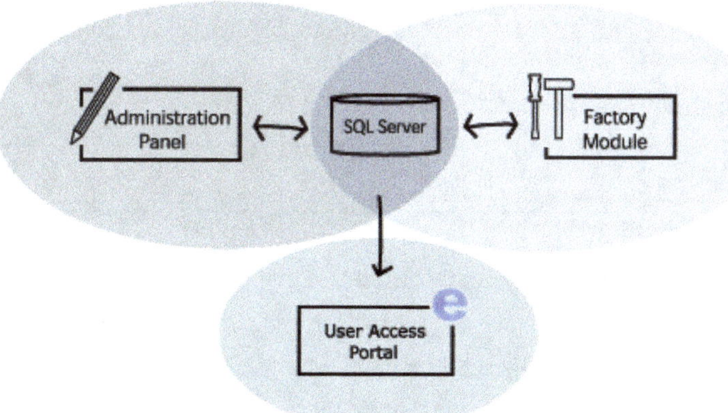

The Factory's tasks were to update the QlikView documents and distribute them in a secure way. On the portal, the users could either download the documents for off-line use or connect to the documents using QlikWeb – which was the name of our server at the time. Finally, the administration panel was used to set the rules for how and when the updates should be made and to whom the documents should be distributed.

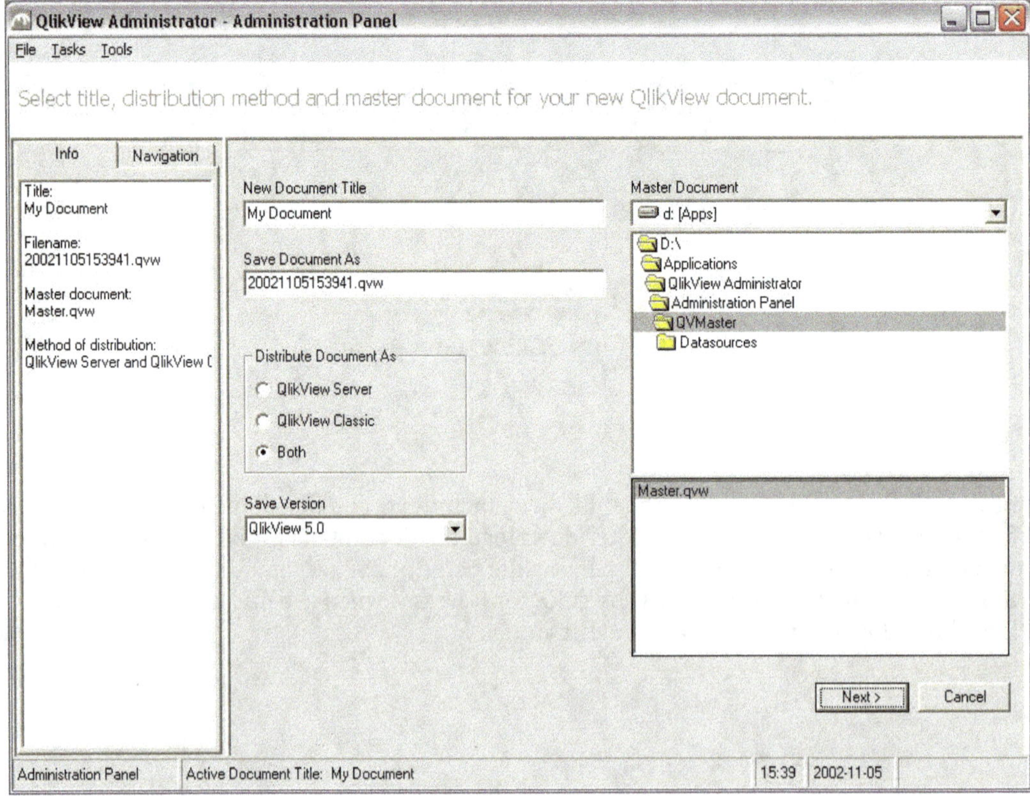

The Administrator was the basic workflow tool that our enterprise customers demanded. It contained tasks, scheduling, data reduction, document categorization, document distribution and it also set the user rights per document. So, it covered all the basic needs.

The name was not quite good, so we renamed it "QlikView Publisher". We also improved the UI and the functionality and when we released version 2 a few years later, it was much richer in features and much more usable.

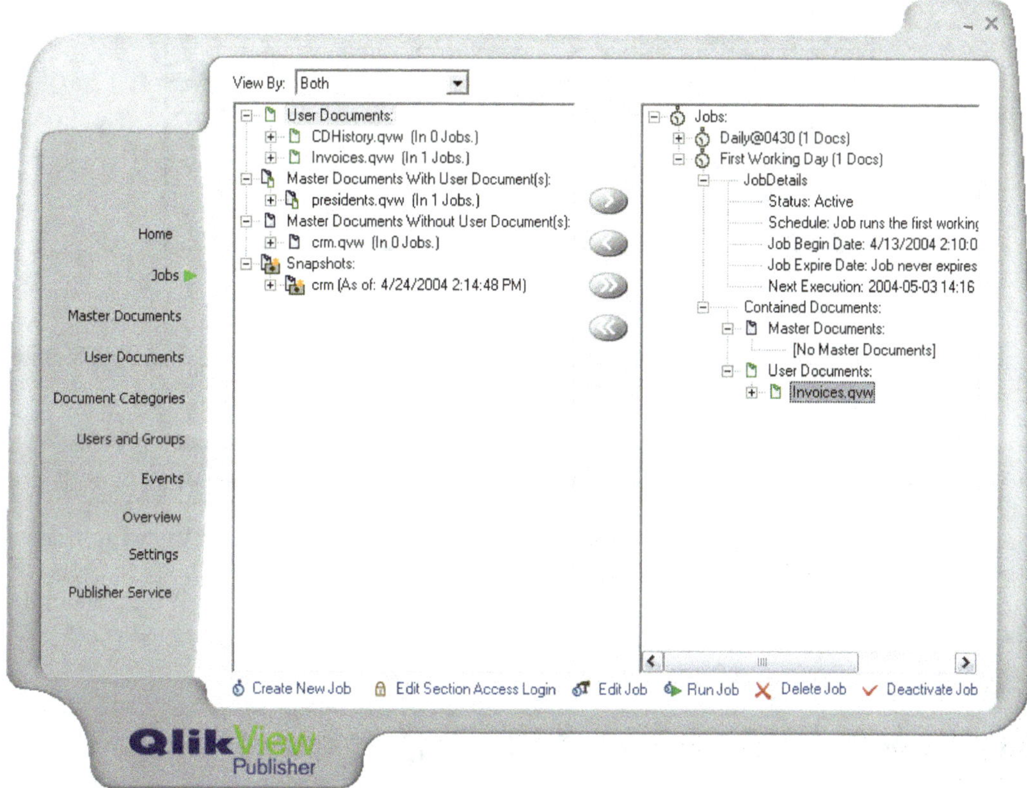

Initially, it was developed in Visual basic 6, but we soon were looking for a more modern development tool and today it is developed in C#.

The version numbers were not in sync with QlikView until QlikView 8. Before that, the Publisher had its own numbering. For QlikView 9 the QlikView Server and the QlikView Publisher were completely merged, with a common management console and a common installation. This also means that some of the original Publisher features became available also without a Publisher license, e.g. the reload of a document.

Publisher version	QlikView version	Year	Developed in
QlikView Administrator 1	QlikView 5	2001	Visual Basic 6
QlikView Publisher 2	QlikView 6	2004	Visual Basic 6
QlikView Publisher 3	QlikView 7.0 - 7.2	2005	Visual Basic .Net
QlikView Publisher 4	QlikView 7.5	2006	Visual Basic .Net
QlikView Publisher 4.1	QlikView 7.52	2006	C# .Net
QlikView Publisher 8	QlikView 8	2007	C# .Net

Although very much has changed since the first Publisher version, the basic concepts for the Publisher remain the same: Security, Distribution and Workflow.

Today, the QlikView Publisher is a mature workflow tool that allows our customers to manage the distribution of information both to off-line and on-line users. It can connect to a large number of directory services; it can be integrated with almost any authentication system and it can use either Windows integrated authorization or the QlikView internal authorization. It can take a master document, refresh it, reduce it so that the user only gets its own data and finally distribute it in any way the administrator wants it. It is an absolute necessity for a company with enterprise demands on security and data governance.

QlikView 7, QVD files and the Aggr() function

Originally posted in the Qlik Design Blog on May 07, 2013

For QlikView 7 we developed a number of features that would enable developers to make even more advanced applications. One such feature was the Buffer prefix – a prefix that you could put in front of a Load or a SELECT that would store the data on the local machine and automatically use the local data when appropriate. With it, you could e.g. load data from a slow ODBC connection just once a day and for other script runs use the buffer.

The buffered data needed to be compact and something that QlikView could load fast. So, the QVD file was invented to solve this need. Today, hardly anyone uses the Buffer prefix, but QVD files created with the Store command are often used.

Another new feature was the Aggr() function. Already for QlikView 4 we had a solution for having an aggregation as dimension. Well, solution is perhaps not the right word … There was a kludgy, hidden feature with which you could use a count of a field as dimension. Internally it was called the Doctors' Special. We solved a customer's problem at the time, but we were not satisfied: we instead wanted a general, good solution for nested aggregations.

Six years later – after much thinking – Håkan (the Inventor) came up with the Aggr() function. It is a general function that can be used both as dimension and as measure. It can be nested and it can internally use any aggregation. In other words: it is a general function for nested aggregations. A by-product was the calculated dimension, which was necessary in order to use the Aggr() as dimension.

The Intel Itanium processor was first released in 2001, but its sales had still not picked up when QlikView 7 was released four years later in 2005. Instead, a new kid appeared on the block: The AMD X64 architecture. The X64 turned out to be both cheaper and faster than the Itanium, and as a consequence it sold better.

We already had an Itanium edition of QlikView and we realized that we also needed an X64 edition. Porting the code was straightforward and QlikView 7 was now shipped in three editions: X86, IA64 and X64.

QlikView 7 also brought the calendar object, the block chart, the box plot, the expression overview, the variable overview, the alerts and the reports.

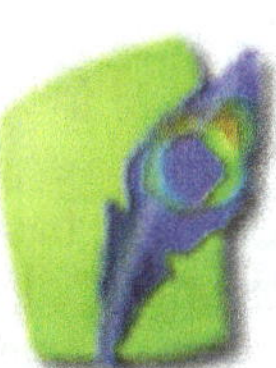

As a curiosity, I can also mention that QlikView 7 was the first version with scroll bars for the sheet. None of the previous versions had had this. We had always had the opinion that scroll bars would steal screen space and not add any relevant functionality. Instead, we had a zoom function so that you could fit the work area to the screen. But – it's never too late to change one's mind …

QlikView 8, Ajax and Set Analysis

Originally posted in the Qlik Design Blog on Aug 13, 2013

QlikView 7 was a great version – the Desktop, the Server and the Publisher all worked fine, but … they were not quite enterprise ready. It was not always simple to integrate all components in an already complex enterprise environment.

So, for QlikView 8, one focus was to drastically improve the enterprise readiness. Hence, QlikView 8 brought us a a number of server components and functions:

- An html-based control panel: The QMC

- A built-in web server: Previously it was necessary to have the Microsoft IIS installed.

- A Directory Services Controller: Previously it was possible to connect to the Microsoft AD only.

- QlikView Server authorization (DMS mode): Previously you could use the NTFS file system security only.

- Server clustering

Another focus was on a light-weight, zero foot-print client – the Ajax client. We had already started to experiment with this in the 7.5 version, but with QlikView 8 we launched it as one of our three basic clients: The C client (Desktop and Plug-In), the Java client and the Ajax client. The three clients had different capabilities – if you wanted full functionality, you chose the C client. On the other hand, there was some effort involved to install this, and if you wanted an install-free environment, you chose the Ajax client. The Java client was somewhere in between.

The Ajax client was, however, not as dynamic as it is today. The web pages had to be created in a manual step and posted on the web server.

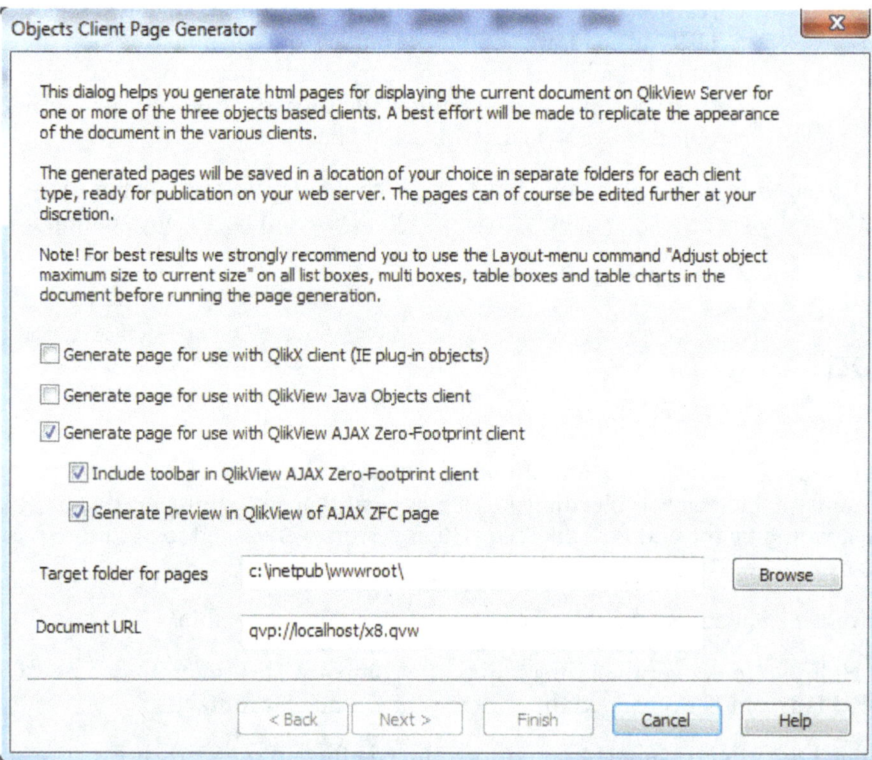

We didn't just add functionality; we also removed some: The Itanium processor had been launched some years earlier, and by now we had realized that its market share would not grow. So, for QlikView 8, we decided to discontinue the Itanium edition of QlikView.

QlikView 8 also brought the Advanced search, the Hierarchy resolution, the Input fields, the License lease and Set Analysis.

And, yes, we got the logo that we use still today.

Finally, QlikView 8 also brought us the first steps towards collaboration. It started with a simple function: the possibility to mail a link with a selection to another user. We already had local bookmarks and now realized that it would not be practical to store an entire selection in a URL. Instead, we should of course store the bookmark on the server, and mail a link to this bookmark. From there, it was only a small step to expand this idea and allow the user to create and share other types of objects also: Visualizations and Sheets.

QlikView 8 was, with the server components, the Set analysis and the collaboration a version that architecturally very much resembled today's QlikView and lay the foundation for Qlik Sense.

Nasdaq

Originally presented at Qonnections in Dallas, May 2015

Around the year 2000 QlikTech was not doing very well. The product was excellent, but the sales were lousy. QlikTech was bleeding and it was clear that something needed to be done, otherwise it would be the end for QlikTech. The investors were asked to put more money into the company.

But the investors demanded change. They demanded a new leadership.

So, Måns Hultman took over the leadership of the company. He also brought a new CFO – Lars Björk. Måns and Lars changed the company and made it profitable.

They changed the sales organization and introduced efficient sales processes. The keyword was *focus*. Focus on companies that use a database that we know well. Focus on controllers that have a real problem that we can solve and are willing to invest to get it done. Focus on mid-sized companies that can make fast decisions.

They didn't change the research and development since this department already worked well.

They also looked for new investors that could help the company grow. The strategy was clear: To go public within a few years. Hence, these were the first steps towards Nasdaq.

New investors were found, and with the new money the company started to transform fast. More people were hired, and training processes were established.

Picture 10: Måns Hultman and Lars Björk.

A mission statement was formulated, and a set of corporate values were defined. These were not defined top-down, but instead bottom-up: People that had been employed long were involved in the process of defining the values. As a result, the values represented the *existing* company culture – *what we already were doing* – and not some fictional state into which the management wanted to transform the company. The company values were NOT corporate BS.

An introductory program for new employees was established – Qlik Academy: All new employees went to Lund in Sweden for a week to get trained, to be taught the values, and to meet other employees from other parts of the world. Networking was important. Anna Kjellberg did a fantastic job organizing this.

Måns and Lars also realized the importance of an organized product management and of the company brand. Anthony Deighton took care of the product management and Pelle Rosell was assigned the task of consolidating the previously confused market communication into something logical and efficient. They both did a great job, and soon the Green – White – Gray was used everywhere in our marketing.

Further, a summit was organized every year. This meant that all employees, new and old, met and had training sessions on values, brand, and products at one single location for four days: Cortina, Cancun, Orlando, Granada, etc.

The importance of the summits and the Qlik Academy sessions cannot be overstated. They helped to keep the company values alive and boosted productivity. The network of individual employees was enormous, which helped individuals in their daily work.

Picture *11: Lining up in the Nasdaq studio.*

Picture *12: Stock development the first hours.*

Ten years later, Qlik was introduced at Nasdaq under the ticker QLIK.

It was a fantastic day in New York – July 16, 2010 – with many representatives from Qlik middle management.

It has been a fantastic journey. Thank you all – Björn, Staffan, Håkan, Sten, Jonas, several Johan, Måns, several Lars, Anna, Pelle, Anthony, Magnus, Henrik, Shima, Karin, Bill, Fredrik, Markus, Patrick, and everyone else who I haven't mentioned – for all the fun, and for making this journey possible.

Picture *13: Evening celebration.*

Since then, Qlik has been acquired by Thoma Bravo and is still today (Jan 2024) privately owned by this company.

Picture *14: Our Brand Manager Pelle Rosell, with green socks.*

Qlik Values and Qlik Academy

Qlik has always been a special company where the attitude of the employees has been positive and helpful. It has led to a pleasant working atmosphere where managers have been approachable, and co-workers have gone to great lengths to help each other.

In 2004, when large investments were made in the growth of Qlik, the investors feared that these values could go lost. So, the QlikTech management made an effort to try to document what was special with the company. Surveys among all old-time employees were made and some core values were distilled from these, and written down:

- Challenge!
    - Challenge the conventional
    - Inspire people to think in new ways
    - Guts to follow our own path

- Move fast
    - Keep it simple
    - Be thorough
    - Innovate where needed
    - OK to make mistakes if we learn from them

- Open and straightforward
    - Open mind to customers <u>real</u> needs
    - Available, no borders, open doors
    - Give and take feedback

- Take responsibility
    - We keep our promises
    - Do it! Actions speak more than words
    - Dedicated and hard working
    - Be cost conscious

- Teamwork for results
    - We are building <u>one</u> QlikTech
    - Help out where needed
    - Friendly and fun
    - Set goals, measure and improve

These values made the company special.

The next step was to make sure that all new hires were exposed to these values and learned how to walk the talk. For this purpose, the Qlik Academy was initiated under Anna Kjellberg's leadership. All new employees went to Lund in Sweden for a week to get trained, to be taught the values, and to meet other employees from other parts of the world. Networking was important.

Picture *15: Anna Kjellberg, who made Qlik Academy a success.*

Qlik Academy made a difference. Still today, years after the Qlik Academy was cancelled, people talk with affection about the Qlik Academy week, and the group to which they belonged. Not only did Qlik Academy boost efficiency in the company, it also forged friendships that will last a lifetime.

A Historical Odyssey

21

Simplicity and Why Qlik is different

All through the development of QlikView and Qlik Sense, the Qlik architects have had *simplicity* as a load star. Everything should be as simple as possible – but not simpler. This goal has clearly helped Qlik make a good product.

But there are other advantages with the Qlik engine: The fact that it is associative – but still not. The idea that all calculations should be on-demand. The multi-table data model. And finally, the architecture that leads to problem separation – an architecture that separates the fundamental pillars of analysis into three separate problems.

This chapter is about the simplicity and the advantages of the Qlik engine.

Relational vs Associative data

Originally presented at Qonnections in Orlando, May 2016

The word "associative" is a word that often is used to describe the Qlik logic. However, it is important to understand that the data model in a Qlik app is *not* associative. It is _relational_.

An associative database (sometimes called an object-oriented database, or a graph database) is quite different. Associative databases do not have tables. Instead, each data item is a node in a graph. Further, the nodes are connected with links that define the associations. By selecting an item, the links will give you the associated items.

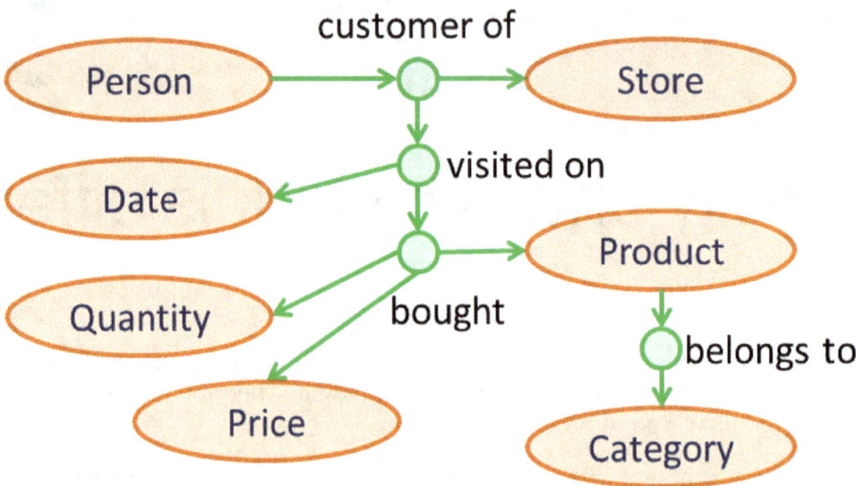

A Qlik app is different: The data storage is relational, meaning that data is stored in tables. The tables have columns and rows, where a column corresponds to a field or attribute, and the rows correspond to records or instances of an object or transaction. Hence, a table is *a list of something*, with an object ID and all object attributes.

The tables are linked through key fields, that define their relations.

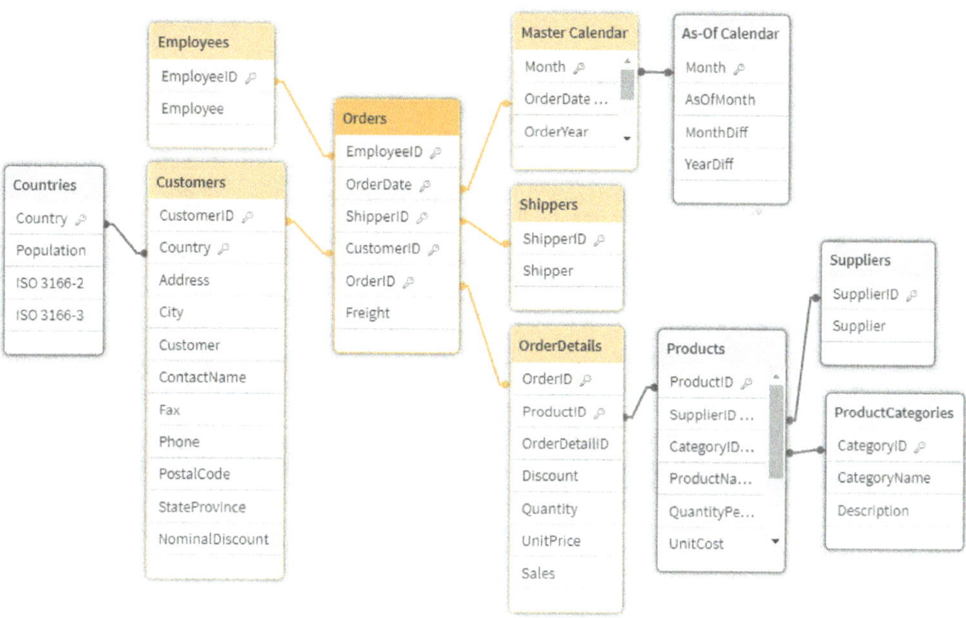

However, the Qlik engine has associative features which makes it behave like an associative database:

- Distinct field values are stored in the symbol tables, together with a corresponding binary index. This is similar to the nodes in an associative database.

- Records are stored as compact data tables containing binary indexes only. This is similar to the links in an associative database.

- By selecting an item, i.e. an item in a symbol table, the links will give you the associated items.

- All fields are equal, and as a consequence, any field can be the starting point for the user. This allows unrestricted exploration in a non-hierarchical way.

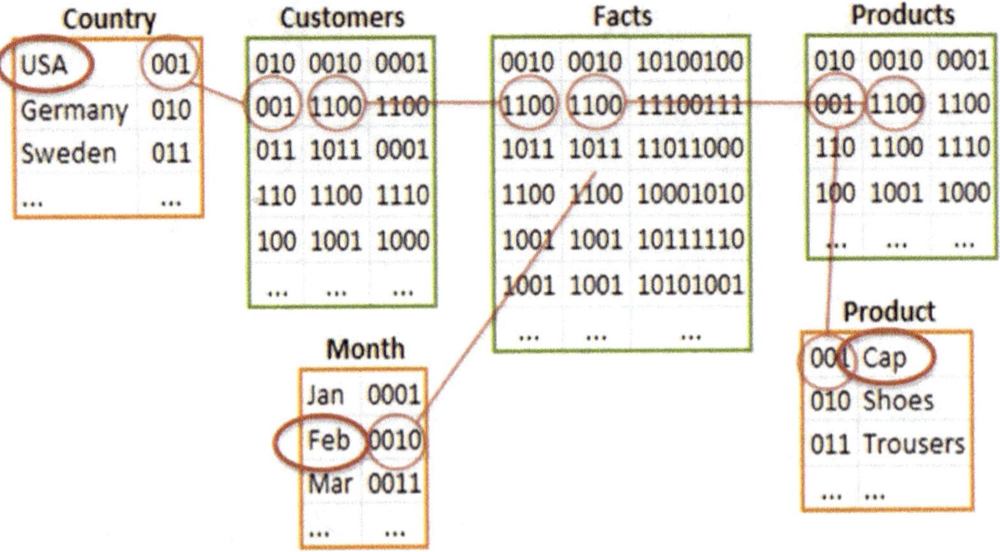

This means that the Qlik engine has the best of two worlds:

- A relational data storage
  - Straightforward to model
  - No hierarchies necessary
- Associative experience
  - Allows any starting point
  - Explore freely in any direction
  - Possible to see excluded values
  - Possible to "turn questions around" – to play with data to understand it
  - Shows the whole story

On-demand calculations

Originally presented at Qonnections in Orlando, May 2016

When a user clicks on something in a Qlik app, two things happen:

1. Logical Inference
2. Calculation of objects

The logical inference (see the Engine chapter) determines which field values it is possible to combine with the selection, and which field values you cannot. Hence, a field value is either "possible" (white or green) or excluded (gray). This is done for all fields in all tables, and the result is stored in the state vectors.

The second step is the calculation of objects. This means that *all* objects – bar charts, pivot tables, other sheet objects – are recalculated to reflect the new selection. They all have content that is determined by the selection in the underlying relational data model. Most charts are hypercubes whose calculations are aggregations, i.e. they loop over many records in the data model. When an object has been calculated, the used memory is returned so it can be used for other calculations. The hypercubes don't retain the information of the data in the data model; they only keep the aggregated values.

In other words: The calculations are aggregations in transient hypercubes.

Note that there are two layers: The data model with the logical inference, the selections, and the state vectors. And the UI layer with objects that are used both for input and output:

A user clicks on a value in an object to make a selection. The selection is sent to the data model layer so that the logical inference can be made. Once this is done, the sheet object uses the output from the logical inference to recalculate.

These two layers create a number of advantages:

- Data model and Logical Inference
  - Marks all field values and all table records as possible or excluded
  - Fast! – No number-crunching
  - Any selection is possible – one item, two items, three items, all items …
- UI layer and calculation of on-demand hypercubes
  - A hypercube = A sheet object = A chart = A visualization
  - Extremely easy to create a hypercube
  - Only visible objects are calculated
  - Multiple cubes are shown simultaneously and "talk to each other": No manual "wiring" necessary.
  - The on-demand calculations are not limited to pre-calculated numbers. Any selection can be calculated.
  - Based on non-aggregated transactional data

Multi-table data model

Originally presented at Qonnections in Orlando, May 2016

How many tables does your BI solution have? And what type of tables?

These may seem like strange questions, but they do in fact matter. Let's look at a couple of examples. First, a standard SELECT statement can have many tables as input – e.g. if joins are used – but the output is always one single table.

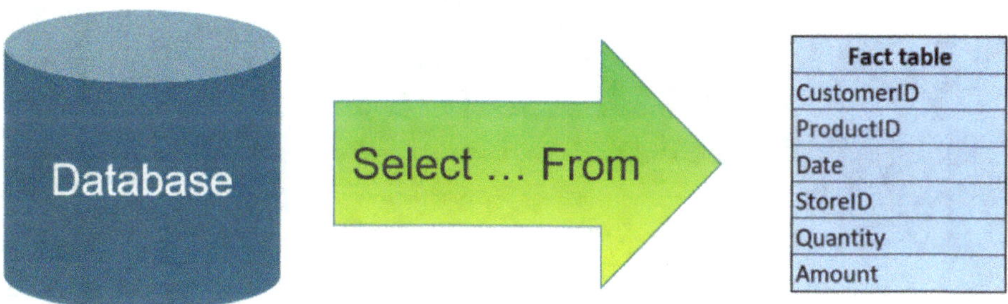

This means that all calculations are made in a table that may be the output of a join. In such tables you often get the problem of double counting, e.g. that the same dollar appears on multiple rows. The reason is that joins sometimes duplicate values.

An example is the below picture: If these two tables are joined, the **"InvoiceFee"** will be calculated five times.

Invoice headers

InvoiceID	InvoiceDate	InvoiceFee
...	...	...
10353	2015-11-08	$10,00
10360	2015-01-16	$20,00
10372	2015-07-30	$10,00
10417	2015-01-10	$10,00
10424	2014-06-17	$0,00
10479	2013-03-14	$20,00
...	...	...

Invoice lines

InvoiceID	ProductID	Sales
...	...	...
10353	38	$3 770,00
10360	28	$1 262,10
10360	29	$4 751,60
10360	38	$807,40
10360	49	$640,15
10360	54	$1 028,44
10372	20	$974,88
...	...	...

A cube in a traditional OLAP tool is similar. The fact table doesn't look very different from above, but now you have additional dimension tables, allowing for hierarchies and additional attributes. There is however often one limitation: Fields that should be used in calculations must be in the fact table, because that is where all aggregations take place. They cannot be in the dimension tables. Note that both Quantity and Amount are such fields.

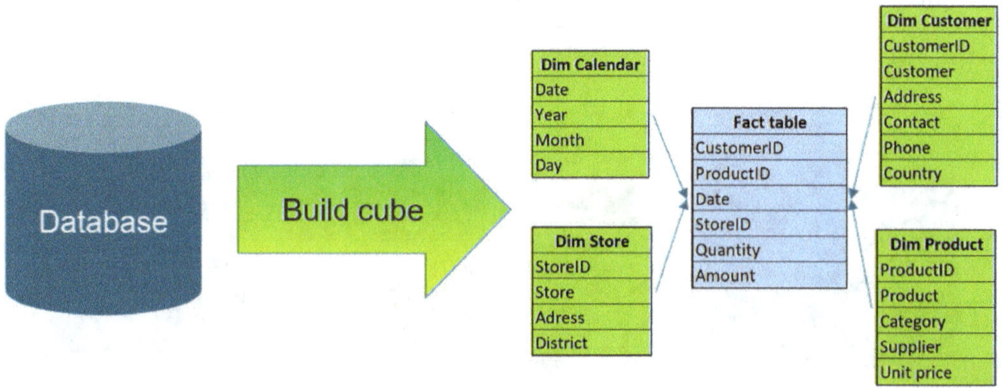

Thus, in a traditional cube, the Fact table has a special position: This is the only place where an aggregation can be made. So, in effect, this is still a single-table model.

A Qlik data model is however different. All tables are equal. There is no table that is more important than the others.

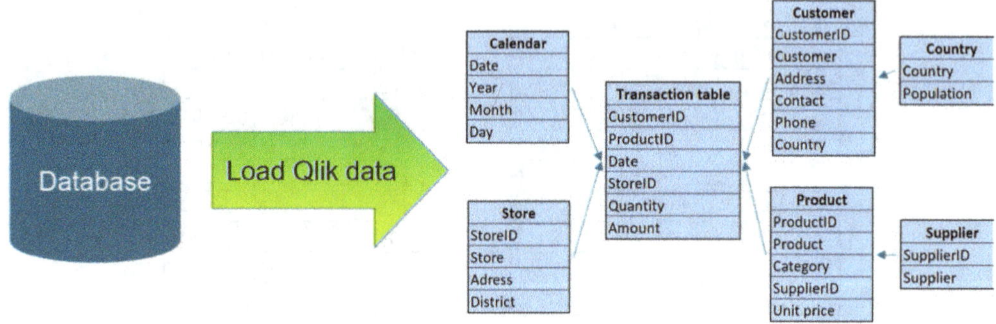

The transaction table – the largest table, in the middle – is still called "Fact table" by many app developers, but this really a misnomer: Facts can exist in *any* table in the Qlik data model.

Hence, there is no dedicated Fact table, and all tables are potential carriers of facts (numbers). And, as a consequence, aggregations can be made anywhere. The engine knows in which table to make the aggregation.

This means that you in most cases don't need to know in advance which metrics you want to calculate. The data model will be the same anyway. It also means that you can easily create composite metrics, e.g. the ratio between the amounts in the transaction table and populations in the country table. This is very useful when comparing how well sales is going in different countries. You would then use the following expression:

```
Sum( Amount ) / Sum( Population )
```

Note that the sum of **Amount** and the sum of **Population** are calculated in different tables: In the transaction table and in the country table, respectively.

Further, tables don't need to be joined, so records are not duplicated. Fan traps are resolved automatically, and all links are bi-directional. You do not need to define the direction.

This approach leads to a number of advantages:

- Aggregations can be made in all tables
  - There is no dedicated table for numbers. The engine "knows" in which table to make the calculation.
  - It is possible to calculate metrics with components from different tables.
- No double counting
  - Joins are not necessary – so record duplication is avoided.
  - Fan traps is a non-problem. They are automatically resolved.
- Allows for any type of data model, e.g.
  - Slowly changing dimensions.
  - Bridge tables (ancestor tables) in hierarchies.
  - Chasm traps, that can easily be solved in the load script.

Problem separation

Originally presented at Qonnections in Orlando, May 2016

When you create a business intelligence solution, there are three fundamental steps that need to take place.

1) Data modelling
2) Metric definitions (measures)
3) Filter definitions

Each of these constitutes a separate challenge, but in many BI tools the three challenges are intertwined and inseparable.

To understand this, we only need to look at the anatomy of a SELECT statement. Here you can clearly see that some parts are data modelling, others are metric definitions, and yet others are filters.

```
SELECT
    Customers.CompanyName, Orders.OrderDate, Sum([Order Details].[Quantity]) AS Qty,
    Categories.CategoryName, Products.ProductName
FROM (Categories
INNER JOIN Products ON Categories.CategoryID =  Products.CategoryID)
INNER JOIN ((Customers INNER JOIN Orders ON Customers.CustomerID = Orders.CustomerID)
INNER JOIN [Order Details] ON Orders.OrderID = [Order Details].OrderID) ON Products.ProductID =
    [Order Details].ProductID
WHERE (((Customers.Country)='Sweden'
    Or (Customers.Country)='USA'))
GROUP BY
    Customers.CompanyName, Orders.OrderDate,
    Categories.CategoryName, Products.ProductName;
```

- Data modelling
- Metric definitions
- Filters

This entanglement makes app development cumbersome.

The problem becomes worse when you realize that the requirements of the different steps often come from three very different user groups:

1) **The data specialists**
   These are typically the content managers of the data warehouse. They know which tables to use, and how to link them in a good data model.

2) **The power users**
   These are typically controllers and other advanced business users. They know which metrics to use, and how to define them. Simple metrics are easy to define. But the more complicated metrics are not as obvious: How do you treat discounts and salesman bonus when you calculate the gross margin? How do you create a supplier scorecard based on product quality and delivery punctuality?

3) **The data consumers**
   These are typically non-technical users, but with very relevant business questions: managers, salesmen, secretaries, etc. They know what data they want to look at, so they know which filters they want to use.

With Qlik, the three steps are separate, but can still be made in one product by one single person:

1) **Data modelling**
   The data modelling is done in the script and results in a data model with multiple tables. Usually, no aggregated metrics are defined here, and filtering is a very rough one just to keep data amounts down. Normally, the app developer will do this, but in large organizations, this step is sometimes delegated to data specialists.

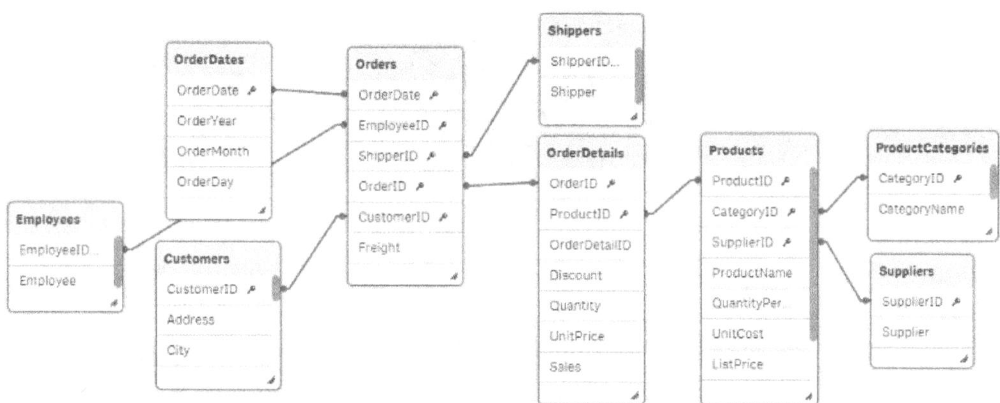

2) **Metrics**
   Metric definitions are made in the UI. The app developer will make the basic ones, but often a power user will define them, either as master measures or directly in a chart.

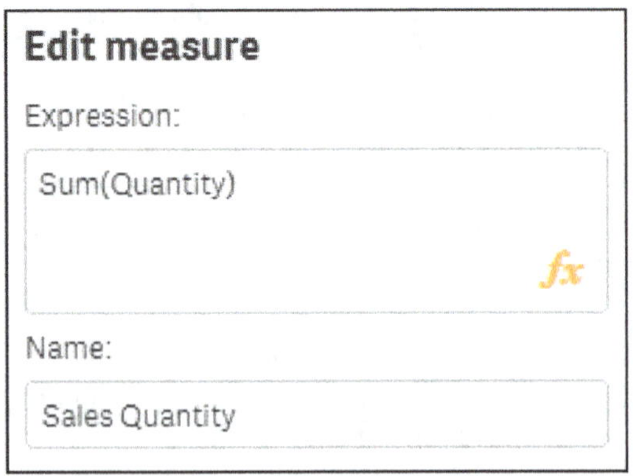

3) **Filters**
   Finally, filtering is made by the data consumers when using the app, either as interactive selections or by using pre-defined bookmarks.

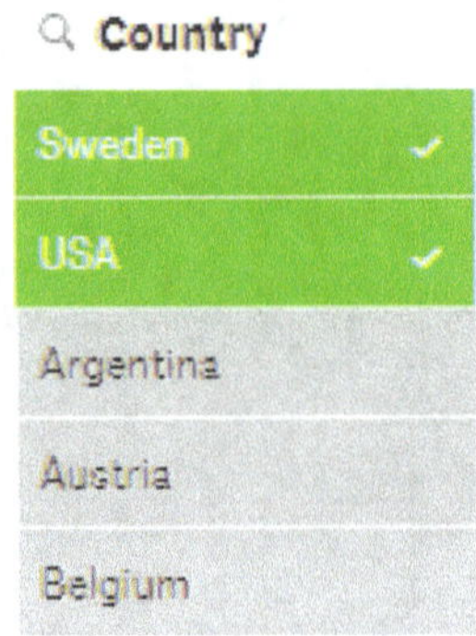

Bottom line: By separating the three challenges, Qlik has made app development and change management easier:

- Problem entanglement
    - In most BI tools the KPI definitions are intertwined with the Data modelling
    - In some tools Filtering is intertwined with the Data modelling
- The Qlik engine separates these three concepts.
    - Leads to simplicity.
    - Gives flexibility.
    - Is easy to create and manage.
    - Allows re-usability: The same data model is used for multiple metrics.
    - Allows step-wise implementation – both in the data modelling and in the metric development.

Let the User Select!

Originally posted in the Qlik Design Blog on Jun 26, 2012

Qlik Sense and QlikView are about empowering the user. Allowing a user to freely choose what to look at and how to look at it is one of the cornerstones of Business Discovery. Another is about simplicity – which often translates into removing unnecessary technical obstacles so that the user can focus on the data and the information that lies hidden in it. This often leads to a situation where you have two different user roles: an application developer and a business user, where the application developer takes care of the data modelling aspects of the analysis and the user interacts with the data, asks questions, and finds new areas of exploration.

In such a situation it is important that the developer treads carefully – he or she must remove technical obstacles *without* limiting the user. However, in an effort to simplify, application developers sometimes complicate things without realizing it. Let me give you a couple of examples.

Macros and ***Actions*** are features that unfortunately sometimes are used to "help" the user make the right selection. I have often seen developers create buttons that make selections and activate other sheets, or triggers that clear selections and make new selections when you leave a sheet. Such constructs are confusing for the user, who doesn't understand why these new selections happen. Macros and Actions often obscure the Qlik logic and prevent the user from learning how to interact with data on their own.

Another area where the power to select can be taken away from the user is when ***Set Analysis*** is used. In set analysis, the developer can define a formula with an arbitrary selection that overrides the one made by the user. Often the new selection is based on the user selection. Set analysis is necessary for calculations that extend outside the user-made selection, e.g., if the user wants to make a year-to-date calculation for the time up to the selected month. Properly used, it is an extremely powerful tool that enhances the user's ability to find information in data. But I have seen cases where set analysis instead ***replaced*** the user's selection and limited the ability to interact with data. To hard code the selection inside a formula is in some cases disrespecting the user's intelligence!

My view is that navigation – choosing a sheet, activating sheet objects, expanding branches in pivot tables, and, most importantly, making selections – ***should as much as possible be left to the user***. Constructions that "help" the user in this area usually have the opposite effect. Instead of helping the user, they often complicate the interaction with data and confuse the user.

I am convinced that macros, actions and set analysis sometimes must be used, but these features should be used with caution. They should never be used for things that the user can do better. We live in an age of empowerment, and users want to be free to explore data in their own way and on their own.

We should allow them to do just that.

Macros are Bad

Originally posted in the Qlik Design Blog on Apr 29, 2014

There are several good reasons _not_ to use macros in QlikView.

First of all, macros are run using Microsoft COM Automation. They will run client-side and work fine if you use the Desktop or the IE PlugIn, which both are Windows executables. But if you use the Ajax client, there are severe limitations since the macros now need to run on the server instead of on the client. For a server, there are both technical limitations and security implications that have forced us to restrict the capabilities of macros.

So, if you want to use the Ajax client, you should avoid macros.

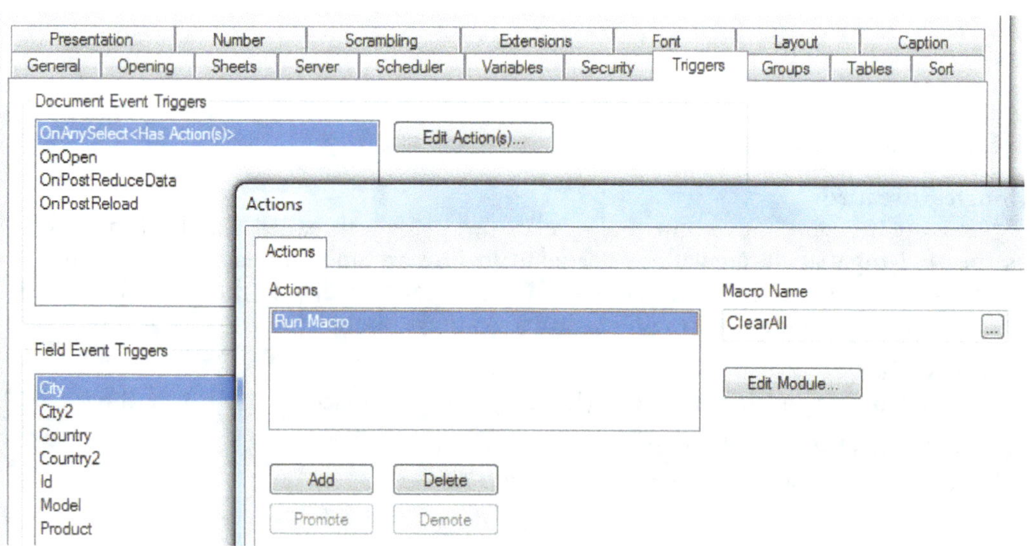

Secondly, a common beginner's mistake is to use macros to build logic into QlikView; logic that almost always works better if QlikView's own out-of-the-box functionality is used. An example is assigning a value to a variable every time a selection is made: In other tools you would use a trigger and a macro, but in QlikView this is not needed: You should instead define your variable using an equals sign and the appropriate expression.

Further, many problems can be solved by using a smart data model instead of macros.

Macros often confuse the user. A user wants a predictable behavior and macros often do exactly the opposite: They create behaviors that exist in some places but not in other. Thisis counter intuitive.

Finally, if the macro is long or complex, it will often push QlikView into an unstable situation. Qlik has often seen this in documents sent to its support organization. The reason is probably a poor fit between the synchronous, sequential execution of a macro and QlikView's internal asynchronous, multi-threaded computation.

From a development perspective, the macro feature is a secondary functionality. In the development process, it will rarely get first priority when compared to the "native" functionality: I.e. in the choice between keeping macro functionality unchanged and improving the out-of-the-box functionality, the Qlik development team will often choose the latter. This means that you can get a changed macro behavior when you upgrade your QlikView installation.

```
1  Sub ClearQlikViewCache
2  ActiveDocument.ClearCache
3  End Sub
```

Some facts about macros:

- **Single-Threaded?**
  Macros are in their nature sequential – i.e. in a way single-threaded. But this is not the same as saying that all calculations started by macros are single-threaded. For instance, if a macro makes a selection that causes a chart to be calculated, both the logical inference and the chart calculation are multi-threaded. As they should be.

- **Clears cache?**
  No. A macro does not clear the cache. (Unless you use the macro in the picture above ...) ☺

- **Clears the Back-Forward stack?**
  No. A macro does not clear the Back-Forward stack.

- **Clears the Undo-Redo stack?**
  Yes, if the macro contains layout changes, the Undo-Redo stack will be cleared.

So, I strongly recommend you don't use macros, unless it is in a QlikView Desktop environment. And there they should be short and concise! On a server you should instead use Actions.

There is however one thing that may confuse the user more than macros. And that is *Triggers*. If a macro or an action is started from a nicely labeled button, then the user will understand what happens.

But if the macro instead is triggered by some other event, e.g. the changing of a variable value, we have a very different situation. Then you will most likely create a non-intuitive behavior.

Macros are Bad, but Triggers are Worse.

The Key to Heaven

Originally posted in the Business Discovery Blog on Feb 4, 2014

"To every man is given the key to the gates of heaven. The same key opens the gates of hell."

[As told to Richard Feynman by a Buddhist monk]

To the Buddhist monk, these words were a general guide to how to live your life.

To Richard Feynman, the words were about knowledge and science: He was convinced that Science, per se, is neither good nor bad. It is just a tool – a tool that can be used for both.

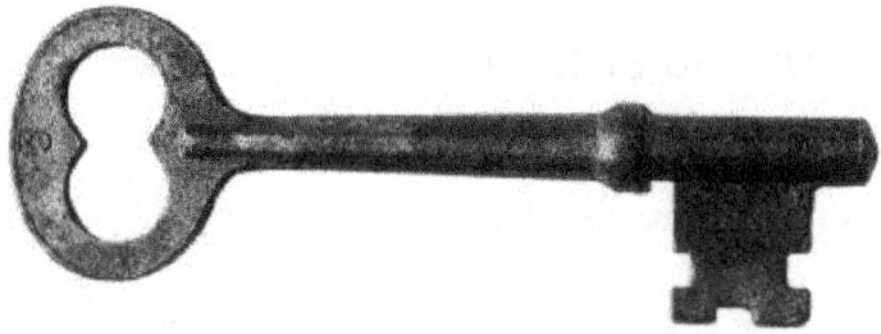

When I see these words, I think of some of the functionality in QlikView and Qlik Sense: Functions and features that were introduced to solve problems that would be difficult or impossible to solve otherwise: Triggers, Actions, Dollar expansions, Set analysis, Alternate states, Show conditions, etc.

These features are all keys to heaven. Correctly used, they can enable you to build an application that calculates and compares immensely complex things, while still presenting the data in a way that a user can understand and investigate further.

However, the very same functions are also the key to making user-hostile and unmanageable applications, e.g. through:

- Set analysis that hard-codes a selection – instead of letting the user select interactively.
- Excessive use of Dollar expansions, Variables and Show conditions, which make the application difficult or impossible to manage.
- Alternate states that are poorly labelled, so that the user gets confused about which selection really is applied.
- Triggers with Actions or Macros that perform navigation or selections that really ought to be user-initiated and not automatic.

Enable the user!

The user will learn to interact with data, if you only let him. Most users have very intelligent questions and want to navigate in data, explore and discover things. Let them do this.

But if you instead obscure the QlikView logic by introducing too much additional logic using any of the above-mentioned features, the user experience will be a very different one. Instead of an active, smart user, you will produce a passive user that doesn't understand how to use Qlik effectively and instead uses the application as a static report.

Some advice:

- Navigation and selections should be left to the user. Don't automate this. Let the user make the selections and interact with data.
- Label fields and charts so that it is clear what they show.
- Avoid hard-coding filters. For example, if you want one graph showing the numbers for 2014 and second graph for 2013, you should not create two separate graphs with the years hard-coded. You should instead use a Trellis chart with year as first dimension.
- Avoid using Triggers and Macros.
- Always ask yourself "How is this going to be managed? Is this a manageable solution?"

Don't let the QlikView functions get in the way of making a user-friendly and manageable application. Instead, use them wisely.

Simplicity.

The Feynman Problem Solving Algorithm

Posted in the Business Discovery Blog on July 16, 2013

Richard Feynman was one of the greatest physicists of the last century. His work spanned many disciplines and his curiosity drove him to explore and understand a variety of problems in the universe. He was awarded the Nobel Prize in physics in 1965.

Feynman, when facing a new problem, used a very simple approach to solve it. He first asked questions and enquired about the details. After that, he retired to think about it, and when he came back, he usually had the solution.

His ability to find the core of a problem and describe it in a simple, yet precise way, was unmatched. The method is summarized (probably by his friend and fellow physicist Murray Gell-Mann) as "The Feynman Problem Solving Algorithm":

1. Write down the problem.
2. Think very hard.
3. Write down the solution.

Intended as a joke, this sounds like a ridiculously simplified workflow for problem solving. One can hardly think that it can serve as an instruction for how to solve a problem.

But it can. In fact, it is even _a very useful approach_.

It can successfully be used when you build Qlik applications. Then you often encounter different problems: Figuring out which data to load, modeling this data and figuring out how to write different complex formulae.

Using the algorithm, you will find that the hardest part is the first point – to formulate the problem. Or rather – to understand the problem in the first place. Points two and three often come automatically if you've done the first point properly. Just formulating the problem in precise words will help you understand the problem. And understanding the problem is the core of all problem solving.

The exercise of formulating the problem in words and explaining it to your users or to your peers will force you to start thinking, which means that you start working on point two. You may even write the first Qlik scripts to test different concepts, which means that you start working on point three.

This only shows that the three points are interconnected and that you will need an iterative approach to get it right. I often start working on all three points in parallel, but all the time I am aware that I need to understand the problem and think hard before I can deliver the final solution.

Some methods that I find useful:

- Listen to your users. They are the best source when it comes to understanding what the application should do; what the goals are. Which measures? Which dimensions? Discuss with them. Ask them questions.

- In data modeling, you should always ask yourself what each table or record represents. Which field, or combination of fields, uniquely defines a record? Study the data. Understand the data.

- Visualize your data model. Draw it on a piece of paper, if needed. Name the tables so that you understand what each record represents. Don't load a table unless you understand what its content is and how it relates to existing tables.

- Start small: Just one or two KPIs and few dimensions. Make sure you understand the data model and its calculations before you expand it.

- A smoker, stuck with a problem, usually takes a break. He stops working and takes a cigarette instead. *He starts thinking.* Taking a break in order to think is a very good habit that also non-smokers should adopt. So, once in a while you should walk away from the computer just to think.

Simplicity. Feynman was a genius.

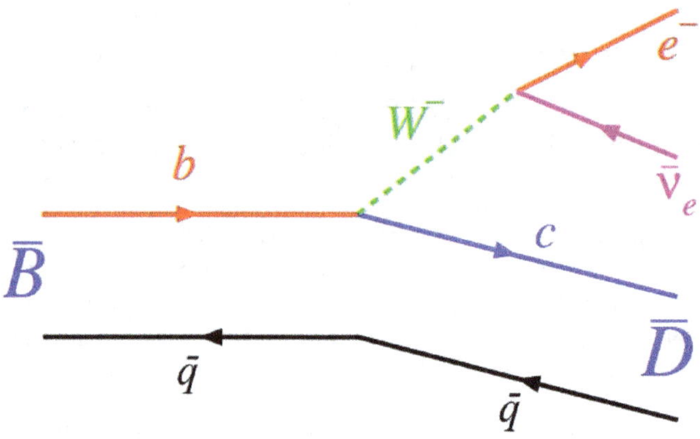

The decay of a B meson depicted in a Feynman diagram.

Illustrations

The author would like to thank the following individuals and institutions who have kindly given permission to reproduce the illustrations listed below. In addition, there are images from Qlik's marketing material and screen dumps from the Qlik products.

- The Unclearly Said
  - Statue of Esaias Tegnér in Lundagård.
    Photo by Anton Holmquist.

- Ancient Gods and Modern Days
  - Statue of Nabû at Nimrud, Mesopotamia. Licensed under Creative Commons International license.
  - Tyr. Illustration from manuscript in the care of the Icelandic National Library.
  - Statue of Venus. Vatican Museums Collection. Photo by Carlos Teixidor Cadenas.

- Roman Emperors and the Month Names
  - Numa Pompilius. Illustration from "Allmän kulturhistoria eller det mänskliga lifvet i dess utveckling, bd 2 (1901)" by Anton Nyström.
  - Julius Ceasar.
    Vatican Museums Collection.

- The Importance of Nothing
  - The statue of Nothingness.
    Photo by Henric Cronström.

- A Historical Odyssey
  - Staffan Gestrelius and Björn Berg.
    Photo by Henric Cronström.

- Three Friends
  - Håkan Wolgé.
    Photo by Johan Asplund.
  - Henric Cronström and Jonas Nachmanson.
    Photos by Johan Asplund.
  - Development team 2015.
    Photo by Johan Asplund.

- Nasdaq
  - Måns Hultman and Lars Björk.
    Photos by Johan Asplund.
  - The IPO at Nasdaq.
    Photos by Henric Cronström.
  - Pelle Rosell at Nasdaq.
    Photo by Henric Cronström.

- Qlik Academy
  - Anna Kjellberg.
    Photo by Johan Asplund.

- The Feynman Problem Solving Algorithm
  - Richard Feynman.
    Photo by the Nobel Foundation.

Illustrations

Index

Index